East Asia:
A New
History

East Asia: A New History

Rhoads Murphey
University of Michigan

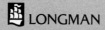 LONGMAN

An imprint of Addison Wesley Longman, Inc.

New York • Reading, Massachusetts • Menlo Park, California • Harlow, England
Don Mills, Ontario • Sydney • Mexico City • Madrid • Amsterdam

Acquisitions Editor: Bruce Borland
Developmental Editor: Carol Einhorn
Cover Designer: Mary McDonnell
Cover Illustration: Sim Sa-jong (1676–1759), "A Boating Party."
  Son Se-gi Collection, Seoul
Photo Researcher: Joanne DeSimone
Electronic Production Manager: Angel Gonzalez Jr.
Project Coordination and Text Design: Ruttle Graphics, Inc.
Manufacturing Manager: Willie Lane
Electronic Page Makeup: Ruttle Graphics, Inc.
Printer and Binder: RR Donnelley & Sons Company
Cover Printer: The Lehigh Press, Inc.

For permission to use copyrighted material, grateful acknowledgment is
made to the copyright holders on pp. 452–453, which are hereby made part
of this copyright page.

Library of Congress Cataloging-in-Publication Data

Murphey, Rhoads, 1919–
    East Asia: a new history/Rhoads Murphey.
        p.   cm.
    Includes bibliographical references and index.
    (alk. paper)
    1. East asia—History. 2. Asia, Southeastern—History,
        I. Title.
    DS511.M95   1996
    950—dc20   96–16976

ISBN 0–673–99350–7
  2345678910—DOW—999897

BRIEF CONTENTS

DETAILED CONTENTS

LIST OF MAPS

PREFACE

East Asia is the single most populous unit of the world, comprising China, Korea, Vietnam, and Japan, together over a fifth of the world's people, more than twice the total of Europe and many times that of the United States. Before the present century, its share of the world's population was much larger. East Asia also contains the world's oldest living civilizations, with an impressively rich cultural history. The area forms an easily comprehensible unit in the sense that the Chinese model of civilization spread to its immediate neighbors in Korea and Vietnam and somewhat later to Japan; in all three the original Chinese imprint is still powerful. East Asia is thus sometimes called the *Sinic* (Chinese) world, but its modern evolution has also included close interaction among its politically and culturally separate parts, as in the Japanese takeover of Korea from 1895 (or 1910), the long Sino-Japanese War from 1931 (or 1937) to 1945, or the spread of Chinese-style communism to North Korea and Vietnam. Japan led the postwar world in rapid economic and industrial growth, and global economic growth rates more recently have been headed by China, Hong Kong, Taiwan, and South Korea.

This is a part of the world which becomes more important every year and which we must try to understand if we are to play a role in world affairs. U.S. trade across the Pacific, predominantly with East Asia, has for many years been far larger than our trade across the Atlantic. We have fought four major wars in East Asia in modern times, beginning with our conquest of the Philippines in 1898–1902, followed by our struggle against Japan from 1941 to 1945 and then by the Korean and Vietnam wars. But equally deserving of our attention is the uniquely long and culturally rich history of East Asia, important and rewarding for itself, and providing invaluable perspective on ourselves, our different traditions, and our own times. East Asian civilization is older than anything in the West and offers a different and fascinating set of answers to universal human problems, as does its modern development, where East Asian societies have worked out their own distinctive solutions. In many cases, these compare favorably with the solutions, or lack thereof, which our own Western societies have evolved to the dismaying problems which confront us. If we can learn from East Asia to improve our own situation, it would not be the first time. Chinese science and technology, including, for example, paper and printing, gunpowder, the compass, coal as fuel, horticulture, metallurgy, and medicine, developed far in advance of the West and later contributed importantly to Western development. Chinese and later Japanese art served as models for eighteenth and nineteenth century Europe, while trade with both played a role in the nineteenth century economic rise of the West. Today our fortunes are linked ever more closely with those of East Asia.

This book is an introduction to the history of this major part of the world, from earliest times to the present. It is designed mainly for use as a textbook in courses on East Asia, but may be supplemented by readings, from those listed at the end of each chapter or from primary materials (in addition to those quoted in the text). Chapters are of approximately equal length. The book can serve alone, or with supplements, for a one- or two-semester course, two quarters, or a full academic year. It draws on the writer's more than forty years' experience in teaching such a course or courses, beginning with apprenticeship as a teaching assistant for my teachers, John Fairbank and Edwin Reischauer, to whose memory this book is gratefully dedicated. Both were pioneers in the development of East Asian studies, and together they wrote a still basic text for it, *East Asia: The Great Tradition*, and *East Asia: The Modern Transformation* (1958 and 1965), followed by the one-volume *East Asia: Tradition and Transformation* (latest edition 1989; Albert Craig replaced Reischauer on modern Japan after the latter became Ambassador to Japan in 1961), all of which built on the highly successful course they had begun at Harvard.

One may well ask why there is any need for a new text, especially given the others now available for the field of East Asian history, in addition to texts dealing with Chinese and Japanese history respectively. No text is perfect, including this one, but each may appeal to the needs of particular instructors and their courses, all of which differ to one degree or another. And despite what already exists, the field is far from oversupplied with texts, especially by comparison with European, American, or so-called world history, despite the greater span of East Asian than of Western history. Our perceptions of what is important in history also change continually, which provides a further case for a new treatment which takes more account of things like the status of women, the life of the common people, the role of cities, the environment, and the newly perceived importance of Korea and Vietnam, often neglected in other texts.

No single-volume history of the vast span of East Asian history can be more than the briefest introduction and, one hopes, an invitation to explore further. Space limits have made it necessary to foreshorten the treatment of every major aspect of East Asian history, and to do less than justice to all of them. Under such restraints, I have tried to apportion space more or less in relation to the size, populousness, and level of development of each area or culture at each period. In addition, especially for the earlier periods, we do not have adequate sources for many areas, by comparison most of all with China, where written records begin by about 2000 B.C. and which provide increasing detail, much of it preserved, for subsequent periods. Thus, for example, Japan before about 1500, Korea before about 1850, and Vietnam before about 1800 are not treated here as extensively as China. On the other hand, none of these countries has ever contained more than a small fraction of China's population or area, and the development of civilization in each, some fifteen hundred to two thousand or more years after China's beginnings, was a direct result of diffusion from the Chinese model, in each case by Vietnamese, Korean, and Japanese choice.

No one really writes alone, and I have drawn heavily on what I have learned from my teachers, fellow students, my own students, friends, and colleagues, plus many others whom I have known only through what they have written, including those to whom the publisher sent the manuscript for review, many of whose suggestions I have gratefully adopted. But I must also thank a host of people in China (where I have lived and worked at different times for many years), Japan (where I have also spent large parts of several years), and Vietnam and Korea (where I have visited more briefly). With few exceptions, I have been treated everywhere in East Asia not only with kindness but with genuine warmth, and have accumulated many friends. Apart from helping me with my work, they have given me an understanding, and a love, of their cultures and societies without which an outsider like myself cannot hope to teach or write adequately about them.

It takes about a year to make a book from a finished manuscript. Thus, events after the completion of the final revision cannot be dealt with, but that is inevitable for any book. East Asian history covers more than 5,000 years; a year or so which lies beyond our view does not seem terribly important. This is a book of history, not of current events, but readers are urged to keep themselves up-to-date through the periodical press.

Rhoads Murphey
Ann Arbor
Fall, 1995

A Note on the Spelling of Asian Names and Words

Nearly all Asian languages are written with symbols different from our Western alphabet. Chinese, Vietnamese, Korean, and Japanese are written with ideographic characters, plus a phonetic syllabary for Japanese, Korean, and Vietnamese. Most other Asian languages have their own scripts, symbols, diacritical marks, and alphabets, which differ from ours. There can thus be no single "correct spelling" in Western symbols for Asian words or names, including personal names and place names—only established conventions. Unfortunately, conventions in this respect differ widely and in many cases reflect preferences or forms related to different Western languages. The Western spellings used in this book, including its maps, are to some extent a compromise, in an effort to follow the main English-language conventions but also to make pronunciation for English speakers as easy as possible.

Chinese presents the biggest problem, since there are a great many different conventions in use and since well-known place names, such as Peking or Canton, are commonly spelled as they are here in most Western writings, even though this spelling is inconsistent with all of the romanization systems in current use and does not accurately represent the Chinese sounds. Most American newspapers and some journals now use the romanization system called *pinyin*, approved by the Chinese government, which renders these two city names, with greater phonetic accuracy, as Beijing and Guangzhou, but which presents other problems for most Western readers and which they commonly mispronounce in a way which is irritating to anyone who knows even a little of the language.

The usage in this book follows the most commonly used convention for scholarly publication when romanizing Chinese names, the Wade-Giles system (with some minor modifications), but gives the pinyin equivalents (if they differ) in parentheses after the first use of a name. Readers will encounter both spellings, plus others, in books, papers, and journals, and some familiarity with both conventions is thus necessary.

In general, readers should realize and remember that English spellings of names from other languages (such as Munich for München, Vienna for Wien, and Rome for Roma), especially in Asia, can be only approximations and may differ confusingly from one Western source or map to another.

For Japanese, the Hepburn transcription system universally used presents few problems, and is relatively easy for a Westerner to pronounce more or less correctly, remembering that spoken Japanese sounds each syllable as written in the Hepburn system and accents all syllables equally. For Korean, the similarly near-universal transcription system is the McCune-Reischauer, but easy pronunciation is more of a problem, as it is also for Vietnamese, where the *quoc ngu* ("national language") system is used. Vietnamese and Chinese are *tonal* languages, standard Chinese with four tones, Vietnamese with thirteen. Each tone, rising, falling, or a combination of inflections, is central to meaning; context often helps, and although both languages are monosyllabic, most words are in fact a combination of two (sometimes more) monosyllables. The McCune-Reischauer system for

Korean often includes some diacritical marks, and some letter combinations and sounds which are difficult for English speakers, but the problems for Vietnamese are even more daunting, with its *ng* and hard *oc* sounds. The only reliable guide to pronunciation of Chinese, Korean, and Vietnamese is to listen to a native speaker and try to reproduce those sounds and inflections. It is to be hoped that readers of this book will have the opportunity to do that through experiencing East Asia for themselves, always the best way to learn about another culture, not as tourists, but as students or participant observers with the chance to make Asian friends and to see the world through their eyes.

Wade-Giles	Pinyin
cha	zha
chai	zhai
chan	zhan
chang	zhang
chao	zhao
che	zhe
chen	zhen
cheng	zheng
chi	ji
chia	jia
chiao	jiao
chieh	jie
chien	jian
chih	zhi
chin	jin
ching	jing
chiu	jiu
cho	zhuo
chou	zhou
chu	zhu
chü	ju
chua	zhua
chuai	zhuai
chuan	zhuan
chüan	juan
chuang	zhuang
chüeh	jue
chui	zhui
chun	zhun
chün	jun
chung	zhong
ch'a	cha
ch'ai	chai
ch'an	chan
ch'ang	chang
ch'ao	chao
ch'e	che

Wade-Giles	Pinyin
ch'en	chen
ch'eng	cheng
ch'i	qi
ch'ia	qia
ch'iang	qiang
ch'iao	qiao
ch'ieh	qie
ch'ien	qian
ch'i	chi
ch'in	qin
ch'ing	qing
ch'iu	qiu
ch'iung	qiong
ch'o	chuo
ch'ou	chou
ch'u	chu
ch'ü	qu
ch'uai	chuai
ch'uan	quan
ch'uang	chuang
ch'üeg	que
ch'ui	chui
ch'un	chun
ch'ün	qun
ch'ung	chong
ho	he
hung	hong
hs	x
hsieh	xie
hsien	xian
hsiung	xiong
hsü	xu
hsüan	xuan
hsüeh	xue
hsün	xun

Wade-Giles	Pinyin
j	r
jih	ri
jo	ruo
jung	rong
k	g
ko	ge
kuei	gui
kung	gong
to	duo
k'	k
k'o	ke
k'ung	kong
lieh	lie
lo	luo
lüeh	lüe
lung	long
tzu	zi
mieh	mie
mien	mian
nieh	nie
nien	nian
no	nuo
nüeh	ne
p	b
pieh	bie
pien	bian
p'	p
p'ieh	pie

Wade-Giles	Pinyin
p'ien	pian
shih	shi
so	suo
sung	song
ssu, szu	si
t	d
tieh	dieh
tien	dian
tung	dong
t'	t
t'ieh	tie
t'ien	tian
t'o	tuo
ts, tz	z
tso	zuo
tsung	zong
ts', tz'	c
ts'o	cuo
ts'ung	cong
tz'u	ci
yeh	ye
yen	yan
yu	you
yü	yu
yüan	yuan
yüeh	yue
yün	yun
yung	yong

About the Author

RHOADS MURPHEY Born in Philadelphia, Rhoads Murphey, a specialist in Chinese history and in geography, received the Ph.D. degree from Harvard University in 1950. Before joining the faculty of the University of Michigan in 1964, he taught at the University of Washington; he has also been a visiting professor at Taiwan University and Tokyo University. From 1954 to 1956 he was the director of the Conference of Diplomats in Asia. The University of Michigan granted him a Distinguished Service Award in 1974. Formerly president of the Association for Asian Studies, Murphey has served as editor of the *Journal of Asian Studies* and *Michigan Papers in Chinese Studies* and currently edits the Association for Asian Studies *Monographs*. The Social Science Research Council, the Ford Foundation, the Guggenheim Foundation, the National Endowment for the Humanities, and the American Council of Learned Societies have awarded him fellowships. A prolific author, Murphey's books include *Shanghai: Key to Modern China* (1953), *An Introduction to Geography* (4th ed., 1978), *A New China Policy* (with others, 1965), *Approaches to Modern Chinese History* (with others, 1967), *The Scope of Geography* (3rd ed., 1982), *The Treaty Ports and China's Modernization* (1970), *China Meets the West: The Treaty Ports* (1975), and *The Fading of the Maoist Vision* (1980). *The Outsiders: Westerners in India and China* (1977) won the Best-Book-of-the-Year award from the University of Michigan Press. At Michigan he is Director of the Program in Asian Studies.

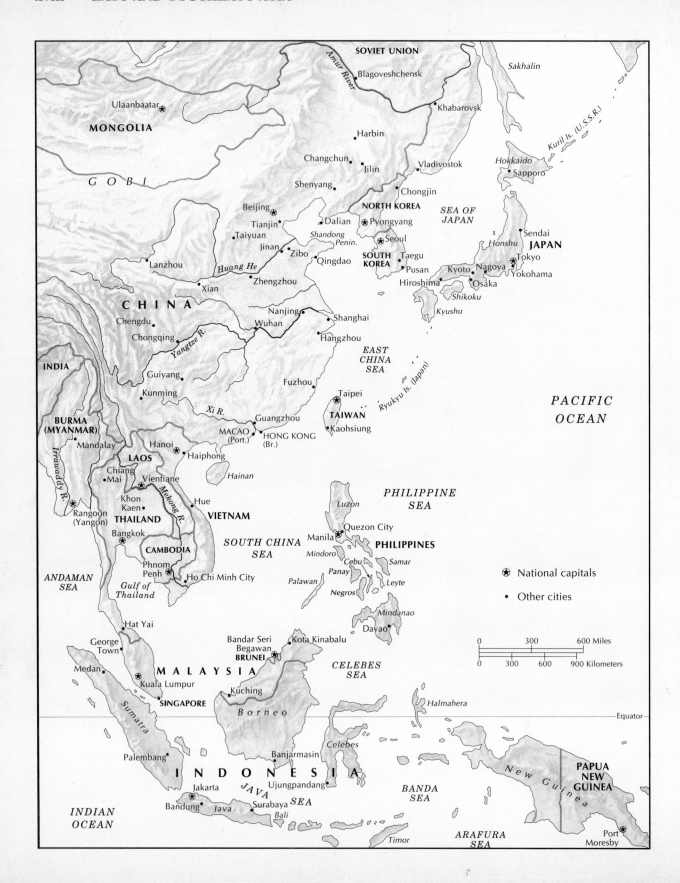

SOVIET UNION

Amur River

Blagoveshchensk

Sakhalin

Khabarovsk

Ulaanbaatar

Kuril Is. (U.S.S.R.)

MONGOLIA

Harbin

G O B I

Changchun

Hokkaido
Sapporo

Jilin

Vladivostok

Shenyang

Chongjin

NORTH KOREA

SEA OF
JAPAN

Beijing

Dalian

Pyongyang

Honshu

Sendai

Tianjin

Shandong
Penin.

Seoul

JAPAN

Taiyuan

Jinan
Zibo

Qingdao

SOUTH
KOREA

Taegu

Kyoto
Nagoya

Tokyo

Lanzhou

Huang He

Pusan

Hiroshima

Osaka

Yokohama

Xian

Zhengzhou

Shikoku

C H I N A

Chengdu

Nanjing

Wuhan

Shanghai

Kyushu

Chongqing

Yangtze R.

Hangzhou

EAST
CHINA
SEA

INDIA

Guiyang

Fuzhou

PACIFIC
OCEAN

Kunming

Xi R.

Taipei

Ryukyu Is. (Japan)

BURMA
(MYANMAR)

Guangzhou

TAIWAN

Mandalay

Hanoi

MACAO
(Port.)

HONG KONG
(Br.)

Kaohsiung

Irrawaddy R.

LAOS

Haiphong

Chiang
Mai

Vientiane

Hainan

PHILIPPINE
SEA

Khon
Kaen

Hue

Luzon

Rangoon
(Yangon)

Mekong R.

THAILAND

VIETNAM

Quezon City

PHILIPPINES

Bangkok

SOUTH CHINA
SEA

Manila

CAMBODIA

Mindoro

Cebu

Samar

ANDAMAN
SEA

Phnom
Penh

Ho Chi Minh City

Panay

Leyte

Gulf of
Thailand

Palawan

Negros

Hat Yai

Mindanao

George
Town

Bandar Seri
Begawan

Kota Kinabalu

Davao

Medan

BRUNEI

CELEBES
SEA

M A L A Y S I A

National capitals

Kuala Lumpur

Other cities

Kuching

SINGAPORE

B o r n e o

Halmahera

Sumatra

Equator

Palembang

Celebes

PAPUA
NEW
GUINEA

I N D O N E S I A

Banjarmasin

New Guinea

Jakarta

JAVA

Ujungpandang

BANDA
SEA

Bandung

Java

Surabaya

Bali

ARAFURA
SEA

Port
Moresby

INDIAN
OCEAN

Timor

0   300   600 Miles

0   300   600   900 Kilometers

Time Chart

	China	Korea-Japan	Southeast Asia	Other Civilizations
3000 B.C.	Yang Shao Lung Shan	Jomon culture in Japan to c. 300 B.C.	Early bronze and agriculture	Sumer and Egypt
2000 B.C.	Hsia (?) Shang	Chinese civilization spreads to Korea	Javanese (?) sailors to Africa	Hammurabi's Code, 1750 B.C. Hyksos invasion of Egypt Trojan War
1000 B.C.	Chou conquest, 1027 B.C. Confucius Warring States Ch'in conquest, 221 B.C.	Yayoi culture in Japan, c. 300 B.C.–A.D. 250	Nam Viet	Homer, Socrates, Plato Greek city-states Aristotle, Alexander Rise of Roman power Julius Caesar
A.D.	Han dynasty, 206 B.C.–A.D. 220 Northern Wei and "Six Dynasties"; Spread of Buddhism Sui, 581–617 T'ang, 618–907 Northern Sung, 960–1127 S. Sung, 1127–1279 Su Shih, Chu Hsi	Paekche, Koguryo, and Silla in Korea Tomb Period, A.D. 250–A.D. 550 in Japan Yamato State c. 550–c. 710 Nara Period 710–784 Heian 794–1185 Lady Murasaki Koryo in Korea, 935–1200	China conquers Nam Viet Early states: Funan, Champa Northern Vietnam free from China T'ang retake N. Vietnam, Sung let it go Pagan kingdom in Burma, 850–1280s	Jesus Christ Roman Empire-Mediterranean and Western Europe Fall of Rome by 410 Muhammed 570–632 Abbasid Caliphate Byzantine Empire Charlemagne, 768–814
1000	Mongol conquest, Yuan dynasty, 1279–1368 Ming, 1368–1644 Cheng Ho's fleets Water Margins, Golden Lotus	Mongol conquest of Korea; Yi, 1392–1910 Kamakura in Japan 1185–1333 Ashikaga 1336–1580 Nobunaga and Hideyoshi	Ankor Thom and Wat, c. 900–c. 1200; Khmer glory and decline Rise of Thai state Borobodur, Sri Vijaya Majapahit, 800–1400	Mayas in Central America Aztecs in Mexico Crusades, 1096–1204 Tamerlane 1136–1405 Incas in Peru Ottoman Empire-Suleiman 1495–1566 W. Renaissance 14th–16th centuries Copernicus, Galileo, Michelangelo

Time Chart

	China	Korea-Japan	Southeast Asia	Other Civilizations
1500	Ming in Decline Manchu Conquest 1644, Ch'ing dynasty, 1644–1911 K'ang Hsi, 1662–1722	Hideyoshi's invasion of Korea Tokugawa, 1600–1868 Expulsion of foreigners Rise of Edo and merchant culture	Southward expansion of Vietnamese Portuguese trade and bases Rise of Dutch power Spanish Philippines, 1521 (1565)–1898 and Spanish America	Rise of the English state Elizabeth I d. 1603 Shakespeare 1564–1616 Louis XIV r. 1669–1715 Peter the Great of Russia, 1672–1725
1700	*Dream of Red Chamber* Ch'ien Lung, 1736–1799 Macartney Mission, 1793 White Lotus Rebellion	Nagasaki as "window on the world" Daimyo hostages at and visits to Edo	New Toungoo state in Burma, 1635–1732 Chakrit dynasty in Siam, from 1782 Further rise of merchants Vietnamese control the South	J. S. Bach, d. 1750 American Revolution Mozart, d. 1791 French Revolution and Napoleon Dutch control Java
1800	Opium in, silver out Amherst mission "Opium War" 1839–1842 Taiping Rebellion, 1850–1865 T'ung Chih Restoration, arsenals French war, 1885 Japan defeats China The 100 Days and the Boxer Rebellion	Tokugawa system under threat Perry to Tokyo Bay, 1853 Meiji Restoration, 1868; rise of Tokyo Japanese industrialization and imperialism in Korea and Taiwan Korea a "protectorate" "Unequal Treaties" end	Penang founded 1786 Singapore founded 1819 1st Burmese war "Culture System" in Java 2nd Burmese war "Unequal Treaties" in Siam French take South Vietnam in 1862, and North in 1885 3rd Burmese war; Dutch take Sumatra and Bali U.S. takes the Philippines	U.S. War of 1812 Waterloo, 1815 Reform Bills in England Abortive revolutions of 1848 in Europe Latin American independence The West enters Africa; U.S. Civil War; German and Italian unification
1900	1911 Revolution Yuan Shih-k'ai and warlords, May 4, 1919 Kuomintang Nanking, 1927–1937; Japan invades Rise of CCP and Civil War The Cold War P.R.C. 1949	Defeat of Russia 1905 Shantung and 21 Demands Rule of Korea and Manchuria; the "China Incident" The Dark Valley Defeat and regrowth	U.S. crushes Philippine "rebels" Rise of nationalism in Burma, Vietnam, Indonesia; Philippine collaboration Ho Chih Minh, Sukarno, Pearl Harbor, 1941 Japanese conquest Independence	Boer War World War I Russian Revolution World depression World War II Korea independent, and at war Manuel Quezon Vietnam War

CHAPTER 1

EAST ASIA: COMMON GROUND AND REGIONAL DIFFERENCES

T he people of East Asia: Chinese, Koreans, Vietnamese, and Japanese, are all closely similar physically. There are some clear physical subtypes within each national population, especially the larger ones of China and Japan, but a random individual might belong to or be mistaken for any of the four. East Asians call themselves "the black haired people," and they share a basic set of other so-called Mongoloid physical characteristics, including what is known as the Mongolian fold around fleshy, narrow eyelids, relatively short limbs, high cheekbones, limited body and facial hair, straight black head hair, flat faces, dark colored eyes, short broad noses, light tan or coffee colored skin, and until recent dietary changes, relatively small stature on average. Each national subgroup is identified mainly by cultural clues: language, of course, but also clothing, gait, hairstyle, and manner. Chinese and Japanese, and to a lesser extent Koreans and Vietnamese, are all racially mixed, China most of all, composed of many originally separate groups which have long intermarried and merged; there is no such thing as a Chinese, Japanese, Korean, or Vietnamese "race."

The Korean language is related to Japanese, suggesting a common origin of both peoples somewhere in northeast Asia, but the connection is far short of mutual intelligibility. Vietnamese is distantly related to Chinese, but spoken Chinese and Japanese are unrelated apart from the many Chinese loan words which have entered Japanese and Korean in the course of long cultural borrowing. East Asia is thus rather like Europe, a population of basically similar physical makeup (where a German or even a Swede may still be mistaken for an Italian or Spaniard despite their respective physical norms), but divided by regional, cultural, and linguistic differences within an overall European mode. Like premodern Europe with its dependence on Latin as the international language of learning and diplomacy and suggesting in both cases an underlying cultural unity, all of East Asia adopted the Chinese system of writing and thus developed a fabric of common culture and communication, the medium through which each area acquired Chinese civilization.

Koreans referred to themselves as Younger Brother to Elder Brother China; Vietnamese and Japanese attitudes were similar in their enthusiastic adoption of nearly all aspects of Chinese culture, like the Koreans. China achieved a highly successful model of civilization early, and it was understandable that in time the rest of East Asia should want to follow the Chinese example. China was rich, powerful, and culturally sophisticated, far in advance of the other areas; to them it made sense to transplant that model to their own home bases, roughly as soon as they were aware of what was happening in China. Korea and Vietnam, right next door, and both incorporated for a time in the expansion of the Chinese empire from the third century B.C. to the third century A.D., were first to remake their cultures along Chinese lines. Japan, isolated by its insularity and by a difficult sea passage, was slower to develop on its own and got only some faint echoes from the Chinese mainland until the eighth century A.D. when under the first effective Japanese political order, a major effort accompanied by successive missions

1

to China brought to Japan the full flood of classical Chinese civilization.

China, as by far the largest unit, bigger than all of Europe or the United States, contains accordingly the greatest regional differences, including the originally separate cultures of Fukien (Fujian) and Kwangtung (Guangdong) provinces plus the still separate cultures of Tibet, Sinkiang (Xinjiang), and Inner Mongolia, and the many small islands of surviving earlier cultures in the south. Most of China's provinces are on the scale of European states, and each has developed its own regional culture, at least as different as, for example, Maine, Alabama, Texas, or California, but with greater regional speech differences. Not only the Chinese written language but a standard form of spoken Chinese became universal, as an accompaniment of empire; indeed the national form of spoken Chinese was long called *kuan-hua* ("official speech"), the language in which officials communicated. What were once separate languages, especially Cantonese and Fukienese (Fujianese, or Min), still exist and are spoken at home, but in all areas education has long been in the national language and there are few who do not know it. Cantonese especially has lost much of its original separateness through long integration within the national whole, and nearly all of its words are derived from standard spoken Chinese, though pronounced differently; the same is true to a lesser degree of Fukienese. Standard spoken Chinese, sometimes called Mandarin (from the Portuguese word for official), is thus common to the whole country, though regional dialects and regional cultures persist.

Boundaries and the Home Base

East Asia as a whole, beginning with China, is set off from the rest of the world by high mountains (including the Himalayas and Pamirs) on the west and northwest and by the steppe-desert of Mongolia on the north, with the Great Khingan (Tajingan) Range enclosing Manchuria on the northeast. Korea is an obvious subunit as a peninsula walled off from Manchuria by the Chang Pai Shan (Long White or Snowy Mountains) and the gorge of the Yalu River. There is easy access from South China to Vietnam, but it in turn is separated from the rest of the Indo-Chinese Peninsula by mountains. Japan's separateness as an island is obvious, but to the east stretches a huge and largely empty ocean, until recently also a barrier. It was understandable that the culture which evolved in Japan should see itself as part of greater East Asia, relating first and most closely to nearby Korea and then through Korea to China, for the Japanese the source of civilization.

This total area as a whole, the warm and generally moist fringe of Monsoon Asia, contains the largest area of high-productivity agricultural land in the world. Agriculture was the source of wealth which fueled Chinese civilization and provided the surplus which supported imperial government and sophisticated culture. It was as agricultural techniques spread from China to the rest of East Asia that Chinese-style culture developed there, together with originally Chinese attitudes about the land and about human relationships to it. In this view, nature had been generous, or as the Chinese said, benevolent, in providing the potential for productive agriculture: a permissive climate of long growing season and generally adequate rains, broad plains, and great river valleys of fertile alluvial soil. East Asians came to see their realm as a favored part of the world, free of the extremes they observed or heard about to the west, north, and south beyond the mountain and desert barriers: too cold, too dry, or too hot and jungly. It was understandable to them that the people of these areas seemed far less highly developed than themselves, most of them preliterate, not yet working metals or building cities, and living as nomads or hunters. To the Chinese especially, who had their own experiences with nomadic groups on their western and northern frontiers, their own domain, the gift of a beneficent "heaven," was clearly the best, where all things were in proper balance.

They called their country the Middle Kingdom, meaning not only geographically central (as all cultures see themselves, in the center of the map), but a place which followed the middle path between the extremes which surrounded them: an Aristotelian Golden Mean. As they saw it, the environment, and hence cultures, deteriorated rapidly as one left this center, and entered frigid Siberia, desert central Asia, or hot steamy Southeast Asia. They had limited knowledge of what lay immediately beyond their mountain barriers to the west, but knew little or nothing about India or the lands beyond it. In their experience, beyond those barriers it was all "barbarism," a perception which of course strengthened their conviction of their own unique superiority. This vision of the world as they knew it might be represented diagrammatically as follows:

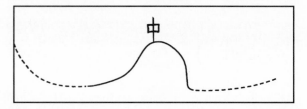

中 is the Chinese character meaning middle or central, and the dashed lines show the ascending curve of "civilization" which the Chinese might have found if they had persisted in their westward probings. The curve is intended to show the level of civilization, peaking in China as the apogee and falling off rapidly beyond the borders of East Asia as the physical conditions deteriorated. Koreans, Vietnamese, and Japanese inherited and shared this view. East Asia was seen in effect as an Eden, a fertile womb sheltered from and more favored than the rest of the harsher world. One of the worst punishments was banishment. Within this protected home base, the Chinese developed by far the most productive agricultural system in the world. Its productivity was the principal basis of China's prosperity, with a level of material well-being far ahead of the rest of the world until some time in the last century, and a technological and cultural level to match it, all supervised by a vast imperial bureaucracy held together by a network of imperial roads and canals and by the medium of the written language.

From all of this grew the Chinese, and subsequently East Asian, attitude toward nature, as something to be cherished and made more fruitful through human effort. Nature was not seen as enemy or object, as in the modern West, nor were people seen as the most important part of the cosmos, but as a small and lesser part of creation compared with the great forces of nature. It was both philosophically and practically necessary for people to adjust to nature rather than to try to fight against it, and to embellish it. It was an attitude which encouraged stewardship of the land rather than its exploitation or despoliation, but unfortunately it did not prevent the progressive deforestation of most of China as population increased. It was done to make room for agriculture, and the rationalization was that it made the earth more productive, but the cumulative consequences were catastrophic, in the form of massive erosion, siltation of streams and irrigation works, drying up of wells, and increased flooding. As long as removal of tree cover made way for agriculture it was considered all right, despite early and repeated warnings from the more far-sighted of the dangers of deforestation. By comparison, mining, robbing earth's body, digging holes in it to extract minerals, was looked down on and those who engaged in it viewed almost as criminals, ostracized from the rest of society.

Attitudes Toward Nature

These admiring or loving attitudes toward nature were of course the views of the literate elite, who left a written (or painted) record (of which more below), whereas it was peasants, the overwhelming majority of the population, who did the work and who to us now are voiceless. But to a considerable extent, peasants echoed the attitudes of the elite and certainly they practiced careful

stewardship of the land; although their circumstances meant that they often had cause to see the forces of nature as something other than benevolent, in general they acknowledged that it was more powerful, and more to be admired, or propitiated, than themselves or than humans as a whole. Where the elite built pavilions in scenic spots for the viewing of nature, the peasants built local shrines to the earth god, made of clay and straw from their fields and decorated from time to time with new paper clothing for the small god figures inside the shrine, to whom offerings of food and flowers were made when times were good and to help ensure good harvest to come. Chinese, Korean, and Japanese painting and poetry are justly famous for their loving portrayal of nature, again an elite matter but one which can still speak to us and which marks the distinctive East Asian character. Here is the Tang dynasty poet Li Po (Li Bo, A.D. 701–762):

If you were to ask me why I dwell among green
    mountains,
I should laugh silently; my soul is serene.
The peach blossom follows the moving water;
There is another heaven and earth beyond the
    world of man.[1]

And here is the painter Kuo Hsi (c. 1020–c. 1090):

Why does a virtuous man take delight in landscape? It is for these reasons: that in a rustic retreat he may nourish his nature; that amid the carefree play of streams and rocks, he may take delight; that he may constantly meet in the country fishermen, woodcutters, and hermits, and see the soaring of the cranes and hear the crying of the monkeys. The din of the dusty world and the locked-in-ness of human habitations are what human nature habitually abhors; while on the contrary haze, mist and the haunting spirits of the mountains are what human nature seeks, and yet can rarely find.[2]

Painting and poetry were different versions of the same view of nature, and indeed from Sung times (tenth century) most poets were also painters and vice versa, while most also, as members of the educated elite, served as officials. Poets and painters urged readers-viewers to lose themselves in the greater world of nature, emptying their minds of the comparatively petty concerns and busyness of the human world. Mountains, where the human imprint was least and nature best preserved, were the places to seek wisdom, and understanding of the cosmos and the human place in it. There the sages lived, as so often shown in paintings, which emphasized untrammelled nature, with a human figure shown, if at all, as a tiny woodcutter, a fisherman, a lone figure leading an ox, or a sage-hermit in his small rustic shelter by a stream near the base of a mountain. The implication was clear: that nature was grander and more important than people, and that human society should seek peace and wisdom from contemplating nature. The bulk of imperial administration was devoted to the care of agriculture, directly or indirectly, and agriculture was the support of state and society to a greater degree than in any other civilized tradition since ancient Egypt. The emperor's most important ceremonial functions were the yearly rites at the Temple of Heaven in the capital, where he ploughed a ritual furrow and interceded with heaven for good harvests. To question or attack nature was to contradict the broader order of the cosmos, and this was particularly disturbing to the profoundly hierarchical social order of East Asia.

Agriculture

As pointed out, none of this prevented people from remaking their environment, probably on a greater scale than in any other part of the world. This involved not only removal of most of the forest but the transformation of the landscape for the growing of wet (irrigated)

rice. Rice as a crop plant probably spread into China from adjacent Vietnam long before the historical era, but as it proved to be highly productive it came to be the dominant crop of south China and of better watered parts of the north, from which it was spread first to Korea and then to Japan. The rice strains originally diffused to China were suited to a warm tropical climate, but as rice moved north other strains were developed which tolerated cold better. Much of this adaptation may have taken place in north China and Korea before rice spread to Japan, but the resulting variety of rice is still called *Japonica*, and indeed the Japanese more recently have achieved the world's highest rice yields.

Rice is however a demanding crop, especially in its water requirements as an originally aquatic plant first cultivated somewhere in the Indo-Chinese Peninsula. It is grown from seed in specially prepared beds and then transplanted by hand with much backbreaking labor and laid out in rows in equally carefully worked flooded fields which have first been ploughed and then stirred and worked after the water has been let in, usually by driving a water buffalo through. The buffalo's hooves "puddle" (compact) the mixture so that the water will not percolate out, to produce a fine muddy

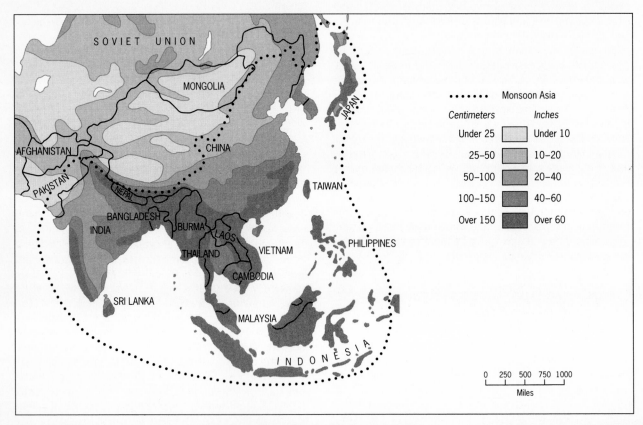

Precipitation in Monsoon Asia

mixture the consistency of thick cream. As the rice plant grows, the water level is artificially raised and then drained in the few weeks before harvest so as to hasten the ripening of the grain heads. Throughout the growing season, the rice is meticulously weeded and fertilized, primarily until very recently with aged human manure or "night soil," as the Western missionaries called it, all by hand. The irrigation systems which fed the rice fields, or paddies, were complex achievements of engineering, but they also required huge amounts of labor, to build and to maintain. Elsewhere, in drier or hillier areas, other crops were more important, mainly wheat, millet, and kaoliang (a form of sorghum), all resistant to drought. But they too were cultivated with intensive hand labor.

It was an agricultural system ideally suited not only to East Asia's climate, soils, and plains but to its large and growing supply of peasant labor. Yields rose with population, as more and more labor was available to increase the intensiveness of cultivation; more people of course produced more night soil, which also helped to raise yields. Increased production (including that from newly cleared land as population rose) supported and probably encouraged the slow rise of population—until late in the day, somewhere around the end of the eighteenth century A.D., when further increases in output were not possible in the absence of new technology such as chemical fertilizers, improved crop strains, and dams and power-driven pumps—the West's achievement in the nineteenth and twentieth centuries. Accordingly the level of material well-being began to fall, slowly at first and then more rapidly in the course of the nineteenth century. Japan escaped from this Malthusian trap by modernizing its entire system after 1869, eagerly seeking Western technological advances in all fields. But the rest of East Asia grew successively poorer and was wracked by famines, rebellions, and ultimately revolutions. Nevertheless, for over 2,000 years East Asian agriculture, like the rest of its civilization, led the world and provided the basis for cultural greatness.

China was fortunate in its extensive plains, as in eastern north China (the flood plain of the Yellow River) and the lower half of the Yangtze (Yangzi) valley, but as population rose cultivation was pushed beyond them onto first gentle slopes and then increasingly steep ones, especially in the hilly or mountainous south as Chinese occupation spread there from the north. Since rice yielded more calories per acre than any other crop then known in East Asia, especially when given the kind of care described above, artificially leveled fields had to be constructed out of the slopes in the form of walled terraces, each provided with water from higher up the slope. The same laborious technique was used in the hilly areas of Vietnam, Korea, and Japan. Next to deforestation and its consequences, terracing has altered the original environment most. Both basically resulted from growing population pressure, and both violated the philosophical regard for nature, but both made it possible to support the world's largest population mass.

Wet rice agriculture, with its heavy applications of night soil and other organic materials such as mud dredged from stream and canal bottoms and crop residues, even house floors with their accumulation of human and animal droppings, was in fact a remarkably stable system. The same fields were able to produce the same crop, and in southern areas two or even three crops a year, for more than 2,000 years and nevertheless to maintain or increase yields over time as growing population totals promoted more intensive cultivation and fertilization. Night soil can be a carrier of disease, but the common practice of aging it in prepared pits in each peasant household, to let the excess nitrogen pass off so as not to burn the plants, produced high temperatures and fermentation which killed most disease germs. From the nineteenth century, many Western observers commented on the concentric rings of heavier crops around the cities and towns, proportional to their populations but limited in radius to about thirty miles for the larger cities and where bulk water transport was available, as it necessarily was for most big cities in order to supply them with food.

Lowland plains and river valleys, especially the deltas of rivers with their rich alluvial soil, still support uniquely high population densities, whereas the mountain areas, which cover most of Vietnam, Korea, and Japan, and well over half of China, remain thinly settled or almost empty, especially where any form of agriculture was impossible or at best marginal. The modern population map shows similar low densities in the drier areas around the western and northern fringes of China, where, until recently, permanent field agriculture was largely absent and the non-Chinese inhabitants supported themselves mainly by the nomadic herding of sheep, plus some irrigated farming in the scattered oases. Chinese civilization has always rested on agriculture. Where that was not possible, Chinese settlement did not spread and the land was occupied by other peoples and cultures, although in the present century Chinese political control of these outer areas and new technology for irrigation and railways has been accompanied by large-scale movement of Chinese people into the steppe-desert margins and into alpine Tibet. In some of the hill and mountain parts of all four countries, shifting cultivation, or slash-and-burn agriculture, was until recently practiced, using the thin poor mountain soils to produce a quick crop for a year or two, nourished by the ash from burning the tree and bush cover; but it was never able to support more than a few people, who supplemented their diet by hunting and gathering in the remaining forest.

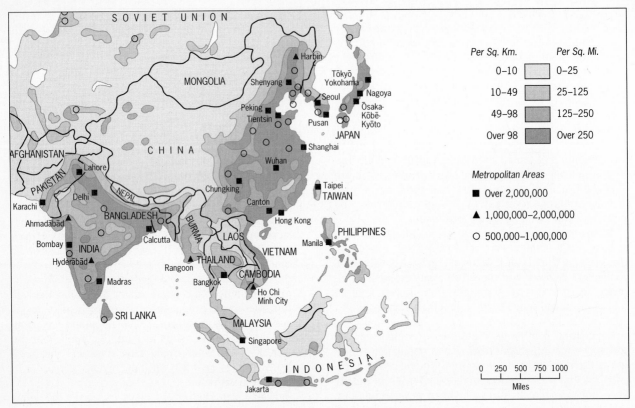

Population Density, Monsoon Asia

In general terms, the East Asian environment was potentially munificent, but especially for wet rice farming it required much organized labor in irrigation, cultivation, and fertilization to make it productive. On the other hand, it repaid these efforts handsomely, with the highest yields in the world. China especially is subject to periodic drought in the north and northwest, something which also happens from time to time in the other parts of East Asia; irrigation, which raised yields in any case, was thus essential. The population tended to increase up to the limit which could be fed by agriculture under optimum conditions; since conditions fell short of optimum periodically in many areas, efforts were made to protect the system against bad years. These were often not sufficient, again especially in north and northwest China, and there were periodic famines, as there were everywhere in the world, and for the same reasons, until the nineteenth century and the coming of the railways in the West. Famine, like drought or flooding, is rarely more than local or at most regional; when crops failed in a given area, people starved because there were inadequate means to move a bulky, heavy commodity like grain from surplus to deficit areas. The state did what it could to distribute grain in famine areas, but lacked the means to cope with major crop failures and consequent suffering.

Rules for Society

Recurrent natural disasters increased peoples' awareness of the power of nature and the puniness of human ability to do much about it. To a degree, peasants, the great majority, reflected elite attitudes toward the natural world and stressed the need to listen and adjust to nature. Confucius (c.551–c.479 B.C.) reflects this in the chief Confucian text, the *Analects*, which describes how moral laws for humans reflect the heavenly order which governs the universe, the movement of the heavenly bodies, and the progression of the seasons. Moral laws, says Confucius,

form the same system with the laws by which all created things are produced and develop each in its order without injuring one another; the operations of nature take

Rice paddies in south-central Thailand. This is typical of warm, wet Asia and of its great river valleys and plains, highly productive agriculturally. (Standard Oil of New Jersey)

South China landscape. This agricultural scene is typical of much of monsoon Asia, where the principal crop is irrigated rice. The rice is grown in fields (paddies) that are finely engineered to hold water within their low embankments, letting it trickle down from higher up the slope to each paddy in turn for constant irrigation. The water level is raised as the crops grow, and then is drained in the few weeks before harvest. The gentler hillsides are terraced, as in this picture, to create a staircase of nearly level irrigated fields. The heavy labor required to maintain this system is repaid by high crop yields. (R. Murphey)

their course without conflict or confusion, the lesser forces flowing everywhere like river currents, while the great forces of creation go silently and steadily on. It is this—one system running through all—that makes the universe so grand and impressive.[3]

East Asians believed that as the universe ran by rules, so should human society. But this conviction was based also on practicality; rules for the conduct of everyone, according to his or her station in life, were thought to be essential to prevent chaos and ensure the Confucian goal of "harmony." This is a very different conception from the Western and especially American view, which emphasizes instead what is loosely called "liberty" or "freedom" and glorifies the individual and freedom of action. The American revolutionaries proudly printed on their banners "Don't Tread on Me," and later generations sang "Don't fence me in," and individualism and competition remain hallmarks of American society.

But in East Asia, absence of rules was seen as producing chaos. There is no word in any of their languages for our concept of "freedom"; the closest equivalent means simply "no rules," and it was understood that this is bad for everybody, leading to gross disorder,

Terraced fields in Szechuan (Sichuan), China. This is typical of the less mountainous areas of south China, with irrigated paddies spread over a gentle slope, here flooded for planting. (Hsueh Tse-chiang)

what the Chinese call *luan*, the most feared of all social catastrophes since everyone suffers from it. In East Asia, individuals prospered or suffered only as members of a group: family most of all, and beyond it clan or lineage (larger kinship networks), village or district, and the wider community of the state, or in modern times the work unit or company (employer), and in Communist China until recently, the Party. Pursuit of individual goals, ambitions, or competition was seen as selfish and disruptive (which of course it often may be), whereas working together the group has great collective power and is best able to further the interest of individuals as group members.

As a traditional Chinese saying has it, "The acknowledgement of limits leads to happiness." One must admit that this still contains much universal wisdom. The group provides help for those who need it, as a kind of mutual benefit and insurance society, and serves also as an advocate for group interests. To East Asians, this has always seemed eminently reasonable, even though the price is the subservience of individual to group interest and the lack of individual freedom. Sons are subject to their fathers and elder brothers, daughters to their mothers (and after marriage to their mothers-in-law), wives to husbands, and all to the eldest male, usually a grandfather, although his place may be taken after his death by a grandmother. Age is given great respect, and males still dominate East Asian society, although their dominance is slowly being somewhat reduced in recent years. The strict hierarchical, rank-ordered nature of East Asian society is easily critized by modern Westerners, but it did serve to minimize conflicts. People accepted their status and did not in general try to challenge the system.

Beyond the immediate family, traditionally three generations living together—parents, children, and surviving grandparents—was the wider network of clan, lineage, and village or district, within which each individual had an agreed place, owing subservience or wielding authority, depending on status. Kin relations were uppermost and were designated in far greater detail than in the West and were far more important, for example, paternal and maternal uncles, a long string of cousins, and others genetically more distant as well as those related only by marriage. Marriage was in fact primarily a contract between families whereby each gained an additional set of family members on whom to depend, to increase the resources of the group. Within kin networks, all were responsible for the behavior of other members, just as all benefited or took pride in individual achievements. If a member of this extended family committed a crime, all members were liable, and often punished, while shameful behavior of other sorts brought shame on all. This form of collective responsibility was in fact a major deterrent to crime or to any socially deviant behavior, as it still is. Indeed East Asian societies still have by far the lowest crime rates in the world, and collective responsibility is often given as the major reason.

The other side of the coin is the glory or benefit earned by individuals which the other members of the group share. This helps to explain, for example, the efforts made within families to promote the education of their children, especially sons, which helps importantly to account for the strikingly greater educational success of East Asian children by comparison with their American peers, as recent studies have shown. In East Asia, education is a family enterprise, and rests also on the conviction that education and learning are by far the best avenues to worldly success as well as to social prestige as they always have been, achievements in which the family shares. Traditionally in China, whole villages or small towns would pool resources to support a promising local boy through the long hard discipline of learning the classics so as to pass the imperial examinations and get the chance to become an official, an accomplishment which could be of great material benefit to his home area as well as shedding glory on it. One can still see memorials erected in the approaches to such places celebrating some local boy who made good. Group effort and its collective power had much to do with the outstanding success of East Asian societies in the past, and goes a long way to explain their achievements in the modern world, where Japan and China are now the second and third largest economies in the world and where China, South Korea, Taiwan, and Hong Kong lead the world in economic growth rates. Japan rose to industrial and technological leadership in the postwar world, with the highest growth rates in history up to that time, in large part as a result of the power of group effort.

The price paid, especially from the Western point of view, is the lack of much individual freedom, and the hierarchical ordering of society which kept most individuals subservient to others. Individual East Asians have always been assigned to well-defined status groups, each with its place in the pecking order. One can observe this at work in the Japanese custom of bowing when meeting anyone; if you look carefully, you can see that one of the two bows lower than the other, acknowledging the latter's superior status, based on gender, age, and position in life. The notion that some people or status groups are somehow superior to others goes back to the early years of Chinese civilization and to Confucius, not an innovator but a codifier of what he saw as the values of traditional society. He stressed the importance of good example, to be set by the "superior" men, and believed that such model behavior would be followed by the lesser orders and would insure social harmony. As he put it in the *Analects*, "If the lord does not behave as a lord should, the subject does not have to behave as a subject should." The lowest groups in the hierarchy, notably nearly all women, including new brides subject to their mothers-in-law and husbands, daughters, and younger sons, suffered under this system as recorded, although only partially, in surviving literature.

The Confucian-East Asian ethic supported thus what seems to us rank injustice and certainly inequality, but it also expected those at the top of the order—fathers, elder brothers, and particularly officials—to act responsibly and "benevolently." As for those in official posts, or those who were educated and literate from whom officials were selected, it was a top-heavy system. The educated group, known in China as the gentry, probably numbered at most about 2 percent of the population. A saving grace is that gentry status could not be inherited and could be won only through passing the first stage of the imperial examinations, while officials were chosen from those who had passed the third stage. For gentry and for those in authority, including fathers, the Confucian stress was on responsibility rather than power; high status brought with it a heavy obligation, to set a good example to those below and to be sensitive to the needs of others. Of course it never worked perfectly, and, especially before the Sung but at every period, hereditary aristocrats and military leaders often dominated society. But the force of the education system, primarily moral, was considerable. The same system spread to Vietnam, Korea, and Japan, with each country modifying the Chinese original to some degree to suit their own originally separate cultures and preferences.

One way to measure its success, despite what seem to us to be its flaws, is the long centuries through which it lasted and was reconfirmed each time there was a break in the political order and the opportunity for basic change, as at the fall of each Chinese dynasty. The basic Confucian system was never successfully challenged or altered, until the whole fabric of society began to fall apart in the last half of the nineteenth century, after 2,500 years or more during which it provided the basic cement of society and a set of values by which most people lived. Traditional East Asia was a brilliant success, even if only in worldly terms, and on the whole society ran relatively smoothly most of the time despite the strains within it, as within any social system. All societies try to strike some working balance between power or authority and justice or responsibility, between controls and human welfare, and to guard against abuses, which seem to come almost automatically with power. The Confucian solution was to humanize or educate the holders of power by imbuing them with a moral sense of responsibility. One must acknowledge that it worked at least as well as other systems, such as our own, in ensuring human welfare and checking the corruption of power. Like Plato in classical Greece, Confucians in East Asia believed that, in Plato's phrase, "Education makes good men, and good men act nobly." They were certainly more successful than Plato or his descendants in achieving social harmony, most of the time for over two millennia.

Village and Town

The primacy of the group and the virtues of collective effort were probably related to the basic place of agriculture in the East Asian system and the pressing need for joint efforts and cooperation, especially in the construction and maintenance of the irrigation systems which were so essential. People also lived very closely together, gathered in villages rather than in separate farmsteads as in the West. This was more practical in East Asia since the fields were small and tended to be grouped around each village within an easy walk each day. They could be small and still support a family or a village of some 30–60 families because the highly intensive cultivation system produced very high yields. There was thus little scope for individual enterprise, or departure from group norms, virtually no alternative avenues, and no individual privacy, given the high population densities in the agricultural areas where nearly all people lived. One was rarely out of sight or sound of other people. This further underlined the need for rules. Six or eight neighboring villages would be linked through a rotating market system, meeting in each village in turn and then repeating the cycle. There and in the market town within one or two hours' walk of nearly every village, peasants could exchange their produce and buy some goods from outside (if they did not make

them in their local area), such as salt, iron tools, cotton cloth, matches (a Chinese invention), or wood. There was often a scribe to read and write for the illiterate, the majority of peasants, and a tea house where those who came to market could relax and exchange gossip.

Most people lived and died within that small village world and never traveled farther than the few miles involved or saw a city. In some market towns there might be a traveling troupe of actors, singers, musicians, or jugglers, who provided most of the few amusements available to peasants. It was also within this village market network that most families sought marriage partners for their sons or daughters, who commonly could not be chosen from the family's own village, where often most people had the same surname and genetic relationships were close. The cities, and most of all the capital, offered a wider world, and it was there and in some of the market towns that the gentry lived as well as the officials, garrison troops, artisans, laborers, shopkeepers, merchants, and the other components of any urban place. There was in fact a good deal of interurban and interprovincial trade and long-distance shipment of rice, salt, wood, metals, cloth, tea, silk, and other goods for the supply of urban populations and their elite. Domestic trade was larger in volume than in Europe until the nineteenth century, and overseas trade, within East Asia, was also large, but it and the merchants who managed it were dwarfed in size by the huge bulk of the agrarian economy. This was largely locally self-sufficient on a subsistence basis except for commercial production near the cities for the urban market, although it did have to pay taxes, largely to maintain the imperial system. That in turn derived its revenues overwhelmingly from the land tax, borne by peasants and small landlords.

Most land was worked by peasant owners, although they might rent some additional land, and the rate of tenancy was relatively low. The average holding was small—something like four or five acres (less in more productive areas, more in others)—and most landlords did not accumulate large blocks of land but survived on the rents from 10 or 20 acres. Leisure was scarce, but highly valued, and when a family, by good luck and good management, acquired enough land to live on the rents, it tended to welcome the chance to enjoy leisure and to pursue the finer arts of living rather than to continue to maximize income. The enjoyment of leisure was indeed developed to a fine art, much celebrated by poets and philosophers, in sharp contrast to the modern West, which the English historian R. H. Tawney labeled "the acquisitive society." For East Asians, life was to be enjoyed, and work (for the fortunate) minimized. Family, food, festivals, and self-cultivation for the elite, were more important than the pursuit of material gain. The gentry wore the long blue scholar's gowns and often let

Lowland Taiwan: intensive hand labor in the permissive climate of warm, wet Asia. Rice, the most productive crop of Asia, is commonly weeded laboriously by hand, as these two are doing. The effort is repaid by very high yields. (Joint Commission for Rural Reconstruction)

their fingernails grow long, in both cases to signal that they did not do manual labor and could spend their time reading, painting, writing poetry, and contemplating the beauties of nature.

There was little fundamental change in this East Asian world for some 2000 years, by comparison with the sweeping changes taking place in the West: the rise and fall of the Roman order, the medieval system which succeeded it, the rise of trade and towns, the blossoming of the Renaissance, and then the scientific, commercial, industrial, and urban revolutions which produced the modern West. East Asians tended to distrust change as disruptive (which it clearly is) and as something which did not necessarily offer an improvement on things as they were. East Asia already led the world, and technical, material, and cultural levels were high. People tended to value the past and reaffirmed its values rather than looking to the future. Agricultural success depended, as everywhere, on close attention to nature and to the example of those who had gone before or who had long experience. Innovation was not seen as a promising way to go. In larger terms, individuals and

groups prospered by working within the system rather than by attempting to challenge or alter it; those who attempted to rock the boat or to change the rules were criticized or ignored, and the glorious past, especially of Chinese civilization, was seen as a golden age which successive generations sought to emulate.

East-West Contrasts

There was nothing like the modern Western belief in "progress" and its orientation to the future. History and time were seen as operating in cycles, good periods and less good ones, corresponding to the political cycles which were so obvious, the rise and fall of dynasties and the periods of invasion or civil war followed by regrowth. Here too the model of nature was cited, as in this commentary on a classical text:

When the sun stands at midday it begins to set.
When the moon is full it begins to wane.

The fullness of heaven and earth wane and wax.
How much more true is this of men.[4]

Such attitudes were accompanied by respect for elders, and veneration of ancestors. The past was looked to as a guide to the present and future. Early in the development of Chinese civilization, ancestors were venerated, not exactly worshipped, but paid respect to in small household shrines where their name tablets were kept, and they were often prayed to for help or guidance. It was a very past-conscious society, with a lively sense of its own history and of its great tradition. Even for the mass of illiterates, there were more or less accurate versions of history in the form of operas and plays, nearly always with historical themes from the great past or telling the stories of famous generals or courtesans. R. H. Tawney tells of talking with peasants in the dark days of the 1930s and their response to his commiserating with them about the hard times and disorder which had overtaken China in their lifetimes. "Yes," they said, "the times are bad, but not as bad as at the fall of the Ming (the 1640s), or for that matter the fall of the Han (third century A.D.)[5]

The modern West followed a different course, actively pursuing change in the name of "progress," attacking nature to get at its secrets, and developing a new science and technology which in a century or two transformed Western society in the progression from steam and steel and railways to the internal combustion engine and nuclear power. East Asia did not make this leap, until the Japanese, impressed by new Western power, determined to replicate it for themselves in the last part of the nineteenth century. China, Korea, and Vietnam (the latter by then under French colonial rule) resisted such catastrophic change as disruptive of all their traditional values and moreover as something of despised "barbarian" origin, until their modern humiliation at the hands of the West and Japan drove them finally to pursue fundamental change. There were some echoes in the West to suggest that the mad rush of industrialization, accumulation, and "progress" was not an unmixed blessing, as in the novels of Charles Dickens, or the lines by Wordsworth, which might have been written by an East Asian:

> *The world is too much with us, late and soon;*
> *Getting and spending we lay waste our powers;*
> *Little we see in nature that is ours;*
> *We have given our lives away, a sordid boon.*

Most of us would now acknowledge that Wordsworth had a point, but industrialization, or "modernization" as it is often called, includes desirable as well as undesirable things and comes as a package, from which one cannot effectively pick and choose: anesthetics and slums, useful and harmful drugs, new wealth and new poverty, longer life expectancy and environmental deterioration. In any case, the positive aspects appeal strongly, especially to those societies which are still behind the West or Japan in these terms.

Their falling behind is a very recent matter, in the long span of East Asian history, something of the last two centuries only. Chinese science and technology have a long and distinguished history, as already indicated, and led the world until some time in the eighteenth century. Early Chinese theoretical inquiry into the nature of physical matter was not followed up consistently in later centuries, but a wide range of empirical discoveries continued to take place, including, for example, iron-shod plows by the sixth century B.C., observation of sunspots and development of cast iron by the fourth century B.C., iron suspension bridges by the first century A.D., use of petroleum and natural gas as fuel by the fourth century B.C., porcelain by the third century A.D., movable type printing by the eleventh century A.D., paper money and the mariner's compass by the ninth century A.D., understanding of the circulation of the blood by the sixth century B.C., inoculation against smallpox in the tenth century A.D., crossbows in the fourth century B.C., rockets in the eleventh century A.D., and guns soon thereafter, to name only a few from the long catalogue of Chinese firsts, all of them many centuries, some well over a thousand years, in advance of Europe. Each period could build on the discoveries of earlier ones, since the Chinese tradition was continuous and preserved records of findings made in the past.

Why such empirical development, or the earlier theoretical investigations, were not continued, or why China never produced an industrial revolution on its own, is one of the great questions of history. It may be more appropriate to ask why Europe did so—breaking with its own medieval tradition and pursuing abstract theory about many things not directly observable—than to ask why East Asia did not. Its human-centered world was perhaps more practical, and less interested in abstract theory. It also felt less need to pursue change or to explore the unknown, complacent in its existing prosperity and achievements. The reasons for Europe's scientific and industrial revolution are many and complex, including the prominence of its merchant group and the expansion of both internal and overseas trade, things which were far less proportionally prominent in East Asia.

The restless Western urge to dominate nature, since at least the time of the first chapter of the Book of Genesis where God directs man to "be fruitful and multiply and replenish the earth and subdue it and have dominion … over every living thing," was also probably part of the reason for Western persistence in, as they put it, "unlocking nature's secrets." East Asian sensitivity to nature may have slowed them down in such endeavors. Another thing which worked against the development of theoretical and experimental science in East Asia was the separation between scholars and artisans. In Europe, scientists like Galileo, who built a telescope and ground his own lenses, or Newton, who designed and conducted his own experiments, were both theoreticians and experimentalists. Theory is necessarily based on experimental evidence and develops as experimental data accumulate. In East Asia the thinkers were members of the elite, who scorned manual labor, while most of the artisans or craftsmen were at best only marginally literate, although they were often highly inventive. Indeed most of the achievements of East Asian technology were produced by such men, usually anonymously as they worked out practical problems. Thus Chinese metallurgists solved problems like the reduction-refining of nickel many centuries before their medieval European opposite numbers found this so difficult that they called the ore "Kupfernickel" ("the Devil's copper") because they thought the Devil's aid was necessary to work with it. Chinese craftsmen invented the wheelbarrow, the sternpost rudder, and watertight ship compartments.

China especially, as a huge country, is richly endowed with the mineral resources used in industrialization, and although the derogatory attitude toward mining as impiety may have affected elite behavior, it never prevented miners and craftsmen from extracting and working a great variety of metals. But the great leap from sophisticated practical technology to genuine science and its fruits which have so enriched the modern West never took place, despite what seem now some close approaches, as for example during the Sung dynasty (see Chapter 6).

The Confucian emphasis was strongly this-worldly, and had little interest in theoretical matters. It admired nature, praised it as a model, but accepted rather than questioned it. The metaphysical Taoists (Daoists), scorned by Confucianists, also used nature as a model but in time became involved in some experimental work in their development of alchemy and the search for an elixir of immortality, in the course of which they did make some useful (as well as lethal—e.g. ingestion of mercury) discoveries. Orthodox Confucian disapproval of Taoist alchemy and "magic" probably helped to discredit experimental work in general. What did survive was the importance attached to natural portents, and the pseudoscience of *feng-shui* ("wind and water") or geomancy. Any unusual natural event—earthquake, flood, eclipse, drought—was seen as a sign of heaven's displeasure, and a reminder for people, especially those in charge, to mend their ways; the emperor would often issue a penitential edict confessing his "lack of virtue" and asking heaven not to punish his people further. *Feng-shui* is still practiced in some areas, whereby buildings and graves are supposedly sited so as to conform to the natural forces or force lines represented by hills, water courses, and exposure to points of the compass. Portents and *feng-shui* appropriately suggest the immaturity of traditional Chinese science and in any case did not yield useful information. It was typical of the long Chinese experience that when astronomers, who had charted the movements of the heavenly bodies and observed eclipses since ancient times, noticed that their calculations were no longer accurate after some 2,000 years, they concluded that "the heavens were out of order" when they should have gone back to the drawing board.

The Traditional System

Personal morality rather than law was the foundation of society. That did not of course always ensure that everyone behaved morally, or that wealth and power for a few did not lead, as everywhere, to corruption and abuse. But for most people most of the time it did mean that society tried to minimize conflict, controlled by the all-powerful family system which settled most disputes and kept people in line. Officials had a fatherly relationship to those beneath them, and the emperor at the top played the role of father to all his subjects. There was no separate or independent middle class of merchants or professionals, so important in the emergence of the modern West. In East Asia, they were subordinate to or integrally incorporated within the state, as were the representatives of religion; there was no separate church power (except for a time in medieval Japan) and no other bases or institutions which could rival the state. The state did develop detailed law codes, primarily for criminal offenses, and magistrates at the local level, reviewed by higher courts at provincial and national levels, followed those procedures, but most cases did not reach the courts because the informal local, family, and lineage networks dealt with them. It was a closely knit system in which any deviance was discouraged or prevented, so much so that it has been called "the self-regulating society." Personal virtue or virtuous behavior as defined by Confucian ethics—honesty, integrity, loyalty, filiality (respect for one's parents), sincerity, and benevolence—were the norms for social conduct. Confucianism thus played some of the role of religion elsewhere (although it lacked a theology or doctrines about a life after death) as well as some of the role of Western law.

This system survived largely unchanged during periods of imperial disintegration and disunity or the change of dynasties, and although in periods of hardship there was understandably an increase in lawlessness, the traditional system emerged again. Presumably this was because it had proven to be successful, at least for the goals which were important to East Asians: social harmony, minimization of conflict, and material well-being through group effort. There was of course a wide gap between the rulers and the ruled. Society was traditionally divided into four ranked classes, with literate scholar-officials (or in Japan literate warrior-aristocrats who were also administrators) at the top, followed by farmers—the chief support of society, then artisans, and at the bottom merchants, who were seen as parasites producing nothing. Farther still down the rank order were soldiers (except in Japan), miners, vagrants, lepers—and of course foreigners. The derogation of merchants was to a large extent window dressing; merchants were numerous, wealthy, and often powerful, but they owed their position, especially the biggest ones, to their connections with officialdom. Most came from gentry or educated families, where one son might be an official while other sons managed the family estates, arbitrated local disputes, promoted local development projects, or taught the classics to the young. Many merchants were also in effect officials, managing state monopolies in the trade in metal, salt, or rice, or carrying out government transport contracts. Army generals, also usually from gentry families, might similarly rise to prominence.

One got ahead in East Asia by working within the system rather than by trying to buck it or to pursue a different course. Working from inside produced ample rewards. Elite families were rich enough to support large households and many sons as well as daughters, but most people, primarily peasants, had to limit their families to what they could support, and the average was only a little over two surviving children, whose families lived necessarily frugally in simple mud-walled and thatch-roofed houses of two or three rooms, often shared with domestic animals, while the timber and tile-roofed elite houses extended to many courtyards where sons and their families lived. Girls became members of their husbands' families at marriage, had no property or inheritance rights, and no status in their new families until they had produced a son. Wives and widows were expected to be chaste and not to remarry on their husbands' deaths, but husbands could take secondary wives and concubines into the household. This striking inequality derived from the basic patriarchal nature of the society whereby family name, all-important to East Asians, and its traditions and continuity descended only through the male line. Women were important primarily as breeders of sons, and were often rejected as wives when they did not produce a male heir. Family considerations dominated; East Asians have always arranged their names with family name first, by far the most important designation, and given names only after that.

The family was security, and there was none outside it. It was thus essential to produce sons, who could support their parents in old age, something the state never attempted and for which there were almost no other institutional provisions.

Regional Differences

The power of the Chinese empire, its wealth and numbers and technological superiority, led it to extend its control over adjacent areas which are as large as China Proper (east of alpine Tibet and desert Sinkiang [Xinjiang] and south of arid Mongolia and cold, dry Manchuria) but still within the outer mountain and desert barrier boundaries of East Asia. These areas were inhabited by other Mongoloid peoples (Tibetans, Mongols, Manchurians—but not the Turks of Sinkiang), whose cultures and languages were fundamentally different from China's. Most of Tibet is too high as well as too dry and cold for agriculture except in a few lower pockets. Traditionally the sparse economy rested mainly on nomadic herding of yaks, a woolly bovine adapted to Tibetan conditions. Tibetan culture was dominated by Lamaistic Buddhism, ruled as a theocracy by the Dalai Lama from his great palace in Lhasa, and as many as half of the adult male population lived as monks in monasteries. Tibet was incorporated into the Chinese empire relatively late, under the Ch'ing (Qing) dynasty in the eighteenth century, and more recently subjected to tighter Chinese control and some settlement of Chinese officials and professionals, but it remains a separate culture despite Chinese efforts to suppress Tibetan distinctiveness.

Sinkiang came under Chinese control much earlier, under the Han dynasty in the second century B.C., in part to protect the trade routes which ran through it from China, including the famous Silk Road, and in part to try to prevent raids on the Chinese settled areas by nomadic tribesmen. Until about the ninth century A.D., Sinkiang was settled predominantly by a fairer-skinned Indo-European people, some of whom were mounted nomads, some farmers in the scattered oases. Both groups were gradually displaced or succeeded by the spread of Turkish groups over almost all of Central Asia, probably originally from farther east, who since about the tenth century have dominated the area, with related Turkish groups as nomadic herders of sheep and goats and as oasis farmers. Since 1950 Chinese managers and settlers have become nearly half the population and built a major industrial sector. Mongolia is a classic steppe, too dry for permanent farming in most areas but with enough rain over most of it to support grass, which with its deep roots can tolerate long periods of drought.

Grass supported the Mongol economy based on the nomadic grazing of sheep and goats, or a tough hybrid of both which could withstand the bitterly cold winter and the hot dry summer and could convert the often sparse, tough pasturage into meat, milk, wool, and hides, which provided not only food but clothing and shelter in the form of the hemispherical tent or *yurt.*

Mongolia attracted Chinese attention at the beginning of the imperial period and as Chinese agricultural settlement spread into the arid northern margins of China Proper, where it was exposed to raids from a variety of steppe nomads. The Great Wall, originally a chain of walls, was built in an effort to keep these raiders out, and although it never worked for that purpose, it still serves as a rough line of demarcation between areas to the south where there is on average enough rainfall for farming without irrigation or outside support, and those to the north where conditions are too arid. The line, or zone, fluctuated with fluctuations in the climate, and there was movement across or through it from both sides, but there was no doubt in anyone's mind that two separate worlds faced each other across the steppe borders. The Mongols emerged as a clear group only under Chinghis (Genghis) Khan in the twelfth century A.D., but their earlier ancestors, with different tribal names, were almost equally effective with their military tactics against the vastly larger Chinese forces, which tried to prevent their raiding and even, unwisely, attempted to invade the steppe, where they and their supply trains were often wiped out by the mounted nomads' superior mobility.

Under Chinghis and his successors, a Mongol confederacy finally conquered China, along with most of the rest of Eurasia, but their rule in China lasted less than a century and their power rapidly declined thereafter. The rise of China in the present century has brought an avalanche of Chinese agricultural settlement into Inner Mongolia, where Chinese now outnumber Mongols by 20 to 1 and traditional Mongol culture is fast fading. Outer Mongolia, now an independent state and never firmly in the Chinese sphere, lies beyond the Gobi and Ordos deserts and is still mainly a herding economy, though now with some commercial and even some small industrial development. In Inner Mongolia, once again attached to the Chinese state, commercialization and industrialization are farther advanced, and irrigation with deep wells and powered pumps has largely displaced traditional nomadism with settled farming and commercial ranching, linked to the China market by rail and motor road.

Manchuria was the last of these outer areas to be settled by Chinese, mainly after about 1900 when the population first reached one million, subsequently mushrooming as immigrants from North China poured in. The moister and warmer southern part in the valley of the Liao River, where agriculture is possible, was Chinese from about the second century B.C. and was incorporated in the Chinese empire at about the same time, although the area had been settled earlier by Tungusic tribes. The rest of Manchuria was inhabited by a variety of non-Chinese people, hunter-gatherers and nomadic herders related to the peoples of Siberia and northeast Asia. A confederation of some of these groups emerged as the Manchus in the sixteenth century and went on to conquer China, where they established the long-lived Manchu or Ch'ing (Qing) dynasty, which ruled all of greater China from 1644 to 1911. As Ch'ing authority crumbled in the last years of the nineteenth century, waves of impoverished peasants from north China poured into Manchuria, averaging a million a year from 1900 to 1940, and rapidly became the overwhelming majority of its population. First under Japanese control from 1905 (de facto) to 1945 and since then once again as part of China, Manchuria, with its rich mineral resources, developed as the premier heavy industrial area of East Asia, as it still is, and also generated a highly productive commercial agricultural system whose exports helped to feed first Japan and then China.

From the beginnings of Chinese history there were tension and conflict between the agriculturists and their political orders of China Proper and the nomadic groups who occupied the steppe margins. Both cultures tended to despise each other. To the Chinese, the nomads were primitive savages, not literate, having no fixed habitations, and wandering about under no obvious control. To the nomads, the Chinese were slaves—to tax collectors, landlords, and officials, tied to the land and rarely going very far from it, and bound to a life of toil, grubbing in the soil. They glorified the freedom of the nomadic way of life, subjected to no masters, robbing the richer areas around them whenever they got the chance, and with the wide open steppe as their roving home. There really was no middle ground, no compromise between their positions, and no mutual tolerance. In armed conflict the nomads usually had the upper hand; their mounted warriors could strike swiftly and without warning and then retreat into the steppe before an adequate response could be prepared. When Chinese armies pursued them, the nomads were usually able to lead them far from their bases and then encircle them until they surrendered. It was a centuries-long shifting contest back and forth across the zone between their territories, but in the long run China's enormously greater numbers plus more modern firepower prevailed. The once fearsome Mongol power was finally put down for good in the nineteenth century, and Chinese settlement began to invade the steppe-desert borders, as already indicated, until in many areas the Chinese outnumbered the natives.

China Proper

China Proper, the roots and body of Chinese civilization, consists essentially of three great river valleys with their plains and deltas and their fringing hills and mountains: the Yellow (Huang) River in the north, the Yangtze (Yangzi) for central China, and the smaller basin of the West (Hsi or Xi) River in the south. Together they still hold the vast majority of China's population, most of its cities, industries, and trade routes, and most of its agricultural land. North China is a brown, semiarid land with long cold winters and extensive level plains in its eastern half. Rainfall decreases and winter temperatures drop in the western half, farther from the moderating influences of the sea, the source also of moisture. But equally important, the land rises into hills and mountains where agriculture is at a severe disadvantage, despite the general fertility of the soil. Most of north China is covered with a fine, wind-laid, calcareous alluvium called *loess*, which is almost inexhaustibly fertile as long as it gets some water, but in many years, especially in the western half, rainfall is precarious or inadequate. The Yellow River is so silted by centuries of erosion in its deforested watershed and so fluctuating in volume that it is mainly not navigable, but since 1950 a series of dams along its course have checked the previously disastrous flooding, generated electricity, and provided irrigation, mainly in its eastern half. Despite its problems of aridity, the Yellow River plain has long been China's largest area of dense population, the combined result of level land and fertile soil, although in the past this also meant periodic famines in poor rainfall years.

The Yangtze basin, where the main stream is fed by a series of tributaries from both north and south, drains half of China proper and has long been its chief commercial and urban area, aided by the river system which can move goods cheaply over the great distances in the basin, from the edge of the Tibetan massif to the river's mouth near Shanghai. The river's delta, from Nanking (Nanjing) to Hangchow (Hangzhou) to Shanghai, crisscrossed by an intricate network of canals, has for centuries been the most urbanized and commercialized part of the country, and the most densely settled on such a scale, supported by productive agriculture on the rich alluvial soils of the delta. Most of China's big cities have grown up along the big river. As in the north, the east is generally level and hence densely populated, while in the western half hills or mountains cover much of the landscape, with correspondingly lower population densities. The Red Basin of Szechuan (Sichuan) in the west, surrounded by mountains and with predominantly red, tropical soils which give the basin its name, looks mountainous internally on the map, but in fact contains many areas of moderate slope and has long been productively farmed and densely settled. Protected against the winter winds from the north and northwest, Szechuan enjoys a semitropical climate with accordingly high productivity. Its commercial sector is fed by several Yangtze tributaries as well as by the main stream, and the provincial name Szechuan means "Four Rivers."

South of the Yangtze watershed there are relatively few breaks in a jumbled mass of mountains, and as a result the West (Hsi or Xi) River with its mouth near Canton (Guangzhou) has a constricted basin but nevertheless has long served as the main artery of populous south China. Its delta, though much smaller than the Yangtze's, is even more intensively farmed, growing three crops of rice a year in this frost-free climate just south of the Tropic of Cancer, which also receives ample rainfall, and accordingly supports China's—and perhaps the world's—highest population densities for an area of comparable size. Canton has long been a major commercial center and overseas port, surrounded by several satellite towns, a smaller-scale version of Shanghai, and the source of most Chinese who have emigrated abroad, including those in the United States. The rest of south China, and especially its western half, is relatively poor and isolated, the more mountainous parts of it inhabited still by originally non-Chinese peoples who have been driven off the few lowland basins by the advancing wave of Chinese settlement over the past 2,000 years.

East and west, north and south China are clearly different places, the east with broad plains (except south of the Yangtze), the west increasingly mountainous (and also increasingly dry, farther from the sea). The north is dry, brown, and essentially treeless, the south moist, green, hilly, and warm. The line of transition from north to south follows roughly the course of the Huai River, a lesser stream more or less halfway between the Yellow and the Yangtze, and continues westward along the line of the Tsinling (Qinling) Range running near the northern borders of Szechuan. This line coincides for the most part with the isohyet (line of average annual rainfall) of 40 inches, which is adequate for unirrigated agriculture most of the time, although irrigation can greatly raise as well as insure yields, especially for rice. Drought is not unknown south of this line, which after all reflects averages, but it can be devastating north of it, where floods are a further risk along the course of the Yellow River and lesser streams in the eastern part, as they are occasionally in the Yangtze basin with its far greater average rainfall. Summers in both north and south are hot and often humid; Peking (Beijing) near the northern edge of north China is at the same latitude as Philadelphia. Northern winters are cold and often snowy, in the grip of the cold outblowing winds from Mongolia and Central Asia, while the south is milder, and Canton, just within the tropics, is at the latitude of Havana.

China is big enough to include great climatic differences, but climate is also largely determined by the monsoon system which dominates all of East Asia. In summer the center of the great Eurasian landmass heats up, and thus draws into it cooler and moisture-laden air from the seas to the east and south; this produces the spring-summer rains on which agriculture depends, but they are far more reliable in the south than in the north, and even more undependable in the far west. The north lies on the edge of the main monsoonal system, which tends to peter out farther from the sea in any case and leaves the steppe-desert borders with only 10 or 15 inches on average, whereas the south usually gets plenty of rain, and in southern coastal areas too much, over 80 inches. In winter the flow of air is reversed as the center of the continent cools down and cold out-blowing air flows especially over north China on its way to the warmer sea, which does not alter in temperature with the seasons nearly as much as the land. These winter airflows are mainly dry as well as cold, and rule out winter crops, whereas the south can often grow some, and gets the spring rains sooner and more dependably than the north. Ironically, rainfall tends to be most variable from year to year where its annual averages are least: "To them that hath shall be given, and from them that hath not shall be taken away."

The same monsoonal system dominates the climate of Vietnam, Korea, and Japan, none of them as large as any of the main regions of China proper outlined above, but only parts of Korea suffer drought problems on the scale of north China, and drought is nearly unknown in Vietnam and Japan, although excessive rainfall associated with typhoons, the fall storms related to our hurricanes, often causes severe damage in Japan. Japan also benefits from the surrounding sea on all sides, and since mountains mean that most population is on the interrupted coastal plain, none of the main settled areas are more than 40 or 50 miles from the sea. Thus, although Japan is fairly far north (Tokyo is at about the latitude of North Carolina and has a similar climate, while Hokkaido, the northernmost Japanese island, is as far north as Toronto), its winters are generally mild, although there is heavy snowfall on the west coast. Summers in Japan are hot and humid, in the path of the in-blowing summer-monsoon. Vietnam is climatically close to southernmost China, Korea to eastern north China.

Relations with Other Areas

China and East Asia grew up largely in isolation from the rest of the world. Beyond the outer ring of mountains and deserts on China's borders rise the towering peaks of the Himalayas, and beyond the Pamirs on the west stretches the vast steppe-desert of Central Asia. It was to the west of course that the Chinese might have found another civilized culture the equal of their own, but they learned only that the people whom they encountered west of the Pamirs were not nearly as advanced as themselves, more nomads and oasis farmers like those of Sinkiang, and nothing to compare with the riches or power of China. India was closer, in a direct line, and its civilization certainly the equal of China's as well as being somewhat older. But the massive barrier of the Himalayas lay between them. There was a tiny trickle of trade through Tibet and Nepal and a little indirectly by sea, but the principal connection was far longer, through desert Sinkiang, thousands of miles from the center of Chinese civilization, and then across the Karakorum range by an 18,000-foot pass into Kashmir, still on the margins of Indian civilization. India and China were barely aware of each other's existence. Little or nothing from China seems to have reached India, and although Buddhism spread from India to Central Asia and from there after considerable delay to China, it brought little with it of Indian civilization beyond art styles. Cotton, native to India and woven into cloth there by the third millennium B.C., did not spread to China until the eighth century A.D. and, despite its superior qualities and cheapness, did not spread widely until the Sung (Song) dynasty in the eleventh century.

There was of course a southern route to India, across Burma from the remote Chinese southwest, already far from the main base of Chinese civilization. There, too, was a trickle of trade, but it was used even less than the route through Sinkiang. It passes through a wild mountain, gorge, and rain forest country where the road or trail climbs and then drops five thousand feet or more in crossing the steep-sided valleys of the Mekong, Salween, Irawaddy, Chindwin, and other rivers where they have cut deep gorges in their courses south from the Tibetan plateau. As if this were not enough deterrent, the rain forest through which this route passes, itself a formidable barrier, harbors a long list of tropical diseases, which were feared more than the physical demands of the route, and was the home of wild tribespeople who had an evil reputation for head-hunting. It is perhaps not surprising that communication with India by this route was at best faint, and similar conditions minimized Chinese contact with areas beyond Vietnam to the south, which the Chinese spoke of with distaste. Later, as part result of the Mongol conquest in the twelfth century, there was a major movement of people from the mountainous southwest into Thailand, primarily the Thais themselves, whose close cousins still live in western Yunnan. The people of Burma, who speak a Sino-Tibetan language, probably also came many centuries earlier from southwest China and the margins of Tibet, but China's relations with them and with Thailand were minimal until the nineteenth century, when large numbers of Chinese, mainly from overpopulated Kwangtung (Guangdong) in the southeast migrated to both mainland and insular Southeast Asia, originally as laborers, and then increasingly as entrepreneurs.

There had been trade between China and Southeast Asia from at least Sung times, including small settlements of traders at Manila in the Philippines, in Java, and in ports in Malaya, what is now southern Vietnam, Siam (Thailand), and Burma, but the major influx of Chinese was attracted by the growth of tin mining and the plantation industry, principally rubber, late in the nineteenth century. By the present century, there were some 15 million Chinese living in Southeast Asia, and Singapore had grown as a major entrepôt for trade managed almost entirely by Chinese merchants, many of whom had grown rich in this expanding economy.

The Vegetable Civilization

East Asia has been called "the vegetable civilization," from the prominence of rice and other cereals in the agricultural system and diet, and the relatively small place of animals, by Western standards. Cereals, especially rice with its high yields, can provide far more food per acre than can a system based on grazing or stall-fed animals. Since population densities were high, nearly all land which could be cultivated was used for grains, with vegetables grown on field borders or on adjacent gentle slopes and little or no place for fodder crops. Draft animals were necessary, especially water buffaloes, to work the wet, sticky soils of the rice paddies or to plough fields in drier areas for wheat, but they were rarely killed for meat, and were eaten, with a show of reluctance, only when they died of old age. In addition to their labor, they provided large amounts of manure for the fields, and were fed on crop residues and grass cut on nearby hillsides by the small boys of the family, who were often their chief tenders. In drier areas where water buffaloes suffered from lack of water for their necessary daily bath, their places were taken by oxen or cows, occasionally by horses or mules, although the latter were more common as pack animals. Buffaloes and cows gave little milk—that was not their function—and there was little room for proper pasture in the East Asian agricultural system. Sheep and goats, voracious and destructive eaters of grass, could not be allowed to graze freely, but a few were kept in penned enclosures and fed on what the small boys could gather on the hillsides, yielding some

milk but mainly meat and wool. These animals, and all milk products, were associated with the despised nomads, but in any case they did not fit into the main East Asian ecological system.

Pigs, chickens, and ducks could however be kept as scavengers, living on the leavings, although the ducks had the best of it since they could manage fine in the flooded paddies. They took something from the fields, in the form of small plants and other fodder, but they also left behind their manure, so they were given free range, after the young rice plants had grown too big for the ducks to damage. Most households outside Japan tried to keep a pig, penned in, under or near the house and fed on scraps. Japan adopted Buddhism via Korea and China, and most Japanese avoided eating any meat, its place in the diet being taken by the great variety of fish and other seafood so plentifully available. Elsewhere in East Asia, nearly every household also kept some scrawny chickens who managed a meager living pecking in the dirt around the house but provided both eggs and meat in small amounts without any drain on the household's limited resources. The overall diet was short on meat, but some protein was available from beans, including soy beans and the curd (dofu, or in Japanese tofu) made from them. Plain, unhulled rice is nutritionally well balanced, but East Asians came to prefer hulled and polished rice, turned in a small drum with a bit of talc to give it a sheen. This of course destroyed the rice germ, the source of B vitamins, and led to deficiency diseases in extreme cases, partially prevented by beans, bean products, and vegetables, including lots of cabbage which could be pickled for winter, supplemented during festivals by small amounts of meat or eggs on occasion.

Other important crops were silk, tea, and vegetable oils for cooking and for lamps, plus cotton from Sung times on. Most silk was produced on a household basis, with intensive hand labor by all family members during the critical period when the silkworms are growing and spinning their cocoons, feeding voraciously on the leaves of the mulberry tree grown by each silk-making household and fed to the worms several times a day. The worms' droppings and their dead bodies were saved as fertilizer, and might also be fed to fish reared in ponds, especially in south China. Pond-raised fish, fed on sweepings and refuse, could produce more calories and faster per acre, and valuable protein, than any other form of land use. Tea, common in China by Tang times (seventh and eighth centuries A.D.) and quickly spread to Korea and Japan from its earlier home in Vietnam via China, also involved a laborious process to produce, but was grown almost entirely on slopes too steep for rice or other cereals since the tea plant requires good drainage and cooler temperatures and is not fussy about soil fertility. In China most of the best tea was grown in the mountainous area between the Yangtze and Hsi basins in the southeast, including the region known as the Bohea Hills in Fukien (Fujian) Province, where it got plenty of rain and cool, cloudy weather. After successive hand pickings of the tender new leaves, they were sorted, roasted or cured, sorted again, reroasted, and finally packed in air-and-water-tight boxes for shipment to distant markets, eventually also to markets in the West, including the tea chests dumped in Boston Harbor in 1773.

Oil seeds included sesame, rape, and oil pressed from the nuts of the t'ung tree, used in paint and varnish and for waterproofing. An early Chinese invention of the fourth century A.D. was the collapsible umbrella, a silk version for the elite and one made of heavy oiled paper treated with t'ung oil for the common people. The latter, especially, spread rapidly to Korea and to rainy Japan, and in all three countries as well as Vietnam can still be seen widely used. It did not reach Europe, where it was readily copied, until much later. Fermentation and distillation were originally developed to preserve fruit, grain, or other vegetable matter. Beer is the earliest form, known in ancient Sumer and by 1500 B.C. in China, but distillation was first worked out in seventh century A.D. China, five centuries before its discovery in twelfth century Italy; wine from fermented rice or other grains made its appearance by 1000 B.C., grape wine by the second century B.C. With the rest of Chinese culture from the eighth century wine from fermented grain spread to Japan, A.D., where it was called *sake*. Otherwise the Japanese diet remained distinctive, with its avoidance of meat and dependence on fish; heavy reliance on rice led also to the development of a variety of pickled vegetables and seaweed to add flavor. The strong Japanese aesthetic sense decreed that the range of colors and textures of different kinds of food be arranged artfully to satisfy visually as well as to provide a range of tastes and flavors.

Larger Regional Differences

East Asia was in larger terms both a physical and a cultural unit, but each national area had its own set of physical characteristics and its own distinctive culture. Korea and Vietnam, closest to China and for a time part of the Chinese empire, followed the Chinese model most closely. Vietnam was physically like south China, Korea like north China, and the Vietnamese people had originally been close cousins of the people of southernmost China, sharing a common language. The origin of the Koreans and their language was different, but the routes to and from China were short and easy for both areas. The spread of Chinese culture to both was pursued mainly by the elites: writing, art forms (including music and literature), philosophy and ethics (especially Confucianism), a set of social institutions (including the centrality of the family and the primacy of the group—although these may have been present earlier and were merely reinforced by the Chinese model), and a set of political institutions modeled on those of China. Like China, Korea and Vietnam stressed the importance of learning and education as the path to worldly success and prestige, and the importance of status within hierarchically ranked groups. As in China, it is this elite legacy which has come down to us through the written record, but it is not a full picture of Korean or Vietnamese culture. There, as elsewhere, most people were not literate, and after the spread of Chinese culture to the elite they continued to follow their traditional ways. Beneath the Chinese-style surface one can still see, and can catch occasional glimpses of from the past, an original and still in many respects different foundation, in addition to language, especially at the village level. Korea, Vietnam, and Japan are treated in more detail in Chapters 9 and 10, where their general geographical and cultural differences are given greater attention.

Despite the physical and cultural differences among the parts of East Asia, it remains an obvious unit, showing more in common than it shows differences, the largest cultural and economic unit in the world. It is important to understand it, but it is also richly rewarding to study its long and distinguished history. Both can provide us with invaluable perspective on ourselves, and both can enrich our lives. Enjoy the trip! It is meant to be enjoyed.

Notes

1. Translation by Robert Payne in *The White Pony.* New York: Mentor, 1960, p. 3.

2. From Kuo Hsi, *Essay on Landscape Painting,* transl. Sakanishi Shio. London: John Murray, 1935, p. 30.

3. After James Legge, *The Chinese Classics.* Oxford: Oxford University Press, 1895.

4. From a commentary on the I-ching, in James Legge's translation of the I-ching, reissued New York: Dover, 1963, p. 259.

5. *Land and Labour in China.* London: Allen and Unwin, 1932, p. 23.

CHAPTER 2

PREHISTORY, BEGINNINGS IN CHINA, AND THE SHANG DYNASTY

T he direct ancestors of the human species seem on present evidence to have evolved first in East Africa some three million years ago. After another million years, more or less, these creatures, known as *Homo erectus*, slightly smaller than modern humans but walking erect, using fire, and making crude stone tools, had spread to Europe and Asia. Finds of *Homo erectus* were made in Java (now in Indonesia) in 1891 and near Peking (Beijing) in 1921, labeled respectively Java Man and Peking Man. Both are dated approximately 500,000 B.C., although other finds suggest that this species was widespread in Asia by 1.5 million years ago. More recently, remains of *Homo erectus* have been found near Sian (Xian) in northwest China dated about 600,000 B.C., and remains dated about a million years ago in Yunnan in the southwest. This early human type merged with later humanoid species after about 300,000 B.C. Given the span of time and the mixing of peoples since, it may not be reasonable to think of these creatures as early East Asians, rather than just as ancestors of modern people in general. However there is some faint evidence that by about 200,000 B.C. they had developed some of the physical features of modern East Asians and thus perhaps that they had become relatively isolated from the rest of the world, although of course we have no evidence of things like hair, skin color, or facial characteristics. They fashioned "fist axes," handheld stone choppers with cutting edges, probably used for chopping, scraping, and digging, and may have ritually eaten the brains and bone marrow of their own dead, for which there is some evi-

dence at the site near Peking where the fossils of a number of individuals were found in a cave at Chou Ko Tien (Zhougodian) together with charcoal from a campfire and cracked human skulls and bones.

The fist axes they made were quite similar and look much the same at sites scattered over East Asia, consistently different from the stone tools made in the rest of Eurasia. Their stone knives were equally distinctive, and again suggest the relative isolation of East Asia. After about 150,000 B.C. a new species called *Homo Neanderthalensis* (from the Neander Valley in Germany where the first finds were made) rose to dominance over all of the Old World of Eurasia and Africa, which suggests that there was some communication between East Asia and the rest of the world. But in the course of the last glaciation and the final advance of the ice sheets, between about 70,000 and 20,000 B.C., Neanderthals were gradually displaced or superseded (although there was probably some interbreeding) by modern humans whom we call *Homo sapiens*. Since that time *Homo sapiens* has been the only human inhabitant of the globe. Physical differences among the various branches are relatively slight; they are most marked in shades of skin color and a few other superficial and external features such as hair color and texture and facial characteristics. Since few of these minor attributes are discernible for long after death, we do not know when the present small racial distinctions emerged, but, as suggested above, the East Asian type may have begun to appear much earlier. People who lived in or migrated to hot, sunny climates or spent much time out of doors in regions of strong sunshine probably retained the original human skin color, which was dark as a protection against sun damage to the skin. Others who moved to or were overtaken by colder or cloudier climates slowly evolved lighter skin colors so as to maximize the beneficial effects of sunlight on the body, especially as a source of vitamin D. The East Asian skin color is a good adaptation to East Asian climates.

Until very recently, Africa, Asia, and Europe—the units of the Old World divided only by the narrowest of water barriers (the Bosporus and the Gulf of Suez) and hence sometimes called "the world island"—were nevertheless largely isolated from each other by great distances and by intervening deserts and mountains. There was a trickle of trade between them, but the minor physical differences we now observe slowly emerged through inbreeding beginning perhaps by about 200,000 B.C. Physical evolution is a slow process on any human timescale. Contemporary humans everywhere show no discernible differences from their ancestors of ten thousand years ago whose skeletons have been found. Modern Egyptians are the same physically as those from the Old Kingdom in the third millennium B.C., and modern Chinese as those from the Shang dynasty of the second millennium B.C. This includes what evidence remains of skin and hair color, tooth and bone structure, vital organs, brain capacity, and so on. The same would almost certainly be true for the people of 20,000 B.C. or even earlier, if we could compare their remains more adequately.

We need not concern ourselves in any detail here with the almost equally slow evolution of culture—how people lived and what they created—during the thousands of years of the Old Stone Age or Paleolithic Era. This lasted from about a million years ago to about 20,000 or 15,000 B.C., during which time people learned to use fire, build shelters or make use of caves, and fashion garments out of skins or furs. Slowly they improved their stone tools and increased the effectiveness of their hunting using stone-tipped spears. Soon after 30,000 B.C. the pace of change began to quicken, probably hastened by the last phase of glacial ice advance and its subsequent retreat. Cave paintings from this period near the edge of the ice sheets show the skill and imagination of the people who created them and suggest a highly developed social organization. Somewhat later rock paintings suggest the same conclusions. Well before this time *Homo sapiens* had migrated from East Asia to the Americas and Australia. The earliest New World finds are dated about 20,000 B.C., but there is good reason to believe that people from northeast Asia had crossed the narrow Bering Strait between Siberia and Alaska, perhaps on the glacial ice, by about 50,000 B.C. or earlier, and had reached Australia by about the same time across what may have then been a more or less complete land bridge from the Southeast Asian mainland.

With the last retreat of the ice in Europe and Asia beginning about 20,000 B.C. but reaching its present limits only about 3000 B.C., forests slowly replaced the ice sheets and the treeless tundra along their margins. The game, such as woolly mammoths, which the Paleolithic people had hunted, also moved northward or became extinct. Basic changes in the environment required basic human adjustment, as had been necessary when the ice sheets were advancing. People developed new techniques, including the bow and arrow, for hunting in the forest; others moved to coastal or riverine sites and lived on fish and shellfish, creating new or improved tools such as needles for sewing and for fishhooks, now made of bone. But far more significant and rapid changes were beginning to take place in drier areas, centered in the region we now call the Near East or southwest Asia.

The Neolithic Revolution

Neolithic is to some degree a misnomer since it means literally "new stone age," referring to the rapid improvement and new variety in finely made stone tools. But while stone tools continued to be made, bone and clay were of increasing importance, and toward the end of the period tools and weapons began to be made of metal. The term "revolution" is more appropriately applied to the beginnings of agriculture. This made possible for the first time large permanent settlements, a great increase in population, the accumulation of surpluses, the consequent need for writing (in part to keep records), and the growth of the first real cities, from which comes our word "civilization," via its Sanskrit, Greek, and Latin roots. In the few thousand years between about 10,000 B.C. and about 4000 B.C.—an extremely short space of time compared with the almost imperceptible pace of change during Paleolithic times—most of the elements of what we call modern civilization emerged.

By 3000 B.C. early cities in Mesopotamia and the Indus valley of northwest India had bureaucrats, tax collectors, priests, metalworkers, scribes, schools, housing and traffic problems, and almost all the features of our own times. As the Old Testament book of Ecclesiastes put it about 200 B.C., a view which we can echo today: "There is no new thing under the sun. Is there anything whereof it may be said, See, this is new? It hath been already of old time which was before us."[1] That is, in fact, a very Asian view. The changes of which we are so conscious in our own times are extremely recent and center on new technology beginning with the steam engine a mere two centuries ago and accelerating rapidly in the second half of the present century. But people, human society, and their problems have not changed much since the building of the first cities some 5000 years ago.

The Neolithic revolution in agriculture and town building transformed the lives of everyone involved, which was most people. The change came about over several thousand years, probably first in the Near East and then spreading to other parts of Eurasia; similar development in East Asia and much later in Mexico and Peru probably began independently. "Neolithic" refers to a stage of development rather than to specific years or centuries. It came later in western Europe and most of the rest of the world; isolated areas like Australia or the tropical rain forest were still in the Paleolithic when they were invaded by Europeans after the eighteenth century.

Archaeological evidence suggests two main areas as the earliest cradles of settled agriculture: the uplands of southwest Asia surrounding the Tigris-Euphrates lowland of Mesopotamia, and the coastal or near-coastal areas of mainland Southeast Asia. There is clear evidence of early agricultural settlement in southern Anatolia (now in modern Turkey), Palestine and Syria, northern Iraq, and western Iran. In these semiarid areas with some winter rainfall grew steppe grasses that include the wild ancestors of wheat and barley. Early Neolithic stone-toothed sickles, dated to about 10,000 B.C., have been found here, which have a sheen from cutting such grasses with their grain heads. Dating from a little later, small hoards of stored grains have been found. It must have been a long process of adaptation from gathering such grasses or grains in the wild to planting them, perhaps originally by accident, in fields which then could be prepared and tended until harvest. Fields growing only the desired grain could obviously yield far more than could be gathered in the wild, but they did require care and hence a permanent settlement of farmers at a given site, usually one where a supply of water was available. Soon after 10,000 B.C. stone mortars appeared, indicating that the grain was milled (ground into flour) and that it helped to support a population already beginning to grow beyond what could be sustained by hunting and gathering.

By about 7000 B.C. there were large and numerous storage pits for grain, and early clay pots for the same purpose and for carrying or storing water. By this time, cultivated wheat, barley, and peas had clearly evolved into more productive forms than their wild ancestors, probably through purposeful selection by the cultivators. Sheep, goats, and dogs were domesticated instead of being used as hunting prey or hunting assistants. A thousand years later cattle and pigs had joined the list of domesticates. There is a reasonably clear record of this evolution at a number of Near Eastern sites including Jericho in southern Palestine, Cayonu and Catal Huyuk

in southern Anatolia, Jarmo in northern Iraq, Hassuna and Ali Kosh in western Iran, and many others.

By about 4000 B.C. or slightly earlier agricultural techniques were far enough advanced and populations large enough to permit an expansion into the different environment of the Tigris-Euphrates lowland, and somewhat later to the Indus valley in what is now Pakistan, the latter based on models transmitted via early agricultural settlements in eastern Iran and Afghanistan. Most of these areas, including Mesopotamia, were desert or near-desert, with a few scattered oases in Iran, but the river floodplains, given their fertile alluvial soils and long growing seasons of high temperatures, were potentially highly productive if they could be provided with water by controlled irrigation. The Tigris-Euphrates and Indus rivers are fed by rains and snowmelt in their mountain source areas and hence subject to seasonal flooding. The destructive aspects of these floods had to be controlled to permit permanent agriculture. There were also problems of drainage to be solved, especially in the lower course of the Tigris-Euphrates, where the two rivers meet and empty into the Persian Gulf together through what was originally a vast swampy delta.

Techniques of irrigation also had to be developed at about the same time in lower Egypt. Soon after 4000 B.C. villages began to grow into small cities at the conjunction of the Tigris and Euphrates and in the lower Nile. Lower Nile sites have since been buried under silt, and we do not know their names or locations; but in Mesopotamia, perhaps slightly earlier than in Egypt, these first true cities included Ur, Nippur, Uruk, and Eridu. Their names are recorded in the world's first written texts, which have been preserved on clay tablets.

The Neolithic revolution was completed with the development of metalworking and the production of bronze tools and, unfortunately, weapons. Copper was the first metal to be worked, in both the Old and New World, because it sometimes occurs at or near the surface in nearly pure form and can be beaten into a more or less rigid shape without refining or smelting, although it will not hold an edge and was used primarily for ornaments. In Mesopotamia by about 4000 B.C., successive experiments mixing copper with tin and lead in varying proportions produced bronze, which was stronger and would take and keep an edge. But it needs to be remembered that it was agricultural surpluses which made possible the division of labor. Some people were able to pursue nonfarm occupations, and there was more leisure time for experimentation and for the perfecting of artisan techniques, including the smelting and working of metal. The need for better tools for farming, clearing trees, and building towns and cities provided further incentives.

Perhaps through the medium of trade, agricultural and irrigation techniques spread east from Mesopotamia and western Iran, and, by at least 3500 B.C., both were fully developed at sites in eastern Iran, Afghanistan, Baluchistan, and the fringes of the Indus valley. By or before 3000 B.C. irrigated agriculture was fully established on the floodplain of the Indus and its major tributaries, where the first true cities of monsoon Asia arose, growing out of Neolithic villages and towns.

Agricultural Origins in Southeast Asia

Rice was almost certainly native to southeast Asia, as a swamp plant around the shores of the Bay of Bengal or in the valleys of the great rivers of the Indo-Chinese peninsula. It may be the accident of which sites have been excavated so far in Southeast Asia which suggests a clustering of early agriculture in northern and central Thailand and northern Vietnam. Subsequent work may fill out the pattern suggested of agricultural beginnings in the upland fringes of river valleys, with perhaps also sites on or near the coast, where gathering and early cultivation could be supplemented by fishing and by collecting from fixed shellfish beds. It is plausible that this area of unbroken growing season and ample rainfall, where both rice and several tropical root and tree crops were native in wild form, should have seen the first transition from gathering cultures to those which planted and tended fields.

Early developments in Southeast Asia probably centered on root crops, easily cultivated in this tropical climate by setting cuttings in the ground. Taro and yams are still grown this way all over Southeast Asia and offer plentiful output for minimal labor. But there is as yet no hard evidence for early beginnings, let alone reliable dating. Rice was probably also first domesticated somewhere in this area, but there too the evidence is elusive and incomplete. All organic material rapidly decays in the humid warm climate, and except for occasional bits of charcoal from fires, little but stone, metal, and perhaps some bone survives even for as long as a thousand years.

What evidence we have suggests that by about 8000 B.C., or probably about as early as in the Near East, a late Neolithic culture called Hoabinhian had evolved in what is now northern Vietnam. Stone tools and other remains left by this culture suggest a move already made from gathering to the beginnings of agriculture, with fixed permanent settlements, some of which also depended on shellfish beds. At later and better-known sites in northern Thailand, there are severe dating problems, given the perishability of organic materials in this wet area, and the estimates for the beginnings of settled rice agriculture and the first bronze implements range

from 4500 B.C. to as late as 2000 B.C. There is also some debate over whether the few identifiable food remains represent wild or cultivated forms, including rice, which is present as impressions in hardened clay pots in the earliest layers. Remains of chickens and pigs, bronze tools and weapons, and the presence of a large cemetery at one of the sites, certainly suggest agriculture to support so large and technically advanced a population.

Sites elsewhere in Southeast Asia, and in closely related south China, may yield firmer evidence. Rice agriculture may be as old in parts of south China as anywhere in Southeast Asia. The extremely fertile volcanic soil of the island of Java and of parts of nearby Sumatra (both now in Indonesia) may well have supported early agricultural beginnings. Pigs (as opposed to the more widely occurring wild boar) and chickens (originally jungle fowl) are native to mainland Southeast Asia and were almost certainly first domesticated there. They spread from Southeast Asia westward to India, Mesopotamia, and Europe, and northward to China, Korea, and Japan, together with the water buffalo, also native to and first domesticated in Southeast Asia.

Other evidence suggests that millet may have been the first cereal actually cultivated in Southeast Asia. Rice could be gathered wild, to supplement the more easily grown and more productive root crops in the tropics. Millet was not native, but was introduced, from northwest China or from central Asia, and hence could be grown only on a tended basis. As an originally arid-climate or steppe grass, like wheat, millet was better suited to uplands or to elevated sites than to the floodplains. This may help to explain why the earliest Southeast Asian agricultural sites so far found are of that sort. It was apparently not until about 1000 B.C., with the development of controlled irrigation, flood management, and the rise of rice as the dominant crop, that farmers began to occupy and increasingly to concentrate in the lower river valleys and deltas, which since then have been the major agricultural areas. Much earlier, wild rice may have invaded root crop fields as a weed and then been domesticated when its potential was realized. Until then, taro, a root crop, may have dominated the agricultural system, since it is a water-loving plant probably domesticated first in upland areas where shallow depressions fill with water each rainy season.

Peoples and Early Kingdoms of Southeast Asia

Most of the modern inhabitants of Southeast Asia came originally from what is now China, mainly from the south, perhaps including Tibet, with minor and later additions from India. The migrations began many thousands of years ago, probably before the Neolithic period, and migrants probably interbred with what may have been still earlier inhabitants of Southeast Asia as well as with other strains, probably including Negrito groups and others from farther south. Ethnically and culturally, however, there is a clear line of demarcation between the Philippines and Indonesia west of New Guinea on the one hand, and the Pacific and Australasian world on the other. The latter include New Guinea, the Solomon Islands, Australia, New Zealand, and the many tiny islands of the South Pacific eastward from there—Melanesia, Micronesia, and Polynesia, the latter reaching as far as the Hawaiian Islands (until their recent overwhelming by American people and culture). Southeast Asia thus ends as a cultural region at the Moluccas, the easternmost islands of Indonesia, although in the 1950s Indonesia took over western New Guinea as part of its territory.

While scholars are not clear about the precise source area, the Philippines, Indonesia, and the Malay Peninsula on the mainland were probably settled by successive groups of migrants who are called Malays and who belong to a common culture and language family. For the most part, the Malays of Malaysia and Indonesia speak the same language, with regional differences, and the many languages of the Philippines are all in that same group. Ethnically and physically, these Malay people are all broadly similar. Malays were probably the earlier dominant inhabitants of all of mainland Southeast Asia as well, but were displaced southward by later migrations of different peoples from south and southwest China, who became dominant in Burma, Thailand, Vietnam, Laos, and Cambodia (Kampuchea). We cannot date either the Malay migrations or those which later followed them, except to say that both began long before the beginnings of written records, and before the emergence of a Chinese state.

Over a long period, mainland Southeast Asia received a series of migrants from the north who became almost the sole inhabitants of Burma, Thailand, Vietnam, Laos, and Cambodia, all of whom speak languages related to Chinese and Tibetan but unrelated to Malay or the languages of India, although Burmese and Thai are written in an Indian-derived script. Migrations probably had begun by 2500 B.C. or earlier and continued in scattered spurts involving different people into the thirteenth century A.D.

However, there may well have been some movement of peoples even earlier from mainland Southeast Asia northward into China. Culturally as well as environmentally, south China was far more closely linked to adjacent Southeast Asia than to environmentally very different north China until the first Chinese empire united most of the present country into a single state in 221 B.C.

Northern Vietnam was in fact part of an early kingdom which included much of southeastern China and whose culture and language were strikingly different from those of the early kingdoms in north China. Chickens, pigs, rice, and water buffalo moved north from their origins in mainland Southeast Asia to Neolithic south China, within what was until quite late a single culture region. In any case, traditional Chinese agriculture is inconceivable without any one of these basic elements derived from the south; some people and other aspects of culture may well have moved north with them. There is relatively easy access between northern Vietnam and southeast China, by river and across a low mountain range, and, until about the third century A.D., there was little or no distinction between the two areas in people, language, and culture.

Burma and Thailand were progressively settled by somewhat different groups coming originally from mountainous south China, but interaction across the present political borders continued until recently. As already indicated, agriculture and bronze technology developed very early in mainland Southeast Asia and adjacent south China. The technology also spread throughout what is now Indonesia, but we have no evidence of true cities in this period. Writing, the other element of what we call civilization, came to all of Southeast Asia except northern Vietnam from India beginning about the second century B.C. as part of the larger spread of Buddhism, Hinduism, and other aspects of Indian culture, and also through the medium of trade. Northern Vietnam's close ties with China ensured that the Chinese system of writing and many other aspects of Chinese culture became dominant there. By the time we have evidence of the first Southeast Asian states or kingdoms they already seem thoroughly Indianized or, in northern Vietnam, Sinicized (based on the Chinese pattern). But in basic social culture, as opposed to the more sophisticated levels of literature, statecraft, elite art, and revealed religion, Southeast Asia retained its far older and distinctive regional character, including such things as the higher status of women, the nature of village organization, patterns of inheritance, the hierarchy of values, popular art forms, folk religion, and so on.

The first recorded kingdoms in Southeast Asia seem to have been based more on trade than on agriculture. Southeast Asia is in effect a series of peninsulas and island chains (archipelagos) lying between India and China across the major sea routes of inter-Asian trade. The first regional states we know about arose around the second century A.D in the narrow waist of the Malay peninsula in what is now southern Thailand and northern Malaysia, where east-west trade by sea had to portage across the isthmus. (There is some archaeological evidence to suggest that some smaller states may have been formed as early as the first century B.C.) In time, however, the much richer agricultural resources of the great river valleys, plains, and deltas supported the emergence of more powerful states, including the Vietnamese kingdom in the valley and delta of the Red River with its mouth near Hanoi, and the kingdoms of Funan and Champa founded by other groups in what is now central and southern Vietnam, on the coastal plain of Annam and in the delta of the Mekong River.

All three were well established, according to Chinese records, by the third century A.D., although the kingdom of Funan is said to have been founded under the leadership of an Indian Brahman in the first century A.D. Funan became the greatest state of Southeast Asia and controlled much of the mainland area until it was superseded by the rising power of Champa in the middle of the fourth century. Both were Indianized Hindu kingdoms, both built large walled cities, and both also depended on their control of maritime trade. Champa remained dominant in the south and extended its control westward into what is now Cambodia and southern Thailand, until the Chams were finally defeated in the fifteenth century by the long progressive southward advance of the Vietnamese. Earlier they had also been displaced by the rise of the Khmer Empire centered in Cambodia beginning about the eighth century.

As indicated above, Burma had been settled by successive waves of migrants from south China, who by the third century B.C. or earlier were in close contact with neighboring India. These migrants adopted much of Indian high culture, including Buddhism, writing, legal systems, and art forms while retaining, like the rest of Southeast Asia, their own distinctive social culture. By at least the fourth century A.D. Indianized kingdoms had been established in the Irrawaddy valley, which forms the central core of Burma. In 849 the first kingdom for which we have detailed information was founded with its capital at Pagan; it unified under its control most of the present state of Burma. Like earlier Burmese kingdoms, it was a Buddhist monarchy, and like them it built magnificent Buddhist temples, or pagodas, as well as cities, based on surpluses from the productive rice agriculture of the Irrawaddy valley. The continued southward movement of Thai people from southwest China was accompanied by periodic destructive raids against the Burmese kingdoms, but the main Thai thrust was against the Khmer Empire, which by the fifteenth century they had largely defeated. From the thirteenth century the Thai kingdom was established in the lower valley of the Chao Praya River, still the heart of the Thai state and the center of its agricultural economy.

China was in trade contact with the Philippines probably by the time of the T'ang dynasty in the eighth century A.D., but there are no detailed records and there was apparently minimal impact on Philippine culture, or cultures. The people of these islands, though all belonging to the Malay family, remained divided into a great many separate groups or tribes, isolated from each other by the mountainous and heavily forested landscape and on the many islands of which the Philippines are composed. Most of the elements we call civilization, including writing, had barely begun to penetrate this area before the arrival of the Spanish in the sixteenth century.

Prehistoric China

The emergence of civilization in China is most clearly documented archaeologically for the north China plain of the Yellow River (Huang He). But because of the probable earlier origins of agriculture and bronze technology in Southeast Asia, and the close cultural and ethnic connection between that area and south China before the rise of the Chinese empire, it seems clear that developments in south-central China may have been even earlier than in the north. Rice, pigs, chickens, water buffalos, and bronze would easily have moved northward from their Southeast Asian origins, following first the several north-flowing tributaries of the Yangtze (Yangzi) River from the northern edge of the Canton (Guangzhou) area. The latter was culturally closely linked to, and from about the third century B.C. or before, politically a part of what is now northern Vietnam, the old kingdom of Nan Yüeh (Nam Viet, or Viet Nam, in Vietnamese) with twin capitals at Hanoi and Canton and sharing a common language, identity, and way of life.

Archaeological evidence is much less complete for south than for north China, for the same reasons which explain its scarcity for Southeast Asia: high humidity, ample rainfall, and high temperatures, which rapidly break down organic remains. But the south has also been much less investigated archaeologically than the north, and future finds may well alter the present picture. Already sites excavated since 1949 have revealed traces of advanced farming, bronze making, and town-building cultures at several places in south and central China, as far as the northern edges of the Yangtze valley, which are about as old as their culturally different equivalents found in north China. There are severe dating problems, but the estimates for the oldest of these sites range from 5500 to 4500 B.C. Their occupants grew a domesticated form of rice and kept pigs and water buffaloes. Excavated sites in the south are too few as yet to demonstrate what may well have been still earlier developments in domesticated root crops, if indeed any evidence remains.

China north of mountain-girt Szechuan (Sichuan) province and north of the lower Yangtze valley, essentially the floodplain of the Yellow River and its tribu-

The bronze age: bronze figure of a warrior from the Dong-Son culture of northern Vietnam, about 400 B.C. (Art Resource/Lauros-Giradou)

from Japan have been dated to about 8000 B.C., and it is unlikely that development there was earlier than on the mainland. Pottery suggests the need for storing surpluses, and hence at least the beginnings of agriculture, but the emergence of farming, here as elsewhere, was no doubt a long, slow transition from earlier gathering and hunting. The dominant, and perhaps the only, early crop plant in north China was millet, like wheat a drought-tolerant steppe grass. It was probably native to the area and domesticated there in two varieties by at least 4500 B.C., or perhaps as early as 5000. Dependence on millet suggests that agriculture in the north was an independent development rather than a diffusion from either the south or from southwest Asia.

A major early northern site has been excavated at Pan P'o (Banpo) near modern Sian (Xian), which was well established as a small village by at least 4000 B.C. Its people grew millet and kept sheep, goats, and pigs, supplementing their diet with river fish and game. Rice and water buffalo probably did not spread widely to the north until about 1500 B.C., after their basic usefulness had long been demonstrated farther south. It was the heavy water demands of rice, rather than the cold winter and shorter growing season, which retarded its spread northward. The first form of rice domesticated from its wild ancestor was, however, a warm-climate plant, and as its cultivation spread northward different varieties were developed which were better suited to colder temperatures and shorter growing seasons. These were the varieties later diffused to Korea, and from there to Japan.

Pan P'o and most of the many other early northern sites are in the loess uplands well away from the main floodplain of the Yellow River. As elsewhere, it was only after the rise of some form of water control that the major farming centers moved into river valleys and deltas. This seems to have begun in north China by about 2000 B.C. but did not acquire full momentum for another millennium. By that time, about 1000 B.C., wheat had replaced the earlier dominance of millet in the north and was supplemented by barley and rice. Rice could now be irrigated, from river water or floods and from shallow wells. Wheat and barley are not native to east Asia and must therefore have been diffused from southwest Asia some time between 4000 and 1000 B.C., joining an agricultural system which was already there and had probably emerged independently.

The Pan P'o people belonged to an early stage of what is called the Painted Pottery culture, or *Yang Shao*, taking its name from a village in Honan (Henan) Province where the major find was made. It lasted as late as 1500 B.C., after which it merged with other late Neolithic cultures to form the first literate and city-building, metal-using civilization, the Shang dynasty. Painted pottery was covered with intricate geometric designs in red and black: there is a wide range of sizes and shapes

taries, is by contrast a semiarid area of precarious and limited rainfall and with a long, cold winter. In these terms it is not all that different from the early cradle of agriculture in southwest Asia, where wild forms of wheat and barley were first domesticated. The great agricultural advantage of north China has always been its highly fertile soil, often found in semiarid areas, in this case deep deposits of wind-laid dust called *loess*, much of it also picked up and redeposited by rivers. It is very easily cultivated and of almost inexhaustible fertility if adequate water is available. The largely treeless plain, open for agriculture and for transport of surpluses and other goods, offered the same advantages as the Nile, Tigris-Euphrates, and Indus valleys, although the heavily silted Yellow River was less useful for navigation.

Neolithic cultures in north and probably south China were most likely producing pottery as early as or perhaps earlier than in southwest Asia; pottery fragments including what are clearly fish and others human faces. It was baked in a kiln, although it was made without the potter's wheel. The culture's original domain extended from Kansu (Gansu) in the northwest eastward into Honan, where it overlapped with another late Neolithic culture called Black Pottery, or Lung Shan (Longshan), from the major type site in Shantung (Shandong) Province, whose domain reached westward from the sea. Central and south China during this period were occupied by other Neolithic cultures, as indicated above, each producing distinctively different types of pots. Black Pottery ware was of fine quality and often elegant in design, wheel-made and kiln-fired at temperatures over 1,000 degrees centigrade. Neither it nor the Painted Pottery ware show any connection with Mesopotamian or Indus pottery. Both these late Neolithic Chinese cultures still used stone tools, including finely worked and polished arrowheads and some smaller bone tools such as needles and fishhooks.

Some scholars suggest that writing began as a limited set of symbols including both ideographs and pictographs inscribed on Neolithic pottery of the Pan P'o period by about 4000 B.C. and that these symbols became the basis for both classical and modern Chinese. But by 2500 B.C. or perhaps a little earlier, a more fully developed writing system had emerged, the direct ancestor of the Shang dynasty script. We have no similar Neolithic pottery from the south, which supported several different cultures, but by about 5000 B.C., at a site

called Homutu in Chekiang (Zhejiang), south of the lower Yangtze valley, people had domesticated pigs, dogs, chickens, and buffaloes and were growing irrigated rice. It seems likely that similar developments were as early or earlier farther south, especially in the Canton delta with its close connections with Vietnam, where these innovations appear to be even older.

By about 2000 B.C., the Lung Shan or Black Pottery culture, perhaps by that time merged in part with the Painted Pottery culture, was building larger and larger villages, now better called towns, and producing the first north China bronze ornaments and weapons, probably for mainly ceremonial use since no bronze tools have yet been found from this period. Many of their settlements were surrounded by thick walls made of successive layers of stamped earth, a technique which was to continue for many centuries of subsequent recorded Chinese history. The later Lung Shan sites included bronze foundries and produced fine black pottery whose quality and shapes closely resemble those of the first historically authenticated dynasty, the Shang, which rose to power about 1600 B.C. Indeed, the Shang built one of their early capitals on the foundations of the late Lung Shan town at Ao, near modern Chengchou (Zhengzhou) in Honan on the floodplain of the Yellow River.

A further practice which links Lung Shan culture to the Shang is the use of animal bones for divination purposes, the so-called oracle bones. Interpretations were based on the cracks made in them when they were

A fine example of Yangshao (Painted) pottery, found in Kansu (Gansu) and dated sometime after 5000 B.C. (Buffalo Museum of Science)

heated. There is thus a clear line of succession from late Neolithic cultures in north China to the beginning of recorded history, with the Shang as the first literate city-building Chinese civilization, according to present evidence. We can only speculate that similarly advanced development may well have taken place as early or earlier in the Yangtze valley and/or the south, and that the relatively sudden emergence of the Shang on the Yellow River plain may have owed much to innovations farther south. What does seem clear is that the rise of civilization in both north and south China owed little if anything to early developments in southwest Asia, Mesopotamia, or the Indus valley. China does not seem to have been in contact with those areas or to have received anything from them until considerably later, when wheat, barley, alfalfa, donkeys, the horse, and the spoked chariot were diffused to China between about 1800 and 600 B.C.

Korea and Japan

Millet-based agriculture, accompanied by domesticated pigs, sheep, and goats, spread from north China to Korea by about 2000 B.C., although some evidence of questionable date suggests millet cultivation in the Han River valley near Seoul as early as 5000 B.C. Rice and bronze entered later, via north China, possibly aided by the flow of refugees from the fall of the Shang dynasty, about 1100 B.C. The development of rice varieties adapted to a colder climate probably continued in Korea, by purposeful selection. The ancestors of the Korean people migrated there from the north via Manchuria, probably from an original homeland in what is now Siberia and northeastern Russia, a migration which continued well into historic times. The clearest evidence for this is the Korean spoken language, unrelated to Chinese and part of the language family of northeast Asia called Altaic.

The early Koreans were tribal peoples with a fishing, hunting, and gathering culture but producing technically advanced pottery and later, after the emergence of agriculture, building large, aboveground tomb chambers of stone blocks, often mounded over with earth. As their culture began to merge into farming, permanent villages and towns arose and bronze weapons and ornaments appeared, probably derived from north China. Korean tradition dates the founding of a Korean state to 2333 B.C. by a ruler who was the son of the divine creator and a female bear in human form, but this is almost certainly far too early, if indeed it can be taken seriously at all. Another myth has it that a royal refugee from the fall of the Shang founded the state of Choson (an old name for Korea). That too seems improbable, though more plausible, and in any case fits with the transfer of much of Shang culture and technology to Korea during the first millennium B.C.

By the third century B.C. iron technology had also spread from China to Korea. The Chinese border kingdom of Yen (Yan), with its capital near modern Peking (Beijing), apparently also had some control over southern Manchuria and northern Korea. In the second century an unsuccessful rebel against the Han dynasty fled to Korea and established, about 194 B.C., a Sinicized state which controlled the northern half of the peninsula. It too was called Choson, with its capital at Pyongyang, still the capital of North Korea. The Han emperor Wu Ti (Wu Di, see Chapter 4) conquered Choson in 109–108 B.C. and added further territory in central Korea under his control. Before the fall of the Han dynasty in A.D. 220 most of the Chinese garrisons had been withdrawn, and from A.D. 220 onward Korea remained an independent state, or states, since it was long divided into rival kingdoms.

Remnants of the Chinese colonies planted under the Han survived in the north and continued to transmit Chinese cultural influences, but by the fourth century A.D. were overwhelmed by Korean insurgents or tribal groups, much as the Roman settlements in Britain and northern Europe were largely extinguished somewhat later by the rise of Germanic, Gallic, and British tribes. Nevertheless, as in Europe but to a much greater extent, influences from what was acknowledged to be a superior civilization continued throughout the later periods of Korean history. Unlike Rome, China successively rebuilt its empire and restored the vigor of its brilliant culture under the T'ang, Sung (Song), Ming, and Ch'ing (Qing) dynasties from the seventh to the eighteenth centuries. Successive Korean states explicitly sought to adopt many elements of Chinese culture and continued to admire it as a model while maintaining their political independence. Three rival Korean kingdoms emerged after the end of Han Chinese control; their history and that of subsequent Korean states is given in Chapter 9.

As an island country—four main islands and many smaller ones 120 miles off the coast of Korea at the nearest point—Japan has preserved a separate identity, and its culture has remained a distinctive variant of anything on the mainland. Isolation and insularity kept Japan free from foreign control until the U.S. occupation from 1945 to 1952, but also helped to retard its early civilized development. Like the Koreans, the present-day Japanese people can be traced back to migrants from northeast Asia or Siberia; these migrants spoke an Altaic language related to Korean but not to Chinese. Their distinction from the Koreans was, however, minimal until well after they entered Japan, some time between about 300 B.C. and A.D. 200 in successive waves, a movement about which we know very little. Other and unrelated groups already inhabiting the Japanese islands were absorbed by intermarriage, and the few survivors of the Japanese invasion were slowly driven northward.

At a much earlier date there were probably also some movements of people into Japan from the Malay areas of Southeast Asia, and perhaps from the South Pacific, as well as cultural influences, although these are hard to trace. Paleolithic cultures were widespread in Japan at least 40,000 years ago, differing little from those of the Asian mainland. By about 6000 B.C., according to present archaeological evidence, a great variety of early Neolithic cultures had arisen in Japan, of which the best known is called Jomon. We know too little about this period to be precise, but it seems likely that the Jomon people were quite diverse and often in conflict. Some groups may have begun to practice agriculture by about 300 B.C. Most of the Jomon people made a rudimentary cord-marked pottery, lived in sunken-pit shelters, and engaged in hunting, gathering, and fishing. They seem, in other words, to have been as advanced as the Pan P'o people of north China, and possibly a little earlier in achieving such a level. But the Jomon people were only very indirectly and partially the ancestors of the Japanese, who as pointed out were much later invaders from northern Asia, via Korea, although they probably merged in part with people already in Japan.

In any case, the Jomon culture was progressively displaced beginning in the third century B.C. by an early agricultural Neolithic culture called Yayoi. The Yayoi used the potter's wheel, cultivated rice, practiced irrigation, and had begun to use bronze and iron, all of these things diffused from earlier developments in China and entering Japan from Korea. A few Chinese coins and polished bronze mirrors found at Yayoi sites show that there was trade between the two areas. Like the Lung Shan, Yayoi bronze objects seem to have been ornamental or ceremonial; the few weapons that have been found are too thin to have been used in combat. By the third century A.D. the Yayoi began to construct large earthen mounds over the tombs of prominent men, a practice presumably derived from Korea; indeed much of Yayoi culture, and its people, may most accurately be seen as provincial Korean.

By the fifth century iron swords and iron armor appeared. These were similar or identical to Korean equivalents, as were the jeweled crowns and other ornaments found in some of the tombs. Houses were now raised off the ground, agriculture was becoming more productive with the help of iron tools, and pottery had become harder and more highly fired, unlike the cruder earthenware containers and stylized clay figures of earlier Yayoi. Now inhabited by people whom we may legitimately call Japanese, Honshu and Kyushu, the two main islands, had reached the technological levels achieved by the Shang in China some 2,000 years before, and by Korea perhaps 1,000 years thereafter. Japan still lacked

writing, and we have no evidence of genuine cities or of the emergence of a true state.

The earliest written accounts of Japan are Chinese, compiled in the third century A.D. and describing the route via Korea. They record that the people of Japan were farmers and fishermen living in a hierarchical and law-abiding society—something likely to attract Chinese approval. The country was shown as divided into a hundred kingdoms—perhaps better called "clans"—of so many thousand households each. The earliest Japanese written accounts, using the characters adopted from China, are the *Kojiki* ("Record of Ancient Matters") and the *Nihongi* ("History of Japan"), which date, respectively, from A.D. 712 and A.D. 720 and are hence strik-

Pottery figure from the Jomon period in Japan, about 500 B.C. The pottery is still relatively crude and is not wheel-made. The impressions were made by rolling twisted cords of different types onto the clay while it was still wet and then firing. Similar cord-marked vessels were made in the Neolithic period in the rest of Asia. (The Granger Collection)

ingly late. Both are a mixture of pious and often contradictory myths, especially for the early periods, with some more factual accounts of later events. Both recount the story of the divine creation of the Japanese islands. Another god descended to earth as the first Japanese emperor, and his grandson or great grandson founded the Japanese state in the Kyoto area, allegedly in 660 B.C., although one must observe again that the predominant ancestors of the Japanese people did not reach Japan for another 400 years!

It does appear that by the late fifth century A.D. the first true Japanese state had emerged, centered in the Kyoto-Osaka area, and that the earlier clan basis of organization was slowly giving way to it, although the state's power seems still to have rested mainly on family connections and was limited in geographical area to the Yamato basin of the Nara-Kyoto-Osaka region. The state was called Yamato and gave its name to the area, as well as, traditionally, to the Japanese people as a whole, who in later times referred to themselves as the Yamato people. The ruler, who from the beginning was called emperor, probably in imitation of the much-admired Chinese system, which was used as a model in so many things, was allegedly descended directly from the sun goddess Amaterasu, unlike the very human-centered and this-worldly Chinese approach. It is significant that Amaterasu, the titular deity of Japan, was a woman; in early Japanese history there are more than a few traces of matriarchy, and even a number of women rulers. The fanciful extension of Japanese history into the distant past in the *Kojiki* and *Nihongi* was, however, designed to give Japanese civilization a long tradition, as in China, and the respectability which came from it. The emperor or empress was both a temporal and a spiritual ruler who presided over the worship of the sun goddess and the forces of nature. In later times this nature worship came to be called Shinto, the "Way of the Gods," but it was never a fully developed religion and had no organized philosophy or moral code.

Immigration from Korea continued into the ninth century A.D., and until the sixth century Japanese retained a foothold on the southeast coast of Korea, facilitating the flow of migrants and perhaps reflecting some form of alliance between groups on both sides of the Straits of Tsushima, which separate the two countries. Large numbers of Koreans lived in Japan, where they seem to have dominated or at least been prominent in the elite structure of Japanese society. In a record of genealogy compiled in A.D. 815, over a third of the Japanese aristocracy claimed Korean or Chinese ancestry, clearly a mark of distinction. Korea was not only more advanced but was the source of Chinese learning and technology. In addition to being members of the Japanese nobility, Koreans served in Japan as skilled artisans, metallurgists, and other technologists.

For some centuries there appear to have been periodic raids or invasions in both directions across the Straits of Tsushima, but by the fifth century A.D. such violent interactions faded. Those remaining in Japan began to move northward from their early base on the island of Kyushu, closest to Korea, and established their major settlements on the main island of Honshu. The central core on the Yamato Plain in the Nara-Kyoto-Osaka area saw the birth of the Yamato state by the fifth century, as indicated above, where the focus of the state was to remain for approximately the next thousand years, although the capital was not moved north to Tokyo until 1868. During the centuries after their first arrival in Japan, the new invaders intermarried with the variety of groups already there, including a physically dissimilar group called the Ainu, who at that time probably occupied most of northern Japan. For many centuries the frontier with the Ainu lay just north of Kyoto, but they were slowly absorbed or pushed northward and now live as a tiny and dwindling minority on reservations in the northernmost island of Hokkaido.

Buddhism seems to have come to Japan from Korea in the sixth century A.D. and brought with it further elements of Chinese and Korean culture. But the pace and scope of such influences accelerated on a major scale with the rise of the T'ang dynasty in China in 618. This new model of cultural brilliance powerfully attracted the Japanese, who had perhaps now, in any case, reached a level in their own development where they were ready to move from an essentially tribal and preliterate stage into a Chinese-style civilization. Successive embassies were sent from Japan to T'ang China beginning early in the seventh century, explicitly to bring back all they could learn about Chinese ways, including writing and city building. Japan thus enters the true historical stage of civilization at that period, surprisingly late, a story resumed in Chapter 10.

The Origins of China

We cannot fix a precise date for the emergence of city-based, literate, metal-using civilization in China. As everywhere else, it happened over a long period of transition out of Neolithic beginnings. By about 2000 B.C., however, the late Neolithic culture we call Lung Shan had begun to build walled settlements larger than villages, to make bronze tools, weapons, and ornaments, and to use a pictographic and ideographic script clearly recognizable as the ancestor of written Chinese. Their towns or cities included large groups of nonfarmers—scribes, metallurgists, artisans, and perhaps officials—and already the Lung Shan people had learned the art of silk making, long an exclusive Chinese skill and trademark. Approximately four centuries later, about 1600 B.C., the first authenticated Chinese dynasty, the Shang, was established in the same area around or near the great bend of the Yellow River, where the major Lung Shan settlements had also clustered, on the north China plain. The Shang probably consolidated or arose from a combination of the previously distinct Lung Shan and Yang Shao (Painted Pottery) cultures, but they and other late Neolithic cultures may well have begun to merge considerably earlier, perhaps to form the dynasty of Hsia (Xia), recorded as such by traditional Chinese texts but not yet confirmed archaeologically.

Whether the Hsia was a real state and dynasty or not, the name was certainly used, and the Shang could not have appeared without a predecessor. The existence of the Shang was also discounted by modern historians, despite its mention in the traditional texts giving the names of kings, as for the Hsia, until archaeological discoveries in the 1920s began to reveal its capitals and inscriptions which listed Shang kings exactly as the traditional texts had them. Hsia may still be a convenient label for late Lung Shan-Yang Shao culture in the last stages of its evolution. By about 2000 B.C. Lung Shan towns were large and were surrounded by pounded earth walls with heavy gates, clearly no longer farmers' villages and possibly organized into some form of kingdom or kingdoms. What may have been a capital from this period near modern Chengchou (Zhengzhou), perhaps of the Hsia and referred to in the traditional histories as Yangcheng, had a rammed earth wall 20 feet high and a mile square, with two bronze foundries outside the walls.

Lung Shan settlements with a similar material culture extended eastward to the sea, northward into southern Manchuria, and southward to the Yangtze valley along the coast. The traditional Chinese texts give the names of five pre-Hsia "emperors" who are recognizable as mythological culture heroes, credited with the "invention" of fire, agriculture, sericulture, animal domestication, calendrics, writing, and flood control, developments which in fact happened over many centuries or even millennia. The last of these "emperors," the great Yü, is said to have founded the Hsia dynasty, which may tentatively be dated 2000–1600 B.C., but we know almost nothing more about it. The earliest texts we have were written down many centuries later. Yü is also credited with "controlling the waters," limiting what had been chronic flooding, presumably from the Yellow River. That this was a huge job is implied by the stories of Yü as a tireless worker who several times in the course of his work passed his own doorway without stopping.

By Shang times in any case, many of the elements of a distinctively Chinese culture are present. There has been a long debate about how much, if anything, Shang or its Chinese predecessors may have owed to earlier achievements farther west, by diffusion from Mesopotamia or India. There seems no question that wheat, and later donkeys, alfalfa, grapes, and some elements of mathematics were carried to China from western Asia but well after 2000 B.C. The horse-drawn war chariot, an important Shang war weapon, seems also to have come in by about 1500, perhaps related to the Aryan migration into India. Rice, water buffalo, chickens, and pigs, also not native to north China, came considerably earlier from their Southeast Asian origins via southern China. Indeed China owed far more to diffusion from the south than from the west, especially if one considers the basic place in its economy which came to be occupied by these originally southern imports.

More recent finds reveal a pattern of cultures in both north and south China, spanning the period from about 5000 B.C. into Shang times and beyond; these seem clearly to have been independent centers of development rather than extensions or offshoots of either Lung Shan or Shang developments. Sites excavated in southern Manchuria, on the margins of the Yangtze delta, and in Szechuan near Chengdu have produced fine glazed pottery, beautifully carved jade, and magnificent bronze sculptures, all strikingly different from Lung Shan or Shang objects and much earlier than the Shang, or probably than at least the mature form of Lung Shan. These cultures, and doubtless others yet to be discovered, were in any case far beyond the Shang domains, although they probably traded with both Shang and Lung Shan people and among themselves, as pottery and bronze technology also spread. These finds make it even clearer that there was no single center of what was to become Chinese civilization, that the south was at least as advanced as the north, and that it is, to say the least, misleading to regard "China" as emerging from the Shang or evolving only out of its cultural or political achievement. China had multiple cultural origins, which came together only with the Ch'in (Qin) conquest of 221 B.C.

The chief crop of Shang China and for many centuries later was not wheat but millet, probably an indigenous grain. There is no aspect of Shang culture which suggests any connection with Mesopotamia or India, including Shang art and two other basic and conclusive elements, writing and bronze technology. Both were earlier developed in Sumer and then in India, but the earliest Chinese writing resembles neither. It seems unlikely that the Chinese would not have adopted or adapted cuneiform instead of the far more cumbersome ideographic characters if they had been in touch with Mesopotamia or had imported ideas or techniques from there. As for bronze, Shang China stands alone in the technical perfection and beauty of its bronze work, sharply distinct from that of any other ancient culture and showing in China a long history of experimental progress, using varying proportions of copper, tin, lead, and zinc until the optimum mix was worked out. The farther one goes from the Shang centers (except southward), the cruder the bronze artifacts become; there is no trail leading from Sumer or Harappa. For these and other reasons it seems clear that Chinese civilization, like Indian, was an independent innovation, which was already well formed before it came into effective contact with other or older centers of equal sophistication. This is also consistent with the Paleolithic and early Neolithic record, where the stone tools of China remained distinct in type from those produced in the area from India westward through central Asia to Europe. Chinese civilization evolved largely on its own, after the much earlier diffusion of some agricultural elements from the south.

The Shang Dynasty

The Shang ruled from several successive walled capitals, first near modern Loyang, then near modern Chengchou (both close to the Yellow River), and finally at Anyang at a city they called Yin. We do not know the extent of the Shang political domains, but cultural remains suggest they were limited to the central Yellow River floodplain, although the Shang had, or claimed, vassals to the west, east, northeast, and possibly the south, who shared much of Shang material culture. By this time wheat was beginning to share prominence with millet, and rice was also grown, though mainly in the Yangtze valley and the south. Hunting remained a subsidiary source of food in addition to domesticated cattle, pigs, and poultry. The Shang kept slaves, mainly war captives from among less highly developed or subjugated groups on the Shang borders, and slaves may

An inscribed oracle bone from the Shang dynasty. Oracle bones bear the earliest known examples of Chinese writing. (East Asian Library, Columbia University)

have been an important part of the agricultural workforce. They were also used extensively to build the cities and palaces, and perhaps as troops. The Shang developed a highly accurate calendar, appropriately for an agricultural people, and an advanced system of astronomical observation which included records of sunspots and eclipses. Their geometry included the precise survey or resurvey of fields and their borders, probably annually, suggesting that many were covered every year by flooding.

Especially at Anyang, monumental building was impressive, and the city may have covered at its peak as much as 10 square miles, with nearly a dozen elaborate royal tombs, complete with a variety of grave furniture. The tombs provide evidence of a surplus production which could support extravagant display, including richly decorated chariots with bronze fittings and caparisoned horses to draw them; the horses had been harnessed, backed into the underground tombs down a ramp, and killed. Royal or aristocratic dead were accompanied in their burials not only by things of use and value but by tens or even hundreds of followers, buried as human sacrifices to serve in the afterlife, and probably also as a mark of the dead man's status. Bronze vessels and weapons of great beauty and technical perfection attest to the high quality of Shang technology.

We have no written texts as such, but there are a great number of Shang inscriptions, most of them incised on the flat shoulder bones of cattle or on lower tortoise shells, and used for divination purposes. A text, usually in the form of a question, was inscribed on bone or shell after heating in a fire or with a hot iron rod until it cracked; the cracks supposedly provided an oracular answer to the question. Others of the so-called oracle bone inscriptions, like the divination texts using characters close enough to classical Chinese that many can be read, provide lists of the Shang kings and brief accounts of royal activities. Many of the characters used in the oracle bone inscriptions have not been deciphered, and we may thus learn more about the Shang in time, although many of the unknown ones are probably personal names. The questions or requests or wishes range widely, from "When will the drought end?" to "Will the queen's toothache be cured?," "Will the royal hunt go well?," to "Will the campaign against (a rival or "barbarian" group) succeed?" The answers or outcomes are given too in many cases, probably in order to form a record. Since the bones were first heated to form cracks and then inscribed, the texts may have been part of a ritual to influence a good outcome.

Altogether this inscriptional material, some of it on bronze vessels toward the end of the period, gives a picture of a hereditary aristocratic society in which warfare against surrounding groups was chronic; archers used a powerful compound bow, there were ranks of spearmen, and nobles and their drivers rode in their light, fast war chariots similar to the chariots of the Indo-Europeans. The royal hunt remained important and was usually a very large affair in which hundreds took part and thousands of animals perished. The inscriptions make it clear that the spirits of royal and perhaps all aristocratic ancestors demanded respectful service from the living and could intercede for them with a supreme deity—the roots of traditional Chinese "ancestor worship." Slaves were not thought to have souls or spirits and thus could safely be killed; the Shang aristocrats seem not to have thought about what might happen to them if they became war captives themselves.

Although those at the top lived in great luxury, the houses of the common people seem to have been quite crude, often simple pit dwellings, certainly not in a class with those of the Indus civilization. Writing continued to develop in complexity and the representation of abstract ideas, and used nearly 5,000 characters by the end of Shang rule. By that time even artisans had their own personal seals and kept their own records, and we have real accounts of events, campaigns, the appointment of officials, and so on. Many of the divination questions ask about the weather and suggest that the north China climate then, as now, was semiarid and prone to both drought and river flooding, but there is little evidence of any large-scale irrigation, apart from what one may assume was the possible use of floodwater. North China was not as dry as the Indus valley, and the agriculture there seems to have been primarily rain-fed except perhaps in small areas adjacent to the river or on a small scale from local wells in long dry spells. Millet is highly drought-tolerant and can produce good yields where other crops might fail. The great agricultural advantage of north China was its highly fertile *loess* soil (wind-laid alluvium), which is also easily worked, and the level expanse of the largely treeless plain, allowing easy transport and exchange.

The Chou Dynasty

Relations between the Shang and their vassals were uneasy, and chronic warfare with other groups on the margins strained Shang resources, as did the extravagant demands of royal building and display, much of it extorted from slave laborers and artisans. The last Shang king is said to have been a physical giant and a monster of depravity who, among other cruelties, made drinking cups of the skulls of his vanquished enemies. The dynasty ended in a great slave revolt about 1050 B.C., which was joined by one of the Shang vassals, the Chou (Zhou, pronounced like "Joe"), who guarded the western frontier in the Wei valley with their capital near modern Sian (Xian). Originally, the Chou were probably a barbarian group taken over by the Shang. These tough

Shang bronzes are technically sophisticated and are dominated by ritual vessels in a variety of forms. This piece, with its removable lid, probably served as a pitcher for pouring ceremonial wine. Like other Shang bronze objects, it shows a mythical beast in abstract form and is covered with abstract designs. (Freer Gallery, Washington)

frontiersmen, in turn, seem to have been awaiting their chance to take over the whole kingdom. By about 1050 B.C. when, together with the slave rebels, they finally succeeded in defeating the last Shang king and sacking Anyang (where the Shang king died in the flames of his own palace), the Chou had acquired most of Shang culture and technology. Their conquest was not merely a plundering expedition but a succession to a new dynasty that continued the cultural and technical evolution already begun. The victorious Chou, now fully literate, gave their own account of the excesses and oppression of the Shang as justification for their conquest and first voiced what was to become a standard Chinese justification for political change: "The iniquity of Shang is full; Heaven commands me to destroy it." In other words, the Shang had lost the "mandate (approval) of Heaven" by their misgovernment, and it was the duty of responsible people to overthrow them. According to the traditional histories, the Shang had used the same argument for their overthrow of the Hsia.

We should not conclude from the self-justifying propaganda of the Chou that all of the Shang was noted for its cruelty and its bad rulers. Indeed it became a truism in the writing of subsequent Chinese history as well that the last ruler of most dynasties was an evil and incompetent person. The Shang had originally displaced the Hsia on grounds of the latter's bad government, and at least for a time they appear to have represented an improvement. Yü, the supposed founder of the Hsia, had come to power when he was selected by his predecessor for his ability and conscientiousness, as was the case with the two preceding Hsia rulers. For about half of the Shang dynasty the succession was from brother to brother rather than from father to son, which may have ensured a greater degree of continuity and perhaps efforts to achieve reputations as good rulers. Up to the end of the Shang most agricultural tools continued to be made of stone or wood, since bronze remained too scarce and expensive for most tools and was used largely for weapons or ornaments. Jade was much admired, but also as an ornament, and money, or its crude form, was mainly cowrie shells, as in so many other early cultures, brought or traded for from the south coast and beyond into the Pacific world. By late Shang the state was well enough organized, with its vassal dependencies, to put 3,000 or more troops into battle.

The story of the discovery of the remains of the last Shang capital at Anyang is exciting. For some years ground-up bones called "dragon bones" were sold by apothecary shops as medicine, and in 1899 Chinese scholars in Peking began to notice that bone fragments had scratched on them what looked like ancient writing. After much perseverance they traced the bones to their source near Anyang and began to study them further. Excavations were begun at Anyang in 1927 and are still continuing, bringing to light still more of the oracle bone inscriptions as well as remains of extensive palaces, tombs, and buried chariots. Thus the traditional histories were vindicated.

Note

1. Eccles. 1:9–10.

Suggestions for Further Reading

Aikens, M. C. and Higuichi, T. *The Prehistory of Japan.* New York: Academic Press, 1982.

Barnes, G. I. *Protohistoric Yamato.* Ann Arbor: Center for Japanese Studies, 1988.

_____. *The Rise of Civilization in East Asia.* London: Thames and Hudson, 1993.

Bellwood, P. *Prehistory of the Indo-Malaysian Archipelago.* New York: Academic Press, 1985.

Chang, K. C. *The Archeology of Ancient China.* 4th ed. New Haven: Yale Press, 1987.

_____. *Chinese Civilization: Anthropological Perspectives.* Cambridge: Harvard Press, 1976.

_____. *Shang Civilization.* New Haven: Yale Press, 1980.

Chard, C. S. *Northeast Asia in Prehistory.* Madison: University of Wisconsin Press, 1974.

Higham, C. *The Archeology of Mainland Southeast Asia.* Cambridge University Press, 1989.

Keightley, D. *Sources of Shang History.* Berkeley: University of California Press, 1992.

_____, ed. *The Origins of Chinese Civilization.* Berkeley: University of California Press, 1983.

Kim, J. H. *The Prehistory of Korea.* Honolulu: University of Hawaii Press, 1978.

Kohl, P., ed. *The Bronze Age Civilization of Central Asia.* Armonk, New York: M. E. Sharpe, 1981.

_____. *Central Asia: Paleolithic Beginnings to the Iron Age.* Paris: Editions Recherchés sur les Civilizations, 1984.

Li Chi. *Anyang.* Seattle: University of Washington Press, 1976.

Masson, V. M., and Sairanidi, V. *Central Asia Before the Achaemenids.* New York: Praeger, 1972.

Nelson, S. M. *The Archeology of Korea*. Cambridge University Press, 1993.

Perason, R. L., ed. *Windows on the Japanese Past*. Ann Arbor, Michigan: Center for Japanese Studies, 1986.

Treistman, I. M. *The Prehistory of China*. Peking: Foreign Languages Press, 1972.

Walker, R. L. *Ancient China*. New York: Watts, 1969.

Watson, W. *China Before the Han Dynasty*. New York: Praeger, 1961.

_____. *Early Civilization in China*. London: Thames and Hudson, 1966.

_____. *Ancient China: Discoveries of Post-Liberation Archeology*. London: British Broadcasting Corp., 1974.

CHAPTER 3

THE CHOU, ITS DECLINE, AND THE AGE OF THE PHILOSOPHERS

The Chou conquest of the Shang and their establishment of a new dynasty did not represent a sharp break in almost any respect. They had come to share most of the characteristics and achievements of Shang culture and were willing to continue it without significant changes. They even confirmed the son of the dead Shang king as the chief official of most of the old central Shang territories, and the Shang royal line continued for some time thereafter. Given their function as guardians of the western border regions against "barbarian" groups, the Chou had become more militarized than the Shang and appear to have developed improved tactics of chariot warfare, with a new kind of harness enabling them to use four horses abreast. Equally important, they seem to have had better leadership, if one accepts the account given in the traditional histories, notably King Wen and his son King Wu who together completed the conquest of Shang, and King Wu's brother, the Duke of Chou, dedicated regent for a boy king (King Wu's son), much praised later by Confucius as a model statesman and philosopher. The Duke of Chou is given credit for the founding and wise management of the new dynasty.

It was understandable that in their frontier region the Chou should have preserved a degree of cultural distinction from the Shang—and perhaps some of the Shang's earlier virtues as opposed to their later degenerate years. Such an analysis fits the standard Chinese conception of each dynasty as founded by strong and upright rulers, only to be brought down in the end by dissolute and incompetent ones. There is much justification in fact for

such a view, and indeed it may be said to fit the rise and fall of most empires or political regimes elsewhere. In any case, it is reasonable to apply it to the decline of the Shang and the rise of the Chou, who preached old-fashioned virtue and the courage and hardihood generated in their frontier base, like the Ch'in who were to succeed them from the same base and to unify China for the first time some 800 years later. It may be of some relevance that the old Lungshan (Black Pottery) culture seems to have survived longest in the Wei valley, almost up to the time of the fall of Shang, although it had by then disappeared everywhere else.

Like the Shang, the Chou shifted their capital several times, mainly within the area around modern Sian (Xian), and surrounded each with stamped earth walls with gates which faced the four cardinal points of the compass. Major buildings, including palaces, were oriented to face south, as the Shang had done. Bronze vessels and ornaments of great technical perfection continued to be made, although now with long textual inscriptions and with some new shapes, including finely wrought animals and birds. Writing continued to evolve, until by mid-Chou it was close to modern or classical Chinese. Oracle bone divination continued to be practiced, as did ancestor veneration. The Chou dynasty lasted with some vigor from about 1050 B.C. to the latter part of the ninth century, or something over 200 years, not a bad record for any political regime, but their system began to weaken and then to fall apart in the eighth century.

Like the Shang, they had chronic trouble with "barbarian" groups around the fringes of their domains, and in 771 B.C. the royal capital in the Wei valley was sacked by invaders from the north in league with dissident Chinese or supposed vassals, and the Chou king was killed. His son was installed as king the next year, but in a new and better protected capital at Loyang (Luoyang), surrounded by long-settled Chinese territory. The hope was that a control point closer to the center of the royal domains would also be more effective in holding the kingdom together, as opposed to the offside base of the Wei valley. But it proved a vain hope, and any effective Chou control over the territories they had conquered from the Shang and subsequently added to ended in 770. Royal authority slowly dwindled to nothing and supposedly dependent vassals became rival states. The period from the conquest to 770 is called Western Chou, and from 770 to the extinction of the dynasty, Eastern Chou, but though the name continued it was little more than that.

The Chou seem to have subdued or controlled a much larger area than they inherited from the Shang, from the Wei valley to the sea, north into southern Manchuria, and south into the Yangtze valley. Mutual interest among evolving kingdoms, or dukedoms as the Chou called them, led them to cooperate in the defense of the "civilized" area against the outer barbarians and to keep order internally. The system the Chou used to ensure this was similar to the Shang's, creating feudatory vassals (dependent allies) linked to the Chou king by oaths of loyalty and acknowledging him as sovereign. Vassals were granted fiefs of land, and titles translatable as duke, earl, baron, marquis, or count, and supplied troops on request from the Chou king for mutual defense as well as gifts.

The parallel with medieval European feudalism is not exact, although Chinese historians also use the term for this period. The major difference is that the Chou system was based on kin (family) ties, which, especially in the Chinese context, was designed to ensure loyalty and cooperation, whereas in Europe other supposedly loyal (but often rival) figures were granted fiefs and bound by oaths, gifts, and ritual submission. Despite the family tie, the Chou system did not last even as long as European feudalism. In time the royal family line declined; originally related families built up their own local or re-

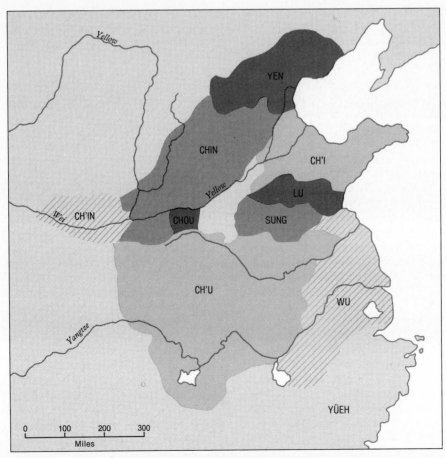

China in the Sixth Century B.C.

gional power, as was perhaps inevitable, and others who were unrelated or had risen as henchmen to the powerful also grew in status. Family-based power was of course hereditary, and successive generations grew increasingly independent. These regional powers, which were in effect evolving states, came to be ruled by people who called themselves kings, a title previously reserved for the Chou rulers, and often disregarded Chou commands. Each of these developing kingdoms was based in a walled city like that of the Chou capital, in effect small city-states, although some of them expanded to control much larger areas of surrounding countryside and what were called townships. Some were absorbed by others, and some new ones appeared along the margins of the original Chou area. By the eighth century there may have been as many as 200 all told.

The basic system, and the reasons for it, were the same as in medieval Europe: a central kingdom with pretensions but without the means, at this early stage of statecraft, to control or administer any large area beyond its immediate territory around the capital city. Agreements were hence made with local chieftains or relatives in a feudal-style compact that extended the authority of the central state, at least in name. For a time, perhaps the first two centuries of Western Chou, it worked reasonably well, based also on what appears to have been an institution like serfdom, by which most land was cultivated under the ownership of hereditary lords. As in medieval Europe, serfs were bound to the lord's land and could not leave it even if the lord died. There may have been some irrigation from shallow wells in a center plot, later labeled the "well field system." The full picture is not clear, but serfs, who were

the property of the lord, supposedly gave priority to cultivating the center plot, whose crop belonged to the lord and was of course the biggest and best since it was presumably most effectively irrigated, and only after that was done could work on the outer plots. Such a system seems plausible, given the level land of most of north China and the need for irrigation in most years or in every year in order to maximize yields. We have no way of knowing what yields or total output may have been, but it seems clear that population rose well above Shang levels. As one measure, toward the end of the ninth century the Chou king is said to have led an army of 30,000 men and 3,000 chariots, many times the numbers they had used against the Shang.

What we know about Chou society comes mainly from a much later text of the fourth century B.C., *The Traditions of Tso*, or *Tso-chuan*, whose accuracy about matters many centuries earlier can obviously not be relied on wholly. The Chou king had the title of Son of Heaven, which all subsequent Chinese emperors carried, and like them was thought to hold his office by divine authority from the Lord of Heaven. The capital in the Wei valley was called Chou-tsung (or Tsung-Chou) and was the chief religious center of the kingdom, with a great temple of deceased kings. Most writing was by now done with brush and ink on silk or on strips of bamboo, but none of these perishable texts have survived and we are dependent on much later copies, possibly substantially altered versions. It is generally assumed that the central body of the Chinese classics originated in early to mid-Chou. These include the *I-ching* (*Book of Changes*—a cryptic handbook for diviners), the *Book of Songs*, the *Book of Rituals* (*I-chi*, or *Book of Rites*), and

Mencius on Good Government

Mencius, the first great follower of Confucius, lived from about 372 to about 289 B.C. and wrote down his own moral precepts and anecdotes. On benevolent government, he recorded the following advice to a certain king of one of the Warring States.

Dogs and pigs in your realm feed on the food of your subjects, but you do not restrain them. People are starving on your roads, but you do not open your granaries. When people die as a result, you say, "It is not my fault; it is a bad year." How is this different from stabbing a man to death and saying, "It is not my fault; it is the sword." If your majesty would stop putting blame on the year, people from throughout the empire would come to you.

Source: After C. O. Hucker, *China's Imperial Past* (Stanford, Calif.: Stanford University Press, 1975), p. 81.

collections of historical documents (*Shu ching*), among them the texts which give the story of the five culture-hero emperors and the Hsia dynasty, as well as a now-confirmed account of the Shang and of the Chou conquest, although later scholarship has shown that the versions we have now are much later forgeries. But already the Chinese were writing history and attaching characteristic importance to the keeping of records.

The *Book of Songs* (*Shih ching*) is probably the earliest, consisting of some 300 songs, or poems, although the music which went with them has been lost. Poetry and music were clearly important, as they were to be to all subsequent generations of educated Chinese. The *Shih ching* includes political poems, love songs, and ritual hymns, all in carefully constructed meter and rhyme. The *I ching* was probably composed at different periods and centers on combinations of three-line "trigrams" of complete or broken lines purporting to read the future; it probably grew out of the earlier practice of divination and was used by shamans, but much more recently became popular, like tarot cards, among the hippy generation in the West, few of whom are aware of its origin. The *Li chi*, as we have it now, is a later compilation of the second century B.C. of earlier materials describing rites and rituals, important for ensuring that the social order ran smoothly, as Confucius stressed. To these four were later added, to complete what are still called The Five Classics, the *Spring and Autumn Annals* (*Ch'un Ch'iu*), a brief record of major events in Lu, the home state of Confucius, from 722 to 481 B.C., but including also the *Tso chuan* (a commentary on the *Ch'un Ch'iu*) with its account of earlier events. Confucius knew this work, but almost certainly did not compile it, although he died shortly after the end of the period it covers. "The Classics" came to mean this specified set of texts which were held in special veneration as coming from a supposed "golden age," in keeping with the general Chinese respect for the past as a model and for the written word.

One may certainly call the *Shih ching* literature, and of relatively high quality, while the *Shu ching* and *Ch'un Ch'iu* are clearly history; to educated Chinese, the *Li chi* is a philosophical description of morals to guide behavior. We are dealing thus with a sophisticated culture, resting on an economic base which had expanded and developed far beyond the levels reached under the Shang. But fundamental changes were at work that were to disrupt and then destroy the entire Chou political structure. As technology improved, iron was slowly becoming cheaper and more plentiful. By the seventh or sixth century B.C., it began to be available, as bronze had never been, for agricultural implements, including iron-tipped plows, which the Chinese were using over a thousand years before the West. Helped by better tools, especially spades and axes, irrigation was spreading,

especially important in semiarid north China, and more and more land was being brought under cultivation. Iron axes speeded the attack on the remaining forests in the hilly margins of the north and in the Yangtze valley. Spurred by rising agricultural output, the population began to grow more rapidly, perhaps reaching 20 million by mid-Chou; the Shang may have totaled 5 to 10 million in the same area. Except for recurrent years of drought and famine, population did not apparently outrun food supply, and surpluses were common, the basis for increasing trade and the rise of merchants and towns.

New agricultural productivity freed increasing numbers from farm labor to serve as artisans, transport workers, soldiers, officials, scholars, and merchants. Towns and cities, now more important as centers of trade than of royal or feudal control and dominated by merchants, began to dot the plain and the richer lands to the south in the Yangtze valley, where easier transport by water further stimulated the growth of trade and of urban centers. Fixed and hereditary serfdom and the domination of a landed aristocracy came to seem less and less suited to the changing conditions, a situation which may have been in some ways similar to that in the later periods of European feudalism with the rise of towns and the revival of trade. At the same time many of the original Chou vassals were evolving toward separate statedom, each with its distinctive and regional culture. After some four centuries of Chou rule, the political, social, and economic structure began to show strains, and eventually it disintegrated.

In 841 B.C., according to the traditional histories, there was an uprising by the people of Chou-tsung, the royal capital, and the Chou king was driven out. His suc-

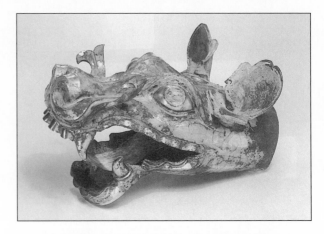

Early Chou bronzes show a trend away from abstraction and toward more lifelike representation, although the pieces remain highly ornamented. (Freer Gallery, Washington)

cessor managed to restore the royal power, using the 30,000 troops and 3,000 chariots referred to above. But less than a hundred years later the capital was invaded by "barbarians," allied with rebellious Chinese groups from among the Chou vassals, who destroyed the city. According to tradition, the Chou king had too often in the past lit the beacon fires to summon aid from his vassals merely to amuse a favorite concubine, and now when the alarm was real no one came to help. But the basic problem was that most previous vassals were breaking away from Chou authority and setting up their own independent and rival kingdoms. Under such circumstances, most of them probably welcomed the fall of the Chou and began to jockey among themselves for position, and for acquisition of the former Chou domains and power.

The sack of the Chou capital in 771 B.C. gives us the first reliable date in Chinese history, although the date given for the earlier uprising in 841 is probably equally accurate. Traditional dates for earlier events are almost certainly undependable, but with the writing of historical accounts (the earliest surviving books come from the ninth century) the dates they give are confirmed by other evidence; by the eighth century astronomical records still preserved describe eclipses of the sun, which in fact did occur exactly when the records state, as we can determine through modern astronomical calculations. From their new capital at Loyang the Chou tried to restore their position as overlord, but it was far too late, as the feudal system they had presided over was breaking up. The old Chou base in the Wei valley was given as a fief to a supposedly loyal noble of the Ch'in (Qin) clan, the new guardians of the frontier. Five centuries later the Ch'in were to sweep away the crumbled remnants of Chou pretension to found the first all-China empire.

Warring States

The Ch'in were in fact the smallest and weakest of the major contenders among the former Chou vassals, at least to begin with. The contest between them lasted nearly 550 years, a period known as the Warring States, although traditional dating has it beginning only in 453 B.C. In addition to Ch'in, the principal rival kingdoms were Chin (Jin) north of the Yellow River, Yen (Yan) to the northeast in the area around modern Peking, Ch'i (Qi) to the east in Shantung (Shandong), Ch'u (Qu) in the central Yangtze valley, Shu in Szechuan (Sichuan), Wu in the lower Yangtze, Yüeh in the southeast, and a number of smaller ones, including Lu in Shantung, where Confucius was born and served for a time as an adviser. It is still too early to speak of any of them, even

of the Chou, as "China." Each was culturally, linguistically, and politically distinct, and for some there were also minor racial differences. China as we know it emerged only under the Ch'in empire in the third century B.C., which united north and most of south China by force. The Ch'in empire put its own overpowering stamp on what was to become the dominant Chinese style in language (both spoken and written), culture, statecraft, and social organization for the ensuing two millennia, as detailed in Chapter 4. Our name *China* comes, appropriately enough, from the Ch'in, the creator of an imperial Chinese identity for the first time.

Until then, there was no dominant strand within the varied assortment of people, cultures, and states which occupied what is now China. They warred constantly among themselves and against the still more different groups around the edges of the cultivated area but still well within the borders of modern China proper. Technology passed easily and quickly from group to group, and by mid-Chou most seem to have shared more or less common achievements in metallurgy, agriculture, irrigation, and other arts. By the end of Chou, furnace temperatures may have reached 2,000 degrees centigrade with the help of an early form of forced draught from double-acting piston bellows, another Chinese first, centuries ahead of Europe. They produced a growing stream of tools, smelted with coal 2,000 years before the West. The Chinese had an early advantage in easily worked iron ores which were high in phosphorous, combined with low-sulphur coal, which made the making of cast iron much easier. But the contending states of this period had their own different scripts and spoken languages and their own cultures. They were at least as different from each other as the evolving states of late medieval Europe, which did share, in spoken and written Latin, a common language for the educated, and a common religious faith and tradition.

The state of Ch'u provides a good example. Its location straddling the central Yangtze valley made it probably the most productive of the rival states as well as the largest; its agriculture benefited from the more adequate and reliable rainfall and longer growing season of central China as well as from greater ease of irrigation. But it was different in character too, in particular in the size and importance of its merchant group and the role of waterborne trade and towns in its economy. Ch'u had evolved far beyond the earlier Shang pattern, where power was held by hereditary landowning nobility and where agriculture worked by slaves or serfs was virtually the sole source of wealth. Literature was highly developed and there was a lively urban culture. Unlike the northern states Ch'u was also a naval power; it had fleets on the Yangtze and its tributaries and adjacent lakes and even larger numbers of trading junks (riverboats). Nevertheless, Ch'u was ultimately defeated by a coalition of northern states in 632 B.C. and again in 301 B.C.; though it continued to exist, its power and further growth were greatly reduced while those of the other states rose. This may have been one of those contests which change the course of history, giving the future to a peasant-based authoritarian empire rather than to a state where trade and merchants were prominent. A China which followed the Ch'u pattern would have been very different from what was established by the final victory of the Ch'in, whose shape is described in Chapter 4.

With increasing agricultural yields and total output, it was now possible to field large armies of men who could be spared from agriculture at least for parts of the year and could be fed on surpluses. Warfare became larger in scale and more ruthless, and its character changed from that of earlier chivalric contests of honor between aristocrats to one of more wholesale conquest and fights for survival. The crossbow with a trigger mechanism, developed by or before this time, greatly increased firepower, range, and accuracy, and by the fourth century B.C. foot soldiers were supported by armed cavalry. Such developments combined to undermine the earlier dominance of hereditary aristocrats, their chariots, and their personal retinues.

What was happening in China paralleled the Indian pattern a century or so before, where a chivalric age gave way to interstate power struggles and the emergence of the Mauryan Empire, based on the spread of iron, improvements in agriculture, and a population boom. As in India, bronze and copper coins minted by the state became common in this period in China, trade and cities grew rapidly, roads were built, standing armies proliferated, and the bureaucratic apparatus of the state began to appear. All of this offered a range of new opportunities for able commoners. For many it was a positive and welcome change, but for others the passing of the old order and the great disruptions and sufferings of warfare offered only chaos and moral confusion. Confucius, who lived at the beginning of the Warring States period, made it clear that his prescriptions were an effort to reestablish order and what he referred to as "harmony," following the values of an earlier "golden age."

Many of the contending states were described in the Chou records as "barbarian," which meant only that their cultures and languages were different from the Chou mode. It seems clear that most of them, such as the state of Ch'u described above, were at least as advanced economically and technologically as the Chou. In general, those on the edges of Chou control tended to be more rather than less developed, perhaps because the remnants of Chou overlordship and the force of tradition retarded innovation, especially in military and economic growth, for the states closer to the center,

which in any case were smaller and more crowded together. The larger states on the periphery were the first to outgrow the old feudal system, as Ch'u had done. Private ownership of land and its unrestricted buying and selling replaced the former communal use, and powerful new families whose wealth came from trade as well as from land replaced the old aristocracy of families linked to feudal lords.

Larger territories also increased the need for more effective political institutions and more centralized power, along with a tax system, regulation of weights and measures, copper coinage, and the first state monopolies of salt and iron production and trade; all were to be mainstays of the empire from its founding in 221 B.C. The round copper coins with a square hole in the middle (for stringing together) first made in late Chou were to remain the basis of the currency system into modern times, known simply as "cash." To administer all this, a swelling bureaucracy began to take the place of the old aristocratic system, and written legal codes increasingly replaced feudal-style personal rule. Armies and military campaigns continued to increase in size, and conquered states tended to be obliterated or absorbed into the territory of the winner.

The Chou had already been troubled by barbarian raids on the part of the nomadic peoples who lived along the northern and western borders of the settled agricultural area. During the centuries after 770, some of the new northern states began to build long walls to protect their territory, forerunners of the Great Wall put together as a consolidation by the Ch'in empire after 221 B.C. Armed cavalry became newly important for defense against the mounted nomads, and Chinese horsemen began to adopt the close-fitting trousers of the nomads as the most practical garb. Although interstate warfare became chronic as well as more ruthless, there were repeated efforts to arrange treaties and even to discuss some degree of disarmament at many interstate conferences, the beginnings of diplomacy. As in Europe later, marriages between the families of heads of state were used to cement alliances, and some states, notably the ultimately victorious Ch'in, made wide use of deception, intrigue, and psychological warfare, the beginnings of what was later called in the West Realpolitik. The state of Chin was broken up in 453 into three components, presumably to weaken its power, and that date is, as indicated above, used to mark the start of the Warring States period. Ch'u demolished Yüeh in 334 (although it was to rise again) and Lu in 249. Ch'i nibbled off still more of former Chou territory in 286, and Ch'in, from its base in the Wei valley exterminated the remnant of Chou power in 256, with no ceremony. Ch'in was emerging as the strongest and best organized of the contenders, despite its small size and offside location. In a series of lightning campaigns Ch'in overwhelmed all the other states between 231 and 221 B.C.

It is understandable that the period of the Warring States should have produced also a set of remedies for the violence, destruction, and anarchy which characterized those centuries. There is a parallel here to the roughly contemporary developments in Greece, where chronic and destructive fighting, especially after the seventh century B.C., was followed or accompanied by the growth of philosophical remedies designed to restore peace and order, notably those of Socrates, Plato, and Aristotle. Like the Greek philosophers and their prescriptions for a better society, the Chinese philosophers failed in their goal. Plato's ideals and his short-lived experiment in government were destroyed by the renewed outbreak of bitter fighting in the Peloponnesian War between Athens and Sparta. The Confucian formula for the restoration of order, like those of his rough contemporaries, was set aside in the heat of battle and the struggles for power. But both the Greek and Chinese philosophers, born in the troubled times they sought to heal, have lived on ever since, and have helped to shape the later evolution of Western and Chinese civilizations.

Confucius, the Sage

Confucius was born about 551 B.C. in one of the smaller states which arose out of the Chou domains in Shantung province, and died about 479. He was thus roughly contemporary with the Buddha and died only a few years before the birth of Socrates. His family name was K'ung, and Chinese refer to him as K'ung Fu-tze (Kongfuzi, "Master K'ung"), which modern Europeans latinized as Confucius. The K'ung family appear to have been rather low-ranking aristocrats in reduced circumstances but were able to arrange for their son's education. This was still more than three centuries before the establishment of the imperial examinations, and Confucius made a career out of teaching, periodically serving as consultant or counselor to various feudal lords. To his pupils he taught not only literacy and the classics but his own philosophy of life and government. Some of his pupils won high-level jobs in state administration, but Confucius himself was never very successful in such terms, and at the end of his life apparently thought of himself as a failure. In fact, he was the founder of probably the most successful philosophical, moral, and ethical system in human history, measured by the number of people in China, Korea, Japan, and Vietnam who followed his precepts for more than 2,500 years and who are still profoundly influenced by them.

We have nothing that the sage himself wrote and not very much information about him or his teachings. All we know for sure comes from a collection of discourses, or sayings, known as the *Analects*, which were put together in a rather unsystematic way after his death by his disciples and are hence probably not wholly accurate. Later commentaries expanded on the meaning and application of his teachings.

The picture we have of the man himself and of his ideas from the *Analects*, while incomplete at best, is of a thoughtful but also very human person. He complained that he could never seem to get the right kinds of students or the kinds of appointments he yearned for. And he is rather transparent in discussing his lack of success: "I don't mind not being in office; I am more concerned about being qualified for it. I don't mind not having recognition; I strive to be worthy of recognition." Yet he complained about being treated "like a gourd fit only to be hung on the wall and never put to use." He seems to have been so anxious to get a post as adviser that he even considered working for rebel groups, believing that, given any kind of opportunity, he could remake men and states in line with his philosophy—an attitude which Plato was to share a century later. But he also had a good sense of the ridiculous and could even enjoy jokes on himself.

The basic message of all his teachings is that people can be molded and elevated by education and by the virtuous example of superiors. "Civilized" people so formed will *want* to do what is morally right, rather than merely expedient, and hence will preserve the "harmony" of society, which is what distinguishes humans from animals. Force and threats are ineffective controls; only internalized values can produce correct behavior. Behavior should also be modeled on that of higher-status people, beginning within the family and extending to the ruler, who thus must match power with responsibility and uprightness. For all relationships, "Do not do unto others what you yourself would not like."

Confucianism is a prescription for benevolence in human affairs and in government, but it is also essentially conservative, placing stress on order. Nevertheless, the focus on benevolence meant that bad government should rightly be rejected, despite the threat to order, a point which the *Analects* repeats in several contexts. The Confucian model is the upright man who unswervingly pursues the right moral course whatever the consequences, even at the expense of his own self-interest. Master K'ung's life seems to have conformed to the model he preached. Perhaps he was too outspoken, like Socrates, to win the favor of the powerful men of his day. But his teachings and his example have far outlived the petty politics of the age he lived in.

Confucius: A Ch'ing dynasty rubbing, made over 2,000 years after the death of the sage, of whom there are no contemporary portraits. (**The Granger Collection**)

HSÜN-TZU

The philosopher Hsün-tzu (Xun Zi—c. 300–237 B.C.), a prominent Confucianist, was opposed to the view that human nature is intrinsically good. He argued that human emotions and desires lead to conflict; they need to be curbed and redirected through education. The teacher was thus seen as a revered figure, an attitude which helped to shape Chinese values for over two thousand years, and which was transmitted with the rest of Confucianism to Vietnam, Korea, and Japan. Hsün-tzu also reacted against the Taoists in rejecting belief in "spirits," although this became a standard elite putdown of folk religion in general. He saw *li*, badly trans-

lated as manners or etiquette (we really have no comparable word or concept, but *li* is an inner sense of what is proper rather than a set of rules), as the supreme guide to good behavior and indeed to all wisdom, and hence stressed the importance of ritual as well as education, and the maintenance of a strict hierarchical order enforced through precepts and punishments. He thus supported what was already becoming a trend toward more authoritarian government. The teachings of Mencius (see below), by contrast, centered on "goodness" (*jen*) or "human-heartedness," "compassion," or responsibility for the welfare of others, qualities which he felt people were born with, although they could be reinforced by proper education. States which are governed by such "goodness" will endure.

It is noteworthy that virtually all of the classical Chinese philosophers were concerned mainly with the right ordering of state and society and with practical politics; many of them served as political advisers, like Confucius and Mencius. It would hardly be accurate to call them politicians, since they were far above that dusty arena of power struggles and immoral behavior, and correctly saw power, like money, as corrupting. All looked back to what they saw as a "golden age" in the remote past (safely long ago enough that they knew few details about it to mar their idealized picture). Certainly they knew disruptive change in their own lifetimes and their response to it, to go back to an idealized past, seems human and understandable. But of course they had a rosy vision of the past, and indeed we know that it too was often violent and chaotic. Confucius especially admired the Duke of Chou as a wise and good statesman; perhaps he was (although we know too little about him and his times to be sure), but that was a highly selective view of the past, and even in his time and under the Chou regime he established, greed, ambition, and the conflict they always generate were surely not absent.

Confucianism

Many would argue that Confucianism is not a religion but merely a set of ethical rules, a moral philosophy. It is true that it specifically avoids any concern with theology, the afterlife, or otherworldly matters. Most Chinese, Korean, Vietnamese, and Japanese Confucianists have apparently found it appropriate to supplement their religious diet with bits of Buddhism, Taoism (see below) or Shinto (traditional Japanese animism or nature worship), which provide what Confucianism leaves out. Perhaps it does not matter whether one calls Confucianism religion or philosophy; it is the creed by which millions of successive generations of East Asians, something like a third of the world, have lived for over 2,000 years. Confucianism has probably had more impact on belief and behavior than any of the great religions, in the sense that most East Asians accept and follow the teachings of the sage more thoroughly than the ethical teachings of any other system of belief. Confucian teachings contain much common sense about human relations, but they are a good deal more than that, reflecting and shaping a highly distinctive set of values, norms, and sociopolitical patterns. Confucianism has its temples too, monuments to the doctrine, though it lacks a prescribed ritual or organized priesthood; for those things, Confucianists turn elsewhere, as indicated, but do not thereby cease to be true and diligent followers of the sage's teachings.

Confucius and Mencius

Confucius became a sometime advisor to various local rulers. He never had a definite official post, and he had no real political clout. Like Plato, he looked for rulers who might be shaped by his advice, but also like Plato, he never really found one. Several of his students became his disciples, though never as organized as in Plato's Academy; after his death they and their students began to write down his teachings and to expand on them. His most famous later follower and commentator was Mencius (the Latinized version of Meng-tzu, c. 372-c. 289 B.C.). Like Confucius, Mencius lived in the chaotic Warring States period and sought means for restoring order and social harmony through individual morality, a parallel to the origins of Buddhism.

Society in East Asia has always been profoundly hierarchical, and the social order was seen as a series of status groups and graded roles, from the ruler at the top through officials, scholars, and gentlemen, to the father of the family, all with authority over those below them but also with responsibility to set a good example. The key element was "right relationships," carefully defined for each association: father–son, subject–ruler, husband–wife, elder brother–younger brother, and friend–friend. Confucius and Mencius provided what became doctrinal support for such a system. It left small place for the individual as such, but at the same time stressed the vital importance of self-cultivation and education as the only true assurance of morality, or "virtuous behavior." To paraphrase Plato, "Education makes people good, and good people act nobly." According to Confucianism, people are born naturally good and naturally inclined to virtue, but need education and the virtuous example of superiors to stay that way. Mencius illustrated natural human goodness by the instinctive action of anyone who saw a child fall in a well and would, without thinking, rescue the child from drowning. Confucius emphasized "human-heartedness," benevolence, integrity, uprightness, altruism, respect for superiors, filial loyalty, "right relations," and learning as cures for chaos, and as the formula for achieving the "great harmony" which was his chief objective. The virtuous man must also have culture and manners (*li*) and must conscientiously observe ritual, while avoiding all extremes. The Chou *Book of Poetry* (*Book of Odes*) says: "To be a man and not have rituals? It would be better to make haste and die." Confucius added: "Uprightness uncontrolled by *li* becomes rudeness."

Inherent Goodness

Like Confucius, Mencius believed in "human heartedness," or compassion.

All men have a sense of commiseration. When a commiserating government is ruled from a commiserating heart, one can rule the whole empire as if one were turning it in one's palm. Why I say all men have a sense of commiseration is this: Here is a man who suddenly notices a child about to fall into a well. Inevitably he will feel a sense of alarm and compassion. And this is not for the purpose of gaining the favor of the child's parents, or seeking the approbation of his neighbors and friends, or for fear of blame should he fail to rescue it. Thus we see that no man is without a sense of compassion ... (which) is the beginning of humanity ... and the beginning of wisdom. ... When left to follow its natural feelings, human nature will do good.

Source: From W. T. deBary, ed., *Sources of Chinese Tradition,* Vol. I (New York: Columbia University Press, 1960), pp. 92–93.

Confucian temple, Yunnan Province, China. This is a modern photograph, but the building's style is traditional. (R. Murphey)

Ritual was accompanied by music, as in much Christian practice; the proper music was thought to help produce proper moral attitudes and behavior. In any culture, ritual and social forms help to inculcate inner attitudes, although the contemporary West seems to have largely forgotten this, unless one chooses to regard some pop or rock music as serving some of the same purpose. According to Confucianism, sanctions and law are no substitute for or guarantee of individual virtue or social harmony, and indeed they were seen as ineffective as well as unnecessary in a properly run society. People must learn to prefer to follow the right path, and that can be achieved only by internalizing morality. When force or punishment have to be used, the social system has broken down. Confucianism is a highly pragmatic, this-worldly, and positive view of humanity and society; it provides little scope for metaphysical speculation, for the supernatural, or for concepts like sin or salvation. And although Confucius and Mencius were certainly conservatives, supporters of a hierarchical social order, their doctrine also allowed for individual ability and dedication, based on the conviction that everyone is born with the seeds of virtue. By self-cultivation and by following virtuous examples, anyone can become a sage. No priests are necessary, only self-development.

This concept was later incorporated in the imperial examination system and the selection of officials from the ranks of the educated, regardless of their social origins. Confucianism also reaffirmed the right of the people to rebel against immoral or unjust rulers who had forfeited the mandate of Heaven by their lapse from virtue; loyalty to superiors was a basic Confucian tenet, but loyalty to moral principle could win out, although this often presented individuals with a severe dilemma: for example, fathers, however unjust, were rarely defied.

In general, Confucianism reflected the basically positive as well as practical Chinese view of the world, where the greatest of all blessings was the enjoyment of a long life, or, more accurately, "the enjoyment of living." This included the particularly Chinese emphases on the pleasures of good food, the production of children, and the attainment of a ripe old age surrounded by one's descendants. These are still notably Chinese values, and the culture built around them has attracted the admiration of successive generations of Western observers, who approach it from the perspective of their own more somber and more theological religious and social tradition with its overtones of original sin, guilt, retribution, and divine judgment. Confucianism was more human-centered and more life-celebrating. Hard work, achievement, and material prosperity and its enjoyment were valued and pursued, but the enjoyment of leisure, of nature, and of what Confucianists called "self-cultivation" were also important goals, far more than in the West. The educated elite obviously had more opportunity for such pursuits, including the chance to write about them and thus to provide us with evidence of their values.

Confucianism and "Heaven"

Although most peasants had a life of toil, they too enjoyed to the full what leisure they could manage, especially in winter with its succession of festivals, including the two-week celebration of Chinese New Year. Those who were fortunate enough to accumulate a bit more than was necessary for survival quickly adopted the lifestyle of the gentry. Rather than continuing to work their land or to amass more wealth, most of them rented the land out to tenants and lived on the rents even at a modest level. Most landlords owned very small amounts of land by Western standards, living on the income from 8 or 10 acres, and did not strive to become richer or to branch out into other enterprises, except for some money lending.

Natural calamities like floods, droughts, or earthquakes were commonly taken as portents of Heaven's displeasure at the unvirtuous behavior of rulers and as pretexts for rebellion, especially since they disturbed the Confucian sense of order and harmony, the greatest social goals. The natural world was seen as the model for the human world, both running by regular rules. Nature was a nurturing power, not a hostile one, grander and more to be admired than human works, something to which people should harmoniously adjust rather than attempt to conquer. But as Confucius said, "Heaven does not speak"; it merely shows us a model of order and harmony to emulate.

The occasional references to Heaven as an impersonal force superior to humankind are about as far as Confucius went beyond the human world. When disciples asked about the suprahuman world or the life after death, he merely said we had enough to do in understanding and managing human affairs without troubling about other matters: "Not yet understanding life, how can we understand death?" Although he did not explicitly say so, he did approve of what is rather misleadingly called "ancestor worship." In folk religion, ancestors were prayed to as if they could intervene as helpers. It may seem strange that the Chinese retained the relatively primitive practice of ancestor worship, although after the Shang "veneration" or "commemoration" may be a better term. It is clear in China by at least 4000 B.C., as it was in ancient Egypt, where, as in China, it was incorporated into state rituals. Both societies were very conscious of their pasts, and China exemplified special respect for age, for parents and grandparents, and for tradition. Formal Confucianism merely extended respect for one's elders to those who had gone before, valuing them as models and performing regular rituals in small household shrines to keep their memory alive. It was the duty of the eldest son to perform rituals on the death of his father, through successive generations, keeping the ancestral chain intact and thus ensuring family continuity. Mencius underlined this by saying that of all sins against filiality, the greatest was to have no descendants, by which he meant male descendants, since women left their parental family at marriage and became members of their husband's family. This attitude still plagues current Chinese efforts to reduce the birthrate, since it clearly favors sons and may influence the parents of girls to keep trying for a boy.

In the twelfth century A.D., many centuries after Confucius and Mencius, the Confucian philosopher Chu Hsi (Zhuxi, 1130–1200) went somewhat further in speculat-

❈ The Confucian Code ❈

Confucius said:

At fifteen I set my heart on learning. At thirty I was firmly established. At forty I had no more doubts. At fifty I knew the will of Heaven. At sixty I was ready to listen to it. At seventy I could follow my heart's desire without transgressing what was right.... I am a transmitter and not a creator.... By nature men are pretty much alike; it is learning and practice that set them apart.... Learning without thinking is labor lost; thinking without learning is perilous. Shall I teach you what knowledge is? When you know a thing, say that you know it; when you do not know a thing, admit that you do not know it. That is knowledge.... A young man's duty is to be filial to his parents at home and respectful to his elders abroad.... and while overflowing with love for all men, associate himself with humanity.... Do not do to others what you yourself would not like.... The gentleman is concerned with what is right, the petty man with what is profitable.... The gentleman is always calm; the inferior man is always worried.... The gentleman makes demands on himself; the inferior man makes demands on others.

Source: Selections from W. T. deBary, ed., *Analects, Sources of Chinese Tradition*, Vol. I (New York: Columbia University Press, 1960), pp. 22–31.

ing about the nature of the universe, where he saw the working of abstract principles (rather like those of Plato) and a Supreme Ultimate, or impersonal cosmic force. From his time on it is appropriate to speak of Neo-Confucianism, which also stresses self-cultivation and the goal of every person to become a sage. Like classic Confucianism before it, Neo-Confucianism spread to Korea, Vietnam, and Japan, where it became the dominant philosophy, especially for the educated.

Because Confucianism never developed a formal priesthood or set rituals, some analysts feel that it is not a religion, although the same can be said to a somewhat lesser degree of Hinduism, Buddhism, and Islam. Faithful Confucianists did build temples in nearly every city and town in China and northern Vietnam, as well as many in Korea and some in Japan. These were cared for by people who were called priests, who did conduct what may be called services, usually in honor of the ancestors or of illustrious local figures of the past. Such services are carried out for the sage himself at the large temple complex erected at his birthplace in Shantung (Shandong) Province. After Confucianism became, in effect, the state religion during the Han dynasty, the emperor of China presided over annual rituals at the imperial capital to intercede with Heaven for good harvests, to pray for rain, an end to floods, pestilence, or civil chaos, or to commemorate the imperial ancestors. Emperors sometimes also issued penitential edicts acknowledging their lack of virtue as a ruler, real or fancied, in order to persuade Heaven to restore prosperity or the broken harmony of society. This stemmed from the Confucian precept that if things went wrong lower down it was the result of the bad example or lack of moral leadership of the "superior men."

Some analysts have attributed the rapid economic growth rates of modern Japan, Korea, Taiwan, Hong Kong, Singapore (a Chinese city), and more recently mainland China to their common heritage of Confucianism, with its stress on collective effort, hard work, education, and the dedication of individuals to the interests of the larger group: family, work unit, or even state. Such an analysis does fit the circumstances and achievements of these societies, as it also helps to explain the long-lasting success of imperial China. Confucianism in general strikes an interesting balance between providing scope for individual self-development or cultivation, and hence achievement, on the one hand, and on the other the subjection of the individual to the greater good of the family and society. Individualism and freedom, basic positive values to Americans, have in East Asia the chief connotation of selfishness and lack of rules. The result of both is chaos and anarchy, from which everyone suffers. Every society evolves its own balance between individual license and the need to protect the group interest and to preserve order through rules. Confucianism persisted because it worked, as the creed

of probably the world's most successful society over so long a time.

MO-TZU

Another philosopher, Mo-tzu (Mo Zi), who was born about or soon after the death of Confucius, was for a time his rival in influence. His teachings are recorded in some essays and dialogues, rather like those in the Confucian *Analects*, where he attacks Confucianism and stresses the need for logic. In Mo-tzu's bitter denunciation of war and his promotion of what he called "universal love," one can see a reaction against the violence of his times, and also against what he called the "graded love" of the firmly hierarchical Confucian prescription. These views probably helped to account for Mo-tzu's popularity, at least for a time, but he also adopted what seemed to most people other quite extreme positions. These included the abolition of all hereditary power (although this was to be accomplished by the Ch'in a few centuries later) and, perhaps more upsetting, the limitation of food, clothing, and housing to bare necessities. He is described as a utilitarian, and thought that all emotions, music, art, funerals, and the ceremony (ritual) so dear to Confucius were wastes of time. The text of Mo-tzu is heavy going, unimaginative, and humorless, perhaps in keeping with his killjoy and antiaesthetic views. But Mo-tzu also said that the interest of society would be best served if "everyone would love others as much as he loves himself," a view which of course corresponds closely with the Christian Gospels and attracted the attention of Western missionaries in the nineteenth century.

By Mo-tzu's time, it would seem that most Chinese, and certainly the social and political systems and their power structures, were too firmly supportive of the Confucian-style hierarchy (which in fact had been characteristic of China from its beginnings, long before Confucius) to consider an egalitarian alternative; that was to wait another 2,500 years, for the Chinese Communist party. Mo-tzu and his ideas, including his interest in logic rather than emotion or simply "human heartedness," were almost wholly rejected by the third century B.C., although they would certainly have enriched Chinese philosophy and perhaps softened some of the more rigid or rank-conscious aspects of Confucianism. Unfortunately, Mo-tzu himself, or his teachings, struck most Chinese as far too rigid and austere for their basically pleasure-loving or life-celebrating nature. Mo-tzu's philosophy also had an authoritarian aspect; he demanded total obedience from his followers, which may have turned off some people, and spoke of a strictly disciplined state which would carry out his teachings. The state would invoke a moral "Heaven"

✠ Reflections on Social Reform ✠

The philosopher Mo-tzu (Mozi), who was born in the fifth century B.C. soon after Confucius, was less of a traditionalist and more interested in reforming society.

It is the sage's business to regulate the world; he must thus know whence disorder comes in order to be capable of regulating it.... The origin is the lack of mutual love.... All the disorders of the world have this cause and this alone.... If mutual love prevailed universally throughout the world, no state would attack another state; no family would trouble another family; thieves and brigands would not exist; princes and subjects, fathers and sons, would all be filial and good. Thus the world would be well governed.... Where do ills comes from? They come from hatred of others, from violence toward others.... The love which makes distinctions among persons causes all the ills of the world.... This universal love is very advantageous, and far more easy to practice than you imagine. If it is not put into practice, that is because the rulers take no pleasure in it. If the rulers took pleasure in it, I believe than men would throw themselves into it.... Nothing on earth could stop them.... To kill a man is called an unjust thing; it is a crime deserving death. To kill ten men is ten times more unjust, to kill a hundred men a hundred times more unjust. Today every prince in the world knows that this must be punished; they declare it unjust. Yet the greatest of injustices, the making of war, they do not punish. On the contrary, they glorify it and declare it just! Truly they do not know how unjust they are.

Source: After H. Maspero, *La Chine Antique* (Paris: Presses Universitaires de France, 1927), pp. 253–254.

---

in handing out appropriate rewards and punishments. Mo-tzu's followers were a devoted band, much better organized than those of Confucius; but like many religious sects it did not long survive his death.

Taoism

The second major moral or religious philosophy of traditional China after Confucianism was Taoism (Daoism). Its answer to the chaos of the Warring States was in effect to withdraw from all worldly matters and to seek solace, and answers, in nature. The Tao (Dao, "the Way") is hard to define since one of the basic axioms of Taoism is silence, even inaction. The observable, rational human world is not what matters. It is from the cosmos one must seek guidance, but this is not the realm of words. As Confucius claimed to be the codifier of the wisdom of an earlier "golden" age, Taoism was probably based at least in part on older ideas, and also referred to a "golden age" of the past. Its emphasis on the natural world may reflect early Chinese worship of nature, like

its mysticism, which some scholars have related to ancient shamanism. The Taoist aim is to achieve "tranquility in the midst of strife" and to assert the independence of the individual, free of the rigid social and political controls implicit in Confucianism. "Tranquility" suggests a reaction against the "strife" of the Warring States period; but where Confucius prescribed the restoration of order through rules, Taoism sought a solution in rejection of the political world and the search for personal peace in the great world of nature. It stresses "doing what comes naturally," noninterference, and personal spontaneity.

The chief text of Taoism, the *Tao te Ching* ("Classic of the Way"), is a cryptic collection of mystical remarks whose meaning even in Chinese is unclear, let alone their meaning in the many hundreds of Western translations. The famous opening line is typical, varyingly translated as "The name that can be named is not the eternal name," or "The Way that can be spoken of is not the true Way, which is inconstant," implying (one supposes) that truth cannot be put into words or, if at all, only through riddle and paradox. Much of its content is attributed to a contemporary of Confucius, known simply as Lao Tzu (Laozi, "The Old One"), although the present text is not older than the third century B.C. and was probably compiled by several hands. Lao Tzu is said to have debated with Confucius and to have disappeared in old age, traveling westward, where he somehow became an immortal.

On one point the *Tao te Ching* is clear: "Those who understand don't talk; those who talk don't understand." This may well have been aimed at the Confucians. Although Taoist figures did occasionally speak or write, it was usually in riddles or in parallels with nature, all making the point that worldly strivings, and especially government, are both futile and wrong. Their message is to relax, go with the flow, stop trying to "improve" things (as the Confucians were always doing), and model yourself on water, flowing around obstructions, adapting to what is, and seeking the lowest places. Whatever is, is natural, and hence good. The ideal of the Taoists was a small state where the dogs and roosters of a neighboring state could be heard but whose people were content never to visit it. Efforts to "improve" invariably bring disaster; law is the cause of crime, as wealth is its source. Mechanical devices are against nature and must be avoided.

The other major figure of Taoism is the philosopher Chuang-tzu (Zhuangzi, died c. 329 B.C.). The text which bears his name also dates from the third century B.C., and is clearly the work of many different hands after his death, consisting of anecdotes about him. In them he further pursues the relativism, mysticism, and amorality already associated with the school; the stories about him are still intriguing. One of the most delightful tells of how he dreamed he was a butterfly and when he woke could not be sure if he was himself or if he was the butterfly, now dreaming he was Chuang-tzu.

Taoism grew into a religion as it merged with folk beliefs, earlier animism and worship of natural forces, belief in the supernatural, and a variety of mystical practices. Taoist priests, temples, and monastic orders developed (however inconsistent with the earlier message), and the original rather esoteric philosophy became a mass religion. Later Taoists, especially after the Han dynasty, practiced magic and alchemy and pursued the search for elixirs of immortality. Such activities put them in bad repute with proper Confucians, as did their habit of irresponsible hedonism or pleasure seeking. However, the Taoist search for medicinal herbs and their varied experimentation contributed importantly to the growth of Chinese medicine and other technology. In this they deviated from their supposed founder's injunctions to accept nature without questioning and began instead ot probe for its secrets.

As it acquired a mass following, Taoism also developed a pantheon of gods and immortals offering help to people in trouble and also easing the way to a Taoist ver-

Scholar Viewing the Moon. **This Ming dynasty painting reflects the Chinese interest in the beauty and wonder of the natural world, which is also the Taoist message. (Seattle Art Museum)**

sion of the Buddhist heaven. It increasingly merged with folk religion and with Buddhism, and even provided the populist religious sanctification for mass movements and rebellions, and for cults centered on faith healing. But as already suggested, Confucianists often found Taoism attractive even though they might scorn its "superstition" and magic. It was aptly said that most Chinese were Confucian when things went well (or when they were in office), and Taoist when things went badly and in retirement or old age—workday Confucians and weekend Taoists. Confucianism's activism

✵ The Tao ✵

The Tao te Ching is hard to fathom, but many of its passages are appealing as a kind of mystic text. Here are some samples.

- There was an ever-flowing something that existed prior to heaven and earth. Silent and shapeless, it stands by itself and does not change. So may it be the mother of heaven and earth.

- The Way is void, yet inexhaustible when tapped.

- Always make the people innocent of knowledge, and desireless, so those with knowledge dare not, and refrain from wrongdoing. Of old, the followers of the Tao did not teach people cleverness. A people difficult to rule is because they are too clever.

- Emptying one's heart in pursuit of the Void, that is the exhaustion of all inquiries.

- Men should be bland, like melting ice, pure and peaceful like a block of uncarved wood.

Two centuries after Lao Tze, Chuang Tze's essays deal with happiness and pain, life and death, with a perspective typical of Taoism.

I received life because the time had come. I will lose it because the order of things passes on. Be content with this time and dwell in this order, and then neither sorrow nor joy can touch you.… The inaction of heaven is its purity; the inaction of earth is its peace.… How do I know that loving life is not a delusion? How do I know that in hating death I am not like a man who, having left home in his youth, has forgotten the way back? … Man's life between heaven and earth is like the passing of a white colt glimpsed through a crack in the wall: whoosh!, and that's the end.

Source: The excerpt from the Tao te Ching was translated by Chao Fu-San. Chuang Tze translated by Burton Watson in *Early Chinese Literature* (New York: Columbia University Press, 1962), pp. 163, 164.

and social reformism were complemented by Taoism's passivism and laissez-faire philosophy. Taoism's intrinsic sympathy with aestheticism as well as with nature meant that poets and painters were usually Taoists in essence, and, after all, even Confucius himself praised the natural order as the proper model for human society.

This dualism appealed also to older Chinese notions of harmonious balance in all things and the principle of *yin* and *yang*, where yang is strong, assertive, intellectual, bright, and male, and yin is soft, gentle, passive, intuitive, aesthetic, and female. Taoists and Confucianists alike agreed that both nature and humans must approximate a balance of yin and yang elements, and agreed also in seeing nature as a model for man. One may say that Confucianists were *yang* and the Taoists *yin*, but since every person should strive for a balance

of the two elements, most Chinese combined both. But where Confucianism sought to shape the world through education, Taoists urged acceptance of things as they are, confident that human meddling could not improve on cosmic truth, compared to which it was in any case microscopically petty. Confucians officially scorned the Taoists, but most Chinese found both attractive, for different reasons. Many members of the educated elite and thus necessarily at least lip-service Confucians, were in practice Taoists at heart, especially artists and poets.

Late in the Warring States period, as it approached its climax with the victory of Ch'in (thought of by the other states as "barbarian"), a new school of philosophy, men who called themselves disciples of Hsün-tzu, was advanced as the only guide for state and society. It was

❇ More from the Tao ❇

We put thirty spokes together and call it a wheel;
But it is on the space where there is nothing that the usefulness of the wheel depends.
We turn clay to make a vessel;
But it is on the space where there is nothing that the usefulness of the vessel depends.
We pierce doors and windows to make a house,
And it is on those spaces where there is nothing that the usefulness of the house depends.
Therefore just as we take advantage of what is,
    we should recognize the usefulness of what is not.

Source: From the Tao Te Ching, as translated in Arthus Waley, *The Way and its Power* (London: Allen and Unwin, 1949), p. 135.

Yin-yang circle

called Legalism, since it asserted that harsh laws, not morality, "goodness," or *li*, should be the only way to ensure order. Of course it quickly won a bad press from Confucianists and followers of other schools, and it did not survive the catastrophic fall of the Ch'in, but it is interesting as an alternate view, another set of prescriptions for the chaos of the Warring States era, and at least some of its ideas were incorporated as a necessary part of the new statecraft of empire. It is best discussed in Chapter 4, dealing with the Ch'in conquest in which it played such a key role.

The Chinese Language

This is the place, however, to discuss the nature and evolution of the Chinese written language, transmitted to the rest of East Asia in the course of the Ch'in-Han creation of empire and in subsequent centuries. It is both a mirror and a shaper of Chinese and East Asian culture, more than language in other areas because of the importance attached to the written word and because of the nature of the characters, or symbols, in which it is written. Writing everywhere began as pictographs, and China is no exception. What is unusual is that this was not succeeded by a set of phonetic symbols as everywhere else. The characters early became too basic and unique a part of Chinese culture to be abandoned when China learned of phonetic systems in use elsewhere. Some saw them as having an inherent almost-magic quality, which they seem to have had on the oracle bones. Inscriptions, such as for weddings or funerals, are still seen as possessing power in the characters themselves, and bad consequences are thought to come from their destruction or desecration. Paper with characters written on it is sacrosanct, even so-called scrap paper, and must be reverently preserved. Characters used for names, both personal and place names, are carefully chosen to convey auspicious meaning. Calligraphy is seen as the supreme art form, even more so than painting, and the work of accomplished calligraphers is cherished in museum collections. By the second century A.D. some 35,000 characters were in use; by the eighteenth century as many as 50,000 were recorded in the biggest dictionary.

The persistence of characters has greatly strengthened the sense of continuity and identity with the origins of Chinese civilization since before the Shang. Some of the characters used on the oracle bones are nearly identical with the modern forms or are easily recognizable. It is as if modern Europeans could read and feel a close connection with the hieroglyphs and culture of ancient Egypt or the cuneiform texts and culture of Sumer. Even Greek is an unknown language to most modern Westerners, despite the clear antecedents of Western civilization in classical Greece. Some sample comparisons between Shang characters and modern ones are given on page 54.

Most Chinese words are monosyllables, and the characters thus help importantly to distinguish words which may sound the same, although in the spoken language this is dependent on the tones in which each word is pronounced: level, rising, falling, or a combination of rising and falling. Most words in the spoken language, and many in written Chinese, are, however, combinations or compounds of two (sometimes three) sounds or characters, so that in practice there is seldom any ambiguity of meaning. This is so despite the absence of inflections—tenses, cases, articles (like "the" or "a")—which seem so important in other languages. In the absence of plural-singular or past-present distinctions, Chinese merely uses the root form and depends on context, or on the addition of another monosyllable to indicate past or plural. Thus "house" may mean "houses" as well, "stream" "streams," "go" "went" or "will go," and so on. There is also only one word which does duty for he, she, or it, so that verb forms do not have to follow gender rules; the addition of "-men" turns these into "they," as "io" ("I") becomes "io-men" ("we"). This great degree of simplicity may suggest that the spoken language has been around a long time and has worn away what are really nonessential ornaments, although this is much debated.

We have few clues to the nature of the spoken language even five hundred or a thousand years ago, still less in Shang or Chou times. Rhymes used in the poetry of each period provide a little help, but we can assume that for spoken Chinese, as for all other languages, continual changes were taking place at every period which made the speech of, say, five hundred years earlier unintelligible. We can easily confirm this for our Western culture by trying to read Chaucer in fourteenth-century English; we even have to struggle a bit to understand parts of Shakespeare in the late sixteenth-early seventeenth century. The great virtue of written Chinese is that it changed relatively little; although new characters were added and a few meanings altered a bit, the cumulative body of characters remained much the same, so that Han, Chou, and even Shang texts can still be read.

This was of enormous value to the Chinese, with their keen sense of history, their valuing of the past, and their respect, even reverence, for the written record. And of course despite the homophonic nature and regional variations of the spoken language, all educated people used and read the same characters, as they studied the same set of "classics" with their Confucian message. One can still see people, often from different dialect areas, clearing up a problem in spoken communication by sketching rapidly on their palms a character or two—"Do you mean this *wu* or that one?" *T'ang* may mean "soup" (first tone), "a pond" or the famous dynasty or "sugar" (second tone) to flow (third tone), or an axle (fourth tone). This sounds more problematic than it is in practice; as one learns a word, one learns its tone, just as we learn its pronunciation.

The administration of a vast empire would have been impossible without a common writing system—and the development to accompany it of a standard speech called "kuan-hua" ("official speech"), the origins of modern standard spoken Chinese now called "kuo yu" ("national speech"). China is a huge country, originally occupied by widely differing cultures with separate languages plus great dialectical differences. Traces of this remain in Cantonese in the Canton area, although nearly all its words are the same as in standard Chinese, just pronounced differently. Originally it was a wholly different language, allied to or identical with Vietnamese, as the two groups shared a common culture and state in the ancient kingdom of Yüeh. The old state of Wu in the Yangtze delta area also had its own speech, some of which remains in Wu dialect. The speech of Fukien (Fujian) Province remains separate from (though related to) standard spoken Chinese, reflecting its relatively late incorporation in the empire and its mountainous and hence relatively isolated base, related more closely to the sea than to the main body of China. Taiwan (Formosa) was settled mainly from Fukien, and Taiwanese, the dominant language of the island, is the same as coastal Fukienese.

Canton has been absorbed into the main body of Chinese culture for so long, since the Ch'in conquest of the third century B.C., and for many centuries served as the chief port for foreign trade; consequently, while its language is still distinctive (and uses *nine* tones—six common and three less commonly used), its close affinity with standard spoken Chinese is clear. Each province has its distinctive regional dialect, something which occasionally or briefly puzzles visitors from another province, but they are all easily recognizable versions of standard spoken Chinese. Szechuanese is probably the most distinctive provincial dialect, but one might be inclined to

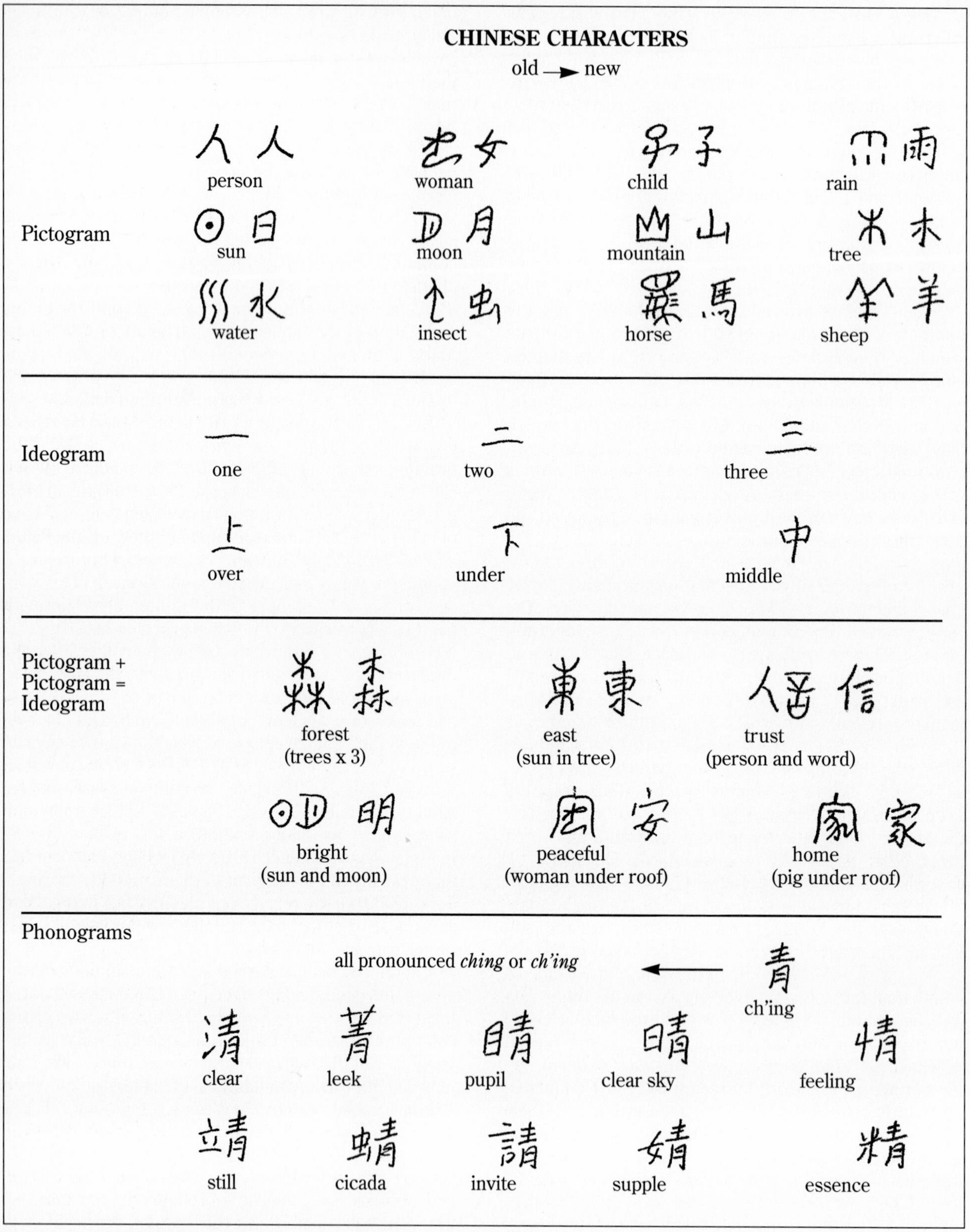

CHINESE CHARACTERS

old ➝ new

Pictogram

人 人 person   㐅 女 woman   子 子 child   雨 雨 rain

⊙ 日 sun   月 月 moon   山 山 mountain   木 木 tree

川 水 water   虫 虫 insect   馬 馬 horse   羊 sheep

Ideogram

一 one   二 two   三 three

上 over   下 under   中 middle

Pictogram + Pictogram = Ideogram

森 森 forest (trees x 3)   東 東 east (sun in tree)   信 信 trust (person and word)

明 明 bright (sun and moon)   安 安 peaceful (woman under roof)   家 家 home (pig under roof)

Phonograms

all pronounced *ching* or *ch'ing*   ⟵   青 ch'ing

清 clear   菁 leek   睛 pupil   晴 clear sky   情 feeling

靖 still   蜻 cicada   請 invite   婧 supple   精 essence

Courtesy of Kenneth Dewoskin

argue that there are no greater dialectical differences in China proper (outside Fukien and the Canton area) than in the United States, remembering the large blocs of Spanish speakers, the development of Black English, and the gap between the speech of a Maine backwoodsman and someone in the Louisiana bayous.

This leaves out of course Tibetan, Mongol, Uighur (in Sinkiang), and some other smaller non-Han language groups also on the fringes not yet wholly displaced by Han Chinese expansion and settlement. But since Han Chinese are something like 95 percent of the total population, one can certainly speak of *the* Chinese language, spoken now by well over a billion people, without having to give it a dialect name such as "Mandarin." The word comes from Portuguese, "mandare," to lead, and was meant to designate the official speech, or *kuan-hua*, but it has long been the speech of most people, and has been especially widely disseminated in a more uniform fashion through the education system, which now reaches nearly everyone.

If spoken Chinese had been inflected, with plurals, cases, and genders like Western languages, it would long ago have been obliged to depend on a more flexible phonetic writing system. Its homophonic and simple nature, free of the ornamentation of other tongues, may have been another powerful reason for retaining the characters with their heavy load of unique tradition and shades of meaning. It may seem a great burden for successive generations to learn to read, but in fact China, and later Japan as well as Korea and Vietnam, achieved what appear to have been the world's highest literacy rates well before modern times, and Japan still leads the world in literacy. The heavy hand of Confucian learning is in part responsible for this with its insistence on memorizing the classics as the only path to worldly success and prestige. Two or three thousand characters must be learned to read even the simplest texts (except those especially designed for younger learners: The Hundred and Thousand Character "Classics"), and five thousand to read a newspaper with any ease. But characters have a beauty and a fascination which phonetic scripts lack, and once learned are seldom forgotten. Most of them are built around a basic "radical" as it is called, such as the sign for water or for tree, to which other strokes are added, sometimes only a few but for complex ones as many as twenty-five.

The premium this places on memorization and on perfecting one's calligraphy as the mark of an educated person has probably hampered the freer development of education, and perhaps of innovative thought. The current regime has simplified many of the characters, part of the effort to spread literacy to all, and we now have computers which can write characters, although without the aesthetic appeal of good calligraphy, written

with black ink made from pine soot and a brush, the same instrument used by painters, who begin their training with calligraphy. Chinese characters carry a rich freight of meaning and subtler qualities than speech. This gives them a condensed vividness in both poetry and prose, which can pack into a few lines a wide range of expression. Poems are usually short, much shorter than any translation can capture while at the same time it must leave out the many shades of meaning which the characters convey. Given their terseness, written texts can be read more quickly than phonetic script; the reader takes in a character at a glance, where combinations of alphabetic letters must be worked out, and the frequent pitfalls avoided; a character is unique, and to a literate East Asian is a unique and integral part of the culture.

If China had developed or adopted a phonetic script, it might well have remained a series of separate national groups, while East Asia would never have evolved as a distinct unit sharing so much in common. Until about a hundred years ago, most books written in Korea and Vietnam and many of those in Japan were in classical Chinese rather than in each national language, even though each of them did develop phonetic systems which represented the sounds of each spoken language. Chinese remained the language of learning. Even now, educated people throughout East Asia can read books in Chinese, although they pronounce the words very differently, and one can still see signs—street names, subway stops, place names, and so on—written in characters, and sometimes personal names for more formal use, which are pronounced as if they were the Japanese, Korean, or Vietnamese names, although the meaning has remained constant and some of the sounds of each language are often indicated in each country's distinctive phonetic syllabary.

The present Chinese government, in addition to simplifying many of the characters for easier learning, has also created and (still "unofficially") endorsed the supposedly phonetic-based *pin yin* system of romanization in Western letters (see the note on romanization systems at the beginning of this book and the *pin yin* equivalents given for most proper names throughout). Both moves are intended to promote literacy, and many official pronouncements are now issued in *pin yin*. But the characters persist, and probably will continue to be used as long as China retains its distinctive identity, of which they have so long been such an important part. All East Asian societies, China most of all, are deeply conscious of their great past. To lose the characters would be unthinkable, and not only for the educated elite. Like other societies outside the modern West, East Asians have had to manufacture or find equivalents for the enormous number of new words spawned by industrialization and technological change in the past two centuries, as the West did when these changes began, often adapting words from Greek or Latin, such as dinosaur ("terrible lizard"), hypotenuse, sine, dynamite, or proton. Some of those coined in East Asia were relatively easy, such as "fire car" for locomotive or train (although that betrays its coinage when all trains were steam-powered); "energy car" for automobile is better, though our word automobile is derived in turn from Greek and Latin.

Other technical or scientific words presented more problems, and, as elsewhere outside the West, many of the original Western words are used instead of relatively awkward artificial constructs based on Chinese words or characters. This has been easier for Japanese, and to an extent for Korean and Vietnamese, with the help of their phonetic syllabaries, and indeed Japanese has a special subsystem used mainly for transliterating words of foreign origin; this has also helped to bring into the language a number of primarily English words in more common use, pronounced Japanese-style but written out intelligibly in the syllabary, remembering that Japanese pronounce every syllable and stress them equally, as we do not. Hence we get basu-ball-u (baseball—very popular in Japan), isu-crem-u (ice cream), bed-u (bed—not known in Japan until after 1870), and even su-ku-way-u-dans-u (square dance), plus many many more, enough to earn the label "Japlish." This kind of flexibility is harder in Chinese, although it is not unknown. The Japanese have long been outstanding in their willingness to adopt or adapt things and ideas of foreign origin wherever they saw them as improvements, beginning long ago with their wholesale adoption of Chinese culture from the eighth century A.D. Chinese have been more enamored of their own great past, and more resistant to influences from abroad, which were commonly dismissed as "barbarian" and hence of no worth to the "civilized" Chinese. Koreans and Vietnamese, deeply in the shadow of the Chinese colossus next door, had similar attitudes until very recently, but then their experiences with foreigners, like those of China, were uniformly bad, unlike Japan, which was never successfully invaded until 1945.

The retention of Chinese characters, like Chinese pride in their own tradition, has probably been in balance a handicap in China's long struggle to come to terms with the modern world, something the Japanese managed with relative ease. But the emotional and aesthetic rewards of written Chinese have also been sustaining, and it is one of the special hallmarks of Chinese and East Asian civilization, clung to as something uniquely their own.

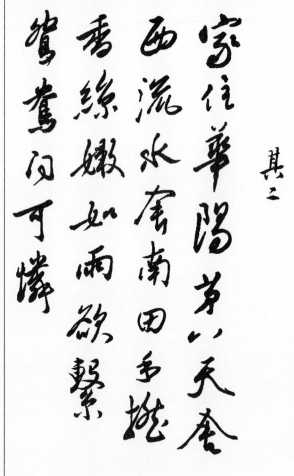

My abode is in Huayang's
Eighth heaven,
On the west a brook,
On the south a field.
I finger the fine silk
Tender as rain—
I long to use it
In match-making for the true lovers.

A sample of fine calligraphy, read vertically from right to left. From Elsie Choy, *Leaves of Prayer.* **Hong Kong: The Chinese University Press, 1933, pp. 174–175. Calligraphy by T. C. Lai.**

Suggestions for Further Reading

Chamberlayne, J. H. *China and its Religious Inheritance*. London: Allen and Unwin, 1993.

Chan, W. T. *An Outline of Chinese Philosophy*. New Haven: Yale Press, 1969.

Creel, J. G. *Confucius: the Man and the Myth*. New York: John Day, 1949.

_____. *What is Taoism?* Chicago: Univ. of Chicago Press, 1970.

Dawson, R. *The Analects*. Oxford University Press, 1993.

Gernet, J. *Ancient China from the Beginnings to the Empire*. Berkeley: Univ. of California Press, 1968.

Graham, A. C. *Disputers of the Tao*. La Salle, Ill., Open Court, 1989.

_____. *Chuang Tzu: The Inner Chapters*. London: Allen and Unwin, 1981.

Hansen, C. and Lindruff, K. M. *Western Chou Civilization*. New Haven: Yale Press, 1988.

Hansen, C. *Language and Logic in Ancient China*. Ann Arbor: Univ. of Michigan Press, 1983.

Hawkes, D. *Ch'u Tz'u: The Songs of the South*. London: Oxford Univ. Press, 1959.

Hsu, C. Y. *Ancient China in Transition*. Stanford Univ. Press, 1965.

Kitagawa, J. M. ed. *The Religious Traditions of Asia*. New York: Macmillan, 1989.

Knoblock, J. *Xunzi*. Stanford Press, 1988.

Legge, J. *The Chinese Classics*, 5 vols., Hong Kong Univ. Press, 1960 (reissue).

Liao, W. K. *The Complete Works of Han Fei Tzu*. London: Probsthain, 1959.

Mair, V. H. *Tao Te Ching*. New York: Bantam Doubleday, 1991.

Morgan, K. W. *Reaching for the Moon: Asian Religious Paths*. Chambersburg, Pa.: Anima, 1991.

Munro, D.J. *The Concept of Man in Early China*. Stanford Univ. Press, 1969.

Overmyer, D. L. *Religions of China*. New York: Harper and Row, 1986.

Peerenboorm, R. P. *Law and Morality in Ancient China*. Albany: SUNY Press, 1993.

Rubin, V. A. *Individual and State in Ancient China*. New York: Columbia Univ. Press, 1976.

Schwartz, B. I. *The World of Thought in Ancient China*. Cambridge: Harvard Press, 1985.

Taylor, R. I. *The Religious Dimensions of Confucianism*. Albany: SUNY Press, 1991.

Thompson, L. G. *Chinese Religion*, 4th ed. Belmont, Calif: Wadsworth, 1988.

Waley, A. *Three Ways of Thought in Ancient China*. New York: Doubleday, 1956.

_____. *The Way and its Power*. London: Allen and Unwin, 1934.

_____. *The Book of Songs*. London: Allen and Unwin, 1954.

Watson, B. *Basic Writings of Mo-tzu and Han Fei-tzu*. New York: Columbia Univ. Press, 1967.

Welch, H. *The Parting of the Way*. Boston: Beacon Press, 1957.

Wilhelm, R. (transl) *The I-ching*. Princeton Univ. Press, 1967.

CHAPTER 4

CH'IN AND HAN: THE MAKING OF EMPIRE

The victory of Ch'in in 221 B.C. marks a decisive turning point in Chinese history, a watershed dividing the ancient feudal past from the imperial centuries which followed until the collapse of the last dynasty, the Ch'ing (Qing), in 1911, almost as long a period as that from the beginnings of Chinese civilization about 2000 B.C. to the Ch'in conquest. Ch'in was one of the poorest, smallest, and most remote of the Chou dependencies; it seemed easily outclassed by the other contending states in the struggle for supreme power. But its frontier location protected it to some extent from the warfare which drained the resources of the others, and from the beginning it was organized on a martial basis. Like the Western Chou before them, the Ch'in were the guardians of the frontier, and warfare was their occupation. They kept their Wei valley base secure against invasion from the other states while they built up their own armies and strictly disciplined their people for war. In other parts of the world too, it was often peripheral groups which eventually succeeded to central power: Upper Egypt in the time of Menes, Macedon under Philip and Alexander, the Germanic tribes in the declining years of Rome, Muscovite Russia from the fourteenth century, and others, all cultivating the arts of war.

The Ch'in also benefited from a succession of able rulers, as the early Chou had done. They made virtues of the state's relative poverty and peasant base and stressed the importance of frugality, hard work, and discipline, free of the degenerative luxury which was growing in many of the other states with the rise of merchant

and urban culture. The Spartan circumstances and directives of Ch'in bred hardiness, as the Spartans, Macedonians and later the Scots and the Gurkhas of Nepal thought about themselves. Agriculture, which the Ch'in saw as the only sound basis of the economy, was also less susceptible to disruption or damage than the trade which had become more important in the economies of other late-Chou states. Merchants and intellectuals were despised, as parasites and as boat-rockers, while peasants could make good soldiers and were more easily commanded. In contrast to the other states, Ch'in had no literature, no music, no theater. It was a grim place.

In a long series of campaigns, the tough armies of Ch'in defeated those of rival states. The mountain-ringed Ch'in base also helped to keep the fighting away from the Wei valley and its agricultural economy, the source of food, taxes, and soldiers, while the more fragile economies of its enemies were often devastated. Opponents saw the menace of rising Ch'in power too late to unite against it and were picked off one by one. Ch'in was originally dismissed as "barbarian," and as too small, weak, and remote to be a serious threat. Ch'in statesmen and generals were masters of strategy and tactics, and used diplomacy, espionage, propaganda, and treachery adroitly. They were adept at psychological warfare and at keeping their enemies guessing, frequently breaking agreements, shifting sides, and suddenly mounting lightning attacks without warning, often after disarming their opponents or weakening their morale by propaganda. Hitler might have taken lessons from the Ch'in, including from their ruthlessness. Other states tried trickery too; representatives from Ch'i urged Ch'in to build huge irrigation works, hoping this would divert them from war and exhaust their resources. But Ch'in followed the advice—perhaps they saw through its supposed purpose?—built the irrigation canal and distributary systems, and emerged stronger than ever, with now a never-failing agricultural base. In the course of the third century B.C. they built not only an army but a state which had the power to win out in a troubled age of contention.

Ch'in's authoritarian character was expressed most clearly in the development of the philosophical school known as Legalism. The Legalists were certainly influenced by Hsün-tzu (whose disciples they claimed to be) and his pessimistic view of human nature, and probably also by Mo-tzu's utilitarianism (which does seem to find more than an echo in Ch'in domestic policies) and his insistence on absolute obedience. The chief text of Legalism is the essays of Han Fei-tzu, who died in 233 B.C., over a decade before the final Ch'in triumph. Li Ssu (Li Si), who survived to witness the collapse of the Ch'in empire and died in 208 B.C., was another prominent member of the Legalist school who served as the prime minister of Ch'in under its last ruler, Prince Cheng, who became in 221 the first emperor, with Li Ssu as his right hand man. Lord Shang, an earlier Ch'in official (died 338 B.C.) and probably the first of the Legalists, summarized state policy in classic totalitarian terms:

> **Punish severely the light crimes ... if light offenses do not occur, serious ones have no chance of coming. This is said to be "ruling the people in a state of law and order"**
>
> **A state where uniformity of purpose has been established for ten years will be strong for a hundred years; for a hundred years it will be strong for a thousand years ... and will attain supremacy....**
>
> **The things which people desire are innumerable, but that from which they benefit is one and the same. Unless the people are made one, there is no way to make them attain their desire. Therefore they are unified, and their strength is consolidated....**
>
> **If you establish what people delight in, they will suffer from what they dislike, but if you establish what they dislike, they will be happy in what they enjoy.**[1]

In other words, in unity is strength, although it must be created by force, and the state knows what is best for people, whatever they may say or choose. Han Fei-tzu also stressed the need for severe laws and harsh punishments as the only way to establish *order*, under the direction of the ruler. He argued that people are naturally selfish (as Hsün-tzu had said), and they must be held mutually responsible for each other's actions. All of this sounds pretty awful, but visitors to Ch'in from other states before 221 B.C. remarked on the positive and confident atmos-

phere they found there and the sense of conviction that the Ch'in represented progress and a political wave of the future. The partial text of the Ch'in legal code, along with a case book and a number of sample cases, have been found which contain also instructions to magistrates. In general, they show a remarkably even-handed justice where rank or status was not the determining factor. The code and the legal practice instructions are quite detailed, and appear to have ensured far more equality under the law than in later dynasties where we have similar information. For example, the penalties for wife-beating under the Ch'in code were the same as for any case of beating. There are also cases from Ch'in courts where a father was punished for beating his son, something which the Confucian society of later centuries condoned as wholly within the father's rights. Nevertheless, the Legalists insisted that "right" was what the ruler wanted, and "wrong" what the ruler did not want, wholly on grounds of expediency. Everyone was held responsible and punished for the actions of everyone else, and informers were rewarded, a vicious system.

Book learning was condemned, and people should be kept "dull and stupid." The law embodies the ruler's will, and the penalties for disobeying it are so harsh that the ruler can relax and enjoy himself. In response to Confucianism, the Legalists said:

> **Goodness alone does not enable a father to keep unruly children in order, still less can it enable a ruler to govern a mass of people to whom he is bound by no ties of kinship. Force can always secure obedience, an appeal to morality, very seldom.... The people are no more capable of understanding the ultimate object of all unpleasant things that are done to them than a baby is capable of understanding why ... its boil is lanced.... The small pain to which it is being subjected will result in a great gain.**[2]

The only qualification for official appointment must be, not "goodness" or learning, but proven ability to do the job efficiently and honestly—not such a bad idea—but the sole aim of the state is to expand its frontiers at the expense of other states. Agriculture and military strength are the only activities worthy of state support. Agriculture is hard work and war is risky, but:

> **If there is no hope of gain except from the soil, the people will work hard in their fields; if there is no hope of fame except through service in warfare, the people will be ready to lay down their lives.... Concentrate the people on warfare and they will be brave; let them care about other things and they will be cowardly.... A people that looks to warfare as a ravening wolf looks at a piece of meat is a people than can be used.**[3]

In less than ten years, Ch'in conquered all of the remaining rival states, finally exterminating Ch'u in 223,

Yen in 222, and Ch'i, the last to fall, in 221. The king of Ch'in now took the title of emperor as Ch'in Shih Huang Ti. He had risen to power in Ch'in supposedly as the son of a favorite dancing girl and a rich merchant named Lü Pu-wei of the state of Wei, near modern Kaifeng (later the capital of the Northern Sung dynasty). According to a Han dynasty account, Lü, who loved to "buy cheap and sell dear," decided to interest an exiled prince of Ch'in in his dancing girl, whom he had already made pregnant; he presented her to the prince, and by bribery managed to get the prince accepted as the Ch'in heir apparent. The prince died, however, in 246 B.C., and the dancing girl's son succeeded him at the age of 13, which gave Lü the chance to consolidate power in his own hands. But when his illegitimate son reached maturity he wanted power for himself, and had Lü poisoned. The tale, part of a collection of stories, is not necessarily accurate, but it shows the future emperor as a ruthless lover of power, fully in keeping with what we do know of him and his future career. The story is also both a Legalist and a Confucian slap at parasitic and scheming merchants.

Thus in 221 north and south China were politically united for the first time as an empire, to which the new regime applied the systems which had built Ch'in power. Further conquests after 221 began the long Chinese absorption of the hillier and remoter south, beginning with the acquisition of the old kingdom of Yüeh centered by then in the Canton delta but including what is now northern Vietnam, where there was a secondary Yüeh capital at Hanoi. Tributaries of the Yangtze and their valleys were avenues of invasion southward, and

also centers of southward moving Chinese settlement. Throughout the new empire, as in the former state of Ch'in, primogeniture (whereby the eldest son inherits all of the father's property and status) was abolished, as was slavery except for minor domestic servants. Land was privately owned and freely bought and sold; the new empire was divided into 36 "commanderies" (later increased to 42 with new conquests), and subdivided into administrative counties (hsien) ruled by an imperial magistrate. Both systems were continued by the Han and all subsequent dynasties. The state levied a tax on all land in the form of a share of the crop. The new Ch'in law code was applied to all subjects without discrimination, ending many centuries of aristocratic privilege, a reform which clearly appealed to most people. Currency, weights, measures, and forms of writing, previously widely varied among what had been separate cultures and states, were also unified by imperial fiat to follow the Ch'in mode, a change essential for empire. An imperial system of roads and canals was begun, and a splendid new capital called Hsian Yang was built near modern Sian (Xian) in the Wei valley. Even axle lengths for carts were standardized, so that all carts would fit the same ruts.

Probably the most spectacular and best known of the new public works projects was the Great Wall, which Ch'in Shih Huang Ti ordered consolidated from a series of much earlier walls along the northern steppe border and reconstructed as a uniform barrier with regularly spaced watchtowers. It and subsequent reconstructions (the remains currently visible date from the Ming re-

The Great Wall was probably Ch'in Shih Huang Ti's most famous project. The wall was built wide enough to allow two war chariots to pass abreast. The sections of it that remain standing date from its most recent major reconstruction under the Ming dynasty in the fifteenth century. (American Museum of Nastural History)

building in the fifteenth century A.D.) constitute probably the largest single works project in human history. The Great Wall was made possible by the new mobility of labor, which could be freed from farming at least seasonally. Reportedly, 1 million men died in building the wall, conscripts working as corvée labor (work performed as part of state tax, equivalent to military conscription). Ironically, the wall was never very effective in its supposed purpose of preventing nomadic incursions; end runs around it, and intrigues which opened the gates, made it often quite permeable. It was seldom easy to distinguish friend from foe, harmless traders or travelers from troublemakers or invaders disguised in small groups. But it did serve as a symbolic affirmation of empire, and as a statement of territorial and sovereign limits. "Good fences make good neighbors," the Chinese might have said, to which the Mongols and their predecessors might have replied, also quoting Robert Frost (however anachronistically), "Something there is which doesn't love a wall." The new and powerful state control over mass labor tempted the emperor, with his megalomaniac tendencies, to plan more and more projects of monumental scope, including the road system, the new canals (useful for transporting troops and their supplies as well as for irrigation), and his own magnificent palace and tomb, in addition to fresh conquests.

Ch'in Authoritarianism

As in the Ch'in state, hardy peasants were available in off seasons for corvée or for the army. Trade and merchants were still regarded as parasitic, and as potentially dangerous power rivals to the state, hence in part the removal of primogeniture, which also reduced the threat from landed power. But the chief target of the Ch'in system was intellectuals, people who ask questions, consider alternatives, or point out deficiencies. China already had a long tradition of scholars, philosophers, and moralists, of whom Confucius and Mencius were honored examples. The Ch'in saw such people, perhaps accurately, as troublemakers and boat-rockers. It was an openly totalitarian state, and its sense of mission made it additionally intolerant of any dissent.

Ch'in Shih Huang Ti persecuted intellectuals, buried several hundred scholars alive for questioning his policies, and ordered burned all books which could promote undesirable thoughts, which meant most books other than practical manuals and the official Ch'in chronicles. The documents destroyed included invaluable material accumulated from earlier periods. There was to be no admiration of the past, no criticism of the present, and no recommendations for the future, except the state's. These policies, more than anything else, especially the

burning of the books, were profoundly contrary to the Chinese reverence for the written word and the preservation of records. They earned the emperor the condemnation of all subsequent Chinese scholars and historians. Certainly he was a cruel tyrant, inhumane, even depraved in his lust for absolute power. But his methods, harsh though they were, built an empire out of disunity, and established most of the bases of the Chinese state for all subsequent periods, including the present.

Much of his policies were in fact the work of his prime minister, Li Ssu. Tight state control over everything was augmented by a greatly expanded state bureaucracy and by rigid supervision of all education. Only those values that supported the state design were inculcated, and practical skills were stressed over critical inquiry. There was a highly developed police system, and a secret service to ferret out and punish dissidents. Another potential source of ferment, travel, within the realm or abroad, was forbidden except by special permit.

Empire building, anywhere and in any form, is a disagreeable business, and one may question its usefulness in any case. Are people better off forcefully unified in an empire, at tremendous cost in lives, than if they had been left to their own regional cultures and states? Unfortunately empire building seems to be a common human failing, as is inhumanity in the name of religion. Both have the appeal, at least for some, of a grand idea, or simply of pride, for which costs are not counted. China once unified, even by such methods, was to cling to the idea of imperial unity ever thereafter. Each subsequent period of disunity following the fall of a dynasty was regarded as a time of failure, and each ended in the rebuilding of the empire. But one must acknowledge also the appeal of the new order which the Ch'in represented. By its time most people were clearly ready to break with their feudal past, and to move toward a system based on achievement rather than birth. The Ch'in believed firmly that their new order was progress; they had a visionary conviction that they were creating a better society. The parallels with Communist China were striking, and indeed Ch'in Shih Huang Ti was praised as a model during the Cultural Revolution in the late 1960s. Sacrifice for an inspiring national goal has its own appeal; the end is seen to justify the means, including treachery, cruelty, and inhumanity toward the people, who are nevertheless seen as supposedly the beneficiaries of the new order. A Ch'in adage used also by the Communists was "A thousand die so that a million may live."

Nevertheless, there was merit in the new equality under the law, and new opportunities for advancement; and ambitious projects have an allure which draws people to support them, perhaps especially those associated with empire building. The best illustration of the more constructive aspects of the Ch'in is the figure of Li Ping (Li Bing), appointed provincial governor of the former state of Shu (Szechuan–Sichuan) and also famed as a hydraulic engineer associated with many of the big Ch'in projects, including control works on the Yellow River. It was Li Ping who announced the best formula for minimizing the floods that had already made the Yellow River notorious: "Dig the bed deep, and keep the banks low." This helped to prevent the build up of silt in the river's bed, which in time raised it above the level of the surrounding country and greatly worsened the destructive consequences of floods that could not forever be retained within the dikes along the river's banks. Li Ping's sound advice was finally acted on effectively only under the present Communist government after 1949. Li Ping is credited with designing and constructing the famous irrigation works at Kuan Hsien (Guanxian) in western Szechuan, diverting the Min River where it emerges from the mountains and enters the wide plain around the capital city of Chengdu. They were reputed to have saved millions of people on the Chengdu plain from drought and famine since their construction. His irrigation works, much visited by tourists, still stand, his statue overlooked by that of his son Cheng Kuo, who completed the project. Like all big projects, they took enormous labor and hardship, mainly from conscript workers under iron discipline. According to the great Han dynasty historian Ssu Ma Ch'ien (Simaqian) writing a century later, toward the end of his life Li Ping said:

> **People can be depended on to enjoy the results, but they must not be consulted about the beginnings. Now the elder ones and their descendants dislike people like me, but hundreds of years later let them think what I have said and done.**

Li Ping's memory is still honored, while that of his emperor is reviled.

Ch'in Shih Huang Ti was buried in a huge underground tomb near modern Sian with an army of life-size clay figures to guard the approaches. Excavations in the 1970s brought them to light again after more than 2,000 years; each figure is a faithful representation of a real individual. (John Henebry)

The Han Dynasty

Ch'in Shih Huang Ti died in 210 B.C., leaving the throne to his eldest son, but Li Ssu and other counselors suppressed the news of his death for fear of uprisings, and then installed the second son as their puppet. The first emperor had built a huge underground tomb with forced labor, still only partly excavated, where 2,000 terra-cotta figures of warriors stood guard, realistic images of actual people, in place of the earlier burial of live or sacrificed followers. But the harshness of Ch'in rule had left the country in turmoil, exhausted the people, drained the treasury, and alienated the upper class. Without their cooperation, the regime was in trouble. The empire was in fact already collapsing into rebellion, and several army commanders deserted. Li Ssu was arrested and killed in 208 by his own police because he lacked the travel permit which his own laws had required of everyone. The empire he had helped to found, to last a thousand years, had collapsed in only 15, like Hitler's "Thousand Year Reich." In 206 B.C. rebel armies occupied the capital and burned the emperor's splendid new palace. Rival forces contended for power in the ensuing struggle and large

groups of soldiers, workers, and former officials roamed the country. By 202 B.C., a new rebel leader, Liu Pang (Liu Bang), emerged out of this chaos; he had risen from peasant origins by his ability, and thus made the point that leadership was no longer the exclusive preserve of the aristocracy. He founded a new dynasty, which he named the Han. Under Han rule China took both the territorial and the political and social shape it was to retain until the present century. The Chinese still call themselves "people of Han," in distinction from Mongols, Tibetans, other domestic minorities, and more distant foreigners, a label which they carry with much pride as the heirs of a great tradition of culture and empire first established in its classic form by the Han. Han dynasty imperial success, and that of later dynasties, depended however on retention of many of the techniques of control used by the Ch'in. The administration of an empire the size of all of Europe, and with a population of probably over 60 million people by Han times, could not have been managed otherwise.

Beginning with the Han, the harsher aspects of the Ch'in Legalist approach were softened by both common sense and the more humane morality of Confucianism. Liu Pang, who took the title Han Kao-tsu ("High Progen-

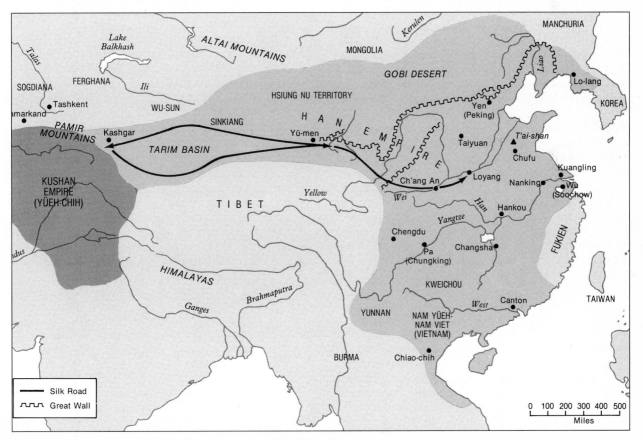

The Han Empire

Rubbing from a Western (Former) Han tomb tile: Tiger and mounted archer with compound reflex bow. (Royal Ontario Museum)

itor") as the first emperor, emphasized the Confucian precept that government exists to serve the people and that unjust rulers should forfeit both the mandate of Heaven and the support of the ruled. He abolished the hated controls on travel, education, and thought, lowered taxes, and encouraged learning so as to build a pool of educated men whose talents, in the Confucian mode, could be called on to serve the state. However, conscription for the army and forced labor for public works such as road and canal building were retained, as was the administrative division of the empire into *hsien* (*xian*, "counties"), each under the control of an imperial magistrate. The imperial state superimposed its model in all things, including currency, weights, measures, script, and orthodox thought, on a vast and regionally diverse area which had long been politically and culturally varied. Under beneficent rule, this was a system which could be made to work successfully and could command general support. Early Han was a time of great prosperity, and of enthusiasm for the new order.

Expansion Under Han Wu Ti

But power corrupts everyone and everywhere, and the new power of the Han empire, on Ch'in foundations and with the boost of new economic and population growth, tempted successive emperors to further conquests and imperial glory. Liu Pang's son and grandson continued his frugal and benevolent model as rulers, but the bitter memories of Ch'in had faded by the time of the emperor Wu Ti (Wu Di, 141–87 B.C.). He first tightened imperial

control, removed the remaining power of the lords created by Liu Pang for faithful service, imposed state regulations on trade and merchants, and set new taxes and new state controls on salt, iron, and the supply of grain. The last measure, which came to be known as the "ever-normal granary system," was intended to prevent famine by state collection of grain in good years or surplus areas, for sale at low, controlled prices when lean years came. It was a good idea and was practiced with some success also by subsequent dynasties but, like Li

Bronze casting continued its development under the Han. This magnificent horse from the second century A.D. shows the sophistication of Han technology and art. (The Granger Collection)

Ping's projects, was not always popular with the local producers, let alone the merchants.

Having put the imperial house in order and increased state revenues and state power, Wu Ti began in 111 B.C. an ambitious program of new conquests, first in the southeast against Yüeh in the Fukien and Canton areas, which had broken away after the fall of the Ch'in. The Yüeh kingdom had included the related people and culture of what is now northern Vietnam, and this was again added to the Chinese empire. Thus began the long struggle of the Vietnamese to reassert and maintain their separate identity despite their absorption of much of Chinese literate culture. In Han times, the southern people and culture of Yüeh were regarded as foreign and were in fact very different from those of the north; more than traces of these differences remain even now, including the Cantonese language and cuisine, but the south has been an integral part of China for 2,000 years and has been largely remade in the greater Chinese image. The people and culture of Vietnam were still more different and regained their independence from China after the fall of Han.

Turning north in 109–08 B.C., Wu Ti's armies conquered southern Manchuria and northern Korea for the empire, while other campaigns established a looser control over the still non-Chinese populations of Yunnan and Kweichou (Guizhou) in the southwest. Southern Manchuria was to remain off and on Chinese territory and in any case solidly a part of the Chinese system, with large originally military colonies planted there by Wu Ti. These became agricultural settlements in the fertile valley of the Liao River.

Similar garrisons were established in northern Korea, and there was heavy Chinese influence from Han times on. But the Koreans, like the Vietnamese, remained anxious to reclaim their national identity and independence. As in Vietnam, Korea had already generated its own civilization and cultural style and was linguistically and ethnically distinct from China despite massive Chinese cultural influence. After the Han collapse in A.D. 220, both areas broke away from Chinese control—Korea as a nominally tributary state, Vietnam to endure later Chinese reconquest under the T'ang and then successive wars of independence until modern times, with a heavy legacy of mutual mistrust reflecting the last 2,000 years. The Vietnamese record of repeated nationalist success in expelling the seemingly overpowering forces of imperial China should have been enough to dissuade the United States from its own misadventure there; ignorance of history imposes a high price.

China's northern and northwestern frontiers had been and were to remain a chronic problem for other reasons. The Great Wall had been built to solve this problem, but it could not prevent infiltrations by the horse-riding nomads who occupied the steppe border zone and who periodically harried Chinese agricultural

areas and trade routes. The major route for international trade was the famous Silk Road through the Kansu Corridor and then running along the northern and southern edges of the Tarim Desert in Sinkiang (Xinjiang, Chinese Turkestan), where there are widely spaced oases fed by streams from the surrounding mountains. The two routes met at Kashgar at the western end of the Tarim and then crossed the Pamirs into central Asia, where the trade passed into other hands on its long way to the Levant and eventually on to Rome. Silk was the main export, a Chinese monopoly since Lung Shan times and in great demand in the West, especially in luxury-loving imperial Rome. The Romans were obliged to pay for it largely in gold, a drain which Pliny and other Roman historians felt weakened the economy and contributed to Rome's ultimate fall. It was profitable to China, and Wu Ti's pride in his new imperial power made him less willing to accept nomad interruptions of the trade and raids on Chinese territory.

The chief nomad group at this period was the Hsiung-nu (Xiongnu), a Turkic people whose mounted mobility and cavalry tactics gave them the kind of military effectiveness later used by the Mongol leader Chinghis Khan. The Han generals complained that the Hsiung-nu "move on swift horses and in their breasts beat the hearts of beasts. They shift from place to place like a flock of birds. Thus it is difficult to corner them and bring them under control." One can understand the Han frustration, but in a series of major campaigns Wu Ti defeated them, drove them at least for a time out of most of Inner Mongolia, Kansu, and Sinkiang, and then planted Chinese military colonies and garrisons in those areas and along the Silk Road, which is still marked by ruined Han watchtowers. Sinkiang and Inner Mongolia were to fall away from Chinese control in later periods whenever the central state was weak, but were reclaimed by most subsequent strong dynasties as part of the empire. Non-Han groups like the Hsiung-nu and the Mongols remained the major steppe inhabitants until the present century. Another Turkic people, the Uighurs, replaced an earlier Indo-European group as the dominant oasis farmers in otherwise desert Sinkiang by the eighth century A.D. The Uighurs later embraced Islam and helped to transmit it to China proper, where there are still a number of Chinese Muslims, concentrated in the northwest.

China and Rome

Wu Ti sent an ambassador westward in 139 B.C., a courtier named Chang Ch'ien (Zhangqian), to try to make an alliance with other nomads against the Hsiung-nu and to scout out the country more generally. He was captured instead by the Hsiung-nu, but escaped after ten years. Eventually, in 126 B.C. he returned to the Han capital at Ch'ang An ("Long Peace") in the Wei valley, where the Ch'in had ruled, with cuttings of the grapevine and seeds of alfalfa. He also brought firsthand accounts of central Asia, including bits of information about India and routes to it, and about a great empire far to the west, where the silk went. This was China's first news of Rome, but they were never to learn much more. Travelers who said they had been to Rome turned up much later at the Han court with their own tales, including a group of jugglers in A.D. 120 and some merchants in A.D. 166, both of whose visits were recorded in the Han annals. The Romans knew China only as the source of silk, and called it accordingly, Seres, the Latin word for silk.

Wu Ti was tempted by Chang Ch'ien's report to move on central Asia and add it to his conquests, partly out of pure vainglory, partly to secure supplies of the excellent horses to be found there, which he wanted for the imperial stables and his cavalry. If he or his successors had done so, the Chinese and Roman empires, or their forward troops, might have met and perhaps learned from each other. In the first century A.D., with the Han still in power and still occasionally probing westward, Rome was at the same time campaigning against the Parthian kingdom in Persia (Iran). If the Romans had conquered Parthia, they might have at least encountered Han patrols, or they might have followed the Silk Road, which they knew about, from central Asia to the borders of China. But both armies were very far from home. Moreover, the Parthians and other central Asian groups were formidable opponents, and were anxious to retain their profitable middleman position in the silk trade, as well as raiding the caravans, rather than letting the two empires meet. Later Han envoys in A.D. 97 reached the Parthians but were advised to return home, advice which they followed. According to the *History of the Later* (Eastern) *Han*, the Chinese were trying to make contact with the eastern part of the Roman empire in Syria and Mesopotamia, about which they had vaguely heard, and hoped to reach it via the Persian Gulf and/or the Red Sea. The Parthians replied:

> **If you meet slow winds it may take you two or three years. There is something about this sea which makes a man homesick, and several have lost their lives. When Kan Ying heard this he immediately decided to return.**

The Parthians obviously feared direct contact between China and Rome, which would eliminate their middleman role, end their caravan raids, and perhaps destroy their independence if the two giants could team up against them.

An extraordinarily lifelike pottery figure from a Han dynasty tomb in Szechuan shows a groom whistling for his horse. (Innervision/Overseas Archaeological Corporation)

Each empire thus remained largely in ignorance of the other except for travelers' tales, although both were of comparable size, sophistication, power, and achievements. China might have developed a different and more open attitude to the rest of the world on the basis of some experience with another empire and culture, Roman or Indian, at their own level of sophistication. Like the Chinese empire, both Rome and Mauryan India were builders of roads, walls, and planned cities, synthesizers of varied cultures under an expansionist and cosmopolitan system, and contenders with "barbarians" along the fringes of their empires. Of the three, the Han empire was the largest and probably the most populous and richest, although its level of cultural and technical sophistication was probably matched by both ancient India and Rome.

Wu Ti's endless campaigns and his impositions on the people exhausted the country's patience and resources. One of his earlier reforms had been the establishment of imperial censors whose job it was to keep officials, even the emperor, faithful to their duty to serve the people. The censors finally convinced Wu Ti that he had neglected this basic precept, and persuaded him to issue a famous penitential edict apologizing for his excesses and promising to be a better ruler, more deserving of the Mandate of Heaven—and less likely to be overthrown by rebellion, which was already brewing. The institution of the censorate remained a regulatory feature of all subsequent dynasties.

Wu Ti's immediate successors, while largely abandoning further conquests, continued to press the Hsiung-nu as a defensive strategy and even sent an expeditionary force across the Pamirs into the Samarkand region in pursuit. There, in 42 B.C., on the banks of the Talas River near Tashkent in central Asia, they defeated a Hsiung-nu coalition which included some mercenary troops, who, from the Chinese description, may have been Roman auxiliaries. These people had learned the Roman *testudo* formation with shields overlapping over their heads to ward off arrows and spears—another near miss at a direct encounter with Rome. Han armies in central Asia, having marched across deserts and high mountains, were farther from their capital than regular Roman troops ever were from Rome. But this was the high point of Han power, and the empire which Wu Ti welded together was not to be significantly enlarged in subsequent centuries, except for the much later incorporation of Tibet (and the loss of Korea and Vietnam as merely "tributaries").

nese civilization. Given the multiplicity and often the mutual hostility of the various cultural groups in central Asia during the ancient and medieval periods, the passage of goods and ideas through this area, in either direction, was necessarily slow and difficult. There was certainly trade from China and India to western Asia, Greece, and Rome. From at least 600 B.C. there was also sea trade, bringing Indian and Southeast Asian spices to the Mediterranean and Europe. But except for the visits of Greek and Roman traders to the coasts of India, and perhaps of Romans as far east as Malaya (where Roman trade goods have been found), plus the travels of a few Indian philosophers to Greece and Rome and the invasion of India by Alexander, there was no direct contact between Eastern and Western civilization from then until the time of Marco Polo in the thirteenth century. Arab ships traded by sea, and a chain of various central Asian peoples transmitted ideas as well as goods across Eurasia, but the transmission was incomplete, and understandably some of the ideas were lost or garbled in the process.

Commerce between China and the rest of Eurasia almost certainly developed later than India's trade with Mesopotamia, and there is no evidence of Chinese exports westward until the beginning of the silk route, probably during the Chou dynasty. Chinese merchants took the silk only as far as the eastern edge of Sinkiang, handing it over at Yü Men (the "Jade Gate") in western Kansu, China's traditional front door, to a long series of central Asian traders who passed it along through the thousands of miles to the shores of the Mediterranean, where Syrian, Greek, and Roman merchants picked it up for transport farther west. This trade continued after the fall of the Han dynasty and was later augmented by the export of porcelain and lacquer goods, all high-value commodities that could bear the very heavy costs of such long-distance transport. The camel caravans carrying them were also exposed to frequent raids from other central Asian groups along the route, risks which further increased the prices charged for Chinese exports when they finally reached their destinations. By the eleventh century much of the Chinese export trade was being carried westward by sea to India, while Indian exports westward—fine cotton textiles, spices, gems, and other goods—continued from the earliest times through the Middle Ages to move mainly by ship, from ports on the Indian west coast. There must have been some return flow of trade by sea from India to China, but apart from the mention of what sound like Indian merchants in ports on the south China coast, we know very little about it.

Wider Trade Patterns

Contacts across Eurasia had been important during and since the prehistoric period. Sumer may have contributed something to the origins of Indian civilization (and vice versa) and perhaps indirectly to the emergence of Chi-

Han Culture

The first two centuries of Han rule were also a time of great cultural flowering, in poetry, painting, music, philosophy, literature, and the writing of history. There was a renewed enthusiasm for books and learning after the Ch'in persecution and destruction. In part as a result, paper appeared by the end of the first century B.C. and was in general use by about A.D. 100. Confucianism was more firmly established in time as the official orthodoxy and state ideology, where the major figures were Kung-sun Hung (Gongsunhung—died 121 B.C.) and Tung Chung-shu (Dong Zhongshu), his younger contemporary, both noted for their moral interpretation of the *Spring and Autumn Annals*. Liu Pang, founder of the Han, had been born a peasant, and the new stress was on ability and education rather than on inherited status. He called for "men of talent to serve the state" and held examinations to select the fittest, a prefiguring of the civil service system institutionalized in later centuries. This approach was to remain a source of strength and effectiveness for the state for the next 2,000 years, and was rightly admired by the modern Western heirs of Plato. Officeholding by the scholar-gentry, who were enriched each generation by new blood rising from peasant or commoner ranks and entering the elite through the imperial examinations, became the most prestigious of all occupations.

Han dynasty scientists in the second century A.D. calculated the value of pi as 3.1622 and developed a highly accurate calendar, the wheelbarrow, and a bronze seismograph for recording earthquakes. The model shown here is based on a detailed description of the original. Eight dragons at major compass points along the outer edges of the vessel respond to tremors from the appropriate direction by spitting a pearl into the mouth of the frog below. (Ronald Sheidan/Ancient Art and Architecture Collection)

The sons of rich or gentry families obviously had strong advantages because their parents could afford to spare them from work and give them a classical education, often with a private tutor. But gentry status could not be inherited; it had to be won through passing the examinations, and many nongentry were able to pursue that route through hard work and the support of relatives and friends. We do not know what the proportion of such new entrants to the gentry class was before Ming times (1368–1644) but it seems to have been significant, if small; by the Ming it has been estimated at 30 percent in each new generation. Upward mobility was necessarily accompanied by the decline of others. Very few rich families kept their position more than two or three generations, after which they lapsed back into the general mass. "Rags to riches in three generations," as well as the opposite, was a Chinese as well as a Western proverb. The prestige of officeholding helped to ensure that able people went into the administration, and preserved the political arena and government service generally from much of the corruption, mediocrity, and ineffectiveness that have plagued political systems everywhere and at every period.

China was far from free of such problems or from other imperfections, but each new dynasty reestablished the system begun under the Han, and on the whole probably managed the task of government better than most other states, perhaps including most modern ones. One may thank Confucius for this, with his stress on duty, learning, "human heartedness," and virtue. Chinese society chose that way among many others and periodically reaffirmed what had been the minor teachings of an obscure consultant to a small feudal lord in the sixth century B.C., long before there was any thought of empire. Great landed-gentry families remained and were periodically nuclei of power, together with court aristocrats, eunuchs,* and ambitious generals—a pattern familiar from imperial Rome, Persia (Iran), and elsewhere. In China, the original Han ideal, however, endured through the rise and fall of successive dynasties and, with all its imperfections, built a long and proud tradition of power combined with service which is still very much alive in China. The Peoples' Republic is the conscious heir of greatness.

By the first century B.C. there were some 30,000 officials, concentrated at the imperial capital and in the provincial capitals but extending down to the imperial magistrate in each *hsien* city, the system the Han took over from the Ch'in. Beyond the *hsien* city, people were

---

*Eunuchs are men castrated as youths and hence without heirs so that they were often used as courtiers who could not intrigue on behalf of their sons. However, they often formed power cliques of their own and seldom used power responsibly.

Pottery figure titled *Balladeer*, part of the grave furniture from a Han dynasty tomb in Szechuan (Sichuan). The afterlife was clearly supposed to be a happy time, replete with worldly pleasures. This figure beautifully captures the human quality of Han folk culture. (Jack Deutsch Studio/Innervisions)

left pretty much to manage their own affairs, as long as they paid taxes, provided corvée labor (usually one month per year, sometimes more for big projects), and did their military service. Corvée was used for an expanded program of road and canal building, to knit the empire together, as well as for local public works projects, while the army carried out the conquests of new territory, the expeditions into central Asia, and the guarding of the frontiers. All of this strained the empire's resources, driven by the megalomania of Wu Ti, until he was finally persuaded to push his people less hard if he was to avoid a rebellion. It was courageous of the censors to rebuke him. In 99 B.C., when the courtier and historian Ssu-ma Ch'ien (see below) tried to defend a general who had been forced to surrender to the Hsi-

ung-nu and had been disgraced as a result, Wu Ti was enraged and had Ssu-ma Ch'ien castrated.

The new bureaucracy was staffed largely by Confucian scholars, who were anxious to replace the harsh rule of the Ch'in with policies more in keeping with the sage's teachings. Even Wu Ti, despite his Legalist tendencies, assigned 50 students to pursue the Five Classics, which he officially recognized. This became in time a kind of state university, which, by the end of the first century B.C., had 3,000 students and provided graduates who passed the imperial examinations and entered the civil service. Confucianism became the official philosophy of the state, and thus helped, like the sponsorship of Confucian learning, to ensure the support of educated people rather than driving them into support of rebellion as the Ch'in had done. Tung Chung-shu (see above) tried to relate the historical events recorded in the Spring and Autumn Annals theories of *yin* and *yang* and the Five Elements (earth, water, fire, wood, and metal) developed in the age of the philosophers in the Warring States period. Thus Confucianism, at least in Tung's work, was absorbing some elements of Taoism as in other respects it also at least took account of the political realities included in Legalism.

Tung was however a typical Confucian scholar in calling Wu Ti's attention to the plight of the poor, who suffered from both excessive rents and from government exactions. In addition to his treatment of Ssu-ma Ch'ien, Wu Ti executed five of his last seven chancellors who had displeased him, but with the courage of the Confucian "upright man" Tung advised him that:

> Ownership of the land should be limited so that those who do not have enough may be relieved and the road to unlimited encroachment blocked. The rights to salt and iron should revert to the people. Slavery and the right to execute servants on one's own authority should be abolished. Poll taxes and other levies should be reduced and labor services lightened so that people will be less pressed. Only then can they be well governed.[4]

Han rule was briefly broken by a palace coup of the usurper Wang Mang, a member of the imperial family who made himself emperor from A.D. 9 to A.D. 23 and announced the founding of the Hsin (Xin) dynasty. As a model Confucian ruler, Wang Mang tried to curb the resurgent power of merchants and of the landowning gentry. He also extended new state controls over the economy, all in an effort to reestablish the egalitarianism he claimed to derive from the sage's teaching. His reforms included the abolition of private estates, which had increasingly avoided paying taxes, and the nationalization of land. Such policies bitterly alienated the rich and powerful, and Wang Mang was murdered by a new rebel group called the Red Eyebrows, who were supported by both distressed peasants suffering from a drought-induced famine and by merchant and gentry groups.

Landowning and its abuses were problems for all ancient and medieval empires, and were to remain a plague for every Chinese dynasty. Ownership of land meant power, and the abolition of primogeniture did not always prevent powerful families from accumulating large blocks of land. Big landowners built up wealth but also threatened the supremacy of the state by their growing political power. By manipulating political influence locally, usually as members themselves of the gentry group with its official and unofficial connections, they managed to reduce or avoid paying state taxes on their lands or got them off the tax rolls entirely, a major problem for most dynasties. Their tenants, the peasants who farmed their land, were often cruelly exploited and hence driven to rebellion. Reformers in government periodically tried to correct these abuses, as in Wang Mang's abortive reforms and many similar efforts in later centuries, but the imperial state was never able to overcome completely the power of landed families.

In A.D. 25, the Han was reestablished, though under new rulers and with a new capital at Loyang (Luoyang), following the earlier model of the Chou and for the same reasons. It is thus known as the Eastern or Latter Han, while the Ch'ang An period from 202 B.C. to A.D. 9, is called Western or Former Han. The new rulers, a succession of strong and conscientious emperors, restored the power, prosperity, and cultural vigor of Wu Ti's time. Learning, philosophy, and the arts flourished once more and elite society reached new levels of affluence, elegance, and sophistication. Peace was reestablished along all the imperial frontiers by reconquest, and in A.D. 97 a Han army marched all the way to the Caspian Sea. Scouts were sent farther west, reaching either the Persian Gulf or the Black Sea before returning, another missed encounter with imperial Rome, then too at the height of its power and conquests. In A.D. 89 a Han army invaded Mongolia and again defeated the Hsiung-nu, probably contributing to the start of their subsequent migration westward and their ultimate role, now merged with other central Asian groups, as invaders of Europe under the name of the Huns. Sinkiang, northern Vietnam, northern Korea, southern Manchuria, and Inner Mongolia were all reincorporated into the empire, trade flourished, and China gloried in its confidently reasserted power and cultural leadership.

After the first century, landlord power and oppression grew again; Wang Mang had been right to try to curb them. There were growing peasant revolts, and imperial relatives and powerful families jockeyed for position or influence. The elite, especially those at court surrounding weak emperors, indulged themselves in luxurious living, heedless of the problems around them—all echoes of the problems Rome was facing at the same time. Palace intrigues grew out of control, and eunuch groups acquired more and more power. Generals in the provinces became rival warlords after suppressing peasant revolts. The entire imperial structure was crumbling, and in A.D. 220 the last Han emperor abdicated.

The power, wealth, and expansion of Han China were based in part on trade with Mongolia, Korea, central Asia, Vietnam, and northern India as well as on the productivity and trade of newly conquered south China. The incorporation of these areas within the empire (except for India and central Asia) gave it secure frontiers, defended

Han Confucianism

Tung Chung-shu, the leading philosophical spokesman of the Confucianism revived under the Han, included this statement in his "discources."

Heaven holds its place on high and sends down its blessings, hides its form and shows forth its light. Because it holds a high position it is exalted and because it sends down blessings it is benevolent. Because it hides its form it is holy and because it shows its light it is bright. Thus to hold an exalted position and practice benevolence, to hide one's holiness and show forth light, is the way of Heaven. Therefore he who acts as the ruler of men imitates Heaven's way, within hiding himself from the world so that he may be holy, and abroad observing widely so that he may be enlightened. He employs a host of worthy men that he may enjoy success, but does not weary himself with the conduct of affairs so that he may remain exalted. Loving all creatures, he does not reward in joy or punish in anger. ... He who is the ruler of men ... considers impartiality as his treasure.... No one sees him act, and yet he achieves success. This is how the ruler imitates the way of Heaven.

Source: From W. T. deBary, ed., *Sources of Chinese Tradition*, Vol. I, (New York: Columbia University Press, 1960), pp. 158–159.

Raised ceramic tile from a Han dynasty tomb showing a festive scene with jugglers, dancers, and musicians. (Private collection, Chengdu, PRC)

by mountain and desert barriers, beyond which there was little incentive to expand farther. But control over all of these regions beyond China Proper was lost with the collapse of the imperial structure. By this time nearly all of the Chinese originally settled in Sinkiang as garrison troops had withdrawn, leaving their watchtowers and fortified bases along the Silk Road to crumble away, like the Great Wall, in succeeding centuries. The loss of trade and revenue contributed to the fall of the dynasty, but the primary cause was self-destructive indulgence and faction fighting at court, as well as local and provincial rivalries. No empire, especially not one based on conquest, has lasted more than a few centuries at best. Regional and provincial counterpressures, and efforts by conquered peoples to reassert their independence, have joined with decay at the center to destroy every empire. The difference in China is that each new group which came to power founded a new dynasty, and strove to rebuild the empire the Han had first established.

Cities in Ancient China

The Shang capitals, and their immediate Lung Shan predecessors, were primarily cosmic, ceremonial centers, symbols of royal authority. The late Lung Shan city on the site of modern Chengchow (Zhengzhou) and the

Shang capitals there, at Loyang and at Anyang, were massively walled and gated. The walls enclosed royal palaces and tombs, royal residences, some quarters for priests, slaves or kept artisans, and military guards, but much of the enclosed area was not built on. Most nonroyal inhabitants, and most of the workers, lived in villagelike settlements outside the walls which, unlike the walled area, apparently were not planned. By at least late Shang, the Chinese character and the spoken word for *city* were the same as those for *wall*, and this has remained so to the present. Cities were in other words designed as statements of authority; the wall was a symbol of state or (later) imperial power, and distinguished cities from unplanned villages or market towns. Apart from the capitals, imperial and provincial, most cities first arose as county seats, the lowest rung of national administration and, from Han times, the base of an imperial magistrate.

Chinese cities were built predominantly of wood and thus very little evidence remains from this early period to show what they or their buildings may have looked like. By Chou times we do at least have some written documents that describe the precise planning of all walled cities and their ritual or symbolic importance, including their exact north-south orientation, and the arrangement and dimensions of the royal or imperial buildings within the walls. Religious cults such as ancestor worship and the worship of what the Chinese called Heaven, or the

Supreme Deity, were represented in every walled city by specific and carefully placed temples.

By the time of the Han dynasty, there had been nearly 2,000 years of urban experience in China; much of it was reflected in the Han capital at Ch'ang An. The site was carefully chosen by Liu Pang (Han Kao-tsu), the first Han emperor, but it was not until the reign of his successor, in 192 B.C., that the city walls were begun, 52 feet thick at the base and 27 feet high, made of pounded earth and over 3 miles long on each of the four sides. The walls enclosed imperial palaces, tombs, and temples to the ancestors among other temples, but as with the Shang, the Chou, and the Ch'in, much of the walled area was not built on, although it remained important symbolically. The government regulated and supervised market areas inside as well as outside the walls, and the city was divided into 160 wards. Straight broad avenues led from each of the major gates at the main compass points, but there was apparently a less planned growth of lanes and alleys in each of the quarters. The ideal city form was a square, which Han dynasty Ch'ang An approximated, with three gates on each of the four sides, one major central gate and two lesser ones on each of the four sides.

The Han now ruled an immense territory, much of it newly conquered, especially in the south. The imperial stamp on these new lands was achieved primarily through the building of walled cities. Once the original inhabitants had been subdued and the land cleared, settled, and farmed, garrison towns or fortresses gave way to or were made over as walled county seats from which the imperial magistrate could keep order, dispense justice, and supervise the collection of taxes and the exactions of corvée and military conscription. In the hilly south such cities often had to accommodate to the terrain and sometimes altered the square shape somewhat, but the imperial model was apparent in all of them, including their official buildings, temples, military barracks, and appointed and regulated market areas inside and outside the walls. One can in fact chart the southward spread of Han occupation and the growth of Chinese-style agricultural settlement by noting the successive establishment of new walled county seats. They appeared first along the rivers leading south from the Yangtze, and then spread progressively inland from the rivers. Cities were linked with each other and with the imperial and provincial capitals by the imperial road system begun under the Ch'in and greatly extended under the Han.

Han Achievements

China by Han times was highly developed technologically as well as culturally. Crop rotation, practiced since Chou times, was further improved, especially with the use of soy beans. Fertilization increased, and yields and output rose. Ch'ang An and Loyang were built mainly of wood, and little has survived to tell us much about them, but what accounts we have suggest that they rivaled imperial Rome in size and splendor. It is symptomatic of this vast bureaucratic empire whose culture also put a high value on learning and education that paper was first made there toward the end of the first century B.C., more than 1,000 years before the knowledge of paper making spread to Europe. Another Han innovation was porcelain (hard, glazed, nonporous ware), one more Chinese gift to the world, known everywhere simply as "china." Water-powered mills were invented in Han China, as was the prototype of the modern horse collar and breast strap which made it possible for draft animals to pull much heavier loads more efficiently and without being choked. Lacquer had made its finished appearance from its origins in late Chou by Wu Ti's time, and samples of beautiful lacquer pieces have been found in Han tombs.

Han dynasty alchemists invented the technique of distillation, not discovered in Europe until the fourteenth century A.D. Ships were built with watertight compartments, multiple masts, and sternpost rudders, and magnetic compasses were in use, a thousand years before the West. Early in the Han, steel was made from cast iron and coal, making possible a great improvement in tools and machinery, especially cutting tools. The circulation of the blood was also discovered in Han China, despite the conventional Western claim to its discovery by William Harvey in the seventeenth century. The wheelbarrow had made its appearance by late Han, much better balanced than its later Western copy, since the single wheel was placed in the middle instead of at one end, enabling greater weights to be transported with less effort. Metallurgy, already far advanced, depended on the further refinement of the double acting piston bellows, something not achieved in the West until the seventeenth century. The square pallet chain pump for raising water, and the suspension bridge, were in use by the Han many centuries before the West.

Probably the greatest literary achievement of the Han was in the writing of history, a consistent Chinese emphasis on preserving the record of the past. Many Chou records destroyed by Ch'in Shih Huang Ti were reconstructed by Han scholars from memory, and the texts we have date largely from this period. New pride in empire and tradition produced the man called China's Grand Historian, Ssu-ma Ch'ien (Simaqien, died c. 85 B.C.). His massive *Historical Records* put together materials from earlier texts in an effort to provide an accurate record of events since before the Shang and added summary essays on geography, culture, the economy, and biographies of important people. A century later Pan Ku (Ban Gu died A.D. 92) compiled a similarly comprehensive *History of the Han Dynasty*, which became the model for the standard

✠ End of an Empire ✠

The poet Wang Ts'an (A.D. 117–217) reflected on the horrors of the revolt of the Yellow Turbans, centered in the eastern part of north China but spreading beyond that, destroying cities and massacring people.

The Western capital lies in sad confusion;
The wolf and tiger come to plague the people.
Whitened bones were strewn across the plain.
Upon the road I saw a starving woman
Abandoning her infant in the grass;
She looked around when she heard its piercing wail,
But, brushing away her tears, would not turn back:
"I do not know at what place death may take me,
What can I do to help the two of us now?
I spurred my horse and left behind that scene;
I could not bear to hear the woman's words.
I turned about to gaze back on Ch'ang An
And thought how many had gone to the underworld,
Sighing a heavy sigh and my heart in pain.

Source: From *The Rise and Splendour of the Chinese Empire* by Rene Grousset, English translation by A. Watson-Gandy and T. Gordon (Berkeley: University of California Press, 1965), p. 95.

histories commissioned by each subsequent dynasty, another respect in which the Han set the pattern for later centuries. Interestingly, Pan Ku worked with his sister Pan Chao (Ban Zhao) in writing the *History*, and she also wrote on her own a classic, much studied in subsequent centuries, called *The Seven Feminine Virtues*.

Han writers set a high standard for historical scholarship that many Western scholars feel was not equaled elsewhere until the eighteenth century in the West. Here is another point of comparison between Han China and imperial Rome, where the writing of history also reached a high standard and reflected a similar pride in accomplishment and the tradition that had led to it. The Roman ideal remained appealing to the European mind and still underlies much of the modern West, but in China the state system, the imperial model, and most of the other institutions and forms first established under the Han endured to shape the course of the next 2,000 years.

Pressures on the Environment

The population total of 60 (or 59.6) million usually given for the Han is not based on a census in the modern sense, although the Han first began the effort, which all subsequent dynasties repeated, to find how many people they governed, and thus to determine tax yields, conscription

quotas, economic needs and potentials, and administrative requirements. It was not based on a full head count and was compiled at the capital mainly from each district magistrate's enumerating, or estimating, the number of households and the totals of fit adult males. Women and children were not counted as such, nor were slaves (perhaps 2 to 3 percent of the population); children, women, and slaves were simply subsumed under households. Non-Han populations were also left out—at that period a far larger proportion than the roughly 5 percent of modern times, although it is not known how large—and estimates for many remoter areas were at best sketchy. Sixty million is thus clearly an undercount, though by how much is hard to say. Figures were also often kept low because they were used as the basis for taxation. The true figure for total population may have been closer to 80 million, although that would represent a peak, probably sometime in the first century A.D. (the official "census" is dated A.D. 2), and there were fluctuations over time, mainly downward during troubled periods. But even 60 million was more than Rome ever controlled.

Population had thus increased six-or-eightfold (or more) since the Shang, and quadrupled or more since the Chou. The human pressure on the environment had already become drastic. Much of the remaining forest cover of the north had been cut by late Chou, especially after the development of iron axes. Even Mencius warned against this and its consequences by citing the traditional proverb "Mountains empty, rivers gorged." He also said:

> The trees of the Niu mountain were once beautiful (but) ... they were hewn down.... Then came the cattle and goats and browsed. To these things is owing the bare and stripped appearance of the mountain, and when people see it they think it was never finely wooded. But is this the nature of the mountain?[5]

There is little reason to think that the climate changed, at least after about 2000 B.C. Plant pollen preserved in the soil can help to reconstruct vegetation cover and hence climate over long past periods; that, and the evidence of relict stream channels, plus whatever we can extract from the texts of the oracle bones, suggest that the Shang climate was much the same as it is now: semiarid and prone to recurrent drought, although the progressive removal of tree and bush cover may, as elsewhere, have increased the proportion of rain which fell as violent thundershowers because of heat reflected from the bare surfaces, most of which runs off into stream channels before it can be absorbed. With tree and bush cover removed, it was very difficult for it to reestablish itself naturally in this dry climate. That left especially the slopes exposed to disastrous erosion, made worse by the porous and easily eroded loess soil which covered most of the north. Well into the Han, and later farther south, fire was widely used to clear forests, for cultivation and to make hunting easier, or to drive away wild beasts. Hunting was still important during the Shang, and the royal hunt used hundreds of people and killed thousands of animals, mostly various species of deer who could survive on the sparse pasturage, as the oracle bone texts recount in great detail, giving the tallies for repeated hunts. Climate fluctuated then as now, and the oracle bones speak of both drought and flood in different years. But it is the nature of climate to fluctuate everywhere, especially in dry areas on the margins of better-watered ones where annual variability of rainfall, for example, may reach 40 percent, as it does in the western half of north China, and where there may be long periods of drought or of less-than-average rainfall which may last as much as a century, balanced by others when rainfall returns to or exceeds the average. This was, of course, the situation which wiped out Chinese agricultural communities which had been tempted north of the line of the Great Wall during a period of more ample rainfall.

As population increased, the assault on remaining forests intensified, mainly to clear land for farming to feed the rising number of mouths. But mouths were accompanied by hands, now armed with iron tools, and there was also a growing demand for wood, as fuel and as building material. The Shang and Chou capitals had devoured huge amounts of wood in their construction, and the building of Ch'in Shih Huang-ti's enormous palace at Hsian Yang in the Wei valley is said to have stripped the trees from at least the lower half of the Tsinling mountains along the border with Szechuan. Han Ch'ang An and Loyang, also built mainly of wood, exacted a further huge toll, and probably completed the deforestation of most of north China except for the more inaccessible mountain areas in Shansi, Shantung, and Manchuria. Cooking and heating were still done largely with wood, or with twigs, branches, and grass gathered or grubbed up from the slopes surrounding most villages, the work of small boys who doubled as buffalo or cattle-tenders, although as supplies became scarcer and the nearby slopes were denuded, all of the family's efforts had to be marshaled. Such repeated clean cutting and subsequent picking over left no chance for seedlings or even grasses to reestablish themselves.

Fortunately the Chinese did not for the most part keep sheep or goats, whose close cropping destroys even grass cover if they are not moved on regularly, as the steppe nomads did. What herbivores the Chinese needed, mainly for draft purposes, were kept in stalls, often in or attached to the house, and fed on what small boys and other family members cut for them, or on what they could graze under close supervision. But the mounting pressures on all vegetation cover were inexorable as population rose, and already by late Chou there was serious erosion. Trees and bushes and grass, but most of all forests, act like a sponge and protective cover on the land, breaking the force of rainfall and absorbing it in their roots and forest litter, preventing its rapid runoff and storing it near the surface or allowing it to percolate into the water table for slow release between rainy periods and thus maintaining soil moisture levels. With the vegetation cover gone or decimated, rains wash unchecked down slopes, and may even cause sheet or splash erosion on apparently level ground. The water table is not adequately replenished, wells run dry, and soil is washed away, to choke irrigation systems and stream channels. This in turn greatly increases the frequency and severity of floods, as normal channels are blocked and cannot accommodate the next rush of water, which overflows and floods surrounding land, or cuts a new channel, which may be even more destructive of life and property.

This is essentially the story of the Yellow River ("China's Sorrow"), and to a lesser extent of all the rivers of north China. Efforts to build up the dikes in order to keep the river in its bed have prevented the escape of floodwaters, but at the cost of allowing the heavy load of silt the rivers carry to be dumped in the bed after the flood peak has passed. The Yellow River bed over much of its lower half has risen progressively until in many areas it is far above the level of the surrounding countryside. But this merely postponed the reckoning, as pent up floodwaters eventually and inevitably breached the dikes and flooded huge areas. The problem has been partially solved only under the present government, but erosion and siltation continue, as deforestation and clearing of slopes continue. Siltation has been disastrous for irrigation works too. The Cheng Kuo canal, built under the Ch'in to bring water from the Wei River to surrounding areas, irrigated 40 million *mou* (6 1/4 million acres) when it was opened in the late third century B.C. By the Tang, that area had shrunk to 10 million *mou*, and by the Sung (eleventh century), to 2 million, entirely as a result of siltation. Erosion and siltation hastened the decline of the Han, and in the longer run the decline of the north as a whole. By the time of the Tang dynasty (618–907) the chief center of population had moved south, into the Yangtze valley and beyond, and half or more of the empire's revenue came from there.

In the warm, moist climate of the south, where rainfall was well distributed through the year and normally without extensive dry periods, the vegetation cover was reasonably lush and more quickly regenerated after cutting. On the other hand, rainfall was far heavier than in the north, far more of the southern landscape was in slope, and much of it was mountains. As population spread southward the originally heavy forest cover was progressively removed to make way for agriculture, and deforested slopes were cut over for brush and grass as fodder and fuel. As in the north, this generated massive erosion, siltation of stream channels, and an increase in flooding. Removal of the forest also limited or destroyed the habitat of many plant and animal species. We have no record of species which became extinct but can guess that the numbers were in the many thousands. China is thought to have contained originally the world's largest range and number of fauna and flora, given the wide range of its climates, soils, and topography. That may still be the case even though so many species have been extinguished. In a few small areas and around temples samples of the original forest cover have been preserved. At Purple Mountain outside Nanking (Nanjing) a larger tract was fenced off around the mausoleum of Sun Yat Sen in the late 1920s. Within 20 years the once deforested mountain, now protected from cutting or gathering, had come to life again with a mixed coniferous-deciduous forest which gives us a reasonable idea of what the original forest cover of central China may have been.

🀫 The Fall of the Han 🀫

The popular Chinese novel Romance of the Three Kingdoms, *first written down in the fourteenth century* A.D., *tells of the fall of the Han and the civil war that ensued. The account begins as follows:*

Empires wax and wane; states cleave asunder and coalesce. When the rule of Chou weakened, seven contending principalities sprang up, warring one with another until they settled down as Ch'in, and when its destiny had been fulfilled there arose Ch'u and Han to contend for the mastery. And Han was the victor.... In a short time the whole empire was theirs, and their magnificent heritage was handed down in successive generations till the days of Kuang-wu, whose name stands in the middle of the long line of Han.... The dynasty had already passed its zenith.... The descent into misrule hastened in the reigns of the two emperors who sat on the dragon throne about the middle of the second century. They paid no heed to the good men of the court but gave their confidence to the palace eunuchs.... The two trusted advisers, disgusted with the abuses resulting from the meddlings of the eunuchs in affairs of the state, plotted their destruction. But the chief eunuch was not to be disposed of so easily. The plot leaked out and the two honest men fell, leaving the eunuchs stronger than before.... [Some years later] the earth quaked in Loyang, while along the coast a huge tidal wave rused in which, in its recoil, swept away all the dwellers by the sea.... Certain hens developed male characteristics, a miracle which could only refer to the effeminate eunuchs meddling in affairs of state. Away from the capital, a mountain fell in, leaving a great rift in its flank.... But the eunuchs grew bolder. Ten of them, rivals in wickedness, formed a powerful party. One of them became the emperor's most trusted advisor. The Emperor even called him Daddy. So the government went from bad to worse, till the country was ripe for rebellion and buzzed with brigandage.

Source: After C. H. Brewitt-Taylor, trans., *Romance of the Three Kingdoms* (Tokyo: Charles Tuttle, 1959), Vol. I, pp. 1–2.

As for animal species, the royal hunt under the Shang accelerated the extermination process, but the growing pressures of population, and the destruction of the original environment, were the major forces. Thus the population of rhinoceros, apparently fairly common in Shang times, was wiped out by the end of the Han; elephants were extinguished in the north and survived in parts of the south, but only for a few more centuries as the growing southern population destroyed their habitat as well as killed elephants for their ivory and to prevent their destruction of crops. Such large animals of course received much attention, but nothing is said about the probably similar fate of thousands of smaller species. Tigers survived into contemporary times, but only just, as an endangered species. In general, the Chinese have altered their original environment more than is the case for any other part of the earth, if only because there have been so many more people at it for so long.

In the wet rice areas of the south the water in the paddies protected the soil from erosion, and as population pressure pushed cultivation onto slopes, terracing was almost equally effective, though at high labor cost in relation to the crop output. Wet rice growing comes close to being a stable system, especially when given organic fertilization as from Han on. In the warm and generally sunny climate of the south the water in the paddies supports a variety of aquatic life—small fish, snails, crabs—which can be harvested or left to decompose when the paddy is drained and thus enrich the soil. Sunlight and high temperatures promote the growth of blue-green algae in the shallow water which are potent fixers of nitrogen, to return to the soil at harvest and thus keep up the nitrogen balance, the main element necessary for plant growth. A variety of nutrients also enters with the slowly moving irrigation water. There was of course a direct relationship between population and production of night soil for use as fertilizer. It does not seem to have been used much if at all before mid-Chou, when population totals reached a new high. Mencius refers to manuring as a common practice in his time, but night soil does not seem to have been used until the Han, when it spread rapidly in both north and south to help feed the new mouths.

But forests continued to be cut, and on the hillsides burned, in part to destroy wild animals seen as predators, in part to deprive bandits or rebels of cover, and in part to obtain with minimal effort fertilizer in the form of ash which the rains could wash down onto the cultivated land at lower levels. Efforts to measure the frequency of flooding and of drought in China since the Chou agree in finding a notable rise in the incidence of both beginning in the Han. Flooding is clearly and directly related to deforestation and the spread of cultivation on slopes in stream watersheds. Even by the time of the mythical Yü, founder of the Hsia dynasty, the floods which he sought to control in "taming the waters" must have been occasioned at least in part by the siltation of stream courses and the great increase in runoff following the beginnings of deforestation on the slopes of loessland. Later, Mencius condemned the practice of many officials of his time in encouraging the clearing of new land. The Han dynasty text *Huai Nan Tzu* (second century B.C.) includes a passage criticizing the widespread practice of burning forests as fuel for metallurgy: "Smoke obscured the very light of heaven and below the riches of earth were utterly exhausted."[6] The move south had to adjust to very different climatic and soil conditions as well as to hilly or mountainous terrain, a process which evolved over successive centuries. It took time to alter the agricultural techniques originally developed on the dry level plains of the north with their deep, fertile loess soil. Manuring and the use of night soil became universal in order to produce acceptable yields from the indifferently fertile and leached soils outside the immediate river valleys and deltas.

In general, the southern landscape was transformed on an even greater scale than that of the north, through its conversion to a vast man-made construct of carefully engineered and irrigated paddies whose soil was also largely artificial. On any but level land, scarce in the south, hillsides were transformed into man-made terraces, while the upper slopes were progressively cleared and used as gathering grounds for grass, twigs, and branches, or periodically burned. The landscape would be largely unrecognizable to people before the Han. Many scholars have wondered how it happened that the Chinese so thoroughly degraded their environment, given their supposed philosophical view of the "harmony between man and nature," which appears to contrast with the Western view since the time of the Book of Genesis, where Adam is told to "have dominion" over the natural world. The major reason seems to be simple population pressure. Our image of the Chinese as seeking a harmonious relation with nature is based on elite rather than peasant views, and it was peasants (plus merchants or their agents supplying a growing market for wood) who cut down the trees, as well as megalomaniacal emperors with their great palaces made of wood. There seems no question that the Chinese have altered their environment more even than Westerners have altered theirs. After all, we still have in Europe and North America extensive heavily forested areas, plus broad stretches of prairie, while Chinese forests are almost entirely gone and the areas of dense population have been almost totally remade to fit the intensive agricultural system.

In this respect, too, the Han marks the beginning of the Chinese system which was to last for some two thousand years in most of its characteristics, many of which are still apparent under Communist rule.

CHAPTER 5

BUDDHISM, BARBARIANS, AND THE T'ANG DYNASTY

he collapse of the Han in A.D. 220, following nearly a century of increasing disintegration of the imperial system and the rise of rival warlords, was a time of disillusionment and disaster. The last major Han figure was Ts'ao Ts'ao (Cao Cao), a former general turned bandit and warlord who sacked Loyang. But by his time the dynasty had become a joke, and the empire increasingly carved up by great landed families into their own satrapies and by rival generals. Three regional states reasserted their independence as separate kingdoms: Shu in Szechuan, Wu in the lower Yangtze valley and the southeast, and Wei in the north. This was the time of the famous Shu statesman, general, and strategist who tried to reestablish the Han tradition of unity, Chu Ko Liang (Zhugeliang, A.D. 181–234) about whom endless stories are still told. Many are recorded in the *Romance of the Three Kingdoms*, still widely read, and others have found their way into Chinese opera and folk tales and ballads. Chu was clever and dedicated, but in the long run he failed to stem the course of disintegration, despite many brilliant victories and the defense of Shu against invasion through the passes in its mountain wall by other states and by both Chinese and barbarian warlords, perhaps a little like the mythical Frankish hero Roland in his vain effort to withstand the supposed Saracen invasion in the eighth century, much celebrated in medieval European ballads. But the Chinese tradition was continuous, and songs and operas about Chu are still widely popular and widely performed, sentimentally attractive perhaps especially as a hero who failed.

Buddhism

Buddhism had come into China in the first and second centuries A.D., transmitted rather slowly from its Indian origins in the sixth century B.C., first to adjacent central Asia, and from there to Han China, spread by traders and by Han contacts with central Asia. The new faith spread slowly at first, but then began to appeal more widely as the political order disintegrated and Chinese, with their traditional distaste for chaos, turned to Buddhism's otherworldly message and its doctrine that the real, observable world of human affairs was illusory and insignificant. Great piety might lift one to a bodiless heaven, or Nirvana, while proper attention to the Buddha's precepts might at least ensure a higher status rebirth rather than a lower status one such as an animal or insect.

This was of course the Hindu doctrine of reincarnation or transmigration of souls, which Buddhism absorbed along with many other aspects of Hinduism such as its commitment to nonviolence and avoidance of taking life even for food, or "reverence for life," as Albert Schweitzer called it. Pious Hindus and Buddhists did not eat any kind of meat or fish and remained strict vegetarians. Hinduism is probably the world's oldest textually based religion, and Buddhism is best seen as an offshoot of Hinduism founded by the historical Buddha in the sixth century B.C. He and other contemporary religious figures in India reacted against the growing ritualization of Hinduism and its dominance by the priestly

Notes

1. From J. L. Duyvendak, transl., *The Book of Lord Shang*. London: Probsthain, 1928, pp. 193–194, 203, 209, 211, 229.
2. Han Fei-tzu, Chs. 49 and 50, p. 68, as quoted in A. Waley, *Three Ways of Thought in Ancient China*. New York: Doubleday, 1956, pp. 155, 164.
3. *The Book of Lord Shang*, transl., Duyvendak, op.cit., Ch. 6, p. 50, Ch. 18, p. 116.
4. From Burton Waston, transl., *Records of the Grand Historian: Chapters from the Shih-chi of Ssu-ma Ch'ien*. New York: Columbia University Press, 1971, pp. 32–33.
5. Legge Translation, Book III, Part I, Ch. 8–31, p. 407.
6. Quoted in J. Needham, *Science and Civilization in China*. Cambridge University Press, 1972, Vol. 4, Part #3, Section 28, p. 245.

Suggestions for Further Reading

Birrell, A. *Popular Songs and Ballads of Han China*. Honolulu: Univ. of Hawaii Press, 1993.

Bodde, D. *China's First Unifier*. Hong Kong: Hong Kong University Press, 1967.

———. *Festivals in Classical China*. Princeton: Princeton Univ. Press, 1975.

Creel, H. G. *The Origins of Statecraft in China*. Chicago: Univ. of Chicago Press, 1970.

Dawson, R., ed. *The Legacy of China*. Oxford: Clarendon Press, 1964.

De Crespigny, R. *Northern Frontier Politics and Strategies of the Later Han Empire*. Canberra: Australian National University Press, 1985.

Gernet, J. A. *A History of Chinese Civilization*. Transl., Foster, Cambridge: Cambridge Univ. Press, 1995.

Hsu, C. Y. *Han Agriculture*. Seattle: Univ. of Washi 1980.

Hulsewe, A. F. P. *Remnants of Han Law*. Leiden: Brill,

Laio, W. K. *The Complete Works of Han Fei Tzu*. Lo sthain, 1959.

Li, Yun-ning, ed. *Shang Yang's Reforms and State Contr* White Plains: M. E. Sharpe, 1977.

Loewe, M. *Everyday Life in Early Imperial China*. New nam, 1968.

———. *Crisis and Conflict in Han China*. London: Unwin, 1974.

Needham, J. *Science in Traditional China*. Cambrid Harvard Univ. Press, 1981.

Owen, S. *Remembrances: The Experience of the Past i Chinese Literature*. Cambridge: Harvard Univ. Press,

Powers, M. *Art and Political Expression in Early Ch* Haven: Yale Press, 1992.

Sage, D. F. *Ancient Sichuan and the Unification of Chin* SUNY Press, 1992.

Sullivan, M. *The Arts of China*. Berkeley: University of (Press, 1977.

Swann, N. L. *Food and Money in Ancient China*. Princetor ton Univ. Press, 1950.

Twitchett, D. and Loewe, M., eds. *The Cambridge History (Vol. I, Ch'in and Han*. Cambridge: Cambridge Univ 1986.

Waley, A. *Three Ways of Thought in Ancient China*. Ne Doubleday, 1956.

Wang, Z. *Han Civilization*. New Haven: Yale Press, 1982.

Watson, B. *Courtier and Commoner in Ancient China*. Ne Columbia Univ. Press, 1977.

———. *Ssu-ma Ch'ien, Grand Historian of China*. New Columbia Univ. Press, 1993.

———. *Records of the Grand Historian*. Vols. I–IV. New Columbia Univ. Press, 1977.

Yu, Y. S. *Trade and Expansion in Han China*. Berkeley: U California Press, 1967.

caste of Brahmins. They urged independent access to truth through meditation and self-denial (both long established Hindu techniques) and urged the equality of all persons, rejecting caste and other hierarchical systems. This may have helped further to gain its acceptance by many in firmly hierarchical China. But Buddhism also grew directly out of the Hindu traditions and shared its beliefs in *dharma* (duty), *karma* (the consequences of one's actions), *samsara* (reincarnation), and *moksha* (nirvana) as well as its belief in the unity of all life, the great chain of being.

GAUTAMA BUDDHA

The founder of Buddhism was born about 563 B.C. in the Himalayan foothill region of Nepal, the son of a minor king (*raja*; compare English "royal") of the Sakya clan. His family name was Gautama and his given name Siddartha, but he was also later called by some Sakyamuni ("Sage of the Sakyas"), as well as Gautama and Prince Siddartha. Until he was 29 years old, he led a conventional life for a prince, filled with earthly pleasures. At nineteen he married a beautiful princess and in due time they had a son, or so says the pious legend elaborated in great detail after his death, as with so many other religious figures. We know that he became an ascetic as an adult, wandered and taught for many years, acquired a number of disciples, founded a religious order, and died at about eighty somewhere between 485 and 480 B.C. This is all we know of his life for certain. The later embroidered story of his life, replete with miraculous tales, is important as it has influenced the lives of so many millions of successive generations of Asians, from India eastward.

According to this story (in its briefest form), Prince Siddartha, filled with nameless discontent, wandered one day away from his walled palace and met in quick succession an old man broken by age, a sick man covered with boils and shivering with fever, a corpse being carried to the cremation ground (Hindus have always burned their dead), and a wandering *sadhu* (holy man) with his begging bowl and simple yellow robe but with peacefulness and inner joy in his face. Overwhelmed by this vision of the sufferings of mortal life, the emptiness of worldly pleasure, and the promise of ascetic devotion, he shortly thereafter left his palace, abandoned his wife and son, and became a wandering beggar seeking after the truth and owning nothing but a crude wooden bowl (to beg the bare essentials of food) and a rag of clothing. For several years he wandered, wasted from fasting, until he determined to solve the riddle of suffering through intense meditation under a great tree. After 49 days, during which he was tempted by Mara, the prince of demons, with promises of riches, power, and sensual pleasures, all of which he ignored, he knew the truth and attained enlightenment. From this moment, he was known as the Buddha, or the Enlightened One. Soon after, he preached

Buddhist Teachings

Many of the teachings attributed to the Buddha are almost certainly later additions or commentaries. Here are two rather striking passages from such Buddhist scriptures, whose closeness to the Christian Gospels is remarkable.

A man buries a treasure in a deep pit, thinking: "It will be useful in time of need, or if the king is displeased with me, or if I am robbed, or fall into debt, or if food is scarce, or bad luck befalls me." But all this treasure may not profit the owner at all, for he may forget where he hid it, or goblins may steal it, or his enemies or even his kinsmen may take it when he is not on his guard. But by charity, goodness, restraint, and self-control man and woman alike can store up a well-hidden treasure—a treasure which cannot be given to others and which robbers cannot steal. A wise man should do good; that is the treasure which will not leave him.

Brethren, you have no mother or father to care for you. If you do not care for one another, who else will do so? Brethren, he who would care for me should care for the sick.

Source: A. L. Basham, *The Wonder That Was India.* (New York: Grove Press, 1959).

his first sermon, near Banaras (Varanasi) in the central Ganges valley, and spent the rest of his life as an itinerant preacher with a band of disciples.

The Four Noble Truths, announced in that first sermon, formed the basis for the new faith: (1) Life is filled with pain, sorrow, frustration, impermanence, and dissatisfaction. (2) All this is caused by desire and attachment, by wanting, and by the urge for existence. (3) To end suffering and sorrow, one must end desire, become desireless—change yourself rather than trying to change the world. (4) Desirelessness can be gained by the eightfold path of "right conduct."

Faithful followers of the path outlined in the first sermon may attain *nirvana*, release from the sufferings of worldly existence by avoiding the cycle of rebirth and achieve blissful reabsorption into the spiritual infinite, as the Buddha did on his death. Such devotion, and such insight into truth through meditation, are however rare, and although the Buddha did not say so, Buddhism incorporated the Hindu concept of *karma*; less dutiful individuals were reborn in successive existences in forms appropriate to their behavior in their most recent incarnations. The "right conduct" of the eightfold path was defined as kindness to all living things, purity of heart, truthfulness, charity, and avoidance of fault finding, envy, hatred, and violence. To these were added specific commandments not to kill, steal, commit adultery, lie, speak evil, gossip, flatter, or otherwise wander from The Path (always capitalized in Buddhist texts and commentaries). Accounts of the Buddha's own teachings were recorded in a collection of texts called the *Tripitaka* ("three baskets"), and there was a growing literature of moral tales about the life of Buddha and related events, plus commentaries on the teachings, all comparable in many ways to the New Testament. The worship of relics, such as alleged teeth or hair of the Buddha, became part of Buddhist practice, as in later Christianity.

As with Christianity, Buddhism remained for its first several centuries a minority religion, but the difficult discipline of the original teachings was softened somewhat so as to accommodate more followers. The conversion of the Emperor Ashoka (r.c. 269–c. 232 B.C.) helped to transform Buddhism into a mass religion, and began its spread from India, first to Ceylon and Southeast Asia, and later to China, Korea, and Japan. Within India, Buddhism survived for many centuries, although its following slowly declined from a peak about A.D. 100. For many, the distinction from Hinduism was gradually blurred, and in general one may say that, except for the several monastic orders and some lay devotees, Buddhism was slowly reabsorbed into Hinduism. Many Hindus saw Buddhism's rejection of the sensory world as "life denying," and returned to their own religion's affirmation of life. The remaining Buddhist centers and monasteries in the central Ganges heartland of the faith were destroyed and the few survivors driven into exile by the Muslim slaughter of the twelfth century, when Buddhism was largely extinguished in the land of its birth.

Hinayana, Mahayana, and the Spread of Buddhism

Soon after Ashoka's time, Buddhism divided into two major schools known as Theravada, or Hinayana ("the lesser vehicle") and Mahayana ("the greater vehicle"). Theravada Buddhism remained closer to the original faith, although it too was necessarily popularized to some extent. As it spread, it came to include more scope for the doctrine of good works as a means of acquiring "merit." Good works could even offset bad conduct in the building of *karma*; for example, one could give money to finance a temple and make up for the bad *karma* which may have been created by unethically acquired money or in other wanderings from The Path. Theravada was the form of Buddhism transmitted to Southeast Asia, where, especially in Burma, Thailand, Cambodia, and Laos (plus Ceylon), it has remained the dominant religion and is still taken very seriously by most of the people of those countries; nearly all young men traditionally spent two years in a Buddhist monastery, as many still do, with shaven heads, a yellow robe, and a begging bowl; as adults, they and most others pay far more than lip service to the Theravada version of The Path.

Mahayana Buddhism developed a little later, during the Kushan period in India between about A.D. 100 and A.D. 200. What had begun as a spiritual discipline for a few became a mass religion for all, popularized, humanized, and provided with a variety of supports, including the worship of relics. The Buddha himself was made into a supernatural god, and there were also innumerable other Buddhas called *Bodhisattvas*, saints who out of compassion delayed their entrance into *nirvana* in order to help those still on earth to attain deliverance. Faith in and worship of a *bodhisattva* also offered comfort to those who felt they needed divine help, for any purpose. This in turn promoted the worship of images, including those of the original Buddha, and the development of elaborate rituals and cults. Such worship by itself could produce salvation, and could also solve worldly problems.

Bodhisattvas became the chief gods of Mahayana Buddhism. The figure called the Buddha Amitabha was originally a bodhisattva, and was worshipped in China as O-mi-t'o-fu, in Japan as Amidha Buddha, the principal "savior" of the Western Paradise. Another bodhisattva, the compassionate Avalokitesvara, came to be worshipped by Mahayana Buddhists as a female Goddess of Mercy, called in China Kuan-yin (Guanyin) and in Japan Kannon. She was much prayed to, especially by women (to whom she was a symbol of fertility), for help in the present world rather than for release from it, as the classical Buddhist doctrine emphasized. Like Theravada, Mahayana Buddhism came also to stress the redemptive power of charity and good works, both to help others and to contribute to one's own salvation.

None of these later developments had much to do with the Buddha's original teachings, but they did relate Buddhism to everyday life, and to everyday people and their needs rather than rejecting this-worldly concerns. Especially in Japanese Buddhism, salvation in some sects might be won simply by faith and devotion, or by reciting the Buddha's or bodhisattva's name. Lamaistic Buddhism in Tibet saw similar developments, including belief in the power of relics and the use of prayer flags and prayer wheels on which a simple incantation was written; it was believed each time the wheel was turned or the winds fluttered the flag, the prayer ascended to heaven and won merit for the one who had turned the wheel or placed the flag. This, plus the worship of many anthropomorphic gods and the doctrine of good works, made the asceticism, self-denial, and "desirelessness" of the original teachings of the historical Buddha less necessary. That was in any case a difficult road for most people, and as Buddhism won more converts it was transformed almost unrecognizably.

Some forms of Mahayana Buddhism acquired a magic overlay: bodhisattvas and their attendants flew through the air; worshippers could obtain sanctity merely by repeating ritual phrases or worshipping supposed relics of the Buddha. The Mahayana school also developed details of a bodily heaven to which the faithful would go, filled with recognizable pleasures and wholly different from nirvana. To match it there was a gruesome hell presided over by a host of demons, where the wicked or unworthy suffered an imaginative variety of hideous tortures. One may again compare all this to the changes in Christianity from its origins to its medieval form. As with Christianity, the popularization of Buddhism, especially in the Mahayana school, led to a flourishing artistic representation in painting, sculpture, and architecture: endless and often profoundly beautiful paintings and statues of the Buddha and his attendants and temples in great variety. The latter included the pagoda form, derived from the earlier *dagoba* of India, originally a hemispherical mound of earth to represent the great bowl of the sky or universe, with a small three-tiered spire on top from which the pagoda evolved.

It was Mahayana Buddhism which was transmitted to China, Tibet, Korea, and Japan because it had by that time become the dominant form in India. It spread first across the Himalayas to central Asia, including Sinkiang and other areas farther west with which the Han were in periodic contact. From there it slowly made its way into China proper. Buddhism appears to have reached Tibet from both India and China, and soon spread from China to Korea, reaching Japan from there probably some time in the fifth century A.D., although in Japan Buddhism grew more rapidly from the eighth century when there was direct contact with China and a long series of Japanese Buddhist monks went there. In Japan and Korea also, Buddhist art flourished in a variety of forms, as in China. Many Mahayana monastic orders and sects developed in China, including the contemplative and mystical school of Ch'an Buddhism, which was diffused to Japan where it was called Zen, the Japanese sound of the character. Other Buddhist schools and monastic orders also flourished in Japan, as described in more detail in Chapter 11.

In China, Buddhism encountered opposition from the T'ang dynasty in the ninth century as a possible rival to state power after temples and monasteries had acquired large tracts of land and much wealth. For the rest of Chinese history, Buddhism survived only as a small minority religion within a dominantly Confucian context. But in Japan, Buddhism remained proportionately more important, especially in the medieval period, and Japan is still listed as a Buddhist country although in fact most Japanese pay relatively little attention to its precepts or discipline in the country's modern and highly secular culture. Vietnam received Buddhism more directly from its Indian source, and is thus better classified under Hinayana or Theravada, although the Chinese form of Mahayana made an impact there too along with Taoism. In Korea there was no parallel to the T'ang confiscation and Buddhism remained proportionately more important, but especially from the fourteenth century, under the Yi dynasty, Confucianism was promoted as the official religion and in time Korea became as thoroughly Confucian as China. In all four countries, but perhaps particularly in Confucian-dominated China, Vietnam, and Korea, Buddhism entered the stream of folk religion, especially for the nonliterate, and its beliefs and practices further mixed with peasant traditions of magic, as was also the case with Taoism.

The End of the Han

Meanwhile at the Han court in its later years, the growing power of the great landed families and endless court intrigues fatally weakened the central state and drained its resources. Many of the big landowners and their private estates paid little or no taxes, leaving an increasingly heavy burden on the peasantry. This provoked chronic banditry and rebellions, and many peasants fled to new lands in the south where taxation was less rigorous. Most emperors of the last Han century were weaklings, and power came increasingly into the hands of court eunuchs, a disastrous pattern which was to plague later dynasties as well. Eunuchs were to begin with trusted because they had no heirs, but this did not prevent them from continual scheming to amass power for themselves and to promote their favorites. Ts'ao Ts'ao, last of the Han warlords, was the son of an adopted son of a court eunuch; like them, he did not use his power wisely, or in the end effectively. Many emperors before him had been obsessed by the quest for immortality, unable to accept the end of their power and grandeur in mortal life. By now there were Taoists as well as Confucians at court, and many of them were also dabblers in alchemy. They recommended to eager emperors that they drink mercury as an infallible elixir of immortality. It killed most of them of course, but the fascination of mercury, which seems almost alive, lived on to tempt many others.

To most Chinese, even in this dark period, life was good, and the greatest of all blessings was a long life. Immortality was best achieved in the form of many descendants, who would honor one's memory. The Chinese love of life probably slowed the spread of Buddhism with its life-denying precepts and its dismissal of the real world as illusory and of no importance. Nevertheless, Taoism seems to have thrived in this period, perhaps because unlike Buddhism it was part of Chinese tradition rather than an alien religion with Indian overtones. Taoism blended more and more with traditional folk religion and folk magic, but it also picked up, perhaps from Buddhism, the doctrine of good works, all of this completely at variance with the original Taoist message but ensuring it a much wider following. In time however, Taoism and Buddhism largely merged, especially for the unlettered but to some extent also among the educated. Thus Taoism picked up from Buddhism the ideas of an immortal soul, a heavenly afterlife, a variety of monastic orders, a priesthood, and semimagical rituals. Its popularity, like that of Buddhism in time, seems clearly related to the disappointing nature of life to many people in the last century of the Han and the chaos which followed its collapse.

The fall of the Han was soon followed, and had been hastened, by new barbarian pressures along the northern steppe frontiers. Those old Chinese enemies, the Hsiung-nu, were on the rampage, and another group whom the Chinese named Hsien-pei (Xian bi) were also active in raiding and minor conquests of border lands. In 316 the Hsiung-nu actually sacked the former Han capital of Loyang, and the whole of the north was in turmoil. The earlier collapse of the Han had been in large part the work of its generals, with their private armies supported by rich landowners. They became in effect warlords, contending among themselves for power; Ts'ao Ts'ao was a good example. But the generals were unable to stem the mounting tide of peasant rebellion, most damagingly that of the group who called themselves the Yellow Turbans, which broke out in force from A.D. 184.

The rebel groups were in most cases led by Taoist cult figures, and practiced many semimagical Taoist rituals; that in itself symbolized their opposition to Confucian orthodoxy and authority.

The rival warlords, and the struggle between Shu, Wei, and Wu, did not, as during the Warring States period, lead to a victory by any of them. Nor were the warlords effective in holding off the Hsiung-nu and other invading groups. The administrative and financial system established early in the Han had fallen apart with the rise of powerful landowning families, runaway corruption by court officials and eunuchs, and a general loss of cohesion and morale. The period between 220 and 290 is called the Three Kingdoms (Shu, Wei, and Wu), but despite its popularity in legend it was a disruptive and sorry time, especially since all of the three were weakened by the same set of problems which had destroyed the Han, financially dependent on their own great landed families.

As for the "barbarians" from the steppe, many of them had settled as semiagricultural groups inside the Great Wall, while many others had been recruited into the Chinese army along the frontiers, another parallel with the later Roman empire and an obvious contributor to ultimate "barbarian" triumph over both empires. After the Hsiung-nu sack of Loyang in 316, rival barbarian groups fought over most of north China, although mountains kept them out of Szechuan and the Yangtze protected the south, to which millions of Chinese fled. For some three centuries there was chaos in the north, including successive futile efforts to establish Chinese dynasties aiming to drive out the barbarians and unify the country. With the imperial structure and its revenue base destroyed, this was a forlorn hope. In the end, progress toward unity, and eventually the re-creation of empire, was accomplished, as after the fall of Rome and the blending of Latins and Germanic tribes, by a mix of "barbarians" and Chinese.

The entire period from 220 to 589 is often called The Six Dynasties; there were in fact many more, but six of them successively established their capitals at Nanking (whose name means "southern capital," although the name is in fact much later). Although they failed to unify even the south and made little impact on the north, the ideal of imperial unity stayed alive through this long period of three and a half centuries, and was ultimately to be reasserted.

Northern Wei

Contending barbarian and Chinese groups, now augmented by invading Tibetans, struggled for power in the north, until by 439 one group, the To-pa (Toba) tribe of the Hsien-pei (Xianbei), emerged victorious and unified most of the north under the dynastic title of Northern Wei. By the late fifth century their rule had become almost entirely in the Chinese manner, and many Chinese were involved in the administration of it, while the court promoted the whole process of Sinification. The capital was moved from Ta-t'ung (Datong) in northern Shansi (Shanxi) to Loyang, with its classical imperial overtones; Chinese became the official court language, and To-pa elite were ordered to wear Chinese dress, follow Chinese customs, and marry Chinese wives. Buddhism continued to flourish, at least as much among the educated elite as among the masses, and was as widespread in the south as in the north. The Northern Wei promoted Buddhism vigorously, and built a number of splendid cave temples with both small and immense statues of the Buddha and his devotees, first outside their early capital of Ta T'ung at Yün Kang (Yungang) and then outside Loyang at Lung-men (Longmen); both are still reasonably well preserved. Their style, though Chinese, reveals the Indian origins of Buddhism in the treatment of the sculptured figures.

It was in this period that there began a long series of Buddhist pilgrims to India, seeking true copies of the Buddhist *sutras*, many of which were brought back to China. The names of nearly 200 such pilgrims, including nine Koreans, are recorded between A.D. 259 and 790, and we may assume that there were in fact many more. Many wrote accounts of what they had seen; the most famous of these were by Fa Hsien (Fa Xian) who visited India from 399 to 414, Hsuan Tsang (Xuanzang) from 629 to 645, and I Ching (Ijing) from 671 to 695. These and other pilgrim accounts of India brought detailed information and often praise about this great civilization across the Himalayas but seem to have made remarkably little impact on the Chinese mind or on their attitudes toward the world beyond their own borders.

Beginning in the last decades of the crumbling Han dynasty, the south was enriched by a flood of wealthy and educated refugees from the north as well as by millions of impoverished peasants. Among those fleeing the north was a group called Hakka who now live in the upland areas of Kwangtung (Guangdong) and whose language betrays their earlier northern origin. Trade and towns, which had flourished under the Han, suffered a sharp decline in this period of disunity and chronic fighting, but, especially in the south, literature, philosophy, and the arts continued vigorously, supported in part by the flight of gentry families from the north. Technological progress also continued, including the invention of gunpowder in this period, refinements in the use of a magnetized needle for indicating north and south (the forerunner of the compass), and the use of coal as heating fuel as well as for smelting ores.

Despite the political chaos, it would be a mistake to see this period of disunity and conflict as a sort of Dark Ages, although of course it had that quality for many who were caught in the barbarian invasion or the civil wars, or who had their homes or families destroyed. And despite the loss of the Confucian order and its Great Harmony, perhaps in part because of that, Taoist philosophy thrived and along with it new attitudes among the literati which were far freer and more unconventional than in the Confucian straitjacket of propriety and its reverence for prescribed ritual. Many people of such persuasions were indifferent to the political world, which was discouraging in any case, and had no Confucian yearning to set things right, but reveled in a free and easy life of spontaneous or even Bohemian behavior, with lots of wine and a dedication to art for art's sake. The group which came to be called the "Seven

A beautiful gilt bronze Buddha from the Northern Wei, dated A.D. 536. (University of Pennsylvania Museum)

Sages of the Bamboo Grove" is the best-known example of such people, beginning in the third century soon after the fall of the Han. Their number included poets, musicians, and painters, and their style spread from Szechuan to Chekiang in the lower Yangze valley and elsewhere. There was in fact no cultural break to coincide with the political break, but then why should we expect one? Chinese culture was already old, and in most respects it went on as before, perhaps even more passionately in the absence of much to be excited about in terms of contemporary affairs or morals.

There was also, equally understandably, a great increase in the contemplation and enjoyment of nature, partly resulting from the new interest in Taoism but at least as much from the solace it could bring in a human world which was falling apart. Most of the literati, no longer in office, wrote nature poems and many also painted scenes from nature, especially mountain scenes where human activity was absent or minimal and where a sensitive person could find peace and inspiration. We begin in this period to know the names of famous painters and poets, most importantly Ku K'ai-chih (Gu Kaizhi, 345–411), a few of whose paintings, or copies of

them, survive. T'ao Ch'ien (T'ao Yuan-ming, 365–427) and Hsieh Ling-yün (Xie ling-yun, 385–433) became well known with their poems in praise of rural and landscape values. In the sixth century critical studies and anthologies began to be published which also included Han period literature and thus give us much of what we know of it as well as of the unbroken literary output which followed the Han. These were matched by similar analytical accounts of painting which cover the productive period between 220 and 589 with the rise of the Sui reunification.

The Move South

One result of the southward movement of the Chinese fleeing trouble in the north was the incorporation of Fukien (Fujian) within the Chinese sphere and its incorporation also into the Sui and T'ang empires as a result. Fukien is a mountainous province whose easiest communications are by sea from its coast, far easier than across the difficult mountainous country along its west-

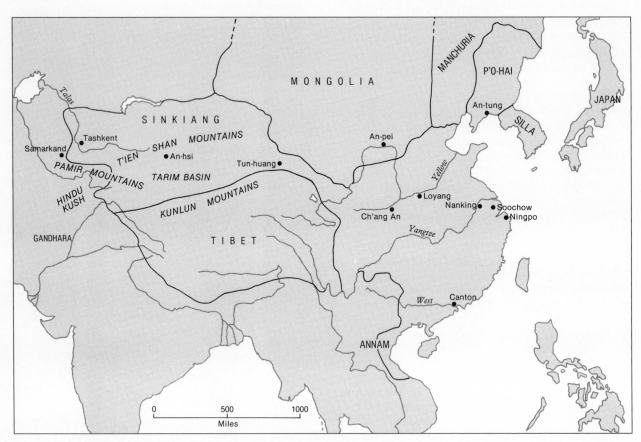

China Under the T'ang

ern boundaries. Its people were among the first to develop trade with Taiwan and Southeast Asia, something which further set them apart from the main body of Chinese culture, as their language still does. The transplanting of rice from seedbeds to irrigated fields had begun under the Han, and now spread south; it greatly increased yields, but also imposed heavy labor demands, all of which helped to attract and then to feed the greatly increased southern population with its pressures on the original non-Han inhabitants, including those in the upland areas of Fukien. New tools suited to wet rice agriculture were developed in this period, including the endless chain fitted with paddles, driven by two men pushing pedals on a crank. Known as The Dragon's Backbone, it was made entirely of bamboo and thus was light enough to be easily portable from one spot to another as needed. It could move greatly increased volumes of water from one field to another at different elevations.

The absorption of Fukien and the reabsorption of the rest of the southeast coast into the empire under Sui and T'ang, including the Canton area, set the stage for the first major expansion of Chinese trade overseas, and for the new rise of the merchant group. Both trends greatly accelerated under the Sung dynasty (960–1279) successors to the T'ang (618–907). The Sui dynasty, even before the T'ang, built a navy and sent expeditions to Taiwan and as far as southern Vietnam and Sumatra, maritime openings which were to become much more prominent under the T'ang and the Sung.

Under the T'ang the emergence, or reemergence, of a prominent merchant group further set the stage for developments under the Sung. The rapid growth of trade between north and south, especially in tea, led to the development of long-distance credit as bills of exchange called "flying money." These were used to pay for commodities bought in the south and elsewhere, including tea, and could be redeemed through the merchants' provincial offices at the capital, marked for payment (less taxes, of course!) in each merchant's home province. This was followed in the ninth century by the issue of negotiable certificates of deposit, the forerunner of paper money, which was to come into its own in the Sung.

Reunification: Sui and T'ang

Most Chinese wanted to see the Han model of imperial greatness restored, but first the country had to be reunited. The Northern Wei had been split in half between rival groups in 534, and then reunified by the western half, called Northern Chou, based in the Wei valley with its capital at Ch'ang An, which in the by-now-classic pat-

tern conquered its northern rivals in 577. Four years later General Yang Chien, who was of mixed Chinese and Hsien-pei descent, took over the throne and founded the Sui dynasty in 581 as Sui Wen Ti (Di), going on to conquer the south in 589 and thus restoring the unified empire. His successor Yang Ti (Di, 604–618) reconquered northern Vietnam and campaigned farther south. He also tried to reestablish Chinese control in north Korea and south Manchuria, both parts of the Han empire, but his armies were badly defeated there in three successive campaigns, and, in an ill-judged effort to subdue a group on the northern frontier known as the Eastern Turks, or T'u-chieh (the Chinese version of "Turk"), were even more thoroughly humiliated. Yang Ti fled south as the empire began to fall apart, and was assassinated in 618.

The Sui dynasty too had its origins in the Wei valley, and its brief rule is full of parallels to the Ch'in. The Sui also rebuilt the Great Wall, at the cost of another million lives, and created an extensive network of roads and canals. Sui Yang Ti is often compared to Ch'in Shih Huang Ti. Sui Yang Ti built a magnificent new capital at Loyang, but at heavy expense, and in general seems to have shared the megalomania of his Ch'in predecessor. Perhaps his most notable project, again at heavy cost, was the building of a Grand Canal from Hangchou (Hangzhou) in the south to Kaifeng on the Yellow River to bring rice from the productive Yangtze delta to feed troops and officials in arid north China. From Kaifeng he constructed canal connections to Ch'ang An in the west and to the Peking area in the east. But his incessant demands on his people caused great suffering to exhausted troops, forced laborers, taxpayers, and tyrannized officials. Rebellion spread, as in the last years of the Ch'in, and there was a brief contest for power among military figures. A frontier general swept away the pretensions of the Sui heir and proclaimed a new dynasty, the T'ang, in 618.

Like the Han, its success rested in large part on the empire building of the Sui, as the Han had rested on Ch'in foundations. But the T'ang was to reestablish the glory of the Han in all respects and to go beyond it, moderating the harsh rule of the Sui by more emphasis on Confucian "benevolence," as the Han had done. The now reconstituted empire reincorporated northern Vietnam, Sinkiang, southern Manchuria, and (after successive hard-fought campaigns) a now-united Korea, though as a vassal or tributary state rather than as conquered territory. Even Tibet was for a time added to the empire, and the northern frontier with the Eastern and Western Turks was pacified. This was much more than the Han had ever controlled.

Li Shih-min, the general who founded the T'ang, was, like the Sui founder, a man of mixed Chinese and "barbarian" blood. He first put his father on the throne, then had him abdicate in 626 and ruled in his own name until 649, taking the title T'ai Tsung (Tai zong, "Great Ancestor"). He is remembered as a wise, honest, conscientious, and humane ruler who was also a good general. His successor, Kao Tsung (Gao zong, "High Ancestor"), completed the incorporation of Korea as a tributary state and was an equally able ruler, remembered like T'ai Tsung for fostering education and encouraging conscientious officials. But his later years were overshadowed by a beautiful concubine named Wu Chao (Wuzhao), inherited from T'ai Tsung, whom he made his consort and empress. After Kao Tsung's death in 683, she ruled alone or through puppets, and then proclaimed herself emper*or* of a new dynasty, the only female emperor in Chinese history. She struck at the old aristocracy, her chief opposition (one can imagine their reactions to her!), and ordered many of them executed, while strengthening the bureaucracy based on merit. The Confucian establishment was clearly antifeminist, but Buddhism had no such bias, and she drew support from the by-now-large Buddhist establishment, which she strongly favored and which declared her to be a reincarnation of the bodhisattva Maitreya, the Buddhist messiah. Wu Chao had become a Buddhist nun after T'ai Tsung's death in 650 but grew restless without greater scope for her undoubted talents. It was under her direction that the cave temples at Lung-men were completed. The Empress Wu, as she is called, was denounced by Chinese historians, although this has clear sexist overtones; she was a strong and effective (if ruthless) ruler, obviously opposed to the hereditary establishment, and promoted its "enemy," the alien faith of Buddhism. To be a woman in addition was just too much, and in 705 she was deposed in a palace coup.

After some jockeying for power among rival contenders, another able ruler emerged in 712, taking the title of Hsuan Tsung (Xuan Zong, "Mysterious Ancestor") and reigning until 756. Under Hsuan Tsung the empire prospered as never before, richer and more populous than ever, especially in the Yangtze valley and the south. Trade and towns had revived, and literature and the arts had a glorious new growth. The greatest painter of this time was the legendary Wu Tao-tzu (Wudaozi), although unfortunately all of his work has been lost. Many stories were told of his lifelike paintings and of how he, after painting a scene on a wall, walked into it and left behind only an empty wall. Relatively little T'ang painting has survived, apart from a few tomb walls, but we have many accounts of the great painters of the time and of fiction writers of whose work we have only the tiniest samples. What has survived in abundance is the magnificent glazed pottery figures used to furnish tombs and adorn houses and palaces, probably the best-known aspect of T'ang art.

Learning and the arts enjoyed a further bloom under Hsuan Tsung and at his elegant but efficient court. But in his old age Hsuan Tsung became infatuated with a son's concubine, the beautiful Yang Kuei-fei (Yang Gueifei); she and her relatives and protégés gained increasing control of the empire, but ran it badly. Rebels (see below) sacked the capital at Ch'ang An in 755, and Hsuan Tsung fled south with Lady Yang, but his resentful guards strangled her as the cause of all the empire's troubles, and Hsuan Tsung abdicated in sorrow. The rebellion was finally put down and order restored, but Hsuan Tsung's reign marks a high point in the glory of the T'ang. Although the dynasty continued for another 150 years it never recovered its earlier power or cultural brilliance.

At its height, for its first century and a half, the T'ang empire was the greatest yet seen anywhere on earth, in area, in population, and in its achievements. This was to be typical of most Chinese dynasties: a first half of new vigor and a second half in which the system began to run down and finally collapse. Like the Han, T'ang rule was broken at its midpoint by rebellion. Regional commanders had built up their power and one of them, a man of Turkish descent named An Lu-shan, had earlier challenged the central government from his strong regional bases. He was a great favorite of Yang Kuei-fei, who even adopted him legally as her son. When he clashed with Yang Kuei-fei's brother, An Lu-shan revolted in 755, and it was his troops who captured Ch'ang An and drove Hsuan Tsung and his lady southward, to her death and his abdication. The brother was also executed: so much for power schemes! The story is still popular and is told and retold in opera and by poets and other writers. The rebellion of An Lu-shan shook the dynasty to its roots, and was symptomatic of its almost total dependence on foreign or barbarian troops, as An himself had been— more echoes of the later Roman empire. An Lu-shan was murdered by his son in 757, and order was restored by loyal armies by 762, but the dynasty was never the same as in its first half. Regional commanders continued to build their power, as in the last century of the Han, while at the court the eunuchs came to dominate successive administrations, with the same evil consequences as in the Han and in later dynasties.

The T'ang System

The Sui and T'ang armies had been led mainly by the old aristocratic families of the north, and their dependents provided the best troops. Like aristocrats elsewhere, they loved fine horses, although the steppe origins of many of them helped to account for this at least as much. The military system was based on a militia, concentrated around the capitals and along the northern and northwestern frontiers. Cavalrymen had to provide their own horses and equipment, and though peasant infantrymen outnumbered them, the main striking force of the T'ang army was its mounted warriors, armed with crossbows as well as with lances and swords. Public stud farms were established which by the middle of the seventh century were able to produce well over half a million horses for the imperial army. Among the sources of the growing military weakness of the T'ang from the eighth century on was the disruption of these stud farms and raids for horses by Tibetan and Turkish forces. The horses used by the T'ang army were hybrid products of crossbreeding between the small but wiry steppe ponies and larger horses imported from Arabia and central Asia, but some horses were also bought directly from steppe tribes. As T'ang control in central Asia collapsed after the mid-eighth century, this source also disappeared. But the T'ang love of horses is evident in their art.

What had built T'ang strength, and was at least partially restored after 762, was the revenue system which was kept in government hands. This was primarily the land tax, plus the old government monopoly in salt, now joined by tea and liquor and by renewed government control of the shipment of grain from the Yangtze region to the capital. The earlier disastrous pattern of private estates and the growth of rich landowning families who evaded most taxation had been broken in the disorder following the fall of the Han, and the tax was now based on specified areas of land rather than on individuals. There thus emerged the system of landowning which was to remain until the Communist era whereby the land tax was paid by peasant-owner farmers, or by a landlord who worked his land with tenants. With the help of an efficient central administration staffed in large part by those who had passed the imperial examinations and absorbed Confucian morality from their essential study of the classics, this was a system which worked well, at least until the last decades of the T'ang. It was further institutionalized by the T'ang, after powerful families had largely perverted it in the dark years after 220. In fact the examinations and the recruitment of officials were made far more comprehensive than under the Han, supported by government schools. A civil service based on merit was one of the greatest achievements of imperial China, and provided probably better government than in other parts of the world.

While not a new idea under the T'ang, it was more thoroughly applied, and indeed had begun to take this shape under the Sui. Officials were forbidden to serve in their native places—the "rule of avoidance"—and their terms were limited in general to three years, after which they were moved to another district, with the idea that this would prevent their becoming identified with local rather than imperial interests. All of this, and the beefing up of the examination system and of merit-based appointments much reduced the power of the great families which had been so disruptive in the past. Unfortunately it was to rise again in the second half of the dynasty, and even in the first half there were still many, perhaps most, appointments made through family connections. The completion of the model of a merit-based bureaucracy was to be the achievement of the next dynasty, the Sung, though on foundations which went back to Ch'in and Han. To assist the work of magistrates but also to consolidate the restored empire, the T'ang issued a detailed

The great bronze Buddha at Kamakura, near Tokyo, completed in 1252 and originally housed in its own temple but now in the open and still visited by millions of tourists, day-trippers, and worshippers every year. It was built with the help of funds raised from the common people of the Kamakura domains, and shows the compassionate benevolence of the Buddha, or Amida Buddha as the Japanese say. (Cameramann, International)

new law code and administrative regulations, with laws divided according to category and lists of appropriate punishments for each criminal offense.

Two magnificent new capitals were built, important as always as symbols of imperial power and majesty, one at Ch'ang An, where the Han had ruled, and one at Loyang, the latter Han capital, both sites reeking with imperial tradition. Ch'ang An is described below; Loyang was somewhat smaller but on the same checker-board plan. They were linked by some transport on the Yellow River and by the canal built under the Sui; but as the south boomed, greatly increased supplies of rice were shipped north by Sui Yang Ti's Grand Canal. This was of course more effective at Loyang, and when famine struck the Wei valley the court and central government officials had to move to Loyang.

To facilitate the administration of this now immense empire, the T'ang rebuilt the road network of the Ch'in and Han, with a system of post stations along them and along the canal system where official messengers could

rest or change horses every ten miles. This too was to be retained by every subsequent dynasty. T'ai Tsung also reestablished the Board of Censors, charged with investigating cases of abuses, misgovernment, or treason and reporting directly to the emperor himself, whom they were supposedly also free to criticize, though only the brave or foolhardy did so. The gradual Sinification of the originally non-Han or barbarian south, below the Yangtze valley, continued apace under new imperial momentum, though the mountainous and remote southwest of Yunnan and Kweichou (Guizhou), home of the Thai and other groups, remained outside the empire.

By late T'ang most Chinese lived in the south and most of the empire's revenue came from there, including the productive Yangtze valley. The north, where empire was born, suffered as always from recurrent drought, erosion, and siltation of the vital irrigation works. But now the south, progressively cleared of its forests, more than made up the differences. Agricultural techniques were slowly adapted to the wetter and hillier conditions

✳ Tax Reform: A Chinese View ✳

Yang Yen (727–781), a high official of the T'ang, wrote a memorial to the throne proposing tax reforms, which were carried out and lasted several centuries.

When the dynastic laws were first formulated there was the land tax, the labor tax on able-bodied men, and the cloth tax on households. But enforcement of the law was lax; people migrated or died, and landed property changed hands. The poor rose and the rich fell. The Board of Revenue year after year presented out-of-date figures to the court. Those who were sent to guard the frontiers were exempted from land tax and labor tax for six years, after which they returned from service. Yet as Emperor Hsuang-tsung was engaged in many campaigns against the barbarians, most of those sent to the frontier died. The frontier generals, however, concealed the facts and did not report their deaths. Thus their names were never removed from the tax registers. When Wang Kung held the post of Commissioner of Fiscal Census during the T'ien Pao period [742–755] he strove to increase revenue. Since these names appeared on the registers and yet the adults were missing, he concluded that they had concealed themselves to avoid paying taxes.... The way to handle all government expenses and tax collections is first to calculate the amount needed and then to allocate the tax among the people. The income of the state would be governed according to its expenses. All households would be registered in the places of their actual residence, without regard to whether they are native households or not. All persons should be graded according to their wealth.... Those who have no permanent residence and do business as travelling merchants should be taxed in whatever prefecture they are located at the rate of one-thirtieth of their wealth. All practices which cause annoyance to the people should be corrected.... Everything should be under the control of the President of the Board of Revenue and the Commissioner of Funds.

Source: W. T. deBary, ed., *Sources of Chinese Tradition.* (New York: Columbia University Press, 1960), pp. 414–416.

The "Ever-Normal Granary" System

Po Chu-i (722–846), one of China's greatest poets, was also a T'ang official. While serving as an imperial censor in 808 he wrote a memorial criticizing the "ever-normal granary" system.

I have heard that because of the good harvest this year the authorities have asked for an imperial order to carry out Grain Harmonization so that cheap grain may be bought and the farmers benefitted. As far as I can see, such purchases mean only loss to the farmers.... In recent years prefectures and districts were allowed to assess each household for a certain amount of grain, and to fix the terms and the date of delivery. If there was any delay, the punitive measures of imprisonment and flogging were even worse than those usually involved in the collection of taxes. Though this was called Grain Harmonization, in reality it hurt the farmers.... If your majesty would consider converting the taxes payable in cash into taxes payable in kind, the farmers would neither suffer loss by selling their grain at a cheap price, nor would they have the problem of re-selling bales of cloth and silk. The profit would go to the farmers, the credit to the emperor. Are the advantages of that commutation in kind not evident? ... I lived for some time in a small hamlet where I belonged to a household which had to contribute its share to Grain Harmonization. I myself was treated with great harshness; it was truly unbearable. Not long ago, as an official in the metropolitan district, I had responsibility for the administration of Grain Harmonization. I saw with my own eyes how delinquent people were flogged, and I could not stand the sight of it. In the past I have always wanted to write about how people suffered from this plague [but] since I was a petty and unimportant official in the countryside, I had no opportunity to approach your majesty. Now I have the honor of being promoted to serve your majesty and of being listed among the officials who offer criticism and advice. [If] my arguments are not strong enough to convince.... order one of your trustworthy attendants to inquire incognito among the farmers.... Then your majesty will see that my words are anything but rash and superficial statements.

Source: W. T. deBary, ed., *Sources of Chinese Tradition.* (New York: Columbia University Press, 1960), pp. 423–425.

and the far longer growing season. The rising use of human manure (night soil) improved the less fertile southern soils outside the alluvial river valleys; the continued increase of population thus provided its own increase in agricultural yields. Many northerners had fled south after the fall of the Han dynasty; now they and their descendants were joined by new streams seeking greater economic opportunity than in the overcrowded and often marginal north. Imperial tradition, and defense of the troublesome northwest frontiers, kept the capital in the north, but the south was flourishing.

Renewed contacts with more distant lands westward revealed, as in Han times, no other civilization which could rival the Celestial Empire. The Son of Heaven, as the emperor was called, was seen as the lord of "all under heaven," meaning the four corners of the known world, within which China was clearly the zenith of power and sophistication. Did not all other people the Chinese encountered acknowledge this, by tribute, praise, and imitation of Chinese culture, the sincerest form of flattery? In fact, even beyond the world the Chinese knew, they had no equal, in any terms. Rome was long gone, and the Abbasid Caliphate was no match for the T'ang or its great successor, the Sung. A coalition of Arabs and western Turks did repulse a T'ang expeditionary force, far from its base, in central Asia at the battle of the Talas River near Samarkand in 751. But the battle is perhaps more significant in that some captured Chinese probably transmitted the recently developed T'ang art of printing to the West, and that of papermaking, widespread in China from the late first century A.D. after its invention a century earlier. From about A.D. 700, printing was done from carved wooden blocks a page at a time but by A.D. 1030, the Chinese, and only slightly later the Koreans, had developed movable-type printing, with individual characters made of wood, ceramics, or metal, all long before its later spread into fifteenth-century Europe.

Paper and printing were typical creations of the Chinese genius, with their love of written records and of learning, literature, and painting. They were also two of China's most basic gifts to the later-developing West, along with cast iron, the crossbow, gunpowder, the compass, the use of coal as fuel, waterwheels, paper currency, the wheelbarrow, wallpaper, and porcelain, to mention only a few. A perfected form of porcelain had appeared by T'ang times and from it were made objects of exquisite beauty never matched elsewhere, although the process finally made its way to Europe in the eighteenth century. Porcelain joined silk, and later, tea, as China's chief exports to a cruder world abroad.

The secret of silk making had been smuggled out of China, supposedly by two monks in the time of the eastern Roman emperor Justinian (reigned 527–565) in the form of cocoons concealed in hollow walking sticks. But later Western silk production in Italy and France never equaled the Chinese quality, which still remains an export staple, although in the nineteenth century the Chinese lost ground to more uniform Japanese and later Korean silk. Tea, largely unknown in Han times, was introduced from Southeast Asia as a medicine and an aid to meditation and began to be drunk more widely in fifth-century China. It became the basic Chinese drink during the T'ang, grown in the misty hills of the south, another Chinese monopoly which later drew Western traders. Seeds and cuttings of the tea plant were smuggled out of China by the English East India Company in 1843, to start plantation production in India and Ceylon, and tea became the world's most popular drink.

Ch'ang An in an Age of Imperial Splendor

The splendor of the T'ang and its empire was symbolized in its capital at Ch'ang An, where the Han and the Ch'in had also ruled. It was the eastern terminus of trade routes linking China with central Asia and lands beyond, and also presided over the largest empire the world had yet seen, exceeding even the Han and Roman empires. People from all over Asia—Turks, Indians, Persians, Syrians, Vietnamese, Koreans (some 8,000!), Japanese, Jews, Arabs, and even Nestorian Christians and Byzantines—thronged its streets and added to its cosmopolitan quality. It was probably also the largest wholly planned city ever built, covering some 30 square miles and including within its massive walls about 1 million people. The imperial census also recorded nearly an-

other million living in the urban area outside the walls.

Like all Chinese administrative centers, Ch'ang An was laid out on a checkerboard pattern, with broad avenues running east-west and north-south to great gates at the cardinal compass points. These were closed at night, and the main avenues leading to them divided the city into major quarters, further subdivided by other principal streets into 110 blocks, each constituting an administrative unit, with its own internal pattern of alleyways. The emperor's palace faced south down a 500-foot-wide central thoroughfare to the south gate, the one used by most visitors and all official envoys and messengers. This arrangement was designed to awe and impress with the power and greatness of the empire all who came to Ch'ang An. Kaifeng and Peking were later designed similarly, and for the same purpose.

Within the city, people lived in rectangular wards, each surrounded by walls with gates closed at night. The West Market and the East Market, supervised by the government, occupied larger blocks to serve their respective halves of the city. There and elsewhere in the city, in open spaces and appointed theaters, foreign and Chinese players, acrobats, and magicians performed dramas, operas, skits, and other amusements. Women of fashion paraded their fancy clothing and coiffures. For men and women alike, one of the most popular pastimes was polo, adopted from Persia; T'ang paintings showing polo matches survive, and make it clear that women played too. As later in India, the wealthy prided themselves on their stable of good polo ponies and their elegant turnout for matches.

Artists and sculptors also found horses popular subjects; despite their apparent mass production, T'ang paintings and clay figurines of horses are still full of life and movement. Another favorite subject for art was the endless variety of foreigners in this cosmopolitan center, depicted faithfully in both painting and figurines so that one can easily recognize, by dress and physical features, which people are being represented.

T'ang culture was worldly, elegant, and urbane, but Buddhism was still in vogue and in official favor. Buddhist temples and pagodas also gave Chinese architects an outlet for their talents, and the first half of the T'ang was a golden age of temple architecture and sculpture, the latter showing clear artistic as well as religious influences from the Indian home of Buddhism. A cosmopolitan center for all of Asia, Ch'ang An was also, like China, the cultural model for the rest of East Asia. Official tributary embassies and less formal visitors and merchants or adventurers came repeatedly from Korea, Japan, and lesser states to the south and west to bask in the glories of Ch'ang An, and to take back with them as much as they could for the building of their own versions of T'ang civilization. Persian Zoroastrians, Muslims, Jews, Indian Buddhists and Hindus, and Nestorian Christians

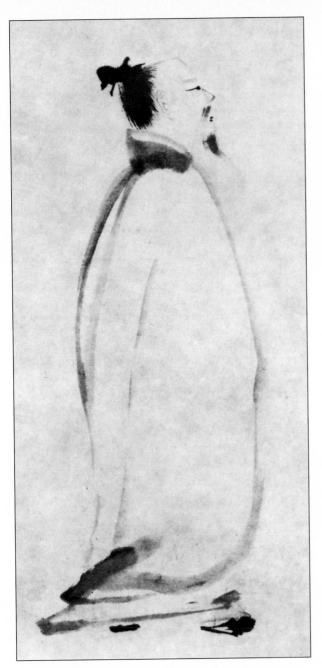

The poet Li Po (701–762), perhaps the most appealing T'ang figure. His poetry is still learned and quoted by successive generations of Chinese. (Tokyo National Museum, through courtesy of the International Society for Education Information, Inc., Tokyo)

from the eastern Mediterranean, representing thus nearly all of the great world religions, were among the city's permanent residents, all welcomed in this center of world culture and all leaving behind some evidence of their presence. Ch'ang An flourished for two and a half centuries, from the early seventh to the mid-ninth, when the capital, like the empire, fell into chaos. But from 618 to about 860 it shone with a cosmopolitan brilliance perhaps never equaled anywhere.

The T'ang is still seen as the greatest period of Chinese poetry, especially the work of Li Po (Libo, 701–762) and Tu Fu (Dufu, 712–770).

Some 1,800 samples of Li Po's 20,000 poems survive, including these lines:

> *Beside my bed the bright moonbeams glimmer*
> *Almost like frost on the floor.*
>
> *Rising up, I gaze at the mountains bathed in*
>   *moonlight;*
> *Lying back, I think of my old home.*
>
>   * * *
>
> *A girl picking lotuses beside the stream—*
> *At the sound of my oars she turns;*
> *She vanishes giggling among the flowers,*
> *And, all pretense, declines to come out.*
>
>   * * *
>
> *Amid the flowers with a jug of wine*
> *The world is like a great empty dream.*
> *Why should one toil away one's life?*
> *That is why I spend my days drinking …*
> *Lustily singing, I wait for the bright moon.*
>
>   * * *
>
> *I drink alone with no one to share.*
> *Raising up my cup, I welcome the moon …*
> *We frolic in revels suited to the spring.*

The legend, almost certainly untrue but appealing, is that Li Po drunkenly leaned out of a boat to embrace the reflection of the moon and drowned, happy in his illusion.

Tu Fu was a more sober poet than Li Po, but equally admired. Here are some samples of his lines:

> *Frontier war drums disrupt everyone's travels.*
> *At the border in autumn a solitary goose honks.*
> *Tonight the hoar frost will be white …*
> *I am lucky to have brothers, but all are*
>   *scattered …*
> *The letters I write never reach them.*
> *How terrible that the fighting cannot stop.*
>
>   * * *
>
> *Distant Annam* sends the court a red parrot,*
> *Gaudy as a peach blossom and as talkative as we*
>   *are.*

---

*Then a Chinese tributary state (central Vietnam), hence the gift of a parrot.

*But learning and eloquence are given the same
   treatment—
The cage of imprisonment. Is one ever free?*

* * *

*The capital is captured, but hills and streams re-
   main.
With spring in the city the grass and trees grow
   fast.
Bewailing the times, the flowers droop as if in
   tears.
Saddened as I am with parting, the birds make
   my heart flutter.
Army beacons have flamed for three months.
A letter from home now would be worth a king's
   ransom.
In my anxiety I have scratched my white hairs
   even shorter.
What a jumble! Even hairpins cannot help me.*

Tu Fu's poetry, concerned as it is with human troubles,
reminds us that the rebuilding of empire exacted a
price, for all its glory. He lived through the rebellion of
An Lu-shan and his occupation of Ch'ang An, and then
through the subsequent fighting between rival generals.
By this time the second half of the T'ang was well
begun, and already there were signs of weakness.

Early in the dynasty the division of the empire into
hsien (xian, counties) begun under the Ch'in had been
reestablished, to which was later added a larger administrative unit, the prefecture, containing several *hsien*, and
above that a grouping of prefectures to form provinces,
first ten and then as the empire grew 15, each under an
imperial governor working in tandem with a military
commander, so that the Han system of commanderies
was no longer necessary as such. At the capital three
newly established institutions divided the work of government under the emperor: the Imperial Secretariat
(policy formulation), the Imperial Chancellery (a review
board), and the Department of State Affairs (which saw
that agreed-on policy was carried out). Such an arrangement worked toward some form of balanced power, and
also as some check on the emperor's otherwise absolute
power. The Department of State Affairs functioned as six
separate ministries, known as Boards: Revenue, Military,
Public Works, Justice, Personnel, and Rites. These Six
Boards were continued by every successive imperial
government until the last one fell in 1911. The Board of
Censors was a separate and additional organ. Up to
about the middle of the eighth century this machinery
worked well, and the empire also operated on a munificent revenue base, enough not only for the normal functioning of government but to pay the heavy cost of military conquest and campaigns. Revenue flowed in from
an economy which had grown well beyond Han levels,
especially in the south, collected by an efficient and generally honest administration.

This was the period of the famous Judge Ti (Dee), an
upright magistrate who developed a reputation for solv-

**Stone relief of the Emperor
T'ang T'ai Tsung's horse, "Autumn Dew," with groom, dated
between A.D. 626 and 649. (University of Pennsylvania Museum, Philadelphia)**

ing difficult cases of criminal behavior which came to his attention and were dealt with in his court; he was assisted, like all local magistrates, by unofficial appointees who helped to ferret out crime and share the regular load of administration, and also by the local military commander. Many stories were told about him, his honesty and sagacity, at first oral tales and then, centuries after his death, written down in the Ming dynasty. These were translated in the 1950s by a Dutch scholar, Robert van Gulik, who became so fascinated with Judge Dee, as he called him, that he then wrote nearly 20 new stories at novel length about this exemplary official and his deeds which still make superb reading, and which give the authentic flavor of his times. Judge Dee was perhaps a bit larger than life, like the subjects of most tales, but was often cited as a model magistrate who later rose to high office in the capital. All officials were not as strictly honest or conscientious, in T'ang China like anywhere else, but for the first century and a half the standard was high, prompted by the Confucian morality which all officials were educated in.

Decline

As in the later Han, the revenue base began to be eroded first by imperial land grants to various notables who largely avoided taxes; this of course had the effect of squeezing everyone else, primarily peasants. Population grew substantially in the peaceful and prosperous first century of the T'ang, but while total cultivated land did increase with new lands in the south, it did not match the new mouths, so that average landholdings began to fall as did incomes and subsistence levels. The recruitment of officials through the examination system was made more complete than under the Han, but although many officials were products of that system, there began to be an increase in the appointment of the sons of high officials without the screening of examinations; this obviously led to abuses. And while the Confucian-based training of would-be officials certainly helped to make most of them honest, responsible, and conscientious, it also tended to discourage initiative and

Pleasures of Solitude

Poetry and painting continued to enjoy a glorious growth during the years of disunity after the fall of the Han. One of the greatest poets of this period was T'ao Chien, usually known as T'ao Yuan-ming (365–427). Like so many of the educated elite, he served for a time as an official, and then retired to live in the country, where he found rewards far preferable to those in government, again like many officials in later centuries. His poetry, like that of others who foresook an official career for a return to nature, celebrates both the beauty and the philosophical rewards of a world untrammeled by human enterprise, but reflects also the prominence of Taoist values among so many people of his time, including many of the elite, although this is a trend in nearly all Chinese poetry and painting from every era. Here is a sample of his verse.

I built my cottage among the habitations of men,
And yet there is no clamor of carriages and horses.
You ask, "Sir, how can this be done?"
"A heart that is distant creates its own solitude."

I pluck chrysanthemums under the eastern hedge,
Then gaze afar toward the southern hills.
The mountain air is fresh at the dusk of day;
The flying birds in flocks return.
In these things there lies a deep meaning;
I want to tell it, but have forgotten the words.

Source: From Liu Wu-chi, *An Introduction to Chinese Literature*. (Bloomington: Indiana University Press, 1966), p. 64.

innovation and perpetuated the split between the small group of the educated and the rest of the population. Reactions to the Empress Wu and her attack on the establishment prompted a strengthening of Confucianism after her overthrow, and with it an increasing rigidity. This was also in part a reaction to what many of the Chinese elite saw as undesirable foreign influences, notably Buddhism but also Islam and other central Asian peoples and ideas, which had "invaded" China since the later Han.

Perhaps especially because Buddhism had become so widespread, it was resented by many of the high status people who had not accepted it, and as early as 836 an imperial decree forbade Chinese to have anything to do with "people of color," by which was meant any sort of foreigner, particularly central Asians, Indians, Arabs, Malays, and so on. The very cosmopolitanism of the T'ang had provoked a backlash. Efforts to adapt Buddhism to Chinese tastes and values, which were considerable, could not conceal its foreign origin, or its implicit challenge to the Confucian orthodoxy, perhaps especially its involvement with doctrines about life after death, its development of a large pantheon of divine or semidivine figures, and its absorption of what the Confucians looked down on as magic practices, often merged with Taoism, Confucianism's old rival. It was certainly a religion of mass salvation, as Confucianism never was, and in its later Mahayana form almost the opposite of what Confucianism stood for, the preeminence

of morality and of this-worldly concerns and the avoidance of theology and "superstition." But what probably most attracted the opposition of the state itself was the growth of Buddhist monasteries and their increasing ownership of tax-free land. Some monasteries also operated as inns for travelers or visitors, and even functioned as primitive banks, issuing their own coins and holding also large stocks of copper and other metals in the form of huge bells and Buddhist statues. Gifts from the pious further swelled their wealth, and they also became involved in moneylending at high rates.

Buddhism and the T'ang

All of this was seen, understandably, as a challenge to the state. At first there were efforts merely to control the Buddhist establishment by limiting the number of monks and monasteries, but such controls were never very effective, and there was growing resentment of Buddhist wealth as the state encountered increasing financial problems with the progressive decay of its earlier revenue system. Even under the northern Wei there were such efforts at control, as under its successor regime in the north. Between 841 and 845 the state moved by confiscating and destroying most of the monasteries, temples, and their lands, an action reminiscent of Henry VIII of England seven centuries later and

Ceramic figure of a court lady playing polo, T'ang dynasty, between A.D. 650 and 700. (The Nelson-Atkins Museum of Art)

✠ Sufferings of the Poor ✠

Over a century after the death of Tu Fu, the latter T'ang produced another outstanding poet, Po Chu-i (Bo Juyi, 772–846), whose work is still greatly admired. Despite the troubles of empire in his time, this was clearly not a moribund period culturally. Like Tu Fu, Po Chu-i was, however, concerned about the sufferings of ordinary people during these years. Here is one of his poems, still a favorite.

An old charcoal seller
Cuts firewood, burns coal by the south mountain.
His face, all covered with dust and ash, the color of smoke,
The hair at his temples gray, his ten fingers black.
The money he makes selling charcoal, what is it for?
To put clothes on his back and food in his mouth.
The rags on his poor body are thin and threadbare;
Distressed at the low price of charcoal, he hopes for colder weather.
Night comes, an inch of snow has fallen on the city;
In the morning he rides his cart along the icy ruts,
His ox weary, himself hungry, and the sun already high.
In the mud by the south gate outside the market he stops to rest.
Suddenly two dashing riders appear:
An imperial envoy garbed in yellow, and his attendant in white;
Holding an official dispatch, he reads a proclamation,
Turns the cart around, curses the ox, and leads it north.
One cartload of charcoal—a thousand or more pounds!
No use appealing to the official taking the cart away.
Half a length of red lace, a slip of damask
Dropped on the ox; payment in full!

(Note: Fine silk often served as currency, and equivalent values were listed for many major commodities, by weight.)

Source: From Liu Wu-chi and I. Y. Lo., eds., *Sunflower Splendor.* (Garden City, New York: Anchor Double-day, 1975), pp. 206–207.

with the same incentives—the need to regain control over lost revenues.

It is possible that Buddhism was already beginning to lose its wide appeal in this new age of imperial grandeur and order, but in any case it never recovered from the confiscations and remained for the rest of Chinese history a minority religion, although, as pointed out above, merged to some extent with Taoism, which as a native Chinese religion was more readily accepted, even by Confucians. Objections to Buddhism included its Hindu-derived practice of burning the dead as well as the original celibacy enjoined on monks. Both were seen as violating the Confucian emphasis on family continuity and on taking care of the body received from one's parents. In later Chinese Buddhism monks were permitted to marry, probably in order to deflect Confucian criticism.

After its official suppression and the reassertion of Confucian dominance, Buddhism remained as an element of folk religion and Buddhist influences are discernible in vernacular literature and many other aspects of subsequent Chinese society. The Buddhist temples, caves, statuary, and painting form a major part of the Chinese artistic heritage, although after the completion of the caves and statues at Yün Kang and Lung Men (the latter actually finished under the Empress Wu), there were no more such massive projects. Another cave site which is of special interest is at Tun Huang (Dunhuang) in westernmost Kansu, really in the desert, where a series of caves were decorated with large and small images of the Buddha and with a remarkable series of wall paintings showing scenes from the Buddha's life and many of his attendants. Work seems to have begun on this complex at Tun Huang in the fourth century A.D. and continued for several centuries thereafter, although it was noted as a key trade center long before, where routes between India, Central Asia, and China converged in a small oasis. In addition to wall paintings and Buddhist statuary, the caves at Tun Huang also contained a very large Buddhist library of manuscripts. The caves, or most of them, were sealed up by the monks in the eleventh century to protect them from raiding, and were not re-opened until 1900, when they revealed treasures from centuries earlier. The painting shows a fascinating blend of Indian, Central Asian, and Chinese art styles, and the manuscripts included many from each of these major culture areas and in their scripts, all befitting Tun Huang's role as a meeting place of cultures as well as the route along which Buddhism reached China.

Along with Buddhist texts, some Indian scholars made the journey to China and are mentioned as among the residents of both Ch'ang An and Loyang. They also supervised translations of Indian texts on astronomy, astrology, mathematics, and medicine, the last two almost certainly more advanced than in China at this period but greatly enriching Chinese practice, although there was also some transmission of Chinese medicine to India. There is evidence too of the introduction of Indian music and dance, although not apparently with lasting consequences. Earlier, in the fourth century, the central Asian monk known by his Indian name as Kumarajiva (350–413—he had studied in India) supervised a team of translators in Ch'ang An, then the capital of one of the short-lived kingdoms of north China, who prepared Chinese versions of a great number of Buddhist texts from the original Sanskrit.

Buddhist art was accompanied by Buddhist literature: stories of the Buddha, accounts of pilgrimages, sermons, and other pious themes. Much of this was written for a popular audience. Popularization also took place on a large scale in art, both painting and sculpture, including large and small statues of a fat Laughing Buddha, totally opposite from the original ideal of asceticism and otherworldliness. After all, Buddhism became a mass religion, and art and literature for the masses were logical accompaniments, along with the development of a great variety of sects and the merging of Buddhism with much folk religion as well as with popular Taoism.

Islam or its followers, probably at first merchants trading to Ch'ang An, reached China by the eighth century, after its seventh-century founding by Mohammed in Arabia and its rapid spread to most of central Asia. The Turks of central Asia were early converts to Islam, and mainly through them it spread also into the Chinese northwest, where it is still prominent. Islam later spread also into the southwest, although during the T'ang the independent (and non-Islamic) kingdom of Nan Chao (Nanzhao) arose in the mid-eighth century, founded by

A sample of perhaps the best-known T'ang art form, in glazed pottery. Horses, like this one, camels, and hundreds of other figures, were turned out in great quantity, but each figure is of superb quality. (Art Institute of Chicago)

Thai people in western Yunnan, which was patterned closely on the T'ang model. One form of literature which was to become important in each succeeding Chinese dynasty had its beginnings in the T'ang, the compilation of local gazetteers for both *hsien* and prefectures (*fu*) which outlined each district's history, natural features, institutions, economy, and biographies of notable people of the district. These gazetteers are still a mine of information, especially since they came to be redone frequently to keep them up to date.

Buddhist Sects

Eight or nine different sects of Buddhism developed by mid-T'ang, although only four of them lasted very long, and were spread to Japan by visiting Japanese monks. These were T'ien T'ai (Tendai in Japanese), Hua-yen (which became Kogon in Japanese), Ch'ing-t'u (Quingtu, Japanese Jodo), and Chan (already mentioned as Japanese Zen). Another, San Chieh (Sanjieh, The Three Sages), was suppressed by the T'ang mainly because its division of history into epochs put the T'ang into the period of decay, which even the Empress Wu could not tolerate. Others were later destroyed in the great mid-ninth-century persecution of Buddhism. A mystic or esoteric sect called Mi was much patronized by Hsuan Tsung, centered on the use of mantras (mystic syllables repeated like a chant to induce a form of trance, or a "clearing of the mind"); it did not long survive his death but reappeared in Japan as the very popular sect of Shingon.

T'ien T'ai, named for a mountain range in Chekiang (Zhejiang) Province, combined various elements of different doctrines and practices and promoted the supremacy of the Buddhist text, the Lotus Sutra, supposedly a sermon preached by the Buddha to a huge audience of saints, bodhisattvas, gods, and other supernatural beings. It is full of magic symbols, and was widely represented in art. The lotus, bearing an ethereal white flower with its roots in the mud of a stagnant pond, is a common Buddhist symbol of transfiguration out of the muck of worldly involvement. Figures of the Buddha are often shown sitting on a representation of the lotus, with his hands in one of the many gestures, or *mudra*, symbolizing different aspects of the Buddha's message. T'ien T'ai argued that all things contain the truth, or the "Buddha nature," even, according to some of its exponents, inanimate things. Hua-yen centered on what it called "the doctrine of emptiness," and the generic interdependence of all things through its doctrine of "reciprocal causation." Ch'ing-t'u, also known as the Pure Land sect, was the school which above all stressed faith as the chief means to nirvana. Ch'ing-t'u was the school which did most to spread and popularize the worship of Amitabha (Amit'ofo in Chinese, Amida in Japanese), who was supposed to reign in the Western Paradise as the Buddha of Infinite Light. What became the female figure of Kuan-yin (Guanyin, Japanese Kannon), the Bodhisattva of Mercy, was another prominent

figure of the Pure Land sect. In Chinese Pure Land, and even more in its later Japanese version, began the practice of repeating the name of Amitabha, or Amit'ofo, as a pious invocation which could in itself win a wholehearted believer a place in Nirvana. One can perhaps understand its wide popularity, really as a form of folk magic. Pure Land also emphasized salvation through faith as the best course for an age of temporal troubles.

Chan (Zen) centered on meditation as the best means for seeing through the illusory observable world and penetrating the Buddha nature inside one's self. Its origin and growth in China were clearly much influenced by Taoism, but Chan rejected the doctrine of good works and the study of the Buddhist scriptures as paths to salvation and stuck to silent meditation, believing that enlightenment, like that of the Buddha himself, might come in a sudden flash—*satori* in Japanese—after years of meditation. Various means were used by Chan monks or their teachers to shock the mind out of its ordinary ruts, including contradictions, conundrums, unanswerable riddles, nonsense phrases, or enigmatic statements, with the idea that these would help the pupil to go beyond everyday, real-world reasoning and to understand the infinite. Probably the best known of these supposed aids to enlightenment is "What is the sound of one hand clapping?" (There is no guarantee that it will produce enlightenment for you, but try it out!)

Increasing Chinese settlement of the south brought new pressures on the indigenous inhabitants, who remained separate from the Han Chinese in language and culture and who were usually less technically developed. They were also divided into a large variety of

Part of the Buddhist caves at Lung Men (Longmen) near Loyang. (R. Murphey).

separate groups, but even their total numbers made it impossible for them to withstand Chinese pressures. Most of the land which they had originally occupied was taken, where it was level or gentle enough to permit agriculture Chinese-style, or if necessary, terracing. The surviving southern natives were progressively driven up into the highlands and many of them slaughtered, although there was probably some intermarriage. This was a process which stretched over many centuries and had begun earlier, in the Han, but the T'ang marked the rise of the south as China's major area of population and production and hence also marked the major assault on the indigenous inhabitants, south of the Yangtze valley.

Collapse

By the end of the eighth century the T'ang system, for all its imperial and cultural glory, was running down, presaged by the rebellion of An Lu-shan and the chaos which followed it soon after mid-century. As already indicated, more and more land passed off the tax rolls through imperial grants, leaving those who did pay taxes, mainly peasants and smaller landowners, with a heavier burden. Total revenues fell, slowly at first and then more drastically, despite new taxes on trade and on households, while more and more peasants turned to

banditry, always a sign of decay in the political, social, and economic order. Corvée labor had originally been required of all fit adult males, but in the course of the eighth century it was no longer enforced, while the armies became more and more staffed by hired mercenaries, which of course cost money. Many of the troops developed their primary loyalty to regional commanders, and in any case they were often recruited from "barbarian" groups whose loyalty to China was uncertain. The regional army leaders tended to become powers in their own right, while at the court the evil power of the eunuchs rose rapidly after Hsuan Tsung's death. The resurgent Turks, who with their Arab allies had defeated a T'ang army at the Talas River in 751, marked the beginning of the end of Chinese power in central Asia. In the following decades the T'ang army as a whole began to lose its effectiveness.

The final stages of the T'ang collapse began with a series of rebellions in the north in 874. Although they were eventually put down by 884, other regional commanders enhanced their power during the rebellion and now more or less openly contended among themselves for supremacy. In 907 one of them usurped the imperial throne and declared the T'ang at an end. Unfortunately this did not end the fighting. Most of the country remained divided among the generals, each claiming to be emperor. This period is called by the official histories The Ten Kingdoms, although there were in fact many more contenders, while in the north five brief efforts to

✠ Against Buddhism ✠

In A.D. 845, the T'ang emperor Wu Tsung issued one of many edicts over several years condemning Buddhism as an alien and undesirable doctrine.

We have heard that up through the Three Dynasties* the Buddha was never spoken of. It was only from the Han and Wei on that the religion of idols gradually came into prominence. So in the latter age it has transmitted its strange ways, instilling its infection with every opportunity, spreading like a luxuriant vine, until it has poisoned the customs of our nation; gradually and before anyone was aware, it beguiled and confounded men's minds so that the multitude have been increasingly led astray.... Each day finds its monks and followers growing more numerous and its temples more lofty. It wears out the strength of the people with constructions of earth and wood, pilfers their wealth for ornaments of gold and precious objects, causes men to abandon their lords and parents for the company of teachers, and severs man and wife with its monastic decrees. In destroying law and injuring mankind indeed nothing surpasses this doctrine.

* This is the period usually known by modern scholars as the Warring States.

Source: From W. T. deBary, ed., *Sources of Chinese Tradition, Vol. I*, op. cit., p. 380.

found dynasties on the part of regional commanders, all of which lasted only a few years, led to the label The Five Dynasties. It is noteworthy that three of the five would-be emperors were "barbarian," two Turkish and a third probably Persian, a good indication of what had happened in the military as it came to be dominated by foreign troops and leaders.

At the same time, the tribes along the northern steppe frontier were on the warpath again, sensing the weakness of China in this period of disunity and seeking to carve out their own territories south of the border. One such group, the Khitan Mongols, did succeed in winning control of 16 border prefectures based on what later became Peking, and went on to take over much of southern Manchuria and the northern part of north China. This was perhaps a foretaste of the great Mongol conquest of China two and a half centuries later. The Khitan gave their mini-empire the dynastic name of Liao, from the Liao River in southern Manchuria, and ruled it from 947 to 1125; after 960, when the Sung dynasty was established, this was confirmed by treaty with the Sung, who paid them in effect an annual tribute. It is probably from the name Khitan that the Russian name for China, Khitai, was derived, and the later European name of Marco Polo's time, Cathay. The T'ang thus ended in chaos and civil war, but the period of disunity was only a little over 50 years, unlike the long division of China after the fall of the Han. The luster of the T'ang, and the by now long-established pattern of imperial unity, had built up its own momentum, and the varied institutions of centralized power were ready to hand. In 960 one of the still contending generals in the welter following the collapse of the T'ang took over the throne in the north and made his conquest stick. This man, Chao K'uang-yin (Zhao Kuang Yin), took the imperial title of T'ai Tsu (Taizi, "Grand Progenitor"), and founded the Sung dynasty.

There were obviously plenty of signs of trouble in the last century of the T'ang and indeed rebels captured and devastated Ch'ang An, especially the troops of the chief rebel leader Huang Ch'ao who in 881 went on a rampage of killing and destruction, after having earlier done the same to most cities in the south. The government troops found only ruins when they retook the city in 883. The remaining T'ang emperors, now the pawns of powerful warlords, largely abandoned Ch'ang An and moved to Loyang. The defense system along the imperial frontiers fell apart, and from about 790 control over central Asia west of Yü Men, the Jade Gate in westernmost Kansu, was lost. Korea, formerly a T'ang tributary, declared its independence. The kingdom of Nan Chao in the southwest mounted expansionist campaigns both north into Szechuan and southeast into northern Vietnam, though only temporarily. Vietnam in fact regained its independence in the last years of the collapsing T'ang, while in the north the Khitan empire had bitten off an important piece of what had once been prime Chinese imperial territory (see the map on page 84).

No doubt it all added up to disaster, but except for those unlucky enough to be caught in the fighting and slaughter, like the people of Ch'ang An and Loyang, Foochow (Fuzhou), and Canton (Guangzhou), the deterioration was perhaps not all that evident to observers or to those in the areas of peace and reasonable prosperity which remained. China was huge, and imperial politics were not the most important part of it, as indeed they never are in any country. Relatively late in the supposed period of steep decline, from 838 to 847, the Japanese Buddhist monk Ennin, one of the many who came or were sent from Japan to study Buddhism nearer to its source, described in his diary of those years a China which impressed him still as well ordered and prosperous. He was especially struck, even at this late date, by the efficiency and responsibility of the bureaucracy and the imperial system of centralized control—so much for perspectives dominated by politics. Every empire, and every political regime, contains the seeds of its own downfall. The vast momentum of Chinese civilization kept it going despite political disaster, almost to the end, and then enabled it to flourish again in an even more impressive manner under the new dynasty, the Sung.

Suggestions for Further Reading

Carter, T. F., and Goodrich, L. C. *The Invention of Printing in China and its Spread Westward*. New York: Ronald Press, 1955.

DeCrespigny, R. *Under the Brilliant Emperor*. Canberra: Australian National University Press, 1985.

Eberhard, W. *Conquerors and Rulers*. Leiden: Brill, 1965.

Fitzgerald, C. P. *Son of Heaven: A Biography of Li Shih-min*. Cambridge: Cambridge University Press, 1933.

_____. *The Empress Wu*. Vancouver: University of British Columbia, 1968.

Hightower, J. R. *The Poetry of T'ao Ch'ien*. Oxford: Clarendon Press, 1970.

Legge, J. *A Record of Buddhistic Kingdoms, Being an Account by the Chinese Monk Fa Hsien of His Travels in India and Ceylon*. New York: Paragon, 1966.

McMullen, D. *State and Scholars in T'ang China*. Cambridge: Cambridge Univ. Press, 1988.

Munro, E. C. *Through Vermillion Gates*. New York: Pantheon, 1971.

Pulleyblank, E. G. *The Background of the Rebellion of An Lu-shan*. London: Oxford University Press, 1968.

Reischauer, E. O. *Ennin's Diary* and *Ennin's Travels in T'ang China*. New York: Ronald Press, 1955.

Schafer, E. H. *The Golden Peaches of Samarkand: A Study of T'ang Exotics*. Berkeley: California Press, 1963.

_____. *The Vermillion Bird: T'ang Images of the South*. Berkeley: California Press, 1967.

Twitchett, D. *The Birth of the Chinese Meritocracy*. London: China Society, 1976.

_____. *Financial Administration Under the T'ang*. Cambridge: Cambridge University Press, 1970.

_____, and Wright, A., eds. *Perspective on the T'ang*. New Haven: Yale Press, 1973.

Waley, A. *The Life and Times of Po Ch-i*. New York: Macmillan, 1949.

_____. *The Poetry and Career of Li Po*. New York: Macmillan, 1950.

Wang Gung-wu. *The Structure of Power in North China During the Five Dynasties*. Stanford: Stanford University Press, 1967.

Weinstein, S. *Buddhism Under the T'ang*. Cambridge: Cambridge University Press, 1988.

Wright, A. F. *The Sui Dynasty*. New York: Knopf, 1978.

Zürcher, E. *The Buddhist Conquest of China*, 2 Vols. Leiden: Brill, 1959.

CHAPTER 6

ACHIEVEMENT AND DISASTER: THE SUNG AND YUAN DYNASTIES, 960-1355

In many ways, the Sung (Song) is the most exciting period in Chinese history. Later generations of Chinese historians have criticized it because it failed to stem the tide of barbarian invasion and was ultimately overwhelmed by the hated Mongols. But it lasted from 960 to 1279, longer than the roughly 300-year average for dynasties, and presided over a period of unprecedented growth, innovation, and cultural flowering. For a long time the Sung policy of defending their essential territories, and appeasing neighboring barbarian groups like the Khitan and the Hsi Hsia (Xixia) of the northwest with gifts, worked adequately. It made all kinds of sense to give up the exhausting Han and T'ang effort to hold Sinkiang, Tibet, Mongolia, Manchuria, Vietnam, and even the marginal arid fringes of north China. These areas were all unprofitable from the Chinese point of view. They never repaid, in any form but pride, the immense costs of controlling them. Most of them were arid or mountainous wastelands thinly settled by restless nomads who took every chance to rebel or raid, and who were very effective militarily.

Although the period of disunity after the collapse of the T'ang was relatively brief, it saw hard fighting among rival groups and generals. The short and incomplete rule from 751 to 760 of what was called the Later Chou dynasty, with its capital at Kaifeng, promised to reestablish an all-China empire, and carried out a major program of economic reconstruction, although its rule was limited to the southern two-thirds of north China. Canals and dikes were repaired, land which had been abandoned was brought back under cultivation, and taxes were moderated, in part through a fresh confiscation of Buddhist monasteries and possessions. With its new strength, the Later Chou under General Kuo Wei (Guowei) began the process of unification by successful campaigns in Szechuan and in the northern fringes of the lower Yangtze valley. The period between the T'ang collapse in 907 and the founding of the Sung in 960 is (rather confusingly) called the Five Dynasties, since five kingdoms divided up the country, the last of which was Later Chou. But its campaign for supremacy was cut short in 960 by another general, Chao K'uang-yin (Zhao Kuang yin), who usurped the throne in the north with the support of his troops, established his capital at Kaifeng, and founded the Sung dynasty, which was to rule most of China until 1279.

In fairly short order, and building on the reconstruction begun under the Later Chou of his rival General Kuo Wei, he conquered the middle Yangtze region of Ch'u in 963, the kingdom of Shu in Szechuan by 965, and had added most of the south by his death in 976, a process largely completed by his successor two years later. The Khitan kingdom and its Liao dynasty, by now thoroughly Sinicized, remained inside the Great Wall in the northeast (see Chapter 5) despite repeated Chinese efforts to dislodge them, while the northwest and Sinkiang remained in other "barbarian" hands, the Hsi Hsia kingdom, against which successive Sung campaigns also failed. In the southwest of Yunnan, the kingdom of Nan Chao, now under new management as the Kingdom of Tali, was too strong to challenge, and a brief campaign against Vietnam in the far south in 981 convinced the Sung not to attempt its reincorporation in the empire after it had broken away in the last years of the T'ang. So the China of the Sung even at its height, which also left Manchuria in Khitan control and abandoned the Chinese position in Tibet (indeed rampaging Tibetans had already in late T'ang occupied parts of the northwest), was considerably smaller than at the height of the T'ang, and also did not attempt to contest the de facto independence of Korea as a "tributary state." This made rational sense, however damaging to Chinese imperial pride, and at least for the time left China stronger, resting on the unparalleled resources of its prime agricultural areas, river valleys, and trade routes.

Vietnam and Korea had been chronic drains on China's military strength; both were determined to fight relentlessly against Chinese control, but willing to accept a mainly nominal tributary status, which protected Chinese pride and avoided bloody struggles. The Sung wisely concentrated on the productive center of Han Chinese settlement south of the Great Wall and east of the dry northwest and even made an agreement, with an annual subsidy or tribute, to accept Khitan control of what is now the Peking area, where the Khitan fixed their capital, plus most of Manchuria and parts of northernmost eastern China. There was a similar agreement with the dominant non-Chinese group in the northwest, the Tanguts and their Hsi Hsia empire, who controlled most of Kansu and adjacent northern Shensi. The Tanguts were a mixed group, part descendants of the Hsien-pei (Xianbei) and intermarried with Toba, Turkish, and Tibetan peoples. Their economy was thus also a mixture of herding and farming, but their area included considerable Chinese population as well. Sung offensives against them failed, but the Hsi Hsia were finally overwhelmed by the Mongols in 1227.

Little of value to China was lost by these agreements to give up economically submarginal border territory to

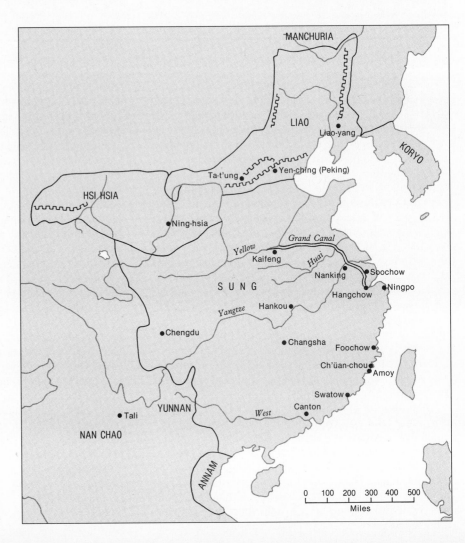

China and Korea in 1050

the Hsi Hsia and Khitans, or by the giving up of Manchuria, Korea, Sinkiang, and Vietnam. Indeed the remarkable flowering of Sung China has much to do with the abandonment of wider imperial ambitions with their great diversion of resources. What remained under Chinese control was still roughly the size of non-Russian Europe and, with a population which reached about 100 million, was by far the largest, most productive and most highly developed state in the world. Any so-called efficiency expert would have strongly recommended such a downsizing policy, and the concentration on developing the tenderloin of China where any investment paid so much greater returns.

In part as a result, and in part because of the rise of civilian control over the military and the decline of the old aristocratic/military ambitions, China leapt forward under the Sung to new heights of economic growth and technological innovation. This period is often regarded as the end of the old medieval order and its apogee under the T'ang and the beginning of what one may call "modern" development. While the T'ang continued and refined many institutions begun under the Ch'in and Han, the Sung saw basic change, perhaps enough to be called a transformation. It is certainly a useful reminder that it is wrong to regard Chinese history and the Chinese system as "changeless," as one sometimes hears. To put a finer point on the changes under the Sung, most of them not only have a distinctly "modern" look, but presage the kinds of changes which were to remake Europe seven or eight centuries later: the rise to dominance of the commercial sector, the boom growth of towns and cities, the expansion of both internal and overseas trade, the rise of an urban culture and of merchant groups, and, especially toward the end, a whole series of technological innovations which look like the early stages of industrialization—waterpowered mills and looms, new explosives, guns, and cannons, movable-type printing and a boom in publishing, clocks with escapements, the beginnings of a factory system, and a long list of mechanical devices or protomachines to aid production.

Northern Sung

The Sung capital was built at Kaifeng, near the great bend of the Yellow River. In addition to its administrative functions it became a huge commercial center and also a center of manufacturing, served in all respects by the Grand Canal, which continued to bring rice and other goods from the prosperous south. There was a particularly notable boom in iron and steel production and metal industries, using coal as fuel. China in the eleventh century probably produced more iron, steel, and metal goods than the whole of Europe until the mid-eighteenth

century, and similarly preceded Europe by seven centuries in smelting and heating with coal. Kaifeng was better located to administer and to draw supplies from the Yangtze valley and the south than Ch'ang An, whose frontier pacification role was in any case no longer so necessary. The Sung army was large, mobile, equipped with iron and steel weapons, and well able for some time to defend the state's new borders. Kaifeng probably exceeded 1 million inhabitants, with merchants and artisans now proportionately more important than in the past, although there were also clouds of officials, soldiers, providers, servants, and hangers-on.

The early Sung emperors prudently eliminated the power of the court eunuchs and the great landed families, and rebuilt the scholar-officialdom as the core of administration. Civil servants recruited through examination had no power base of their own but did have a long tradition of public service and could even check the abuses of the powerful. In each county and at each higher level the emperor appointed both a civil administrator—a magistrate or governor—and a military official, each with his own staff, who with other officials such as tax collectors and the imperial censors or inspectors had overlapping jurisdiction and could check on each other. It was an efficient system, which insured good administration most of the time. The growing spread of mass printing promoted literacy and education and opened wider opportunities for commoners to enter the elite group of the scholar-gentry from whom officials were recruited, or to prosper in trade.

It was in many ways a golden age of good government, prosperity, and creativity. Paper promissory notes and letters of credit, followed by mass government issue of paper currency, served the growth of commerce. Government officials distributed printed pamphlets and promoted improved techniques in agriculture: irrigation, fertilization, ingenious new metal tools and protomachines, and new improved crop strains. Painting had a glorious development, often patronized by rich urban merchants as well as by the Sung court. Literature also flourished, boosted by the spread of cheap printing. Fictional tales proliferated, some now in the vernacular. The most famous Sung literary figure is the poet-painter-official Su Shih, also known as Su Tung-p'o (Su Dongpo, 1037–1101), perhaps the best known of all China's long tradition of poetic nature lovers. It was a confident, creative time.

Su Shih was, like so many of the scholar-gentry, a painter as well as a poet. In several of his poems he tries to merge the two media, inviting the reader to step into the scene and lose him/herself in a mind-emptying union with the great world of nature. He also used dust as a symbol for both official life (dead files, lifelessness, etc., as in our own culture) and for the capital on the dusty plains of the north, where he served for many years as an official:

Life along the river near Kaifeng at spring festival time. This scene comes from a long scroll that begins with the rural areas and moves through suburbs into the capital, giving a vivid picture of the bustling life in and around Kaifeng, at the time the largest city in the world. The painting, by Chang Tse-tuan, was done in the early twelfth century. (Werner Forman Archive, London)

*Foggy water curls and winds around the brook
    road;*
*Layered blue hills make a ring where the brook
    runs east.*
*On a white moonlit shore a long-legged heron
    roosts.*
And this is a place where no dust comes.
An old man of the stream looks, says to himself:
*"What is your little reason for wanting so much
    to be a bureaucrat?*
You have plenty of wine and land;
Go on home, enjoy your share of leisure!"

* * *

*A boat, light as a leaf, two oars squeaking
    frighten wild geese.*
*Water reflects the clear sky, the limpid waves are
    calm.*
*Fish wriggle in the weedy mirror, herons dot
    misty foreshores.*
*Across the sandy brook swift, the frost brook
    cold,*
The moon brook bright.
*Layer upon layer like a painting, bend after bend
    like a screen.*
*Remember old Yen Ling long ago—"Lord,"
    "Minister"—a dream,*
Now gone, vain fames.

*Only the far hills are long, the cloudy hills
    tumbled,*
The dawn hills green.

* * *

*Drunk, abob in a light boat, wafted into the thick
    of flowers,*
*Fooled by the sensory world, I hadn't meant to
    stop here.*
*Far misty water, thousand miles' slanted evening
    sunlight,*
Numberless hills, riot of green like rain—
I don't remember how I came.

Chao K'uang-yin, the general who founded the Sung in 960, took the imperial title of T'ai Tsu (Taizu, another Grand Progenitor like Han Kao Tsu). He had succeeded in large part because, having come to power himself as a military man, he knew well the threats to order from regional commanders (as he had been). He pensioned off most of them, and over time replaced the regional commanders with civilian officials. Generals were moved around periodically and troops rotated as a further check against warlordism. The old aristocracy of T'ang times had been largely destroyed in the chaos of the ninth century and the fighting of the tenth after the dynasty's collapse. This removed a major problem for the central control of the army, and also made possible the growth of an administrative regime dominated by an elite based on education, products of the examination system steeped in the Confucian morality of responsibility and service. The entire army was put firmly under the control of the government. The work of consolidation was completed by T'ai Tsu's brother and successor T'ai Tsung (Taizong, another "Grand Ancestor" like T'ang T'ai Tsung, 976–997), especially after he completed the reconquest of the south by 978. Another source of imperial strength was the development of close control over tax revenues and the disappearance of tax evasion by large estates, most of which had in any case been broken up in the fall of the T'ang and the disorder following it. This was not to last, but for the time it made a big difference.

The administrative divisions of government begun under the T'ang were continued and amplified, with the addition of a Finance Commission to manage the Treasury, the tax system, and the government monopolies. The Sung thus learned from the weaknesses of the T'ang and developed effective means to prevent them in most respects. The big exception was the army, which despite its size was never very effective in dealing with the aggressive barbarian groups along the northern and northwestern frontiers, and in the end failed to prevent the loss of north China and the final disaster of the Mongol conquest. The Sung was the age of civilian government by Confucian scholars who tended to look down on the military. Civilian control was fine, but it also led to chronic factionalism and divided counsels as well as to a general demoralization of the army. But for a time, all went well; the imperial treasury had a large surplus and by the early eleventh century was taking in nearly three times what the T'ang had done at its highest point.

The Civil Service

Perhaps an even more important change was the development under the Sung, for the first time, of a civil service recruited for its higher posts almost entirely from the educated group who had passed the three levels of the imperial examinations. Under the T'ang, when recruitment through examination was developed well beyond its Han origins, such people filled at most a third of the civil service jobs. Under the Sung this system, one of the chief glories of imperial China, reached its peak. Imperial relatives were barred from any important positions (another source of big trouble in the past), and eunuchs, an even greater plague, were kept out of any political power. There was a small amount of selling of offices (an abuse which was to become much greater in later dynasties), and upper-level officials could recommend people for junior posts, but nearly all higher posi-

tions were filled by graduates. To help insure impartiality, candidates were identified by number rather than by name and their examination papers were copied out by scribes so that the calligraphy could not be recognized.

Something less than 10 percent of the candidates passed the first examinations held at the prefectural level and went on to the capital to take the second level. About 10 percent of those passed, and were then given the third screening in the palace itself. Many aspiring candidates took the examinations many times in hopes of eventual success. Failure of course led to frustration, and in troubled times such people might be tempted to join rebel groups. But passing the first level meant the acquisition of gentry status, a considerable advantage as well as a distinction, and those who did not progress beyond that or who did not succeed in the examinations at the capital had nevertheless acquired an extensive education in the classics, which many of them used to advantage, including serving as teachers to upcoming generations of aspirants.

Once in office, officials were regularly rated for merit—mainly honesty and efficiency—and promoted or passed over accordingly. Higher officials who nominated lower ones for promotion (although they were forbidden to nominate their own relatives) were responsible for the performance of those they recommended, and could be punished if their protégés were found to be inept or dishonest. Officials were also checked on by the imperial censors, who often toured local districts, sometimes incognito, to detect malfeasance in office. A bad report from a censor could end a man's career, or even lead to his execution or banishment. The positive aspects of this system were mainly its insurance that only dedicated and able people, according to the standards of the time, would wield power, and that able men from any background could rise to office, not only the sons of the rich and well connected. Lists of successful candidates from the mid-eleventh to the mid-twelfth centuries include up to a third or more from families which had never produced an official before during three preceding generations. This is a truly remarkable degree of upward mobility, in any premodern society and perhaps even now anywhere. It clearly helped to ensure good government and stability, and at the same time served as a sort of escape valve for ambitious men, who could find a prestigious career within the system rather than seeking alternative routes or trying to overturn the system.

Unfortunately, before the end of its first century the Sung began to encounter the familiar problems of dynastic decline in financial matters. As population probably doubled under the peace and prosperity of the Sung, from its low point in late T'ang, tax revenues did not keep pace. In addition, the old pattern of big landowners evading taxes surfaced again, leaving the peasants more and more pressed. With the great increase in population, farms became smaller and less able to support families, many of whom then became tenants or simple laborers on large estates, and there was a growing group of both rural and urban poor. Meanwhile expenditures continued to rise, especially for the increasingly desperate defense of the northern and northwestern frontiers in several campaigns. By the mid-eleventh century the army absorbed nearly 80 percent of the government's total budget, a disastrous imbalance. Nevertheless, despite its swollen size, the army made no progress against the barbarian threats. It was made up largely of people recruited from the poorer classes, who had difficulty making a living in the new circumstances. But they had to be paid and equipped, although their striking power was inadequate to deal with the Khitan, Hsi Hsia, and other border groups. The subsidy payments in silk and silver to the Hsi Hsia and Khitan, intended to ensure peace, were a further drain on Sung resources, and had to be increased before the first century was out. The bureaucracy was divided on the best policies to pursue.

Reform

In 1068 a new young emperor, Shen Tsung (Shenzong), appointed the head of a reformist faction as Chief Councillor, Wang An-shih, who tried to rearrange the whole sphere of government policies, especially in financial matters. His earlier proposals for reforms in 1056, aimed mainly at stabilizing the deteriorating situation in the northwest, had attracted favorable attention. Wang has earned a reputation as a socialist through his policies of government control over the economy, but the system was in growing crisis and he did his best to check the decline and restore the dynasty's financial solvency. He went beyond the "ever-normal granary" arrangement

and had the government buy special products of some areas, to be sold in other regions at stable prices, at the same time making a profit. He tried more generally to control prices, and to cut out usurious moneylenders by offering government loans to poor peasants at lower rates. In 1072 he set up a state trading organization to break the monopoly of big merchants and to deal directly with smaller firms, who were offered government loans. New land surveys tried to get rid of long-standing injustices favoring the rich and well connected, and taxes were adjusted accordingly, based on the productivity of land. All personal property was assessed for taxation, and corvée service was commuted into money payments. These were all reasonable measures designed to promote the general welfare as well as the imperial treasury, but they not surprisingly aroused the bitter opposition of larger landowners, merchants, moneylenders, and those with vested interest in the existing system, including of course the conservative bureaucracy.

In other areas, Wang tried to get each district to provide quotas of trained militia and to supply them with arms, another reform much in order to help strengthen the quality of the army. The Sung heretofore had had very few cavalry units, in part because they had lost control over the chief horse breeding areas in the north and northwest. This had been a serious weakness in battles with the steppe people and their mounted warriors. Wang attempted to correct it by buying up horses for distribution to peasant families in the north, with the understanding that a member of each family would be available, with his horse, as part of an imperial cavalry when needed. On the civil side, he also greatly expanded the number of government schools, open to anyone of ability, to offer education and a chance at office-holding to those who could not afford to obtain this in the private academies which still were predominant. He

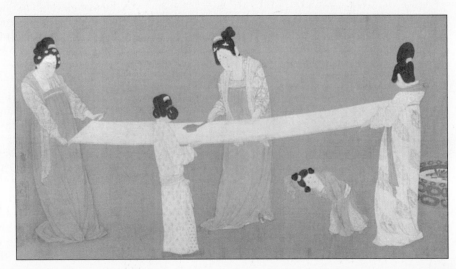

Court ladies preparing a roll of silk, painted by the Sung Emperor Hui Tsung. (Courtesy, Museum of Fine Arts, Boston)

also urged that the imperial examinations should include practical problems of administration and tests of aptitude rather than being so heavily concentrated on memorization of the classics. This too was a forward step, but of course it drew the resistance of the Confucian bureaucracy also, men who had risen to power by the old system and were wedded to it.

Perhaps Wang An-shih tried to push for more change and faster than these political realities might have suggested. In fact, most of his "new" policies were simply revivals of things which had been advocated or pursued under the Han and the T'ang, and none could be called revolutionary. The brief career of Wang Mang (see Chapter 4) suggests many parallels, although he probably enraged the traditionalists still more by declaring himself the emperor of a new dynasty, whereas Wang An-shih was simply a determined and far-sighted official appointed by the emperor to deal with obvious pressing problems. Apart from the strong opposition of vested interests who saw themselves as damaged by Wang's policies, most of the Confucian bureaucracy was also against him. His determination and his strong views alienated many, and not only among the traditionalists and conservatives. The bureaucracy, as well as Confucianism itself, had grown increasingly rigid over the centuries since the Han, and was to do so still more in later centuries. Its instinctive reaction against change was perhaps its greatest weakness, and Wang An-shih's reforms in the end crashed on that rock, plus the inertia of any large established system. The issues are still hotly debated among Chinese historians. The conservative group at court forced him out in 1076, but he was recalled in 1078. When Emperor Shen Tsung died in 1085, Wang was summarily dismissed and his reforms canceled or destroyed; he died the following year.

It is certainly possible that if Wang An-shih or his policies had been retained the Sung might have been sufficiently strengthened to surmount its problems, including its relations with the Hsi Hsia and the Khitan, or even to have been able to resist the final Mongol assault. Such speculation is tempting, but not very profitable. In any case the debate went on between the conservatives and those favoring more radical policies such as Wang's, but no decisive action was taken. It was these inconsistent or even contradictory policies which contributed importantly to the ultimate collapse of the Sung in the face of the overwhelming problems which confronted it, none of which were ever effectively dealt with. Bitter factionalism among rival groups at court critically weakened the dynasty just when a united front and truly national effort had become most critical. Conservatism, including its inflexible Confucian form, is seldom an appropriate response to crisis. It says something about this that most Chinese historians continued to criticize Wang An-shih in subsequent centuries, including those

in the nineteenth century when China faced an equally threatening series of crises as the Ch'ing dynasty lost effectiveness and pressures from an expansive West and Japan progressively humbled the proud Chinese tradition, still resisting change even to save itself.

Culture and Conquest

As so often even in the declining years of a dynasty, the arts continued to flourish, especially under the emperor Hui Tsung (Huizong, 1100–1125), who was himself an accomplished painter as well as a patron of the arts. The luxurious style of his court imposed further burdens on the state's treasury. The largely unaddressed problems which Wang An-shih had tried to confront, including the continued impoverishment of the peasantry, led to an outbreak of popular uprisings. Hui Tsung founded new schools, but also spent fortunes in further embellishing the imperial palace and gardens. The rebellions were ultimately put down, with great loss of life, but at the same time fresh trouble was brewing on the northern frontier. An originally nomadic group, the Jurchen of northern Manchuria, ancestors of the Manchus, spilled over into southern Manchuria and attacked the Khitan empire there in 1114. They soon adopted the Chinese dynastic name of Chin (Jin), and the Sung unwisely made an alliance with them against the Khitan, anxious to regain the north China border areas ceded to the Khitan two centuries earlier. The warlike Jurchen demolished the Khitan empire by 1125, in alliance with the Hsi Hsia, but the Sung army had no such sweeping successes.

The Jurchen were not impressed by the effectiveness of their Sung allies, and the Sung foolishly treated them as inferiors, and complained about their meager share of the spoils of victory over the Khitan. The Jurchen response was to invade north China, and in a devastatingly rapid advance captured the Sung capital at Kaifeng in 1126. Almost nothing remained to testify to the grandeur of the Northern Sung, and the destruction was completed by the Mongols just over a century later. The mobile mounted Jurchen forces pushed on south and even crossed the formidable barrier of the Yangtze. The great southern cities of Nanking and Hangchou (Hangzhou) were taken and sacked in 1129–1130, along with most other cities and towns in central China. But the Sung army regrouped, for once under superb leadership by a gifted general, Yüeh Fei, and drove the Jurchen northward. Unfortunately he was adamantly opposed by a counterfaction of conservatives at the new court in Hangchou, and died in prison in 1142 after he was dismissed and jailed. Yüeh Fei is still much celebrated as a hero betrayed. Given the sorry events which followed his dismissal and death, and his accomplishments as a military commander, one is strongly inclined

Parakeet on a flowering almond tree, another painting by Emperor Hui Tsung (r. 1101–1125). (Maria Antoinette Evans Fund. Courtesy, Museum of Fine Arts, Boston)

to take his side. This was perhaps the biggest example of many of the fatal consequences of factionalism within the government, but there had been and were to be many more.

A peace treaty was agreed to in 1142 which fixed the boundary between Jurchen and Sung territories along the course of the Huai River, about midway between the Yangtze and the Yellow, but it also required the Sung to pay an annual tribute even larger than they had paid to the Khitan and the Hsi Hsia. The capture of Kaifeng in 1126 marks the end of the Northern Sung, as it is consequently called. The Southern Sung fixed its capital at Hangchou, at the southern edge of the Yangtze delta, while the Chin empire of the Jurchen moved its capital from northern Manchuria to Peking in 1153. Like the Khitan (Liao dynasty), the Jurchen adopted Chinese administrative systems, economic forms, and culture on a wholesale basis, and employed large numbers of Chinese in their administration, including high officials. But the Jurchen triumph was to be short-lived. The Mongol onslaught captured Manchuria and the Peking area by 1215, and overran all of the Jurchen and Hsi Hsia empires by 1238, as a prelude to their conquest of the whole of China. The Sung had lost the north, but now they could focus on China's economic heartland, the Yangtze valley and the south, where most Chinese now

lived and which was highly productive. Another century of brilliance in art and technical innovation ensued, with the briefest loss of momentum.

The Southern Sung Period

Cut off from normal land trade routes through the northwest, the Sung turned in earnest to developing sea routes to Southeast Asia and India. Permanent colonies of Chinese merchants grew in many Southeast Asian trade centers. Ports on China's southeast coast, from Hangchou south, flourished, including large numbers of resident foreigners, mostly Arabs, who lived in special quarters under their own headmen. Foreign accounts agree that these were the world's largest port cities of the time. Taxes on maritime trade provided a fifth of the imperial revenue, unheard of in the past.

There was a striking advance in the size and design of oceangoing ships, some of which could carry over 600 people as well as cargo, far larger than any elsewhere until modern times. The earlier Chinese invention of the compass was a vital navigational aid, and these ships also used multiple masts (important for manageability as well as speed), separate watertight compartments (not known elsewhere until much later), and, equally important, the sternpost rudder instead of the awkward and unseaworthy steering oar. In all of these respects Sung ships and their Han dynasty predecessors predated modern ships by many centuries. Ironically, they helped make it possible much later for Europeans to make the sea voyage to Asia using the compass, rudder, and masts—plus gunpowder of course—originally developed by China, and to record their conquests and profits on Chinese-invented paper.

Domestically also commerce and urbanization flourished. The Yangtze delta and the southeast coast had long been China's commercial center, with the help of high productivity and easy movement of goods by river, sea, and canal. The proliferation of cities included for the first time several as big or bigger than the capital and many only slightly smaller. Suchou (Soochow, Suzhou) and Fuchou (Foochow, Fuzhou) each had well over 1 million people, and according to Marco Polo there were six large cities in the 300 miles between them. An immense network of canals and navigable creeks covered the Yangtze and Canton deltas, serving a system of large and small cities inhabited increasingly by merchants managing a huge and highly varied trade. Hangchou, the new capital, with its additional administrative role, may have reached a population size of 1.5 million, larger than cities became anywhere until the age of railways; water transport made this possible for Hangchou and other big cities, including Pataliputra, Rome, Ch'ang An, Istanbul, Edo (Tokyo), and eighteenth-century London. Chinese medicine became still more sophisticated, including the use of smallpox vaccination learned from Guptan India and usually attributed by provincial Westerners to the Englishman Edward Jenner in 1798.

We know a good deal about Hangchou, both from voluminous Chinese sources and from the accounts of several foreigners who visited it, including Marco Polo, who actually saw it only later, toward the end of the thirteenth century under Mongol rule after its great period had long passed. Nevertheless he marveled at its size and wealth and called it the greatest city in the world, by comparison with which even Venice, his hometown and then probably the pinnacle of European urbanism, was, he says, a poor village. The great Arab traveler Ibn Battuta 50 years later, in the fourteenth century, says that even then Hangchou was three days' journey in length and subdivided into six towns, each larger than anything in the West. His rough contemporary, the traveling Italian friar John of Marignolli, called Hangchou "the first, the biggest, the richest, the most populous, and altogether the most marvelous city that exists on the face of the earth."

These were all men who knew the world; even allowing for the usual hyperbole of travelers' tales, they were right about Hangchou. Its rich merchant and scholar-of-

ficial community, and its increasingly literate population of shopkeepers, artisans, and the upwardly mobile supported a new bloom of painting, literature, drama, music, and opera, while for the unlettered, public storytellers in the ancient Chinese oral tradition abounded. Southern Sung (and the Yuan or Mongol dynasty which followed it) is the great period of Chinese landscape painting, a celebration of the beauties of the misty mountains, streams and lakes, bamboo thickets, and green hills of the south.

Innovation and Technological Development

The Southern Sung period was also an exciting period of technological innovation, and even of what seem like the first steps toward the emergence of modern science. The philosopher Chu Hsi (Zhuxi, 1130–1200), the founder of what is labeled Neo-Confucianism, was in many ways a Leonardo-like figure, interested in and competent at a wide range of practical subjects as well as philosophy. This was in the pattern of the Confucian scholar-gentry, but Chu Hsi and some of his contemporaries carried what the sage called "the investigation of things" still further, into the area of what one is tempted to call scientific inquiry. Chu Hsi's journals record, for example, his observation that uplifted rock strata far above current sea level contained marine fossils. Like Leonardo, but three centuries earlier, he made the correct deduction and wrote the first statement of the geomorphological theory of uplift. Chu Hsi argued that through the Confucian discipline of self-cultivation, every man could be his own philosopher and sage, a doctrine similar to Plato's.

In agriculture, manufacturing, and transport there was rapid development, on earlier foundations, of a great variety of new tools and machines: for cultivation and threshing, for water-lifting (pumps), for carding, spinning, and weaving textile fibers, and for windlasses, inclined planes, canal locks, and refinements in traction for water and land carriers. Water clocks were widespread, as were waterpowered mills, to grind grain and to perform some manufacturing functions. It all looks reminiscent of eighteenth-century Europe: commercialization, urbanization, a widening market (including overseas), rising demand, and hence both the incentive and the capital to pursue mechanical invention and other measures to increase production.

Would these developments have led to a true industrial revolution in thirteenth-century China, with all its profound consequences? We will never know, because the Mongol onslaught cut them off, and later dynasties failed to replicate the details of the Sung pattern. The great English historian of early modern Europe, R. H.

Tawney, warns us against "giving the appearance of inevitableness by dragging into prominence the forces which have triumphed and thrusting into the background those which they have swallowed up." It is tempting to think that if the Sung had had just a little longer—or if Chinghis Khan had died young (as he nearly did many times)—China might have continued to lead the world unbrokenly and the rise of modern Europe might never have happened as it did. Nothing is "inevitable," and historians dislike the word. The seeds of the present and future are of course there in the past, but they seldom dominate it; each period has its own perspectives, and does not see itself simply as a prelude to the future—nor should we. We know what has happened since, but we must avoid the temptation to see the past only in that light, and must try to understand it in its own terms.

Southern Sung was in fact far wealthier than Northern Sung, for all its accomplishments, had been, and it

Sung landscape painting by Ma Yuan, early thirteenth century. Chinese painters have always been fascinated by mountains and by nature that is unblemished by, or towers over, human activity. In nearly all such paintings, however, there are tiny human figures, as here near the bottom of the painting, emphasizing the harmony between people and nature, with humans appropriately in a minor role, accepting and drawing wisdom from the far greater and more majestic natural world. Landscape painting had its greatest flowering under the Sung dynasty and its brief successor, the Yuan (Mongol) dynasty. (Boston Museum of Fine Arts)

had a larger budget and a larger bureaucracy, supported by its booming economy. Even though it controlled only about half of China Proper, its half was by far the richer and more populous, and became more so under its rule. This did not make it immune to the administrative and financial problems inherited from Northern Sung, or from the more general pattern of slow dynastic decline, but its ample financial base and its highly developed civil service kept it functioning reasonably effectively until it was destroyed by the Mongol advance. The big and finally fatal exception was the vital sector of military defense, where vacillating policies further weakened the effort to repel the Mongols, as they had done for earlier efforts to defend China against the Khitan, Hsi Hsia, and Jurchen pressures. But for all its faults, in the end mortally destructive, Southern Sung presided over and encouraged a new economic boom and a new cultural flowering far beyond what had been achieved earlier. This made China unquestionably the world leader in both respects, and enormously impressed the few Europeans who saw it, although they did not see it until it had already declined from its Sung height under the brief Mongol rule.

For about half a century the Mongol empire imposed its own form of peace and order (at terrible human cost) on most of Eurasia. It was possible for the first time for people to travel unmolested from Europe to China through central Asia. Marco Polo and his father Niccolo and uncle Maffeo were given great heavy silver passes stamped by the Mongol Khan as a sort of passport, which they had only to show along their long land route from 1271 to 1275 to obtain food, accommodation, fresh horses, and the protection of the Mongol order, through an area otherwise notorious for attacks on caravans and travelers by its nomadic inhabitants. In any case, we now have European as well as Chinese accounts of Sung China, and they make impressive reading.

Kaifeng and Hangchou

Much of these accounts deals with the bigger cities, but it was an age of great urban growth at all levels. Kaifeng, the northern capital, outgrew both its inner and outer walls and spilled over into large extramural developments. Ch'ang An had been mainly an administrative and ceremonial center, but in Kaifeng industrial and commercial developments became predominant, while the bursting population supported a great variety of formal and informal entertainment. The curfew, previously enforced in most Chinese cities, was abolished in Kaifeng in 1063, and people were free to move around at night as they liked. Some businesses and many places of entertainment stayed open until dawn. The same was true in the southern capital of Hangchou, whose commercial development and popular culture were on an even higher level. Merchants were organized into guilds and displayed an enormous variety of goods, from all over the Southern Sung empire and from abroad, since Hangchou was also a major port for foreign trade.

Favorite diversions included a wide range of restaurants, teahouses, public baths, and what we would call nightclubs. Marco Polo's journal also praises the "ladies of the evening," who offered a wide range of entertainment, as without equal anywhere, a judgment echoed by other foreign visitors. Fortune-tellers, puppeteers, actors with musical accompaniment, and storytellers who specialized in different kinds of stories were to be found in many parts of the city. There was a multitude of shopkeepers, druggists, large and small merchants, transport coolies, artisans (now largely independent of court or aristocratic patronage), and employees of the many bookshops attendant on the boom in printing and the rise of a popular readership, and even pet shops. In addition were the workers in the many metal, ceramic, and paper factories, printing establishments, inns and teahouses, plus other types typical of any big city: salesmen, con men, thieves and pickpockets, and a host of domestic servants of various grades from stewards and household managers to cooks, gardeners, their many assistants, and maids in the great houses of the rich.

Outside the city, at the beautiful West Lake (partly artificial, but very artfully so) with mountains on the near horizon surviving Buddhist temples offered the goal of an excursion; the less energetic strolled along the lake or went boating, or attended grand parties of an evening. Pavilions for the contemplative viewing of nature were located at special vantage points, and could offer shelter from a sudden shower. West Lake is still a popular tourist spot, and one can imagine what it must have been like under the Southern Sung. This urban and urbane culture was a far cry from the aristocrat-dominated society of the T'ang, and it also included large numbers of lower-class or working people and even illiterates. This was a new audience for the

✠ The Confucian Revival ✠

The Sung poet, official, and historian Ou-yang Hsiu (1007–1070) was one of several leading figures who promoted the revival of Confucianism and criticized Buddhism as alien.

Buddha was a barbarian who was far removed from China and lived long ago. In the age of Yao, Shun, and the Three Dynasties [the golden age of China's remote past], kingly rule was practiced, government and the teachings of rites and righteousness flourished…. But after the Three Dynasties had fallen into decay, when kingly rule ceased and rites and righteousness were neglected, Buddhism came to China [taking] advantage of this time of decay and neglect to come and plague us…. If we will but remedy this decay, revive what has fallen into disuse, and restore kingly rule in its brilliance and rites and righteousness in their fullness, then although Buddhism continues to exist, it will have no hold upon our people…. Buddhism has plagued the world for a thousand years…. The people are drunk with it, and it has seeped into their bones and marrow so that it cannot be vanquished by mouth and tongue…. There is nothing so effective in overcoming it as practicing what is fundamental…. When the way of Confucius [is] made clear, the other schools [will] cease. This is the effect of practicing what is fundamental in order to overcome Buddhism…. These days a tall warrior clad in armor and bearing a spear may surpass in bravery a great army, yet when he sees the Buddha he bows low and when he hears the doctrines of the Buddha he is sincerely awed and persuaded. Why? Because though he is indeed strong and full of vigor, in his heart he is confused and has nothing to cling to…. If a single scholar who understands rites and righteousness can keep from submitting to these doctrines, then we have but to make the whole world understand rites and righteousness and these doctrines will, as a natural consequence, be wiped out.

Source: W. T. deBary, ed., *Sources of Chinese Tradition.* (New York: Columbia University Press, 1960), pp. 442–445.

rapid growth of popular and vernacular literature, now made much easier with the development of mass printing, for a mass culture as well as for the educated elite. All of the Sung cities had an active street life well into the night. Comedians and acrobats performed daily or nightly, usually in the open at spots where it was easy to gather a crowd. A lower-class culture was emerging, although much of it could be and was enjoyed by all sorts of people. As in almost all cities there were also masses of urban poor, prime recruiting grounds for the army.

Fires in the cities were frequent, and in the close-packed concentration of wooden houses could spread disastrously. Special measures were taken to deal with them, including guard stations and watchtowers manned by firefighters armed with buckets, axes, ropes, and protective clothing. One problem which also accelerated in the new crowded urban conditions was epidemic disease, especially under the jammed and primitive circumstances of a siege, such as the disastrous epidemic at Kaifeng in 1232. We do not know what precisely it was, but it is said to have killed as many as a million people. The south was the home of many warm-climate diseases not so prevalent in the north: filariasis (insect-borne blood parasites), schistosomiasis (a liver fluke), and malaria, as well as many others, all generated especially in the irrigated paddies which now dominated the landscape and were universally enriched with night soil, which carried a variety of intestinal parasites. Other waterborne diseases, such as the various forms of dysentery, cholera, and typhoid, thrived in the southern environment.

In the cities infection of any kind could spread much more easily within close-packed populations who dis-tributed their night soil to nearby farms whose products they ate, and who drank untreated water into which all household sewage ultimately went. What saved the Chinese from far worse contagion was undoubtedly their practice of avoiding cold water for drinking (its coldness was said to gripe the bowels, a good description of dysentery, cholera, or typhoid) and instead drinking tea, made with boiling water, or, for the poor, "white tea," plain water just boiled. Typhus, spread by body lice, was another scourge of crowded populations, especially in winter, and hence more common in the north while nearly absent in the semitropical south. During the cold months people wore padded or quilted clothing which they rarely removed and even more rarely washed themselves, in the absence of piped water or a warm and private room. Lice found a warm protected environment on the skin and in the clothing and hair, but could easily jump from an infected person to others under crowded conditions.

At Ch'ang An merchants and all commercial activities were kept under close control, but at Kaifeng, and even more at Hangchou, they were far freer, and proportionally far more important among the urban populations. Instead of being confined to appointed quarters, commercial and craft businesses were spread all over the Sung cities, and districts were no longer walled and gated. Street names appeared instead of district names, where enterprises of a given sort often clustered together for easier comparison shopping. All county towns (*hsien* capitals) were walled, as a symbol of the imperial authority they represented, where an imperial magistrate held his court. This was the lowest level of imperial administration, which did not much touch the

Part of a garden near Suchou (Soochow, Suzhou) originally laid out in the Southern Sung. (R. Murphey)

far vaster rural areas but was a dominating presence in the walled towns, with an average population between 5,000 and 20,000. The north gate was usually kept closed (an inauspicious direction: cold winds plus invaders), but along the roads or paths leading to the other gates a varied assortment of commercial enterprises grew up outside the walls: sellers of fruit, vegetables, sugarcane, fried, grilled, or steamed goodies, and candies of many sorts, fortune-tellers, beggars, barbers, and, among many others, scribes for the illiterate, who would for a fee write a letter or read one the client had received.

Inside the walls, stone-paved streets ran between the four gates. Where they met in the center was usually a cluster of official buildings housing the magistrate, his court, quarters for his (unofficial) assistants, and a barracks for the small garrison of soldiers. Often nearby was a drum tower of four or five stories which was used as an observation post—for fires or riots—and a place from which to sound alarms or make announcements. In the same central area was usually a Confucian temple, and near it some bookstores. In the more prosperous towns there might also be a private academy where the sons of the well-to-do could learn the classics. The rest of the town was mainly narrow alleys fronted by houses crowded together, with the larger ones, occupied by the gentry, grouped around an inner court but closed off from the street by heavy solid gates. Gutters down the sides of the streets carried an odorous mix of water, sewage, and human filth, flushed by the rains when they came. Some streets were more commercial than others and many were specialized, as in the bigger cities, in particular lines: the street of the barrel makers or furniture makers and so on, plus the main markets for grain, coal, charcoal, wood, cooking and lamp oil, fish, meat, vegetables, fruit, and poultry. There were over a thousand such walled *hsien* capitals, of varying size, throughout the empire, usually sited where they could command easy access, in the south often on navigable water, but, ideally at least, surrounded by hills or mountains separating them from adjoining *hsien* and offering some protection.

Rise of the South

The move south, beginning on a major scale under the T'ang and then accelerating in the Sung, especially with the shift of the capital to Hangchou in Southern Sung, brought an acceleration also in the growth of southern agriculture, primarily irrigated rice. The south was immensely more productive than the north, and could not only support a far larger population but could also free more people from farming, to staff the urban trades and professions and to pursue the arts, the growth of tech-

nology and metallurgy, the boom in printing, literature, painting, and philosophy, or the game of politics. Already under the Northern Sung the Chinese had imported from southern Vietnam varieties of rice which ripened early, some of which reached maturity in early winter. These were systematically distributed by the government through each *hsien*, and made possible in many areas the raising of two rice crops per year; in the far south a third crop could be obtained, while in the Yangtze valley farmers began to grow a third nonrice crop in winter: beans or mulberry (to feed silkworms), cotton, or wheat. Cotton had reached China from its Indian home under the T'ang and began to spread more widely under the Sung, as the cheapest and in many ways best material for clothing, especially in a hot, humid climate like south China's. It slowly replaced the cruder hemp and ramie used by the poor, while silk continued to be used mainly by the rich.

The government was active in building and encouraging landowners to build new and more sophisticated irrigation works, and in disseminating all kinds of new agricultural technology, including the use of new machines for moving water such as the "dragon's backbone" described in Chapter 5 and for speeding the laborious process of soil preparation, threshing, winnowing, and milling. The great increase in agricultural output fed the doubled population and also supported the wider growth of the economy as a whole, including its urban sector. Many towns specialized in the manufacture of pottery and porcelain for distribution, like cotton cloth, rice, and manufactured goods in general, throughout the empire, especially along the multiple waterways of the south.

The Yangtze was the main stream of regional exchange, but its several major tributaries were almost equally important. The delta area, and the delta of the West River in the far south, had been developed earlier as the country's most highly productive agricultural areas as well as, under the Sung, the most highly commercialized and urbanized. Both were crisscrossed by a vast network of canals supplementing the natural creeks and distributary streams and linking every place with every other place by water, often the only linkage. Altogether this was by a huge margin, including the Yangtze system, the largest network of navigable waterways anywhere in the world, as it still is. This played an important role in enabling the commercialization and interregional trade which boomed under the Sung, since water transport is far cheaper and easier than any alternative. In addition to porcelain from Hangchou, Fukien, and from Ching Te Chen (Jingdezhen) in Kiangsi (Jiangxi), now at a new level of perfection, there was a large interprovincial trade in specialties like lacquer (much of which, like porcelain, moved out also into overseas markets) and in iron and metal products, sugar, paper, and printed books, among many other commodities. The highly indented coastline of south China with its numerous good harbors was also heavily used for trade along the coastal route.

Most of the trade goods went to the booming cities, and especially to the growing number of rich families there, who built grand houses which they decorated lavishly and where they laid out extensive gardens. Foreign trade brought in tropical goods such as ivory and sandalwood, paid for in part in copper coins, which are found all over East Asia from Sung times as well as in Southeast Asia. But most of the balance was made up by Chinese exports of silk, tea, lacquer, and porcelains, which are also found from this period throughout East Asia and even as far as India and the east coast of Africa, although it was Indian or Arab middlemen who carried Chinese goods to Africa in the Sung. As part of this expansion of both domestic and overseas trade, the state established workshops, enough to be called factories, run by civil servants. Some of the private and official workshops employed as many as 3,600 workers, true factories.

All of this was part of the general trend toward commercialization. Much of the government's revenue now came from taxes on manufactured goods and on trade, and the empire's main new wealth was generated by those sectors of the economy. This was a situation approaching that of modern states everywhere. Under the Southern Sung the yield from commercial and industrial taxes far exceeded what the state realized from the land tax. Revenue included income from the continued state monopolies in salt, tea, and alcohol, plus customs duties on foreign trade. In part because it was so profitable to the treasury, the state for the first time actively encouraged foreign trade, maintained or improved harbors and canals, built warehouses and navigational aids, and even organized inns for foreign merchants and those from distant provinces. This too was a source of profit, along with sales taxes on transactions, transit taxes, license fees, and port duties. There was also a head tax, and income from the substitution of cash payments for corvée labor.

As much of the new agricultural production as well as other trade goods moved to the cities and towns to feed the growing urban population, it entered into the commercial system, yielding tax revenues along the way and supporting brokers, transporters, merchants, and shopkeepers. But along with the new wealth inevitably came new corruption, and the growth of a new rich group, while most peasants suffered; as they were squeezed harder by both landlords and the state (rich landowners continued to slip off the tax rolls and the peasants had to make up the difference), most lacked the means for bribery (by now widespread) or other forms of influence; some of them turned to banditry, but in any case their material standards of living declined. They and others of the smaller fry were also hurt by inflation. As

the role of a cash economy rose, the government began to issue paper money in 1024, and its volume increased rapidly. This of course greatly assisted the spread of commercialization and was far preferable to the heavy and bulky copper coins, even collected into "strings" of a hundred or more as they were. But in time paper money was overdone, with too large an issue not backed by or redeemable in silver, and lost the confidence of the people. As government faced growing financial problems, it was, as always, tempting just to print more money, but that of course created in the end disastrous inflation. By the end of the dynasty this aggravated the disorder in the years before the Mongol conquest. More credibly, bills of exchange, begun under the T'ang, continued to be used but on a much greater scale, as did promissory notes equivalent to bank checks, and of course massive minting of copper coins.

By the Southern Sung overseas trade had become far larger than in Europe until as late as the nineteenth century. It was in the Sung that the various techniques used in large oceangoing ships were perfected, although ships nearly as large had long plied the Yangtze and its tributaries as well as the coastal routes. It is in this period also that for the first time many Chinese merchants lived overseas, primarily in the Philippines and Java but also elsewhere in Southeast Asia, including what are now Vietnam, Thailand, and Malaya. It was the Sung who set the stage for the celebrated maritime expeditions of the early Ming and their huge fleets, which reached as far as Africa. In Sung and Ming times, China was indisputably the greatest naval and maritime power in the world; the Mongols were to make use of that power and its parallel development in Korea in their huge but unsuccessful expeditions to conquer Japan and Java.

Wood-block printing, begun under the T'ang, had the advantage of reproducing an entire page at once, and of including illustrations as well as characters and special calligraphy, and books produced by this method became widespread in the tenth and eleventh centuries. It could also be used to print bills of exchange, promissory notes, and then paper money. In the 1040s began the use of movable type, a piece for each character, made of some hard material—porcelain, and later metal (tin or copper, or a harder alloy). This was widely used, and founts of type were cast and kept in cases for easy access, as later in the West, where the technique spread. In Europe it caught on rapidly and largely drove out the wood block method which had earlier spread from China. But in all of East Asia where the Chinese writing system was used, movable type did not offer such a clear advantage. Foreign observers a few centuries later noted that Chinese printers required no more time to engrave (carve) their wood-block pages than European printers took to compose a page of type, and most read-

Advice to a Chinese Emperor

The Sung official Ssu-ma Kuang (1019–1086) was also part of the Confucian revival and wrote a monumental general history of China. Here is part of one of his memorials to the emperor, urging the abolition of Wang Anshih's reforms.

Human inclinations being what they are, who does not love wealth and high rank, and who does not fear punishment and misfortune? Seeing how the wind blew and following with the current, the officials and gentry vied in proposing schemes, striving to be clever and unusual. They supported what was harmful and rejected what was beneficial. In name they loved the people; in fact they injured the people. The crop loans, local service exemptions, marketing controls, credit and loan system, and other measures were introduced. They aimed at the accumulation of wealth and pressed the people mercilessly. The distress they caused still makes for difficulties today. Besides, they were frontier officials who played fast and loose, hoping to exploit their luck. They spoke big and uttered barefaced lies, waged war unjustifiably, and needlessly disturbed the barbarians on our borders.... Officials who liked to create new schemes which they might take advantage of to advance themselves ... changed the regulations governing the tea, salt, iron, and other monopolies and increased the taxes on families, on business, and so forth, in order to meet military expenses.... They misled the later emperor, and saw to it that they themselves derived all the profit from these schemes....

Now the evils of the new laws are known to everyone in the empire, high or low, wise or ignorant. Yet there are still some measures which are harmful to the people and hurtful to the state. These matters are of immediate and urgent importance, and should be abolished. Your servant will report on them in separate memorials, hoping that it may please your sage will to grant us an early decision and act upon them.... The best plan is to select and keep those new laws which are of advantage to the people, while abolishing all those which are harmful. This will let the people of the land know unmistakably that the court loves them with a paternal affection.

Source: W. T. deBary, ed., *Sources of Chinese Tradition.* (New York: Cambridge University Press, 1960), pp. 487–489.

ers were much better pleased with the result, on largely aesthetic grounds. Engraved wood-blocks could be reused many times, could be corrected, and when they had worn too much from making too many copies, could be recarved as needed. It was also cheaper than printing from type, and remained so until relatively recently with the development of fully mechanized printing technology. So although movable type was invented in China (and then perfected in Korea), it made far more impact on European society once they learned of it than in China or the rest of East Asia.

However in China too, the development of both forms of printing was accompanied by a huge increase in the number and variety of books written and published, and in the much wider dissemination of knowledge and of literature. In addition to individual sales and bookshops, the Sung saw a new growth of both government and private schools and the spread of libraries, from the imperial palace collection to libraries in most other cities and larger towns. The literary output was great enough to prompt the appearance of anthologies, and encyclopedias also began to be produced as compendia of the published learning now so widely available. Wood-block printing, in addition to being perfectly adapted to illustrations, was also just right for printing maps. Under the Sung, cartography reached a new height of precision and accuracy. Although this was partly the result of the dynasty's expanded interest in the world overseas, the maps made of the empire, both north and south, were a great deal more accurate than those made in Europe until the nineteenth century. They used a grid of coordinates, and relief maps were also made, as well as a wheeled device for measuring distances by road.

Many of these maps were used in books of illustrated geography and in a 200-chapter geographical encyclopedia. There were also scientific treatises on various subjects, illustrated collections of painting and calligraphy, historical works, books on medicine, and books on architecture. Mathematics was further developed in the Sung, including the appearance of algebra and the use of the zero, probably influenced by the earlier origin of both in Guptan India but possibly worked out to a degree independently. (Our word *algebra* is Arab, but the Arabs borrowed the technique from India.) At Kaifeng in 1090 astronomers built a mechanical model of the heavens with a chain drive, turned by a wheel powered by water through an ingenious system of pivoted cups with a controlled escapement, and later developed an astronomical clock. Historical writing included most importantly *The Complete Mirror for the Aid of Government* by Ssu Ma Kuang (Guang, Wang An-shih's chief opponent and his successor as head councilor), a worthy successor to Ssu Ma Ch'ien, the great Han historian. Like Ssu Ma Ch'ien's work, it relied on a careful collecting of all available sources, and a critical use of them. The *Complete Mirror* was an admirable effort to cover the history of China from 403 B.C. to A.D. 959; it was the subject of many subsequent commentaries and rearrangements to make it easier to consult by topic.

"The sad thing, if it catches us, is that no one will know we invented the motorcar in 1227."

This cartoon, adapted from one in the *New Yorker* magazine for May 29, 1978, speaks for itself. (Drawing by W. Miller; © 1978 The New Yorker Magazine, Inc.)

Neo-Confucianism

Not surprisingly, given the ascendancy of the scholar-elite under the Sung, there was a new revival of Confucianism and a renewed interest in the Chou period classics, before the stream of Chinese thought was sullied, as many of the Sung philosophers felt, by Buddhism. Chu Hsi, among many others, reexamined the canonical classics and added his own philosophical commentary. He was the chief figure in what came to be called Neo-Confucianism, which also spread to Korea, Vietnam, and Japan as the dominant school. In all three, but especially in China, Neo-Confucianism became the only accepted orthodoxy and tended over time to have a rigidifying effect on thought, especially under the Ming and Ch'ing dynasties of the fourteenth to the twentieth centuries, when flexibility and openness would have been more appropriate to the changing circumstances and the new challenges which China faced. By the end of the nineteenth century, Confucianism (which meant really Neo-Confucianism) was seen by those who agonized over China's weakness as the chief villain of the old society, closing its mind and making it resist change of any sort while perpetuating the injustices implicit in what was, after all, the highly elitist and pointedly antifeminist positions of Confucianism.

But the Sung philosophers are not to be held responsible for what later generations did with their work, which at the time gave fresh new life to Confucianism. They settled once and for all the old debate between those who followed Hsün Tzu in seeing human nature as potentially evil and hence needing strict control—a support for totalitarianism—and those who favored Confucius and Mencius in their conviction that people were naturally good and needed only education and the virtuous example of superiors to improve themselves and to further their own development. The Neo-Confucianists also stressed the importance of "the five relationships" as first enunciated by Mencius: ruler–subject, father–son, husband–wife, elder brother–younger brother and friend–friend as the basic rules for behavior to ensure a harmonious society. It was clearly hierarchical, and all but friend–friend were of course between superior and inferior, relationships of authority and obedience, but within a benevolent context. This restatement of Confucian principles, and the continued emphasis on morality and responsibility in government, the priority of service over private or personal interest, was the heart of Neo-Confucianism. The revival of Confucianism stimulated the growth of many new schools, both government-run and private academies like the famous Academy of the White Deer Grotto, presided over for a time by Chu Hsi himself. Students were urged to pursue the Confucian goal of "self-cultivation," or as we might put it, "learning for learning's sake," rather than merely to study in order to pass the examinations and get a job as an official. We are still battling in our own time to get that message across.

Unfortunately, it was also in the Sung that the practice of binding the feet of young girls, supposedly to make them more attractive to men, is first mentioned, although at that time it was confined to only a few of the upper classes and did not become widespread, as a mark of upper-class status, until much later. Foot fetishism is hard for us to understand, but the notion became established that a woman's foot should be tiny, a so-called lily foot, as a sex object which could be fondled and used as a turn-on. Much was written (by males of course) about the delights of "lily feet" and the erotic pleasures associated with them, although again this comes almost entirely from later periods. In fact, a bound foot was prevented by tight wrappings from growing normally, causing great pain to the growing girl, and distorting it by bending in the toes and in effect breaking the arch, to produce a weird abortion like a bird's claw. This also made walking painful and reduced even mature women to a hobble. Their place was thought to be in the bedchamber as a toy for men, not walking around outside the household or its courtyard subject to the curious gazes of other men.

It underlines the rarity of this barbaric practice in Sung times that China's most famous female poet, Li Ch'ing-chao (Li Zingzhao, c. 1094–1152), whose life spanned the end of Northern and the beginning of Southern Sung, never mentioned footbinding and seems to have been free of it herself. Her attractive descriptions of married life with her husband are probably more typical of the elite, centered on the mutual enjoyment of paintings and other works of art. But Li Ch'ing-chao is almost the exception which proves the rule, that published women writers of any kind, like women painters, were extremely rare in this male-dominated society, although among the elite many of them were educated well beyond literacy. Polite female accomplishments did include music, both playing and singing, and some decorous dancing, but by far the most prominent practitioners of these and other arts were the courtesans, or high-class prostitutes, as in so many other premodern societies. We will meet them again in Chapter 8.

Painting and Porcelain

Under the Sung, Chinese painting largely took the forms it was to retain for the rest of the imperial period, especially and most impressively the painting of landscapes. (Painting also included portrayals of palace and other architecture, but, sadly, nothing of what had once been the architectural glories of Kaifeng, Hangchou, and other Sung cities survived the Mongol holocaust.)

Noted painters included Fan K'uan (died about 1023), who tried to encompass in his landscapes the full range of the observable cosmos, including not only mountains, streams, and trees but also small human figures, in their appropriately minor place against the grandeur of untrammeled nature which provides the backdrop. With Fan K'uan we also begin to see Chinese-style perspective introduced, where the large scene is shown in what are in effect three focuses: distant for the mountains, middleground for lesser hills, forests, and streams, and foreground through which a road or path usually runs, inviting the viewer (as in the poetry of Su Shih) to enter the painting.

Many paintings were made on fans, or on long scrolls or screens which would reveal successive scenes as the scroll unwound or the screen was studied in its different panels, again suggesting the illusion of tempting the viewer to step into these scenes, while at the same time telling a story. Perhaps the most famous of these, among many, is the scroll showing the approaches to Kaifeng along the Grand Canal, first in the rural countryside, then into the gradually more congested suburban developments outside the wall, and finally to the great gate of the city, with boats along the way carrying goods to the capital and clustered especially thickly as the city is approached. The banks of the canal, and many arched bridges across it, are crowded with people, especially closer to the city gate. Country houses and buildings, townhouses, palaces, teahouses, peddlers, vendors, sedan chairs, and a variety of carriages, are shown in lifelike detail. The scroll, by the artist Chang Tse-tuan (Zhang Zeduan), is titled "Spring Festival on the River" and remains one of the treasures of Chinese art. The emperor Hui Tsung was, as pointed out, a gifted painter himself as well as a connoisseur. His edict on painting was well realized by most of the Sung artists: "Painters are not to imitate their predecessors but to depict objects as they exist, true to color and form. Simplicity and nobility of line is to be their aim."[1]

The enforced move south after the Jurchen captured the north saw the continued development of landscape painting. Painters had more opportunity to observe and capture the far more rugged southern scenery, especially mountains, rivers, and forests. They also painted, in a style which remained typical of Chinese art, a scholar or hermit contemplating the beauties of nature from a rustic shelter or pavilion, something which implies more than an echo of the Taoist view. The best known artists were Ma Yuan (c. 1160–c. 1225) and Hsia Kuei (Xia Guei) (whose major works were done between about 1190 and 1230). Both produced masterpieces of landscape scenes, distinctively Chinese in their feeling for the grandeur of unsullied nature and still regarded as the pinnacle of Chinese landscape painting, famous for their subtle brushwork. Both also

---

✠ Criticism of Merchants ✠

Hsia Sung (Xia Song, 985–1051), a high official of the Northern Sung, was a reformer concerned about the rise of merchants.

Since the unification of the empire, control over merchants has not yet been well established. They enjoy a luxurious way of life, living on dainty foods, owning handsome houses and many carts, adorning their wives and children with pearls and jades, and dressing their slaves in white silk. In the morning they think about how to make a fortune, and in the evening they devise means of fleecing the poor. Sometimes they ride through the countryside behaving haughtily, and sometimes they inveigle rich profits from the poor. In the assignment of corvée duties they are treated much better by the government than average rural households, and in the taxation of commercial duties they are less rigidly controlled than commoners. Since this relaxed control over merchants is regarded by the people as a common rule, they despise agricultural pursuits and place high value on an idle living by trade. They also want to sell farm tools in exchange for carts and vessels, letting the land lie waste and meeting at markets.

Source: From J. W. Haeger, ed., *Crisis and Prosperity in Sung China*. (Tucson: University of Arizona Press, 1975), p. 43.

---

were equally admired in Japan, and helped to influence the growth of Japanese landscape painting in the Chinese style. Painters, who usually began their artistic training with calligraphy, itself regarded as a high form of art, used, like simple scribes, a hair brush and black ink made from pine soot dried and compressed into a small slab and moistened with water for each stroke. Strokes could be broad or narrow, straight or gracefully curved. Much of the painting was in simple black and white where the artistry of the brushwork is the heart of the painting. Bamboo, primarily a southern plant, especially lent itself to such a technique, and some of the most celebrated paintings are of its angular and curving but graceful shapes which despite the absence of color are extraordinarily lifelike. Calligraphy and the painting of bamboo were closely allied.

Sung porcelains, so widely distributed through East Asia and as far as Africa in trade, were brought to a new peak of perfection, to some tastes the finest ever produced, with a wide range of shapes, colors, and different glazes as well as the basic clay material from which they were made. Some are decorated with painting or enameled design, some not, but perhaps the finest, made primarily for the imperial court and household, are the pieces called celadon, usually bluish green, sometimes shades of milk white or gray, small, delicate, and exquisitely shaped, a fitting symbol of the elegance of Sung culture as a whole.

The Mongols

The Mongols overran Southern Sung because they were formidable fighters, and because of a series of drastic Sung errors. The Mongol armies probably represented the apogee of mobile mounted warfare. This had always given the nomadic tribes, who depended on horses for their basic economy of herding and thus were consummate riders, a strong advantage over the numerically superior sedentary empires which they raided and eventually invaded. The relative poverty of the steppe increased the temptation represented by the rich surpluses of the agricultural areas, and they also profited from raiding the trade caravans which passed through their home domains. The Han dynasty had chronic trouble with the Hsiung-nu, as the T'ang and Sung had with the Turks, Toba, Hsien-pei, Tanguts, Khitan, and Jurchen. By the fourth or fifth century A.D. these people, probably first the Turkish tribes, had developed the stirrup, which gave the rider a much firmer seat on his horse and enabled him to fire his arrows from any angle, or while turning in the saddle.

The Mongols were much better armed than the earlier nomadic groups which had harried the Chinese empire and even before they conquered China their conquests included most of Eurasia as far as the Ukraine, Poland, and Hungary. Each mounted warrior wore a hel-

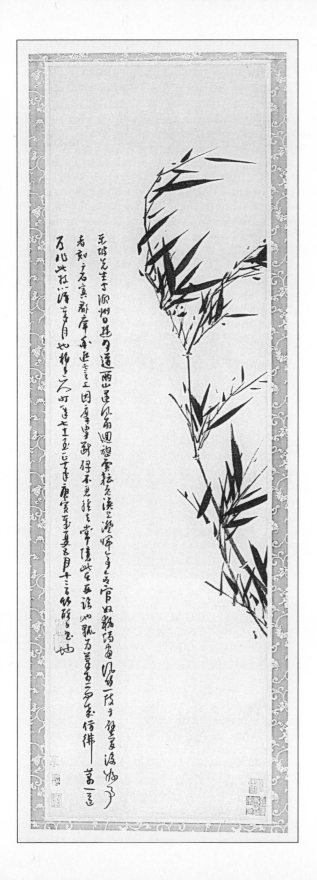

met and a coat of mail and carried bows and arrows, clubs, battle-axes, and dried milk and grain as field rations. Even their horses were protected by coats made of hides or metal. Against the Sung with its great scarcity of horses, they were much better supplied with horse-drawn carts for their supply train, and riders had a fresh horse to ride every day, with half a dozen or so in reserve following on a string. The horse is a steppe animal, and the Mongols controlled the major breeding grounds. Their mounts were in fact more the size of ponies, native to the central Asian steppe and used to its extreme cold and sparse pasturage. They were tough, wiry animals with more stamina than full-size horses.

The great military advantage of all the nomadic groups was their mobility, and hence unpredictability in sudden lightning strikes against a much slower moving army of their opponents, encumbered also by its far larger supply train. They had earlier dealt with Han efforts to subdue them by drawing the Han armies out into the steppe away from their supply bases, and then surrounding them or cutting them off. By the time of the Mongol assault on China, they had also developed battle tactics centered on fast-moving cavalry units, manipulated in battle by the ingenious use of signal flags. After an initial attack, in a hail of arrows, they would often wheel away and appear to be in headlong retreat. With their opponents strung out in pursuit, they would then turn in the saddle and fire devastating volleys at their pursuers, or sometimes turn sharply and attack the enemy's flank or rear. Each movement was planned and coordinated, beginning with the discharge of four or five arrows at high velocity, then withdrawal to reload and attack pursuers, or form another charge before retiring to their own lines, passing on the way a fresh contingent of their fellow warriors with filled quivers riding to a new attack. The nomads were also adept at leading a pursuing enemy into an ambush, but in any case these were battles of rapid movement and maneuver. The Mongols made their own bows and arrows, often by each warrior for himself, in the short but powerful

Bamboo, **by Wu Chan (Yuan dynasty). Chinese artists loved to paint the graceful fronds of bamboo, each leaf created with a single stroke of the brush, in black ink. The techniques of bamboo painting were akin to those of calligraphy, and hence such paintings often include gracefully written text. (Freer Gallery, Smithsonian Institution)**

compound reflex form shaped like a cupid's bow, which had great firepower but was small enough to be easily managed on horseback. It was made of composite layers of horn, bone, wood, and sinew, materials the Mongols had ready to hand from their own pastoral economy, and was less liable to damage than a longer bow.

Chinghis (Ghengis) Khan (1155–1227), the Mongol leader who united previously separate Mongol clans and planned the conquest of most of Eurasia as far as the Balkans and European Russia, turned his attention to China, the old Mongol enemy. He first attacked the Jurchen territories in the north, capturing their capital at Peking in 1215, and then the other non-Chinese groups in the northwest, including the Hsi Hsia empire, which he crushed in 1227, the year of his death. The several Mongol campaigns were carried on after his death by able successors, to the west under Batu Khan and others as far as Poland and Austria, and into Korea and China more or less simultaneously under Ogodei Khan (1229–1241). In 1232 the Sung made an alliance with the Mongols ("he who sups with the devil needs a long spoon"!) to crush the remnants of the Jurchen and within two years reoccupied Kaifeng and Loyang. A year later they were desperately defending north China against an insatiable Mongol army, fresh from its victory over Korea.

For 40 years the fighting raged in the north, where the heavily fortified Chinese cities were both defended and attacked with the help of explosive weapons, which the Mongols had by that time learned about from their great neighbor. Gunpowder had been invented and used much earlier in China, both for fireworks and as an explosive "fire powder." Fire arrows using naphtha as a propellant were known in the Han, and by the tenth century fire lances, spear-tipped bamboo tubes filled with a gunpowder propellant, were used. By Sung times there were repeating crossbows, flamethrowers, and armored vehicles. Given its innovations in ship design, the Sung also developed a substantial navy, including paddleboats driven by a crank through a system of connecting rods, for use on the Yangtze, which for some time was the front line against the Mongols. Naval ships on the Yangtze mounted these and other weapons, including catapults hurling explosive grenades which had been used earlier against the Jurchen and helped to hold back the Mongol tide. Unfortunately, the Mongols quickly acquired most of these new weapons. By the mid-twelfth century with the campaign at its height, both sides were using mortars and longer cast-metal barrels in which gunpowder propelled a tight-fitting projectile, the first certain occurrence of cannon in warfare. This devastating new technology quickly spread to Europe by the early fourteenth century. But the Sung continued to be weakened by factionalism, divided counsels, and inconsistent, often faulty strategy.

By 1273 the Mongols had triumphed in the north. They soon poured into the south, where Hangchou surrendered in 1276. Resistance continued in the Canton area until 1279, when the Sung fleet was defeated in a great sea battle off the coast by a fleet the Mongols had forced Chinese and Koreans to build and man for them; they had somehow mastered the art of naval tactics. Thus, even the originally great lead the Sung enjoyed in technology as well as numbers could not in the end save them. During much of the long struggle it was touch and go, but the Mongols made few mistakes and the Sung made many. One false move against an enemy like the Mongols was usually all it took. But the Sung put up a far more effective and longer resistance to the Mongols than did any of their many other continental opponents except the Delhi Sultanate of north India with its largely Turkish mameluke troops. (The Mongol seaborne expeditions to Japan and Java left them at a serious disadvantage; their fleets were scattered by major storms at critical times, and their invasion attempts were abandoned.)

The Mongols could never have conquered China without the help of Chinese technicians, including siege engineers, gun founders, artillery experts, and naval specialists. Their triumph was completed under Chinghis' grandson Kubilai (1260–1294), who fixed his capital at Peking as early as 1264 before the campaign in the south had even begun, and adopted the dynastic title of Yuan. The Mongol armies rolled on from south China to invade Vietnam, and also extinguished the Tali kingdom of largely Thai people in the Chinese southwest, welding it to the empire for the first time and sending a stream of refugees south across the mountains, probably the major beginnings of the Thai state. Vietnam managed to resist strongly enough to be allowed to settle for tributary status and the Mongol campaign in Burma failed thanks in part to the Burmese war elephants (after dreadful carnage and destruction), although the Burmese and Thais in Thailand had to accept the same theoretically subordinate tributary relationship as the Vietnamese.

It is astonishing that such a vast area, most of Asia and as far as eastern Europe, could be conquered by a people who probably numbered only about a million in all, with a few allies from other steppe tribes. The simple answer is that they were uniquely tough warriors, used to privation and exposure and welded together into a formidable fighting force by the magnetic leadership of Chinghis Khan, who consolidated the many warring Mongol and related clans into a single weapon. Chinghis was born clutching a clot of blood in his tiny fist. The Mongols in his time were Shamanists (animists and believers in magic) and his mother hurriedly called a soothsayer, who declared: "This child will rule the world." His armies, used to wandering the steppe as herders in all weathers, like their horses (or ponies), could cover 100 miles a day in forced marches, carrying their own spartan rations of parched grain, dried milk, and mares' milk in their saddle bags. When pressed, they knew how to open a vein in the necks of their spare mounts and drink some blood, closing it again so horse and rider could continue next day. Those who resisted their attacks were commonly butchered to a man and their women and children raped, slaughtered, or enslaved.

The terror of the Mongol record demoralized their opponents, who described them as inhuman monsters. They were certainly expert practitioners of psychological warfare, and even employed spies or agents to spread horrifying stories of their irresistible force, and their ruthlessness toward any resisters. Chinghis, as a true steppe nomad, especially hated cities and city dwellers and made a series of horrible examples of them, often leaving no one alive. Chinghis is said to have remarked that "the greatest pleasure is to vanquish one's enemies … to rob them of their wealth, and to see those dear to them bathed in tears, to ride their horses and clasp to your bosom their wives and daughters." The Mongols loved the violence and pride of conquest, but had little understanding of or interest in administration, and their empire began to fall apart within a few years of its acquisition.

Their rule in China, the so-called Yuan dynasty (1279–1368), lasted a little longer only because by that time they realized that they could not possibly manage China without employing many thousands of Chinese. They also used many foreigners whom they felt they could better trust, including the Venetian Marco Polo, who served as a minor Mongol official in China from 1275 to 1292. Marco's famous journal, like all medieval tales, includes some supernatural stories, and it was also dismissed by many because it speaks in such extravagant terms about the size and splendor of Yuan China. Indeed he soon became known as "Il milione," someone who told tall tales of millions of this and that. But when his confessor came to him on his deathbed and urged him to take back all those lies, Marco is said to have replied, "I have not told the half of what I saw."

Yuan China

The Mongols ran China largely through Chinese officials, plus a few Mongols and foreigners, and the Chinese bureaucratic system was retained, leaving the military entirely in Mongol hands. For the brief years of Mongol rule, Chinese culture continued its growth on Sung foundations, once the country had recovered from the immense devastation of the Mongol conquest. In particular, the glories of Sung landscape painting were restored and extended by a new list of great Chinese artists, and there was a new and notable flowering of drama and vernacular literature. People, especially the scholar-gentry-official group, were understandably disheartened by the political scene and turned for solace to art and literature. Mongol rule from their new capital at Peking was exploitative and often harsh, though it became much looser under Kubilai and less harsh. Chinese were severely discriminated against and forbidden to possess arms. Artisans and laborers were kept virtual prisoners, especially in the saltworks. Most Chinese (those who survived the slaughter) grew rapidly poorer under Mongol rule, though a few collaborators won new wealth. Taxation was oppressively heavy and workers were forced to labor without pay on large state projects. The Mongols ran a newly efficient postal service based on relays, and once again issued paper money. But the country as a whole suffered. The Mongols rebuilt the Grand Canal, neglected since the fall of Northern Sung, and extended it to feed and supply Peking, but at heavy cost in lives and revenue.

Kubilai proved an able ruler of his new empire but concentrated on China and became almost entirely Chinese culturally. Marco Polo gives a flattering account of his sagacity, majesty, and benevolence, a portrait which was probably as accurate as his more general accounts of Yuan China. But Kubilai was followed on his death in 1294 by increasingly inept figures. Smoldering Chinese hatred of their conquerors had flared into widespread revolts by the 1330s, and by 1350 Mongol control of the Yangtze valley was lost, while factions of their once united front fought one another in the north. A peasant rebel leader welded together Chinese forces, chased the remaining Mongols back into the steppes north of the Great Wall, and in 1368 announced the foundation of a new dynasty, the Ming, which was to restore Chinese pride and grandeur.

Dynastic Cycles and Continuity

Chinese history readily divides into dynastic periods, and into what is called the dynastic cycle. Most dynasties (but not the Yuan) lasted about three centuries, sometimes preceded by a brief whirlwind period of empire-building such as the Ch'in or the Sui. The first century of a new dynasty would be marked by political, economic, and cultural vigor, expansion, efficiency, and confidence; the second would build on or consolidate what the first had achieved; and in the third vigor and efficiency would begin to wane, corruption would mount, banditry and rebellion would multiply, and the dynasty would ultimately fall. A new group coming to power from among the rebels would rarely attempt to change the system, only its management and supervision.

✠ Escapist Poetry ✠

The Yuan dynasty was a hard time for most Chinese. Here is a series of short poems by Chinese of that period.

Ch'ao T'ien-tzu

Be unread, To get ahead
Be illiterate and benefit!
Nowadays, to gain men's praise just act inadequate.
Heaven won't discriminate, Between the wicked and the great,
Nor have we ever had Rules to tell the good from bad.
Men cheat the good, They scorn the poor.
The well-read trip On their scholarship.
So practice no caligraphy, *Great Learning* or epigraphy!
Intelligence and competence Now count for less than copper pence.

Yu-chiao Chih

Among the hills, Beneath the forest shade,
A thatched hut, sheltered window, made For elegant solitude.
The pine's blue, Bamboo's deep green,
Combine to make a scene For artists' brush.
Nearby threads of smoke From hearths of huts unseen—
And I drift through my pleasant dream As blossoms fall through air—
Insipid as chewing wax, That bustling world out there,
To a heart that's proof against desire, What matters a head of whitened hair?

Ch'iao Chi

State honor rolls will lack my name, As will biographies for men of fame.
I have from time to time Found sagehood in a cup of wine;
Now and then, Some verse of mine
Has contained one brilliant line Enlightening as *zen*.
Drunken Sage of lake and stream, With a Doctorate in Sunset Skies,
I've laughed at all of those who strained At great official enterprise.

Ma Chih-yuan

Gold in piles, Jade in heaps—Then there comes a single day Old Death sweeps them all away!
What use are they? The cloudless hour The day benign, Salute with carven cup and amber wine;
With swaying waists, With flashing teeth and eyes—Ah, there's where pleasure truly lies.

Source: Translated by J. Crump.

Culture was continuous, even during the political chaos following the fall of the Han. By T'ang times most of the elements of contemporary Chinese culture were present. Especially with the rise in importance of the south, rice was now the dominant element in the diet. This was supplemented or replaced in the more arid parts of the north by wheaten noodles (brought back by Marco Polo in the thirteenth century as the origin of spaghetti) and steamed bread, or, for poorer people by millet. Food was eaten with chopsticks, a model adopted early by Korea and Japan, while the rest of the world ate with its fingers. The Chinese cuisine is justly famous, including as it does such a wide variety of materials (the Chinese have few dietary inhibitions), flavors, and sauces. What went on the rice—vegetable or animal—was sliced small so that their flavors were maximized and distributed and also so that they could cook very quickly over a hot but brief fire. There was a progressive shortage of fuel as increasing population cut down the forests and people were reduced to twigs, branches, and dried grass for cooking. The universal utensil was the thin, cast-iron, saucer-shaped pot (*wok* in Cantonese), still in use, which heated quickly but held the heat and distributed it evenly—the technique we now call "stir-frying."

The Chinese landscape became more and more converted into an artificial one of irrigated and terraced rice paddies, fish and duck ponds, villages, and market towns, where the peasants sold their surplus produce or exchanged it for salt, cloth, tools, or other necessities not produced in all villages. From T'ang times, teahouses became the common centers for socializing, relaxation, and gossip, and for the negotiation of business or marriage contracts. Fortune-tellers, scribes, bookstores, itinerant peddlers, actors, and storytellers enlivened the market towns and cities, and periodic markets with similar accompaniments were held on a smaller scale in most villages.

All this made it less necessary for people to travel far from their native places, and most never went beyond the nearest market town. Beyond it they would have found for the most part only more villages and towns like those they knew, except perhaps for the provincial capital, and of course the imperial capital. In the south most goods and people in the lowlands moved by waterways, in the dry north by pack animals, carts, and human porters, which also operated in the mountainous parts of the south. The wheelbarrow and the flexible bamboo carrying pole were Chinese inventions which greatly enhanced the ability to transport heavy weights, balanced as they were by each design and hence enabling porters to wheel or trot all day with loads far exceeding their unaided capacity. All these and many other aspects of Chinese culture have remained essentially unchanged until today, as has the deep Chinese sense of history, and of the great tradition to which they are heir.

Notes

1. Translation by Arthur Waley, quoted in R. Goepper, *The Essence of Chinese Painting*. Boston: Boston Book and Art Shop, 1963, p. 106.

Suggestions for Further Reading

Allen, T. T. *Mongol Imperialism*. Berkeley: Univ. of California Press, 1987.

Barfield, T. J. *The Perilous Frontier*. Oxford: Blackwell, 1989.

Cahill, J. *Hills Beyond a River: Chinese Painting of the Yuan Dynasty*. New York: Weatherhill, 1976.

Chaffee, J. W. *The Thorny Gates of Learning: A Social History of Examinations in Sung China*. Albany: Suny Press, 1995.

Chan, W. T., ed. *Chu Hsi and Neo-Confucianism*. New York: St. Martins, 1987.

Crump, J. *Chinese Theater in the Days of Kubilai Khan*. Ann Arbor: Center for Chinese Studies, 1980.

_____. *Songs from Xanadu* and *Song-Poems from Xanadu*. Ann Arbor: Center for Chinese Studies, 1983 and 1993.

Dardess, J. W. *Conquerors and Confucians*. New York: Columbia Univ. Press, 1973.

Davis, R. L. *Court and Family in Sung China*. Durham: Duke Univ. Press, 1986.

Ebrey, P. (transl.) *Family and Property in Sung China*. Princeton: Princeton Univ. Press, 1984.

_____. *The Inner Quarters: Women in the Sung*. Berkeley: California Press, 1994.

Franke, H. *China Under Mongol Rule*. Aldershot: Vanoram Press, 1994.

Gernet, J. *Daily Life in China on the Eve of the Mongol Invasion.*, transl. H. M. Wright. London: Macmillan, 1962.

Haeger, J., ed. *Crisis and Prosperity in Sung China*. Tucson: Univ. of Arizona, 1975.

Hymes, R. *Statesmen and Gentlemen: Elites of the Southern Sung*. Cambridge: Cambridge Univ. Press, 1986.

Lee, T. H. C. *Government Education and Examinations in Sung China*. Hong Kong: Chinese Univ. Press, 1986.

Liu, J. T. C. *Reform in Sung China: Wang An-shih and His New Policies*. Harvard Press, 1959.

_____. *China Turning Inward: Intellectual and Political Changes in the Early 12th Century*. Cambridge: Harvard Press, 1988.

McKnight, B. E. *Law and Order in Sung China*. Cambridge: Cambridge Univ. Press, 1993.

_____. *Village and Bureaucracy in Southern Sung*. Chicago: Univ. of Chicago, 1972.

Morgan, D. *The Mongols*. Oxford: Blackwell, 1986.

Needham, T., et. al. *Heavenly Clockwork*. Cambridge: Cambridge University Press, 1960.

Olschki, L. *Marco Polo's Asia*. Berkeley: Univ. of California Press, 1960.

Philip, E. D. *The Mongols*. New York: Scribner, 1969.

Rossabi, M. *China and Inner Asia*. New York: Pica Press, 1975.

————. *Kubilai Khan: His Life and Times*. Berkeley: Univ. of California Press, 1987.

Shiba, Y. *Commerce and Society in Sung China*. transl. Elvin. Ann Arbor: Center for Chinese Studies, 1969.

Shih, Chung-wen. *The Golden Age of Chinese Drama*. Princeton: Princeton Univ. Press. 1979.

Spuler, B. *History of the Mongols*. Berkeley: Univ. of California Press, 1972.

Twitchett, D. *Printing and Publication in Medieval China*. New York: Bell, 1983.

CHAPTER 7

NEW IMPERIAL SPLENDOR IN CHINA: THE MING DYNASTY

With the expulsion of the Mongols in the mid-fourteenth century, the Chinese imperial tradition was reasserted with the founding of the Ming dynasty in 1368. Pride in regained power and wealth led to the building of magnificent new capitals, first at Nanking (Nanjing) and then at Peking (Beijing), as well as to the resumption of the tributary system whereby lesser Asian states sent regular missions to China, acknowledging its superiority and prostrating themselves before the Son of Heaven. Ming armies reconquered the empire of the T'ang and the Sung, and early in the dynasty a series of seven naval expeditions toured Southeast Asia, India, the Persian Gulf, and as far as the east coast of Africa, acquiring new tributaries, trading in Chinese products, and bringing back curiosities from afar. The growing commercialization of the economy, aided from the sixteenth century by imports of silver from the Spanish New World, greatly stimulated urban growth and a rich merchant culture. Literature, philosophy, and the arts flourished, and popular culture also expanded into vernacular writing, opera, plays, and wood-block prints.

For at least its first two centuries, Ming administration was effective and the country was prosperous. But the dynasty became increasingly conservative and traditional. It was plagued by court intrigues, and a series of weak emperors sapped its vigor. Popular unrest mounted as government became less and less able to provide an equitable order, or to move with the times. Rebels took Peking, and then were replaced by a new set of alien conquerors, the Manchus from Manchuria,

who inaugurated the Ch'ing dynasty in 1644. Manchu rule, nevertheless, rested consciously and purposefully on the Ming heritage, and most of the trends which began under the Ming continued with little break once order was restored.

The Founding of the Ming

By the early 1300s Mongol control of China was weakening under the ineffective successors of Kubilai Khan (died 1294). Mongol power was enfeebled by chronic feuding within the imperial clan and pressures from rival clans, and by 1330 there was open civil war. Beginning in 1333 successive drought-induced famines racked north China, worsened by unchecked flooding in the Yellow River where the dikes had been neglected. Most Chinese interpreted these natural disasters as portents of divine displeasure and the loss of the Mandate of Heaven by the Yuan dynasty, a response typical of the declining years of all dynasties but further fed in this case by bitter Chinese hatred of the alien Mongols and their oppressive rule.

Banditry and rebellion spread rapidly in nearly every province, and rebel leaders vied for Heaven's Mandate in efforts to eliminate their rivals. Many rebel groups were aided by or belonged to secret societies, which recruited supporters from among poor peasants and drew on anti-Mongol sentiment. Many had Buddhist rituals that dated back to the Sung, including the Red Turbans,

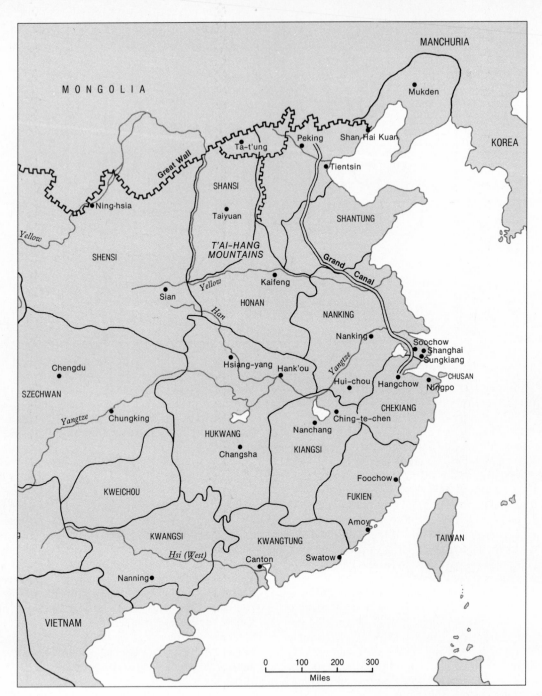

Ming China

so called for their distinctive headdress; they played a major role in the lower Yellow River plain.

One of the rebel leaders, Chu Yüan-chang (Zhu Yuanzhang, 1328–1398), rose to a commanding position in the 1350s and went on to found a new dynasty. His forces swept the Yangtze valley by the end of the decade, set up a government at Nanking in 1356, and in 1368 captured Peking, proclaiming the Ming ("brilliant") dynasty, which was to last until 1644. The Ming achievement in rebuilding the empire and restoring Chinese pride ushered in a period of unprecedented economic and cultural growth, on Sung foundations but going far beyond where the Sung had left off. The population probably rose by at least 50 percent by the end of the dynasty, stimulated by major improvements in agricultural technology promoted by the state. There was also rapid commercialization of the economy as a whole, an accompanying rise in the number and size of cities, and perhaps a doubling of total trade.

HUNG-WU: THE REBEL EMPEROR

Chu Yüan-chang, the victorious rebel leader who became the first Ming emperor, took the title Hung-wu ("great military power"); he is known mainly by this name and by his official dynastic title Ming T'ai-tsu (Taizu, "Great Progenitor"). Life had been hard for him up to that point. Like Liu Pang, the founder of the Han dynasty, he had been born a peasant, in 1328. Orphaned early in life, he entered a Buddhist monastery where he became literate, and at age 25 joined a rebel band, where his native ability soon brought him to the top. As emperor his strong personality and high intelligence made a deep and lasting impression on the first two centuries of the Ming, whose foundations he largely built. He was an indefatigable worker, concerned with all the details of administering his new empire, but he had few close associates or friends and led an austere lifestyle that reflected his difficult and impoverished youth. He was notoriously frugal, and often a pinchpenny in his disapproval of expenditures proposed by others. Having risen to power over rebel rivals, he became paranoid about supposed plots against him, and was given to violent rages of temper, during which he often ordered harsh punishments or tortures for suspected disloyalty or for trivial offenses.

Irritated by continued Japanese piracy along the China coast, Hung-wu also wrote to the Ashikaga *shogun* (see Chapter 11): "You stupid eastern barbarians! Living so far across the sea … you are haughty and disloyal; you permit your subjects to do evil." The Japanese replied, two years later, in a more Confucian mode, but doubtless partly tongue-in-cheek: "Heaven and earth are vast. They are not monopolized by one ruler."[1] Hung-wu's reaction, perhaps fortunately, is not recorded. In his last will, he wrote of himself: "For 31 years I have labored to discharge Heaven's will, tormented by worries and fears, without relaxing for a day."[2] One wonders if he felt that the winning of the Dragon Throne had really been worth it!

Hung-wu increasingly concentrated power in his own hands, trusting no one, and in 1380, after suppressing a plot for which he blamed his chief minister, abolished the Imperial Secretariat, which had been the main central administrative body under dynasties of the past. The emperor's role thus became even more autocratic, although Hung-wu necessarily continued to use what were called the Grand Secretaries to assist with the immense paperwork of the bureaucracy: memorials (petitions and recommendations to the throne), imperial edicts in reply, reports of various kinds, and tax records.

The emperor Hung-wu (1328–1398), also known more formally as T'ai-tsu ("Great Progenitor"), in a caricature by an unknown fifteenth-century artist, one of a series of caricatures of notable emperors. Hung-wu's rather piglike face, commented on by many of his contemporaries, was pockmarked from smallpox, which had nearly killed him as a younger man. The caricature conveys Hung-wu's forceful personality. (National Palace Museum, Taipei, Taiwan)

This group was later more regularly established as the Grand Secretariat, a kind of cabinet, but in Hung-wu's time he supervised everything and made or approved all decisions. He was concerned about the power of the eunuchs, remembering the trouble they had often caused in earlier dynasties, and erected a tablet in the palace which read, "Eunuchs must have nothing to do with administration."[3] He greatly reduced their numbers, forbade them to handle documents, insisted that they remain illiterate, and got rid of those who so far forgot themselves as to offer comments on government matters. Some eunuchs were considered necessary as guards and attendants for the imperial harem, which the emperor was thought to need so as to ensure male heirs. In time the eunuchs were to reemerge as closely connected and scheming insiders at court, until in later Ming they were once more a scourge on good government.

One policy of Hung-wu's that shocked the Confucians was his resumption of the Mongol practice of having officials publicly beaten when they had displeased him. Confucian doctrine held that corporal punishment was only for the ignorant masses; the "superior man" was to be exempt because one could reason with him and expect him to mend his ways by following the virtuous example of those above him. Hung-wu was a tough ruler and demanded complete submission, despite his praise for the Confucian classics, which he saw as a prop for the state. But as a peasant by birth, he never lost his envy and distrust of intellectuals. He also reorganized the army around a new system of elite guards units stationed at strategic points throughout the empire and along the frontiers. While some of his policies seemed extreme to many and his personality forbidding or fearsome rather than benevolent according to the Confucian ideal, Hung-wu was a strong emperor whose work provided the Ming with a momentum of imperial power and effectiveness which lasted far beyond his time. His concentration of power in the emperor's personal hands worked well when the emperor was as able and dedicated as he was. When weaker and less conscientious men occupied the throne, the empire was in trouble, as was to happen disastrously in the last decades of Ming rule. To be successful, despotism had to be enlightened; the late Ming emperors were no match for Hung-wu.

When Hung-wu died in 1398 the provinces within the Great Wall were secure and Chinese power was again dominant in eastern Sinkiang, Inner Mongolia, and southern Manchuria. Vietnam, Tibet, Korea, and Japan accepted tributary status. Hung-wu built a splendid new capital at Nanking with a city wall 60 feet high and 20 miles around, the longest city wall in the world, intended like most Chinese city walls more as a symbolic affirmation of imperial power than for defense. Indeed the Chinese word for "city" also means "wall," to distinguish it from a mere town. Peking was passed over as a capital because of its association with the Mongols, and its location on the northern fringe of the country, far from major trade routes and unable to feed itself in this semiarid area on the edge of Mongolia. The Yangtze valley had long been the economic heart of the empire, and it made sense to put the capital there.

The third Ming emperor, Yung-lo (Yong-le, reigned 1403–1424), seized the throne after defeating his nephew, the second emperor, in a civil war. He was also an able and conscientious administrator. Continued prosperity, plus the new southern emphasis of the Ming, stimulated the further expansion of trade, including its maritime extensions. Commerce and city life grew rapidly. Ports on the southeast coast acquired new importance as links with the colonies of overseas Chinese in Java, the Philippines, Vietnam, and elsewhere in Southeast Asia.

The Ming Tributary System

To mark the resurgence of empire after the brief Mongol eclipse, the traditional tributary system was enlarged and made more formal. This was mainly a device to feed the Chinese ego, but it also helped to keep peace along the extensive borders, and to assert Chinese overlordship. In theory, Chinese political and cultural superiority was a magnet for all lesser peoples or states, who would willingly acknowledge its greatness and would model themselves on it, "yearning for civilization," as the official Chinese phrase put it. In practice, there was just enough truth in this to warrant saying it. Although of course non-Chinese states and cultures had their own pride and their own sense of superiority, like all peoples, all of them also freely recognized that Chinese civilization was more advanced than their own and had a great deal to offer them, in trade, culture, and technology. The Chinese capital and other cities were exciting and profitable places to visit, and near-neighbors such as Korea or Vietnam, and later Burma, Laos, Tibet, and even Mongolia had reason to fear Chinese military power and hence to accept tributary status. Recognizing China's supremacy cost them little; as long as they did not try to challenge it, they were left to manage their own affairs.

The required ritual obeisance to the Son of Heaven was probably not seen as humiliating, but in keeping with the way in which they had to deal with their own monarchs at home, and in any case the proper way to be received by any exalted person. Once that was completed, they could learn and profit, and return home without feeling they had given anything away, since their own states were in fact fully sovereign. Tributary states sent regular missions every few years to the imperial capital, where they knelt before the Son of Heaven in a series of prescribed prostrations known as the *k'e t'ou* (later Westernized as *kowtow*, literally "bang head," on the floor, as a token of respect). They presented a long list of "gifts," and in return were given "presents" which were often greater in value and amount. The missions were in part a polite cloak for trade, combining mutual benefit with diplomacy, and the prestige of association with the Celestial Empire. It also of course fed the Chinese bias about themselves as the only imperium, the only true civilization, the center of the world, compared with which all other people were mere barbarians. This was a long-standing attitude since at least Han times when the tribute system which reflected it came to include over 50 central Asian "barbarian" groups.

At its modern height, first under the Ming and later in early Ch'ing, the tributary system involved over 40 states, including Korea, Vietnam, Tibet, Japan, Java, the Philippines, Burma, Siam, Ceylon, Malacca, and a number of others, in addition to many central Asian kingdoms. The renewed Chinese interest in the wider world was a feature of the first few decades of the Ming, although the tributary system continued into the nineteenth century. The last half or more of Ming rule was in contrast a period of retrenchment, of preoccupation with the defense of the land frontiers, and cultural conservatism. Such a shift fits the pattern of the dynastic cycle discussed in Chapter 6. All dynasties tended to be open-minded, cosmopolitan, and expansionist in their first century, complacent in their second, and overwhelmed by problems in their third and last, when the effectiveness and vigor of the imperial government deteriorated, corruption mounted, and rebellion spread. The Ming were no exception to this recurrent pattern, and the memory of the Mongol conquest tended in any case to make them xenophobic, conservative in their determination to reaffirm the Great Tradition of the *Chinese* past, and inward-centered. All this was understandable, and probably benefited the country, at least in the short run, as much or more than foreign adventuring. China was a huge and productive world in itself. Until late in the 1500s things continued to go well, and general prosperity kept most people content.

Japanese and Korean pirate raids at places all along the coast did worry the Ming, and not only because of what the pirates stole or destroyed. The raids demonstrated that the Chinese government could not keep order locally or defend its people. The raids were regarded as equivalent to rebellion, and the government also knew that a good many renegade Chinese were involved, masquerading as Koreans or Japanese or in league with them. After much pressure from the Chinese court, the Ashikaga shogunate in Japan, formally a Ming tributary, suppressed some of the Japanese pirate activity, and sent some captured pirates to Peking for execution. A Ming document addressed to the Ashikaga in 1436 acknowledged this, and went on to say, in the customary language of the tributary system and with its pretentious assumptions:

> Since our Empire owns the world, there is no country on this or other sides of the seas which does not submit to us. The sage Emperors who followed one another had the same regard and uniform benevolence for all countries far and near. You, Japan, are our Eastern frontier, and for generations you have performed tributary duties. The longer the time, the more respectful you have become.[4]

Ming Maritime Expeditions

What distinguished the early Ming, but fit the pattern of early Han, T'ang, and Sung, was the outreach of imperial pride, especially in their remarkable maritime expeditions. Using the nautical technology inherited from the Sung, the eunuch admiral Cheng Ho (Zhenghe) mounted seven naval expeditions of Chinese fleets between 1405 and 1433, with up to 60 vessels. They toured much of Southeast Asia, the east and west coasts of India (including Calicut, where 90 years later Vasco da Gama was to make his Asian landfall), Ceylon (Sri Lanka), the Persian Gulf and Hormuz, Aden, Jidda (from where seven Chinese went to Mecca), and on to east Africa. Some ships may have gone as far as the Cape of Good Hope, or even around it. They brought back giraffes, zebras, and ostriches to amaze the court, and tributary agreements with gifts from a host of new states. When the king of Ceylon was considered not deferential enough, he was arrested and taken back to Nanking, where Yung-lo appointed a new king in his place.

Cheng Ho's many-decked ships carried up to 500 troops, but also cargoes of export goods, mainly silks and porcelains, and brought back foreign luxuries such as spices and tropical woods. The economic motive for these huge ventures may have been important, and many of the ships had large, private cabins for merchants. But the chief aim was probably political, to show the flag and command respect for the empire, as well as to enroll still more states as tributaries.

Some of the ships were larger than anything previously built in the world, 400 feet long and of 500 tons burden, with four decks. They were reported nevertheless to be faster sailers than the Portuguese caravels or Spanish galleons of a century or two later, especially with a favorable wind. They were designed in accordance with the well-known monsoonal wind patterns of Asia and the Indian Ocean. Properly timed voyages could count on going with the wind for about half the year almost anywhere in that vast region, and then returning with the opposite monsoon in the other half of the year. Cheng Ho's ships, like those of the Sung, were built with double hulls and up to a dozen separate watertight compartments. Despite their far-flung voyages and their many encounters with storms and unknown coasts, few were ever lost. They were provided with detailed sailing directions, at least for the waters nearer home, as well as compasses.

Such exploits of seamanship and exploration were unprecedented in the world. Their grand scale and imperial pretension, as well, perhaps, as their commercial ambition, were an expression of new imperial pride and vigor. But they contributed little to the economy except temporary employment for shipbuilders and crew, and made no lasting impression on the Chinese mind, except to further confirm their sense of superiority as the only civilized empire.

The expeditions were very expensive, and were stopped after 1433, perhaps mainly for that reason, although abuses and corruption in procuring shipbuilding materials and in contracts with shipyards also attracted official criticism. Cheng Ho was a Muslim as well as a eunuch, and this may have generated prejudice against him in the orthodox and highly Confucian court. The emperor may have felt that he had made his imperial point, and it is unlikely that trade profits covered the costs. Another factor was his decision to move the primary capital to Peking in 1421 (Nanking was kept as a secondary, southern capital), to better command the

chronically troubled northern frontier, where there was an attempted revival of Mongol power, as well as to bring the Ming into line with what was by now the hallowed tradition of a northern capital. The monumental building of Peking also competed with the shipyards for shrinking sources of timber, and for construction workers, as well as for treasury allocations.

But the abandonment of the maritime expeditions, like the move to Peking, was a symptom of the Ming's basic conservatism once the first half-century had passed. There were understandable fears of a Mongol resurgence and deep concern about the Central Asian conquests of the Turkish leader Tamerlane (1336–1405), who they had reason to fear was planning to invade China. His death ended that threat, but the Mongols were still active. Yung-lo personally led five expeditions out into the steppe to combat the Mongol revival and remained preoccupied with his northern defenses, for which there was ample precedent in Chinese history. Newly reorganized Mongol tribes continued to harass the border areas and to raid across the frontier until the mid-seventeenth century. The Ming also promoted the spread of Lamaistic Buddhism to the Mongols in an effort to pacify them, a strategy which seems

✠ A Ming Naval Expedition ✠

Here is part of a text engraved on a stone tablet in 1432, commemorating the expeditions of Cheng Ho.

The Imperial Ming dynasty in unifying seas and continents ... even goes beyond the Han and the T'ang. The countries beyond the horizon and from the ends of the earth have all become subjects.... Thus the barbarians from beyond the seas ... have come to audience bearing precious objects.... The Emperor has ordered us, Cheng Ho ... to make manifest the transforming power of the Imperial virtue and to treat distant people with kindness.... We have seven times received the commission of ambassadors [and have visited] altogether more than thirty countries large and small. We have traversed immense water spaces and have beheld huge waves like mountains rising sky-high, and we have set eyes on barbarian regions far away hidden ina blue transparency of light vapors, while our sails loftily unfurled like clouds day and night continued their course, traversing those savage waves as if we were treading a public thoroughfare.... We have received the high favor of a gracious commission of our Sacred Lord, to carry to the distant barbarians the benefits of his auspicious example.... Therefore we have recorded the years and months of the voyages. [Here follows a detailed record of places visited and things done on each of the seven voyages.] We have anchored in this port awaiting a north wind to take the sea ... and have thus recorded an inscription in stone ... erected by the principal envoys, the Grand Eunuchs Cheng Ho and Wang Ching-hung, and the assistant envoys.

Source: J. J. L. Duyvendak, "The True Dates of the Chinese Maritime Expeditions in the Early Fifteenth Century," *T'oung Pao*, Vol. 24 (1938): 349–355.

in the end to have been more effective than military confrontation.

The cost of the anti-Mongol campaigns on top of the building of Peking was a strain, and the extravagant oceanic adventures were a logical item for retrenchment. Cheng Ho's voyages had been supported by his fellow eunuchs at court, who were strongly opposed by the Confucian scholar-officials; their antagonism was in fact so great that they tried to suppress any mention of the naval expeditions in the official record.

China's relations by sea had always been given a far lower priority than her land frontiers, and this ancient pattern was now reasserted. The expeditions discovered nothing worth the effort, and conquest was never part of the plan. Nevertheless the scale of Cheng Ho's voyages remains impressive. While the Portuguese were just beginning to feel their way cautiously along the west African coast in sight of land, Chinese fleets of far larger ships dominated the Indian Ocean and the western Pacific and traded in most of the ports. They did not try to cross the Pacific or continue westward to Europe, which they were clearly capable of doing,* only because to their knowledge there was nothing in either direction to make such a voyage worthwhile.

If they had reached Europe, they probably would have been no more impressed by it than by what they saw in Southeast Asia, India, the Persian Gulf, or Africa, nor any more than they were to be a century later by the early European arrivals in China, still to their way of thinking crude barbarians. Fifteenth-century North America would have seemed to them too primitive even to mention. As with some earlier Chinese innovations in science and technology, these maritime achievements were not followed up. The conquest of the seas, global expansion, and a sea-based commercial revolution were left to the poorer and less complacent Europeans, who, from both their own and the Chinese point of view, had more to gain thereby—and less to concern them or to take pride in at home. The chief early goal of the European expansion overseas was in fact China, whose riches and sophistication had attracted Europe's mind and ambitions since the Roman imports of Chinese silk, that symbol of luxury and wealth.

Prosperity and Conservatism

Meanwhile the Ming turned inward from their new capital at Peking, rebuilding the Great Wall and its watchtowers in the form they still have today, and promoting the development of their own home base. Such domestic concerns had always been the center of Chinese attention. Since Shang times they had called their country the Middle Kingdom, meaning not only that it was the center of the world but that it combined the advantages of a golden mean, avoiding the extremes of desert, jungle, mountains, or cold around its borders. In whatever direction one went from China, the physical environment deteriorated: north (too cold), south (too hot and jungly), west (too mountainous or dry), or east (into a vast and, in cultural or economic terms, empty ocean). The Chinese attributed the lack of civilization they noted in all "barbarians" to their far less favorable environment (in which there was of course some truth) as well as to their distance from the only center of enlightenment.

China was indeed the most productive area of comparable size anywhere in the world, especially its great river valleys and floodplains. The empire was bigger than all of Europe in size, more populous, and with a far greater volume of trade. The Chinese saw their interests best served by further embellishing their home base rather than by pursuing less rewarding foreign contacts. As the Italian Jesuit missionary Matteo Ricci reported early in the seventeenth century, "Everything which the people need for their well-being and sustenance ... is abundantly produced within the borders of the kingdom."[5] Domestic and interprovincial trade, between provinces the size of many European states, was far greater than foreign trade and served the world's largest market. Revenues now went increasingly to nourishing the domestic scene and glorifying its rulers.

There was thus a growing turn to conservatism even before the end of the Ming's first century. Partly this reflected a determination to reestablish the traditional Chinese way in all things after the Mongol humiliation, but it also stemmed from enhanced prosperity. With everything going so well, there was less incentive to seek change or to be innovative, at least in terms of official policy. The emperors who followed Yung-lo were less and less able or imaginative and tended to leave policy and administration to the intrinsically conservative Confucian bureaucracy, once again entrenched in power. The imperial censors were revived (they had been understandably reluctant to speak out under Hung-wu!) to keep officials honest and responsible and to keep the capital informed of actual or potential problems. On the whole, this tried-and-true system worked well for another century. In time it became increasingly rigid and less able to respond to change or the need for change, but until the last decades of the Ming, as with other dynasties, it was an impressive form of government, which kept order and insured justice to an admirable degree.

Nor did official conservatism and Confucian-based anticommercialism prevent the basic changes at work in

*In fact there is some evidence that they may have reached the California coast—anchors of Chinese design and appropriate age have been found in shallow water off Santa Barbara.

the economy. As for every Chinese dynasty, agriculture was regarded as the predominant source of wealth and as something to be officially promoted. Under Hung Wu there was a major reconstruction effort to rebuild agriculture in the extensive areas devastated by the Mongols and the rebellions against them. Many thousands of reservoirs and canals were built or repaired, and depopulated areas resettled by mass transfers of people. Many thousands of acres of farmland were newly reclaimed. There was also a major campaign of reforestation. There were many new government projects to extend irrigation, build new canals and paved roads, stock public granaries, and construct flood-prevention works.

Rice yields rose with the use of new more productive and earlier-ripening varieties introduced from Southeast Asia and actively promoted by the state. New irrigation and better manuring, as well as new land brought under cultivation to feed the growing population, produced a major rise in total output and a marked improvement in average material well-being. In the sixteenth century new crops, most importantly maize (corn), sweet and white potatoes, and peanuts, reached China from Spanish America via the trade connection with the Philippines. All of these imported plants increased output still further since they did not need irrigation and for the most part they did not replace rice or wheat but fitted into the system using hilly or sandy areas little cultivated before.

The Ming government and most of its Confucian magistrates cared about the welfare of their people, at least until the final collapse, and even reformed the tax system to make it less burdensome for peasants, although the bulk of imperial revenue now again came from taxes on land and grain, plus the official monopoly taxes on salt, tea, and such foreign trade as was officially recognized. Regular labor service was also required of all districts and households, for public works of general usefulness, including the building and maintaining of irrigation and flood-prevention systems and of the imperial road network. The roughly 2,000 local magistrates, forbidden to serve in their native provinces lest they show favoritism, were necessarily but effectively assisted by a

Magnificent paintings of nature continued under the Ming in the now long-established Chinese tradition. This lovely spray of white magnolia is part of a larger painting by the master Wen Cheng-ming (1470–1559). (Metropolitan Museum, New York, bequest of John M. Crawford, Jr.)

large staff and also by local degree-holding gentry. Local gentry were often the major factors in keeping order and ensuring that official policy and projects were carried out. Imperial censors traveling on circuit from the capital watched for irregularities and reported directly to the emperor. A newly comprehensive code of administrative and criminal law was published in 1397.

Food crops were still considered of prime importance, but there was a boom in commercial crops also, encouraged by the state, such as mulberry (for silkworms) and cotton. Silk was produced principally in the densely populated Yangtze delta area, where its dependence on intensive hand labor could rest on family members as a household enterprise, especially women and older children. The Canton area, equally densely populated, and the similarly populous Red Basin of Szechuan, were other important silk-making regions. All three were close to major urban markets and to navigable waterways to distribute their output at low cost throughout the empire. Under the Ming cotton became for the first time, after its earlier diffusion from India, the predominant fabric of daily clothing for most people. It was cheaper and more durable than silk and displaced coarser or more laboriously made hemp and linen. Silk remained a luxury item for the wealthy, more numerous than ever before, but cotton became a far larger crop, grown and woven most importantly in the lower Yangtze, eastern north China, and central China, adding to the income of farmers and providing new employment for weavers and merchants. It was a peaceful, confident, prosperous time for most people, and Ming culture reflected it.

Commerce and Culture

For all the ambitiously revived system of imperial bureaucracy, it remained a thin and superficial layer at the top, administered by a relative handful of officials—about 4,000 outside the capital—which barely touched most aspects of daily life in this vast country with a population by now well over 100 million. Commerce was officially disparaged, except for its taxation, but the most significant changes taking place in Ming China were in the expanding commercialization of the economy. Cheng Ho's expeditions were past, but trade with most of the places he had visited continued to increase, especially with eastern Southeast Asia. Although the largest trade was domestic, new supplies of silver and silver coins came into China to pay for the exports of silk, tea, porcelain, lacquerware, and other goods, and heightened the pace of commercialization and monetization. More and more production was undertaken for sale, in agriculture and in manufacturing. Most of it was consumed in the rapidly growing cities, but some found its way to Korea, Japan, Java, the Philippines, and farther abroad.

Some of the silver flowing back came from Japan, but increasingly it came from the new Spanish base at Manila by the end of the sixteenth century, where it was brought from the mines in Peru and Mexico. Spanish-minted silver dollars began to circulate widely in the China market. By about 1450 silver coins, bars, and smaller ingots had driven paper money out; it was abandoned as people came to prefer silver, which by then was plentiful, to a paper currency that could not be exchanged for metal; after its value deteriorated beyond recall, it was given up. Taxes began to be commuted from a share of the grain harvest and periods of labor on public works projects to cash payments in silver. A sweeping reform in the sixteenth and early seventeenth centuries known as the "single lash of the whip" attempted, with considerable success, to simplify the tax system. The reform lumped what had previously been a great variety of exactions into a few categories and collected them at fixed dates, in silver, a major step toward modern revenue systems. At least for a time, this greatly reduced both the confusion and the corruption or evasion that had bedeviled the former system. It also increased the government's net income.

Merchant guilds acquired new though unofficial power in many Chinese cities, especially in the lower Yangtze and the southeast coast, the country's most urbanized and commercialized areas. Guilds controlled much nonagricultural production, marketing, and long-distance trade, informally and often through family or native-place networks, but very effectively. Merchants were still considered parasitic rather than productive and were formally subject to officials and periodically to special government exactions. But they had their own less formal official connections, usually through a degree- or office-holding gentry member of an extended family, as protection, access to favors, and indeed the only secure basis for commercial success in this bureaucratic society. Despite the Confucian disdain, at least on the surface, many merchants grew rich in this expanding economy, and some were able to buy gentry rank, although those who purchased rank were almost never permitted to hold office. In any case, their money enabled them to live in the style of the scholar-gentry, as literate connoisseurs of sophisticated art and literature in their great townhouses in the fashionable quarters.

After about 1520, capital investment increasingly moved away from the ownership and rental of land and into commercial enterprises: trade and artisan production. Prices for land continued to fall, and coastal piracy did not apparently discourage the increase of maritime trade as charges rose to cover those risks, although the biggest growth was in domestic commerce. In agriculture too, commercial or industrial crops such as cotton,

Love of unsullied nature remained a prominent theme for Ming painters. Like the white magnolia for spring, white lotus for summer represented purity, regeneration, and tranquility, as in this peaceful scroll by Ch'en Shun, who lived from 1483 to 1544. (The Nelson-Atkins Museum of Art, Kansas City)

indigo (for dyeing fabrics), and vegetable oil for illumination became more important. Handicraft production of tools, furniture, paper, porcelain, and art objects for wider sale grew rapidly, and large specialized workshops became common, distributing finished products to a regional or even national market. Some of them employed several hundred workers—another step toward industrialization.

There was a major cluster of porcelain workshops at Ching Te Chen (Jingdezhen) in the central Yangtze valley which made magnificent pieces for the imperial household and the court, but also for the domestic market as a whole and for export. Iron and steel were made in many places, especially in southern Hopei, in what amounted to factories. Large cotton mills producing cloth in major urban centers in the lower Yangtze valley and the highly commercialized delta area sold their output nationwide. There were 50,000 workers in 30 papermaking factories in Kiangsi province alone at the end of the sixteenth century. Skilled workers were in great demand, and were recruited over a very wide area. A national labor market developed, with the equivalent of hiring halls in major regional centers. Silk, porcelain, and tea especially, among other products, were exported in growing volume and with great profit. For example, Chinese silk sold in Japan at five or six times its price in the domestic market, and it continued to be sold in the West at even higher prices.

As would happen two centuries later in Europe, growing commercialization, a widening market, and rising demand for goods provided incentives for improving and speeding up production and the development of new technology to turn out more goods. In the last cen-

tury of the Ming a number of technical handbooks and treatises were published which show impressive progress in production technology. Some of the new techniques are reminiscent of those which appeared in eighteenth-century Europe, where the increase in trade and demand helped lead to technological innovation, rising output, and the beginnings of the Industrial Revolution. In Ming China, such innovations included mechanical looms with three or four shuttle winders for producing larger amounts of silk or cotton cloth in less time and without increasing labor requirements. New techniques emerged for the printing of woodblocks in three, four, and five colors, to feed the booming market for books and prints, and further improvements were made in movable type. An alloy of copper and lead was developed which made the type sharper and more durable so that it could be used for many more copies, and could be reused many more times. New procedures were worked out even for the manufacture of specially refined grades of sugar, to suit the tastes and the pocketbooks of the greatly increased numbers of the wealthy.

Suspension bridges using iron chains carried the booming trade over rivers. Originally developed in Han and T'ang times, the bridges were widespread under the Ming and greatly impressed the early European observers, although they were not successfully copied in Europe until the eighteenth century. The use of a mast and sail on wheelbarrows, important carriers of trade and raw materials on a local scale especially on the north China plain with its wide expanses of level and treeless areas with often strong winds, also attracted European attention. The practice was soon copied at home

✳ A Ming Play ✳

Verse drama became very popular under the Ming. Here is part of the play "Peony Pavilion" by the dramatist Tang Hsien-tzu (1550–1616), translated by Ma Rui-fang.

Maid: I open the door of the west wing and smooth the eastern couch. Purple iris in the vase, incense of aloes in the censer. Have a rest, young mistress, while I go to the old lady.

Liniang *(female lead):* We come back from enjoying the spring, And my loveliness is fresh as the spring itself. Ah, spring! After sporting with you, how shall I console myself when you are gone? How true it is that spring makes the heart sad! I am wasting my youth as time slips by. Though I am as pretty as a flower, my fate is as uncertain as a wind-blown leaf. Spring yearnings are hard to bear, and in secret I long for a lover. But as daughter of a prominent family, I must make a suitable match. So my youth is wasted. No one knows the languor I feel, and I blush to think of my dreams…. I am tired. Let me have a short nap here at the table. *(She falls asleep.)*
Enter, the ghost of her former lover, Liu:

Liu: In warm sun the orioles warble, in clear weather mortals smile. Following the fallen petals in the stream, I am come to fairyland. I have followed Young Mistress here from the garden. Where is she?—Ah, Madam! I have been searching for you everywhere. Madam, I am madly in love with you, because you are fair as a flower, and youth is slipping away like running water. Now I find you in your chamber alone. Let us take a stroll. I have so much to say to you!

Liniang: Where do you want to go?

Liu: Past the terrace of peonies, by the piled-up rocks, that you may share my ardour for a while.

Together: Somewhere we have met before; we are not strangers. *(He carries her off.)*
Enter, the God of Flowers, in a gown decked with flowers.

God of Flowers: Loving the flowers, I make them blossom early. The work of another spring is nearly done; petals fall like rain and grieve the hearts of men. But the lovers dream on beneath the clouds of blossom.

Source: Based on James Crump.

by the Dutch. The wheelbarrow itself had been invented in Han China and sails added soon thereafter.

A huge network of rivers and canals linked most places from the Yangtze valley south by cheap water transport. The Jesuit Matteo Ricci's journal comments on the immense traffic by water and the great numbers of people who lived on their boats, concluding that there were as many boats in China as in all the rest of the world put together. In agriculture, building on Sung foundations, new machines were developed under the Ming for cultivating the soil, for irrigation, and even for mechanical sowing, planting, and harvesting. Productive New World crops continued to add to total agricultural output. After Hung-wu and Yung-lo, Ming population figures are increasingly unreliable—another symptom of the decline in governmental efficiency—but total population probably increased to something like 130 million by the end of the dynasty.

To serve the needs of an increasingly commercialized economy, guilds of money changers and bankers became more important, and some of them developed a national network, with representatives in most major cities and at the capital. Techniques for transferring money through the equivalent of letters of credit, referred to as "flying money," had been used in the Sung dynasty, but were further refined and greatly expanded in the second half of the Ming, as were other aspects of banking and the financing of trade. These developments too suggest comparison with what was happening in Europe along similar lines. The Marxist historians of China in the 1970s identified these trends in the Ming as "early sprouts of capitalism," a description which seems quite reasonable despite the official downgrading of trade and merchants and the state regulation of commerce. Many of the richest merchants in fact grew wealthy through managing what were officially state enterprises or monopolies: supplies for the army, the shipment of rice to feed the capital, and the trade in salt.

Patronage and Literature

Wealthy merchants patronized literature and the arts, decorated their houses lavishly with art objects, and supported an elegant urban culture. Vernacular literature, too, which had had its major beginnings under the Sung, took on new dimensions and variety, appealing now to a growing mass of urban readers. Ming painting was in general less imaginative or innovative than that of the Sung, and tended to rework older themes and styles, but later Ming produced its own great painters, especially gifted in their exquisite representations of birds and flowers. Ceramics reached a new level of perfection, and beautiful pieces were part of every rich merchant household. This was the period of the famous Ming blue-and-white porcelain, samples and copies of which were prominent among Chinese exports to the West.

Yung-lo commissioned an immense encyclopedia of all knowledge, on which 3,000 scholars worked for five years. It was followed later in the fifteenth century by a great medical encyclopedia, and others devoted to geography, botany, ethics, and art. The medical volumes, completed in 1578, listed over 10,000 drugs and prescriptions, most of them unknown in the West, and recorded the use of inoculation to prevent smallpox, far in advance of this discovery in eighteenth-century Europe. A handbook of industrial technology printed in 1637, just before the dynasty collapsed, described methods and tools or machines in the production of rice, salt, porcelain, metals, coal, weaving, ships, canal locks, paper, weapons and many other fruits of Chinese industry and ingenuity. Science and technology in Ming China still led the world.

In the more popular realm, the theater flourished, but the major advance of Ming literature was in long-popular novels and other stories of adventure and romance. They still make excellent reading and give a vivid picture of the life of the times. Perhaps the best known now is titled *Water Margins* (translated by Pearl Buck as *All Men Are Brothers*), which tells the story of an outlaw band and their efforts to correct the wrongs done by unjust officials. Bandits of the Robin Hood variety had the same romantic appeal in China as in the West, and their life as "men of the greenwood" (a phrase identical to that used in medieval England), meaning of course the forest where they had their protected bases, was idealized. Many centuries later, Mao Tse-tung (Mao Zedong) said that *Water Margins* (the title came from the marshes that surrounded the outlaws' base) was his favorite book, and of course it did glorify those attempting to defy and if possible replace the existing government. Another still widely read Ming novel, *The Golden Lotus*, an often pornographic satire about the amorous adventures of a druggist with servants, neighbors, and other peoples' wives, seems as fresh as today's best-sellers.

Street people of the Ming: beggars and hawkers, painted by Chou Ch'en (active c. 1500–1535). (Cleveland Museum of Art, 1994, John L. Severance Fund)

The West as a whole has still not acknowledged that the novel, in much the same form as we know it today, originated in Asia, as did detective stories. But a few Westerners were less parochial in their awareness and their tastes. Here is a conversation between the famous German writer Johann Wolfgang von Goethe (1749–1832) and a friend in 1827:

"During the days when I did not see you," he said, "I have read a great deal, in particular a Chinese novel with which I am still occupied."

"A Chinese novel," I said, "that must be rather curious."

"Not as curious as one might be tempted to think," replied Goethe. "These people think and feel much as we do, and one soon realizes that one is like them."

"But," said I, "perhaps this Chinese novel is a rather exceptional one?"

"Not at all," said Goethe, "the Chinese have thousands of the kind, and they even had a certain number of them already when our forebears were still living in the woods."[6]

Popular Culture

By the sixteenth century there was a large and growing number of people who were literate or semiliterate but who were not members of any elite, or of the very small numbers of official Confucian-style gentry, who probably never exceeded at most 2 percent of the population. These nonelite literates and semiliterates lived in that vast Chinese world which was little touched by the imperial system and its canons, most of them outside the big cities and the circles of the rich merchant elites. Popular literature, stories, novels, and plays produced by and for them probably exceeded in volume, and in circulation, the more proper output in the orthodox classical mode, extensive and varied as that was. Much of it was also read, in private, by the elite, who would hide any "undignified" book under the pillow if someone entered the room. For us today, too, most of it is more fun than the restrained, polished, or formal material which the scholarly gentry were supposed to read and write.

In addition, as part of popular culture, were the numbers of puppet shows, shadow plays, mystery and detective stories (four or five centuries before they appeared in the West), operas, ballads, the oral tradition of itinerant storytellers, and a wealth of inexpensive wood-block prints, many of them dealing with aspects of daily life, others with mythology or folk religion. Opera, which combined, as now, drama, music, dance forms, singing, and gorgeous costumes, could of course appeal also to illiterates, still probably the majority, as could storytellers, balladeers, and the various forms of plays. (Ming China may have been the world's most literate or semiliterate society, like the Sung before and the Ch'ing after it.) Performances in all of these media were offered everywhere, even in small towns, by itinerant groups. Storytellers would often be accompanied by musicians, or would provide their own music; they would end each recital at a moment of suspense: "Come back next time if you want to hear the next episode," or "Pay now if you want to know how it all came out!"

Over 300 different local or regional genres of opera have been identified, intended mainly for nonelite audiences. Many operas, plays, and stories centered on the adventures of heroes and villains of the rich Chinese past, not always historically accurate in every detail but always entertaining, and appealing to the deep and consistent Chinese interest in their own history. Most of the common people learned their history from opera, theater, and storytellers, and they learned a great deal of it. The connection with folk religion was close, including folk versions of Buddhism and Taoism as well as local animist cults and deities, and many of the operas, plays, and stories focused on it. Operas were commonly performed at festivals celebrating a local god or as part of temple rituals, and many of them and of the shadow plays had an explicitly religious or ritual content, like the medieval miracle plays of Europe. Still others satirized daily life: henpecked husbands, jilted or faithless lovers, grasping merchants, corrupt officials, overprotective or authoritarian parents, tyrannical landlords, and so on—set in villages or towns rather than in the more sophisticated and urbane world of the cities.

They formed in effect a countertradition to the elite culture, and expressed strong sympathy for the powerless, the oppressed, and the underdogs, including especially women, who were often the major figures. They show a contempt for wealth without compassion, for power without responsibility, and for all forms of hypocrisy, opportunism, and moral compromise. Of course, such failings are endemic in all societies, including our own, but especially common among the elite, even in a Confucian China, many of whose supposed values are in fact faithfully mirrored in the popular literature. In this extensive genre, as later in the Ch'ing dynasty, individuals are, however, valued and respected for their achievements and their moral virtue regardless of their social position, unlike the hierarchical ordering of individuals which Confucian doctrine came to support. Through this rich and varied literature we can catch far more than a glimpse of what has been called the "little tradition," present in all societies and often at odds with, or showing a very different perspective on, the great tradition. It was of course already old in China, but with the expansion of printing and literacy under the Ming, these various literary and artistic forms began to be recorded on a much greater scale. It has a universal flavor, and many parallels in the popular culture of most other societies around the world, past and present. But it also reveals the basic good sense, the humor, and the appealing human qualities of the common people of Ming China.

Elite Culture and Traditionalism

In monumental architecture the Ming created new glories in their capitals at Nanking and Peking and in temples in every city and many towns, a further indication of prosperity. But in general, and particularly after their first century, the Ming looked to the past for guidance. This accounted for their interest in encyclopedias, collecting the wisdom and experience of previous generations as guardians of tradition. Most Ming scholars and philosophers were traditionalists, mistrusting speculation or innovation. There were exceptions, of course, but orthodoxy tended to dominate thought, as it did the imperial examinations. As one Ming writer put it: "Since the time of Chu Hsi (the Sung Confucianist) the truth has been made clear. No more writing is needed. We have only to practice." There were nevertheless some important developments in philosophy, especially in the thought of Wang Yang-ming (1472–1529), a scholar-offi-

cial who went beyond the neo-Confucianism of Chu Hsi in urging both a meditative and intuitive self-cultivation, much influenced by Buddhism, and an activist moral role in society. Wang's most famous aphorism stresses the organic connection between knowledge and behavior: "Knowledge is the beginning of conduct; conduct is the completion of knowledge"—a maxim still much admired by Confucianists in China, Korea, and Japan, and one which makes excellent sense to any thoughtful person.

Before Wang's time, Hung-wu had issued six brief imperial edicts which were posted in all villages and towns in 1397, a year before his death. They ordered people to be filial, respectful to elders and ancestors, to teach their children to do the same, and to peacefully pursue their livelihoods. Local gentry, those not in office but functioning as local elites and keepers of order and morality, helped to see that these prescriptions were carried out. The revived orthodox Confucian denigration of trade and merchants and their subordination to officialdom helped to strengthen official disinterest in commerce. Foreign trade was left largely in private hands or was managed by powerful eunuchs at court, which further devalued it in Confucian eyes.

Grain had to be hauled north from the Yangtze valley to feed the cloud of officials, garrison troops, and com-

✠ Every Man a Sage ✠

Wang Yang-ming (1472–1529) was the most noted philosopher of the Ming. Like Chu Hsi in the Sung, whose approach he mirrored, he believed that the way to sagehood is open to everyone.

The highest good is the ultimate principle of manifesting character and loving people. The nature endowed in us by Heaven is pure and perfect. The fact that it is intelligent, clear and not obscured is evidence of the emanation and revelation of the highest good. It is the original nature of the clear character which is called innate knowledge. As the highest good emanates and reveals itself, one will consider right as right and wrong as wrong. Things of greater or less importance and situations of grave or light character will be responded to as they act upon us.... We will entertain no preconceived attitude; in all this, we do nothing that is not natural. This is the normal nature of man and the principle of things. There can be no question of adding to or subtracting anything from them.... How can anyone who does not watch over himself carefully, and who has no refinement and singleness of mind, attain to such a state of perfection? Later generations fail to realize that the highest good is inherent in their own minds, but each in accordance with his own ideas gropes for it outside the mind, believing that every event and every object has its own definite principle. Thus the law of right and wrong is obscured [and] the desires of man become rampant.

Source: From W. T. deBary, ed., *Sources of Chinese Tradition, Vol. I.* (New York: Columbia University Press, 1960), pp. 518–519.

Wild Geese and Tree Peonies in Moonlight, a painting on silk by Lu Chi (active in the late fifteenth and early sixteenth centuries). Mists drift across the moon in this poetic and decorative but deeply restful painting, where the detailed plumage of the geese is balanced by the simple and naturalistic brush strokes of the tall grasses. (National Palace Museum, Taipei, Taiwan)

moners, as well as the elite of Peking. Japanese and Korean piracy prompted Yung-lo to restore the Grand Canal, which had silted up and fallen into disrepair, and to abandon the coastal route by sea after 1415. Fifteen locks were constructed and the canal dredged. The cost was high but the canal helped to stimulate further increases in interregional trade, and in artisan and other consumer goods production to supply a now-enlarged market. It also stimulated the growth of cities along its route. Soochow (Suzhou), in the Yangtze delta just west of Shanghai, was

until the nineteenth century the major city and port of that productive area after Nanking. It became a national financial and commercial center near the canal's southern end and was noted for its fine silk goods, distributed to the wealthy all over China but especially in fashionable Peking. Cotton cloth, lacquer, magnificent porcelain pieces, iron cooking pots from Canton, and a long list of other goods were distributed, mainly by water routes, to an increasingly national market. Hankou (now part of the city of Wuhan) on the central Yangtze grew as a major junction of rivers and a national distribution center as well as a major market in itself. Private Chinese merchants went to Southeast Asia in great numbers and managed an increasing overseas trade from bases on the southeast China coast such as Canton, Amoy (Xiamen), Swatow (Shantou), and Foochou (Fuzhou), despite official discouragement. Tientsin (Tianjin), the port of Peking, grew also as the chief port for trade with Korea. Other booming cities included Chengdu, the capital of agriculturally rich Szechuan with its many rivers, and Changsha, the capital of Hunan on the Hsiang (Xiang) River, a tributary of the Yangtze flowing through the productive lowlands of central China known as "China's rice bowl."

But increasingly conservative official attitudes were reflected in the Ming imprint on the imperial examination system. In 1487 a set form was established for the writing of examination papers under eight categories with no more than 700 characters altogether, following a prescribed style of polished commentary on the Confucian and neo-Confucian classics. This was the famous "eight-legged essay," which clearly and probably intentionally inhibited individual thought or innovation and encouraged a past-centered orthodoxy. Government-supported schools at the county and prefectural levels, originally established by Hung-wu, offered classical education to able boys, the best of whom were brought to the capital for further study, and for training as apprentice officials. On an earlier Sung model, private academies and tutors for the sons of the wealthy (daughters were given no such formal education) passed on the distilled wisdom of the past to those fortunate enough to attend, and shaped their instruction to prepare aspiring youths to conform to what the examinations now required.

Candidates had to pass preliminary examinations at the *hsien* (county) level. Success there enabled the student to compete in exams at the prefectural city, where he could obtain the lowest principal degree, the *hsiu ts'ai* (*xiu cai* or *sheng-yuan*). That constituted admission to the gentry class, with among other things exemption from labor service and from corporal punishment. The second level of exams was held in each provincial capital; it lasted several days during which time each candidate was walled into a tiny separate cell and provided with food and water. Only about one in a hundred passed, earning the degree of *chü ren* (*ju ren*) and the right to compete in the final exam every three years at the imperial capital. Success there brought the designation *chin shih* (*jin shi*) and then a final test interview with the emperor himself, who could then appoint those he chose to an official post. The lowest or *hsiu ts'ai* (*sheng-yuan*) degree could be purchased, especially as the dynasty declined and needed money, but such buyers—merchants or landlords—did not serve as officials. The sale of these degrees also served to some extent as a concession to wealthy families which might otherwise become discontented or restive, a kind of co-optation.

Both the state-financed schools and the private academies multiplied after Hung-wu's time. But although learning and the examinations became more rigidly orthodox, the basic Confucian message of responsibility and "human-heartedness" continued to be stressed, with its conviction that human nature is fundamentally good and moldable by education and by the virtuous example of superiors. The ultimate deterioration and collapse of the Ming, and in 1911 of the entire imperial system, should not obscure its positive aspects, especially during its many centuries of relative vigor. Even up to the last years of the Ming, corruption and ineffectiveness at court were not much reflected in the continued operation of the system elsewhere in the country, which rested far more on the basic Chinese social fabric of family, gentry, and Confucian principles than on the management or intervention of the few imperial officials.

The lives and values of most people had their own momentum. "The emperor is far away," as the traditional saying went, expressing a wealth of meaning. Local freedom and good order had little to do with imperial politics and much to do with the traditional Chinese system of the self-regulating society. Local gentry directed and raised money for public works, especially irrigation, roads, canals, bridges, and ferries. Often they organized and funded schools and academies, orphanages, care for old people, and relief measures in hard times or after floods. Many of them compiled the local histories or gazeteers, which are still a mine of information about local conditions, events, and notable local people. This was all done as part of Confucian morality, and without pay or official appointment. When all went well, perhaps half or more of the time during the 2,000 years of dynastic rule, the local gentry were thus a major supplement to government and an important cement for society.

Imperial Peking: Axis of the Ming World

When Yung-lo decided to move the capital back to the north, Peking was the obvious choice, primarily for its nearness to the most threatened frontiers. It is only about 40 miles from the mountains that surround and protect the city on the west, north, and northeast. The Great Wall runs through the mountains, crossing a narrow lowland strip of coastal plain east of the city leading to Manchuria called Shan Hai Kuan ("mountain sea gate"). Passes to the northwest lead directly into Mongolia. Both areas were accurately seen as by now the chief trouble spots along the frontier, and it was mainly to guard against them that the Great Wall was rebuilt, at tremendous cost.

The Hsiung-nu menace that had plagued the Han had been replaced by that of the Mongols farther east, and by the early signs of what was to become the next alien conquering group, the Manchus of Manchuria. The gradual west-to-east progression of China's capital from Chou, Ch'in, Han, and T'ang Ch'ang An (Sian) to Loyang, the Sung move to Kaifeng and Hangchou, and now the Ming choice of Peking reflected these changes. The location of the capital was also affected by the growth of the south, the drought and agricultural deterioration of the northwest, and the provision of canals to bring food from the surplus areas of the Yangtze to feed successive northern capitals.

The new Peking was designed to make a statement of imperial power and majesty. The pre-1850 center of the city today is largely a Ming creation, replacing what was left of the Mongol capital but on a much larger scale. The main outer city walls were 40 feet high and nearly 15 miles around, forming a rectangle pierced by nine gates with watchtowers and outer gates to further deter attackers, check permit papers, and awe all those who entered. Inside was the Imperial City, within its own walls 5 miles in circumference. These enclosed in turn the red inner walls of the Forbidden City, which contained the palace of nearly 10,000 rooms and was surrounded by a moat 2 miles around. Successive courtyards inside the Forbidden City, dominated by throne halls for different purposes, were set on terraces of white marble and with gleaming gold-tiled roofs. These led along a north-south axis to the palace. Outside the Forbidden City (so called because it was closed to all except those with official business), a similar succession of elegant stone-paved courtyards, terraces, and audience halls led to the main gates. The outermost walls enclosed gardens, artificial lakes, and even an artificial hill.

The orientation of the city as a whole was based on astronomical principles and followed throughout a north-south axis, to reflect and draw authority from the supreme correctness of the universe. The whole plan and all its details were designed to awe and impress all who approached or entered its series of walls and courtyards. It still has that effect, and partly for that reason part has been restored by the People's Republic as the centerpiece of their capital. The Ming design was accepted and further embellished by their successors, the

The Imperial Palace, Peking. (R. Murphey)

still be seen. The majestic Imperial and Forbidden Cities were formally ordered on a grand scale, in sharp contrast to the unplanned alleys and irregular streets of the city around them, but above all Peking was—and remains—an imperial statement in wood, stone, brick, and tile, which dominated the entire urban area physically as well as symbolically.

Complacency and Decline

Peking was built in the days of power and pride, but as the decades went by, complacency replaced new achievements, and was less and less appropriate to a number of growing problems. Japanese and Korean pirate attacks on the coast proved impossible to control, and the government's ultimate response was to order the removal of all settlement 30 miles inland and officially forbid maritime trade, although the ban was widely ignored. Guns had been in use for centuries, but China had begun to fall behind advances in Western gunnery. When, late in the fifteenth century, a touring censor asked a garrison to demonstrate their obviously long-neglected cannons, the commander said, "What, fire those things? Why, they might kill somebody!"[7] This may be an unfair example, however humanly appealing, and during most of the dynasty the Ming armies were reasonably effective in keeping the long peace at home and on the frontiers, maintaining an order which encouraged economic prosperity. But the failure to control raids by supposed "tributaries" was worrying.

China also had to deal with Westerners. The Portuguese reached the south China coast by 1514, but their aggressive and barbarous behavior led to their expulsion from Canton in 1522, where their envoy died in prison. To the Chinese, they were just another lot of unruly pirates, like the Dutch who followed them later, and their numbers and ships small enough to be brushed off. The Chinese also found them hairy, misshapen, and very smelly, and although a few military commanders noted that their guns were superior to China's, no one in the government could take them seriously, still less learn anything from them.

The Jesuit missionary effort of the sixteenth-century Counter-Reformation in Europe soon had its eye on China as an immense potential harvest of souls (as all missionaries were to do until the present century) and sent a series of missioners there beginning with Matteo Ricci in 1582 (see Chapter 12). He and his successors, notably Adam Schall von Bell and Ferdinand Verbiest, were learned men with a good working knowledge of the rapidly developing science and technology of post-Renaissance Europe. Complacent Chinese pride kept

Ch'ing (Qing), as serving their similar purposes admirably. That part of Peking remains one of the best preserved and most impressive planned capitals anywhere. Its splendid courtyards, the gracefulness and yet strength of architectural and roof lines in all of its buildings, and the lavish use of colored glazed tiles make it aesthetically as well as symbolically overwhelming.

A less planned city of course grew up outside the walls, where most of the common people lived, and it soon housed most of Peking's residents. The total population, inside and outside the walls, was probably a little over a million under both the Ming and the Ch'ing, fed in part with rice brought from the Yangtze valley by the Grand Canal. Some space was left clear immediately around the outer walls, for better defense, and there were large military barracks. A maze of streets, alleys, and small courtyards covered most of the extramural area, including the small, walled compounds with their tiny gardens and living space for extended families for which Peking became famous and some of which can

China from learning from the Jesuits what would have been most useful: new European advances in mathematics, geography (their own picture of the world was still woefully incomplete and inaccurate), mechanics, metallurgy, anatomy, surveying, techniques and instruments for precise measuring and weighing, and even gunnery.

The court was instead fascinated by the clocks and clockwork gadgets or toys that the Jesuits also brought, to ingratiate themselves to the Chinese, while their real potential contribution was passed over. Von Bell, a trained astronomer and mathematician, was able to figure out and explain the use of some remarkable astronomical instruments built under the Yuan dynasty in Peking; by late Ming the Chinese had lost the secret of these instruments. Their own astronomers had noticed that their calculations no longer accurately predicted the movements of the heavenly bodies, but instead of questioning their assumptions and methods, they concluded that "the heavens were out of order." All these were symptoms of an increasing tendency to ignore new ideas

or troublesome problems, such as foreigners, or to gloss them over with confident-sounding pronouncements.

At the capital, there was a clear decline in administrative effectiveness by the end of the sixteenth century. The court was filled with intriguing factions, including the eunuchs. This was to become a curse of the imperial system. Hung Wu had set a pattern of secrecy, harsh authoritarianism, plotting, and counterplotting. Because they had no heirs, eunuchs were often trusted, given the care of imperial sons, and had ready access to the emperor and to powerful wives and concubines. They were also given command of the palace guard, and often won high military posts as commanders or served as imperial inspectors in the provinces. They controlled the workshops which made luxury products for the court, and supervised the tribute sent by the provinces and foreign countries. Eunuchs were also often appointed as heads of official missions abroad.

All this gave them limitless opportunities for graft, which they used to enrich themselves. Eunuchs also

✠ A Western View of China ✠

Here is an excerpt from the journal of Matteo Ricci, who observed Ming China from 1583 until his death there in 1610.

The Chinese are a most industrious people, and most of the mechanical arts flourish among them. They have all sorts of raw material and they are endowed by nature with a talent for trading, both of which are potent factors in bringing about a high development of the mechanical arts.... Their skill in the manufacture of fireworks is really extraordinary, and there is scarcely anything which they cannot cleverly imitate with them. They are especially adept in reproducing battles and in making rotary spheres of fire, fiery trees, fruit, and the like, and they seem to have no regard for expense where fireworks are concerned. When I was in Nanking I witnessed a display for the celebration of the first month of the year, which is their great festival, and on this occasion I calculated that they consumed enough powder to carry on a sizeable war for a number of years.... Their method of making printed books is quite ingenious. The text is written in ink, with a brush made of very fine hair, on a sheet of paper which is inverted and pasted on a wooden tablet. When the paper is thoroughly dry, its surface is scraped off until nothing but a fine tissue bearing the characters remains on the wooden tablet. Then with a steel graver the workman cuts away the surface following the outlines of the characters until these alone stand out in low relief. From such a block a skilled printer can make copies with incredible speed; turning out as many as fifteen hundred copies in a single day.... The simplicity of Chinese printing is what accounts for the exceedingly large number of books in circulation here and the ridiculously low prices at which they sold. Such facts as these would scarcely be believed by anyone who has not witnessed them.

Source: M. Ricci, *China in the Sixteenth Century: The Journals of Matthew Ricci, 1583–1610,* trans. L. J. Gallagher (New York: Random House, 1953), pp. 18–21.

came to control the fearsome secret police, and used their power to blackmail and corrupt as well. This was a burden on the treasury as funds were siphoned off from normal revenues. Another serious drain was the huge allowances paid to the endless relatives of the imperial family and the nobility, altogether many thousands of people and their dependents. By the late sixteenth century these allowances alone consumed over half of the revenues of two provinces, which provides some measure of their gargantuan scope. The heavy expenses of the expedition to Korea to expel the invasion of the Japanese warlord Hideyoshi (see Chapter 11) drained financial resources still further. Subsidies to Mongol and other central Asian princes, to keep them quiet and to deter them from new uprisings or raids on Chinese territory, further increased financial strain. The already high taxes were raised still more, and there were both urban and rural revolts. The burden fell disproportionately on the poor, since many families with money and connections had managed to get their names off the tax registers. Peasants also had to perform heavy labor service, including the rebuilding of the Grand Canal and the Great Wall. Many became so desperate that they just melted away into the countryside or the towns, or became bandits.

Strong rulers, like Hung Wu, could check these abuses, and could control the eunuchs, but under weaker emperors eunuchs often became the real powers, and they did not use their power responsibly. Hung Wu had warned his ministers: "Anyone using eunuchs as his eyes and ears will be blind and deaf." After Yung-lo there was a succession of undistinguished emperors, most of whom kept to the pleasures of their palaces and left the running of the empire to the eunuchs and bureaucrats. This was a disastrous pattern in a system where authority and responsibility had been so heavily centralized in the person of the emperor.

Banditry and piracy mushroomed, largely a response to growing poverty, as always, but also to the still growing trade, especially with Japan. Japanese often alternated as traders and as pirates or "privateers," like their rough contemporaries Drake and Hawkins in Elizabethan England. When the government in 1530 canceled permission for the official Japanese trading missions to Ningpo (Ningbo, on the coast south of Shanghai), piracy and smuggling multiplied. Pirates and smugglers had their major base for the central coast in the Chusan Islands off the mouth of the Yangtze River, conveniently near Ningpo, then the dominant maritime trade center for populous and highly commercialized

Social Customs in Ming China

Ricci also described a variety of social customs, as in these excerpts.

When relatives or friends pay a visit, the host is expected to return the visit, and a definite and detailed ceremony accompanies their visiting. The one who is calling presents a little folder in which his name is written and which may contain a few words of address, depending on the rank of the visitor or the host. These folders or booklets consist of about a dozen pages of white paper, with a two inch strip of red paper down the middle of the cover.... One must have at least twenty different kinds on hand for different functions, marked with appropriate titles.... Men of high station in life are never seen walking in the streets. They are carried about enclosed in sedan chairs and cannot be seen by passers-by, unless they leave the front curtain open.... Carriages and wagons are prohibited by law.... The whole country is divided up by rivers and canals. People here travel more by boat than we in the West, and their boats are more ornate and more commodious than ours.... Sometimes they give sumptuous dinners aboard their yachts and make a pleasure cruise of it on the lake or along the river.... Because of their ignorance of the size of the earth and the exaggerated opinion they have of themselves, the Chinese are of the opinion that only China among the nations is deserving of admiration. They look on all other people not only as barbarous but as unreasoning animals.

Source: M. Ricci, *China in the Sixteenth Century: The Journals of Matthew Ricci, 1583–1610,* trans. L. J. Gallagher (New York: Random House, 1953), pp. 61, 81, 167.

central China. Other pirate and smuggling bases were scattered along the much indented-coast of the south in the innumerable small harbors there, shifting from one to another as government pressures or other circumstances required.

This coast, from the Yangtze southward, was almost impossible to patrol adequately, and it had a long history of piracy. Mountains come down to the sea in most of this area, which meant that there were limited opportunities for agriculture or trade on land, but ample forest cover for concealment and to provide timber for ships. Like the shores of much of the Mediterranean, the Dalmatian coast of the Adriatic, or the Caribbean, it combined motives and bases for piracy with tempting opportunity: a golden stream of seaborne trade passing just offshore. In fact, piracy along the south China coast was not finally put down until after 1950, and smuggling continues there still.

As an early twentieth-century report by the Chinese Maritime Customs put it, speaking of the south coast, "Piracy and smuggling are in the blood of the people." When hard-pressed by the authorities of law and order, pirates and smugglers from Amoy or Swatow southward could cross the border into nearby Vietnam, where they could find sanctuaries, supplies, and Vietnamese colleagues. Hainan Island off the coast opposite the border

was long notorious as a pirate and smuggling base for desperadoes from both countries, and even the People's Republic has had trouble preventing large-scale smuggling there. The people of the south China coast were China's principal seafarers in any case, and many earned their livings as fishermen and traders. The fleets of Cheng Ho were built there in those harbors, from local timbers in yards on this coast, and their sailors recruited there. As the power of the central government weakened under the later Ming, including its naval strength and efficiency, and as poverty worsened after the fifteenth century, piracy and smuggling grew once again out of control. By late Ming, most of the pirates were not Japanese or Korean but Chinese.

There was a great and briefly successful effort at reform led by an outstanding minister, Chang Chü-cheng (Zhang Zhu zheng), who became Grand Secretary from 1573 to 1582. The emperor Wan-li had ascended the throne as a boy in 1572, and was guided for some time by Chang Chü-cheng, who as a distinguished Confucian scholar stressed the need for economy, justice, and responsibility. Chang tried to increase the now shrinking imperial revenue by once more reforming the tax system to get exempted lands and families, which had slipped off the rolls after the earlier tax reform, back on again. He also tried to limit the special privileges and extravagant expenses of the court and the imperial family, and to rebuild the authority of the censors to report on and check abuses. But after Chang's death in 1582, Wan-li abandoned all pretense at responsibility and indulged in more extravagance and pleasures while leaving the court eunuchs to run the empire. He avoided even seeing his own ministers for many years and refused to make appointments, conduct any business, or to take note of or react to any abuses.

Unfortunately, he lived and reigned until 1620, and the fifteen-year-old who succeeded him on the throne was mentally deficient and spent most of his time tinkering with carpentry in the palace. He gave over control of the government to an old friend of his childhood nurse, a eunuch named Wei Chung-hsien (Wei Zhongxian) who had been a butler to his mother. Wei then almost certainly poisoned the emperor, although it was never proved; by then people were reluctant to challenge him. Wei put together a small eunuch army to control the palace and set up a spy network all over the empire. Earlier he had been a wastrel and built up huge gambling debts. He had himself castrated, confident that as a eunuch he could get a job in the palace. Although he was illiterate, and despite his poisoning of the boy emperor, he was given an official position by the new emperor. By unscrupulous plotting and force he eliminated all of his enemies—most of the Confucianists at court—filled their places with his opportunist supporters, and extorted new taxes to pay for his luxurious lifestyle. There

A sample of the famous Ming blue-and-white porcelain. (The University Museum, Philadelphia)

was a general persecution of intellectuals as "conspirators" and many hundreds were executed. Most of the academies were closed. Half the government offices were left vacant, and petitions went unanswered. There was of course Confucian resistance, and a group of scholars calling themselves the Tung Lin (Donglin), from the name of a famous academy, attempted a moral crusade against these evils. Wei responded with terror tactics after the Tung Lin leader accused him of murders, the forced abortion of the empress, and 24 other "high crimes." In the end, Wei's unscrupulous power won out and most of the Tung Lin scholars were disgraced, jailed, or beaten to death by the time of Wei's own death in 1628 at the hand of an assassin.

It was late for reform, and the eunuch stranglehold was now too strong to break. But as already pointed out, factionalism, corruption, heedlessness, irresponsibility, and moral rot at the capital did not mean that the same problems dominated the rest of the country, which went on under its own momentum until the very end, although with less vigor or success in the last years. Eunuch power at court undercut and then virtually eliminated the power and even the role of the imperial censors. Many were killed when they dared to speak up. By the 1630s most of the country had lost its former confidence in the imperial order and the smooth working of the traditional system. Palace eunuchs went on making most policy, or not making it, after Wei's death. The state treasury had been exhausted by the heavy expense of assisting the Koreans to repel Hideyoshi's invasion (see Chapter 11) and never fully recovered, with

disastrous results for the efficient operation of all state systems. Inflation greatly worsened the problem. There were major droughts and famine in Shensi (Shannxi) Province in the northwest in 1627–1628, and spreading revolts, soon covering most of the north.

Officials and local magistrates had to cope with a much larger population, and one which was increasingly troubled by discontent, banditry, and even rebellion. Their salaries were increased and special allowances given to discourage them from diverting official funds or taking bribes, but none of this made up for inflation or for the far heavier demands, which necessitated their hiring larger and larger staffs to assist them. These "aides," although essential, were not official employees and their wages were not provided by the state, leaving magistrates and other officials to meet the costs out of their own inadequate salaries and allowances. The inevitable result was increased corruption and bribery, since the greatest of all traditional Confucian virtues was responsibility for one's own family. More and more, the rest of Confucian morality disappeared as individuals and families strove simply to survive.

The Ming army did not distinguish itself in Korea. It drove the Japanese back, but then was ambushed near Seoul, the Korean capital; the rest of the campaign was largely a stalemate, until Hideyoshi providentially died and his army promptly returned to Japan. A few years later, Matteo Ricci found the Ming army unimpressive: "All those under arms lead a despicable life, for they have not embraced this profession out of love of their country or love of honor but as men in the service of a provider of

Cells at Nanking where candidates were walled in to write their answers to the questions on the imperial examinations; the structures were repeated in the other provincial capitals. (Sidney Gamble, as reproduced in J. K. Fairbank, E. O. Reischauer, and A. M. Craig. *East Asia: Tradition and Transformation*. Boston: Houghton-Mifflin, 1989)

employment." Ricci added that the army's horses were poor worn-out things which fled in panic at the mere whinnying of the steppe horses of their opponents. By this time the Chinese saying was common: "Good iron is not used for nails, or good men for soldiers."

Much of the Ming army by this time was composed of ex-prisoners, drifters, former bandits, and idlers. Its size had doubled since the beginning of the dynasty, but its effectiveness had sharply declined. Military contracts had become an open and expanding field for graft and corruption, and the quality of equipment and other supplies had greatly deteriorated, as had military morale and leadership. One of the reasons for the failure to drive the Japanese out of Korea was what had become the inferiority of most Chinese weapons, including swords, spears, and guns. The Japanese had quickly noted and copied the Portuguese improvements in cannons, and the development of an early version of the rifle, the arquebus (harquebus), a cumbersome muzzle-loading weapon too heavy to hold and fire accurately and hence usually propped up on some support, but devastating in close combat.

At the capital under the dissolute Emperor Wan-li, and progressively elsewhere in the empire, there was a similar decline in effectiveness and morale. Despite Chang Chü-cheng's brief reforms, corruption had again removed much land and other wealth from the tax rolls, and the new taxes imposed by the eunuch Wei and his successors, together with continuing population increases, created widespread economic hardship and a rapid growth of tenancy, lawlessness, and local famine. Banditry, local revolts, and secret societies planning rebellion, always a barometer of impending collapse, multiplied. There was open talk that the Ming had forfeited the Mandate of Heaven.

The now incompetent and demoralized government, almost without a head, had to face two major revolts. The famine in Shensi Province in the northwest in 1628 led to arbitrary government economies instead of the needed relief. A postal clerk named Li Tzu-ch'eng (Li Zicheng) was laid off, and joined his uncle who was already a bandit in the mountains. Li and his forces raided widely among three or four adjoining provinces, attracted more followers, set up a government, distributed

✠ An Earthquake at Peking, 1626 ✠

The Chinese interpreted earthquakes and other natural disasters as symbols of Heaven's displeasure. When they coincided with popular discontent and dynastic decline, they were seen as warnings. Here is a description of an earthquake in 1626 at Peking, in the last corrupt years of the Ming. The partisans referred to were palace eunuchs.

Just when the ... partisans were secretly plotting in the palace, there was a sudden earthquake. A roof ornament over the place where they were sitting fell without any apparent reason and two eunuchs were crushed to death. In a moment there was a sound like thunder rising from the northwest. It shook heaven and earth, and black clouds flowed over confusedly. Peoples' dwellings were destroyed to such an extent that for several miles nothing remained. Great stones hurtled down from the sky like rain. Men and women died by the tens of thousands [a phrase which in Chinese means "a great many"]. Donkeys, horses, chickens, and dogs all had broken or cracked limbs. People with smashed skulls or broken noses were strewn about—the streets were full of them. Gunpowder that had been stored in the imperial Arsenal exploded. This alarmed elephants, and the elephants ran about wildly, trampling to death an incalculable number of people. The court astrologer reported his interpretation of these events as follows: "In the earth there is tumultuous noise. This is an evil omen of calamity in the world. When noise gushes forth from within the earth, the city must be destroyed.... The reason why the earth growls is that throughout the empire troops arise to attack one another, and that palace women and eunuchs have brought about great disorder."

Source: C. O. Hucker in D. Lach, *Asia on the Eve of Europe's Expansion.* (Englewood Cliffs, N.J.: Prentice-Hall, 1965), p. 133.

food to famine victims, appointed officials, and proclaimed a new dynasty. Early in 1644 he advanced on Peking, meeting only weak resistance. The last Ming emperor, deserted by his officials and driven to despair by news that the city had already fallen, hanged himself in the palace garden where he had lived a life of ease and irresponsibility, after failing to kill his oldest daughter with a sword.

A rival rebel leader named Chang Hsien-Chung (Zhang Xianzhong) had meanwhile been raiding and plundering over much of north China with hit-and-run tactics that the Ming armies were unable to cope with. In 1644 he invaded Szechuan, set up a government, and moved to claim the throne himself. His power plays and his terror tactics, however, lost him the support of the gentry, whom he saw as rivals for power, and without them on his side his cause was lost. But the Ming had really defeated themselves, by ignoring the basic function of any government, namely, to govern and to serve their subjects.

The Manchu Conquest

Beyond the Great Wall in Manchuria, a non-Chinese steppe people, the Manchus, descendants of the Jurchen who had conquered the Northern Sung, had risen to power despite earlier Ming efforts to keep them divided and subdued. A strong leader, Nurhachi (1559–1626), united several previously separate tribes and founded a Chinese-style state, taking the title of emperor and promoting the adoption of the entire Confucian system and its philosophy. His capital was established at Mukden (now called Shenyang) in southern Manchuria, where his two sons, also capable people, succeeded him and continued the Sinification of the Manchu state and culture.

By 1644 the Manchus were politically and culturally largely indistinguishable from the Chinese, except for their spoken language, and they controlled the whole of Manchuria as far south as Shan Hai Kuan. Their administration and army included large numbers of Chinese, who accurately saw them as a coming power and as a far more effective state than the Ming had by then become. The Manchus made vassals of the Mongols of Inner Mongolia and of the Koreans, after expeditions had conquered both. They were consciously building their power to take over China, and in 1644 they had their opportunity.

A Ming general, Wu San-kui (Wu sanguei), confronted with the rebel forces of Li Tzu-ch'eng, who now occupied Peking, invited the Manchu armies waiting on the border at Shan Hai Kuan to help him defeat the rebels. Having done so handily, the Manchus remained to found the Ch'ing (Qing) dynasty, rewarding a number of Chinese collaborators with grants of land. Some of these collaborators later rebelled, but were suppressed in heavy fighting. Finally, in 1683, the new dynasty conquered the offshore island of Taiwan (Formosa), which had clung to the defeated Ming cause, a situation with parallels in the twentieth century. It thus took nearly another 40 years after 1644 before all Chinese resistance to this new conquest was eliminated by another originally steppe people. But unlike Mongol rule, it ushered in a long period of domestic peace and unprecedented prosperity.

The Manchus called their new dynasty Ch'ing, a title adopted by Nurhachi's sons and continued by his great-grandson, K'ang Hsi (r. 1661–1722), who was only six years old in 1644 and thus "ruled" through a regent, until 1661, when he ascended the throne. *Ch'ing* means "pure" and the name was intended to add legitimacy to what was after all alien, even barbarian, rule. But the Manchus had learned their Chinese lessons well. They honored and continued the Ming tradition, and with it the Chinese imperial tradition, and could legitimately say that they were liberators restoring China's glorious past. While this made them, like the Ming, conservative stewards rather than innovators and in time helped to harden them against any change, they too presided over a brilliant period in Chinese history for their first two centuries. Ch'ing was the China most Westerners first knew well. Although then in its declining years in the nineteenth century, Westerners still found it impressive, built on a long foundation of imperial greatness before it.

The Ming dynasty thus ended in ineptness and disgrace, but the more positive aspects of its achievements were valued and preserved by its successors. Having begun with great vigor and success, the Ming went on to administer effectively for two centuries or more a new wave of prosperity, cultural growth, commercial and urban development, and the further refinement of sophisticated taste. Popular culture, aided by cheap printing, enjoyed a notable boom, and in the larger cities rich merchants patronized and took part in elite culture. Although the dramatic maritime expeditions of Cheng Ho were abandoned, private Chinese trade multiplied with Southeast Asia, and domestic commerce thrived. Agriculture was made more productive, in part under state direction, and the population increased substantially. Ming Peking still stands as a monument to the dynasty's wealth and power. But the highly centralized system of government begun under Hung-wu helped to sap administrative effectiveness under later and weaker emperors, while power came increasingly into the hands of court eunuchs, with disastrous results. The Ming ceased to serve their subjects, the country was torn with revolt, and in the end was easy prey for the far better organized Manchus, who had learned the Confucian lessons that the Ming had forgotten.

Notes

1. J. K. Fairbank, E. O. Reischauer, and A. Craig, *East Asia: Tradition and Transformation* Boston: Houghton Mifflin, 1978, p. 197.
2. Ibid., p. 182.
3. Ibid., p. 182.
4. Quoted, in translation, in W. Bingham, H. Conroy, and F. Ikle, *A History of Asia* Boston: Allyn and Bacon, 1964, Vol. I, p. 459.
5. *The Journals of Matteo Ricci,* transl. L. Gallagher, New York: Random House, 1953, p. 10.
6. Quoted in Jacques Gernet, *A History of Chinese Civilization,* transl. J. R. Forster, Cambridge University Press, 1985, p. xxvii.
7. Quoted in C. O. Hucker, *China's Imperial Past,* Stanford: Stanford University Press, 1975, p. 139.
8. J. Gernet, *A History of Chinese Civilization* (op. cit.) p. 431.

Suggestions for Further Reading

Berliner, Nancy. *Chinese Folk Art.* New York, 1986.
Birch, Cyril. *Stories From a Ming Collection.* London, 1958.
Boxer, C. R., ed. *South China in the Sixteenth Century.* London, 1953.
Chang, S. H. *History and Legend: Ideas and Images in the Ming Historical Novels.* Ann Arbor, 1990.
DeBary, William T., et. al. *Self and Society in Ming Thought.* New York, 1970.
Duyvendak, J. J. L. *China's Discovery of Africa.* London, 1949.
Eberhard, W. *Moral and Social Values of the Chinese.* Taipei, 1971.
Fairbank, John K. *The Chinese World Order: Traditional China's Foreign Relations.* Cambridge, Mass., 1968.
Farmer, E. L. *Early Ming Government: The Evolution of Dual Capitals.* Cambridge, Mass., 1976.
Hayden, George. *Crime and Punishment in Medieval Chinese Drama.* Cambridge, Mass., 1978.
Hsia, C. T. *The Classic Chinese Novel.* New York, 1968.

Huang, R. *Taxation and Government Finance in Sixteenth Century Ming China.* Cambridge, 1974.
Hucker, C. O., ed. *Chinese Government in Ming Times.* New York, 1969.
Idema, W. L. *Chinese Vernacular Fiction.* Leiden, 1974.
Johnson, A., Nathan, A., and Rawski, E., eds. *Popular Culture in Late Imperial China.* Berkeley, 1985.
Lach, Donald, F. *China in the Eyes of Europe: The Sixteenth Century.* Chicago, 1968.
Levenson, J. R. *European Expansion and the Counter-Example of Asia, 1300–1600.* Englewood Cliffs, New Jersey, 1967.
Loewe, M. *The Pride That Was China.* N.Y.: St. Martins, 1990.
Meyer, J. F. *The Dragons of Tien An Men: Beijing as a Sacred City.* Columbia, SC: University of South Carolina Press, 1991.
Mote, F. W. and Twitchett, D., eds. *The Cambridge History* Vol. 7, *The Ming.* Cambridge University Press, 1987.
Parsons, James B. *The Peasant Rebellions of the Late Ming Dynasty.* Tucson, 1970.
Perkins, D. H. *Agricultural Development in China, 1368–1968.* Chicago: Aldine, 1969.
Rawski, E. S. *Agricultural Change and the Peasant Economy of South China.* Cambridge, Mass., 1974.
Ricci, Matteo. *China in the Sixteenth Century.* Transl. Gallagher. New York, 1953.
Rossabi, M. *China Among Equals: The Middle Kingdom and its Neighbors.* Berkeley: University of California Press, 1983.
So, K. W. *Japanese Piracy in Ming China During the Sixteenth Century.* East Lansing, Mich., 1975.
Struve, L. *The Southern Ming.* Yale University Press, 1984.
Tsai, S. H. *The Eunuchs in the Ming Dynasty.* Albany: SUNY Press, 1995.
Van Gulik, R. *The Chinese Bell Murders.* Chicago, 1984; and other detective novels set in the Ming and closely modeled on Ming originals.
Waldron, A. *The Great Wall: From History to Myth.* Cambridge: Cambridge University Press, 1990.

CHAPTER 8

THE CH'ING IN PROSPERITY AND DECLINE

Scattered groups of Ming loyalists and others, including a rebellion by some of the original Chinese collaborators with the Manchus who had been granted fiefs in the south, fought against the new conquerors until the 1680s. Wu San-kuei, the Ming general who had invited the Manchus in to help suppress the rebellion of Li Tzu-ch'eng (Chapter 7) was rewarded with large grants of land in the southwest, and enriched himself through trade monopolies. When he rebelled against the Ch'ing in 1673 with his large army, he was joined by two other Chinese former collaborators who controlled most of the rest of south China. The fighting became a major civil war known as the Revolt of the Three Feudatories, and the Ch'ing did not consolidate their power over the entire country until 1681. The island of Taiwan (Formosa), which the Ming had tended to ignore and which no previous Chinese government had attempted to control (there was no significant Chinese settlement there before the seventeenth century in any case), had supported a Ming loyalist regime under Cheng Ch'eng-kung (Zheng Chenggong, 1624–1662) and his family. Known to foreigners as Koxinga (a corruption of the title given him by the refugee Ming court at Nanking and Foochou), Cheng controlled most of the coast of Fukien from his base at Amoy from 1646 to 1658. Repelled in his effort to capture Nanking from the Ch'ing, he retreated to Taiwan in 1661, driving out the Dutch who had established trading posts and forts there. After his death in 1662 his son succeeded him, and ultimately joined the Rebellion of the Three Feudatories. With its suppression, the Ch'ing turned their full attention to Taiwan and in 1683 occupied the island, thus completing their conquest after nearly 40 years of fighting.

The Manchus had been ruthless in conquering central and south China, but once resistance had been crushed the new dynasty made a genuine effort to win not only Chinese support but actual partnership. This was a far more successful approach than that of the alien Mongol dynasty four centuries earlier. The Manchus established the only long-lasting dynasty of conquest and the only one except the Mongols to rule the entire country. It is sometimes said that China has been ruled by dynasties of conquest for nearly half of its history, but this is highly misleading. Only the Manchus and the Mongols conquered the whole country, and Mongol rule of China lasted for a good deal less than a century. The other originally nomadic groups which established Chinese-style dynasties conquered only a small part of the north; the Northern Wei-Toba and its immediate "barbarian" successors from 439 to 581 is the only significant exception in that for a short time it ruled most of the north, unlike the Khitan Liao and Hsi Hsia empires in their marginal bits of the north from late T'ang to 1225, although the brief Jurchen empire, which they called by the Chinese dynastic name of Chin, covered more of the north. Unless one wants to regard the Chou as non-Chinese, or the T'ang because of its small degree of blending with Turkish strains, China was ruled by non-Chinese for only a tiny part of its history, primarily the 267-year span of the Ch'ing, although it might be more accurate to begin that period, as indicated above, in 1681 or 1683 rather than in 1644, hence only some 228 years.

The non-Chinese conquerors of China or parts of it, even Khubilai Khan, become Sinicized, because they saw Chinese civilization as the only imperial model. For practical reasons also, Chinese experience with empire made it necessary for each of these "barbarian" regimes to employ large numbers of Chinese, and to use the services of many technical experts. Until the Ch'ing they also used the Chinese written language, having none in their own traditions and finding it essential to administer their states. The Mongols, although they used Chinese characters for most records, felt the need to develop a script of their own so as to preserve their

China Proper Under the Ch'ing

separate identity. They adopted or adapted the script of the Uighurs, the Turkish inhabitants of the Sinkiang oases, and the *Secret History of the Mongols* was written in it, purporting to tell the story of the rise of Mongol power, the career of Chinghis Khan, and the acquisition of empire.

Like the Khitan and Jurchen before them (and indeed they too came from the same area of northern Manchuria), the Manchus had adopted most of Chinese civilization well before their final conquest of China. Their leader Nurhachi even took the title of emperor and moved the capital of his newly united Manchu confederacy south to the Liao valley. By his time the Manchus had largely made the transition from herding and hunting to settled agriculture, although they retained the military skills of their mounted frontier ancestors. Under Nurhachi, who fixed his capital at Mukden (Shenyang) in 1625, and even more under his son and successor Abahai (1627–1643), the process of Sinification accelerated, including the wholesale adoption of Confucianism and the employment of many Chinese as advisers and technicians. It was Abahai who changed his peoples' name from Jurchen to Manchu in 1635, and in the next year adopted the Chinese dynastic name of Ch'ing. The Manchus kept their spoken language after their conquest of China for use among themselves, and also their written language, derived from the Uighur script, in which they kept for some time parallel records to those kept in Chinese. They too were understandably anxious to preserve their separate identity, as a conquering people ruling over a vastly more numerous Chinese population. Even though they had become so completely Chinese culturally by 1644 and were to become even more so, they totalled only some 1 percent of the empire, or a little over one million people. But with Chinese collaboration on a large scale especially after the 1680s, the Ch'ing gave China good government, order, and tranquility under which it prospered as never before.

Abahai was succeeded as leader of the Manchus by a younger son of Nurhachi, Dorgon (1612–1650), who was thus in command of the invasion of China. Dorgon was a highly competent figure, but out of deference to his father Nurhachi, and following the Chinese model of filiality, he refused the title of emperor and served instead as regent for Abahai's son Shun-chih. K'ang Hsi, (Kangxi), was only six years old at the time of the conquest but matured rapidly and was in firm control before he officially became emperor in 1661. In time the members of the imperial Manchu clan were kept out of administration, although they served in a state council designed in part to keep eunuchs from wielding power and in part to ensure that strong rulers succeeded to the throne. For nearly two centuries that goal was effectively achieved. Nurhachi had reorganized what were originally tribal fighting men into companies called "banners," which operated more in the bureaucratic tradition of the Chinese army. To these were slowly added Chinese companies, and by 1644 there were 278 Manchu, 120 Mongol, and 165 Chinese companies, an army of close to 170,000, which was less than half Manchu. Abahai made the Korean kingdom of Yi his vassals after two hard-fought campaigns, and did the same with the Mongols and what remained of their state power. Expeditions northward incorporated the Amur River valley, later to be contested with the Russians. Late in the seventeenth century under K'ang Hsi the Ch'ing also conquered Outer Mongolia, beyond the Gobi Desert, and in the eighteenth century K'ang Hsi reconquered Sinkiang and imposed a "protectorate" on Tibet. Thus China once again became a major power in central Asia, now with the advantage of artillery for use against traditional nomadic mounted power. China under the Ch'ing was the largest empire by far in the world of that time.

Chinese collaborators filled about 90 percent of all official posts throughout the dynasty. Manchu aristocrats kept the top military positions, but the army, militia, and police were predominantly Chinese, as were many generals. Provincial administration was headed by two-man teams of Chinese and Manchu governors working in tandem—and of course checking on each other. The gentry, who provided unofficial leadership and authority at all local levels, remained almost entirely Chinese. The gentry continued to supply from their ranks of men educated in the Confucian classics nearly all of the officials through the imperial examination system, which was retained and expanded by the Manchus. At the capital in Peking (Beijing), the Grand Secretariat, the various ministries, and the imperial censorate were staffed equally by Chinese and by Manchus. Ch'ing China was thus administratively at least as Chinese as Manchu, in fact much more.

The Manchus, even before 1644, had been after all an outlying part of the Chinese empire. They came from an area where pastoral nomadism in northern Manchuria merged with Chinese-style intensive agriculture in the Liao valley, where the Chinese cultural model in all respects was at least as old as the Han dynasty. To protect their homeland, and their identity, they tried to prevent further Chinese emigration to Manchuria, and to keep northern Manchuria as an imperial hunting preserve. In their administration of China, they continued the now long-established imperial structure and its institutions. The emperor appointed all officials down to the level of the county magistrates, and presided over a mobile body of civil and military servants who thus owed direct loyalty to the throne. He was accessible to all his officials, who could send confidential memoranda (known as "memorials") to the emperor alone, and to which he would reply in confidence to the sender only. The

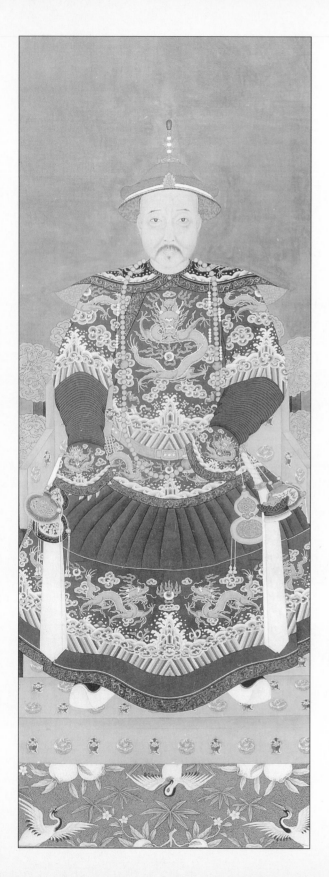

emperor had to approve all policy matters, to sign all death sentences, and hear appeals.

It was a top-heavy structure, but on the whole it worked well, for the first two centuries under strong emperors. Each official had his own extensive unofficial staff to help with the otherwise unmanageable burden of administrative and paperwork. But even so it was a thinly spread system—about 30,000 imperially appointed officials, including by far the biggest cluster in Peking and secondary clusters in the 18 provincial capitals, for a population that rose from some 150 million to over 400 million. Most of China, still over 90 percent rural, continued to govern itself through the Confucian system of the "self-regulating society." But there was a huge amount of imperial administrative business too. Communication was essential among the widely scattered provinces and districts of this enormous empire, considerably larger than the modern United States and far more populous, and between each of them and the capital, where most important decisions had to be made or approved. The Ch'ing established some 2,000 postal stations along the main and feeder routes of the imperial road system, many of which were paved and which extended into Manchuria, Mongolia, Sinkiang, and Tibet. Less urgent communications and shipments traveled by water wherever possible—most of the populated areas from the Yangtze valley southward—but for emergency messages or documents, mounted couriers using relays of fast horses could cover 250 miles a day or more. This still meant at last a week of travel from Canton to Peking, but it was almost certainly faster than anything in the West, rivaled only by the Roman courier system for parts of their empire at its height.

We know more about Ch'ing China than about any previous period, partly because its recency means that far more of the documentation is still available. But we also have a great many foreign accounts, especially after the late eighteenth century, including early Jesuit descriptions. The Europeans were fascinated by China, and they can give us a perspective, and a comparative dimension, lacking for earlier periods. Their accounts help to establish a picture of Manchu China as the largest, richest, best governed, and most sophisticated country in the world of its time. European thinkers of the Enlightenment, including Leibniz, and later Voltaire and Quesnay, were much influenced by what they knew of Ch'ing China. They were struck in particular by its emphasis on morality (as opposed to revealed religion) and on selection for office of those who were best educated—or best

Official court painting of the emperor K'ang Hsi (1661–1722) wearing the imperial dragon robes, by an unknown artist. (The Metropolitan Museum, New York)

✠ Adam Smith on China ✠

The founder of classical Western economics and advocate of the free market, Adam Smith, commented on China in his Wealth of Nations, *published in 1776 and based on the accounts of Europeans who had been there.*

The great extent of the empire of China, the vast multitude of its inhabitants, the variety of climate and consequently of productions in its various provinces, and the easy communication by means of water carriage between the greater part of them, render the home market of that country of so great extent as to be alone sufficient to support the very great manufactures, and to admit of very considerable subdivisions of labor. The home market of China is perhaps in extent not much inferior to the market of all the different countries of Europe put together.

Source: A. Smith, *The Wealth of Nations, Vol. 2.* (New York: Dutton, 1954), p. 217.

"humanized" in the Confucian tradition—through competitive examination. China, they thought, thus avoided the evils they ascribed in Europe to an hereditary nobility and a tyranny of the landed aristocracy. To them, China seemed close to the Platonic ideal never achieved in the West, a state ruled by philosopher-kings.

The Ch'ing compiled a vast new law code, dealing mainly with criminal offenses since most civil disputes continued to be handled locally through family, clan, and gentry networks. It too impressed European philosophers and legal scholars, particularly the application of law on the basis of Confucian ethics. Admiration of China led also to a European vogue for Chinese art, architecture, gardens, porcelains, and even furniture and wallpaper (another item in the long list of Chinese innovations), all of which became the height of fashion for the upper classes, especially in France and England. The foreign perspective on China began to change in the nineteenth century as China declined and the West began its steep rise. But the change in attitudes was slow, and traces of the original admiration remained for those of a more open mind, less blinded by the disease of Victorian imperialist arrogance.

Prosperity and Population Increases

The first 150 years of Ch'ing rule were an especially brilliant period, marked by the long reigns of two exceptionally able and dedicated emperors, Kang Hsi (Kang Xi, r. 1661–1722) and Ch'ien Lung (Qian Long, r. 1735–1796). As a consequence of the order and prosperity they established, population began an increase which was to continue until after 1900, probably tripling from approximately 1650. But until late in the eighteenth century production and the growth of commerce more than kept pace. Even by the 1840s and 1850s, when per capita incomes had probably been declining for two generations or more, British observers agreed that most Chinese were materially better off than most Europeans. A particularly well informed traveler and resident in China writing in 1853 provided a one-sentence summary of many such accounts by saying, "In no country in the world is there less real misery and want than in China."[1] One must remember that he wrote from the perspective of the industrializing England of Charles Dickens and knew the bad working and living conditions for most Westerners at that time. But his judgment was probably accurate about China, and is confirmed by other contemporary Western observers.

The massive growth of population, and of production to match it until late in the eighteenth century, is a good measure of the orderly beneficence of Ch'ing rule and the confident spirit of the times. Government officials diligently promoted improvements in agriculture, new irrigation and flood-prevention works, roads, and canals. More new land was brought under cultivation to feed the rising population, and more new irrigation projects constructed, than in the whole of previous Chinese history put together. The Ch'ing period also saw the completion of Chinese agricultural occupation of the cultivable areas of the south and southwest, at the expense of the remaining non-Han inhabitants, in essentially the pattern of today. Much of the new tilled land was in the hilly south, where terracing was often pushed to extremes, driving the indigenous people into still more mountainous areas, especially in the southwest. In the southeast, concentrated in the mountainous area which forms the watershed between Yangtze and West River drainage, especially in Fukien (Fujian) Province, large tracts were cleared for tea plantations (see Chapter 1). Large new acreage was also brought under the plow in the semiarid margins of north China. Yields everywhere rose with new irrigation, more fertilization, better seeds, and more intensive cultivation.

Merchants were also allowed a larger scope under the Ch'ing, larger even than under the Ming. Trade with Southeast Asia, and permanent settlements of Chinese merchants there, grew still further. Foreign trade as a whole seems clearly to have been larger than Europe's. Domestic commerce, larger still, and urbanization reached new levels and remained far more important than overseas connections. Merchant guilds proliferated in all of the growing Chinese cities and often acquired great social and even political influence. Rich merchants with official connections built up huge fortunes and patronized literature, theater, and the arts. Fleets of junks (Chinese-style ships) plied the coast and the great inland waterways, and urban markets teemed with people and goods. General prosperity helped to insure domestic peace. Silver continued to flow in to pay for China's exports, including now tea and silk to the West, and there was a large, favorable trade balance. Cloth and handicraft

production boomed as subsistence yielded to more division of labor and to increasing market forces.

Along with silver, other New World goods entered the China market through the Spanish link via Manila, most importantly new and highly productive crops from the Americas, including sweet and white potatoes, maize (corn), peanuts, and tobacco. These were all unknown in Asia before the late Ming, and in many cases they supplemented the agricultural system without displacing the traditional staples of rice, wheat, and other more drought-tolerant cereals such as millets and sorgums grown in the drier parts of the north. Potatoes could be raised in sandy soils unsuited to cereals, white potatoes in the colder areas, sweet potatoes in the south. Both produce more food energy per unit of land than any cereal crop. Corn yielded well on slopes too steep for irrigated rice. Peanuts and tobacco filled other gaps and added substantially to total food resources or to the list of cash crops, like cotton.

Early ripening rice introduced from Southeast Asia in the Sung and Ming was further developed under the Ch'ing and the period from sowing to harvest progressively reduced. In the long growing season of the south, this meant that more areas could produce two crops of rice a year, and some could manage three. Transplanting of rice seedlings, after starting seeds in a special nursery bed and then setting the young plants out in spaced rows in a larger irrigated paddy, first became universal in the Ch'ing. This greatly increased yields, as well as further shortening the time to harvest.

Ch'ing glory: the Altar of Heaven, just outside the Forbidden City in Peking, originally a Ming structure but rebuilt by the Ch'ing. Here the emperor conducted annual rites to intercede with Heaven for good harvests. The temple roofs are covered with magnificent colored and glazed tiles. (Northwest Orient Airlines)

As population increased and demand for food rose, agriculture was pushed up onto steeper and steeper slopes, as in this photograph from the southwestern province of Yunnan. Terracing required immense labor but could create only tiny strips of level land, and water for irrigation was a major problem. Terracing was necessary because by the late Ch'ing period all gentler slopes had been occupied, while the population continued to rise. This is an extreme example, but such terraces were not uncommon. (R. Murphey)

Food and nonfood crops such as tea and cotton were now treated with the kind of care a gardener uses for individual plants, fertilized by hand, hand weeded at frequent intervals, and with irrigation levels precisely adjusted to the height and needs of each crop as the season advanced. The use of night soil (human manure) now also became universal, and the amounts applied increased as the population rose, providing both the source and the need for more intensive fertilization. Rice yields probably more than doubled by a combination of all these methods, and the total output rose additionally as the result of double and triple cropping and newly cultivated land. Improvements in rice agriculture, China's major crop since Han times, plus new irrigation and other intensification of the traditional system, were probably the chief sources of food increases. Rising population totals provided the incentive, and the means, for greater intensification, but it was a process pushed also by the Ch'ing administra-

tion and its local magistrates, as well as by local gentry. The irrigation system for rice was a finely engineered affair, permitting the altering of water levels as needed and the draining of the paddies in the last few weeks before harvest. It all required immense amounts of labor, but it paid handsomely in increased yields, and a prosperous China continued to provide the additional hands needed.

These changes, improvements, and additions to an existing highly productive agricultural system help to explain how an already huge and dense population could double or triple in two centuries and still maintain or even enhance its food and income levels. Agriculture remained the heart of the economy and the major source of state revenue, but its surpluses created a growing margin for both subsistence and commercial exchange. The population figures compiled by the Ch'ing, like those of earlier dynasties, were not designed as total head counts, and were based on local

---

✠ **Why China Downgraded Science** ✠

Jean Baptiste du Halde published in 1738 A Description of the Empire of China, *based on earlier Jesuit accounts. In that volume, he wrote:*

The great and only road to riches, honour, and employments is the study of the *ching* (the classical canon), History, the laws, and morality, and to learn to do what they call *wen-chang,* that is to write in a polite manner, in terms well chosen and suitable to the subject. By this means they become Doctors *(chin-shih),* having passed the third level of examinations); soon after they are sure to have a government post. Even those who return to their provinces to wait for posts are in great consideration with the mandarin of the place; they protect their families against all vexations and enjoy a great many privileges. But as nothing like this is to be hoped for by those who apply themselves to the speculative sciences, and as the study of them is not the road to honours and riches, it is no wonder that these sorts of abstract sciences should be neglected by the Chinese.

Source: From Jean Baptiste du Halde, *A Description of the Empire of China Vol. II* (London: E. Cave, 1738), p. 124.

---

reports by village headmen enumerating households and adult males fit for military service. Land and its owners and output were also recorded, for tax purposes, and for a time, as in previous centuries, there was in addition a head tax. Since everyone knew that these figures were used for calculating taxes and for conscription or corvée labor, there was an understandable tendency for local headmen and households to understate their numbers.

Early in the dynasty it was announced that the head tax would never be raised, and it was later merged with the land tax and with taxes in the form of a share of the crop. At the same time the Ch'ing made it plain that reports of population increase were welcome evidence of the prosperity resulting from their reign. Reports showing little or no gain would reflect on the effectiveness of the local magistrate. For these and other reasons having to do with the imprecision, inconsistency, and incompleteness of the count (which often but not always excluded women, servants, infants, migrants, and non-Han people), Ch'ing population figures must be used cautiously. However, the long-term trend is clear. From roughly 150 million in the late seventeenth century, the population had reached 400 million or possibly 450 million by 1850, and 500 million by 1900. The official figures, almost certainly an undercount to begin with, and possibly an overcount after about 1750, show 142 million in 1741 and 432 million in 1851. It was strong evidence that all was well, but in time it became a burden which the system could no longer carry successfully and which produced spreading poverty and disorder.

By mid-Ch'ing (mid-eighteenth century), this had become a common sight in any Chinese town or city; the problems posed by the mushrooming population were unmistakable. This is a late nineteenth-century photograph of a crowd of famine refugees in a mission courtyard. (Keystone View Company)

KANG HSI AND CH'IEN LUNG

The Emperor Kang Hsi, completely Chinese in culture and even a poet in that language, encouraged literature, art, printing, scholarship, and artisan production. He revived and enlarged the Imperial Potteries, which turned out great quantities of beautiful porcelain, originally for the palace and court, then for rich merchants, and even for export. A patron of learning, Kang Hsi himself studied Latin, mathematics, and Western science with Jesuit tutors at his court, and corresponded with European monarchs. Toward the end of his reign he lost patience with the sectarian quarreling of the Catholic missionaries, and was incensed that a Pope in "barbarian" Rome should presume to tell the few Chinese Christian converts what they should and should not believe. But he remained interested in a wide variety of things, and is described by his Jesuit tutors as insatiably curious, as other Jesuits had earlier described the Mughal emperor Akbar.

Kang Hsi was a conscientious and able administrator of boundless energy who tried to ensure honesty in government and harmonious partnership among Chinese and Manchu officials. He went on six major state tours around the empire and showed a great interest in local affairs. He commissioned an ambitious new encyclopedia of all learning, updated and greatly expanded from Yung-lo's compilation under the Ming. At 5,000 volumes, it is probably the largest such work ever written anywhere. The huge dictionary of the Chinese language that he also commissioned and that still bears his name remains the most exhaustive and authoritative guide to classical Chinese up to his own time. He also supervised the compilation of a voluminous administrative geography of the empire. He encouraged the further spread of private academies for the sons of the gentry, and of state-supported schools for worthy but poorer boys, both of which multiplied far beyond what they had been in the Ming, to spread classical learning and open the way to office for those who mastered it. Older scholars and retired officials were sent around the empire at government expense to lecture to the populace on morality and virtue.

Kang Hsi was equally effective in military affairs. He supervised the reconquest of Taiwan, restored Chinese control over Mongolia and eastern Sinkiang, and in 1720 mounted an expedition to put down civil war in Tibet, where he then established firm Chinese authority. His armies had earlier chased the expanding Russians out of the Amur region of northern Manchuria. He then negotiated the Treaty of Nerchinsk in 1689 with the Tsar's representatives, confirming Chinese sovereignty in the Amur valley and southward. This was China's first significant engagement, and her first treaty, with a Western power. It was a contest in which the Ch'ing clearly emerged as the winners, successfully defending China's traditionally threatened landward frontiers.

Far less attention was paid to the sea barbarians—the Portuguese, Dutch, English, and others—already attempting to trade at Canton and to extend their efforts farther north along the coast. The Westerners were regarded as troublesome but were put in the same category as bandits or pirates. They were certainly not to be seen as representatives of civilized states with whom China should have any dealings. These differing responses reflected the long-established Chinese concern about their continental borders, the source of so much trouble in the past and where any challenge to their authority must be met and subdued. Their lack of concern about the maritime frontier, which had never presented any major problem for them in the past, was ultimately to prove critical. Their defenses, their front doors, and their military priorities faced the other way.

When K'ang Hsi died in 1722, the son whom he had designated as his heir to the throne became mentally deranged and there was conflict among his many other sons. Yung-cheng (Yongzheng), one of the sons, was fortuitously in Peking when his father died, with army contingents there to support him. He simply announced himself as the new emperor, imprisoned five of his brothers (who died in prison) and destroyed or undercut all opposition to him, with the help of a network of spies and informers. It was Yung-cheng who first established as the top decision-making body what came to be called the Grand Council, which met with the emperor daily at dawn. Yung-cheng, like his father, was conscientious and able. He intervened with an army in a civil war in Tibet in 1728 and established a Ch'ing resident and a military garrison at Lhasa to keep a watchful eye on what had become a chronic trouble spot, as earlier during the T'ang and Sung. Worried by the disputes over the succession on his own father's death, he kept the name of his heir-designate in a sealed box in the throne room and thus smoothed the accession of Ch'ien Lung when Yung-cheng died in 1735.

Ch'ien Lung, Kang Hsi's grandson, succeeded him in 1735. He might have reigned officially even longer, but filial piety, that greatest of Chinese virtues, prompted him to formally retire in 1796 after 60 years so as not to stay on the throne longer than his grandfather. However, he remained the real power until his death in 1799 at the age of 89. Less austere and more extroverted than Kang Hsi, his grand manner has often been compared to that of Louis XIV of France. But comparison with Louis XIV does Ch'ien Lung far from justice. Until his last years he was a diligent and humane ruler who continued his grandfather's administrative and patronage model in all respects. Not wanting to seem to rival Kang

Hsi, instead of an encyclopedia he commissioned a collection and reprinting of an immense library of classical works in over 36,000 volumes. But he also ordered the destruction of over 2,300 books which he thought were seditious or unorthodox, a censorship and literary inquisition which deeply marred his otherwise admirable record of support for learning.

Ch'ien Lung was, of all Chinese emperors, probably the greatest patron of art. He built up in the imperial palace a stupendous collection of paintings and other works of art from all past periods as well as his own. Most of it is still intact, and Ch'ien Lung also spent huge sums on refurbishing, embellishing, and adding to the imperial buildings inherited from the Ming.

Militarily, he too was an aggressive and able leader. Despite Kang Hsi's expeditions against them, the Mongols had remained troublesome. Ch'ien Lung completely and permanently destroyed their power in a series of campaigns in the 1750s, after which he reincorporated the whole of Sinkiang into the empire and gave it its present name, which means "new dominions." A revolt in Tibet shortly afterward led to a Ch'ing occupation which fixed Chinese control there even more tightly. Punitive expeditions invaded Nepal, northern Burma, and northern Vietnam and compelled tributary acknowledgment of Chinese overlordship.

Until the 1780s Ch'ien Lung, like those before him on the Dragon Throne, dealt personally with an immense mass of official documents and wrote his own comments on them. One of the Grand Council secretaries remarked, "Ten or more of my comrades would take turns every five or six days on early morning duty, and even so would feel fatigued. How did the Emperor do it day after day?"[2] But as Ch'ien Lung grew older he became more luxury-loving and surrounded himself with servile yes-men. For most of his life an astonishingly hard worker, in old age he left matters increasingly in the hands of his favorites. His chief favorite, the unscrupulous courtier Ho Shen (He Shen), built up a clique of corrupt henchmen and truly plundered the empire. When he entered the palace in 1775 as a handsome young bodyguard of 25, Ho Shen had impressed the emperor, then 65 years old. Within a year he had risen to become Grand Counsellor. At his fall after Ch'ien Lung's death, the private wealth Ho Shen had extorted was said to be worth some $1.5 billion, an almost inconceivable sum for that time and probably a world record for corrupt officials. From this exalted post and

❊ Imperial Putdown ❊

Ch'ien Lung's letter to George III reflected China's sense of superiority.

You, O king, are so inclined toward our civilization that you have sent a special envoy across the seas to bring our court your memorial of congratulation on the occasion of my birthday, and present your native products as an expression of your thoughtfulness.... As to the request to send one of your nationals to stay at the Celestial Court to take care of your country's trade, this is not in harmony with the state system of our dynasty and will definitely not be permitted.... This is the established rule (and) this is indeed a useless undertaking. Moreover, the territory under the control of the Celestial Court is very large and wide. There are well-established regulations governing tributary envoys from the outer states and limiting their coming and going.... Now is you, O King, wish to have a representative in Peking, his language will be unintelligible and his dress different from the regulation.... The Celestial Court has pacified and possessed the territory within the four seas. Its sole aim is to do the utmost to achieve good government and to manage political affairs.... The various articles presented by you this time are accepted by my special order, in consideration of their having come from a long distance. (But) there is nothing we lack.... We have never set much store on strange or ingenious objects, nor do we need any more of your country's manufactures.

Source: From J.K. Fairbank and S.Y. Teng, *China's Response to the West* (Cambridge: Harvard University Press, 1954), p. 19.

with the emperor's support he concentrated all power in his own hands, holding in time as many as 20 different positions simultaneously. He betrothed his son to the emperor's daughter and clearly intended to take over the dynasty.

Ho Shen's rise was symptomatic of Ch'ien Lung's growing senility. But it also showed the deterioration of the administrative system as a whole with no responsible figure on the throne, the chief liability of the top-heavy imperial structure. With Ho Shen in charge and giving most of his attention to building his own fortune, the efficient running of the empire was neglected, including the army. This had a good deal to do with the inconclusive sparring action against a major rebellion of the White Lotus sect erupting in 1796. The rebels were finally put down only after Ho Shen's fall under the new emperor Chia Ch'ing, who reigned officially from 1796 to 1820 but did not acquire any real power until Ch'ien Lung died in 1799, when he quickly moved against Ho Shen.

Ho Shen's career also illustrates the importance of personal connections in imperial China, a tradition still vigorous in China today. With Ch'ien Lung's death his connections were destroyed and he was soon stripped of his power and wealth. Corruption, connections, and nepotism were aspects of China, and of all Asia, that Westerners criticized as being more widespread than in their own political and economic systems. Westerners were at least embarrassed by it at home; Asians supported it as proper. Family loyalties and the ties of friendship were the highest goods. Anyone with wealth or power who did not use it to help relatives and friends was morally deficient. The family was the basic cement of society and its support system of mutual aid was blessed by Confucius and by Chinese morality as a whole. The family was a microcosm of the empire where the emperor was properly the nurturing father of his people, and all his officials right down the pyramid were enjoined to behave similarly. The connections of friendship were also part of the sanctified "five relationships" and took precedence over other considerations. Political office was relatively poorly paid, and it was expected that officials would use their position to provide for their families and friends by diverting funds or contracts and receiving "presents." People of rank were expected to live well, in keeping with the dignity of their position. Even now one hears repeated the traditional saying, "Become an official and get rich." Ho Shen broke the rules only by grossly overdoing it.

Before we examine the later decline of the Ch'ing, it is appropriate here to look at East Asian society at the height of the imperial period, when the system, for all its injustices from our modern point of view, was still in good order.

Traditional Society in East Asia

Family and Marriage

Family continuity had a semireligious aspect, as for example in the context of Chinese, Korean, Vietnamese, and Japanese "ancestor worship." The oldest surviving son had the responsibility in all of these cultures to conduct funeral services for his parents, and annual and periodic rituals thereafter, theoretically forever, so as to ensure the well-being of the departed spirits and their continued help from the hereafter. In China each generation's eldest son might thus be responsible for rituals on behalf of past generations of ancestors, by name, over many preceding centuries. In Vietnam, Korea, and Japan similar practices developed, although continuity with the ancestral past was less extensive and rituals usually did not name ancestors for more than a few generations back. But the general Asian belief in the basic importance of family and generational continuity and in the permanence of family and personal identity was a further expansion of the central role of the family as the anchor for all individuals and their place in the temporal and spiritual worlds. It also underlined and gave a critical aspect to the importance of producing sons, who could carry on the family and could perform the rituals for those who had died, which were seen as essential for both the dead and the living.

A new East Asian bride was the servant of the husband's family and was often victimized by a tyrannical mother-in-law. More so than in the West, girls could be married against their wishes and had little or no right of refusal—except through suicide. An entire genre of Chinese stories was devoted to this theme. In a typical story, a bride was carried in an enclosed cart or sedan chair to her new husband's family; when the curtains were opened, an unwilling bride would sometimes be found to have killed herself. The larger society offered few support mechanisms. Without a family or descendants to care for them, the sick, poor, and elderly could not survive. The production of offspring, especially sons, was the overriding goal for simple self-preservation. Those who did well in life were bound to help not only siblings but uncles, aunts, cousins, and *their* families. The average age at marriage was lower than in the medieval or early modern West (and lower than it has since become in Asia): approximately 21 for males and 17 for females in traditional China, and 20 and 16 in Japan.

Marriage was patrilocal: that is, the bride, who was almost invariably recruited from another village to avoid inbreeding, left her family and became a member of her husband's family. Under this patrilocal arrangement, she was the lowest status member until she had borne a son. She might visit her parents occasionally, but she was lost to them as a family member or helper and might cost them heavily in dowry. Girls were often loved as much as boys, but on practical grounds they were of far less value, although girls did much of the household work. Sons were essential for family continuity and security. Since life was an uncertain business and death rates were high, especially in the early years of life, most families tried to produce more than one son. Girls on the other hand might be sold in hard times as servants or concubines in rich households. The childless family was truly bankrupt, and might even pay relatively large sums to acquire a son by adoption. A wife who failed to produce a son after a reasonable amount of time was commonly returned to her parents as useless, for the prime purpose of marriage was perpetuation of the male line. It was not understood until quite recent years that the sex of a child is determined by the father, or that childlessness may result from male as well as from female sterility. But the woman was always blamed. In time, however, most women became willing and even enthusiastic members of their husbands' families, passing on these attitudes to their children. Eventually they might sometimes achieve considerable power.

In China and Korea bride and groom had usually not met before their wedding. Sometimes they might be allowed to express preferences, although these might be overruled in the family interest. Compatibility was rarely considered, and love marriages were extremely rare, although affection might grow in time. Divorce was rare, but though it was difficult, it was still just possible. Remarriage was even more difficult, if not impossible, and that knowledge probably helped people try harder to make their marriages work. It doubtless helped too that romantic expectation levels were not as high as in the modern West. People were trained to put individual wants second to family interest. There is abundant evidence from biographies, memoirs, popular literature, and legal records that most marriages were successful within these terms, and that husbands and wives valued and even loved one another and worked together in the family unit to reproduce the dominant social pattern.

Child Rearing

In East Asia children were taught to obey, boys as well as girls, but until about the age of seven boys were especially indulged, as were infants of both sexes. Given the pressing need for sons, boys were clearly favored, but children in general were welcomed and loved and much fuss made over them. They were often not formally named until they were about a year old and their sur-

vival was more assured; to give them a name earlier was often thought to be tempting fate. Parents sometimes made loud public complaints, for the folk religion gods to hear, about how ugly or ill-favored their child was, hoping that this might preserve it from the early death that excessive pride or pleasure in it could invite. Girls were trained early to accept their lowly place in the hierarchy of the family and of the larger society, and there seems to have been little or no possibility of rebellion.

Some modern psychological studies have in fact shown that females, at least in the modern West, are far less inclined than males to think and act hierarchically or to accept such ranking as appropriate, but we lack comparable modern studies from Asia. Women's much lower level of literacy than men also tended to mean that their voices remained unheard, including whatever objections they may have had in the past to their general subjugation. However, boys were not free of what we would call oppression, especially at the hands of their fathers, older brothers, and other male relatives. The great indulgence that boys were accustomed to often came to an abrupt end when they were seven years old. Some autobiographies suggest that this was commonly a traumatic time for the male child, no longer waited on and coddled but subjected to an often harsh discipline, especially in Japan and China.

Nevertheless, the early years of life were made as easy and pleasant as possible, and by the modern consensus that is the critical period for the development of an individual. Babies were commonly nursed by their mothers until they were at least two or three and were carried everywhere, first on their mother's back in a sling, and later in her arms or those of an older sister. Babies and younger children were handled, played with, touched, and kept close to mother, father, or siblings until they were about five or six, and given lots of love. Fathers often looked after the babies and young children. With such a start on life, it may be that the seven-year-old had become emotionally secure enough to withstand the trauma of adulthood training.

In any case, Western observers (and many modern Asians) find that the Asian adult male, especially an oldest son, remains heavily dependent on others throughout his life. He tends readily to accept the hierarchy of society and his place in it but also assumes that people will take care of him—especially his wife but also society in general, his superiors, his friends, and so on. This extreme dependency has been most remarked on in the cases of Japanese adult males, who some observers have said never grow up, or remain in practical terms helpless, expecting their wives, or others, to do almost everything for them except performing their specific professional or occupational roles. Of course there is a range of such behavior in all societies, and dependent adult males are far from unknown in our own society.

But this trait does seem to be related to East Asian child-rearing practices. While we can of course observe it best in contemporary terms, there is plenty of evidence to suggest that the patterns described above have a very long history and were part of traditional Asian societies.

The Status of Women

Although many women might have been powers within their families, their role in general was highly subordinate. There is no question that theirs was a male-dominated world, and that their chief claim to status was as breeders of sons. Females were subject first to their fathers and brothers, then to their husbands, and to their husbands' male relatives. Most East Asian widows were not supposed to remarry or even to have male friends. Given the high death rate and the unpredictable fortunes of life, many women—often no more than girls—were thus condemned to celibacy, loneliness, and penury for most of their lives. "Chaste widows" were praised, and though some managed a little life of their own, most conformed to the expected model and suffered. The suicide of widows was not uncommon.

As in the West, in hard times female infants were sometimes killed at or soon after birth, so that the rest of the family could survive. Female babies were also sold as servants or potential concubines. The selling of children seems especially heartless, but such a girl might have a better life as a slave-servant or concubine in a wealthy household than starving to death with her own family. Women were rarely permitted any formal education, and although some acquired it, they were primarily instructed by their mothers and mothers-in-law in how to be good, subservient wives, mothers, and daughters-in-law.

Power within the family brought women rewards which were especially important in this family-centered society. Their key role in ensuring family continuity brought much satisfaction. In most families women, as the chief raisers of children, shaped the future. More directly, they managed most families' finances, as they still do in Asia. Some women achieved public prominence as writers, reigning empresses, and powers behind the throne as imperial consorts or concubines. In China and Vietnam a few women became rulers in their own right. Admittedly these were a tiny handful within Asia as a whole, but Vietnam shows its links with Southeast Asia in the much more nearly equal status afforded to women. And in Japan, women writers were important, and accepted.

Among the peasantry, the overwhelming mass of the population, women played a crucial role in agricultural labor, and were usually the major workers in cottage industry, producing cloth and other handicraft goods for sale or barter. In reality, for most people, women were as important as men, even though their public rewards were far less and they suffered from discrimination.

✖ The Chinese View of Foreigners ✖

The Chinese found the Western barbarian at least as "inscrutable" as Westerners found the Chinese. Officials spoke of England as "naturally a country of barbarians with the nature of dogs and sheep, fundamentally ignorant of rites and modesty; how can they then know the distinction between ruler and subject, upper and lower? ... Their legs and feet stretch out and bend with difficulty, and at night their vision is confused.... Barbarian troops and chieftains take elephant skin (rubber) and copper strips and wrap the upper parts of their bodies for protection, so that the edge of a sword cannot wound them; the volunteers of Canton take long cudgels and bend down to strike their feet, and immediately they all fall down.... The barbarians' cunning is manifested in a hundred ways; their ships separate, and some go north and some south ... and their number changes constantly. They take troops that have been captured on successive occasions (i.e., prisoners) and successively send them back. Although they take trade as their excuse, they do not wait for an answer but suddenly raise anchor and sail away—all sorts of craft and secrecy. One cannot get any clue to it.

Source: From J.K. Fairbank, *Trade and Diplomacy on the China Coast*. (Cambridge: Harvard University Press, 1964), pp. 19–20.

Upper-class women lived a generally idle life, and commonly turned their children over to nurses or tutors. Of course there were women of strong character—as many as men—and many did become dominant within their husbands' families. Publicly they were supposed to behave submissively, but inside the household it was often different, especially for older women who had produced grown sons, or whose husbands were weaker people.

Sexual Customs

Asian women were expected to be modest and chaste. Upper-class women seldom appeared in public, and any open display of affection with their spouses was taboo, as it still tends to be. At the same time, the elite Asian cultures are famous for their erotic literature and art, and for the development of a courtesan (prostitute) tradition older than in any other living civilization. The geisha tradition of Japan and its original, the "sing-song" or "flower-boat" women of China, are well known, and formed part of T'ang culture so eagerly transported to Japan in the eighth century. Courtesans were often highly educated and accomplished. But this behavior was reserved for the privileged few. Asian courtesans were however also patronized by the elite as witty and learned conversationalists, and even poetesses, steeped in the classics and able to match wits and learning with their patrons or to cap a classical quotation with a brilliant extempore invention. Sex was only part of the courtesan's role, often a small part. Prostitutes dealing only or largely in sex were a different class, but even so there were clear grades among them, reflected in their price.

All of this—the pleasures of the elite dallying with their concubines, sing-song girls, erotic pictures and stories—was far beyond the experience of most people. For the great mass of the population, sex was a brief and often furtive pleasure after dark (which brought only a minimum of privacy), and centered on procreation. Most people lived close together, and most households included three generations sharing at most two small rooms. Privacy was nonexistent, and one was almost never out of sight or sound of other people. In Japan especially at the village level, premarital sexual experience was tolerated or even encouraged. In China, any bride discovered not to be a virgin was commonly rejected. There was, as in the West, a double standard after marriage. Wives were strictly forbidden to commit adultery and often very harshly punished for it, while male sexual infidelity was often tolerated. In practice, as pointed out, such philandering or the visiting of sing-song girls or other prostitutes was largely limited to the elite, who could afford such indulgences, as they could afford additional wives, plus concubines.

Despite the fact that they did not attend regular schools, women sometimes acquired literacy from their brothers or fathers or occasionally on their own. The best evidence is probably the respectable number of female authors, including the famous Lady Murasaki, Japanese author of the world's earliest psychological novel, *The Tale of Genji*. Court ladies such as Lady Murasaki had the leisure to learn to read and write. Literacy was expected of them, as were accomplishments in music, painting, and dance.

Law, Crime, and Punishment

In general terms, Asian thought made no place for the Judeo-Christian concept of sin, let alone "original sin," hence the image that, as has been proverbially said, "Eden was preserved in the East." Correction of deviant behavior, and if possible reform through reeducation or renewed piety, were stressed more than retribution or punishment, although these were certainly used and frequently harsh. The incidence of crime or social deviance was almost certainly less in Asia than in other areas, thanks to the self-regulating mechanism of the family and the deterrent power of the shame which individual misbehavior might bring on the group. It is sometimes said that while Western societies emphasized sin and guilt, the East stressed the unacceptability of antisocial behavior and used shame to enforce moral codes. Guilt and shame are of course similar, and interrelated, but guilt tends to be more permanently internalized while shame can to a degree be expiated or washed away, by punishment, retribution, and compensatory behavior. In addition to the social stigma of misbehavior, public shaming was commonly used as an official punishment. Criminals were publicly exhibited or executed, and were often paraded through the streets carrying placards or wearing labels indicating their offenses.

Banditry was a common response by those reduced to absolute poverty. Banditry was especially frequent in periods of political disorder; its incidence rose and fell in China with the changing effectiveness of the imperial government and the levels of peasant distress. Bandits operated most successfully on the fringes of state-controlled areas, or in frontier zones between provincial jurisdictions, areas which were often mountainous or forested. In south coastal China, coastal Korea, and Japan banditry took the form of piracy. These were areas that combined local poverty or overpopulation with opportunity: rich coastal or ocean trade routes passing nearby, local forests for shipbuilding, and ample small harbors along indented coastlines far from state power centers, which made evasion or concealment easier. Pirates and bandits often further increased the poverty of those on whom they preyed. Although their prime targets were the rich and the trade routes, these were often better protected than the common people and their villages.

Some bandit groups turned into rebels, who built on the support of the disaffected majority to overthrow the government and found a new order that could better serve mass welfare. A large share of popular fiction dealt with the adventures of bandit groups, often depicted as Robin-Hood-type figures but in any case regarded as heroes rather than as criminals. Criminals operated in towns and cities too, and in the larger cities, especially major trade centers, a genuine criminal underworld existed, as well as highly organized beggars' guilds. Controlling urban crime was often difficult because people were packed into overcrowded alleys, streets, and shanties in warren-like districts.

The incidence of banditry or piracy was often taken as a barometer of the vigor and justice of the political and social order, as well as a measure of economic hardship. It was certainly related to all of these factors, perhaps especially to economic hardship; people in general often interpreted increased banditry or piracy as a sign that the sociopolitical system was breaking down, the greatest of all disasters, and in China that the ruling dynasty had lost the "Mandate of Heaven." Of course natural disasters, commonly blamed on unvirtuous rulers, were often followed by a rise in banditry in the areas most affected. Many bandit groups and most rebellions adopted a non-Confucian or anti-Confucian religious and magic mystique. They followed secret rites, usually Buddhist or Taoist, the obvious antidote to establishment Confucianism. Dissent often began within secret societies, which had their own rituals and underground organizations; as secret societies joined or emerged in banditry or rebellion, this aspect of their origins was retained, including blood oaths of loyalty and rituals purporting to give their members invulnerability to the enemy.

Criminals were tried and laws and punishments enforced by civil courts run by the state and presided over by magistrates, rulers or their representatives, community elders, or learned men. There was no prior assumption of guilt or innocence; judgment was made and sentences arrived at on the basis of evidence, including the testimony of witnesses. East Asians had no lawyers standing between people and the law; plaintiffs and defendants spoke for themselves. In China and most of the rest of Asia, those charged with criminal behavior could be found guilty and punished only if they confessed their guilt. If they refused to do so despite the weight of evidence against them, they were often tortured to extract a confession.

It should be noted that torture was also used in medieval and early modern Europe, sometimes to extract a confession, sometimes simply as punishment. Trial by ordeal was also used in Asia, as in Europe, where the accused might prove his or her innocence by surviving a prolonged immersion under water or by grasping redhot metal. Asian law, like its European counterpart, was designed to awe all who appeared before its majesty. Plaintiffs, defendants, and witnesses knelt before the magistrate or judge; they could be whipped if they were not suitably reverential—another expression of a strongly hierarchical and authoritarian society. Apart from that, flogging was a common punishment.

As in Europe, punishment for major crimes was almost invariably death, commonly by beheading or strangulation. For especially dreadful crimes such as parricide (killing of one's parents), treason, rebellion, or other forms of filial or political disloyalty, more gruesome punishments were used: dismemberment, the pulling apart of limbs from the body by horses, or the Chinese "death of a thousand cuts." These punishments were no less gruesome than those used in Europe such as dismemberment by drawing and quartering. Punishments were seen as deterrents to would-be criminals, and as bringing shame on their families or groups. The heads of executed criminals were exhibited on poles until they rotted; this was also true in Europe until late in the eighteenth century. For all Confucianists, the body was thought to be held in trust from one's parents, and to have damage inflicted on it was regarded as unfilial, thus increasing the shame of any penal disfiguration or dismemberment, including of course beheading. (This attitude tended to prevent surgery, autopsies, or the development of anatomical and other medical knowledge which might have been gained through the dissection of corpses.)

In China a common punishment was being forced to wear a heavy wooden collar, or *cangue*, so shaped that the criminal could not feed himself and had to depend on the pity of others, to his greater shame. Prisons were, again as in Europe, dreadful places where inmates might starve if they were not brought food by relatives. For what we might call misdemeanors, Asian law tended to stress reeducation and reform. (The Communist Chinese were accused of "brainwashing" when in fact they were following a long-established Asian practice.) Criminality, or at least misbehavior, was seen as a failure of society and potentially correctable, especially with family help. Individuals were to be redeemed by reeducation wherever possible, and by the model behavior of their "betters." The long-standing East Asian concept of mutual and collective responsibility whereby every member of a family or other group such as a village or guild was held accountable for the behavior of other members provided a strong deterrent to criminality, as it still does.

People naturally worried about falling afoul of the machinery of the law and the courts, especially in criminal cases. Two important points need to be made: probably about 90 percent of all disputes and minor crimes—and probably most crimes of all sorts—never reached the courts since they were settled or recompensed through family, village, gentry or other unofficial elite or local networks. Secondly, modern Western scholars conclude that justice was probably achieved more consistently than in the West and perhaps just as successfully even as today, when Western legal justice is far from perfect. The Asian record in this respect is creditable. Most magistrates and other dispensers of justice were diligent with evidence, judicious, and concerned to see justice done, not only to avoid the censure that could ruin their careers but also because of the sense of responsibility which they bore.

But there was, as often in the West, a double standard of justice which tended to be harder on the poor, whose crimes generally stemmed from poverty, than on their social superiors. Punishments for lesser crimes were also lighter for those of higher status, or for "white collar criminals," an injustice still characteristic of modern Western law. Laws were made and administered by elite groups, whose interest in the preservation of their privileged status and property was often at least as great as their devotion to justice. Nevertheless, dishonest, disloyal, or ineffective officials were often severely punished, and even exiled or executed, although such punishments might often result from a change of rulers or from arbitrary and sometimes unfair censure.

The Later Ch'ing: Decline and Inertia

By the 1750s the dynasty was already well into its second century. The eighteenth century saw the pinnacle of Ch'ing glory, prosperity, and harmony, but even before the death of Ch'ien Lung decline had begun. Prosperity remained for most, and with it a major output of art and literature. This included new vernacular novels such as *Dream of the Red Chamber*, which prophetically deals with the decline and degeneracy of a once-great family and is still widely read. Except for the disastrous interval of Ho Shen, government remained well organized and efficient. But despite the still rising population, there was only a small increase in the number of official posts, perhaps 25 percent as against a doubling and later a tripling of total numbers. This had an obviously negative effect on governmental effectiveness, and was also bad for morale. A prestigious career in the bureaucracy, once a reasonable ambition for able scholars, became harder and harder to obtain. At the same time, the imperial ex-

aminations became still more rigidified exercises in old-fashioned orthodoxy and the memorization of "correct" texts. These were to be regurgitated and commented on in the infamous eight-legged essays (see Chapter 7), allowing no scope for imagination or initiative. "Men of talent," as they had been called since the Han, were often weeded out. The examination failure rate climbed rapidly, as the system lacked the flexibility to accommodate the ever-greater numbers of aspirants.

Disappointed examination candidates, and others who passed but were not called to office, became a larger and larger group of able and ambitious but frustrated men. Educated, unemployed, and frustrated intellectuals are a worrying problem in all societies. In China the problem was only made worse by the earlier Ch'ing efforts to expand education and to open it to larger sections of the population. Learning had always been the key to advancement. Now it was far from necessarily so. The system had hardened just when flexibility was most needed. Instead of preserving the Great Harmony, it bred discontent. Degrees, and occasionally even offices, once attainable only by examination, began to be sold. Failed candidates and disappointed office seekers provided the leadership for dissident and ultimately rebellious groups, whose numbers increased rapidly after about 1785.

The lack of firm leadership and virtuous example, under Ho Shen and after the death of the Emperor Chia Ch'ing (Jiaqing) in 1820, aggravated the burdens of overworked officials. They now had to manage districts whose populations had more than doubled. A magistrate of the Sung dynasty 500 years earlier was responsible for an average of about 80,000 people in his county. By the end of the eighteenth century the average county, still administered by a single magistrate and his staff, numbered about 250,000; many were larger, and the average rose to about 300,000 in the nineteenth century. Local gentry, landlords, merchant guilds, and sometimes dissident or even criminal groups began to fill the vacuum. There was increasing anti-Manchu sentiment, for the Ch'ing was after all an alien dynasty of conquest.

By the last quarter of the eighteenth century population growth had probably outrun increases in production. Per capita incomes stabilized, and then began slowly to fall. The poorest areas suffered first, and there was a rise in local banditry. By the end of the century there were open rebellions, which increasingly marred the remainder of Ch'ing rule. The secret society of the White Lotus, revived from its quiescence since the fall of the Mongols and the Ming, reemerged in a major uprising in 1796. Its reappearance tended to suggest to many Chinese that once again the ruling dynasty was in trouble and perhaps was losing its grip on the Mandate of Heaven. The secret, semi-Buddhist rituals of the White Lotus, and its promise to overthrow the Ch'ing, attracted many followers, drawing on the now widespread peasant distress. The rebels defied the imperial army until 1804 from their mountain strongholds in the upper Yangtze valley along the borders of three provinces. The enormous expense of suppressing the White Lotus bled the treasury, and fed corruption in the military and its procurement. The unnecessarily long campaign also revealed the decline in the effectiveness of the army, who in the end, even after the fall of Ho Shen, had to depend on the help of some 300,000 local militia.

New Barbarian Pressures

These problems were still just beginning to appear as the Ch'ing approached its third century. Even into the nineteenth century the problems remained manageable, and the traditional system continued to impress European observers, now in far greater numbers than ever before. China was still able to overawe Westerners who tried to deal with the Dragon Throne as an equal or to obtain trading privileges. Like all foreigners, they had from the beginning been fitted into the forms of the tributary system, the only way China knew how to deal with outsiders. At Canton, the only port where Westerners were permitted to trade from the mid-eighteenth century, they were not allowed to stay beyond the trading season of about six months, and were forbidden to bring in firearms or women, to enter the city proper within its walls, or to trade elsewhere on the China coast. They were obliged to deal only with the official monopoly which controlled all foreign trade, a restraint which they found galling given their image of China as a vast market filled with a variety of merchants. The Westerners were viewed as barbarians, but wilder and more uncouth than most, potential troublemakers and perverters of Chinese morality. They should be kept on the fringes of the empire and walled off from normal contact with its people.

Various attempts by the English and the Dutch to trade elsewhere or with other merchants were rebuffed. In 1755 the English trader James Flint had sailed into several ports north of Canton, including Shanghai and Tientsin, in an effort to establish trade there. He was jailed and then deported, but the emperor ordered execution for the Chinese who had served as his interpreter and scribe. By the 1790s the restrictions at Canton seemed intolerable, especially to the British, then in their own view the greatest mercantile and naval power in the world and tired of being treated like minor savages.

In 1793 George III of England sent an embassy to Ch'ien Lung led by a British nobleman, Viscount Macartney, to request wider trading rights and to deal with China as an equal nation. He brought with him as presents samples of British manufactures to convince the Chinese of the benefits of trade with the West. The articles he brought were not yet highly developed enough to impress the Chinese; they included samples of the contemporary pottery of Josiah Wedgewood, hardly likely to appeal to the inventors of porcelain. The Chinese could still make most of the things Macartney brought better and cheaper, and saw no need for his samples. The whole mission was a comedy of errors on both sides, since both were still profoundly ignorant of one another and lacked any standard of comparison. The Chinese interpreted the visit and the presents as a standard tribute mission, although from an especially distant (they had only the dimmest of notions where England was) and hence backward group of barbarians, too far from China to have picked up any civilization. Chinese politeness obliged them to accept the presents, but with the kind of inward attitude which a kindly parent might feel for the work of children.

They expected Macartney to perform the *k'e t'ou* (kowtow) or ritual submission, as all tribute missions, including kings, did before the Son of Heaven. Macartney, as a typical pompous Georgian aristocrat in his satin knee breeches and also suffering from gout, refused. He offered instead to bend one knee slightly, as to his own sovereign, rather than prostrating himself and banging his head on the floor as the Chinese ritual prescribed. Macartney said that he was "sure the Chinese would see that superiority which Englishmen, wherever they go, cannot conceal." One can almost hear him saying it! As a result, he never had a proper audience with Ch'ien Lung, only an informal interview in which the emperor did not face him, although he was kept waiting in Peking for over a month, and all his requests were refused. Ch'ien Lung sent him a letter for George III which was a masterpiece of crushing condescension, imperial Chinese style:

> I have already noted your respectful spirit of submission ... I do not forget the lonely remoteness of your island, cut off from the world by intervening wastes of sea ... [But] our Celestial Empire possesses all things in abundance. We have no need for barbarian products.[3]

One can imagine the reaction of George III and Macartney.

In 1793 it was still possible for China to get away with such haughty behavior, and it was true that China was happily self-sufficient. A Dutch embassy of 1795 which also asked for better trade conditions was similarly rejected, even though the Dutch, less concerned with power or dignity than with profits, vigorously performed the kowtow several times as they lined up at court with other representatives from barbarian countries sending tributary missions. A later British embassy under Lord Amherst in 1816 had a similarly humiliating experience.

Amherst had the bad luck to turn up just when the British in India were fighting the Gurkhas of Nepal, a Chinese tributary since 1792, and was ordered out of the country by the emperor without an audience.

Foreign trade remained bottled up at Canton under the same restrictions, increasingly frustrating to Western traders. They were now beginning to feel the new strength and pride that industrialization at home was starting to give them. Nevertheless, the accounts of China given by members of the Macartney and Amherst parties as they traveled south from Peking to Canton, nursing their rage at the way they had been treated, were still strongly positive. They found it prosperous, orderly, and agriculturally productive, with immense trade flows and with numerous large cities and bustling markets. Here are a few samples from the diary kept by a member of the Amherst mission in 1816:

> **Tranquility seemed to prevail, nothing but contentment and good humor ... It is remarkable that in so populous a country there should be so little begging ... Contentment and the enjoyment of the necessities of life [suggest that] the government cannot be a very bad one ... The lower orders of Chinese seem to me more neat and clean than any Europeans of the same class ... Even torn, soiled, or threadbare clothing is uncommon ... All the military stations are neatly white-washed and painted and kept in perfect repair, and instead of mud cabins the houses of peasants are built in a neat manner with brick. The temples are also handsome and numerous.[4]**

Ch'ing Glory, and Technological Backwardness

China may have declined from its eighteenth-century peak, but it was far from being in ruins. Although the emperors after Ch'ien Lung fell somewhat short of his or Kang Hsi's brilliance, they were conscientious and honest. The corruption which had marred Ch'ien Lung's last years was greatly reduced, his scheming favorites disposed of, and a renewed atmosphere of responsibility and service established. The official salt monopoly, which had become semiparalyzed by corruption, was totally reformed in the 1830s. This was one of many pieces of evidence that even the imperial bureaucracy still had resilience and the power to correct weaknesses. Urban culture continued to thrive as merchant wealth spread more widely and city dwellers could read the new vernacular literature, enjoy the art of the time, and attend plays. It remained a sophisticated society as well as a prosperous one, and still generally confident, even complacent. Imperial slights to barbarian upstarts like the British were in keeping with what most Chinese thought.

But all was not well domestically. The state really had no adequate long-run means to respond to the inexorable pressures of increasing population. Decline was slow at first. China was immense, and its society and economy, largely independent of state management except for the official monopolies, took time to decay. Signs of trouble here and there did not mean that the whole system was rotten—not yet, at least. Nor did governmental or military inefficiency or corruption among some officials mean that the whole administration was in trouble. Most of the Chinese world lay outside the political sphere in any case and continued to flourish after political decay was far advanced. Government was a thin layer. Both foreign and Chinese critics were often misled by signs of political weakness into wrongly assuming that the whole country was falling apart.

The basic problem was rural poverty in some areas, as population rose faster than production. Traditional agricultural technology, already developed to a peak of efficiency, had reached its limit, as had usable land. Further growth in production of any sort could be won only with new technology. China was now rapidly falling behind the West and showed no signs of realizing this, or any readiness to try new ways. There was little interest in the now superior technology of Europe, and especially not in the disruption which must inevitably accompany its spread. China continued to protect itself against such things, and against any ideas or innovations of foreign origin. It strove to preserve the Great Harmony; it was complacently and even narcissistically proud of its glorious tradition and mistrusting of anything that might threaten it. There might have been a different sort of response from a new and vigorous dynasty, but the Ch'ing were now old, rigid, and fearful of change. As alien conquerors, they were also nervous about departing in any way from their self-appointed role as the proponents and guardians of the ancient Chinese way in all things.

The still-growing commercialization of the economy and the rise of urban-based merchants were not accompanied by the developments which these same trends had produced in Europe. Individual or family wealth came not so much from increasing production as from acquiring a greater share of what already existed, through official connections or by managing the state monopolies. Merchants and their guilds never became an independent group of entrepreneurs, or sought to change the system to their advantage, as their European opposite numbers did. In the Chinese view, they prospered by working within the existing system and had few incentives to try to alter it. For longer-term investment, land was the preferred option since it was secure and offered also social prestige. Capital earned in trade went into land, to moneylending at usurious rates (always a symptom of capital shortages), or into luxurious living;

only rarely did it go into enterprises that could increase productivity, such as manufacturing or new technology.

Leisure and gracious living in gentry style were more valued in China than in the modern West, and there was less interest in further accumulation for its own sake. The gentry and the scholar-officials dominated Ch'ing China as they had since at least the Han dynasty, leaving little separate scope for merchants, who were officially looked down on as parasites and who depended on their gentry or official connections to succeed. They neither could nor wanted to challenge the Confucian bureaucracy, and were instead content to use it for their own ends. All of this discouraged or prevented the rise of private capitalism and the kinds of new enterprise and investment which were such a basic part of the commercial and industrial revolutions in the modern West. But it made perfectly good sense in the Chinese context.

In science and technology China had been an outstanding pioneer. In the eighteenth century China seemed again to be on the threshold of new technological and economic change. The Sung and post-Sung achievements are closely similar to what was worked out in eighteenth-century Europe. Until some time in the later seventeenth or early eighteenth century China remained ahead of the West in most respects. But Chinese accomplishments were primarily a catalogue of cumulative empirical discoveries, as in medicine and pharmacology, and their adaptations, rather than the result of systematic or sustained scientific inquiry. Confucianism made little place for abstract theorizing or for speculation about what was not directly perceivable. Learning concentrated on the Confucian classics, and on records of the past as the proper guide for the present and future.

The tradition of the learned man as a gentleman also created a deep division between those who "labored with their minds," as Mencius put it, and those who worked with their hands. Chinese artisans were highly skilled and ingenious but rarely engaged in theory or experiments, and most were not even literate. Scholars saw all manual work as beneath them, even experimental work. It was the joining of theory, design, experiment, and practice that produced the achievements of modern Western science and technology. This did not happen in China, which rested on its already high level of development.

It seems easier to understand why China did not move into capitalism or push on from its early successes in science and technology than to understand why Europe did. The West's abrupt break with its own past and the explosion of modern science are harder to explain. China was too successful by Ch'ing times to conceive of possible improvements or to seek change. To a poorer and less developed Europe, change and new enterprise were more compelling, as the means to "progress." In any case, by the nineteenth century China had fallen critically behind the West, and was also ruled by a dynasty old in office and suffering from the common dynastic pattern of complacency and loss of efficiency. The timing was bad, since it coincided with the rapid rise of Western power. The weakened government faced two unprecedented problems: a population bigger than ever before and now sliding into economic distress, and the threat posed by militant Westerners. Neither was ever adequately dealt with.

Corruption is endemic in all systems; its seriousness is only a matter of degree. As the nineteenth century wore on in China, it became a growing cancer sapping the vigor of the whole country. Confucian morality began to yield to an attitude of "devil take the hindmost." People and families with good connections had their lands and fortunes progressively removed from the tax rolls, as in the last century of all previous dynasties. This of course put a heavier burden on the decreasing number who still had to provide the state's revenue, mainly peasants. The strain on their already marginal position led many of them into banditry and rebellion. In all of these respects, late Ch'ing China was especially unprepared to meet the challenge of an aggressive, industrializing West. It was hard also to readjust Chinese perspectives, which had always seen the landward frontiers as the major area of threat. China was slow to recognize that external danger now came from the sea and along the coast, or to take these new hairy sea barbarians seriously. Their pressures continued to be treated as China had always treated local piracy or banditry, not as a basic challenge to the entire system.

Opium, and War with Britain

Opium imports rose dramatically after about 1810, and by the 1820s the favorable balance of trade that China had enjoyed in the seventeenth and eighteenth centuries was reversed as more and more silver flowed out of the country to pay for it, which was worrying. Most of the opium was grown in British India, though some came from Turkey and Iran. The English East India Company encouraged its cultivation as a cash crop to pay for its purchases of tea and silk in Canton and British ships dominated the opium trade.

Opium had been imported from Persia and was later grown in China for many centuries. It was widely used for medicinal purposes but began to be smoked as an addictive drug on a large scale in the late eighteenth century. Chinese addicts and their merchants and middlemen created the market for imported opium, which was thought to be superior to the domestic supply which had earlier provided the major source. Although the imperial government declared opium smoking and trade a capital offense, the profits of the trade were high

The Opium War: the British steam-powered paddle wheeler *Nemesis* destroying a Chinese fleet in a battle on January 7, 1841, near Canton. *Nemesis,* aptly named, was one of the first iron-hulled steam vessels; it was designed with a shallow draft so that it could attack inland shipping. Its guns had far greater range and accuracy than those of the Chinese ships or shore batteries, and its easy success made it a symbol of Western naval and military superiority. (Hulton Deutsch Collection Ltd., London)

for both Chinese and foreigners and the ban was ineffective. No foreign pressures were necessary. Westerners, including Americans as well as European traders, some of whom bought their opium in Turkey and Iran, merely delivered it to Chinese smugglers on the coast, who then distributed it throughout the country through a vast network of dealers. It was in short a Chinese problem, although foreign traders can hardly be exonerated. Most of the fortunes won by early American traders to China rested on opium. Its spreading use was a symptom both of the growing despair of the disadvantaged and of the degeneracy of a once-proud and vigorous system, including many of its now self-indulgent upper classes.

Meanwhile, opium provided the occasion for the first military confrontation with these new sea barbarians in the first Anglo-Chinese war of 1839–1842, the so-called Opium War. Nearly 50 years had passed since Ch'ien Lung's rebuff of Macartney and his refusal of all of the British requests. British patience was wearing thin, and new power from industrialization was ready to seek a different solution. Opium was the immediate issue that sparked the outbreak of hostilities, but much larger matters were involved. Britain and other Western trading nations wanted freer trading opportunities with the huge Chinese market, as well as direct access and recognition, as equals, by its government. They saw China as rigidly out of step with a modern world where free trade and "normal" international relations were the common ground of all "civilized" nations. They could no longer tolerate being looked down on or ignored and excluded, and

✠ Opium ✠

The imperial commissioner, Lin Tse-hsu, sent to Canton in 1839 to stop the opium trade, wrote a letter in the same year to the young Queen Victoria that read in part as follows:

Magnificently our great Emperor soothes and pacifies China and the foreign countries.... But there appear among the crowd of barbarians both good and bad persons, unevenly.... There are barbarian ships that come here for trade to make a great profit. But by what right do they in return use the poisonous drug [opium] to injure the Chinese people? ... Of all China's exports to foreign countries, there is not a single thing which is not beneficial.... On the other hand, articles coming from outside China can only be used as toys; they are not needed by China. Nevertheless, our Celestial Court lets tea, silk, and other goods be shipped without limit. This is for no other reason than to share the benefit with the people of the whole world.

Source: S. Y. Teng and J. K. Fairbank, *China's Response to the West* (Cambridge, Mass.: Harvard University Press, 1963), pp. 24–26.

they now had the means to do something about it. China's resistance to such demands was taken as proof of its backwardness; Westerners were inspired in part also by their sense of mission to use force if necessary to bring China into the modern world, for its own benefit as well as their own. Chinese and Western arrogance, though resting on somewhat different grounds, were approximately equal, and in 1839 they met head-on.

An imperial Commissioner, Lin Tse-hsu (Lin Zexu), was sent to Canton in 1839 to stop the illegal and damaging traffic in opium. Lin ordered destroyed the accumulated stocks of the drug stored there, most of which was technically the property of British merchants. Although they had no right to keep opium on Chinese soil under Chinese law, the British used the incident as a pretext to declare war. A small, mobile force sent mainly from India soon destroyed the antiquated Chinese navy, shore batteries, and coastal forces. With the arrival of reinforcements it attacked Canton, occupied other ports northward on the coast, including Shang-

hai, and finally sailed up the Yangtze to Nanking to force the still stalling Chinese government to negotiate a treaty which would grant what the British wanted. Distances, supply problems, and the unwillingness of the Chinese government to face facts made the war go on, in fits and starts, for over three years. It was a disconnected series of separate actions, each one ending in a Chinese rout and demonstrating the overwhelming superiority of Western military technology. The Chinese finally capitulated in the Treaty of Nanking, signed in 1842 on board a British naval vessel. This was the first of a long series that the Chinese came to call "the unequal treaties." Western imperialism had come to China.

The victorious British in 1842 found at Amoy (Xiamen) a nearly finished copy of a British man-of-war with 30 guns and several more on the way, and at Shanghai new paddle-wheel boats and brass guns nearby mounted on recoiling carriages, all faithful and high-quality copies of the ships and guns which had humbled China.

Notes

1. Robert Fortune, *Three Years' Wanderings in the Northern Provinces of China.* London, 1853, p. 1 6.

2. Quoted in J. K. Fairbank, E. O. Reischauer, and A. Craig, *East Asia: Tradition and Transformation.* Boston: Houghton Mifflin, 1978, p. 228.

3. From J. L. Cranmer-Byng, ed., *An Embassy to China.* London, 1962, pp. 212–213.

4. George Stanton, *Notes of Proceedings During the British Embassy to Peking in 1816.* London, 1824, pp. 153, 186, 201–202, 205, and 225.

Suggestions for Further Reading

Elman, B., and Woodside, A., eds. *Education and Society in Late Imperial China.* Berkeley, U of California Press, 1994.

Fay, P. W. *The Opium War.* Cambridge: Cambridge University Press, 1975.

Greenberg, M. *British Trade and the Opening of China.* Cambridge: Cambridge University Press, 1951.

Guy, R. K. *The Emperor's Four Treasures: Scholars and the State in the Late Ch'ien Lung Reign.* Cambridge: Harvard University Press, 1987.

Ho, P. T. *Studies on the Population of China, 1368–1953.* Cambridge: Harvard University Press, 1959.

Hsia, C. T. *The Classical Chinese Novel.* New York: Columbia University Press, 1968.

Johnson, L. C. ed. *Cities of Jiangnan in Late Imperial China.* Albany: SUNY Press, 1993.

Kahn, H. L. *Monarchy in the Emperor's Eyes: Image and Reality in the Ch'ien Lung Reign.* Cambridge: Harvard University Press, 1971.

Kessler, L. *K'ang Hsi and the Consolidation of Ch'ing Rule, 1661–1684.* Chicago: University of Chicago Press, 1976.

Ko, D. *Teachers of the Inner Chambers: Women and Culture in Seventeenth Century China.* Stanford: Stanford University Press, 1994.

Metzger, T. *The Internal Organization of Ch'ing Bureaucracy.* Cambridge: Harvard Press, 1973.

Miyazaki, I. *China's Examination Hell,* transl. Schirokauer. New York: Weatherhill, 1976.

Naquin, S. and Rawski, E. D. *Chinese Society in the Eighteenth Century.* New Haven: Yale Press, 1988.

Oxnam, T. B. *Ruling from Horseback.* Chicago: University of Chicago Press, 1975.

Perkins, D. *Agricultural Development in China, 1368–1968.* Chicago: University of Chicago Press, 1969.

Polachek, J. M. *The Inner Opium War.* Cambridge: Harvard Pres, 1992.

Rawski, E. S. *Education and Popular Literacy in Ch'ing China.* Ann Arbor: Michigan Press, 1978.

Rawksi, T. G. and Li, L. M., eds. *Chinese History in Economic Perspective.* Berkeley: California, 1991.

Ross, J. *The Manchus.* New York: AMS Press, 1973.

Rozman, G., ed. *The East Asian Region: Confucian Heritage and its Modern Adaptation.* Princeton: Princeton Press, 1993.

———. *Urban Networks in Ch'ing China and Tokugawa Japan.* Princeton: Princeton Press, 1973.

Skinner, G. W., ed. *The City in Late Imperial China.* Stanford: Stanford Press, 1977.

Smith, R. J. *China's Cultural Heritage: The Ch'ing Dynasty.* Boulder: Westview, 1994.

Spence, J. *Ts'ao Yin and the K'ang Hsi Emperor.* New Haven: Yale, 1988.

Van der Sprenkel, S. *Legal Institutions in Manchu China.* London: University of London, 1962.

Wakeman, F. *The Great Enterprise: The Manchu Reconstruction of Imperial Order in Seventeenth Century China.* Berkeley: California, 1986.

Will, P. E. *Bureaucracy and Famine in Eighteenth Century China.* Stanford: Stanford Press, 1990.

Wong, R. B. and Will, P. E. *Nourish the People: The State Civilian Granary System in China, 1650–1850.* Ann Arbor: Center For Chinese Studies, 1992.

Wu, S. H. L. *Communication and Imperial Control in China.* Cambridge: Harvard, 1970.

CHAPTER 9

PREMODERN VIETNAM AND KOREA

The people and civilizations of Vietnam and Korea, so deeply in the shadow of China (and in Korea more recently of Japan) tend to be dismissed by these two East Asian giants as of minor importance. In fact they are bigger than any European nation except the recently reunited Germany, and each has a very much older history. When the ancestors of modern Europeans were living in the forests of northern Europe in preliterate tribal cultures, Vietnamese and Koreans were highly advanced. Vietnam saw one of the earliest developments of agriculture and of metallurgy (see Chapter 2) in the world. Korea helped to pioneer the wide use of printing. From or before the time of the Han dynasty in China, both countries adopted most of Chinese literate civilization, while retaining at the village level a distinctively indigenous culture. But the wholesale adoption of many elements from China did not weaken either country's strong sense of separate identity, or their determination to assert and then to maintain their political independence from the Chinese colossus. Each country's history is important for itself; in a European context, each would be a major power and an essential focus of specialized study, like French, British, Italian, or German history. As it is, both have been totally overshadowed within East Asia by China (and latterly by Japan), so that very few scholars outside the countries themselves have troubled to study their history or culture. This is a serious deficiency, although there are reasons beyond simple Chinese- or Japanese-centered myopia.

Although most premodern Korean records are in Chinese (the East Asian language of learning) and for recent decades in Japanese, Korean is a separate language, related to Japanese but not accessible on that basis. Vietnamese is distantly related to Chinese, and records there were kept in Chinese for the same reason as in Korea, with more recent records in French and in phonetically transcribed Vietnamese. The overwhelming scholarly effort on East Asia has been devoted to China and Japan, where learning the relevant language (ideally both, given the close interaction between the two countries and the vast literature written in each) is in itself virtually a lifetime work. To learn Vietnamese or Korean on top of that is a task which perhaps understandably very few have been willing to undertake. We badly need more work on the history of both countries. Apart from their own importance in themselves, comparative study invariably brings new perspectives. We can understand China and Japan better, if that is our goal, by examining the Vietnamese and Korean experiences, each representing a different variant of the East Asian totality.

Early Vietnam

Early Vietnamese history is summarized in Chapter 2. As indicated there, archaeological work, especially on the origins of agriculture, is hampered by the rapid decay of

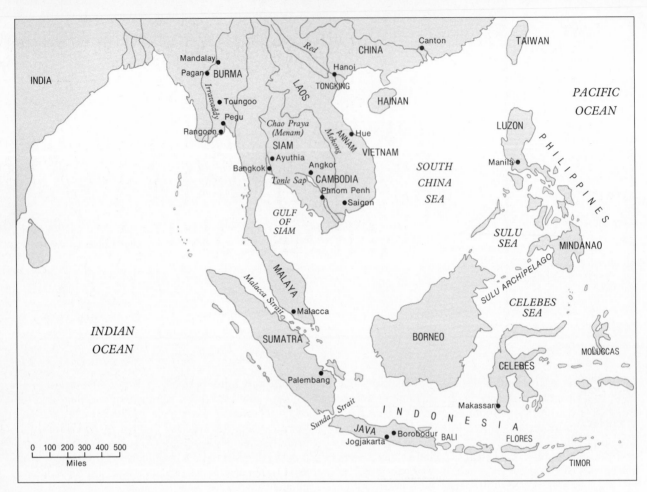

Southeast Asia

all organic remains in this hot, wet climate. Nevertheless it seems likely that as early as 8000 B.C. the Hoabinhian culture of what is now northern Vietnam had made the transition to agriculture. People lived in fixed permanent settlements where they accumulated and stored food surpluses and made Neolithic stone tools. Not long thereafter these people were keeping pigs and chickens (both native to mainland Southeast Asia), and perhaps by 4500 B.C. working bronze, as in the Dongson culture named for a site in northern Vietnam. The nature of their agriculture is unclear; it probably centered on root crops, and somewhat later on rice (also native to Southeast Asia) and on millet, diffused from China. In any case, the Neolithic revolution seems to have taken place as early in Vietnam as anywhere in the world.

As mentioned in Chapter 1, the Vietnamese people are a closely related part of the greater East Asian whole, especially close to the people of southern China but genetically related also to Koreans and Japanese.

Their language also suggests that they came originally from the general area of south China, like the people of Burma, Thailand, Laos, and Cambodia, but if so, long before the beginning of written records. There are no significant physical barriers between Vietnam and China—low mountains at best—and climatically also there are few differences from south China. Both areas were equally suited to the early development of rice cultivation, although that probably spread northward from Vietnam rather than southward from China, along with pigs, chickens, and the water buffalo. By the time of the Ch'in-Han conquest, northern Vietnam and southern China were closely similar culturally, and formed part of the single state and language of Yüeh, with twin capitals at Canton and Hanoi. We do not know how long this state, or the cultural unity it exemplified, had existed before that time, nor do we know how long the people we call Vietnamese had inhabited the area. The valley of the Red River, with its mouth near Haiphong (the port of

The eighth-century Buddhist stupa at Borobodur in central Java, chief remaining monument to the Indianization of Southeast Asia before the arrival of Islam. (Brian Brake/Photo Researchers)

Hanoi), was the major center of Vietnamese agriculture and the heart of Vietnamese culture, and later, the Vietnamese state. But it is unclear when agriculture moved down onto the river valleys and deltas of this part of East Asia from its probable origins in the adjacent highlands; perhaps this took place at about the same time as in the Indus valley of northwest India, roughly about 3000 B.C.

Despite its close connection with south China, however, Vietnam shows equally close connections culturally with the rest of Southeast Asia, of which in a larger sense it is a part. This may suggest trade and other ties well before the building of the Yüeh state and the subsequent Chinese conquest, although we have no concrete evidence. Most of the rest of the people of Southeast Asia apparently came originally from China too, and in the course of their migrations southward may have built or left interregional bonds of some sort. As described in Chapter 1, elite, literate Chinese culture was in effect superimposed in Vietnam onto a far older peasant-village base (probably at the same time superseding the earlier elite Vietnamese culture, of which we know little), which still shows by far its strongest affinities with the Southeast Asian world.

This is still evident at the village level, and apparent for the culture as a whole. As in the rest of Southeast Asia, women have always been far more nearly equal to men than in the rest of East Asia. Women could inherit, often retained their own family names at marriage, and passed them on to their children. Property often descended through the female line, divorce was relatively easy, and males often paid a bride-price to obtain a wife, the reverse of the East Asian pattern elsewhere. Marriage was usually matrilocal; the new family commonly moved to the wife's village or household, and property was held jointly. Women took an active part in courtship and lovemaking, and were commonly entrusted with the management of family finances and also of business affairs more widely. Women often served as diplomats, and many women became political rulers, of whom there are many examples in Vietnam. Even the habit of chewing betel leaf, an Indian and Southeast Asian trait, was to be found in Vietnam too. Buddhism spread to Vietnam along with the rest of mainland Southeast Asia far earlier than to China, and may have antedated the adoption of Confucianism. Most Vietnamese were Hindu-Buddhist, as in Cambodia and Indonesia, although the Vietnamese elite had adopted Confucianism by the sixteenth century. Other originally Indian aspects of culture spread there too at about the same time and tended to predominate in law, politics, and kingship.

The Chinese Connection

But in the valley and delta of the Red River rich alluvial soil and warm, moist climate, ideal for the growing of rice, supported very early a productive agricultural system and an accompanying density of population which matched on a smaller scale the similar developments in China. The southward extension of Chinese influence, and finally the Ch'in-Han conquest, spread relatively easily into this adjoining microcosm of China, far more so than into the mountainous majority of south China, whose incorporation within the empire, settlement by Chinese, and absorption into Chinese culture were long

Goddesses from a frieze at Angkor Wat. Despite its clear Indian origins, Southeast Asian art diverged early into its own styles, as these beautiful and unmistakably Cambodian figures suggest. (Black Star)

delayed. The Chinese referred to Vietnam as Nam-viet, the name it carried among the Yüeh-speaking Cantonese of Ch'in times. In standard Chinese Nam-viet was simply "south Yüeh," whose principal capital was at Canton. It was understandable that this first creation of empire by the Ch'in should conquer first the Canton area and then its adjoining partner and close equivalent in the Red River valley. Nam-viet, or Vietnam, fell away from Chinese control with the collapse of the Ch'in, but remained an independent though Chinese-style bureaucratic state until 111 B.C., when Han Wu Ti's campaigns reclaimed it and reestablished a Chinese government under three commanderies. The Chinese writing system came with the Han conquest, together with Confucianism and the bureaucratic apparatus of the imperial state.

Neither the Chinese conquest nor the earlier Nam-Yüeh state included the mountain areas which fringe the Red River valley and the western edge of the narrowing coastal lowland southward, which continue to the present to be inhabited by ethnically and culturally different peoples in considerable variety, whom the French were later to call simply "Montagnards" (mountain people). Their economy is still relatively undeveloped, and they never became part of the irrigated rice economy of the lowlands, subsisting instead on shifting (slash and burn) agriculture, hunting and gathering, and a little dry or upland rice growing. Primarily as a result the mountain areas have remained very thinly settled, but as the Vietnamese state matured and expanded it tried to bring

them under some degree of control, or at least to tie them into (largely nominal) tributary relationships.

South of the Red River valley was the Indianized kingdom of Champa, much involved with maritime trade (through which it acquired Indian influences) and also with piracy, in part because it seems not to have developed a central state and instead remained a separate set of coastal kingdoms, often in conflict with each other, and periodically or chronically with the Vietnamese. Han rule in the Red River valley of the north was naturally resented, and provoked what one may call the origins of Vietnamese nationalism. There was a major uprising in A.D. 39 which produced the first of many women heroes. The Chinese had executed a Vietnamese lord on suspicion of disloyalty, and as a warning to other restive Vietnamese leaders, but his widow and her sister, Trung Trac and Trung Nhi, raised an army and briefly drove the Chinese out. On the return of Han conquest and control after two years the sisters jumped into the river and drowned themselves, but their memory is still honored, and celebrated by Vietnamese girls every year on Hai Ba Trung Day in March.

Even before the final fall of the Han in A.D. 220, Vietnam had broken away from Chinese control, and like China in the same period became involved in civil war as well as continuing struggles against Champa. Indian influences were renewed as Indian merchants and Buddhist monks strengthened both the religious and the legal-political ties with India, as with the rest of Southeast

Asia, an area which had always been notably open to trade by sea, and, along the trade routes, to cultural influences. With the rise of the T'ang, Chinese control was reasserted over Vietnam, but only as far south as the 17th parallel, about halfway to the southern part, which was then the limit of Vietnamese occupation. The T'ang reconquest strengthened the hold of Chinese-style elite culture, but also brought in Mahayana Buddhism, to merge with the Hinayana or Theravada version which had been established in Vietnam earlier. As in China, Buddhism, Confucianism, and Taoism also tended to merge with each other, and most Vietnamese followed aspects of all three. The meeting of Indian and Chinese influences was reflected strikingly in Vietnamese art and architecture: both stupas (dagobas) and pagodas as well as an amalgam of the two, palaces and painting which were a blend of Chinese and Indian styles, and together with the other earlier Indian influences such as betel chewing, a culture which was a compound of both plus the indigenous Southeast Asian base.

Vietnam broke away once again from Chinese control with the collapse of the T'ang, and from that time on was able to maintain its political independence despite repeated Chinese attempts at reconquest. When one considers the huge size and weight of numbers of China and its position right next door, this is an amazing feat. It reflects the determination of the Vietnamese, like the Koreans, to remain their own people, however much they admired Chinese civilization and eagerly adopted it. The Sung wisely accepted tributary status from Vietnam, but when the Mongols overran China they sent three successive expeditions to conquer Vietnam, in 1257, 1285, and 1287, each of which the Vietnamese repulsed. Given the Mongol record everywhere else (again not counting Japan and Java), this is even greater testimony to the fierceness with which the Vietnamese defended their country. The Mongols took Hanoi in the course of each expedition, but were soon forced to withdraw by determined Vietnamese resistance, and in the end followed the Chinese pattern of accepting tribute instead.

When T'ang control of Vietnam ended, the country was unified for the first time under its own rulers, unlike the period of fragmentation and civil war after the fall of the Han. Unification was primarily the work of Dinh Bo Linh, who declared himself emperor in 968. Dinh accepted tributary status with the Sung but at the same time organized effective resistance against further Chinese pressures and the early Sung effort at reconquest. A dynasty which is called later Li, or Le, to distinguish it from earlier Vietnamese regimes, ruled the country after Dinh's death, from 1010 to 1225, very much in the Chinese institutional style, including a civil service recruited through a Confucian-based examination system. The Le were succeeded in 1225 by the Tran dynasty, which ruled Vietnam until 1400. Their chief, and remarkable, accomplishment was the successful defense of Vietnam against the Mongol hordes, which was all the more remarkable given the devastating Mongol conquest of Korea, which in addition was farther from the Mongol base and much more easily defended given its mountain and gorge barrier boundaries and the mountainous nature of the country as a whole.

Southward Expansion

The Han and T'ang had divided Vietnam into the Red River valley and delta, which they called Tongking ("eastern capital") and the narrow coastal plain south of it which they labeled Annam (or Annan—"peace in the south"), like many Chinese names a euphemism. Annam was a T'ang tributary, but to its south was the kingdom or kingdoms of Champa, as indicated already, occupied by a different people, the Chams. They were part of the larger Malay family and spoke a version of Malay, but had been heavily Indianized, adopting Sanskrit and many other aspects of Indian culture, including Hinduism and Buddhism, or an amalgam of both. They were more or less chronically at war with the Vietnamese, and for a time controlled parts of Annam. But with the rise of the independent Vietnamese state and after their victory over the Mongols, the tables were turned. In a great battle in 1471 the Chams were overwhelmingly defeated and their power greatly reduced. Champa was finally absorbed by an expanding Vietnamese state in 1720. Some of the surviving Chams fled to Cambodia, but probably as many were absorbed into the Vietnamese population and are still discernible as a small element in the south.

Farther south beyond Champa was the kingdom of Funan, to give it its Chinese name, like Champa heavily Indianized but probably related to the neighboring Khmers of Cambodia. We know relatively little about Funan, but it seems likely that it was, like Champa, a loose association of local states rather than a single kingdom. The people of Funan were maritime traders and shipbuilders who ranged widely over Southeast Asia by sea, and even exchanged diplomatic missions with China. Funan fell to the southward advance of the Chams, then to the conquering Khmer empire in the course of the sixth and seventh centuries A.D., and ultimately to the southward expansion of the Vietnamese state.

In the north, where the Vietnamese state originated, population pressures in Tongking probably contributed to expansion southward; the north was blocked by China, and mountains to the west offered little attraction. Champa piracy often provided another motive. A new "later" Le dynasty came to power in 1428 which was to rule until 1789. The Tran regime had fallen to a usurper in 1400, and the then new Ming emperor Yung-lo sent an army to intervene. It had occupied Hanoi by 1406, but patriotic Vietnamese resistance exploded in 1418, and in 1427 Yung-lo's successor concluded that the enormous Chinese effort was not worth it as well as unlikely to succeed. Chinese forces were withdrawn and Vietnam was once again independent, though retaining its tributary status. The leader of the Vietnamese struggle against the Chinese, Le Loi, established the second Later Le dynasty in 1428, under whose direction the Chams were conclusively defeated. Le Loi also accepted Chinese tributary status, but while sending tribute, Le Loi insisted that "We have our own mountains and rivers, our own customs and traditions," and he too took the title of emperor, the ruler of Dai Viet (great Viet), a distinction based on the Chinese label for their own dynasties.

With the Chinese expelled, Le Loi's successors, ruling from Hanoi, administered their country firmly on the Chinese model, with provinces, prefectures, and counties. There were nine ranks of officials, civilian and military, for which men were selected through a Chinese-style examination system. Military colonies were established on the expanding southern frontier, and a detailed new law code promulgated. The emperor also issued, very much in the Chinese style as well, a moral code which, as in the Ch'ing practice, was read aloud and commented on from time to time in every village and town. The Le supported literature and compiled its own dynastic history, all written in Chinese. Thus the Chinese style totally dominated at least the educated sector in Vietnam. To some degree the borrowing of Chinese-style administration represented an overkill, for a country which even as it expanded southward was only a small fraction of China's size. And the wholesale adoption of Chinese culture, including dress, tended to separate the governing elite even more sharply from the nonliterate village masses who were after all the great majority of the population, as everywhere else in East Asia. However the legal codes did reflect the totally different status of women in Vietnam, as in the rest of Southeast Asia.

As the Vietnamese expanded southward, they acquired the former Cham capital of Hue near the southern border of Annam, not long before their final victory in 1471. But in 1527 General Mac Dang Dung seized power at Hanoi. Through Chinese mediation as "elder brother" in 1540, General Mac was recognized as ruler in Tongking, while the Le and Nguyen family coalition withdrew to Hue as their capital. The Mac regime in Tongking did not last long, and in 1592 the head of the Trinh family overthrew it and usurped the throne in the name of the Le dynasty, bringing the nominal Le emperor from Hue to Hanoi, an arrangement which the Chinese accepted. The Trinh family were in fact bitter rivals of the Nguyen family and continued to try to eliminate their power in Annam; the civil war between them

lasted until 1674. By the 1670s the Trinh regime was mortally weakened, although it continued in nominal power; the Nguyens completed the conquest of the far south of the Mekong delta, known as Cochin China. This was largely at the expense of the weakening Khmer empire and its people; most of those who survived fled to Cambodia, although as with the Chams many of their descendants are still recognizable in southern Vietnam. This southernmost area was taken or absorbed by 1740, and by the end of that century virtually all of modern Vietnamese territory had been acquired. This history of expansion by conquest has made the Vietnamese both respected and feared as a power by their neighbors in Laos, Cambodia, and especially Thailand, and it still contributes to bitter tensions in the area.

Both rival families, Trinh and Nguyen, continued to claim loyalty to the Le emperor, and both continued the earlier almost carbon copy of Chinese administration and literate culture in the areas they controlled. Nevertheless, in the course of the fifteenth century the Vietnamese developed their own writing system, better suited to indicate the sounds of their spoken language. It used new Chinese-style characters invented for this purpose, most of them combining a Chinese character which had a sound (such as *k'o,* "mouth"), with another, or a newly minted one, which gave the meaning. It was rather cumbersome in practice, but it had the key virtue of giving the Vietnamese their own system as a way of asserting their distinctiveness despite their heavy use of other aspects of Chinese culture. As in the later periods of Chinese dynasties, large landed families tended over time to accumulate wealth and power, in effect at the expense of state power and revenues, and as in China they did not use it well, or for the welfare of the people at the village level. Nevertheless the economy continued to grow, and with it the population, which increased from about three and a half or four million in 1400 to about nine million in 1800. Urban centers and interregional trade developed accordingly and the economy became more commercialized and monetized.

Vietnam has often been called the "Lesser Dragon," a reference of course to China, of which it was, one might say, a pocket-size version (although it is much larger than the whole of the British Isles). But it was far from being a reduced carbon copy. In some ways it is ironic that, having fought for and won their independence with the fall of the T'ang (as during the centuries between the fall of the Han and the rise of the T'ang, and in the centuries before 111 B.C.), the Vietnamese adopted Chinese forms, in administration, literature, and Confucian morality even more enthusiastically than in the past. As we will see, the same was true in Korea, especially after the Mongol debacle. But both countries never wavered in their determination to maintain their separate distinctiveness and their political independence. Vietnam's ties with the greater Southeast Asian world in fact probably helped to make it even more distinctive from China than was the case with Korea, although such things are hard to measure. In any case, both offer different versions of the Chinese model. Apart from being important to study for themselves, they can give perspective on China and on greater East Asia, if only by showing which aspects of the Chinese model were present and which absent, and thus provoking the question of why in each case. Vietnam's circumstances were both similar to and different from China's, and the same is true for Korea.

Korea

Korea offers another variant of the Chinese pattern, but as in Vietnam, elite, literate Chinese culture was superimposed on a very different and distinctively Korean base which still shows through clearly. As in Vietnam, Korean culture had a long history before it developed close relations with, and ultimately conquest by, the Chinese in the time of the Han dynasty. Early Korean history, or what little we know of it, is summarized in Chapter 2 and need not be repeated here, including its mythical component. The fact that Koreans developed these myths about their origins and about the early beginnings of civilization there, however unreliable they may be, is an indication of their sense of separateness from China and their pride in their own tradition. We do know that a Korean state called Choson, the traditional name for the country, was in existence in the first millennium B.C. with its capital at Pyongyang, or so Ssu-ma Ch'ien tells us in the *Shih Chi* (see Chapter 3), and according to the *Shih Chi* three successive dynasties ruled from there. It does seem clear that a Chinese-style state was established well before the Han conquest of Korea, or the northern two thirds of it, in 108 B.C. Such developments, separate at least politically from China, did however rest on the spread of agriculture and iron tools from the great neighbor to the south, and before it of bronze. Bronze daggers and spearheads are found in Korean tombs and burial sites from the ninth century B.C. on, and by the fifth century iron and then copper coins in the shapes of knives and spades, closely similar to the forms made in mid-Chou China and in the state of Yen centered on modern Peking and hence almost next door. Both bronze and later iron implements seem to have been made in Korea rather than simply imported from China, since some of the molds from which they were made have been found there as well.

Technology spreads relatively easily, but as it does so does not obliterate the cultures to which it spreads. Chinese accounts of Han times describe the Koreans as earthy, frank, direct, robust, spontaneous, and some-

Yi Dynasty, Korea

times, by Chinese standards, even vulgar, as opposed to the proper and ritually constrained behavior of elite Chinese Confucians. Many of these characterizations still fit Korean culture, which, especially below the top elite level, seems refreshingly open and good-humored by contrast especially with Japan but also with China. Korean culture has remained full of a robust vitality with a ready sense of humor and even what we might call horseplay; this and the persistence of Korean folk religion beneath the Confucian veneer have led some observers to compare the Koreans with the Irish. But Korean culture preserved other perhaps more important traits which still help to distinguish it. Probably the most important was the persistence of hereditary privilege and the dominance as a result of an aristocracy of birth, something which was discarded in China under the Ch'in. For quite different reasons, since there was no connection with Southeast Asia, Koreans also preserved their original patterns of matrilocal (instead of patrilo-cal) marriage, and an inheritance system which nor-mally left half of what was inherited to females; even the eldest son got only half. This was changed only in the sixteenth century when the Yi dynasty (1392–1910) im-posed a massive Sinification and in effect forced Kore-ans into the Chinese pattern.

Food and dress, fundamental to most cultures, re-mained distinctively Korean, as did house styles and in-deed most of what one may call the bases of everyday life. No Korean meal, house, or clothing outfit could be mistaken for Chinese or Japanese, at least until recent times in the avalanche of "modernization," which too often means simply "Westernization," among a few urban people. For example, white is the color of mourn-ing in China, but was the common color of Korean gar-ments, with usually a loose cut darker jacket worn over it. Men wore the distinctive stovepipe hats, and much more often than Chinese sported beards. Dance, includ-ing the use of masks and syncopated music, was and re-mained far more prominent in Korean than in Chinese culture, and so on.

As pointed out in Chapter 2, the Koreans probably came from somewhere in north central Asia, via Manchuria; their language, in the Altaic family like Japanese, suggests this, though we have no other evi-dence, and no information to show how long they may have inhabited the Korean peninsula, although they probably entered over many centuries and their migra-tion continued into early historic times. Comb-marked pottery was being made there by at least 4000 B.C., probably earlier, but we have no clues to who the mak-ers may have been. The principal physical distinction from China is the dominance of mountains in Korea, and the colder winter climate, especially in the north-ern half. This was and is a less munificent agricultural base than China's, made still less so by periodic drought, in common with much of north China and Manchuria. Only a little over 16 percent of the land area is cultivated even now, the rest being in slope too steep to use. Primarily for this reason, Korea, like Japan, de-veloped agriculture later and remained considerably poorer materially than China or Vietnam. Mountains also fragmented the country economically and politi-cally, and, again like Japan, it was politically unified rel-atively late. Nevertheless it seems clear that a distinc-tive Korean culture had developed long before it came into effective contact with China, and that it retained its distinctiveness under Chinese rule and despite what became sweeping Sinification.

Korea is larger than Britain, hardly a small country by European standards. A central mountain spine runs down the center of the country from the Ch'ang Pai Shan ("long white mountains") which mark the border with Manchuria. Easiest communication with China was often by sea to and from the Shantung peninsula, and there are plenty of good harbors along the west and south coasts, where the coastal plain is a good deal wider than on the east, although most communication with Japan was understandably from ports on the south-east coast, especially Pusan. The southern coastal plains have remained the major rice-producing areas, since with the help of the surrounding sea their climate is warmer and moister. Northward the peninsula widens somewhat, winters are long and cold, and agriculture is much less productive. The fact that the Pyongyang area, in the north, was apparently the center of the earliest Korean states suggests the prominence of Chinese in-fluence, and perhaps also the longer Korean settlement of the north than of the south as they moved into the peninsula from Manchuria and northeast Asia.

Han Conquest and After

In 109–108 B.C. the expansionist campaigns of Han Wu Ti conquered the early Korean state of Choson and in-corporated roughly the northern two-thirds of the peninsula, with Chinese-style commanderies under the overall supervision of the northern one based at Py-ongyang, referred to by the Chinese as Lo-lang. There was substantial Chinese settlement, as military gar-risons and as permanent residents, and the total Chi-nese population may have reached half a million. Promi-nent Chinese families built splendid tombs in which they left samples of Han art, including beautiful lacquer-ware. Chinese occupation and rule outlasted the fall of the Han even after the Han garrisons were withdrawn, but by the fourth century, with north China under "bar-barian" rule, Korean groups overran the Chinese colonies and from thenceforth the country as a whole was politically on its own, although divided internally for many subsequent centuries.

Chinese rule had been extended at least as far south as the Han River valley, where Seoul now lies, and, both there and farther north, families of Chinese descent ap-pear to have hung onto positions of prominence for some time. All of this suggests comparisons with Roman Britain, both before and after the Roman garrisons were withdrawn, over more than four hundred years in which Britain was incorporated in the Roman world both politi-cally and culturally, only to be reclaimed in the end by the British tribes. But as in Korea, Britain even under in-digenous rule retained much of the cultural heritage of Rome, and the Roman presence in Britain, like the Chi-nese in Korea, left behind a major legacy which helped to shape the subsequent growth of both cultures, as well as many monuments: palaces, temples, patrician houses, and so on, more of which are still being discov-ered by archaeologists.

A masterpiece of Korean art in bronze from the Silla period, sixth or seventh century A.D. This seated figure is Maitreya, Buddha of the future. (National Museum of Korea, Seoul)

Three Kingdoms

In the wake of the Chinese retreat and collapse in the fourth century, three rival Korean kingdoms emerged, sharing dominance over the peninsula: Koguryo in the north, Paekche in the southwest, and Silla in the southeast, the last two separated to an extent by the central mountain spine. Koguryo originated as a confederation of five tribes of mounted warriors who dominated the mountain areas along the border with Manchuria and then spread their power southward, supporting themselves in large part by raiding agricultural communities on both sides of the border. They were obviously opponents of the Chinese establishment in Korea, and in chronic conflict with them. Despite punitive raids against them and the repeated sacking of their home base and capital region on the Yalu River, they survived as a power, and it was largely their victories which ended the life of the Han commandery of Lo-lang. In the course of the fourth century Koguryo became the rulers of roughly the same northern two-thirds of Korea that the Chinese had incorporated in their empire, adding other tribes to their numbers in the process.

The south had remained outside Chinese control, and especially in the southeast was far more in touch with Japan than with China. Other tribes, originally related to the ancestors of Koguryo, who had migrated southward, developed a rival state in the southwest which they named Paekche, while in the southeast still another group of tribes fought off Koguryo control and established their kingdom, which they named Silla. On the south coast, yet another tribal grouping joined together to form what is referred to as a league, called Kaya, which had especially close ties with early Japan, probably blood ties which related them to "cousins" who had migrated to Japan and whose help could be summoned in Korean internal struggles. Since it seems likely that the people we now call Japanese entered those islands from Korea, and probably over a longish period, such ties would make sense. They were close enough also, as presumably were trade links, that the early Japanese even kept a garrison and for a time what was in effect a piece of Japanese property at the port they called Mimana on the highly indented south coast of Korea.

The Kaya league was never an effective contender for control of all of Korea, however, which until the late seventh century was contested instead among the larger rival states of Koguryo, Paekche, and Silla. Although Chinese rule had ended, much Chinese cultural influence remained and continued to spread in Korea, while at the same time the chaos following the fall of the Han spawned a stream of Chinese refugees, not only into south China (most of them) but also northward into Manchuria and Korea. The three rival Korean kingdoms each cultivated a Chinese connection in the hope of using Chinese influence, or possibly even intervention, to strengthen their side. Koguryo even accepted Chinese tributary status by agreements with the successive "barbarian" regimes which ruled north China, and with the southern dynasties as well, an obvious play for Chinese help. Such connections greatly assisted the further spread of Chinese influence in Korea, including the introduction of Buddhism by a Chinese monk sent in A.D. 372 from the short-lived Chin dynasty in north China to Koguryo. At about the same time the knowledge and use of Chinese characters spread to Korea. Koguryo set up what they called a university to teach the Confucian classics, and began work on a Chinese-style code of law. There were no earlier written records in Korea and the first texts still preserved are from the twelfth century; what we know about Korea before then comes from Chinese records, before, during, and after the Han.

In 427 Koguryo decided to move its capital from its early base on the Yalu to Pyongyang, where the Han had ruled the Lo-lang commandery. Slowly Koguryo developed a Chinese-style government, with corvée labor, agricultural taxes, military garrisons in newly conquered areas, and a bureaucratic system. By this time there was enough surplus from the growing Korean economy to build splendid stone, aboveground tombs, adorned with wall paintings like those of the Han and Northern Wei. Meanwhile the state of Paekche, which had developed China connections by sea, received Buddhism from south China by the late fourth century, only a little after its introduction to Koguryo, and with it Chinese characters. Silla was more isolated, but it too sent an embassy to China in 381. Conflict between Koguryo and Paekche, occasioned mainly by Koguryo efforts to expand its control southward, intensified about the same time. Paekche forces repulsed a Koguryo invasion in 369, and then invaded its northern rival and killed the Koguryo king in 371. Paekche was strengthened by its control of the most productive agricultural land in Korea, in the valley of the Han River and the coastal plain to the south of it. But it never became as politically well organized, or in the longer run as militarily effective as Koguryo. Paekche tried to strengthen its hand by alliances with Silla and even with Kaya and its Japanese connections, but as the contest wore on Koguryo won the upper hand. Paekche was forced to shift its capital southward twice, from a little north of the Han River to the vicinity of modern Kwangju and then farther south again to a city called Puyo.

Silla, with its capital at Kyongju in the southeast, was less advanced economically than the other two rivals, and less enriched by Chinese cultural influences. It had a hard struggle to resist unrelenting pressures from the other two larger and wealthier states, but it may be that the lesser influences of China helped to preserve its early tribal aristocratic governing structure and that this was a source of strength. Originally a confederation of tribes, like the Kaya league, under the rule of tribal leaders, with the sixth century Silla began to evolve a more unified structure under a monarchy, whose rulers called themselves king (*wang* in Chinese). King Pophung (514–539) accepted Buddhism as the official religion, and strengthened his own position as the primate in effect of the Buddhist church. Later in the century Silla began the same process earlier promoted by Koguryo of adoption bit by bit of the Chinese bureaucratic system, which further strengthened its administration and its control over local areas. Silla created 17 grades, known as "bone ranks," within the government bureaucracy but, unlike China, strictly on the basis of the hereditary aristocracy. The top two were kept for the widespread and numerous royal clan, who also monopolized the first five grades of the bureaucracy. The army, unlike in China, was not peasant conscripts but young aristocratic warriors.

The ornaments worn by the Silla aristocracy, many of them preserved in their tombs, were often magnificent, made of gold and jewels. They suggest at least some level of prosperity, as well as artistic talent. In any case, Silla, allied with Paekche, campaigned successfully against Koguryo in the mid-sixth century, occupying the upper Han River valley by 551, and then turning against Paekche and taking from it the lower Han valley, with its easier access to China. By the late sixth century Silla had eliminated Kaya and its Japanese foothold. This was of course the time of the Sui dynasty in China (Chapter 5) and of the three successive Sui efforts to conquer Korea, in the footsteps of the Han. But Korea was no longer the relatively easy prey it had been for Han Wu Ti, and all three Sui expeditions were defeated by Korean forces, mainly from Koguryo, a catastrophe which contributed importantly to the collapse of the Sui in China. The T'ang tried again, but when its expeditions too failed, the T'ang made an alliance with Silla against Paekche and sent a fleet to the west coast with a large army in 660. The alliance with Silla destroyed the power and even the existence of Paekche, and also defeated a Japanese force sent to help Paekche.

Silla Victorious

Together Silla and T'ang forces campaigned against Koguryo and by 668 had destroyed it, after an existence of some seven centuries. The T'ang had of course planned to include Korea within the new Chinese empire, in the model of the Han. But as soon as this was apparent Silla, now assisted by fellow Koreans from the two rival and defeated states who nevertheless were at one in their fierce opposition to the T'ang attempt to record in holding off the Chinese colossus (although Vietnam succumbed to the T'ang while it lasted) and in maintaining their independence and their pride in it. Since the seventh century and the repulsion of the T'ang, Korea has remained a unified state, though periodically wracked by internal conflict and factionalism, governing essentially the same area, people, and culture as today, far older than any unified states elsewhere in the world except for China.

Union with the former states of Koguryo and Paekche under single Silla rule, and the now easier connections with China from the west coast and overland, accelerated the spread of Chinese civilization and political institutions. As a tributary, Silla Korea sent the usual annual tribute embassies to the Chinese capital; they and increasing numbers of Korean students and Buddhist pilgrims, most of whom spent many years in China, brought back with them a much more important freight of Chinese culture to Korea. This included the further spread of Buddhism, introduced after the fall of

Korean painting in Chinese style, including its theme of fisherman and woodsman, from the mid-Yi dynasty. (National Museum of Korea, reproduced in J. K. Fairbank, E. O. Reischauer, and A. M. Craig, *East Asia: Tradition and Transformation.* Boston: Houghton-Mifflin, 1989)

Stone pagoda at the Monastery of the Buddha Land, near Kyongju and founded in A.D. 751. (U.S. Army photography, reproduced in J. K. Fairbank, E. O. Reischauer and A. M. Craig, *East Asia: Tradition and Transformation.* Boston: Houghton-Mifflin, 1989)

reimpose Chinese colonial rule, fought bitterly against the T'ang. After some ten years they managed to drive the Chinese out of all but the immediate frontier area north of Pyongyang. The T'ang were obliged to settle for tributary status for the newly unified Korean state, but did not try again to interfere in Korean affairs. This accomplishment must stand with the Vietnamese the Han, which became almost universal in Korea, and the continued adoption of Chinese institutions, enough so that where Vietnam came to be called "The Lesser Dragon" for its adoption of the Chinese system, Korea was sometimes called a "Little T'ang."

Some of the refugees from the destruction of Koguryo founded another Korean state in northern Manchuria in 713 called P'o-hai, which included Tungusic tribes related to the Koreans and in the area from which they had originally come, or migrated through. Koreans still think of it as part of their tradition, and like the states in Korea itself P'o-hai became thoroughly Sinicized and even produced a literature in Chinese as well as Buddhist monasteries. As it prospered its control spilled over the border into northern Korea, but with the rise of the Khitan empire (see Chapter 5) it was conquered and disappeared into the Khitan domains, as all of Manchuria later did under first the Jurchen and finally the Manchus. Some Koreans remained identifiable as such in Manchuria into contemporary times.

Under Silla rule Korea itself prospered as well. Following the Chinese pattern, the country was divided into provinces, prefectures, and districts or counties, like Vietnam. The original Silla capital at Kyongju was the principal seat of government, but its offside location in the extreme southeast led to the establishment of five subsidiary capitals. Kyongju itself became a large city with much architecture in Chinese style, but we have no evidence as to its population. The old Korean tribal society was thus gradually superseded, or overlaid, by the Chinese model, but traditional Korean hereditary structure persisted. Officials were selected from the "bone ranks," and government was dominated by the extensive royal and other aristocratic clans. Perhaps in part because of Korea's relative poverty and less productive agricultural system, most peasants received little benefit from the growing wealth and sophistication of the aristocracy and remained essentially bound to the local lords whom they served. However, Buddhism, in its Mahayana Chinese version, spread widely with its offer of otherworldly salvation, and Buddhist art began to be produced in Korea on a level equal to China's, including large numbers of huge pagodas and both stone and bronze statues of the Buddha, many of them profoundly beautiful.

Koryo

Like all political regimes, Silla rule began to lose its luster and its cohesion by the end of the eighth century. Rich families increasingly contended with each other for power, and in 780 the Silla king was assassinated. Twenty successor kings briefly won and lost the throne in the following century, and there were widespread revolts, manned by the impoverished peasantry

but often led by ambitious aristocrats. By now there was a rising merchant group, some of whom also became involved in the political struggles. The old kingdoms of Paekche and Koguryo were briefly revived as Silla power disintegrated, but by 935, with China in turmoil after the fall of the T'ang so that Chinese intervention was not a possibility, a former merchant named Wang Kon, who had seized control of the new Koguryo kingdom, took control of the entire peninsula, eliminating both Silla and Paekche to found a new state which he named Koryo. This was just a shorter form of the name Koguryo, his first domain, but it is the origin of the modern name Korea. Wang Kon was given after his death in 943 the Chinese-style title of T'aejo, the Korean equivalent of T'ai Tsu, who was his rough contemporary as emperor of the Sung. The Koryo capital was

A bas-relief of the eighth century in the Sokkuram Grotto near Kyongju. (Ministry of Foreign Affairs, Bureau of International Relations, Republic of Korea, reproduced in J. K. Fairbank, E. O. Reischauer, and A. M. Craig, *East Asia: Tradition and Transformation.* Boston: Houghton-Mifflin, 1989)

fixed at Kaesong, near the coast just north of the Han River, and thus closer to the most productive and populous part of the country than either Pyongyang or Kyongju, the Silla capital. Kaesong was built on the T'ang pattern with a checkerboard plan and a great palace facing south. Pyongyang and Kyongju were retained as subsidiary capitals.

During the reign of T'aejo (Wang Kon) a strictly Chinese-style administration was set up along T'ang lines, and an examination system, plus government schools to teach the Confucian texts. But early on Koryo had to deal with the expanding Khitan power, which invaded Korea and in 1010 even sacked the capital, forcing Koryo to become a tributary of the Khitan Liao dynasty centered in southern Manchuria. Koryo forces regrouped and defeated the third Khitan invasion in 1018. After that victory the Koreans built a defensive wall running east-west from the mouth of the Yalu through the mountains to the sea on the east coast. Eventually the Khitan threat was destroyed by the advance of the Jurchen, although they too made Koryo a tributary for the relatively brief period before the Mongol avalanche overwhelmed Korea between 1231 and 1273.

Despite the beginnings of a Chinese-style examination system and civil service, the bureaucracy remained completely dominated by the hereditary aristocracy, who excluded all others. The schools which had been established were limited to the sons of the aristocracy, and those of the highest rank were given government appointments without passing through the examination system. As so often in China, over time the private estates of the wealthy aristocrats paid no taxes, and in consequence the government grew weaker and weaker, while the great bulk of the population remained tied to the soil as virtual slaves or worked in government-run mines or porcelain factories, plus those who served as transport workers or as kept artisans to serve the court. Merchants, earlier much more important, as in the background of the Koryo founder, lost most of their former prominence. What wealth there was, mainly supported by land rents collected by the upper classes, was concentrated in the capital at Kaesong. But the rural areas remained very poor, even backward, and as one measure of poverty what trade there was seems to have been done largely on a barter basis at periodic markets.

Although movable type printing had first been used in Sung China, it may have had its largest use in Koryo, as well as a massive printing from woodblocks of the Buddhist Tripitaka in the eleventh century, and after the blocks were destroyed by the Mongols, another major printing from new blocks in the thirteenth century. The Korean version of Buddhism incorporated early animistic, shamanistic, and Taoist elements, as well as including the T'ien T'ai sect (from China) and later a version of what became Zen in Japan, which in time became

dominant. The Koryo period saw the peak of Buddhism in Korea, including many tombs and monasteries endowed with large landholdings, and even Buddhist monks who served as government advisers. There was also a very large-scale printing of the entire Buddhist tripitaka in the eleventh century, an effort repeated after the Mongols destroyed the original woodblocks. But as Buddhism lost favor in China, it declined in Korea too, and most religion was increasingly a mix of indigenous Korean animism-shamanism-Taoism with some ritual elements of a degenerate Buddhism. Landscape painting, closely following the Chinese pattern, was however joined by superb porcelains, notably the Korean version of Sung celadon, every bit as magnificent as the Sung original but distinctively different. Toward the end of this period, fortunately before the Mongol onslaught, a scholar-official named Kim Pu-sik put together in 1145 the first history of Korea of which we still have copies, titled *History of the Three Kingdoms* (Paekche, Koguryo, and Silla).

Mongol Conquest and After

The Mongols sent a major expedition against Korea and in 1231 besieged the capital at Kaesong. Korea agreed to their demands for heavy tribute and was obliged, as the price for a (temporary) end to the fighting, to accept Mongol garrisons and provincial governors throughout the country. Such conditions were obviously bitterly resented, and into the 1270s there was widespread guerrilla warfare against these hated and oppressive conquerors. The Mongols carried out the usual antiguerrilla strategy of brutal reprisals and terrorism, and in the one year of 1254 alone took away over 200,000 Korean captives to work as slave labor. The Koryo court had retreated to an island off the west coast of Korea for better protection against Mongol raids, but in 1259 they formally surrendered, although guerrilla resistance continued, especially in the mountains, for another decade or more. Through forced marriages of their "princesses" to Korean kings, the Mongols tried to legitimate their rule as well as to Mongolize it, and tried to supplant Korean aristocratic culture with their own.

Korea was also forced to build some 900 ships and provide them with crews and supplies for the two Mongol expeditions against Japan in 1274 and 1281. The country as a whole was devastated, and its common people further impoverished. Korea suffered terribly under the Mongol heel grinding it into the dirt, but its ordeal was mercifully brief in the long span of Korean history, lasting only a little more than a single lifetime, from the 1230s to the 1340s. Given the fact that the Mongols had in effect propped up the Koryo dynasty and used it as their tool, it collapsed soon after the Mongol power was on the retreat in China from the late 1340s. Under Mongol domination, the Koryo system continued the decline which had begun earlier, especially the loss of revenue control to noble families, and the latter's oppression amounted almost to enslavement of the peasants on their estates.

Anti-Mongol Chinese forces entered Korea, and even captured Kaesong briefly in 1361. When the new Ming dynasty was established in 1368, there was disagreement at the Koryo court about the best policy, with some favoring a continuation of the old Mongol-imposed system and some supporting, more realistically, some form of alliance with the Ming. When Koryo forces were sent against the Ming army on the northwestern Korean frontier in 1388, the general in charge, Yi Song-gye, realized when he saw the Ming strength that it was foolish to try to fight them. He marched his troops back to Kaesong, captured the court, and usurped the throne in 1392, putting an end to Koryo and founding a new dynasty which bears his name, the Yi.

Yi Korea

General Yi quickly established tributary relations with the Ming, and his dynasty remained a faithful subject of the Ming in that role for its unprecedentedly long life, which ended only in 1910, after the Japanese takeover. Tribute missions went regularly, first to Nanking and then to Peking, and acted as an additional channel for Chinese influence in everything. The Yi were loyal to China not only through the conventional tributary forms but in their eagerness to replicate every aspect of Chinese civilization, at least at the elite level. This included a special emphasis on Confucianism, mirroring the Confucian revival in China after the defeat of the hated Mongols. What came into Korea during this period, to a greater extent than ever before, was of course the Sung development of Neo-Confucianism, and with it came also a renewed interest in Confucian learning and scholarship, along with a more successful effort to establish a Chinese-style examination system based on mastery of the Confucian classics. In some ways, Korea became even more Confucian than China, and Buddhism declined greatly, preserved as a minority religion as in China and merging with folk religion especially among the illiterate population, although some monasteries survived where Buddhist texts were still studied.

East Asians generally have long been noted for their devotion to education, but in Yi Korea this reached new heights—and is still to be observed in contemporary Korea. It was also in this period that the surviving matriarchal characteristics of Korean society were replaced by Confucian-sanctioned male dominance, filial piety, especially to fathers, the chastity and seclusion of women and wives, and a ban on widow remarriage. Such officially promoted changes never penetrated completely to all levels of Korean society, however, and the lower orders continued to retain much of the original Korean values and forms. As Confucianism hardened and rigidified in Ming and Ch'ing China, so it did in Korea, probably more so. But it was accompanied, as in China, by an impressive scholarly output, in Chinese of course, including the typically Chinese combination of encyclopedias, local and national geographies, medical compendia, and many histories, still important as sources for the study of Korea and well up to the high standard set by Chinese historians. Korean works included the *History of Koryo*, printed in 1451, and the *Complete Mirror of the Eastern Country* in 1484.

General Yi was followed on the throne by able successors, again typical of the first century of most Chinese dynasties, and it is in part due to their work in establishing an effective Chinese-style political and administrative system that the dynasty had such a vigorous beginning, and a momentum which kept it flourishing for so long. The capital was moved from Kaesong to Seoul (where it still is), farther up the Han River and thus still closer to the productive and populous heart of the peninsula. The country as a whole was divided into eight Chinese-style provinces, and they in turn into prefectures and local districts. The Yi finally were able to make good the traditional Korean claim to northern boundaries along the Yalu and Tumen Rivers, and the frontier zone, so often a source of trouble in the past, was pacified and garrisoned. Having first adopted the Ming criminal code, the Yi produced a complete Korean law code in 1485. Even the Censorate was adopted from China, and appears to have worked perhaps even better in Korea—perhaps too well (see below)—operating as two and finally as three boards. But since the examinations were in Chinese and depended on a thorough knowledge of the Confucian classics, also in the same foreign language which could be learned by Koreans only with long years of study, the Chinese system worked out in Korea so as to limit those who passed into the bureaucracy entirely to the sons of the wealthy aristocrats. No others, especially given the poverty of the lower orders in Korea, could hope to enter that upper circle. In this crucial respect, therefore, the long-established Korean pattern of hereditary privilege and status was retained.

Those who passed through the examinations and joined the bureaucracy, in its civil or military branches, thus came from the ruling class which had always dominated Korea. Military officials were recruited through a separate set of examinations in Chinese, and nearly all civil and military candidates first attended government and later private schools where they acquired the necessary learning. Those who succeeded came to be called *yangban* ("two groups"—i.e. civil and military), in a way the equivalent of the Chinese gentry. Like the gentry in China, they also, or their families, became the dominant landowners. Some of these families had been given land grants by T'aejo, and his successors continued this practice. Over time most of the country was divided up into large *yangban* estates, and as in China landowning became a further mark of status. This new group was much larger than the old Koryo aristocracy, and more widely distributed around the country, where some lived on their estates. Below the *yangban* was a much smaller and less well-defined class called *chungin* ("middle people"), most of whom were lesser government workers and lower-level technicians, but still a privileged and hereditary group. The great bulk of the population was, of course, peasants, who were lumped with other manual workers as commoners, or *yangmin*. As before, peasants were bound to the land as virtual serfs, but the Yi, unlike earlier regimes, did try to fix rents which could be charged as a proportion of the productivity of the land in question, a provision which, needless to say, was often ignored. Nevertheless the government attempted to guarantee rights to the land to the cultivators, a situation different from serfdom, to the extent that this was observed.

At the bottom of the social scale were the "base people" or *ch'onmin*: slaves (of which there were still more than a few, both government and private), industrial workers, miners, butchers and leather workers (discriminated against from earlier periods because of the Buddhist prohibition on the taking of life), actors, and lower-class courtesans, not merely prostitutes but singers, dancers, and entertainers like the Chinese flower-boat women and, later, the Japanese *geisha*.

It was probably a more rigid system in general than that in medieval Europe or even than caste in India, since not only was it based on birth but there were no means by which either individuals or groups could es-

Han'gŭl Chart

HAN'GŬL CHART

Vowel pairs: ㅏ a ㅑ ya, ㅓ ŏ ㅕ yŏ, ㅗ o ㅛ yo, ㅜ u ㅠ yu, ㅡ ŭ ㅣ i.

Some consonant pairs: ㄱ k ㅋ k', ㄷ t ㅌ t', ㅂ p ㅍ p', ㅈ ch ㅊ ch'.

Some other consonants: ㅅ s, ㄴ n, ㅁ m, ㅇ ng.

Syllables: * Chosŏn 조 선 Taedong 대 동

ch'ŏnmin 천 민 T'aejong 태 종

Puyŏ 부 여 *yangban* 양 반

P'yŏngyang 평 양

Source: From J.K. Fairbank, E.O. Reischauer, and A.M. Craig, *East Asia: Tradition and Transformation* (Boston: Houghton-Mifflin, 1989), p. 311.

cape from it or could gradually enhance the group's status, as Indian caste groups could. This rigidity was also a reflection of Korea's poverty, especially for the lower orders, and the persistence of slavery or semiserfdom for many. Trade was minimal, and as pointed out, was often managed through barter. Merchants were further degraded because of the Confucian prejudice against them. What manufacturing there was, largely luxury goods for the court and nobility, was government-owned and the workers kept as near or actual slaves. The capital supported a sophisticated culture of considerable luxury, but the rural areas belonged to a different world. Roads were miserable or nonexistent and little or nothing of the splendor of the capital, including simple awareness of it, reached the mass of the people. Peasant houses were mud and thatch huts with no amenities, where people commonly slept on the floor and had almost no other furniture. They were bitterly cold in winter and baked in summer. Famine was common, and many diseases endemic.

What has come down to us of Yi culture is, understandably, the achievements of the literate elite. This is true of course for China too, and indeed for nearly all premodern societies, but in China we have more than a few glimpses of the life of the common people and, equally important, the Chinese state and elite felt a responsibility to do what could be done to improve the welfare of the masses: famine relief, agricultural improvements, and even moral uplift, through the example of Confucian officials at every level, plus the system of traveling lecturers on morality and the itinerant players, opera performers, and other amusements at local fairs and markets. Despite the Korean enthusiasm for Confucianism, too little of this aspect of it—the message of "serve the people"—seems to have been carried out there. Yi Korea, or its first 300 years, is contemporary with Ming China. Any examination of the Ming, even so superficially as in Chapter 7, can show a vast difference from what we know of Yi Korea, although it is certainly true that our knowledge of the later, especially below elite levels, is far less adequate.

Probably the best-known accomplishment of Yi Korea, in addition to the continued use of movable type and extensive printing projects, is its invention of a phonetic system for transcribing spoken Korean. For all its adoption of Chinese civilization, including written characters, Korea asserted its distinctiveness in this form too. The *han'gul* system, as it is called, could also be used to give the sounds of Chinese characters and thus to write any text in either language. It was developed by scholars at the capital in 1443, early in the dynasty when the flood of adoption from China was in full spate—and perhaps for that very reason. *Han'gul* has been called the best, most accurate system of writing anywhere in the world; although it is phonetic rather than ideographic, it combines the virtues of an alphabetic script with those of a syllabary by grouping individual letters into syllabic groups, like the similar Japanese *kana* system. At first it was used mainly to put Chinese texts into Korean form, but in time it was used for all purposes, although Chinese continued as the language of government and many of the elite looked down on *han'gul* as vulgar.

Yi rule began to weaken as a result of the large land grants each king felt obliged to make to ensure *yangban* support. The *yangban* soon became as powerful as the king, unlike the situation in China, and the government suffered from too little revenue, from the lands that were left to them. This, as in China, increased the squeeze on peasants living on the remaining government lands, and built up pressures for rebellion and banditry. The problem was realized early, notably by King Sejo (1455–1468), but his efforts to correct it through a land survey and by reducing the power of *yangban* families were defeated by massive opposition from the privileged. From this time on Korean politics was increasingly characterized by bitter factionalism, first between the throne and *yangban* groups defending their position, and then among rival *yangban* officials and leaders, including those in the Censorate who quite correctly called to account all who fell short of the Confucian ideals.

Members of the Censorate felt both the right and the duty to criticize officials, and did so continually. Since this included most of the elite, it was bound to provoke contention. Faction fighting, which often crippled the Yi government, became perhaps the major characteristic of the Yi period especially after its first century. Hostility between the factions persisted over successive generations and became in effect the birthright of each new generation, a little like the clan feuding characteristic of the Scottish Highlands. More and more this infighting paralyzed Korea's political will and made a shambles of the Yi government. Even where the disputes were over particular pieces of policy, it was considered to be part of the Confucian way to equate criticism of a man's political views with denunciation of his moral virtue. The middle ground, or what we sometimes call honest agreement to disagree among civilized people, was squeezed out. In the chronic Korean contention, the king ultimately lost almost all power despite the efforts of some kings to reestablish their authority.

All governments are troubled by factionalism and by ongoing contests between those who favor different policies. One must acknowledge that such rivalries usually also have baser motives, the rivalry for positions and power in the political system, of whatever sort. In China, factions at court, as in the time of Wang An-shih, were usually kept from debilitating the state by the power and if necessary intervention of the emperor, although in the worst case, the inconclusive sparring over defense policies under the Southern Sung, the state was indeed critically weakened by division and inconsistency. In Korea the Yi king, unlike a Chinese emperor, began more or less on an equal footing with the *yangban* and then was unable to maintain his supposed original higher authority over them. One might have expected regionalism to be a divisive force in China, and on occasion it was. But in far smaller Korea it became much more so as *yangban* leaders in different provinces used their geographic and familial connections to strengthen their side in the fighting at the court. Victorious factions purged officials who had supported a rival group, and even executed many, thus perpetuating the bitterness among those in subsequent generations.

By the end of the sixteenth century the bureaucracy was split primarily into two opposing factions, the "Easterners" and the "Westerners" (not a reference to their geographic origins but to the districts in Seoul where their respective leaders lived). The "Easterners" came out on top, but then they themselves divided into "Northerners" and "Southerners." When the "Northerners" prevailed, they in turn split into "Great" and "Small" factions. It is all a sorry tale, including the end of any effective or coherent government authority or leadership. With Korea thus enfeebled, the Japanese warlord Hideyoshi launched an invasion of the country as the first step in his planned conquest of China. When his request for free passage through Korea was refused, he sent an army of about 160,000 men in 1592. Korea was in effect a rudderless ship, and it had also fallen far behind in the technology of warfare, which the Japanese had begun to acquire some of from the Portuguese, Dutch, and English who had been trading in Japan since the middle of the sixteenth century. Hideyoshi's forces easily took Seoul in the first month and then spread out over most of the country.

The Ming came to the aid of their tributary "younger brother" (see Chapter 7), and despite some severe reversals achieved an eventual stalemate, with the help of the gifted Korean Admiral Yi Sun-sin. His ingeniously designed "turtle ships," covered with overlapping iron and copper plates so that they were almost invulnerable, were armed fore and aft with metal prows shaped like beaks. They were powered by rowers under the protection of the outer "turtle shell," and could ram and sink any ship by being rowed forward or backward—the first armored warships. Admiral Yi repeatedly defeated Japanese naval detachments and disrupted their supply lines, while the Chinese continued to engage and pin down the Japanese land forces. Providentially, Hideyoshi died in 1598, and the Japanese promptly returned home, but Korea never recovered from the immense devastation of the fighting. The decline of the Yi dynasty continued or accelerated, still picked away at by perennial faction fighting.

The process of recovery from Hideyoshi's destructive invasion was slowed by the rise of Manchu power in Manchuria soon afterwards. They invaded Korea in 1627 and again in 1636 and 1637, forcing the Yi to shift their allegiance from the Ming to their newly founded Ch'ing dynasty, on the eve of their conquest of China. Domestically, new factions appeared, disappeared, and reappeared, but little changed. Nevertheless two relatively strong kings emerged in the eighteenth century, Yongjo (1724–1776) and his grandson Chongjo (1776–1800), who were able to reestablish a workable tax system and a revised legal code. In their time there was a new burst of printing, especially historical records and encyclopedias, and a general patronage of learning in the long-standing Korean tradition. Economically the devastation of Hideyoshi's war was gradually repaired and agriculture improved with new irrigation and the introduction of new, more productive strains, including early ripening rice via China so that some areas could now grow two crops a year, including winter crops of wheat and barley. Population accordingly grew, from an official figure of about five million in 1669 to nine million by the late eighteenth century. Artisans who had worked as kept servants to the court and nobility were freed and began to produce for the general market. That such a market now existed indicates that the economic level in general was slowly rising. Merchants also became freer of earlier restrictions and began to manage internal and external trade, with both China and Japan. Money, minted by the government, began to displace barter, and taxes were increasingly commuted into cash payments, developments which had taken place in China many centuries earlier.

Partly as a result, the rigid traditional class system of Korea began to soften somewhat as the government sold class status and even official posts to anyone who could pay, and as merchants, formerly despised, rose in status. In time, many of them acquired the *yangban* distinction as they also acquired Confucian education, and as many of the older *yangban* families also became involved in trade as a source of income. By the mid-nineteenth century roughly half of the total population claimed to belong to the *yangban* group, including some who were just farmers but who clung to ancestral *yangban* heritages. At the same time, most of those who had been slaves escaped by becoming soldiers in the now largely voluntary professional army. Some bits of Western influence seeped into Korea through contacts between tribute missions to Peking with the Jesuits there, and in 1795 a Chinese Jesuit convert, Chou Wen-mu, came to Korea as a missionary.

Christianity soon came under government persecution for its disapproval of many aspects of Confucianism. Chou Wen-mu was executed in 1801, but the new religion spread in secret in the provinces, encouraged by fresh Chinese missionaries and then after 1836 by French missionaries. Korea was beginning to be drawn into the wider world, and despite conservative resistance, into Westernization and "modernization." "Practical Learning," as the new Western knowledge was called, stimulated a new movement among intellectuals which pressed for reform across the board, adoption of new scientific ideas despite their foreign origin, and an increase in social equality. Thus the stage was set for the final Korean confrontation with the world beyond China, the weak and ineffective government response, and the ultimate takeover by a resurgent Japan in 1895.

Suggestions for Further Reading

Vietnam

Coedes, G. *The Indianized States of Southeast Asia.* ed. W. F. Vella, Honolulu: East-West Center Press. 1968.

Gesick, L., ed. *Essays on the Classical States of Southeast Asia.* New Haven: Yale, 1983.

Hall, D. G. E. *A History of Southeast Asia.* London: Macmillian, 1981.

Marr, D., and Milner, A. C., eds. *Southeast Asia in the 9th to 14th Centuries.* Singapore: Heinemann, 1986.

Osborne, M. *Southeast Asia.* New York: Harper Collins, 1991.

Sar Desai, D. R. *Southeast Asia Past and Present.* Boulder, Colo.: Westview, 1989.

Tarling, N., ed. *The Cambridge History of Southeast Asia.* Cambridge Univ. Press, 1992.

Taylor, K. W. *The Birth of Vietnam.* Berkeley: California, 1983.

Whitmore, J. *Vietnam.* New Haven: Yale, 1985.

Woodside, A. *Vietnam and the Chinese Model.* Cambridge: Harvard Press, 1988.

Korea

Deuchler, M. *The Confucian Transformation of Korea.* Cambridge: Harvard Press, 1993.

Eckert, C. J. et al. *Korea Old and New: A History.* Cambridge: Harvard Press, 1991.

Han Woo-keun. *The History of Korea,* transl. K. Y. Lee. Honolulu: Univ. of Hawaii, 1971.

Henthorn, G. *History of Korea.* Glencoe Ill.: Free Press, 1971.

Kang, H. W. ed. *The Traditional Culture and Society of Korea.* Honolulu: University of Hawaii Center for Korean Studies, 1975.

Lancaster, L. R., and Yu, C. S., eds. *Introduction of Buddhism to Korea.* Berkeley: Asian Humanities Press, 1989.

Lee, K. B. *A New History of Korea,* transl. E. Wagner. Cambridge: Harvard Press, 1985.

Macdonald, D. S. *The Koreans.* Boulder, Colo.: Westview, 1990.

Palis, J. B. *Politics in Traditional Korea.* Cambridge: Harvard Press, 1991.

CHAPTER 10

BEGINNINGS IN JAPAN: PATTERNS AND ORIGINS

Composed of four main islands (and many smaller ones) off the southern tip of Korea, the nearest part of the mainland, Japan had been protected by its insularity from turmoil on the mainland, and also to a degree isolated from the process of development. The Straits of Tsushima between Korea and Japan are about 120 miles wide, and although Japan has been periodically involved in interaction with the mainland, the connection has never been as close as between Britain and Europe, separated by only some 21 miles across the Straits of Dover. Nor has it been nearly as varied, since East Asia remained dominated by the culturally monolithic civilization of China as opposed to the multiplicity of both cultural and ethnic strands of Europe. Japan has had the advantage of a clearly separate identity and of a large degree of cultural and linguistic homogeneity resulting from insularity and from its relatively small size, no larger than an average Chinese province. The Japanese have been able to make their own choices at most periods about what they wanted to adopt from abroad; what came in was what the Japanese wanted to have.

Overall, Japan is smaller than France or California and larger than the British Isles, but it is mainly covered by mountains. Settlement has thus remained heavily concentrated on the narrow coastal plain, mainly between modern Tokyo and Osaka, in a series of disconnected basins over an area roughly equivalent to the coastal corridor between Boston and Washington in the United States. In practice, this makes Japan an even smaller country, since so much of it (in the mountains)

is very thinly inhabited. Hokkaido, the northernmost island, was effectively occupied by the Japanese very late, mainly after the first world war. Mountains retarded Japanese economic development and political unification, as in Korea, and political unification came very late, in 1600, after many centuries of disunity and chronic fighting among rival regionally based groups.

In part because of these regional divisions and attendant warfare, an hereditary aristocratic warrior class became dominant in Japan and enforced an essentially feudal system with strict class distinctions. Where China emerged out of its version of feudalism by the third century B.C., Japanese feudalism continued until the 1860s, along with hereditary status. Japan was torn by fighting until the seventeenth century, which also retarded its development. As late as the ninth century A.D., the total population was less than four million, less than 20 million by 1600, and less than 30 by 1870, reflecting an economic level which left most people (peasants) in poverty, although this also reflected Japan's agricultural handicaps.

The dominance of an hereditary warrior-aristocracy meant that Japanese society was relatively authoritarian and that people were accustomed to direction. This was to prove in the longer run a strong advantage when after 1869 Japan determined to adopt Western technology and was able to create basic change from the top down. Insularity promoted a strong sense of Japanese national-cultural identity, which was a further asset, especially by comparison with China's long struggle for modern unity and the national strength to cope with the challenges of foreign pressures. The outstandingly beautiful natural

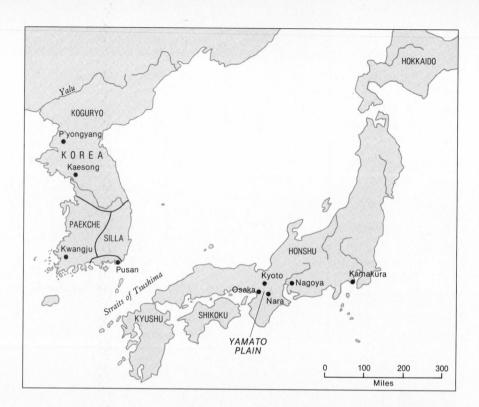

Korea and Japan,
c. 500–1000

landscape of Japan further underlined Japanese identity, and was intimately involved in the content of Shinto, the Japanese nature religion, which also became a part of Japanese nationalism in the modern period. Early in the period of heavy Japanese borrowing from the Chinese model, from the seventh to the ninth centuries, Japan considered but soon rejected the system of meritocracy through examinations which was the basis of Chinese status and officialdom in favor of its traditional hereditary and hierarchical patterns. That was an important factor in the evolution of Japanese society, but equally important was the very experience of borrowing ideas and institutions from abroad. Where the Chinese, Koreans, and Vietnamese tended to regard other cultures as "barbarian" and rejected the notion of learning anything from them, the Japanese recognized early that they could acquire much of value by adopting elements from abroad. They were probably influenced by their awareness that China in particular was far richer and more advanced than they were, while China haughtily looked down on other cultures as inferior and resisted any change, especially of foreign origin.

To the Japanese, change continued to mean the possibility of improvement, an attitude which stood them in good stead not only for the first great wave of borrowing from China but in the face of the nineteenth century Western challenge, which Japan met with brilliant success while China resisted, and floundered. Japan's rela

tively small size was also a strong advantage in enabling rapid change, especially since the great majority of its small population was so highly concentrated as well as being linked together by cheap, easy, coastal routes. Given the basic differences between Japan and the mainland, it is remarkable that so much of Chinese culture was successfully transplanted there.

Agriculture too has been hampered by the shortage of level land, and even now only some 17 percent of the total land area is cultivated, a situation close to Korea's. Japan's great agricultural advantage is its mild maritime climate, the gift of the surrounding sea which keeps it well watered and with a mild winter, largely free of the droughts which plague especially north China. Coastal sea routes have also helped to link settled areas and carry trade, while the sea provided fish and other seafood which has always made an important part of the diet, especially convenient since the bulk of the population lives close to the sea. Soils in Japan are of relatively low natural fertility, but have been improved by centuries of use and fertilization. This is a volcanic archipelago, and most soils are the product of weathered lava and ash. Sometimes, as in Java, this is the basis of high fertility, but in Japan the product of vulcanism is mainly acidic rather than basic, and most soils are also rather thin. Mountains are steep and come down to or close to the sea, so that nowhere are there extensive plains where alluvium can build up, as in China. Rivers are

Mountains and sea. With population so concentrated close to the coasts, even these steep slopes are terraced for agriculture. (R. Murphey)

✠ A Chinese Account of Japan ✠

The earliest accounts of Japan we have are Chinese. The most valuable was written about A.D. 297 and follows the standard Chinese usage in referring to Japan as Wa.

The land of Wa is warm and mild. In winter as in summer the people live on raw vegetables and go about barefooted. They have houses, father and mother, elder and younger, sleep separately.... Whenever they undertake an enterprise or a journey and a discussion arises, they bake bones and divine in order to tell whether fortune will be good or bad ... then they examine the cracks made by the fire and tell what is to come to pass.... In their meetings and in their deportment there is no distinction between father and son or between men and women. Men of importance have four or five wives, the lesser ones two or three. Women are not loose in morals or jealous.... There is no theft, and litigation is infrequent. In case of violation of the law, the light offender loses his wife and children by confiscation; as for the grave offender, the members of his household and also his kinsmen are exterminated. There are class distinctions among the people, and some men are vassals of others.... When the lowly meet men of importance on the road, they stop and withdraw to the roadside. In conveying messages to them they either squat or kneel, with both hands on the ground. This is the way they show respect. When responding, they say "ah," which corresponds to the affirmative "yes."

A later Chinese account of about A.D. 580 noted that

"They have no written characters and understand only the use of notched sticks and knotted ropes. They revere Buddha and obtained Buddhist scriptures from Paekche (Korea). This was the first time that they came into possession of written characters."

Source: From Conrad Totman, *Japan before Perry.* (Berkeley: University of California Press, 1981), pp. 7–9 and 43.

short and swift, carrying most of their silt loads into the sea rather than depositing them along their lower courses or deltas.

Largely for this reason, Japan has become the largest user of chemical fertilizers in the world, and it has been able to support a quadrupling of its population since the eighteenth century despite the disadvantages of its agricultural base, and without disproportionately heavy food imports. In the modern period the Japanese have achieved the highest rice yields in the world through a combination of heavy fertilization and the development of improved crop strains. All of this rested on Japan's remarkable success in industrialization and technological development, primarily since 1870. The modern image of Japan as industrially and technically advanced is accurate, but it represents a fundamental change which has come about mainly in the last 100 years, and hence is not an appropriate sample of Japan for most of its history.

The origins of the Japanese people are summarized in Chapter 2, so that it is unnecessary to present that here. As pointed out there, agriculture seems to have come relatively late to Japan, perhaps not much before, perhaps in the course of, the migration of the people we may call Japanese from somewhere in northeastern Asia, via Korea. The Neolithic Yayoi culture which emerged about the third century B.C., cultivating rice and using first bronze and then iron, may well have been stimulated if not created by these immigrants from the mainland, bringing with them all of these aspects of new technology through contact with Chinese civilization in the course of their movement through Korea. We know that there was trade, perhaps indirect via Korea, between the Yayoi people and China, judging from Chinese coins and polished bronze mirrors which have been found at some Yayoi sites.

Ties With Korea and Tomb Builders

The connection with Korea was clearly a close one. The later Yayoi built large aboveground tombs covered with earthen mounds very like those built in Korea slightly earlier, and used both bronze and iron weapons, when the latter appear in the third century A.D., closely resembling those made in Korea, as do late Yayoi jeweled ornaments. By this time one may certainly call the people Japanese, but, as mentioned in Chapter 2, it may be equally accurate to think of them as provincial Koreans or Korean cousins. The Yayoi people made pottery on a potter's wheel instead of the coil-made pottery of Jomon, the culture which preceded it, which seems to have spread over the whole of Japan including Hokkaido, or at least Jomon sites have been found there as well as in Okinawa far to the south. The potter's wheel presumably entered from China via Korea, along with bronze, iron, and rice. With the coming of rice agriculture, population increased substantially and there was probably some surplus, as evidenced by the large tombs built from the third century A.D. and the many bronze bells, some of them quite large and similar to Korean forms, although already distinctively Japanese. Yayoi culture from the third to the sixth centuries A.D. is labeled the tomb period; some of the tombs, or the mounds erected over them, were built in an interesting keyhole shape. Pottery figures found arranged, perhaps as guardians, around these tombs include those of people, warriors, animals, and houses, and are known as *haniwa*. They are certainly attractive, but seem still relatively primitive.

The tombs, presumably built for aristocrats, show strong similarities with Korean forms, as do the Yayoi weapons, helmets, and armor. Remains of this tomb culture have been found as far as the Tokyo area and in the

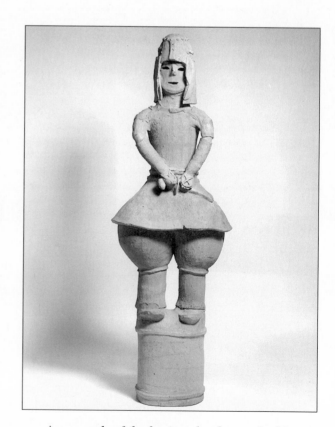

An example of the *haniwa* clay figures, in this case a warrior, from the sixth century A.D. (Asian Art Museum of San Francisco, The Avery Brundage Collection)

southwestern island of Kyushu, although the original and chief center was the area between Kyoto and Osaka, soon to be known as Yamato. People now lived in wood and thatch houses supported off the ground on pilings or stilts instead of the pit dwellings of Jomon times, and there were similar structures for storing grain. The first Chinese written account of Japan, the *Account of the Three Kingdoms,* compiled about A.D. 290, described Japan as a sort of appendage to Korea (hence the title of the work, which clearly refers to Korea), talked about routes from Korea to Japan, and said that the Japanese were a law-abiding people (likely to attract Chinese approval) who depended on agriculture and fishing and observed strict social differences which were marked by tatooing. Japan was said to be divided into a hundred "countries" of a few hundred households each—clans is probably a better word—some ruled by kings and some by queens. Thus in Japan too the original social pattern seems to have been matriarchal, merging at this period into a patriarchy of male dominance. The *haniwa* figures include some which seem to represent female shamans, who probably played an important role. The Chinese *Account of the Three Kingdoms* tells us that the Japanese were much involved with divination and ritual, and speak of an unmarried queen who as a kind of high priestess ruled over several "kingdoms," or clans, and was considered important enough to have one of the largest tombs and mounds erected for her on her death.

Mythical Histories

The first Japanese written records are much later, and are not reliable or even consistent on this early period. These are the *Kojiki* (Record of Ancient Matters) of A.D. 712 and the *Nihon shoki*, or *Nihongi* of 720 (*Nihon* is still the Japanese word for their country). Their purpose seems to have been to give the contemporary ruling family a long history comparable to China's (from whom the Japanese were then eagerly adopting its literate civilization), put together from various contradictory myths. These begin with creation myths about a divine brother and sister, Izanagi and Izanami, who between them created the Japanese islands—in one version as the drops from the goddess's spear—and also gave birth to the sun goddess, Amaterasu. Amaterasu's grandson, Ninigi, descended to the earth, according to the myth, and supposedly brought with him three imperial regalia, still the symbols of imperial authority in Japan: a bronze mirror (symbol of the sun), an iron sword, and a necklace made of curved jewels somewhat in the shape of bear's claws. All three, but especially the last two, are identical with regalia found in Korean tombs of early Silla date, again suggesting the close tie

between Korea and early Japan. The myths recount how Niningi's grandson moved up from Kyushu, conquered the lowland area around Nara known as the Kinai region, and founded the Japanese state there on the Yamato plain—but in 660 B.C., when it seems reasonably clear that the people whom we call Japanese had not yet entered the country and were not to begin doing so for another three centuries or more! This was an effort at respectability and legitimacy, to give the state an ancient lineage following the Chinese model.

Ninigi's grandson, the conquerer of Kinai, is called the first "emperor," and is given a Chinese-style title as Jimmu, the "Divine Warrior." We know that by the fifth century A.D. the emerging state in the Kinai region, which also called itself Yamato, had extended its control into Kyushu and northward in Honshu, the main island, to the vicinity of modern Tokyo. In the same period, the Japanese won—or continued to maintain?—a coastal foothold in southeastern Korea, a colony which the *Kojiki* refers to as the work of the priestess-queen Himiko, whose name means "Sun Princess," although its dates for this are far too early. When the people we may call the Japanese entered the islands the dominant occupants, at least of Honshu, were an unrelated people called the Ainu, apparently a branch of Caucasians whose physical characteristics differed markedly from the Japanese, including larger amounts of facial and body hair, enough so that they were often referred to as the "hairy Ainu."

As Japanese occupation and conquest moved northward and eastward from Kyushu, their first center since it was closest to Korea, they did so at the expense of the Ainu, and perhaps of other groups as well about whom we know little. Japan had been settled by people, presumably from somewhere in Asia, since at least 100,000 B.C., and these had first to be conquered, enslaved, absorbed, or driven eastward and northward. For a long time the boundary with the Ainu was along Lake Biwa, just north of Kyoto. Gradually the Japanese prevailed, although there was a good deal of intermarriage or interbreeding, evidenced in the modern population by more facial and body hair than in China. Indeed the Chinese in their superior attitude toward all other people called the Japanese "hairy sea dwarfs," since they were also shorter than the Chinese norm (probably a result of a low-protein diet?) and were more aggressive and effective seagoers, including their role in piracy. The earliest Chinese name for the Japanese was *wa*, which means simply dwarf. The Ainu remained dominant in northern Honshu well into historical times, and now exist as a tiny and dwindling group on reservations in the northernmost island of Hokkaido.

By about A.D. 200 iron tools and weapons were being made in Japan rather than being imported, and thus became far more widespread. This doubtless helped to increase agricultural productivity still more, and with it population totals, giving the Japanese a further advantage in their contest with the Ainu, who were in any case technologically less developed. Japanese pottery improved in the tomb period beyond the Yayoi stage, and in particular was more thoroughly fired and hence more practical for everyday use. Close interaction continued with Korea, and in a genealogical list of A.D. 815 over a third of the Japanese nobility claimed Korean descent, clearly a mark of superiority. Many Korean artisans, metallurgists, other technologists, and scribes (the Japanese were still preliterate) lived in Japan, as well as Korean nobles and perhaps even rulers. There were also invasions and raids in both directions, including some Japanese efforts to hold or expand their small coastal base in southeastern Korea, until by about 400 such violent interactions faded. By this time, Chinese accounts and various Japanese traditions begin to coincide factually and on at least rough dates, although true Japanese historical records in any detail do not begin for another 400 years, after the time of the mythical and mixed accounts given in the *Kojiki* and *Nihongi* in the early eighth century.

The Uji

The Japan we can begin to see somewhat more clearly by the fifth century, long after the fall of the Han, was still a tribal society, divided into a number of clans called *uji* ruled by hereditary chiefs and worshipping the clan's ancestor. The lower orders were farmers, fishermen, potters, and some who seem to have been diviners, although we do not know how many by this time were still women. Some *uji* expanded at the expense of others, but in any case they were the hundred "countries" referred to in the Chinese accounts. The Yamato state seems to have emerged as a consolidation of various *uji* groups in the area, headed by the Yamato *uji* and indeed it may be a bit inaccurate to refer to it as a "state," despite its continued conquest or absorption of other *uji* clans. It did try to organize the *uji* through the creation of ranks, of which the largest were *Omi* and *Muraji*, respectively lesser branches of the ruling family of Yamato, referred to as the "sun line," and unrelated but important *uji*. Headmen were appointed for each, eventually government ministers. Already there had begun the designation of the ruler, later the emperor, as descending from the sun goddess Amaterasu and hence in himself (or herself) divine.

Both *uji* and Yamato rulers combined religious and political functions, as did the Chinese emperor, although he never claimed divinity but merely acted as the per-

former of state rituals while serving overwhelmingly a political function, a sort of temporal head of Confucianism which itself was a very this-worldly affair. These early Japanese rulers were also in effect priests (or priestesses) and were very active in building or recognizing and ranking a great number of local shrines to Amaterasu. This had by now merged with early Japanese animism, the worship of nature and natural forces. Such worship is characteristic of all early societies everywhere, but in Japan it was retained, or merged with the worship of the mythical Amaterasu as the sun goddess rather than being displaced, as everywhere else, by a textually based religion of greater sophistication. The Japanese landscape is exceptionally beautiful, which may have helped the Japanese to identify with it so personally, but Japan also has its dramatic and awesome reminders of the power of nature: active volcanoes, occasional tidal waves, frequent earthquakes, and the yearly visitation of typhoons in late summer and fall which can do enormous damage. Mountains, waterfalls, big trees, and even rocks were thought to contain or to embody a divine spirit, or *kami*. Emperors were of course *kami* too, and sometimes notable *uji* rulers. At many natural beauty spots, plentiful in Japan, shrines were built to the local *kami*. Nature in Japan was seen as productive, as in China, although such a perception long antedated the influx of Chinese influence. To celebrate or worship this beneficent force, there were phallic cults, a common focus of the belief in the central importance of fertility, and also shrines to the god of rice.

Shinto

These practices, centered around the worship of nature, were later called *Shinto*, "the way of the gods," primarily to distinguish them from Buddhism when it reached Japan. Shinto, probably a consolidation of local nature worship cults, has remained into contemporary Japan as a particularly Japanese religion, with its own priesthood and temples. It is an interesting survival of what is still readily recognizable as a primitive animistic cult or cults typical of most preliterate societies but overlaid or extinguished elsewhere long ago. Shinto has never been an organized body of thought or even what we might call a religion. It never developed a clear moral code or coherent philosophy, but did preserve early notions of ritual purity. Physical dirt, death, childbirth, illness, menstruation, and sexual intercourse were all seen as polluting and had to be ceremonially cleansed or exorcised by a priest. Priests also acted as diviners and mediums, like the shamans of Korea. Modern Japanese society is still notable for its insistence on cleanliness, at least at home and in what is referred to as "private space," if not always in "public space." Water, especially running water, is still seen as pure and purifying—hence the tiny spring (sometimes artificial) and pool with dipper provided in the forecourt of every temple and shrine (not just Shinto ones) where the worshipper or tourist can cleanse him/herself before entering the sacred area proper. This is a very Shinto notion, and it is possible that the Japanese fondness for bathing, especially for hot baths as the proper close to a day, may go back to early Shinto or pre-Shinto origins. This is still more plausible when one considers the great number of natural hot springs in this volcanic country, still much visited and used for bathing, and the obvious power of nature which they represent, a kind of opening into the navel of the earth where titanic forces were generated, as in volcanic eruptions, which of course are closely linked to hot springs.

All over Japan one can still see beautiful Shinto shrines, beautiful because they celebrate nature and because they are located in natural beauty spots, but also because of their classically simple architectural style. Worship of nature, combined with insistence on cleanliness, may have nudged the Japanese early toward the spare, clean lines of their traditional architecture, something which they carried over into their adaptations of Chinese architecture, however faithfully they tried to copy the T'ang originals. Most of the shrines are in the original village *uji* centers, dedicated to the local *uji* god and surrounded by tall trees, others are tiny things the size of a large birdhouse with natural bark-covered roof, dotted in the mountains, far from human habitation. The most famous shrine-temple is at Ise, on the peninsula which stretches south from the Kyoto area. Ise is the chief center of the sun goddess cult, and the shrine's graceful simple lines are designed to fit in without a discordant note to the trees and nearby stream. It was probably built some time in the sixth century A.D., but is lovingly rebuilt every 20 years on precisely the same pattern and thus gives us a glimpse of what early Japanese temple architecture must have been like. In the approaches to every temple and many shrines is a *torii* or simple open gateway to signal sacred ground ahead. Worship at Shinto shrines and temples is equally simple: clapping the hands to attract the god's attention, bowing, and usually leaving a small gift as sacrifice. At the same time, shrines and temples are often the sites of festivals with a carnival atmosphere, booths selling food, large and sometimes noisy crowds, and various amusements, often with a good deal of drinking and accompanying high jinks. The persistence of Shinto can be seen as an assertion of Japanese distinctiveness despite the waves of Chinese and later Western influences, but also as a celebration of the Japanese landscape and the bounty of nature.

✠ Japanese Love of Nature ✠

Sir George Sansom, the distinguished British historian of Japan, offers the following interpretation of the early Japanese attitude toward nature.

It may be that, to wayworn tribes from arid regions of Korea and northern China or inhospitable Siberian plains, the genial climate of Japan, with its profusion of trees and flowering shrubs, its fertile soil, and its wealth of running streams, was so pleasing as to make upon them a profound impression, stored up in the racial consciousness as a pervading sense of gratitude. Certainly their religion was … a religion of love and gratitude rather than of fear, and the purpose of their religious rites was to praise and thank as much as to placate and mollify their divinities. The very names given in their mythology to their country—the Land of Luxuriant Reed Plants, the Land of Fresh Rice Ears of a Thousand Autumns—and to their gods—the Princess Blooming Like the Flowers of the Trees, and Her Augustness Myriad Looms Luxuriant Dragonfly Island—testify to their strong sense of the beauty and richness of their environment.

Source: G.B. Sansom, *Japan: A Short Cultural History*. (London: Cresset, 1946), pp. 46–47.

Part of the Ise shrine, like the rest of it, made of Japanese cypress and left bare without decoration. (Consulate General of Japan, Chicago)

The Link with China

By the middle of the sixth century (officially in 552) Buddhism had reached Japan from Korea, although the Japanese were aware of it through their continued close contact with Korea and their foothold in the south there in the Kaya League. Kaya was absorbed by Silla in 562, and thereafter the Japanese had no territorial base in Korea, although the flow of Koreans into Japan continued until the early ninth century, not as conquerors (nor had the Japanese been in Kaya) but as closely related people who moved across the straits, probably in both directions, and as allies or associates rather than as invaders. Buddhism was at first opposed by many as an alien religion, but was championed by the Soga *uji*, which vanquished many of its rival *uji* in a war over the succession in 587 and then established Buddhism at the Yamato court, where it seems to have appealed to many as a powerful new magic. Buddhism served as a vehicle for Chinese influence, and Japanese began to adopt many aspects of Chinese civilization, in a move which was over the next two centuries to transform the country. The rise of the Sui dynasty in China and the subsequent reunification under the T'ang offered a powerful model, just as the old *uji* system and its clan-based values and limited organizational force or control over even local areas was proving inadequate to the needs of an emerging state.

With the Soga dominant at the Yamato court this process was accelerated. It is noteworthy that the Soga chief installed his niece on the throne as empress, a late assertion of the old matriarchal system, and appointed her nephew, Prince Shotoku, as regent. In 604 Shotoku issued a document later dubbed the "Seventeen Article Constitution," which promoted the supremacy of the ruler, the establishment of an officialdom on the Chinese pattern, based on ability, the central power of government, and a set of court ranks for officials. Shotoku's "constitution" also decreed reverence for Buddhism by all Japanese, but at the same time praised Confucian virtues, a combination which was to endure in Japan into modern times. The hereditary ranks of the *uji* were slowly replaced by the new official ranks as the chief marks of status. These new designations were divided into senior, junior, upper, and lower groups, in keeping with the Japanese passion for graded hierarchy, altogether 26 such divisions.

Shotoku was the first Japanese ruler to send large-scale official embassies to China, in 607, 608, and again in 614, although some had been sent in earlier centuries. These became still larger later, and by the next century included five or six hundred men in four ships, which by that time, as a result of friction with Korea and civil war there, had to go by sea, some 500 miles of open ocean on which there were many founderings and shipwrecks. Despite the risks, the Japanese were determined to tap the riches of Chinese civilization at their source and to bring back to Japan everything they could learn or transplant. Students, scholars, and Buddhist monks rather than traders were the dominant members of these embassies, and their numbers included even painters and musicians. The missions generally lasted for one year, but many stayed on for another year or more and returned to Japan with later returning embassies. Over time this constituted one of the greatest transfers of culture in world history, with the added distinction that it was all by official plan and management.

Taika, Nara, and Heian

When Prince Shotoku died in or about 622, the surviving Soga rulers provoked a revolt in 645 against their high-handed administration and their aggressive promotion of Buddhism, which was resented by many who saw it as an alien rival to Shinto. The victorious rebels installed a new "emperor," Tenchi (then a youth), supported and advised by a rising aristocrat who took the new family name of Fujiwara (formerly Nakatomi). Their leader, Fujiwara Kamatari, was to found a long line of nobility which played a major role at the Japanese court for many subsequent centuries. The two allies, Tenchi and Fujiwara Kamatari, began a major movement of reform designed to sweep away what remained of earlier forms of government and to replace them on a wholesale basis with Chinese forms, assisted by returnees from earlier embassies to China. To aid this restructuring, which is called the Taika Reforms, five more embassies were sent between 653 and 669. "Taika," meaning in Japanese "great change," was adopted as the name of the new year period in Chinese style, and decreed as having begun with the success of the rebels against Soga in 645. One of the first great changes was the laying out of a new capital on the Chinese model at Naniwa (now within the modern city of Osaka), complete with government ministries and on a checkerboard pattern, but without the walls around all Chinese cities. A census was carried out in 670 (although the population totals it reported are not clear), and on that basis a Chinese form of taxation. A Chinese-style law code was issued, and efforts made to impose a uniform centralized rule. Not long thereafter, following the death of Tenchi, the capital was moved in 710 to Nara, farther from the sea (see the map on page 190), known at the time as Heijo, farther north on the Yamato plain. The law code had been reissued with some changes in 702, and for the next 75 years while Nara remained the capital there were even greater efforts to replicate the Chinese pattern.

Nara, the first real city in Japan, was built as a direct copy of Ch'ang An, the T'ang capital. It was laid out on the same checkerboard pattern but at about a quarter Ch'ang An's size, though it included an imperial palace facing south, plus many large Buddhist temples. Here too there were no walls, as at Naniwa, and even at this reduced size Nara's plan was never filled in; something like half of it was never built. Japan was still a small country, even tinier at that period before the spread of Japanese settlement and the apparatus of the state much beyond the Yamato area. Nara seems to have been dominated, both physically and politically, by its many Buddhist monasteries and temples, some of which still remain. In 784 a new emperor, Kammu (781–806), decided to move the capital from Nara, first just a few miles northward, perhaps to escape the Buddhist domination of Nara. This was not followed through, and in 794 he began the building of a new city called Heian (modern Kyoto) at the northern end of the plain just south of Lake Biwa. It was larger than Nara but on the same Chinese plan, and also lacked walls. The original checkerboard layout is still apparent in modern Kyoto, which remained the capital of Japan and the seat of the emperor until 1868.

The emperor's role was modeled on that in China, a figure who combined all power over a centralized state. He had been given a Chinese-style title from the time of Prince Shotoku, *Tenno* ("heavenly ruler," like the "son of heaven" in China). In fact the Japanese emperor, at least after Kammu's time (he seems to have been a forceful person), played mainly a ceremonial and symbolic role, as he still does. This was partly because, as a divinity, he could not be expected to involve himself in the rough and tumble of everyday politics, but primarily because real power came increasingly to be wielded by great aristocratic families at court. The emperors were also busy with their ritual function as the head figures of the Shinto cult, and perhaps in keeping with their exalted position far above the noise and dust of *realpolitik*, most of them came to retire early. One of the consequences of the Sinification of Japan, especially in its political forms, was however the end of female power and rulers, which had clearly been important in the past but which now clashed with Confucian notions and Chinese precedents. There was one reigning empress, who favored Buddhism, like the T'ang Empress Wu a century or less earlier, and during her reign a Buddhist monk who had influence with her tried to take over the throne. This may have prejudiced people against her, but in any case on her death in 770 the monk was exiled.

In other respects the Japanese altered the Chinese model of government wherever they saw it as necessary, to fit Japan's quite different society and its far smaller size. Once again the entire area occupied by the Japanese was divided into provinces and districts, although the provinces were far smaller than in China. As in the T'ang, there was a Grand Council of State, and

Part of the temple complex at Horyuji near Nara, the oldest wooden buildings in the world, although nearly all have been periodically repaired, carefully following the original plans. The Chinese model is clear. (R. Murphey)

below it eight (rather than six) ministries or boards, including one to supervise the imperial household and another in charge of the Shinto cult and its many shrines. At the court in Heian there was an effort to replicate the behavior and rituals of the T'ang court, including its court music and dance forms, long since gone in China now but still preserved in relict form at the Japanese court to the present. One of the fascinations of Japan lies in their transplanting and then preserving a great deal of T'ang culture, including its architecture but including also many other things, even the famous "Japanese" tea ceremony, taken lock, stock, and barrel from T'ang China at this period, complete with the rather bitter and sludgy green tea used, the simple bowls, and the elaborate ritual ceremony around which it is built. In these and many other respects, if one wants to get a glimpse of what T'ang China was like, one must go to Japan.

Officials at the local level in Heian times, and for a long time thereafter, were not, as in China, imperially appointed magistrates but local leaders, comparable to headmen. Nevertheless land was thought to belong to the central state, and peasants paid taxes based on the land they owned, primarily in the form of rice but also in textiles (where they could be produced), and in corvée labor, as in China. The hereditary aristocracy dominated the local areas, and also provided troops as needed: themselves with their weapons and their retainers or followers, and later horses. Otherwise it was a Chinese-style system, although it seems likely that much of it was on paper rather than followed in practice. It is only reasonable to expect that such sweeping changes could not be carried out overnight, or that the Chinese model could be made to fit Japan in every respect. Although the power of the central state clearly did increase, at the local level it seems likely that much of the earlier *uji* values, forms, and social organization persisted and were only slowly absorbed into the new state. The regular flow of tax revenues strengthened the central government, and between the late eighth and early ninth century its control expanded to encompass all of Kyushu, and also pushed Japanese control eastward and northward against the Ainu, whose power was finally broken in northern Honshu, although the area north of modern Tokyo was effectively settled by Japanese only slowly. They had begun their occupation in northern Kyushu, almost semitropical, and northern Honshu was cold and snowy. Japanese culture had adjusted to a mild winter climate and hot summers: houses which could be easily opened to breezes, minimal heating, and loose-fitting clothing; it is possible that some elements in the population had come originally from tropical or subtropical south China, and southern Kyushu was truly subtropical.

In Nara and Heian times, despite the growth of the central state, Japan was still not only small but poor, especially by comparison with China, and economically retarded. The elegant court life of Heian, which is what we know most about because it was literate, is far from representative of the way most people lived. As in Korea, barter was still the principal basis of trade, such as it was, and government issue of copper coins in 708, in imitation of the Chinese model, made little impact. One of the chief achievements of the T'ang and subsequent dynasties, the bureaucracy based on merit as measured in the imperial examinations, was briefly toyed with, but all official posts and all political power, even at the lower levels, remained with the hereditary aristocracy. As in

Korea, and in further imitation of China, a government university was established, but instead of offering education as a means of social mobility it educated only the sons of the court nobility. Peasants do seem to have escaped from the serfdom of the *uji* system and became taxpayers to the central government, but this was not necessarily accompanied by any major improvement in their economic well-being. And it would again be logical to assume that the old *uji* aristocracy did not abdicate all their former power, or their wealth. Their aristocratic status continued to be recognized, as "outer" ranks, and they probably retained much of their wealth as well as their superior position over the peasantry. Since they were no longer the chief powers, however, they did not begin to match in their local areas the splendors of Heian and its sophisticated culture.

CHINESE AND BUDDHIST ART

Buddhism continued to act as a vehicle for Chinese culture, including Buddhist art. This gave a new opportunity for the expression of the Japanese artistic genius. Craftsmen worked mainly in wood, where in China many had worked in stone, but given the Japanese faithfulness in preservation (and the fact that most images were housed in roofed temples) a great deal of the Buddhist art of this period still survives. Bronze and lacquer were further media which the Japanese used to perfection, as fine as anything in China or Korea and closely resembling these earlier forms, but already by Heian times distinctively Japanese. This is equally true of architecture, both in palaces and in temples, on Chinese lines but beautifully done. Here too one can see still preserved many buildings in the T'ang style built in the seventh and eighth centuries, including the temple and monastery complex begun by Prince Shotoku at Horyuji not far from Nara and then rebuilt a few decades later, probably the oldest wooden buildings in the world and as close as one can get to T'ang period architecture. Inside the buildings are Buddhist images and wall paintings from this period which are an aesthetic treat. Only a little later in age is the great Todaiji temple at Nara itself, built to ensure good fortune for the new imperial state and imperial and aristocratic families. Subsequent emperors were patrons of Buddhism, endowed many temples and monasteries, and ordered the mass printing of Buddhist charms. Inside the Todaiji is an enormous bronze figure of the Buddha dedicated in 752, still one of the largest in the world. A nearby storehouse (*Shosoin*) contains imperial treasures from the eighth century: rugs, paintings, screens, weapons, and musical instruments, many of them imported from T'ang China.

Buddhism and Literacy

By the ninth century Buddhism, promoted by the court, had spread throughout Japan, and tombs were no longer built. Following Buddhist and Indian practice, Japanese began to burn their dead, although the ashes were often given a burial or an enshrinement in an urn. Diet gradually became vegetarian, in keeping with Buddhist ideas against the taking of life, although fish continued to be eaten and provided a vital source of protein. Since practically all of the Japanese population lived on or near the sea on the narrow coastal plain, fish were widely available, either fresh or dried and salted, together with dried seaweed, which continues to be an important element in Japanese food. The few who lived in the mountains often could not obtain, or afford, fish, and probably continued to eat some local game; birds were referred to as "mountain fish," but for the most part the mountain people too observed the Buddhist ban on meat. Buddhism offered, as Shinto did not, doctrines on the afterlife, text-based rituals and theology, the promise of salvation, and emphasis (in this Mahayana version imported from China and Korea) on good works as the means of acquiring merit and thus increasing one's chances of higher status in the next life. Shinto cults were tolerated, and came to be regarded as minor and local versions of Buddhist deities. The sun goddess Amaterasu was eventually identified as Vairocana, the universal Buddha, and she is the one represented in the large bronze figure in the Todaji. Since Shinto had no theology and little in the way of doctrine, it offered no real contest with Buddhism, and most Japanese continued to follow both, a little like the persistence of Taoism in China in the face of both Confucianism and Buddhism. Indeed, Taoism and Shinto had much in common, especially in their admiration of nature and their feeling about it as the best guide for people.

Japanese monks returning from visits to China brought with them many of the Buddhist sects which had arisen there. The Shingon sect was brought to Japan in 806 by the monk Kobo Daishi, with its magic formulas and incantations, which had a broad mass appeal as it had in China. Kobo founded a monastery on Mt. Koya, near Nara, most of which still exists and is a reminder of the grand scale of Buddhist building in that period. Many stories and myths were generated about Kobo and his wanderings and achievements, and he became a popular religious hero. In 805 the T'ien T'ai (Tendai in Japanese) sect was brought to Japan by another returning monk, Dengyo Daishi, who established the sect's headquarters in the mountains northeast of Kyoto at Enryakuji, near the top of Mt. Hiei, where one can still visit the extensive area and buildings, although none date from this period in their present form. Tendai was a highly eclectic faith, taking elements from many sects as well as echoes of Taoism and even Hinduism, which were reconciled by the simple and easy assertion that each belonged to different levels of truth, or as the Hindus later put it, "There are many ways to *moksha* (nirvana)." A later Enryakuji abbot was the monk Ennin, whom we have already met in Chapter 5 and whose travel diary is such a rich source on T'ang China. Tendai became the dominant sect in Japan in part because of Ennin's combination of its teachings with those of the more esoteric Shingon sect.

The coming of Buddhism accelerated the spread and use of Chinese characters, not only for Buddhist texts but for other purposes as well. Along with the characters, even though they were mainly given a Japanese sound, came also many thousands of Chinese words, which remain in the language still, some of them quite straightforward like the word for three—*san* in both languages—and others less directly equivalent but easily recognizable. To begin with, as in Korea, Japanese used Chinese characters for all their writing, and produced an extensive literature in Chinese, foreign and difficult language though it was. This of course put a premium on education, which was virtually equated with knowledge of Chinese, and further strengthened the position of the upper classes, the only people who had the time and education to master it. The adoption of characters, along with so much of the rest of Chinese culture, also stimulated the first Japanese writing of history, beginning with the *Kojiki* in 712. It was a mark of respectablitity and civilization to keep records, as the Chinese did, and to compile accounts of the past. The *Nihongi* in 720 was followed in the ninth century by five further histories on the Chinese model. The Japanese also began in the eighth century to produce equivalents to the Chinese local gazetteers called *fudoki*, accounts of local geography, history, economy, legends, politics, and notable features. As in China, calligraphy was regarded as the highest form of art and as the mark of an educated person. Poetry and prose were written both in characters and in Japanese phonetic syllables. Another echo of China was the development of short poems, mainly about nature and its reflection in human affairs, or lack thereof, much like many of the Chinese originals. This short form in the Heian period was called *tanka*, and in a later version is perhaps the form of Japanese literature best known in the West, the *haiku*.

The Heian period is usually dated as running from 794 to 1185, and even more than the briefer Nara period before it saw a new flood of Chinese influence which remade most of at least the upper levels of society and many of the forms of government. But with the last century of the T'ang, China was falling into chaos, and the glories of Ch'ang An were no longer so attractive a model. At the same time, the very different Japanese circumstances and traditional forms began to reassert themselves. Embassies to China were discontinued, although individual monks and traders continued to go in smaller numbers, but China was no longer a magnet. Within Japan, the political system founded so squarely on Chinese lines began to encounter the same problems as the Chinese original had done as each dynasty grew old in office.

The Heian aristocracy included the descendants of *uji* rulers with their large landholdings, and the new or higher aristocracy were often given land grants in recognition of their rank or special services. Much land was also granted to Buddhist monasteries and the major Shinto shrines. These paid no taxes, and many of the aristocracy managed to avoid or at least to minimize them. With the slow rise of population (we have no accurate numbers for this period), much new land was opened for rice cultivation, which had to be cleared, and then drained or irrigated. Some of it was reclaimed from the sea or from lakes, but it all cost money. The court encouraged this, reasonably enough, and allowed those who brought new land into cultivation to keep it under their ownership, at first for one generation but soon thereafter permanently. The only groups who could afford the heavy expense of the original development were of course the small upper classes, and so there developed a situation very like that in the declining years of most Chinese dynasties: more and more land slipping off the tax rolls and becoming concentrated in the hands of the rich.

The Shoen System

This of course also fit the long-established patterns of Japanese society, dominated by a small hereditary aristocracy which held all power as well as most wealth. Private estates (*shoen*) began to emerge, which more and more acquired some of the aspects of small local states. Powerful families at court, like the Fujiwara, patronized and protected the *shoen* ruling families, and in some cases became estate owners themselves. Estate owners began to assert their virtual independence from the central government, declaring themselves immune to government inspection or jurisdiction. The *shoen* were not large, single blocks of land like the European manor but often discrete pieces of farmland which might be scattered around a wider area while being run as a unit, and almost always under the ownership of an aristocratic family, with court patronage and protection. They in turn hired local managers but left the job of farming to small peasant farmers and workers attached to them. One interesting aspect of this system, which seems in other respects retrograde, is its provision for income from the estate and inheritance of it to go to women as well as to men. Perhaps this was a modest revival of earlier Japanese forms, as indicated above, but it also reflected the decline of the Chinese-style state, its imposition of Chinese social forms, and thus the reversion in this period to something closer to the original Japanese patterns.

Over time the *shoen* came to occupy the great bulk of the agricultural land; although most were not very large, there were thousands of them and they dominated not only the landscape but the entire society and polity, as their owners, many of them related to the imperial family, became the chief local and even regional powers. Even in the remaining state-owned lands, perhaps about half of the total, aristocrats who served there as officials became in many ways similar to the *shoen* owners, and in time their positions also became hereditary. By the twelfth century, Japan was falling apart in terms of effective central rule. All of this reflected the declining power of the central state, although its power had never been very effective outside the immediate capital area. More and more as time went on power was exercised primarily by the great aristocratic families, and by the large Buddhist monasteries, both in the capital area and in the provinces. The emperor became increasingly a figurehead, as he was to be for nearly all the rest of Japanese history. In this longish period the Fujiwara family dominated court politics and even exiled an emperor to Kyushu who had dared to appoint an official of whom they disapproved in 901. In 1069 another emperor attempted to establish a land records office with the aim of confiscating estates which had come into being in the preceding 20 years, but in 1045 the Fujiwara blocked this obviously overdue effort at reform. Another emperor, Shirakawa, was somewhat more successful in challenging the Fujiwara after he formally retired in 1086 by working through lesser and non-Fujiwara aristocrats. But by his time the central government had been fatally weakened, in large part because it had lost most of its earlier revenues. The Fujiwara were split into factions, and there was widespread more general violence, even in the capital itself.

Heian Culture

But despite political disintegration, economic and cultural development continued, as in China under similar circumstances. The political scene, in both countries, was only one aspect of society, and in both a relatively superficial one. Even in the chaotic centuries after the fall of the Han, Chinese culture and economic and technological growth continued. In Japan, the *shoen* system was perhaps in fact more conducive to regional development than the earlier effort at central control had been, and clearly it was based in and tended to further the in-

terests of local areas, including those far from the capital. It was in this period, between the ninth and twelfth centuries, that the plains area around what was to become modern Tokyo was effectively occupied and put to use for an increasingly intensive agricultural system. Honshu, farther north, the area later known as Tohoku, was first filled in by Japanese settlement and made productive where it could be, producing a great deal of local wealth in the hands of aristocratic families, including branches of the Fujiwara. At the same time, the Chinese cultural model spread from the capital at Heian, where it had been cultivated like a hothouse plant, to the rest of Japan. Heian court culture became even more refined, centered on intellectual and aesthetic self-cultivation in the Chinese mode. Court nobles, who by now had no real political role but did have income from their estates, pursued an exaggerated form of the Chinese elite lifestyle, composing classical-style poems at wine parties and taking enormous pains with their refined manners (*li*) and their clothing, which was suited to each formal or ritual occasion.

Clothing offered an opportunity for the characteristically Japanese aesthetic sensitivity, with its combinations of colors and textures. By all odds the most famous of the literary works of this period is *The Tale of Genji*, written by a court lady, Murasaki Shikibu, which is considered below. In it there are many scenes in which clothing is described in loving detail, and in one such scene a high-born lady is sighted in her carriage. She casually but artfully shows a bit of her forearm on the sill of the carriage window; the successive layers of her clothing thus revealed are noted instantly by the gentlemen who are watching, who comment on the superb taste displayed by the combinations of texture and color in this tiny sample, and conclude that this is indeed a lady worth knowing, and worth making a conquest of. Much of the *Genji*, and other literature of the time, deals with amorous affairs among the court aristocrats, in a setting where such dalliance was clearly acceptable socially and where marriage was not seen as confining.

Much of the literary output was in fact the work of female authors. In addition to Lady Murasaki, there were a number of other court ladies who wrote both poetry and prose. Probably the best known of them is Lady Sei Shonagon, whose *Pillow Book*, written about A.D. 1000, is a collection of comments on court life, by turns witty and caustic. Several other court women wrote novels, and most of them kept diaries, in which they also included poems, reflecting on the changing moods of the seasons and on the foibles of humanity. Court ladies were apparently less conventional than the men and freer to express themselves. The absence of harems and of extensive concubinage in Japan also left them a wider scope than in China. It is indeed remarkable that women writers dominated the literary ouput of Heian Japan, but

Samples of *Genji*

The following samples convey something of the flavor of The Tale of Genji.

"The lady, when no answer came from Genji, thought that he changed his mind, and though she would have been very angry if he had persisted in his suit, she was not quite prepared to lose him with so little ado. But this was a good opportunity once and for all to lock up her heart against him. She thought that she had done so successfully, but found to her surprise that he still occupied an uncommonly large share of her thoughts."

. . . .

"He had come in a plain coach with no outriders. No one could possibly guess who he was and, feeling quite at his ease, he leaned forward and deliberately examined the house. The gate, also made of a kind of trellis work, stood ajar and he could see enough of the interior to realize that it was a very humble and poorly furnished dwelling. For a moment he pitied those who lived in such a place, but then he remembered the song: "Seek not in the wide world to find a home, but where you choose to rest, call that your house.... Monarchs may keep their palaces of jade, for in a leafy cottage two can sleep." There was a wattled fence over which some ivy-like creeper spread its cool green leaves, and among the leaves were white flowers with petals half unfolded like the lips of people smiling at their own thoughts.... It was a most strange and delightful thing to see how on the narrow tenement in a poor quarter of the town, they had clambered over rickety eaves and gables and spread wherever there was room for them to grow. He sent one of his servants to pick some. The man entered at the half-open door and had begun to pluck the flowers when a little girl in a long yellow tunic came through a quite genteel sliding door and, holding out toward Genji's servant a white fan heavily perfumed with incense, she said to him: "Would you like something to put them on? I am afraid you have chosen a wretched looking bunch," and she handed him the fan."

Source: From *The Tale of Genji,* translation of Arthur Waley (New York: Doubleday, 1955), pp. 58.

this provides little clue to the more general status of women outside the exalted circles of court life. The aristocratic women who lived there were generally idle otherwise but were highly educated, in both cases unlike women in the rest of Japanese society, a kind of rarified and small inner group. Nevertheless their output is impressive, and their literary prominence unmatched in any premodern society anywhere.

MURASAKI SHIKIBU (LADY MURASAKI)

Lady Murasaki's birth date is not known precisely, though it was probably about A.D. 978, and we are also not sure of the date of her death, probably about A.D. 1015. We do not know her real name, since in Heian Japan it was considered improper to record the personal names of aristocratic women outside of the imperial family. It is known that she came from a junior branch of the great Fujiwara clan, and that her father was a provincial governor. The name Murasaki may derive from that of a major figure in her novel, *The Tale of Genji*, or from its meaning of "purple," a pun on the *Fuji* of Fujiwara, which means "wisteria." "Shikibu" refers only to an office held by her father.

Lady Murasaki's journal is our only source of information about her life. It is casual about dates, but records that she was a highly precocious child, and became literate early: "My father was anxious to make a good Chinese scholar of (my brother), and often came to hear him read his lessons.... So quick was I at picking up the language that I was soon able to prompt my brother.... After this I was careful to conceal the fact that I could write a single Chinese character." But she acquired a wide knowledge of both Chinese and Japanese works and also became a talented calligrapher, painter, and musician, suitable training for an aristocratic girl. At about age 21 she was married to a much older man, a distant Fujiwara cousin, and bore a daughter. The next year her husband died, and in her grief she considered becoming a Buddhist nun, but turned instead to reflection on the problem of human happiness, especially for women. Around that time, approximately the year 1001, she began work on her masterpiece, *The Tale of Genji*, which was probably nearly finished when, some six years later, she became a lady-in-waiting at the imperial court.

Like the *Genji*, her journal describes the refined and colorful life at court, as well as its less glamorous aspects of rivalries and intrigues. Both are the subject of her great novel, which combines a romantic as well as psychological approach with realistic detail and subtle insight into human behavior, still praised as the chief masterpiece of all Japanese literature. Her people are real, despite the highly mannered world in which they lived, and through

her journal we also have a picture of her as an extraordinarily alive, imaginative, and even compelling person. A collection of her poems has also survived, which further mark her as an accomplished stylist.

Genji deals with the life of a prince and his seemingly endless affairs with various court ladies, including careful attention to the details of manners, dress, and court politics—not perhaps the most rewarding of subjects, but in the author's hands they become so. Although the hero is idealized, this is far more than a conventional romantic tale, including the subtle portrayal of Genji as he grows older. Toward the end of her own journal, Lady Murasaki gives us a candid glimpse of herself: (People think) "I am very vain, reserved, unsociable … wrapped up in the study of ancient stories, living in a poetical world all my own…. But when they get to know me, they find that I am kind and gentle." Perhaps she was all these things. But

This Edo period (seventeenth century) painting illustrates a scene from the *Tale of Genji* entitled "Yugao" (evening faces). (Harvard University Art Museum)

A Very Human Person

Sei Shonagon, author of The Pillow Book *and a contemporary of Lady Murasaki, seems to have been a happy person who enjoyed her life.*

"When I make myself imagine what it is like to be one of those women who live at home, faithfully serving their husbands—women who have not a single exciting prospect in life yet who believe that they are perfectly happy—I am filled with scorn. Often they are of quite good birth, yet have no opportunity to find out what the world is like. I wish they could live for a while in our society (i.e. court), even if it should mean taking service as attendants, so that they might come to know the delights it has to offer."

Shonagon also, in a long essay, compiled a list of "Hateful Things" which makes her seem very human:

"One is in a hurry to leave but one's visitor keeps chattering away.... A man who has nothing in particular to recommend him discusses all sorts of subjects at random as though he knew everything.... One is just about to be told some interesting piece of news when a baby starts crying.... An admirer has come on a clandestine visit, but a dog catches sight of him and starts barking. One feels like killing the beast.... One has been foolish enough to invite a man to spend the night in an unsuitable place—and then he starts snoring.... A mouse that scurries all over the place.... A person who recites a spell himself after sneezing. In fact, I detest anyone who sneezes, except the master of the house.... I cannot stand people who leave without closing the panel behind them.... Ladies in waiting who want to know everything that is going on."

Source: From *The Pillow Book of Sei Shonagon,* translation by Ivan Morris. (New York, Columbia University Press), 1967, Vol. I, passim.

whatever her personal character, she was a gifted and inspired writer.

Art and Gardens

During the Heian, or Fujiwara, period, from 794 to 1185, the graphic arts continued to follow a more clearly Chinese path, including the prominence of calligraphy and the painting of scrolls and many-paneled screens (*shoji*). But Japanese art had already begun to distinguish itself from its original Chinese model with its greater attention to simple line drawing of flat surfaces, often telling a story. Palace architecture became less massive than the earlier copies of T'ang palaces had been, lighter and with more open pavilions, now usually set in artfully recreated "natural" surroundings of carefully designed ponds, gardens, and trees, which greatly enhance the buildings' appeal and express the particular Japanese appreciation of nature. We know little of domestic architecture at this period, but the emphasis on openness apparent in Heian temple and palace architecture already suggests the later evolution of the traditional Japanese house, with its sliding panels which could be opened to the summer breezes and to reveal a garden and/or pond, sometimes very small but designed as a microcosm of the greater natural world. That is perhaps a good example of the Japanese adaptation of an originally Chinese style, as is the Japanese garden. The Japanese are justly famous as gardeners, but nearly all of the plants used were originally developed in China, including even what became the imperial flower, chrysanthemum, the showy tree peonies which the Japanese, like the Chinese, loved to paint, camellias, flowering fruit trees, and many others. Even the Japanese art of *bonsai*, the artificial dwarfing of trees and shrubs grown in pots or tubs through careful and repeated pruning, was originally Chinese; the intent of course was to keep these microcosms of nature down to manageable size so that they could decorate living space or a tiny garden and still serve as reminders, miniaturized samples of a larger world, like the Japanese garden as a whole.

The garden style of Japan, where carefully placed trees and shrubs dominate rather than tended flower beds, usually grouped around a pond, was originally de-rived from T'ang China, like so much else of Japanese culture, but we can see its Chinese origins only in the Sung, and even there, in any living form, probably in a much altered version. Most Japanese gardens were on a smaller scale. Gardens of course are always changing as plants and trees are replaced over time, but garden styles change too, and what we can see of Chinese gar-dens now makes them look quite different from contem-porary Japanese gardens, although one can certainly see the connection, including the often purposeful re-tention of a dead tree, partly to complete the picture of nature, partly to serve as a contrast with the living forms. The gardens originally laid out in the Sung in the city of Suchou (Suzhou/Soochow) west of Shanghai have probably been preserved closer to their original form than other Chinese gardens, although there have doubtless been changes there too. In the Suchou gar-dens, grouped around a pond and with many open pavil-ions and galleries for viewing them at different seasons, one is much closer to the modern Japanese garden style, and indeed it is possible that much of the latter was originally based on the Sung rather than the T'ang model, about which we unfortunately know very little and of which there are no surviving examples except for a few plantings or preserved growth around temples. But it is in China, referred to as "the mother of gar-dens," that one must look for the sources of this, like so many aspects of Japanese culture, which we tend to think of now as particularly Japanese. The Japanese have indeed made it their own, like their graphic arts, ceramics, literary and political forms, the institution of the emperor, the writing of history, even the tea cere-mony, all taken directly from China and woven into Japanese culture, although in each case (some more than others) these imports were refashioned to suit Japanese tastes and circumstances.

Kana and Monastic Armies

One of the early assertions or expressions of separate Japanese identity was the development of a system of phonetic symbols to transcribe the sounds of the Japan-ese spoken language, unrelated to Chinese. Although Chinese characters continued to be used, and are still used by educated Japanese, more and more texts came to be written in this syllabary, known as *kana*. At first the Japanese sounds were in effect spelled out by using the characters' phonetic sound, but during the ninth century, with the borrowing from Chinese civilization still at its height, the phonetic elements of Chinese char-acters were simplified into a new set of symbols. This was relatively easy for Japanese, even though it is not

monosyllabic like Chinese, since each sound syllable is distinct and each is fully pronounced. Most poems came to be written in *kana*, since sound is such an important element of poetry, although in many other texts, and sometimes in poetry, *kana* was mixed with characters, as it still is, especially to write words borrowed from Chinese. Cumbersome as this sounds (and of course it meant learning both systems), it made writing much easier, and more authentically Japanese. Lady Sei Shonagon's *Pillow Book* and Lady Murasaki's *Tale of Genji* were both written primarily in *kana*, although both authors were also fully literate in Chinese.

As Buddhism, also of course introduced from China by both Chinese and Japanese monks, spread more widely beyond court circles and merged with Shinto, Pure Land Buddhism, imported in the ninth century, be-came the most popular sect. Like the original message of the Buddha himself, it focused on the doctrine of re-birth and hence escape from what it asserted was a "de-generate age," into the Pure Land Paradise presided over by the Buddha Amida. It was thus a form of belief in magic, which had a wide appeal to the uneducated. At the court the more elaborate rituals of Tendai and Shin-gon remained more favored. In Japan at large, great Buddhist monasteries grew up to rival those in the capi-tal area, and the different sects became armed rivals. The monasteries drew revenues from the lands they owned, and became powers which also rivaled the de-clining central state and the rising *shoen*. Many monas-teries developed armed bands, and then genuine armies, originally to protect their lands but later to en-gage in large-scale warfare with rival sects and their armies. By the end of the eleventh century these nomi-nally Buddhist armies became the major military pow-ers in Japan and even threatened the capital, a sad se-quel to the teachings of the original Buddha and his doctrine of nonviolence.

Heian court culture was no doubt delightful, but its elegance and refinement were far removed from the real world of most of Japan. The Fujiwara had tried to hold the country together through links with other aris-tocratic families and through extensive patronage, but it is hardly surprising that in time this indirect means of control proved inadequate. The *shoen* and the Buddhist monasteries increasingly became the real powers, and some of the *shoen* were owned by families who also built up their own armies, to rule lands they had originally guarded for court-based families or had acquired through patronage. Some of these armies, together with the new group of warriors called *samurai*, an hereditary aristocratic group who were both educated and trained in the arts of war—"gentlemen warriors," as they have been called—had developed out of the frontier wars as Japanese settlement spread north beyond the Yamato area. Monastic armies also sometimes intervened in factional conflicts and thus became power brokers. By the end of the Heian period, contending armies dominated politics and had become the real powers.

Pressures on the Environment

As in China, decay at the center did not necessarily mean that the country as a whole suffered economically, although the rise in violence and disorder was certainly harmful or fatal to many. We have no real population figures for this period, but by A.D. 1000 the total population is estimated as about five million. This represents a considerable increase from the even rougher estimate of about two million or perhaps a bit more as of about A.D. 550, and indicates that cultivation was spreading over larger areas. As mentioned before, the soils of Japan are mainly thin and poor and are easily eroded. Efforts at fertilization seem to have been limited largely to the use of green manure—leaves, grass, weeds, and branches cut in the surrounding woodlands. The use of human manure, or night soil, seems not to have begun until later (although this is unclear), but the intensiveness of farming, especially the spreading use of controlled irrigation, certainly contributed to steady increases in the total food supply, enough to feed the increase in population and perhaps a bit more. But Japan remained poor and underdeveloped by comparison with China, and perhaps even with Korea, and its population totals unimpressive by such measures. One Japanese asset was its mild and generally well-watered climate, and the surrounding sea provided a major increment to the diet which, as already indicated, was easily available to almost the entire population, given its overwhelmingly coastal distribution.

Nevertheless, as population grew, pressures on the environment increased. These were most evident, and potentially most serious, in the progressive cutting of the forests, primarily for building material but also to clear land for agriculture. Given the thin soils and steep slopes of Japan, good forest cover is essential to prevent or limit erosion, and also the siltation of irrigation systems on the limited area of lowlands. The influx of Chinese influences on a large scale, beginning in the eighth century, led to the building first of Naniwa, then of Nara, and finally of Heian (Kyoto), which created an enormous new demand for wood, increased still further as population rose and needed housing. At the same time, and even more in succeeding centuries, the many very large Buddhist temples and monastery complexes consumed cumulatively even larger amounts of wood. Iron tools after about A.D. 200 speeded the assault on the forests, and also brought new demands for wood and charcoal for smelting. The beginnings of shipbuilding brought further uses for wood, but the major forest depredations were caused by the building of the two successive capitals at Nara and Heian, and the Buddhist temples and monasteries. Since all building was in wood, fires were frequent, often could not be adequately controlled, and hence necessitated frequent rebuilding.

Even the *uji* leaders had built wooden-stockaded bases, and the firing of the *haniwa* pottery figures required large amounts of wood or charcoal fuel. As provincial headquarters developed too, their building required increasing amounts of wood. In this moist climate wood deteriorated rapidly, and palaces and temples or shrines were rebuilt roughly every generation, or with a change in rulers. By the time of the building of Nara, accessible timber in the southwestern part of the Yamato area was largely gone, and trees had to be hauled from relatively far away. In the eighth century the rulers, now called emperors, felt it appropriate to build two capitals, one for the reigning emperor and another for the heir. The building of Heian, on a much greater scale than Nara, could to begin with draw on still largely untapped forests nearby to the northwest and around Lake Biwa. Hundreds of thousands of workers were employed in the construction and in the felling and hauling of timbers. But for all the scale of building at Heian, Buddhist and Shinto construction was probably larger still, including the buildings at Horyuji, the Shinto shrine at Ise, and hundreds of others. The monumental scale of much of this construction ate deeply into remaining accessible forest stands, beginning with the building of the great Buddhist temple at Nara, the Todaiji. Like the palaces, most temples required frequent rebuilding as well as repair. By the tenth century, all of the accessible forests of and around the Yamato area had been cut, and inroads begun into mountainous areas despite the high costs of getting the trees to where they were needed. It is possible that the slow deterioration of Heian was at least partly the result of the difficulty in obtaining wood for construction.

One consequence was the development of a less extravagant form of building, including domestic architecture, which emphasized open instead of enclosed or solid walls, which could be closed by sliding screens covered with translucent rice paper. Some roofs began to be covered with tile instead of wood, far more durable and also fire-resistant, although many roofs began to be made of bark. Floors were covered by rush or grass mats, *tatami*, which could be laid over rough boards but which produced an equally attractive surface, if not more so, as well as welcome insulation and a degree of springiness, important since Japanese have always slept on the floor. This is of course the nature of the traditional Japanese house as one can still see it and as it is represented in art from the past. Houses also became

❈ The Japanese Aesthetic ❈

Here is one of many passages in Lady Murasaki's diary which, like those in Genji, *dwell on the typically Japanese fascination with colors and textures and with the aesthetics of good taste.*

"On that day all the ladies in attendance on His Majesty had taken particular care with their dress. One of them, however, had made a small error in matching the colors at the opening of her sleeves. When she approached His Majesty to put something in order, the High Court nobles and senior courtiers who were standing nearby noticed the mistake and stared at her. This was a source of lively regret to Lady Saisho and the others. It was not really such a serious lapse of taste; only the color of one of her robes was a shade too pale at the opening."

Source: From Ivan Morris, *The World of the Shining Prince.* (New York: Penguin, 1969), p. 206.

smaller, and the building of large palaces largely came to an end in the course of the ninth century.

One indication of the continued development of Japan was the building of ships, made of course entirely of wood. The continuing interaction with Korea required relatively large seaworthy vessels, and with the beginning of direct interaction with China, especially by the sea route, even larger and sturdier vessels were needed. New ships were usually built for each of the many embassies sent to China, commonly four, sometimes more. By the ninth century timber for shipbuilding had become so scarce that an imperial order of 882 tried to prevent tree felling in the area where the most suitable ship timbers grew except for shipbuilding. As another indication of the growing scarcity of wood, the kind most favored for the thousands of large statues which adorned Buddhist temples had apparently become so scarce in the course of the eighth century that sculptors began to work instead in other less suitable woods. By the eleventh century, with the unavailability of large logs, sculptors began to build their images out of separate pieces of wood joined together.

Japanese winters, especially in the Yamato area, are fortunately relatively mild, but there was nevertheless a demand for fuel which rose with population numbers. Charcoal burners cut large swaths through many forests; they could convert heavy, bulky wood, which presented enormous transport problems, into much lighter bundles of charcoal, and could also use a large proportion of branches and even twigs. But charcoal was in great demand to smelt iron, and relatively little of it could be used for heating, mainly in the imperial palaces. Other users of wood included those who evaporated seawater to make salt, who used large amounts of

fuel, and potters for their kilns. Disputes over cutting rights in the remaining forests were chronic. Peasants cut or collected what wood they needed for various purposes in the forests near their villages, but the monasteries and the aristocracy tried to preserve forest stands for their own purposes and tried to keep out especially peasant woodcutters. Even peasant subsistence cutting tended to prevent the regrowth of the forests, and the larger scale cutting for urban and monastery building purposes was often done on a wholesale basis, removing all the trees in the cutting area, especially on slopes. Selective cutting, which for the long run is better management, was too cumbersome and expensive in the mountains, and many areas were stripped clean. Peasants, potters, and charcoal burners did use the remaining litter but also attacked new growth. Many areas once heavily forested thus reverted to spindly brush and coppice growth or were invaded by weeds and wild grasses which inhibited any new tree growth. In combination, these developments increased the incidence of disastrous fires, which often started in forest litter left after clear cutting, and greatly increased the destruction of wooded areas. Charcoal burners had to use fire of course, and often this spread out of control.

Successive emperors tried to control cutting, and to keep peasants out of imperial woodland, as the *shoen* owners and the great monasteries tried to keep any but their own loggers or collectors out of their lands. It seems to have been realized that good forest cover was essential for the stability of rivers and streams. An imperial order of 821 declared as follows:

The fundamental principle for securing water is found in the combination of rivers and trees. The vegetation on

mountains should always be lush. The reason for this is that while the origin of great rivers is always near thickly vegetated mountains, the flow of small streams comes from bald hills. We know the amount of runoff depends on mountains. If a mountain produces clouds and rain, rivers will be full for 9 *ri* (about 5 miles). If the mountain is stripped bald, the streams in the valley will dry up.[1]

This is closely similar to many earlier Chinese remarks as long ago as Mencius on the importance of forests on slopes, and is of course especially applicable to Japan with its steep slopes and thin soils. There were apparently a few efforts at reforestation in this period, and it was clear that forests were vital both as a source of universally demanded wood and as a form of protection. But it is not known how effective these efforts may have been, or how much impact resulted from the various attempts to keep cutting out of certain areas, or to pursue more selective cutting. In any case, by the end of the Heian period, the classical hearth of Japanese civilization in the Kinai area (from Lake Biwa northeast of Kyoto to the Inland Sea beyond modern Osaka) and its surrounding hills and mountains had been largely stripped of its originally lush tree cover. As the chief center of political control moved northeastward, to Kamakura, some of these originally forested areas did recover somewhat through natural regrowth, and Japan was saved the disastrous consequences of the deforestation which continued in China without a break. Japan's mild, moist climate, where trees grow rapidly, was an important asset, assuring that forests would recover when human pressures lessened. But the seemingly unbroken mantle of forest which covers Japan's mountains today is the result primarily of determined conservation and reforestation programs since the late 1940s.

Note

1 Quoted in Conrad Totman, *The Green Archipelago*, Berkeley: University of California Press, 1989, p. 29.

Suggestions for Further Reading

Borgen, R. *Sugawara no Michizane and the Early Heian Court.* Cambridge: Harvard University Press, 1986.

_____. *The Cambridge History of Japan*, Vols. 1 and 2. Cambridge: Cambridge University Press, 1993 and 1994.

Davis, W. *Japanese Religion and Society.* Albany: SUNY Press, 1992.

Hall, J. *Government and Local Power in Japan.* Princeton University Press, 1966.

_____. ed. *The Cambridge History of Japan.* Cambridge: Cambridge University Press, 1992.

Hane, M. *Premodern Japan.* Boulder: Westview, 1990.

Kitagawa, J. *Religion in Japanese History.* New York: Columbia University Press, 1966.

Miki, F. *Haniwa* (as adapted in English by Roy Miller). Tokyo: Tuttle, 1960.

Morris, I. *The World of the Shining Prince.* New York: Penguin, 1969.

Pearson, R. *Ancient Japan.* New York: Braziller, 1992.

Pollack, D. *The Fracture of Meaning: Japan's Synthesis of China.* Princeton: Princeton University Press, 1986.

Soper, A., and Paine, R. *The Art and Architecture of Japan.* New York: Penguin, 1975.

Totman, C. *Japan Before Perry.* Berkeley: University of California Press, 1981.

_____. *The Green Archipelago.* Berkeley: University of California Press, 1989.

Waley, A., transl., *The Tale of Genji.* London: Allen and Unwin, 1975.

CHAPTER 11

WARRIORS, MONKS, AND CONFLICT: MEDIEVAL JAPAN

The period from the fall of the Heian regime in the 1180s to the final unification of Japan in 1600 is a confusing one. Japan was divided into warring factions as aristocratic and rising provincial families contended with each other, with only brief dominance by any one of them. In this ruthless age, warriors became the dominant groups, and Japanese society became more and more a culture of warfare. Throughout this troubled period, the pretense of imperial authority was preserved. Contending warrior groups and their short-lived rule all acknowledged the reigning emperor even while they manipulated him and his supposedly sacred office to legitimize their power. On several occasions they placed their own candidates from the imperial line on the throne and exiled or eliminated others. A few shreds of imperial authority remained, and court ceremonials continued, but real power had shifted irrevocably to the *bushi*, or warriors.

The Collapse of Heian

Fujiwara court culture was out of touch with political reality in the rest of Japan, despite its patronage links with the *shoen*. The Fujiwara were large estate owners too, but like most, they did not live on their estates but employed a manager and lived in the refined setting of Heian. The central government became more and more symbolic rather than effectively operating, and among other things did not even attempt to keep order in the areas outside the capital. *Shoen* and other local groups came into conflict over land and offices, which began to take the form of armed struggle. There was also a rise in banditry, and on the Inland Sea piracy. *Shoen* developed their own armies to defend their lands or to acquire those of their rivals. Officials appointed by Heian for the provinces which had been created and who tried to supervise the state lands also built up their armies, and in time were given military titles to indicate what had become a prime function. These changes were taking place from the late ninth century until the end of the Heian period in the late twelfth century, and as such local groups increased their power they became in effect the dominant political and military elements. Some of them banded together for mutual protection, and increasingly they ignored the remaining facade of central government in Heian.

Most of the *shoen* had been founded by families, and the provincial officials appointed by the court were also bound by family ties through the patronage network. The defense groups which began to form thus largely followed family lines, but these could not provide enough fighting men and thus other and unrelated dependents, many of them recruited from the managerial and supervisory staff of the estates who had a subordinate connection with the controlling aristocrats, became increasingly prominent among the local forces. In time they increased their power and influence and became a kind of provincial warrior group. The Fujiwara family was prolific, and places could not be found at the court for all of the sons of branch Fujiwara families, or of the imperial line. Periodically in the ninth and tenth centuries extra imperial descendants were cut off from the family line and given new family names, of either Minamoto or Taira. They and lesser Fujiwara kin sought their fortunes in the provinces, as officials or as owners or managers of *shoen*. With the prestige of their ancestry, they became the top level of the provincial aristocracy, instead of those who claimed descent from the old *uji* aristocrats.

These figures, and the surviving provincial *uji* aristocracy, dominated and usually led the military forces which were emerging from the need for *shoen* and government lands to defend themselves under the newly chaotic conditions. Such roles in warfare required armor, weapons, and a horse as well as dependent followers as foot soldiers, who sometimes had to be provided with weapons by their lord. It was all rather like medieval European warfare, led by a mounted knight in armor. The Japanese equivalents of knights were called *bushi* ("warrior") or *samurai* ("retainer"), both groups descended from and now constituting an hereditary aristocracy where, as in medieval Europe, military prowess was equated with and largely monopolized by the nobility. The equipment needed was expensive, and again as in Europe tended to exclude all but the aristocracy except for the footmen. *Bushi* and *samurai* developed their own new code of behavior in its stress on loyalty and honor, like the chivalric code of medieval Euopean knights in its stress on loyalty and honor, and warfare in both cultures was more a matter of contests between individual knights or *bushi/samurai* than of large troop maneuvers. *Bushi* and *samurai* carried bows and arrows rather than the lances of medieval Europe, a short sword, and a longer, slightly curved sword made of fine tempered steel, an art which the Japanese brought close to perfection (whereas the best steel for swords in medieval Europe was imported via the Arabs, as in Damascus or Toledo blades, from India). That in itself demonstrates the importance attached to fighting in medieval Japan, and is probably the period's most notable technological achievement. Japanese swords developed a reputation for quality and began to be exported even to China.

This new warrior aristocracy, descended in part from the old *uji* clans with their emphasis on fighting and their military tradition, also developed a light and flexible armor made of overlapping thin steel or hardened lacquer plates held together by thongs and ribbons, which were often colored as decoration and as a mark of group or clan identity. Helmets were elaborate, and as in medieval Europe bore clan crests as easily identifiable symbols, although they were often so large that they must sometimes have been a liability, and a convenient target. In the course of the twelfth century this warrior class rose to dominance in Japanese society and what re-

Samurai armor from the Kamakura Period (The Metropolitan Museum of Art, Fletcher Fund, 1928)

mained of political authority centered primarily on land rights. There are obvious parallels with medieval Europe: the weakness of any central authority, and the consequent growth of local or regional powers which achieved what integration they could manage through essentially feudal and family ties: lord-vassal relationships, and family loyalty, although since there was no one dominant family or clan, this helped to generate chronic intergroup conflict. Medieval Japan and medieval Europe, whose circumstances were thus similar, produced a similar set of solutions which we may appropriately label as feudal in both cases.

Even before the final disintegration of what authority the Heian court had been able to establish, intergroup struggles between armed provincial bands had begun to dominate the scene. In the Kanto region around modern Tokyo a Taira leader, trading on his original imperial connection, tried to set up his own kingdom in the early tenth century, but was destroyed by rival groups in 940. Westward from Kyoto, around the Inland Sea where Heian authority was at best feeble, the leader of a Fujiwara branch made his own bid for regional power, but he too was defeated by 941. The other supposedly imperial line, the Minamoto, then built their power in the Kanto area and farther north in Honshu, defeating a revival of Taira power in 1031 and then moving north at the expense of other local clans. The Kanto plain with its relatively large (for Japan) agricultural areas could provide revenue to support military operations, and northern Honshu had a military tradition in any case as a result of the long campaigns against the Ainu. This was not however the end of the Taira, who used their imperial connection not only to stay alive but even to become a military presence at the Heian court, supposedly as guardians of the emperor, with whom they claimed kinship. This brought with it court ranks, official posts, and control over patronage networks as well as a stake in both the *shoen* system and government lands.

Twelfth century struggles in Heian itself showed the new importance of military men. Contending groups accused their rivals of rebellion against the Heian court, which by this time cut little ice outside of Heian itself. When a retired emperor died in 1156, his two sons were supported as rivals for the throne by contending claimants for the leadership of the Fujiwara, Minamoto, and Taira clans. The victorious Taira leader, Kiyomori, managed to win out over the Minamoto factions and executed most of them. But one of the Minamoto sons had joined Taira Kiyomori's side, and was disgruntled with his share of the spoils. With the help of similar malcontents among the Fujiwara, he and his warriors seized Heian in 1159, but they were soon destroyed by Kiyomori and his superior forces. These armed struggles in the capital are called the Hogen and Heiji wars, from the names of the "year periods" in which they took place. Despite Kiyomori's victory and his now solid authority, he continued to maintain the emperor and his ceremonial role while at the same time building his power and

A House as Art

After the end of the Heian period, conventionally dated as 1185, much of Heian culture survived despite the political turmoil and fighting of the warrior age, including the literary tradition. A bakufu *official at the imperial court, still in Kyoto, who was also a poet, in the elite East Asian mode, named Kenko (1283–1350), who later became a Buddhist monk, recorded his rambling thoughts which in English are titled "Essays in Idleness." The work is rather like Sei Shonagon's* Pillow Book. *Here is a sample.*

"A house, I know, is but a temporary abode, but how delightful it is to find one that has harmonious proportions and a pleasant atmosphere. One feels somehow that even moonlight, when it shines into the quiet domicile of a person of taste, is more affecting than elsewhere. A house, though it may not be in the current fashion or elaborately decorated, will appeal to us by its unassuming beauty—a grove of trees with a indefinably ancient look; a garden where plants, growing of their own accord, have a special charm; a veranda and an open-work wooden fence of interesting construction; and a few personal effects left carelessly lying about, giving the place an air of having been lived in. A house which multitudes of workmen have polished with every care, where strange and rare Chinese and Japanese furnishings are displayed and even the grass and trees of the garden have been trained unnaturally, is ugly to look at and most depressing."

Source: From Donald Keene's translation of *The Tsurezuregusa of Kenko* as included in P. Lopate, *The Art of the Personal Essay.* (New York: Doubleday, 1994), p. 32.

placing his relatives in key positions in what remained of the central government. Other followers were given posts in the provinces and on the estates. Kiyomori married his daughter to the emperor, and in 1180 was able to have his grandson declared emperor, under a Fujiwara as regent. But for all his power in Heian and his patronage networks elsewhere, Kiyomori had little or no control over the warrior groups in the rest of Japan, or over the Buddhist monasteries even in the capital region, let alone in the provinces. Kiyomori's ascendancy also naturally sparked jealousy and resentment among rival *bushi* groups, especially when he had his grandson declared emperor.

In 1180 there was a rebellion, originally called forth by an imperial prince who felt he had been bypassed, as indeed he had. The Minamoto clan had remained powerful in the Kanto area and their leader, Yoritomo, joined the rebel cause. His younger brother, Yoshitsune, seized Heian and chased the Taira forces westward to the end of the Inland Sea, where he destroyed them in a naval battle in 1185. Yoritomo was meanwhile moving against Fujiwara elements in the north, and by 1190 had destroyed them as well. Thus most of Japan now came under more or less single Minamoto rule, and the Heian period was succeeded by what was called the Kamakura era, taking its name from the new center of Minamoto power in the fortified coastal town of Kamakura (now a Tokyo suburb). Heian (Kyoto) was no longer the center of power, but continued to be recognized as the capital since it remained the seat of the emperor, whom all of the rival warrior clans claimed to support.

The Kamakura Period

Yoritomo's and Yoshitsune's triumphs over the Taira and the Fujiwara marked the final domination of the provincial warrior class, and at least for a time brought Japan under single control, although that was not to last. Yoritomo set up a new administrative structure to match his military control, theoretically centered in Kamakura, although that was relatively far from the center of Japanese population, especially at this period. The court in Kyoto recognized the new political reality by giving Yoritomo court rank and official posts as well as titles, including that of *Seii-tai-shogun*, or "Barbarian-subduing General," which had formerly been used to designate military leaders against the Ainu. Shortened to *shogun* it soon became the title of the major military commander, and since Japan was dominated by its military aristocracy it was also the title of the country's real ruler. Theoretically the *shogun* was the emperor's military adviser or chief of staff, but in fact he was the effective head of state, a situation which continued until

1868. The Kamakura era is thus often called the Kamakura Shogunate.

The administration established by the shoguns was referred to as the *bakufu* (literally, "tent government"), to distinguish it from what remained of the civil administration presided over by Kyoto; henceforward *bakufu* was in practice equivalent to "government," although the name continued to show its military origins. The shogun's power depended on his warrior followers and vassals. Yoritomo took over control of the former Taira lands and those of his followers, and used them to reward his own followers, who were thus bound to him by ties of obligation and feudal loyalty. He also appointed many to provincial positions with the same object, nominally on behalf of the emperor. Other provincial leaders, especially those outside the center of Minamoto power in the Kanto area, formally "gave" their lands to Yoritomo and as his vassals acknowledged him as their feudal lord, in an effort to safeguard their positions. Yoritomo extended his control by appointing stewards for each estate, who often did most of the administration and also collected a military tax. A new office was created of military supervision of groups of provinces.

All of this was of course an assertion of the normal functions of the central government, at least in theory, and it was resented. In 1221 a retired emperor mounted a rebellion against Kamakura with warriors from the capital and nearby monasteries, but it was easily defeated and the retired emperor exiled from Kyoto. Kamakura victory brought control over more lands and posts confiscated from the losing side, especially in central and western Japan where its power had previously been weakest. Two Kamakura offical residents were established in Kyoto to keep an eye on the court. At Kamakura Yoritomo had already set up before his death in 1199 an Administrative Office and council to formulate policy, and an Office of Inquiry which acted as a court of appeal, kept land records, and enforced decisions. In 1232 a new code of law and civil administration was issued better suited to the new circumstances than the old Taiho code of Nara. Despite these manifestations of government, the illusion was preserved that the emperor and the civil government in Kyoto were supreme, and their ceremonial role continued to be observed. But Kamakura power was firmly established over nearly all of Japan, and after the rebellion of 1121 the country saw about a hundred years of relative peace and order domestically, a period in which economic growth could resume.

This firm control was based in part on ruthlessness as well as on feudal ties. Yoritomo hunted down his brother Yoshitsune, jealous of his military success and fearful of his potential rivalry. Other close relatives met the same fate. Yoshitsune became a popular hero when, surrounded by his brother's forces, he killed his wife and family and then himself. Yoritomo at his death left two sons, one considered too young and the other, at 17, considered too wild and irresponsible. Both were thus displaced by a rising branch of the Taira family, the Hojo, who had joined Yoritomo's cause in his triumph over Kiyomori but now took power into their own hands. They forced the eldest son to abdicate and make way for his younger brother, who then was assassinated in 1219, bringing the main Minamoto family line to an end. Interestingly enough, Masako, the daughter of the Hojo leader Tokimasa and the widow of Yoritomo, was instrumental in engineering this coup. Her brother Yoshitoki became the dominant Hojo figure on his father's death, but instead of taking on the title of *shogun*, he and his Hojo successors exercised power indirectly through Fujiwara puppets, much as the Fujiwara themselves had done in Heian by manipulating successive emperors and marrying their daughters into the imperial line. A young Fujiwara who was also descended from Yoritomo through his mother was declared *shogun* in 1126, and in 1152 an imperial prince succeeded him. The appearance of feudal loyalty, both to Yoritomo and to the emperor, was thus preserved. Senior members of the Hojo clan served as joint regents of successive puppet *shoguns*.

The Mongol Invasions

All of this manipulation at the Kamakura base was overshadowed by the two Mongol attempts to invade and conquer Japan. The Mongols had taken over Korea by 1258 and had launched their campaign in south China under Kubilai, who demanded that Japan submit to him in 1268. The Hojo treated the Mongol emissaries roughly, beheaded some, and sent back others, minus their ears, with an insolent reply. It was symptomatic of Kamakura independence of Kyoto that although the court was terrified by the Mongol image and would have quickly agreed to their demands, Kamakura took a far tougher *bushi* line. Kubilai was still busy with the conquest of south China, but he was of course incensed and immediately began preparations for an expedition to humble the haughty Japanese, requisitioning ships and sailors from Korea and from China.

By 1274 the expedition was ready and sailed from Korea, probably about 30,000 Koreans, Mongols, and Chinese, plus horses, in about 900 ships. They landed first, took and sacked the island of Tsushima between Korea and Japan, and then landed in November near Hakata on the north coast of Kyushu, the nearest point from Korea, where they were met by Kamakura and vassal forces. The Mongols had superior weapons, especially their powerful reflex bows, and also were equipped with rockets and catapaults hurling gunpowder missiles. Their battle tactics were also superior to

anything the Japanese had yet evolved, but the resistance was fierce and determined. The Mongols were at a disadvantage as the invaders, and many of their horses were still seasick and weak from the voyage so that, especially in the confined space of their beachhead, they could not be used in the usual devastating cavalry attacks. While the battle was still raging indecisively, a late autumn storm blew up which scattered the Mongol fleet and decided them to withdraw to Korea, feeling that they had made their point. Misjudging the Hojo, Kubilai sent further envoys in 1275 and following years up to 1279, they met the same fate as the earlier mission of 1268 except that the Japanese beheaded all of them.

Kubilai was now *really* infuriated, and in 1281 he sent a far larger expedition of about 100,000 Mongols, 20,000 Koreans, and as many as 50,000 Chinese, in two fleets, about 4,500 ships all told. By now the Mongol conquest of the Southern Sung was complete, and they had a large Chinese fleet at their disposal. One fleet sailed from China and one from Korea, meeting off the Japanese coast and landing in June, once again at Hakata. This was a mistake, since the Japanese had been busily preparing for what they realized would be a renewed Mongol attack, and had built a heavy stone wall around Hakata Bay, anticipating that this would again be the Mongol landing place. The invaders were thus contained on a small and narrow beachhead for nearly two months, and at a serious disadvantage. Once again they could not make effective use of their cavalry, while smaller and more mobile Japanese ships diverted and damaged the Mongol junks. Under these circumstances the Japanese were able to hold their own against a greatly superior force. Then on August 1 a great typhoon struck, blowing up out of the southwest and typical of the storms which yearly wrack Japan from midsummer to late fall. Many of the Mongol ships were driven on shore and wrecked; Japanese ships fell on them and completed the disaster. Other ships of the Mongol fleet were driven out to sea and capsized; altogether perhaps over half of the invading forces were destroyed by this *kamikaze*, or "divine wind." Those that remained withdrew in the surviving ships, and the invasion attempt was abandoned. The Japanese understandably regarded this as divine deliverance and were confirmed in their feeling that theirs was a special country.

When Kubilai heard the news he was furious, and insisted on a third expedition, which was planned for 1288. New preparations were begun and more men, money, and ships demanded from both China and Korea. By this time however, luckily for everyone including the Japanese, the Mongol empire was already beginning to collapse. Korea was exhausted from the previous demands, on top of the Mongol conquest of their country, and could provide little, while in China rebellion was beginning to spread even before Kubilai's death in 1294.

Under these circumstances, the expedition against Japan was reluctantly postponed, and was finally abandoned only by the end of the century, although until then the special department established "for the invasion of Japan" remained on the Yuan government's books. The Japanese had been given a severe shock, and of course could not know that there were to be no more Mongol efforts against them; indeed their spies continued to report the new Mongol plans. The Hojo prudently maintained a military alert, while the Buddhist and some of the Shinto establishment and their temples claimed credit for the repulse of the Mongols through their prayers and incantations (Buddhism was still in large part a matter of magic in the minds of many), which had called forth the "divine wind."

The effort against the two Mongol invasions greatly weakened the Hojo and the entire Kamakura hold on the country. The bulk of the fighting and of the losses had been borne by the men of Kyushu and their families, and they demanded some compensation, especially since victory had brought no spoils in the form of conquered lands. The Kamakura *bakufu* had drained its own resources and had little to offer in response to these demands, with the result that its Kyushu vassals were increasingly discontent. This was to be the beginning of the collapse of Kamakura authority, which came to an end in 1336. But its imposition of order had, as indicated, enabled continued economic development and a degree of prosperity. Technical growth such as iron working, the making of fine swords and armor, and papermaking spread more widely from their earlier centers in the Kansai region, and trade with China and Korea increased substantially. At the same time, the culture which had developed in Heian, at first limited to the court, began to spread as well, even while the *bushi*-dominated culture of Kamakura, in some ways its total opposite, also flourished.

Warriors and Monks

Yet there were some points of similarity between these two different worlds. *Bushi* and *samurai* were as devoted to aesthetics, that quintessentially Japanese trait, as were the Heian courtiers, and in addition many became literate later, a skill needed for their growing administrative functions, and in time articulately so in works of literature, although this happened only in later periods. One thing which strikes Westerners is the association of these tough military men with the cherry blossom, which they adopted as their emblem. Cherry blossoms have a short life and drop to the ground with the first wind or rainstorm; just so, the *samurai* gives his life to his lord with no regrets. This is not really inconsistent with the ideals and ethics of medieval European

chivalry, who despite their prominence in warfare were also, like the *samurai*, aristocrats whose tastes were refined and many of whom wrote poetry or epic ballads, as many of the *samurai* did. Even though at this period many warriors were still illiterate, they maintained the traditional East Asian respect for learning, and later took pains to acquire it, becoming what have been called "gentlemen warriors," since learning has always been the mark of the gentleman in Asia.

The other and dominant *samurai* emblem or symbol was the sword, the focus of their profession and the center of what became virtually a cult. *Samurai* were nothing without their swords, and it became a badge of their rank. They did not hesitate to use them in the service of their lord, or to turn them on themselves rather than to surrender or to compromise. The sword was in part also a symbol of feudal loyalty, and one finds similar cult-like beliefs centered on famous swords among the medieval European knights, such as Arthur's Excalibur or Charlemagne's Joyeuse. Feudal loyalty, rather than any contractual arrangements, was the cement of the entire system, although it was also of course its weakest link, since it depended on individuals, and there were many cases of treachery or simply of changing sides at critical junctures which marked many of the military contests of medieval Japan. *Samurai* cultivated their skill in archery, swordplay, and horsemanship, and prided themselves on their acceptance of physical hardship and bravery, a simple and frugal lifestyle, and their disdain of pain, suffering, and death.

In all of this they resembled the Spartan warriors of classical Greece 1,500 years earlier. Suicide as the course of honor when faced with defeat or when caught in a web of conflicting loyalties was ennobled as a part of the *bushi* code. It became a ritual known as *seppuku* ("disembowelment"), also known more fancifully as *harakiri* (literally, "stomach-cut"), where the warrior sits cross-legged on the floor in the ritual position and slits open his stomach so that his insides spill out in a slow and agonizing death, signaling a triumph over physical pain. A loyal vassal would even sacrifice his own family if called on to do so, something unthinkable in Confucian China. Defeated *bushi* were usually decapitated by their victors, and the heads presented as proofs of victory.

Despite the macho culture of the *bushi*, more than an echo remained of the importance of women in early Japan. In this medieval period women could inherit property and even held official or semi-official positions, like Hojo Masako, who with her father engineered the demise of the Minamoto. Women were far from being shrinking violets, and were often called on to show the same loyalty, bravery, and stoicism expected of their men. As in Heian times, these aristocratic women were not representative of the population as a whole, but we know too little of the lot of average people to generalize about it, except to say that as in earlier times there was an immense gulf between the life of the relatively small aristocratic world and that of the great mass of the people. Most Japanese remained poor and bound to a life of toil, where, among other things, women did probably more than their share of the physical work of farming and of household chores, as they still do. In all of this Japan was like most of the rest of the world.

Like medieval Europe, medieval Japan was an age of faith, and religion was basically important. This period also saw the founding of many new Buddhist sects, including those which promoted the notion that the age of fighting and disorder underlined the Buddhist message that mortal life is suffering and can be escaped through salvation and entry into the Buddhist nirvana or other forms of paradise. The spread of Buddhism beyond its original focus in the capital district meant that many of its doctrines became popularized, or even vulgarized, as it became a mass religion, especially the Pure Land Sect (see Chapter 10). Somewhat paradoxically, the warrior group turned to the contemplative sect of Zen (originally Chinese Chan), which had been known in Japan some time earlier but was brought from China specifically by the monk Eisai in 1191 after Chan had become the dominant school of Chinese Buddhism. Other versions of Chan (Zen) were brought by later monks. Like Taoism, Zen centered on simplicity, without the need for priests or temples, and on the quiet contemplation and acceptance of nature, but retained, despite its adoption by the *bushi*, the Buddhist and Taoist emphasis on individual salvation and at least an echo of the original Buddha's testimony against violence and the world of action in general.

Rather like the Taoists also, Zen avoided dependence on written texts, perhaps conveniently for the still largely illiterate *bushi*, and stressed instead disciplined and single-minded meditation as the path to enlightenment, which might come after years of practice in a sudden flash of intuition, *satori*. The Zen adherent would sit for hours or even days motionless, focusing on nothing and rising above the insistent demands of the body or of the conscious mind. This was often done in natural surroundings, in any case in a quiet and peaceful place, where meditation might be aided by placing a single flower in a plain vase to one side—interesting preoccupations for a warrior! Zen required a strict discipline, which was in keeping with the warriors' code, and it obviously did not preclude action and violence when the time was right or when worldly duty called. Specifically Zen temples were built at Kamakura and at Kyoto (no longer called Heian, but still the capital), and became centers of learning (by literate priests) and even of literature and art.

With the spread of Buddhism to the masses we begin to know a bit more about their lot, through Buddhist paintings and through some of the Kamakura-period literature. Commoners even became religious leaders as well as monks, and wrote in simple Japanese in *kana* rather than in Chinese characters, addressing a more plebian audience. Buddhist scriptures began to be translated into vernacular Japanese. One of the appeals of Buddhism everywhere it spread was its message of the equality of all people, including women as well as people of the lower orders. This had tended to be obscured earlier in Japan while Buddhism was largely an aristocratic or court preserve, but it now helped to account for the more nearly universal spread of the faith, which in turn made this original aspect of Buddhism much more prominent. Salvation, primarily through simple faith, was open to anyone, whatever his or her condition in life.

The Pure Land Sect (see Chapter 10) was founded by the monk Honen in 1175, and quickly attracted followers, especially since its formula for salvation and escape from a degraded world to the Pure Land Paradise of Amida Buddha was simple: endless repetition of the name Amida Buddha. There was no need for temples, priests, rituals, or any religious institution; salvation was a game which anyone could play. The monk Shinran, originally a follower of Honen, helped to spread the sect still further, and it was he who insisted that a single pronouncement of Amida's name, as long as it was truly from the heart, was enough for salvation. He urged that there was no need for worldly virtue or the "merit" built up by good works. Shinran paid little or no attention to the Buddhist scriptures, and disdained the Buddhist church and its monasteries while urging priests to marry and thus to be better positioned to understand and help most people. In time, Shinran's gospel became the dominant Buddhist sect in Japan, which is understandable given its easy and populist apeal, and it became known as the True Pure Land, or simply True Sect.

The monk Nichiren, born of humble parents, founded yet another populist branch of Buddhism in 1253 which still carries his name. He emphasized the Lotus Sutra, a major text of Buddhism, or rather just its title, as the center of faith and urged followers to chant its name rather than that of Amida Buddha as the means to salvation. This, and other Buddhist sects of the time, seem to us now rather simple-minded, but one must remember that they were truly populist movements with more than a touch of magic, and that we have some parallels now in our own contemporary society. Nichiren was an evangelist who preached to street crowds in a revivalist style, and was scornful of all other varieties of Buddhism, prophesying tragedy if his views were not accepted. He and others saw the Mongol invasions as confirming such prophesies, not quite the end of the world but certainly something which could be interpreted as a warning of some sort. Apart from the echoes one can find in contemporary American society, these medieval Japanese Buddhist sects also suggest parallels

Buddhist Devotion

Nichiren, founder of a popular Buddhist sect in 1253, asked for total trust in the Lotus *sutra.*

If you desire to attain Buddhahood immediately, lay down the banner of pride, cast away the club resentment, and trust yourselves to the unique Truth.... Has not Buddha declared "I alone am the protector and savior?" There is the power! Is it not taught that faith is the only entrance to salvation? There is the rope! ... Devote yourself wholeheartedly to the adoration of the Lotus of the Perfect Truth, and utter it yourself as well as admonishing other to do the same. Such is your task in this human life.

Source: From R. Tsunoda et al., eds., *Sources of Japanese Tradition, Vol. II.* (New York: Columbia University Press, 1958), pp. 222–223.

Traditional Japanese stone garden at the Ryoanji Temple, Kyoto. Originally from T'ang China, this orderly and peaceful form of landscaping became characteristically Japanese and is still widely practiced. (Jack Deutsch)

with Christianity; some of their ideas, like salvation through faith or through meditation, were part of the original Buddhist message in sixth century B.C. India, and others, like the addition of a heaven and a hell, part of earlier developed Mahayana Buddhism. But the populist style, the stress on translations into the vernacular, the encouragement of marriage for the priests (clergy), and the growing centrality of congregations rather than of the monasteries, all seem similar to European Christianity of the Reformation.

Literature and the Arts

The court aristocracy at Kyoto continued to produce literature much like that of the Fujiwara period, primarily poetry and diaries, plus some novels, but nothing to match the *Tale of Genji* or Sei Shonagon's *Pillow Book*. A new anthology of poetry called *The New Ancient and Modern Collection* appeared in 1205, whose poems continue the Heian tradition. The new warrior culture of Ka-

✠ Impermanence and Truth ✠

An attractive setting of the Buddhist message is in the opening lines of The Tale of Heike.

"In the sound of the bell of the Gion Temple echoes the impermanence of all things. The pale hue of the flowers of the teak tree shows the truth that they who prosper must fall. The proud ones do not last long, but vanish like a spring night's dream. And the mighty ones too will perish in the end, like dust before the wind."

Source: From Donald Keene, *Japanese Literature.* (New York: Grove Press, 1955), p. 78.

makura began to produce its own literature, mainly stories of the wars of medieval Japan, including the *Tale of the House of Taira,* the *Tale of the Hogen War,* and the *Tale of the Heiji War.* All are still popular in Japan, and with their fresh and vivid descriptions help to bring this period to life. The same events were recounted again on a larger canvas in the mid-thirteenth century *Record of the Rise and Fall of the Minamoto and Taira,* better known as the *Tale of the Heike.* As Kamakura culture matured, it also produced historical writings, including *The Mirror of the Eastland* covering events up to 1266 and based on the shogunate's government records, in the tradition of Ssu Ma Ch'ien. On the Kyoto side, perhaps the outstanding work is *The Confessions of Lady Nijo,* an autobiography of some 36 years of her life which appeared in 1307, toward the end of the Kamakura period. She comments, often critically, on the stultifying effects of the obsession with rank at the court and the struggles over the imperial succession (even though that had become a relatively trivial matter by her time). She also gives a useful account of the Kamakura *bakufu,* including their continued respect for the imperial office, expressed through ceremonial visits to Kyoto.

But her chief focus is the lifestyles and values of Kyoto aristocrats, of whom of course she was one herself. They maintained their intense interest in aesthetics, including the composition and reciting of poetry and the performance of music, song, and dance in court style. Even more than in *Genji,* Lady Nijo describes in great detail what court ladies like herself wore on different occasions. As in earlier times, robes were in many layers of different colors and textures, all chosen with exquisite care. Her accounts of male-female relationships make it clear that monogamy was not widespread among the aristocracy and that both men and women engaged promiscuously in many affairs, in addition to males having one or more wives or consorts and several mistresses. Women apparently also helped men they ad-

mired to find other sexual partners, although women were often treated roughly by male lovers, including Lady Nijo herself. Her picture of court life makes it seem by our standards degenerate or even depraved, the self-indulgence of idle aristocrats who filled their otherwise empty lives with endless pleasure-seeking, but who often found it, predictably, unsatisfying.

Many of those involved turned to Buddhism as an escape from the material world and an attempt to shed earthly desires, and some became recluses. Lady Nijo, however, includes censorious comments on the hypocrisy of the Buddhist clergy, such as in the case of one of her lovers who was a high priest and had thus broken his vow of celibacy. Another courtier had an affair with a high priestess. Celibacy was still enjoined on many priests and priestesses, especially in the capital area, although this had already begun to change among the populist sects and at Kamakura. Lady Nijo found the warriors of Kamakura crude and uncivilized by comparison with the sophistication of the Kyoto court, and was shocked that they used falconry, like the knights of medieval Europe and the Middle East, to kill large numbers of birds as well as hunting wild animals, all in total violation of the Buddhist ethic.

Artistically, Buddhism continued to inspire the sculpting of thousands of images both in Kyoto and in Kamakura, although by far the most impressive is the giant 52-foot bronze Buddha cast at Kamakura in the mid-thirteenth century, which remains one of the largest freestanding bronze sculptures in the world. In general, painting followed Heian styles, but the subjects reflected the Kamakura period as an age of the warrior. Long picture scrolls showing successive scenes illustrated the *Tale of the Heike,* and others portrayed the Mongol invasions. Some scrolls included imaginative impressions of the Buddhist hell, the lives of saints, or the histories of the great monasteries. Artists came over from Sung China, and in the capital area there was a great rebuilding of the Nara temples, including the To-daiji, which had been badly damaged in 1180 in the course of the wars of the late twelfth century, leaving most of it a pile of ashes. Landscape painting became newly important, perhaps as the result of Sung influences, and at its best was superb. The painting of portraits was also in fashion, of the nobility of course but also of famous poets and even of oxen who pulled the carriages of aristocrats. Ceramics, which was to become one of the greatest accomplishments of the Japanese artist, received a new stimulus also from Sung China when a noted Japanese potter went to study there early in the thirteenth century and on his return set up a kiln. The introduction of the originally T'ang Chinese tea ceremony, also practiced in the Sung, came to Japan with tea drinking in this period, and stimulated the production of simple but beautiful bowls.

The End of the Kamakura Shogunate and the Rise of the Ashikaga

The repulse of the Mongols had put a great strain on the Kamakura *bakufu*, and when it was unable to provide what they regarded as adequate compensation to those in Kyushu who had borne the brunt of the Mongol assault, its control over them, and over other outlying clans far from Kamakura, was seriously weakened. The earlier success of the Kamakura regime had softened the Spartan discipline and frugal habits of many of the warriors as they adopted more aristocratic lifestyles. Some *samurai* even became writers, poets, and painters. The absence of primogeniture meant that all sons inherited the status and the obligations of warrior-aristocrat fathers but had to share his lands and incomes among them. More and more of successive generations of warriors had trouble even maintaining their *bushi* equipment, and many became impoverished. Under such circumstances, bonds of loyalty tended to fray, especially for those who lived far from Kamakura, whose loyalties tended to be to local or provincial figures. These local leaders began to constitute a new class which tended to displace the version of the nationwide system which the Kamakura shogunate had constructed.

A combination of events led to the shogunate's collapse in 1333. A new and vigorous emperor, Go-Daigo, came to the throne in 1318 and tried to give the emperor's position real power. Kamakura tried to force him to abdicate in 1331, upon which he began a revolt, with the support of armed monks from the monasteries of the Kyoto area, plus some local military leaders who were already moving away from subservience to Ka-

makura and now took the chance to join the emperor's cause. Forces from Kamakura captured Go-Daigo and tried to exile him, but more local military groups joined the revolt on his side and helped him to escape. The Kamakura general sent to recapture him deserted the Kamakura cause and captured Kyoto, in the name of the emperor. The turncoat general was Ashikaga Takauji (1305–1358), who founded the Ashikaga shogunate. He took the title of *shogun* in 1338, but already in 1333 former Kamakura vassals in the Kanto region revolted and captured and burned Kamakura, ending the rule of the Hojo. Meanwhile Go-Daigo continued his efforts to rebuild imperial control, but Japan was now too fragmented into separate and often rival regional military groups. In an effort to bypass Ashikaga Takauji, Go-Daigo tried to join forces with some of his rivals, but Takauji took Kyoto again in 1336 and put a new emperor on the throne from another imperial line. Go-Daigo managed to escape from Takauji's forces and set up his own rival court at Yoshino in a well-protected mountain site near Nara. Surprisingly enough, this effort lasted until 1392, but never acquired real power.

The Ashikaga shogunate was now based in Kyoto, but Takauji and his successors were never able to achieve central control over what had by now become contending military groups all over Japan, each with its landholdings and feudal vassals or retainers. The shogunate was in fact an uneasy coalition among some of these groups in the Kyoto area. More distant groups became increasingly independent in practical terms; although the Ashikaga tried to reestablish the forms of a central government, it remained largely on paper. The persistence of Go-Daigo's rival court at Yoshino, kept in being by his successors, made occasion for repeated local wars between adherents of rival imperial lines, although the fighting was often more about rights to landed estates. Finally, in 1392, the Ashikaga persuaded Go-Daigo's descendants to return to Kyoto, with the understanding that members of their line would alternate on the throne with those from the rival line, although this was in fact never done. This was the work of Ashikaga Yoshimitsu, the third *shogun* (1358–1408), who also built up his power against other clan-military groups to the west, but still far short of central control. As should be clear from the above, the emperor was now manipulated as a symbol by whatever group had most power.

In 1378 the shogunate fixed their headquarters in a district of Kyoto called Muromachi, and from 1392 with the end of the rival court at Yoshino the remaining period of the Ashikaga is also called Muromachi. Yoshimitsu's modest increase in power was not to last long. When his grandson died in 1428, the shogunate's authority was waning, and in 1467 there was a dispute over the succession in which other prominent families joined. For ten years there was chaos and heavy fighting, known as the Onin War, in the course of which Kyoto itself was destroyed and what little remained of Ashikaga power with it. Provincial military figures had been building their power since the latter part of Kamakura rule, and now they took more and more of the local revenues for themselves and their establishments. The old court families, including the Fujiwara and even the imperial family, deprived of most of their former income, lost whatever power they had once had and in many cases just faded away into the larger population. At the same time, provincial warrior families built their strength, not only from their control over local revenues but through restoring most of the system of primogeniture so that one son would succeed to most of the father's holdings as well as his rank. A father still could choose one of his sons as his heir, or could adopt one, usually from another branch of the family. This of course helped to ensure that the most able individuals inherited power and the means to support it. The status of women continued to decline during this age of warfare, although there were a few exceptional individuals, like Lady Nijo and Hojo Masaka (see above).

The Onin War, and Economic Growth

The Onin War from 1467 to 1477 was, despite its destructiveness, in some ways merely the overture to a following century of chronic warfare without a break, mainly over rights to land among local military groups. The Ashikaga *shoguns* were powerless to check this, and in fact their role was so negligible by now that no one took much notice when the last of them was deposed in 1573. The local lords whose power rose during this pe-

The Onin War

In the course of the Onin War of the fifteenth century, the fighting engulfed and made havoc in the imperial capital at Kyoto. A bakufu *official of the time described the ruin of the city.*

The flowery capital we thought would last forever to our surprise is become the lair of wolves and foxes. In the past there have been rebellions and disasters, but in the first year of Onin (i.e., 1467) the laws of gods and kings have been broken and all the sects are perishing.

Source: Quoted in George Sansom, *A History of Japan, 1334–1615.* (Palo Alto: Stanford University Press, 1961), pp. 225–226.

The fifteenth-century Annals of Yoshitsune, *or* Gikeiki, *is a more elaborate retelling of events in the Onin War, including a passage where Yoshitsune mistakes his retainer Benkei in the dark for an opponent and issues a challenge in the* bushi *style.*

"Who are you? Name yourself or be cut down," he demanded, advancing toward Benkei. Benkei proclaimed aloud "Let those who are far away listen to what is said of me! You who are close, behold me now with your own eyes! I am Saito Musashibo Benkei, the eldest son of the Kumano abbot Bensho, who traces his ancestry to Amatsukoyane. I serve Yoshitsune and I am a man in a thousand!"
"Very amusing," said Yoshitsune. "You should save your jokes for more suitable occasions." "Very well—only you told me to identify myself, so I did," Benkei replied, not in the least abashed.

Source: From H.C. McCullough, translator, *Yoshitsune: A Fifteenth Century Japanese.* (Tokyo: University of Tokyo Press, 1966), pp. 148–149.

riod built their virtually total control of local areas into little kingdoms. Most of them were heads of new warrior families rather than the old families which had dominated Japan in earlier centuries. From this period on they were called *daimyo* (feudal lords), supported by their *samurai* vassals. The *daimyo* took over what had earlier been local and provincial administration, staffing their positions with *samurai* vassals, most of whom now became literate. The age of chivalric combat yielded, as in Europe and elsewhere, to armies of pikemen and bowmen under *samurai* leadership. *Daimyo* administration did not penetrate far into village life, and peasants managed most of their own day-to-day affairs, although they did have to pay taxes. These village units also coordinated the use of local water and the increasingly complex irrigation systems, as well as maintaining local shrines, and well into modern times were in effect the main administrative elements of rural Japan.

Merchants and artisans, centered in the relatively few towns, most of them clustered around the *daimyo* headquarters soon to be marked by a fortified castle, were controlled and taxed by the *daimyo* administration, which also requisitioned labor for army transport and for construction. Both taxes and labor went primarily to build each *daimyo's* military power, which was used in the constant fighting and to expand each little feudal kingdom's land and revenues at the expense of others which were less strong or less efficiently organized. The *daimyo* domains varied greatly in size as well as over time; some were the size of modern prefectures or even larger, others far smaller, but most were about the size of an English, Chinese, or American county. Some areas were still fragmented among several smaller warrior families, while the major monasteries retained their extensive estates, many of them larger than the average *daimyo* holding, which they too protected with their armies. With the rise of the foot soldier as the most important element in warfare, commoners could rise in society, and under their own warrior patrons or leaders were even able to challenge local feudal powers. Thus various villager and townsmen groups took the opportunity of the virtual absence of a central government to riot against their supposed feudal overlords and to demand reduction or cancellation of their feudal dues and accumulated debts. A few towns began to grow with the rise of trade, and the town of Sakai (now a part of Osaka) even made good a large measure of independence from feudal or monastic groups. Among the Buddhists, the True Sect won military control over the west coast province of Kaga for nearly a century from 1488, while other members of the True Sect carved out smaller areas of control.

Despite the chaos and chronic warfare of the Ashikaga period, economic development continued. *Daimyo* and other landowners had every incentive to increase local production on which their own revenues depended. This meant that they invested in new irrigation, promoted improved farming techniques, and opened or reclaimed new lands. Best guesses suggest that productivity per acre at least doubled during the Ashikaga period, plus net output from newly cultivated lands. Despite the chronic disorder, trade increased as regional and local specialization developed, including handicrafts, all of which entered both local and interregional markets. Port towns, such as Sakai was, also grew, dealing in both coastal and foreign trade, primarily with Korea and China. Barter, which had earlier been the chief medium of exchange, began to be replaced by a money economy. Since there was no effective central government to produce coins, these were imported from China, supplemented in time by letters of credit for the transfer of larger cash transactions. The Buddhist establishment, which were also major landowners, were part of all these developments, and also began to act as moneylenders. As in China and medieval Europe, producers of goods or services for sale began to form guilds, in part to protect themselves and their trade from arbitrary taxation by the multiplicity of land-based units, to whom they paid a fee as protection and from whom they obtained recognition in a form like charters, which also helped them to assert the monopoly of certain trades, at least in their own region.

Kyoto remained the only real city in terms of population, perhaps 200,000–300,000 or more—larger than any European city of this period—and hence it was the major market and the chief center of artisan production. Certain commodities began to be traded on a seminational basis, especially *sake* (beer made from fermented rice or other grain, as the Chinese had long done), which for a time served as a kind of substitute for money, and locally produced paper with special qualities. Salt could be produced only on the coast, by evaporation of seawater, but was in universal demand and hence was shipped over relatively long distances, although the dominantly coastal distribution of population made this much less of a problem. Carpenters, transport workers, and even actors (many of them itinerants) also formed their own guilds. In Kyoto and the scattered "capitals" of *daimyo* and monastic domains, merchants were closely controlled by these feudal lords, and most artisans worked directly for them, in effect as captive producers. Sakai, as it became a largely merchant-dominated town with its own walls and its own army, was free of such controls, but had few or no parallels elsewhere in Japan.

Trade and Piracy

Some Japanese merchants had been part of the earlier missions to China and the interchange with it and with

Korea, but with the rise of the Sung dynasty trade with both countries greatly increased, and was only relatively briefly interrupted by the Mongol onslaught. Such trade was related to, and often only dimly distinguished from, piracy, for which the Japanese, especially on the coast of Kyushu, developed a reputation. The Chinese and Koreans called them *wako* and learned to fear their lightning raids on coastal areas (see Chapter 7) and on merchant ships. Kyushu especially was ideally situated for piracy, close to the major trade routes off the coasts of China and Korea and with numerous small and large harbors on its own coast, backed by easily accessible forests for shipbuilding timbers, yet far enough from most existing centers of control that there was little fear of government intervention. Koreans and Chinese tried to undercut Japanese piracy by moving toward a larger officially approved trade instead of tempting pirates by trying to restrict it. Korea even granted the Japanese the right to establish permanent settlements of merchants in port towns on the southern Korean coast, in some ways a throwback to the much earlier Japanese footholds there before 562. In China, the Ming tried to get the Ashikaga *shoguns* to control piracy, but they really lacked the power to do so, especially in distant Kyushu. The Ming also fitted the Japanese traders into the tribute sytem, allowing them to send official trade missions every ten years, in return for Yoshimitsu's acceptance of tributary status.

But although the Japanese in fact sent many more trade missions than provided for and many more ships, many of them dispatched by local lords and Buddhist monasteries, it was never enough to cut the ground out from under piracy, which became so great a problem for the Chinese that, as recounted in Chapter 7, the Ming ultimately ordered the evacuation of the coastal areas. Illegal trade with China also flourished, a symptom of economic growth in Japan, and increased demand for Chinese luxury goods. The Japanese paid for their imports of fine porcelains, silks, books, paintings, and large amounts of copper coins (cash) with raw sulphur and copper (both increasingly scarce in China), silver, and some manufactured goods. These included primarily the fine swords which had become famous Japanese specialties, but also folding fans with scenes painted on them and some picture scrolls. Japan was beginning to catch up with its teacher, although Japanese pirates probably did better all in all than peaceful Japanese traders.

MUROMACHI CULTURE

At the Ashikaga court in Kyoto, despite its political and even economic weakness, new economic growth helped to support vigorous new cultural growth, beginning in Yoshimitsu's time when he collected in Kyoto a group of scholars, writers, and artists, in part to legitimize his new power in the old Heian city. For them he built in 1397 perhaps the most beautiful and most photographed building in Japan, the Golden Pavilion, on the northern edge of Kyoto, where in what he designed as a monkish retreat he presided over his coterie of artists and intellectuals. A later *shogun*, Yoshimasa, built the equally beautiful Silver Pavilion on the eastern edge of the city in 1483; although by his time Ashikaga power was largely gone, he could still assert Kyoto's cultural primacy. The court also extended official patronage to the major Zen temples and monasteries of Kyoto and Kamakura. Zen monks became the dominant artists, scholars, and writers, and were also used as official advisers. It is in this period that the tea ceremony became fully established as a specifically Japanese ritual, carried out with exquisite taste and aestheticism and providing the means to tranquility. It is conducted with a few sensitive connoisseurs in a plain, simple room free of distractions and set in beautiful natural surroundings, a kind of artificial simplicity of sophisticates, but truly Japanese in its perfect taste. Even the bowls used for the tea are purposely simple, even crude, but very tastefully so, a reminder of the need to imitate and stay close to nature.

The disciplined simplicity and refined aestheticism of the tea ceremony are very Zen, but during the Ashikaga period elite Japanese culture was in some ways just Zen culture. Another, really untranslatable Zen/Japanese concept is *shibui*, the understated, simple, subtle yet beautiful aesthetic effect produced by a master artist or craftsman, although it can also be applied to all taste, including that of an especially fine persimmon or the subtle combination of flavors, colors, and textures in both clothing and food. Despite the political and military chaos and turmoil of Ashikaga/Muromachi Japan, it was a period when the distinctive Japanese artistic genius found full expression. Most of the population were still relatively poor, and their circumstances relatively crude, but that probably did not distinguish them from most of the rest of the world at that time, perhaps with the exception of south and central China. What did distinguish Japan was its understanding that, in the modern phrase, small can be beautiful, and the Japanese ability to make much of little, including the tasteful arrangement of space and objects in the spare setting of the Japanese house or its garden. Modern Japan has moved on from such circumstances, and much of traditional Japanese culture has been overwhelmed by massive urbanization and industrialization. But more than a few traces remain of a distinctively Japanese perception and values. One of these is surely what we have come to recognize as the quest for perfection, something which early Western visitors to Japan also noted and which still

The Golden Pavilion in Kyoto: Japanese adaptation of a Chinese original, with careful attention to the blending of architecture with landscaping. This beautiful building dates from 1397, in the Ashikaga period, but has had to be restored several times after fires. (Cameramann International, Ltd.)

underlies the phenomenal modern Japanese success in the new world of technology. It was apparent in the superb quality of those Japanese swords which were so widely acclaimed, in the intricately constructed folding fans (which may well have been a Japanese invention), beautifully decorated in miniature with landscape paintings, and in most of Japanese art.

In Muromachi times, Japanese artists mastered the Sung style of landscape painting and made it their own. As in Chinese landscapes, the focus is on nature itself, with human constructions or figures in a minor role, as befits the East Asian conception of nature as far greater than the human world and as something to which people should turn to seek meaning and understanding. Architecture became even more artfully blended into surrounding gardens and trees, as so superbly achieved with the Golden and Silver Pavilions in Kyoto. But perhaps the most distinctive Japanese form was/is the garden of rocks and sand or gravel, as at the Ryoanji in Kyoto illustrated on page 216. Here, and in many others like it, spareness, simplicity, and the arrangement of shapes and textures against the white plaster walls and grey tiled roofs, each forming their own shapes and patterns, and the carefully raked patterns of fine sand or gravel say it all, again a message of tranquility, like the effect aimed at in living gardens. Most of the temple gardens were designed by Zen monks, and indeed do express the Zen spirit effectively.

Most Zen monks continued to write in classical Chinese, but others wrote in *kana* in Japanese, including works of history and new commentaries on Shinto which tried to increase its respectability by arguing that both Confucianism (oddly enough, not Taoism) and

Buddhism were originally derived from Shinto ideas, a little like the *Kojiki*'s invention of great antiquity for the imperial line. There were also new stories of the incessant wars of the time, and the beginnings of a popular literature, which included tales of magic, romance, and comedy. But probably the most significant new form was the Noh drama, which began to take form at the court of Yoshimitsu in the late fourteenth century. The Noh stage is largely bare, but the chief actor and his assistant are dressed in elaborate costumes and are usually masked. A chorus supports the action on the stage and provides commentary. Lines are chanted rather

Flower arranging is an art in Japan, known as *ikebana*. Here is a contemporary woman practicing this ancient art in the traditional way.

than spoken, and are in verse or in poetic prose, accompanied by music with a pronounced beat. The performance is slow and highly stylized, and usually ends with a symbolic formal dance by the principal actor. The Noh has often been compared with the theater of classical Greece, where all the above elements except the final dance were present. The Noh also, like Greek drama, dealt with the affairs of gods, Shinto and Buddhist, and famous human figures who interacted with them.

An actor in a *Noh*, with mask and traditional costume. (Four By Five, Inc.)

The traditional Japanese style. Tatami (grass mats), sliding rice paper doors, tea, and a garden view—the recipe for tranquility. (Sumitano Industries)

Noh actors were often "possessed" by spirits of the gods or of the dead, perhaps a throwback to the importance of shamans in early Japan. Noh is still performed in Japan. It was not directly derived from Zen, but its highly disciplined and formal aesthetics are very much in keeping with the Zen ideal. The combination of chanted lines, dance, costumes, and carefully calculated gestures can communicate to the initiated (foreigners often find it hard to enjoy) rich meaning, emotion, and even passion. Every step and every movement are precisely measured in a state of controlled tension, a slow-moving concentrated experience of understatement, but with a heavy freight of feeling and of disciplined expression. Noh and the tea ceremony were perhaps the conscious counterparts or antidotes to the bloody and often ruthless life of the times.

Renewed Civil War

By the 1570s Ashikaga authority had declined even more completely, and Japan was torn by fighting between rival clans and their armies until the end of the century. In 1568 a minor feudal lord, Oda Nobunaga (1534–1582), won control of Kyoto, where he broke the military power of the major Buddhist monasteries and their fortified strongholds in the capital area, including the great fortress of the Shin (Shinran or True) sect at Osaka. The Portuguese had moved on to Japan in search of trade and converts less than 50 years after Vasco da Gama's arrival in India in 1498 (see Chapter 12), and in 1543 had reached an island off the southern coast of Kyushu. By 1545 they were trading actively in ports elsewhere in Kyushu, and in 1549 the Jesuit Francis Xavier began a major missionary effort in Japan. Many Japanese were eager to take part in the trade, and some of the Kyushu *daimyo* favored the missionaries in the hope that this would attract Portuguese traders, while others adopted Christianity with the same hope. One of the smaller *daimyo* took this step himself in 1562, and established the port of Nagasaki on the west coast of Kyushu, which soon became the chief center of trade with the Portuguese. Other *daimyo* also accepted Christianity, and the new religion spread even to Kyoto. By 1615 perhaps as many as half a million Japanese had become converts, although probably many of them were motivated by their interest in trade and their general curiosity rather than by genuine religious conviction. Nevertheless there were increasing numbers of sincere Japanese Christians, and equally important, a new opening on the wider world.

Nobunaga (commonly known by his personal rather than his family name of Oda) encouraged the Portuguese as a counterweight against the Buddhist power, and was also attracted to them by the hope of trade profits. In 1573 he drove the last Ashikaga *shogun* out of Kyoto and thus ended that historical period. In the effort to consolidate his power, he destroyed the great Tendai monastery of Enryakuji on Mt. Hiei east of Kyoto where Ennin had ruled, and forced the submission of most of the other monastic centers and their strongholds in the capital region, including the True Sect and their fortified headquarters at Kaya on the west coast. He laid siege to their Shin branch castle at Osaka and captured it, as indicated, in 1580. Having demolished these major power rivals, he continued his campaigns against other feudal lords and began the construction of a great castle as his headquarters on the eastern shore of Lake Biwa just beyond Kyoto. Nobunaga's tactics against his opponents were ruthless, including the burning alive of captives and the slaughter of noncombatants. He was murdered by one of his own generals in Kyoto in 1582, but his power was seized by another of his generals, Toyotomi Hideyoshi.

Hideyoshi (also commonly known by his personal name) was typical of the changes of preceding centuries which had enabled commoners to rise to important positions. Indeed he was the son of a peasant and as such had no family name, adopting the surname of Toyotomi only after he had achieved some status. As Nobunaga's successor he continued the campaigns against the other feudal lords and in 1585 conquered the island of Shikoku. Tokugawa Ieyasu, a *daimyo* of eastern Japan, agreed to become Hideyoshi's vassal in the following year, after which, with his rear protected, Hideyoshi invaded Kyushu with a huge army of 280,000 men. This was the largest field force yet in Japanese history, and it swept the whole island. Impressed by Hideyoshi's power, the northern *daimyo* of Tohoku (northern Honshu) also accepted vassal status, and by 1590 Japan was finally unified politically, on a larger scale and more effectively than ever before, including the early Kamakura system under Yoritomo.

Having established his power in Japan and with a large and impressive fighting force at his back, Hideyoshi seems to have succumbed to megalomania. He planned the conquest of China, however grandiose and totally impractical (as the Japanese were to discover during the second world war). The route lay of course through Korea, and when the Koreans refused free passage to his army, he sent an armed expedition there in 1592 with 160,000 men. The Japanese had acquired the latest firearms via the Portuguese and the Dutch and drove the Koreans far into the north. At this point the Ming came to the rescue of their tributary, forced the Japanese to retreat southward to the coast, and obliged them to negotiate, a story already told in Chapter 9. These talks went on from 1593 to 1596, when a peace was arranged, but the Chinese envoys were not deferential enough to suit Hideyoshi, who renewed the attack in

---

✠ Hideyoshi Writes to His Wife ✠

Hideyoshi wrote to his wife while he was besieging a daimyo castle in the spring of 1590.

Now we have got the enemy like birds in a cage, and there is no danger, so please set your mind at rest. I long for the Young Lord [his son], but I feel that for the sake of the future, and because I want to have the country at peace, I must give up my longing. So please set your mind at rest. I am looking after my health. . . . There is nothing to worry about. . . . Since as I have thus declared it will be a long siege, I wish to send for Yodo [his concubine]. I wish you to tell her and make arrangements for her journey, and tell her that next to you she is the one who pleases me best. . . . I was very glad to get your messages. We have got up to within two or three hundred yards and put a double ditch around the castle and shall not let a single man escape. All the men of the eight eastern provinces are shut up inside. . . . Though I am getting old, I must think of the future and do what is best for the country. So now I mean to do glorious deeds and I am ready for a long siege, with provisions and gold and silver in plenty, so as to return in triumph and leave a great name behind me. I desire you to understand this and to tell it to everybody.

Source: G. B. Sansom, *Japan: A Short Cultural History*, rev. ed. (New York: Appleton-Century-Crofts, 1962), p. 410.

1597. When he mercifully died in 1598, his troops in Korea, who had never had his leadership in the field there and may well have resented him as well as suspecting, like most other Japanese, that Hideyoshi was mentally unbalanced, immediately returned to Japan. They brought with them some captive ceramicists and printers, both representing arts which were still more highly advanced in Korea than in Japan, but apart from the considerable Japanese casualties, the invasion had few other effects on Japan, although it devastated Korea.

Hideyoshi rose to power in a period of change and instability; he saw it as threatening to him, and tried to check it. A peasant by birth, he tried to disarm all non-*samurai* so as to ensure that all commoners would be kept down and unable to challenge his authority. As a self-made man, he feared the possible rivalry of others like himself. His famous "sword hunt" among all commoners in which houses were methodically searched and all swords confiscated reestablished rigid class lines, and was accompanied by harsh new laws prohibiting farmers or common soldiers from becoming merchants or even laborers, a freezing of social divisions which he saw as necessary for stability. Hideyoshi at first welcomed the Christian missionaries and the profitable trade with the Portuguese, but in 1587 he turned against them and banned missionaries, although this order was not enforced for some years. He seems to have feared that the spread of Christianity was becoming a disruptive influence in Japanese society and also a political menace.

The foreigners were rivals with each other in both trade and missionary efforts, and they became involved in taking sides in internal conflicts. Japanese converts also developed loyalties to a foreign pope (the Protestants were not yet involved in missionary work in Japan), and the Catholics were split between various orders: Franciscan, Dominican, Augustin, and Jesuit, who often contested with each other. The Spanish, already established in the Philippines, tended to support the Franciscans, the Portuguese the Jesuits, and all four orders quarreled bitterly with each other. Following their usual strategy, the Jesuits concentrated on the elite, and even converted some of the *daimyo*, and later some of those around Hideyoshi. Spaniards intrigued against Portuguese, and both against the Dutch and English, who had now reached Japan to seek a share of the trade and were in both cases mortal enemies of the Spanish. It was understandable that Hideyoshi feared that the foreign missionaries were an advance guard for foreign political aggression. In 1597 he proscribed Christianity and crucified six Spanish Franciscans, three Jesuits, and 17 Japanese converts, although many Jesuits remained in hiding. He did not go beyond this and overlooked the missionaries who remained and their converts, probably for fear of losing out in the trade with the Por-

tuguese, which had become important also as a source of technical knowledge, especially about firearms, and as the supply route for Chinese goods.

Hideyoshi refused the title of *shogun*, out of disdain but also because he was really not eligible since he could not claim Minamoto ancestry, but he patronized the imperial court and tried to use it to bolster his legitimacy. He managed to claim Fujiwara descent and with that boost took the title of *kampaku*, which had earlier been used for Fujiwara regents, although "warlord" is probably a better label. He built a huge new castle on the site of the Shin monastery in Osaka which had been destroyed by Nobunaga, and a splendid palace at Momoyama just south of Kyoto. His own domains resulting from his conquests stretched eastward as far as Nagoya. The *daimyo* of the rest of Japan outside this central core had accepted his overlordship, but he kept their wives and eldest sons as hostages, and also moved some of the *daimyo* around to strengthen their loyalty to him rather than to the people of their local areas. This included Tokugawa Ieyasu, who was moved to the then village of Edo (modern Tokyo), where he ruled the whole of the Kanto area in place of a local lord whom Hideyoshi had defeated. The *daimyo* domains were becoming like little states; they administered their own areas, but had to provide Hideyoshi with troops on request and labor for his huge building projects plus a share of the costs. Hideyoshi now began to mint copper, silver, and gold coins, to regulate foreign trade, and to act in many ways like a head of state.

Like Nobunaga before him, Hideyoshi, especially given his humble origins and swift rise, reveled in his new power and wealth and spent it lavishly, sometimes garishly. Castles and palaces were elaborately decorated, and walls or sliding panels and screens covered with bold, even gaudy paintings in bright colors and with much use of gold leaf. This style of art was in fact the forerunner of the Tokugawa style, but the Japanese sense of good taste kept it from mere vulgarity. In many ways, Hideyoshi was indeed a warlord, and showed many of the gangster characteristics of our own day. He controlled his subordinates and his vassals mainly through ruthlessness and fear. When he died, he left only an infant son as heir, whom he arranged to leave under the protection of Tokugawa Ieyasu and four of his other major vassals. Ieyasu, with his new domains in the Kanto, in fact controlled more area and revenues than were covered by Hideyoshi's own central core. Domains were measured in *koku* (about 5 bushels) of rice, which was of course the predominant crop and the basis of tax yields, and Ieyasu's domain was by far the largest in Japan; he also had more vassals and minor *daimyo* under his direct control. Accordingly the other *daimyo* tended to look to him as the logical successor to Hideyoshi, but a coalition of western clans in Kyushu and western Honshu challenged him. In 1600, Ieyau's combined forces defeated them at the battle of Sekigahara, in a strategic pass through the low hills between Nagoya and Kyoto. He absorbed or gave to his trusted vassals the lands of most of the defeated *daimyo*, and obliged the others to sign written oaths of loyalty. Soon after his victory, in 1603, he assumed the title of *shogun*, with a decree from the court at Kyoto which gave him additional legitimacy.

The Tokugawa shogunate which he founded was to last until 1868, the first truly unified national government in Japan. Ieyasu allowed Hideyoshi's child heir to keep the castle his father had built at Osaka with considerable lands around it, but realized that opponents or power rivals might try to use this, and the heir's presumptive status, against him. He therefore besieged Osaka castle in 1614, and in 1615 took and destroyed the last challenge to his supremacy. The experience helped to convince him that, since the succession to power was a perennial problem, it would be prudent to prevent what he had built from falling into the hands of another family line. The memory of the sixteenth-century wars was still vivid, and many old interfamily rivalries were still active. He therefore decided in 1605 to resign as *shogun* and hand over the office to a grown son whom he trusted, Hidetada, while keeping real power for himself until his death in 1616. He had built at Edo a massive castle in the style of the time, surrounded by a series of walls and moats, which survives today and since 1869 has been the seat of the emperor, a striking reminder of the grim age which produced it, now surrounded by a huge modern city. From 1605, Hidetada thus ruled from Edo castle while Ieyasu formally retired to the capital of the area where Tokugawa family power had originally been based, near modern Shizuoka, but continued effectively in charge.

Hidetada followed his father's example by retiring in 1623 in favor of *his* adult son, who ruled as *shogun* until 1651, by which time the shogunate was firmly established. Tokugawa military power and the feudal support they had built among the other feudal lords was certainly enough to have established a strong central government of the sort which by this time had largely been achieved in England and France, sweeping away the remains of the rule of local lords. From the Tokugawa point of view, that seemed unnecessary; the system they set up worked well, and there was no threat from abroad. In many ways, it was easier, especially given the difficulty of communications and the lack as yet of an extensive bureaucracy under central control, to leave local administration in the hands of the various *daimyo*. The Tokugawa supervised them carefully, watchful for any sign of boat rocking or tendencies to break away or rebel, and for 250 years there was for the first time in Japan internal peace under the authority of a central power. This encouraged continued economic growth, and fed in agricultural taxes which, at least to begin with, were enough to keep the machinery of government functioning.

Suggestions for Further Reading

Asakawa, K. *Land and Society in Medieval Japan*. Tokyo: Tokyo University, 1965.

Berry, M. E. *Hideyoshi*. Harvard Press, 1986.

_____. *The Culture of Civil War in Kyoto*. California Press, 1994.

The Cambridge History of Japan, Vols. 3 and 4. Cambridge University Press, 1990 and 1988.

Dobbins, J. Jodo *Shishu: Shin Buddhism in Medieval Japan*. Bloomington: Indiana Press, 1989.

Dumoulin, H. *Zen Buddhism*. New York: Pantheon, 1989.

Duus, P. *Feudalism in Japan*. New York: McGraw Hill, 1993.

Farris, W. W. *Heavenly Warriors*. Harvard Press, 1992.

Friday, K. S. *Hired Swords*. Stanford Press, 1992.

Hall, J. W., ed. *Japan in the Muromachi Age*. California, 1977.

King, W. L. *Zen and the Way of the Sword*. Oxford University Press, 1994.

LaFleur, W. R. *The Karma of Words: Buddhism and the Literary Arts in Medieval Japan*. California, 1983.

McCullough, H. C. (transl.), *The Taiheiki: A Chronicle of Medieval Japan*. New York: Columbia University Press, 1988.

_____. *Yoshitsune*. Stanford University Press, 1971.

Mass, J. P. *The Kamakura Bakufu*. Stanford Press, 1976.

_____. *Warrior Government in Early Medieval Japan*. Yale Press, 1974.

Pirgrim, R. *Buddhism and the Arts of Japan*. Chamberburg, PA: Anima, 1993.

Shinoda, M. *The Founding of the Kamakura Shogunate*. New York: Columbia University, 1960.

Smith, B., and Ellison, G., eds. *Warlords, Artists, and Commoners*. Honolulu: University of Hawaii, 1981.

Totman, C. *Early Modern Japan*. Berkeley. California Press, 1993.

Varley, H. P. *Imperial Restoration in Medieval Japan*. New York: Columbia, 1971.

_____. *The Onin War*. New York: Columbia University Press, 1967.

Waley, A. (transl.), *The No Plays of Japan*. Rutland, VT: Tuttle, 1976.

CHAPTER 12

THE WEST ARRIVES IN ASIA

The impact of the West is probably the dominant feature of the history of modern Asia. Although we should not overemphasize it, it represents a new force not present before which profoundly influenced the evolution of every Asian society. For over three centuries after Vasco da Gama reached India in 1498 Westerners remained marginal in most of Asia, especially east of India. Even after the West won a form of supremacy as the outcome of the Anglo-Chinese war of 1839–1842, China, by far the largest unit of East Asia, continued to respond much more to its own internal dynamics and cumulative problems. China and Japan were never taken over by the West as pieces of colonial property, but were obliged to submit to foreign domination under the "unequal treaties," China until 1944, while Japan, by acquiring new strength from its wholesale adoption of Western technology, freed itself of these intrusions on its sovereignty early in the twentieth century. Japan went on to become an imperial power in its own right by taking over Taiwan, Korea, and Manchuria as Japanese colonies, while the French conquered Vietnam. But although the West never triumphed in China and Japan, the Western presence and example had far-reaching effects on both countries. It is thus an appropriate introduction to the modern section of this book to consider the arrival of Westerners in Asia, and to trace the course of Western activities there during the period before Western domination.

Independent Development

Despite Marco Polo's spectacular trip to China and India late in the thirteenth century, and his widely read journal, Europe and monsoon Asia, the two major poles of world civilization, remained largely isolated from each other until late in the development of each. The chief exception was India, but its early contact with the Graeco-Roman world of the Mediterranean was largely broken after about the fourth century A.D. with the decline of the Roman order. From the seventh century the Arab and Islamic conquest of the Middle East and central Asia also imposed a formidable barrier. European civilization arose out of the Roman collapse without any but the dimmest awareness of what lay beyond the Arab realms, and without the benefit of Asia's far older and more sophisticated model of civilization. The Arabs transmitted westward a few samples of Asian science and technology: Indian mathematics and numeration system, Indian medicine and steelmaking technology, Chinese silk, paper, and printing. But medieval Europeans tended to call most of these "Arabic" and either never knew or ignored their Asian origins, especially after the end of direct Roman connections with India and the interposition of an Arab monopoly on the trade with India and China, by sea, and by land across Central Asia.

At the more-or-less contemporary height of both the Roman and the Han dynasty empires, between the second century B.C. and the second century A.D., both empires were reaching out in search of conquest or probing beyond their frontiers. The Romans ran a long campaign in Central Asia against the Parthians of Iran (*Persia* and *Parthian* have the same root). Roman legions were fighting in western Persia while at the same time Chinese were making contact with related groups in eastern Persia. The two armies, or their scouts, might well have met, and the two empires perhaps planned a joint campaign again their common enemy. If they had, or if they had made direct contact in other ways, it would have made a great difference in the subsequent shape of

both Chinese and Roman civilizations. Both empires knew about each other, but only very vaguely, and neither seems to have realized that they were in approximately the same class in power, organization, wealth, and sophistication.

Many centuries before Alexander invaded India in 326 B.C., the civilizations of Asia had developed independent of connections with the ancient and classical West. Cathay, as Marco Polo called China, was the land that lay beyond the deserts and mountain barriers of Central Asia, so far that no Europeans before the Polos had ever been there, or had probably talked to anyone who had, a kind of Land of Oz. The West did not learn much more about it, except as the source of silk, than Herodotus

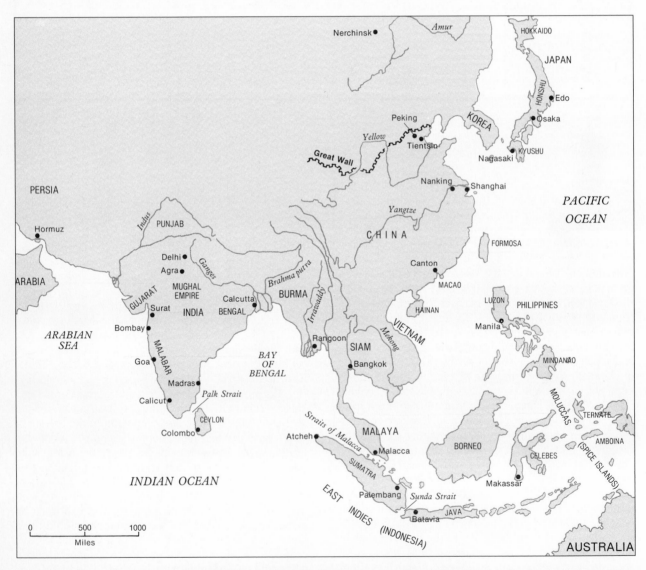

Asia in the Age of Early European Expansion

knew in the fifth century B.C., which was very little. "As far as India," he wrote, "the country is peopled, but beyond that no one knows what sort of country it is." The Chinese at their end of Eurasia appear to have heard travelers' tales about a great empire somewhere far to the west, on the shores of a great western ocean, and that this was the destination of much of the silk China exported.

But there was a long series of Central Asian middlemen, and little or no information about Rome filtered through to China. The Nestorian Christians, Jews, and other groups from westernmost Asia who reached T'ang China (see Chapter 6) probably had never seen or known the Roman empire in its days of greatness and were in any case Asians themselves, most likely from the eastern margins of what had once been the Roman empire. Chinese silk had to be paid for in Rome in gold, like most of India's exports, since the Romans had or produced little or nothing to exchange for it which the Chinese or Indians wanted or didn't produce themselves.

Perhaps the greatest consequence of the medieval European Crusades was their stimulus to the revival of trade, between Europe and the eastern Mediterranean, and then northward from Italy with the rest of Europe, and within northern Europe. Towns began to grow again, some to become trading cities like Genoa, Florence, Venice, Antwerp, or Amsterdam, and a money-based economy began to replace the local subsistence or barter which had dominated most of the European Middle Ages. A revival of trade had begun slowly even before the Crusades, and clearly added to the motives of many of those who took part. They were especially

✠ European View of Asia ✠

Asians did not think much of Europeans, especially in this period when they could so easily be seen as a bunch of crude ruffians. An Italian traveler to early seventeenth-century India, Nicolò Manucci, recorded Indian views that agreed closely with those of Chinese, Japanese, and other Asians. They believed that Europeans "have no polite manners, that they are ignorant, wanting in ordered life, and very dirty." The Europeans, however, were far more positive about Asia, which they had come so far to seek, in terms of both its wealth and its civilization. Here are samples of a Jesuit account of China in 1590.

There are such a number of artificers ingeniously framing sundry devices out of gold, silver, and other metals … and other matters convenient for man's use, that the streets of cities being replenished with their shops and fine workmanship are very wonderful to behold…. Their industry does not less appear in founding of guns…. To these may be added the art of printing … and with marvelous facility they daily publish huge multitudes of books…. You may add two more, that is to say navigation and discipline of war, both of which have been in ancient times most diligently practiced…. The people of China do above all things profess the art of literature, and learning it most diligently, they employ themselves a long time and the better part of their age therein…. Graduates of the second degree are elected in each province, and a certain number … ascend to the highest pitch of dignity…. Out of this order the chief magistrates are chosen…. Magistrates bear office for the space of three years, yet for the governing of each province men of another province are selected … [so that] judges may give sentence with a far more entire and incorrupt mind than if they were among their own kinsfolk and allies…. Over and besides all these there is an annual magistrate [the imperial censor] … whose duty it is to make inquisition of all crimes, and especially the crimes of magistrates…. Hence it is that all magistrates … are kept within the limits of their callings.

Source: N. Manucci, "An Excellent Treatise of the Kingdome of China," in *The Principal Navigations*, Vol. 2, ed. Richard Hakluyt (London, 1598–1600), pp. 88–97. The manuscript was written in Macao and captured by the English on its way to Lisbon.

anxious to extend their trading to include the rich eastern Mediterranean, and to win access to the ports and merchants there which were the western ends of the long trade routes, by sea and by land, which originated in India, China, and Southeast Asia.

The European Context

Europe north of the Mediterranean was agriculturally marginal: cold, wet, and most of it heavily forested. It was hence chronically troubled by banditry, especially in the absence as yet of any large or strong states and the prevalence of local feudal-style sovereignties which were often unable to keep order or to control more than small areas around their fortified castles, a far cry from the great Asian empires which were their contemporaries. But by the fourteenth century trade was an increasingly important source of wealth. Towns began to grow more rapidly, roads and river traffic improved and increased, and a new class of merchants and townspeople began to emerge.

Europe began to acquire the techniques of commerce developed earlier in India and China, such as bills of exchange and letters of credit. Commercial development of this sort was earlier and more advanced in Asia (see Chapter 6), and even included the issue of paper money. Asian trade, both domestic and foreign, was far greater than Europe's, as were Asia's overall production, population, and wealth—which made the Europeans anxious to establish direct contact with them, especially after Marco Polo's return from China and India in 1293 and his fascinating tales of the riches of Asia.

In seeking contact with other cultures and areas, Europe had certain advantages which Asia lacked. Europe is in effect a series of peninsulas jutting out into the ocean, inviting maritime trade, providing plenty of harbors, and promoting contact among its different parts. Each peninsula or island group, Norway-Sweden, Denmark, Great Britain, France, Spain, Italy, Greece, developed its own separate culture, and ultimately national state, but interchange among them was facilitated and encouraged by the regional differences which rewarded exchange. This is in sharp contrast to the great continental empires of Asia. Although Asia did develop an extensive trade by sea, it was a small fraction of their total trade, and tiny as a proportion of an economy dominated by agriculture. They tended to be more landward and inward oriented. Their great river valley and plains agricultural areas were surrounded by high mountains, and by vast deserts beyond the mountains. Asian states and economies centered on the management of their domestic resources, which were so much larger and more productive than those of early modern Europe. Except for

their trade with Southeast Asia and Japan, they knew only that their Central Asian neighbors, for hundreds or even thousand of miles westward, were more to be looked down on or feared than regarded as promising trade partners. Asians were in general more complacent, proud of their own rich and sophisticated civilizations, whereas Europeans realized early that their own domestic base, and, by the Middle Ages, their level of development, lagged behind, and that wealth could be won through trade abroad.

The Portuguese Reach Asia

In the end, it was the Portuguese who pioneered the direct sea route to the East. Columbus, though a Genoese, sailed under the Spanish flag, but his objective was Polo's Cathay, which he believed could be reached by sailing westward on a round earth. Until his death he thought that the coasts and islands he encountered in the New World were outposts of Asia, perhaps the islands of "Cipangu" (Japan). But the Spanish entered the competition relatively late, delayed in large part by their long effort to eject the Moors, which was finally successful only in 1492. The Portuguese were first as the culmination of a long and determined effort to pursue the route around Africa. Portugal's position on the open Atlantic, and their long tradition of seafaring and fishing in its stormy waters, gave them an advantage in this enterprise.

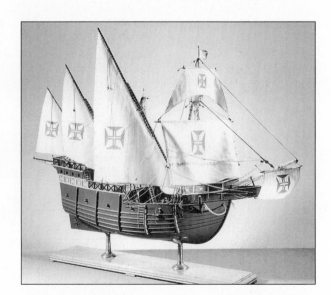

This model of a four-masted caravel illustrates the triangular lateen sails combined with square sails for sailing with the wind. (National Maritime Museum, Greenwich, England)

The Portuguese, like the Dutch, had long since necessarily developed more seaworthy craft and had begun to build small ships which benefited from some of the Arab experience riding the monsoon winds in the Indian Ocean, especially the large triangular lateen sail. The Portuguese combined it with an adjustable square sail and then with a kind of jib, so that it was possible to move better on an angle off the wind instead of only with it. This was the origin of the Portuguese caravel, illustrated on page 230. By the thirteenth century the much earlier Chinese invention of the compass had been spread to Europe by the Arab traders and was adopted early by the Portuguese together with multiple masts and the sternpost rudder (instead of the awkward and unseaworthy steering oars) developed first in Han and then in Sung China (see Chapter 6).

By the late fourteenth century, after the Chinese inventions of gunpowder and cannons had spread to Europe, the Portuguese and the Dutch began a slow improvement in naval warfare, with guns designed for use at sea and taking advantage of the greater maneuverability of their vessels with their combinations of sails. Guns were now used to destroy enemy ships or shore fortifications instead of the traditional method of ramming or grappling and boarding to enable hand-to-hand fighting, as the Greeks, Romans, and Venetians had done, although Venetians and Turks were also early users of cannon at sea. But Europeans made their way to Asia with the help of a variety of originally Asian nautical and military technology—and came to record their conquests, profits, and colonial management on Chinese-invented paper.

The Portuguese had played only a minor role in the Crusades, partly because they did not have a major commercial interest at that time, but they were fervent Roman Catholics and saw themselves as "Defenders of the Faith." They too had been conquered by the Islamic Moors, and Islamic North Africa lay just across the Gibraltar Straits. All Muslims were seen as the archenemies—and also as blocking the routes to the East and fattening on their control of the trade with Asia. Since early medieval times there had been tales of a Christian ruler, Prester ("Priest") John, somewhere east of Europe, who had withstood the Arab onslaught and would make a valuable ally against the common foe. Indeed the pope of the time gave Marco Polo letters to be delivered to Prester John, whom some thought might be Kublai Khan.

After a century of Portuguese effort to find a sea route around Africa, an expedition of four ships was prepared under Vasco da Gama which sailed from Lisbon in 1497 with India as its objective. Both da Gama and Columbus had been inspired by Marco Polo's journal and carried copies of it with them. Europeans were still a bit vague about the location of Cathay, "the Indies," or the Spice Islands, and about the distances and differences between them, or between Europe and monsoon Asia. Hence though Columbus thought he had reached

---

✠ Convenience Marriage ✠

An early seventeenth-century Dutch traveler to the Malay peninsula remarked on the Southeast Asian practice of "temporary marriage" to accommodate foreign visitors.

When foreigners come there from other lands to do their business ... men come and ask them whether they do not desire a woman; these young women and girls themselves also come and present themselves, from whom they may choose the one most agreeable to them, provided they agree what he shall pay for certain months. Once they agree about the money (which does not amount to much for so great a convenience), she comes to his house, and serves him by day as his maidservant and by night as his wedded wife. He is then not able to consort with other women or he will be in grave trouble with his wife, while she is similarly wholly forbidden to converse with other men, but the marriage lasts as long as he keeps his residence there, in good peace and unity. When he wants to depart he gives her whatever is promised, and so they leave each other in friendship, and she may then look for another man as she wishes, in all propriety, without scandal.

Source: A. Reid, *Southeast Asia in the Age of Commerce: The Lands Below the Winds* (New Haven, Conn.: Yale University Press, 1981), p. 155.

the margins of Cathay, he called the people he encountered there Indians.

Arab, Indian, and Chinese ships had long been trading across the Indian Ocean to East Africa. When da Gama, after rounding the Cape of Good Hope, arrived in East Africa early in 1498, he commandeered an Indian Gujerati pilot who had made the voyage many times before to guide him to the port of Calicut on the southwest coast of India. With such help, he reached there easily in May of 1498, after a voyage of nearly a year from Lisbon. The Indian merchants and local rulers realized immediately that the Portuguese represented a threat to their own position in the spice trade, and soon found them to be ruthless competitors. When the authorities at Calicut tried to stall him off in his requests for trade, da Gama bombarded the town and took Indian hostages. In the end he got his cargo of spices, which on his return to Lisbon in 1499 were said to have brought a 3,000 percent profit and to have paid the full costs of his expedition 600 times over. By 1503 the price of pepper in Lisbon was about a fifth of its price in Venice. Portugal's part in the European discovery of the New World was an incident of the second expedition to India in 1500, when Pedro Cabral's ship was blown westward in a great storm off West Africa and reached Brazil, which he claimed for the Portuguese crown.

The Portuguese Commercial Empire

In 1502 da Gama returned to Calicut, which he again bombarded, and then defeated or destroyed Indian and Arab ships sent against him. The Portuguese explored the whole of the Indian west coast plus Ceylon, and in 1510 settled on Goa (page 233) as their principal Asian base, from which they enforced their monopolistic control of all trade westward. It was already clear that the West's new power at sea, thanks to recently improved guns, ships, and naval tactics, could win for them the upper hand, at least as far as the coastal areas within range of their guns. Chinese and Indian ships had carried cannon for some time, most of them larger and heavier than those of the Portuguese, and their ships were generally much bigger. But they were also less easily maneuvered, especially in changing wind conditions, and their guns were usually fixed so that they could not be aimed. In any case, in repeated encounters after 1498, Western ships resoundingly defeated Indian and Chinese ships and by the early years of the sixteenth century had won control of the sea lanes as well as of strategically located trade bases. Even the dreaded Asian pirates were usually no match for them. Soon after the Portuguese arrival, Asian shipbuilders on the Indian west coast began to adopt a Western-looking rig in the hope of scaring off pirates, and sometimes added dummy gun ports for the same purpose.

Meanwhile another Portuguese sailor, Ferdinand Magellan (1480–1521), in the service of Spain, tried to reach Asia as Columbus had done, by sailing westward. He negotiated the stormy and dangerous straits at the tip of South America which still bear his name and sailed across the Pacific to the Philippines, where he and 40 of his men were killed after he had first claimed the islands for Spain. The survivors took the two remaining small

Portuguese Slavers

Especially after the great period of their trade dominance in Asia had passed, the Portuguese increasingly became pirates—and slavers, as this sixteenth-century text makes clear.

The Arakan [north coastal Burma] pirates, who were both Portuguese and native, used constantly to come by water and plunder Bengal. They carried off such people as they could seize, pierced the palms of their hands, passed thin slips of cane through the holes, and shut them huddled together under the decks of their ships. Every morning they flung down some uncooked rice, as we do for fowl.... Many noblemen and women of family had to undergo the disgrace of slavery or concubinage.... Not a house was left inhabited on either side of the rivers.... The sailors of the Bengal flotilla were so terrified of the pirates that if a hundred armed boats of the former sighted four of the latter their crews thought themselves lucky if they could save themselves by flight.

Source: M. Collis, *The Land of the Great Image* (New York: Knopf, 1943), p. 85. The author is quoting the sixteenth-century Mughal historian Shiab-ud-din Talish.

ships to the Moluccas and loaded a cargo of cloves, returning from there in one of them after great hardships with a skeleton crew of only 18 men, who sailed across the Indian Ocean and around Africa rather than daring again the dangerous passage through the Straits of Magellan. This was the first circumnavigation of the globe, which took some three years and cost the lives of most of those who took part; on the long passage across the Pacific the crew suffered terribly from scurvy and were forced to eat rats, hides, and sawdust, a fate which befell mariners on long voyages for several centuries thereafter.

By the 1520s, however, the Portuguese, spreading their control rapidly eastward from India and Ceylon, had won a strong position in the East Indies (what is now Indonesia), and in 1529 the Spanish sold their claims to the Moluccas or Spice Islands in eastern Indonesia to Portugal. Spain retained the Philippines, and Manila was made the colonial capital in 1571, after earlier Spanish bases and settlements elsewhere in the archipelago had been established. Spain's colonial conquests in the Americas took its major attention, but the Philippines nevertheless became the first major Western colonial territory in Asia, and the longest lasting of all large colonial dominions, since Philippine independence was not won until 1946.

The Spanish in the Philippines

Manila prospered as an interisland entrepôt as well as the colonial capital, and provided an important link be-tween Spanish America and Asia, primarily through trade with China. The Manila galleon, as it was called, carried annual shipments of Mexican and Peruvian silver from Acapulco to Manila, much of which went on to China to pay for exports of silk, porcelain, and lacquer back to both New and Old Spain. New World silver flowed into the China market, with major consequences for the economy of the Ming and Ch'ing (1644–1911) periods and their growing commercialization, as well as into Japan. Productive New World crops previously unknown in Asia, especially maize (Indian corn) and potatoes, also entered Asia via Manila and helped to support the subsequent major increase in China's population. Spanish control of the Philippines was relatively loose and did not extend effectively into the more remote or mountainous areas, especially on the larger islands like Luzon (where Manila lies on an extensive bay) or Mindanao in the south.

But it was accompanied by a determined missionary effort to win the inhabitants to Catholic Christianity, which by the later periods of Spanish domination had converted most Filipinos except for some of the mountain tribes and the remaining Muslim groups in southern Mindanao (see Chapter 16). The Philippines became the only Asian area where Christian missions had any substantial success, due largely to the absence there of any literate or sophisticated indigenous religious tradition, unlike India, China, Korea, Japan, or the rest of Southeast Asia. When the Spanish arrived Islam had just begun to penetrate Mindanao, but most of the archipelago remained at an essentially tribal level culturally, practicing a great variety of animistic beliefs and

The harbor of Goa, with craft much the same as those that used it in the fifteenth and sixteenth centuries. (R. Murphey)

without written texts or philosophical/theological traditions. Spanish also became the language in which educated Filipinos communicated with each other, since there was previously no common language and great regional linguistic variety. The missionary effort included schools, and a new educated elite began to emerge, among whom in time the seeds of nationalism were to grow, as elsewhere in Western-dominated Asia.

"Christians and Spices"

Conversion to Roman Catholicism was a major motive of the Portuguese and Spanish drive overseas from the beginning, which they saw as a new Crusade. Da Gama, and Cortez in Mexico, like all the Spanish and Portuguese expeditions, carried missionary priests as well as soldiers in their ships, and saw their goal as winning souls (or killing heathens) as much as winning trade profits. When da Gama reached Calicut, according to a widely repeated story, he is said to have replied to questions about what he sought, "Christians and spices," a neat summary of the two aims of both the Iberian states abroad. The Portuguese did encounter the Christians of south India, but soon dismissed them contemptuously as "heretics," and they also freely slaughtered Hindus as well as Muslims, both of whom they saw as enemies. The Portuguese and Spanish were after all the heirs of the Inquisition (thirteenth through sixteenth centuries) and its persecution or execution of all alleged "heretics" or infidels. Such people and their beliefs were seen as the work of Satan, and those who had the correct "truth" had a sacred duty to destroy them and to spread the "true word."

By the early 1500s, with the beginnings of the Protestant Reformation in Europe and widespread criticisms of the Roman Catholic Church, the Catholic European powers began to mount a counteroffensive, notably Spain and Portugal, a movement which came to be known as the Counter-Reformation. This was designed to regain ground lost to the Protestants, and included renewed efforts to spread Catholicism abroad. In 1534 Ignatius Loyola founded the Society of Jesus, also called the Order of the Jesuits, dedicated to reaffirming and teaching the Roman Catholic faith and to winning new converts. Asia became the major target, because of its huge populations and because of the Catholic (and later Protestant) conviction that Hinduism, Buddhism, and Confucianism were not legitimate or adequate religions at all and hence should easily yield to the superior message of Christianity. Islam remained the archenemy, against which European Christendom had been at war for centuries. There was thus added a new drive, and a new urgency, to Portuguese and Spanish efforts in Asia, and one which profoundly colored their impact.

Strategy and Bases

But for over two centuries after Europeans had made contact with Asia by sea, they remained insignificant on the Asian scene, a handful of people dismissed by Asians as crude barbarians, and completely outclassed in power on land by the great Asian empires or more local states. At sea and along the Asian coasts they had the upper hand, but their power on land extended little beyond the range of their naval guns. The Portuguese and later the Dutch built a strong position in the spice trade and were rivals for the monopoly of its export to Europe, but within Asian commerce as a whole, even its seaborne component, their role was minor. They bought spices and a few other goods in preexisting markets at established ports, such as Calicut, where they had already been collected by Asian traders, and then hauled them to Europe. The Portuguese never and the Dutch only much later had any involvement in production, and both continued to compete as traders with numerous Chinese, Indian, Southeast Asian, and Arab entrepreneurs, who did the bulk of the assembly. Only in the transporting of Asian goods to Europe did they have a monopoly, and there the Portuguese in time faced intense competition from the Dutch and English (see below).

As if to emphasize their role as ocean carriers with their improved ships for long voyages, the Portuguese developed a highly profitable trade between China and Japan, carrying Chinese silks and porcelains (and some Southeast Asian spices) from the Canton area to Nagasaki in southwestern Japan, and bringing back Japanese silver and copper for China. They, and later the English, also found profit in hauling Southeast Asian and Chinese goods to India and exchanging them for the Indian cottons which had an even larger and more eager market in Europe. Recognizing their weakness on land or in trade competition with Asian and Arab merchants, Europeans built on their strength at sea by occupying and fortifying coastal footholds at key points along the sea routes. Ideally these were in areas on the fringes of the great Asian empires, or where the local power was weak or could be persuaded to grant privileges in return for favors. The latter often included Western naval help against pirates, rebels, or small rival states.

A commercial empire stretching another 6,000 miles east by sea, through all of Southeast Asia (except the Philippines) and on to China and Japan, required other bases too. The most obvious control points over the sea lanes eastward from India were Colombo in Ceylon (now Sri Lanka) and Malacca in Malaya. The Palk Strait between India and Ceylon was too shallow for shipping, and the route around Sumatra and through the Sunda Strait between Sumatra and Java added extra miles and was plagued by reefs and currents, with no safe harbors along the Sumatran west coast. Traffic to and from East Asia was therefore funneled through the Straits of Malacca. The Portuguese seized the town of Malacca, commanding the Straits, in 1511, but Malaya at that period was thinly settled and relatively unproductive. Malacca's role was primarily strategic, although it did some entrepôt business to and from insular Southeast Asia. Colombo, which the Portuguese also fortified after establishing themselves there about 1515, was able to draw on the nearby production of cinnamon, predominantly a Ceylonese product produced from the bark of a rain forest tree, and thus played a commercial role as well.

For trade with China and Japan, the Portuguese somewhat later established their chief base at Macao, at the seaward edge of the Canton delta. There they could be a little freer of the restrictions imposed on foreign merchants at Canton by the Ming government and be tolerated by the Chinese authorities, enough to permit modest fortifications and a small, permanent settlement. From the Chinese point of view, these unruly and barbaric foreigners were in any case better shunted off to such a remote neck of land and closed off by a wall (which still stands) where they could not make trouble or corrupt the Chinese, and where they could govern

A traditional Chinese junk. These vessels were seaworthy and fast sailers with the monsoonal winds; many were large and had far greater cargo capacity than European ships until the eighteenth or nineteenth centuries. Like the Ming fleets of Cheng Ho, they were built with separate watertight compartments. (New York Public Library)

themselves according to their own strange customs. In the sixteenth century the Ming were still close to the height of their power and effectively excluded all foreigners except for tribute missions and a handful of traders at the fringes.

The shape and nature of the Portuguese commercial empire is clearly defined by its emphasis on strategically located ports, most of them already long in existence, and on domination of the sea lanes. They controlled no territory beyond the immediate area of the few ports named, and traded in the hundreds of other ports in competition with Asian and Arab traders. Even so, their effort was overextended and by the latter part of the sixteenth century they could no longer maintain what control they had earlier established. Their home base was tiny as well as poor; it could not provide either manpower or funds to sustain the effort required to maintain their overseas stations against competition. As the century ended they were rapidly being ousted by the Dutch in Southeast Asia, and were soon to be eliminated as serious competitors in the rest of the Asian trade by the other rising European power, the English.

Many Portuguese stayed on, picking up crumbs of trade and also operating as pirates. As in Africa, they had from early days married local women, and from the seventeenth century virtually all of them in Asia were Eurasians, though commonly carrying Portuguese names and retaining the Catholic faith to which they had been converted. To this day Portuguese names such as Fernando or de Souza are common in coastal South India, Sri Lanka, Malacca, dotted throughout the Indonesian archipelago, and in Macao. As Portuguese power faded, their bases were no longer a threat, so that Portugal retained formal sovereignty over Goa until it was forcibly reclaimed by India in 1961. Amazingly enough, the fiction of Portuguese control is maintained even now for Macao, an arrangement which suits the convenience of the Chinese government at least for the present.

The Chinese remained aloof from Western maritime and commercial rivalries, and kept European traders at arm's length at Canton, where they were not even permitted to enter the city but did their business outside the walls during the six-month trading season and then were obliged to depart until the next year. Successive Portuguese, Dutch, and English efforts to break these restrictions by trading elsewhere on the China coast were repelled, as Europeans did not have the means to challenge the Dragon Throne. The sixteenth-century missionary effort to penetrate China was more successful, at least for a time. For the Jesuits, as for all later missionary groups, China was the chief goal, if only because of its immense population, its sophisticated culture, and the knowledge that it lacked an indigenous religion of salvation. Successive Jesuit efforts to enter the country failed after Francis Xavier died off the south

An Indonesian dancer in Banda, wearing, as many still do for ceremonial purposes, a replica of a Portuguese helmet of the sixteenth century. (Kal Muller/Woodfin Camp and Associates)

China coast in 1552, still cherishing the dream of converting China's millions.

MATTEO RICCI: MISSIONARY TO THE MING COURT

The pioneer of the Jesuit effort in China was Matteo Ricci. He was born at Ancona in 1552, where he soon demonstrated his scholastic ability and magnetic personality. At the age of 16 he went to Rome to study law, and at 19 entered the Society of Jesus, where he distinguished himself in mathematics and geography. In 1577 he determined to pursue his career in the East, and arrived in Goa the following year. After finishing his religious training he taught in the college there until 1582, when he was called to Macao to prepare himself for the challenge of China. There he began diligent study of written and spoken Chinese, and in 1583 became the first Jesuit to enter China, although at first only as a "guest" in Kwangtung province near Canton. There he continued his study of the Confucian classics, and in 1589 built a church in Chinese architectural style. By this time he had discovered that priests of any kind were associated with the now-despised Buddhists, and he therefore adopted the dress as well as the manner and education of a Confucian scholar.

Ricci was a compelling person, tall and vigorous with flashing blue eyes, a curly beard (which assured the Chinese of his sagacity), and a resonant voice. What impressed them most, however, was his remarkable learning, combining as it did most of contemporary Western achievements, including cartography, and a thorough mastery of the classical Chinese corpus. He also had a phenomenal, almost photographic memory, and made use of a variety of mnemonic devices to assist it. This was a tremendous help to a scholar, especially for learning Chinese characters. Ricci was accordingly much sought after by Chinese who wanted to succeed in the imperial examinations, or wanted their sons to do so. This enhanced his acceptability, as did his success in dissociating himself entirely from the Portuguese traders at Macao. In 1595 he and his missionary colleagues were permitted to move north to the Yangtze Valley, and in 1601 to establish their permanent base at Peking.

The reigning emperor, Ming Wan-li, had become incompetent and concerned only with pleasures; the court was corrupt and full of scheming factions. Ricci finally caught the emperor's fancy by presenting him with two clocks and a clavichord, a precursor of the piano. When asked to demonstrate it, he composed some "edifying" madrigals for his majesty to sing. Later he was given a special imperial stipend and accepted at court as an outstanding and useful scholar. As the first missionary to China and one who fully understood how the hierarchical Chinese society worked (see Chapter 8), Ricci concentrated on the well-placed. To avoid alienating them and to make Christianity more understandable and appealing, he represented it as a system of ethics similar to and compatible with Confucianism, leaving out such potentially upsetting parts as the crucifixion, the virgin birth, and equality of all persons. He also avoided discussion of Christian theology.

This abbreviated version of the faith got the Jesuits in trouble with Rome later on, but it made excellent sense if the aim was to interest the Chinese. Ricci avoided preaching or overt efforts at conversion, and when he died in 1610 he was buried at Peking in a special plot granted by the emperor. He and his colleagues won few converts, but they saw their role as preparing the ground for a later assault by easing the Chinese into accepting the less controversial parts of Christianity, and by masquerading as Confucian scholars. With his sharp mind, vast erudition, and winning personality, Ricci was an ideal person for such a role, but interest in him as a scholar never led to an equivalent interest in the religion he came to China to plant.

Such success as Ricci and his successors achieved was largely the result of their use of some of the new fruits of the European Renaissance as a lure, especially early clocks, improvements in the calendar, maps of the world, astronomy, and glass prisms. Such things intrigued the Chinese and ingratiated the Jesuits at court as learned men. By now they had necessarily learned not only the Chinese language and the Confucian classics but the full deportment of the Confucian scholar as the vital credential for acceptance. They also understood that in this hierarchical society the key to missionary success was to convert those at the top, especially the emperor, and that preaching to the masses would only label them as troublemakers. Aided by their Confucian guise as men of learning and their useful Renaissance knowledge and interesting inventions, they made

some converts among gentry and court officials, but though they interested successive emperors, they never converted many Chinese. Western technology was more appealing than Western religion, as was to be so into our own times.

In the end, the Jesuit effort was undermined by the pope, who refused to permit their softening of Catholic doctrine or the acceptance of some Confucian rites in order to avoid offending potential converts. The controversy simmered for years, but the ground had been cut out from under the Jesuits and they were ultimately expelled in the early eighteenth century. Meanwhile their accounts of China became an important source of Western knowledge, and contributed to the European Enlightenment as a picture of a state of "philosopher-kings." European admiration of China and India, and what people like the French philosophers Voltaire and Montesquieu wrote about it, influenced the American heirs of the Enlightenment who framed our republic in the Jeffersonian vision of an educated citizenry. During much of this period there was a Western craze for things Chinese: paintings, furniture, gardens, flowered wallpaper, in addition to admiration of the Confucian order.

Matteo Ricci with his most prominent convert, Li Paulus, who translated European works on astronomy from Latin into Chinese. Li Paulus is wearing the winged cap of a high Chinese official, which he was, and Ricci the gown of a Chinese scholar. (New York Public Library)

The Russian Advance in Asia

Russian expansion across Siberia was slow, but involved permanent Russian occupation and domination of these vast territories and their technologically less-developed peoples, whose numbers were also small. By 1637 the Russians had reached the Pacific north of what is now Vladivostok, but they were behind the west Europeans in making direct connection with China. Early Russian explorers followed the major Siberian rivers, but these flow northward into the Arctic. Gradually a network of fortified garrisons and trading posts spread eastward. When the Amur River was reached, it was eagerly used as an easier route leading to more productive areas and to the sea. Russian presence in the Amur valley came to Chinese attention when northern Manchurian tribes, tributary vassals of the Ch'ing dynasty, appealed for help. Mongol groups were also trading with the Russians, which additionally alarmed the Chinese. Two successive Russian embassies to Peking, in 1654 and 1676, requesting trade privileges, refused to perform the required prostrations before the emperor and were sent away. By the 1680s, the Ch'ing, now having consolidated their power within China, began to establish new routes and military colonies in the Amur region and put naval ships on the river itself. The Russians were quickly chased out, and a large Ch'ing army besieged the one remaining Russian fortress. The Russians now agreed to negotiate, and sent an ambassador to their major post at Nerchinsk, on an upper Amur tributary but still within Siberia.

The treaty concluded there in 1689 confirmed the Amur region as Chinese, and obliged the Russians to destroy their remaining fortress, but accepted limited Russian trade rights by camel caravan to Peking, in part because the Chinese court wanted to maintain the supply of fine Russian furs from Siberia. A later treaty in 1727 excluded Russia from Mongolia and further delimited the boundary between Russia and China, leaving the Russians only Siberia. The Ch'ing emperor K'ang Hsi would not deal directly with "barbarians," still less go to them, so he sent as his representatives two Jesuits from the court, whom he deemed appropriate agents for the management of such affairs. Nevertheless, the Treaty of Nerchinsk treated both sides as essentially equal sovereign states. It was the only such treaty agreed to by China with a Western state until the nineteenth century, when China was forced to abandon the pretense of political superiority and accept inferior status. Until 1842, the various "sea-barbarians" could be treated as savages, though Russia as a rival and adjacent land power had to be dealt with differently. Fear of Russia and its ambitions remained a fixture in the Chinese mind, and was later intensified by Russian expansion into Manchuria.

Japan's Christian Century

The Japanese, as a small, remote, and, in their own view, less developed people, were far more open than the Chinese or the Indians to new ideas, even of foreign origin. Where Chinese, and often Indians, with their immense cultural pride and self-confidence, tended to dismiss anything foreign as crude and undesirable, the Japanese remained curious and sought opportunities to learn, as they had done from T'ang China. The sixteenth century, sometimes called "Japan's Christian Century," saw significant numbers of Christian converts as well as a flourishing trade with Europeans, centered in Nagasaki but also at Osaka, Edo (Tokyo), and other ports. After missionary work in Goa and the East Indies, Francis Xavier spent two years (1549–1551) in Japan preaching, teaching, and disputing with Buddhist monks. But Christians were soon seen as troublemakers. Rival Catholic religious orders contended with one another, often violently, as did the Portuguese, Spanish, Dutch, and English. Their ships and arms were often used in domestic Japanese factional fighting and intrigue, and Christianity was also seen as corrupting the Confucian loyalty of the Japanese and making converts potential subversives. Earlier Portuguese missionaries in Japan were told that if Christianity was, as they asserted, the only true religion it would long have been

❈ A Japanese View of the Dutch ❈

The Japanese were characteristically curious about the Westerners who came to Japan.

The men of the countries of Europe sail at will around the globe in ships which recognize no frontiers. In Holland, one of the countries of Europe (though a small one) they consider astronomy and geography to be the most important subjects of study because unless a ship's captain is well versed in these sciences it is impossible for him to sail as he chooses to all parts of the world. Moreover, the Dutch have the excellent national characteristics of investigating matters with great patience until they can get to the very bottom. For the sake of such research they have devised surveying instruments as well as telescopes and helioscopes with which to examine the sun, moon, and stars. They have devised other instruments to ascertain the size and proximity of the heavenly bodies.... Scholars write down their own findings and leave the solution for their children, grandchildren, and disciples to discover, though it may require generations.

Source: From R. Tsunoda et al., eds., *Sources of Japanese Tradition,* Vol. II. (New York: Columbia University Press, 1958), p. 41.

Western traders arriving at Nagasaki. A contemporary painting of the seventeenth century. (Tokyo National Museum)

known to and adopted by the Chinese. This helped to convince the Jesuits to try to convert the Chinese, as a key to the rest of East Asia, but as indicated above that effort failed. In Japan, the contending missionaries were increasingly seen as disruptive. Christianity was suppressed by 1640, thousands of converts crucified, and all foreigners expelled. The Japanese were forbidden to go abroad, and contact with the world beyond China was limited to one Dutch ship a year, allowed to trade only on an island in Nagasaki Harbor.

The first burst of Western activity in Asia thus ended with only minor success. It was the Europeans who sought out the East, because Europe, poor and backward by comparison with the riches of Asia, was eager for contact. In terms of power the Europeans were no match for the great Asian empires or even for lesser states, and they had nothing desirable to offer in trade with the more sophisticated economies of the East. This was to inhibit European contacts for several more centuries. The Europeans had to be content with a few tiny and insecure footholds on the coast, where they competed with Asian and Arab merchants. Sometimes they were thrown out at the whim of the Asian states and their goods confiscated.

Only at sea were the Europeans powerful—hence in part the Dutch success in controlling most of the trade of insular Southeast Asia—and there they tended to cancel each other out as rivals. Their chief commercial advantage was in the carrying trade, where their ships made them competitive but where they served mainly

Asian markets. Although Portuguese power subsequently faded in the face of Dutch and English competition, often forcing the Portuguese into piracy, the Asians continued to acknowledge Western superiority at sea. As the first British Consul at Shanghai was to remark over three centuries later in 1843: "By our ships our power can be seen, and if necessary, felt."[1] This was to remain the major basis of Western success in Asia throughout the centuries from 1498 to the end of colonialism in the ashes of the Second World War.

In the early period, Asians saw Westerners as clever with ships and guns but ignorant, dirty, contentious, drunken, uncivilized, and treacherous—all understandable descriptions of the European adventurers of the time. The habit of regular bathing did not come to Europe until well into the nineteenth century, with the advent of piped water and more adequate domestic heating. The smell of the Westerners who arrived in Asia during the first three centuries of their contact, after several months cooped up on board their tiny ships, disgusted the far-cleaner Asians, especially Indians and Japanese with their practice of scrupulous daily bathing and Indian daily toothbrushing. Westerners were also generally bearded, unkempt, knew (or observed abroad) few manners, and often brawled with each other as well as fighting with rival Western nationals.

The Chinese, noticing their greater amount of body hair, smell, and strange features as well as wild behavior, reasoned that they must be more closely descended from apes. They were certainly by Asian standards an

---

✠ To Convert the Chinese ✠

At the beginning of the eighteenth century Father Louis Le Comte (1655–1728), a missionary from the Bordeaux area, suggested the following methods for converting the common people of China: 1. The use of stories and parables. 2. The attribution of great importance to ornaments, processions, chants, and the noise of bells—ceremonies. 3. the inculcation of respect for images, relics, medals, holy water. 4. Concentrating on the instruction of children.

In essentials, these were the same procedures adopted by Buddhist priests in China fifteen hundred years earlier.

Source: From Jacques Gernet, *A History of Chinese Civilization*, translation by J. R. Foster. (Cambridge University Press, 1985), p. 456.

---

unimpressive, impetuous lot of ruffians, adventurers and pirates by their own accounts, as well as religious bigots. The only qualities which made them viable in a far more civilized Asia were their naval skills, and their ruthlessness. Nevertheless, and to Asia's later cost, they were largely ignored. That seemed reasonable enough in the splendid and confident context of Mughal India, Ming and Ch'ing China, and Tokugawa Japan (1600–1869), and it remained so for another two or three centuries. But one after the other, the Asian political orders declined, while by the late eighteenth century Europe began to ride the wave of new industrial, economic, and technological power.

The Dutch and English in Asia

The union of Portugal and Spain in 1580 did not materially strengthen what was now their joint effort in the East, but it did highlight the enmity and rivalry between them as Catholic powers and the rising Protestant states of the Netherlands and England. All of the Iberian positions overseas became attractive targets, and Portuguese profits newly tempting. The Dutch were the first to pick up this challenge effectively in Asia. At this period the Netherlands was a more important center of trade and shipping than was England, and Dutch ships had the upper hand in the English Channel. There were more of them, backed by merchant capital earned in trade, and in the course of the sixteenth century they became larger and more powerful, as well as more ma-

neuverable, than the Portuguese caravels. Dutch seamen had traveled east on Portuguese ships and learned what they needed to know about sailing to Asia and about trading there: what and where to buy and sell most profitably.

The Dutchman Jan Huyghen van Linschoten sailed on a Portuguese ship to Goa and spent some six years there from 1583 to 1589 in the service of the Portuguese archbishop. After his return to Holland he published in 1595–1596 an *Itinerario*, a geographical description of the world as he knew it, his observations in Asia, and a set of sailing directions for reaching most of the major Asian ports. This was exactly what the Dutch (and the English, where the book was soon translated) needed. The Dutch had earlier made determined efforts to find a northeast passage around the north of Russia, but found (as the English were to do) that this was not possible. Now a better path east lay open, and the Dutch also knew that the Portuguese trade empire was overextended and weakening. A Dutch fleet under Cornelis de Houtman sailed in 1595, using Linschoten's sailing directions, and this was followed by a series of trading expeditions financed by various Dutch syndicates.

They found the Portuguese generally disliked, especially in Southeast Asia, and they quickly broke the Portuguese spice monopoly. Their ships and sailors were better and could accomplish cheaper and quicker passages to and from Europe. The first real battle between Dutch and Portuguese ships off Bantam in west Java in 1601 led to a decisive Dutch victory; even though the Portuguese ships and men outnumbered the Dutch, the Portuguese guns were inferior and their ships were less able at maneuvering. As the seventeenth century opened, Dutch ships already outnumbered the Portuguese in Asia and had established their own semimonopoly of the spice trade, concentrating their Asian effort on what is now Indonesia (the "Spice Islands") and adjacent Malaya. They also ousted the Portuguese from Ceylon beginning in the 1640s, and captured Malacca in 1641, both of them strategic points whose passing to Dutch control signaled the end of the Portuguese position and the rise of Dutch power.

Unlike the Portuguese, the Dutch concentrated on trade and avoided all missionary efforts or religious conflict. But they were a hard lot, and enforced their new monopoly ruthlessly, against both Asian and European rivals. The several rival Dutch companies organized for trading to Asia were amalgamated into one national organization in 1602, the Dutch East India Company, to which the government gave a monopoly of all trade with the East. It was empowered to make war or treaties, seize foreign ships, build forts, establish colonies, and coin money, under loose government supervision from home. The new Company's chief rivals were now the English, whom the Dutch progressively drove out of their new domains in what is now Indonesia. Their monopoly was far more effective than that of the Portuguese had been, and they had better means to maintain it by force. English ships were driven off by gunfire, and a small group of ten English merchants who had begun to buy spices in the Moluccas, at Amboina, were accused of conspiracy, tortured to extract confessions, and then executed in 1623. This was the final blow to English hopes in the islands of the East Indies, and thereafter they concentrated their efforts on India. The Dutch retained some trading posts on the Indian east coast and Bengal, in mainland Southeast Asia, and in Formosa (Taiwan), and had a small part in the trade with Canton and Nagasaki (in Japan), but their major focus was the East Indies, and especially the productive island of Java.

Dutch success was due in part to their highly able governor-general Jan Pieterzoon Coen, appointed in 1618, who fixed the naval and administrative capital of the Dutch East Indies at Batavia (now Jakarta) in west Java, where it could guard the Sunda Straits. Dutch ships patrolled the waters and ports of Southeast Asia south of the Philippines and excluded Western competitors, while recognizing that the long-established trade of Asia would remain largely in Asian and Arab hands. They realized that greater profits could be won by taking whatever part in it they could win competitively, and by hauling Asian goods, mainly spices, to the European market. Governor-general Coen turned what had been a network of trading posts into a chain of strongholds, and ruled this new commercial empire with an iron hand, like his successors.

The Dutch drove hard bargains and eliminated rivals wherever they could. Many of the local rulers began to

regret their earlier willingness to exchange the Portuguese for the Dutch, but Coen and his successors gave them little choice. On their own company ships, the standard punishment for fighting among the crew was to nail to the mast one hand of the man judged guilty; thirst in the hot sun might eventually drive him to tear his hand loose, unless he was taken down sooner. For a second offense the punishment was keelhauling: tying one end of a rope to the man's feet and the other to his hands while the crew pulled on the rope so as to pass him under the ship's keel, a procedure which not many survived.

The Dutch acquired territory in Asia slowly and reluctantly; they were interested in profits only and resented the labor and cost of administration or involvement in local politics. But if they were to protect their bases and forts and to enforce their monopoly, they realized in time that some of their attention and resources would have to be diverted from making money to safeguarding it. The vicinity of Batavia came under direct Dutch rule, as did the other major ports. Slowly their grip on west Java, Ceylon, and the Moluccas strengthened, first by treaties with local rulers, then by joining one side against the others, and finally, by the eighteenth century taking over more or less full control; many Dutch-controlled territories in the East Indies were ostensibly headed by a native "regent," or were managed as "protectorates," or as "allies," with a Dutch resident appointed as the ruler behind the scenes.

Trade profits were augmented by tribute exacted from the local states, as well as by forced deliveries of commodities at artificially low prices. The Dutch introduced coffee growing to Java in the late seventeenth century; they compelled the Javanese to grow it, and in the eighteenth century it became the island's largest export to Europe. They also encouraged the production of sugar and indigo, and both became highly profitable exports. Almost as much as the Portuguese, however, the Dutch in Asia freely married local women, although such wives were often discriminated against, as were their children. The Chinese, with their commercial experience, were welcomed by the Dutch, but lived in their own areas at each port and under the administration of their own headmen, as had been the case for most foreigners throughout Asian history.

The Dutch East India Company slowly began to regulate production in order to maintain prices, and to impose their direct control on the areas which produced the most valuable crops. Indonesians in the areas ruled directly by the Dutch were subject to forced labor, most often for construction and harbor improvement projects. Spices remained crucially important to the Company, and the island of Amboina in the Moluccas and the Banda Islands were wholly Dutch-run. Production was adjusted to market demand, and in some years trees

✠ A Chinese View of Ricci ✠

The few Chinese scholars who accepted both Christianity and Western science believed that the latter made up for the shortcomings of Confucianism and that Christianity was preferable to Buddhism. A late Ming writer argued:

T'ien-chu kuo [Lord of Heaven country, i.e., the Catholic state, presumably Italy] lies farther to the west from the Buddhist state [India]. Their people understand literature and are as scholarly and elegant as the Chinese. A certain Li-ma-tou (Matteo Ricci) came from the said state and after four years reached the boundary of Kwangtung by way of India. Their religion worships T'ien-chu [Lord of Heaven] just as the Confucianists worship Confucius and the Buddhists Buddha. [Ricci's message] explains the truth by comparison with Confucianism but sharply criticizes the theories of nothingness and emptiness of Buddhism and Taoism.... I am very much delighted with his ideas, which are close to Confucianism but more earnest in exhorting society not to resemble the Buddhists, who always like to use obscure, incoherent words to fool and frighten the populace.... He is very polite when he talks to people and his arguments, if challenged, can be inexhaustible. Thus in foreign countries there are also real gentlemen.

Source: Quoted in J. K. Fairbank and S. Y. Teng, *China's Response to the West*, (Cambridge: Harvard University Press, 1954), p. 13.

were actually cut down to avoid surpluses which might depress prices. Production of other crops was "encouraged" by various pressures, including later the imposition of taxes which obliged previously subsistence growers of rice to grow sugar or other cash crops in order to pay the taxes, but crops could be sold only to the Company. Indigenous traders and shipbuilders were driven out by Chinese and Dutch competition, and the Javanese especially became largely a group of cultivators and laborers. It was their misfortune that by the sixteenth century the Muslim conquest had undermined the earlier Hindu-Buddhist civilization of Java, and that the whole archipelago, as well as Java itself, was divided into a great number of small rival kingdoms which were easily outmaneuvered and in the end subdued by the determined, highly organized, and persistent Dutch.

The English in Asia

Like the Dutch, the English first tried to find a northeast passage, and a company was formed in London in 1553 to open up trade with "Cathay" by that route. They sent an expedition of three ships under Sir Hugh Willoughby and Richard Chancellor. Willoughby and his men died on the north coast of Scandinavia in their two ships, but Chancellor went on to Russia and obtained a formal trade agreement from the czar, Ivan IV. Subsequent efforts to find a sea route to the East around Russia, and northwest around North America, all failed, but Francis Drake's return from his circumnavigation of the globe in 1580 and his successful penetration of the Moluccas (after an earlier landing at San Francisco) rekindled English interest in the southern route or routes. In 1583 Ralph Newberry and Ralph Fitch sailed to Syria and thence went overland to the head of the Persian Gulf, where they found a Portuguese ship to take them to Goa, the first Englishmen to reach India. Newberry died there, but Fitch traveled widely in the subcontinent for over two years, and then shipped on to Burma and Malacca before returning to England, via the Persian Gulf and Syria, in 1591.

Soon after his return he wrote an account of his travels, including what he had learned about China from the reports of others. Its descriptions of Asian wealth whetted English appetites still further, and contributed to the founding of the English East India Company in 1600. Meanwhile, Thomas Cavendish duplicated Drake's circumnavigation and his successful raiding of Spanish and Portuguese ships in the Pacific from 1586 to 1588. In 1589, the year after England's victory over the Spanish Armada's attempt to invade the home island, a group of London merchants began to seek support for an ambitious trading venture to the East using da Gama's route around Africa. "Great benefit," they said "will redound to our country, as well as for the annoying of the

Spaniards and Portugalls (now our enemies) as also for the selling of our commodities."[2] Continued seizing by English freebooters like Drake and Cavendish of Portuguese and Spanish ships loaded with valuable Asian cargoes provided new reminders of the profits to be won, and fired the English imagination.

Especially with the defeat of the Spanish Armada and the surge of national feeling and ambition, the last decade of Queen Elizabeth's reign (r. 1558–1603) saw an almost feverish interest in extending English shipping and trade overseas, as their old rivals the Dutch were already doing so successfully, following the Portuguese lead. English ships were already beginning to get the upper hand, not only against the larger and far less maneuverable Spanish and Portuguese galleons and caravels but were pulling up equal to the earlier developed Dutch. The relatively small Dutch home base now began to tell against them in the competition with England with its far larger, rapidly developing, and expansionist economy and population, including the eager merchants of London and Bristol.

This was also the time of William Shakespeare (1564–1616), whose last play, *The Tempest*, written about 1614, reflects the wide contemporary English interest in the new overseas discoveries. *The Tempest* also foreshadows to an almost uncanny degree what were much later to become the dominant European attitudes toward Asians as "inferior" people fit only to serve the conquering Westerners. In fact, although Elizabethan and Shakespearean England exuded confidence and pride, the handful of Westerners in Asia remained awed by Eastern power and wealth and were confined to precarious tiny footholds on the fringes of the great Asian empires until the late eighteenth century in India and Java and the mid-nineteenth century in the rest of Asia. Most of them acknowledged that the Asian civilizations were superior to their own. But racial and cultural differences have nearly always been occasions for prejudice when different peoples have confronted each other.

Shakespeare seems to have understood that (see also, for example, *Othello* and *The Merchant of Venice*), and somehow to have anticipated the attitudes which became prominent in the Western mind two centuries or more after his death. He clearly had read and heard accounts of the new discoveries of exotic lands and people, and set *The Tempest* on an isolated island where Prospero, an exiled duke, had been shipwrecked with his daughter Miranda. There by his special powers of magic (new Western technology?) Prospero made the only two native inhabitants his servants: Caliban, a brutish "savage," and Ariel, an elfin-like wood spirit. These two characters seem to personify the later Western image of Asia as "uncivilized" (i.e., different), but also, as in Ariel, graceful, intuitive, and charming, even "child-like." Nearly three centuries later Rudyard Kipling probably had Caliban and Ariel in mind when he put it even more explicitly in "The White Man's Burden," written for the Americans in 1899 as they took over colonial administration of the Philippines from the defeated Spanish (see Chapter 16). Kipling offers them the advice of an older colonial power, and details what to expect in trying to govern "your new-caught sullen peoples, half devil and half child."

Such attitudes were still far in the future, despite Shakespeare's accurate vision, when Queen Elizabeth on the last day of December 1600 signed a royal charter to

---

✠ Chinese and Barbarians ✠

The Chinese long tried to keep all foreigners at arm's length, even at Canton, and forbade foreign efforts to trade elsewhere. In the early stages of their interaction, they obliged the Portuguese to leave the city of Canton every night during the short trading season, as recorded in Ralph Fitch's Journal *in the late sixteenth century.*

When the Portugalls come to Canton in China to trafficke they must remain there but certain days. And when they come in at the gate of the city they must enter their names in a booke, and when they go out at night they must put out their names. They may not lie in the towne all night, but must lie in their boats without the towne. The Chinians are very suspicious and doe not trust strangers.

Source: From the *Journal of Ralph Fitch, 1583–1591*, in W. Foster, ed., *Early Travels in India*. (London: H. Milford, Oxford University Press, 1921), pp. 41–42.

a group of London merchants organized into an East India Company for trading with all of Asia. For all the enthusiasm for overseas exploration and trade, England was still primarily a country of farmers, and the scale of its enterprise in Asia was for some time relatively small. The Dutch had little trouble in repelling English efforts to break their monopoly in the East Indies, but the English hung on as minor players at some of the mainland Southeast Asian ports, and in India after primary Dutch attention shifted to the more profitable East Indies.

Efforts to trade in China were largely blocked by the Chinese authorities at Canton, and by the Portuguese at Macao. Even the determined Dutch had little or no success in their repeated attempts to break through this system. The English captain John Weddell fought his way up the river to Canton in 1637 and took back some English merchants who had been imprisoned there, but was denied permission to trade as well as harried by the Portuguese at Macao. Much the same fate befell subsequent English ventures to China, including an effort in the 1670s to succeed the Dutch in Taiwan after their expulsion by the Ming loyalist Koxinga in 1661, but by 1683 the Ch'ing dynasty (see Chapter 8) had conquered Taiwan and all foreigners were told to trade at Canton. By the early eighteenth century trade by Westerners slowly became easier at Canton, but the English did not get permission to establish a regular trade base there until 1762—a story told in more detail in Chapter 8.

Meanwhile there was a brief English adventure in Japan. Will Adams, an English shipmaster and pilot, was appointed pilot-major to a fleet of Dutch ships bound for the East Indies in 1598. They were scattered in successive storms, and only the ship captained by Adams appears to have survived the passage around Cape Horn, arriving in Kyushu in southwestern Japan in the spring of 1600. Foreigners and their ships were still uncommon, and Adams was summoned to Osaka by Tokugawa Ieyasu (see Chapter 13), who was about to become the effective ruler of the entire country. Again the Jesuits and the Portuguese, already well entrenched in Japan, tried to persuade Ieyasu to execute Adams as an intruder; he did spend some time in prison, and then was ordered to bring his ship around to Edo (now Tokyo), where Ieyasu was beginning his rule as *shogun*. After the Japanese had carefully studied it, the ship was confiscated and Adams and his Dutch crew forbidden to leave the country without permission. Adams settled down in Japan, learned the language, and married a Japanese woman. At Ieyasu's orders he built a couple of small Western-style vessels, and in return was granted an estate near Edo.

Adams' story made its way back to London via Holland, and the English East India Company, anxious not to be outdone by the Dutch (for whom Adams had after all been working) sent three ships in 1611 with a letter from King James I requesting trade privileges; two loaded spices in Southeast Asia and returned home, but the third reached Hirado, on an island off the westernmost tip of Japan some 50 miles from Nagasaki, in 1613, where a trading warehouse was provided. Adams came down from Edo to talk with his compatriots, and accompanied them to Ieyasu, who gave them full permission to trade. When the ship sailed home later that year, seven Englishmen were left at Hirado to promote trade. Adams decided to remain in Japan, although Ieyasu had given him permission to leave, and he died there in 1620. The English trade begun in 1613 lasted only about a decade and never became very profitable, partly because of continued Portuguese and Dutch resentment and competition (including their own imports of Indian cottons). After the death of Ieyasu in 1616 there were increasing pressures against foreigners, culminating in

✠ Protecting China ✠

When James Flint attempted an end run and sailed north from Canton to trade at various ports in 1755, he was rebuffed and expelled, and the following imperial edict issued:

The products of China are abundant; what need have we for the small and insignificant goods of the distant barbarians? Just because you wanted to trade we have had compassion for men from afar and did not prohibit [you from coming]. Now you are not able to keep your place and obey the laws…. The laws will be upheld and feelings will be pacified. Everyone will return to harmonious cooperation.

Source: Quoted in R. Murphey, *The Outsiders*. (Ann Arbor: University of Michigan Press, 1977), p. 10.

their complete expulsion (see Chapter 13), but the English company was not impressed with trade prospects there and withdrew its people and enterprises in 1623.

This was just as well, since the Tokugawa were already turning against foreigners. In the years following Ieyasu's death in 1616 all missionaries were killed or expelled, and all traders expelled by 1638. The Portuguese kept trying, but their emissaries were executed. The Tokugawa simply closed Japan to outside contact and even forbade the building of ships able to go overseas. One (sometimes two) Dutch ships per year were allowed to trade at the island of Deshima in Nagasaki Harbor; the Dutch were free of the missionary taint, and as a small state did not present a great power threat. The Tokugawa were aware that it was prudent to keep at least this small window on the larger world, and a surprising amount of information reached them through this Dutch channel, including samples of the by then rapid advances in Western technology. A few Chinese ships were also permitted to trade; the connection with China remained too important to sever completely. But for all other foreigners, Japan was closed. Before this happened, the Portuguese had introduced tobacco (a New World plant) about 1590, which became widely popular as a smoke, and in 1615 the English at Hirado had brought in via the Spanish connection even more important New World plants, sweet and white potatoes, which extended the potential of the agricultural system as they had done in China (see Chapter 8), although maize did not become widespread in Japan and never acquired even the limited importance it won in China.

China was able to keep the Westerners at arms length until 1842, and even after it had been repeatedly beaten in successive wars refused to acknowledge that this latest set of "barbarians" had anything of value to offer to the Celestial Empire. Western learning and technology went on being rejected until late in the nineteenth century, while China fell farther and farther behind. The first three centuries of Westerners in Asia did not presage their ultimate triumph, with the possible exception of the British in India, but even their dominance there was only beginning by the end of the eighteenth century. Until then, and later in East Asia, Westerners were present only on the fringes of the great Asian empires, and were excluded from Korea, Japan, and Vietnam. As late as 1700 or 1750, let alone 1600 or 1650, it would have been hard to foresee that the tiny groups of Western traders would ultimately impose their dominance. They lacked the means to challenge any of the Asian states or empires, and hung on at their mercy to their small coastal footholds, or in Japan and Korea were denied any form of access.

But as the eighteenth century entered its second half, great changes were at work in Europe which would produce strong new nation-states with overseas ambitions, and with new means to pursue them as technological and scientific breakthroughs set the Industrial Revolution in motion. The West acquired overwhelming power as well as wealth, and in the course of the nineteenth century brought this to bear on Asia and established Western hegemony.

Notes

1. Quoted in R. Murphey, *The Outsiders: The Western Experience in India and China.* Ann Arbor: University of Michigan Press, 1977, p. 21.
2. Quoted in W. Forster, *England's Quest for Eastern Trade.* London: A. and C. Black, 1966, pp. 127–128.

Suggestions for Further Reading

Andrews, K. R. *Trade, Plunder and Settlement: Maritime Enterprise and the Genesis of the British Empire, 1480–1630.* Cambridge: Cambridge University Press, 1987.

Boxer, C. R. *The Dutch Seaborne Empire, 1600–1800.* London: Knopf, 1965.

_____. *The Portuguese Seaborne Empire, 1415–1825.* New York: Knopf, 1969.

Chaudhuri, K. N. *The Trading World of Asia and the English East India Company, 1600–1760.* Cambridge: Cambridge University Press, 1978.

Cipolla, C. M. *Guns and Sails in the Early Phase of European Expansion, 1400–1700.* London: Collins, 1965.

Crosby, A. W. *Ecological Imperialism: The Biological Expansion of Europe, 900–1200.* Cambridge: Cambridge University Press, 1986.

Diffie, B. W., and Winius, George D. *Foundations of the Portuguese Empire, 1415–1580.* Minneapolis: University of Minnesota Press, 1977.

Honour, H. *Chinoiserie: The Vision of Cathay.* New York: Harper, 1973.

Kling, B. B., and Pearson, M. N., eds. *Europeans in Asia Before Dominion*. Honolulu: University Press of Hawaii, 1979.

Mungello, D. E. *Jesuit Accommodation and the Origins of Sinology*. Honolulu: University of Hawaii Press, 1989.

Nowell, C. E. *The Great Discoveries and the First Colonial Empires*. Ithaca, NY: Cornell University Press, 1954.

Parry, J. H. *The Age of Reconnaissance*, 2nd ed. Berkeley: University of California Press, 1981.

_____. *The Establishment of European Hegemony, 1415–1715*. New York: Harper & Row, 1961.

Ricci, M. *China in the Sixteenth Century: The Journals of Matthew Ricci, 1583–1610*, trans. L. J. Gallagher. New York: Random House, 1953.

Ronan, C. R., and Oh, B. C. *East Meets West: The Jesuits in China*. Chicago: Loyola University Press, 1988.

Schurz, W. L. *The Manila Galleon*. New York: Dutton, 1959.

Souza, G. B. *The Survival of Empire: Portuguese Trade and Society in China and the South China Sea, 1630–1754*. Cambridge: Cambridge University Press, 1986.

Spence, J. D. *The Memory Palace of Matteo Ricci*. New York: Viking, 1984.

Tracy, J. E., ed. *The Rise of Merchant Empires*. Cambridge University, 1990.

CHAPTER 13

TOKUGAWA JAPAN

Tokugawa Ieyasu's victory at Sekigahara in 1600 brought Japan the longest period of peace and stability in its history, which lasted until nearly the end of the Shogunate in 1868. A major result was economic and commercial growth far beyond anything in the Japanese past, and the wider spread of what had previously been the exclusively urban culture of the elite. Such developments brought the country closer to the modern world and helped make it possible for Japan to leap ahead under new management after 1868. But it was not yet part of that world, since the Tokugawa closed the country to foreigners and even forbade the Japanese both to go abroad and to build ships capable of making such a voyage. In at least one other respect, the Shogunate's rule was sharply regressive; it rested on a continuation of the feudal system which had evolved in preceding centuries, the chief difference from earlier periods being that it was made still more rigid and more effectively controlled from the center of the *shogun's* power, which had moved to Edo (modern Tokyo) with Ieyasu's triumph.

To strengthen their control still further, the Tokugawa also outlawed all guns, which the Japanese had learned of from the Europeans in the sixteenth century and had used themselves in internal wars and in Korea, with devastating effect. A gun can make anyone who has it of course a severe threat to authority or just to the civil order. The Tokugawa were obsessed with order and control, and guns were an obvious menace to both, an invitation to disorder or rebellion. As weapons improved, this was in effect the next step beyond Hideyoshi's sword

hunt, and was undertaken for exactly the same reasons, and to prevent the vassal *daimyo* from building up enough force to challenge their Tokugawa overlords. Peasants were again made to surrender their swords and other weapons to the *bakufu*, and the hereditary warrior class of the *samurai* was left in complete charge of military affairs. Swords were reaffirmed as the badge of the *samurai*, a mark of aristocratic birth and status which symbolized their role as "gentleman warriors." The *bakufu* eagerly studied Dutch reports of European advances in firearms via the limited trade at Deshima, but for more than two centuries Japan was free of the terrible damage they continue to do in modern society. Unarmed peasants were thus even less able to challenge *samurai* swords.

Japan was now composed of a central area around the Kanto plain ruled directly by the Tokugawa, and a number of feudal dependencies known as *han* administered by *daimyo*, all of whom owed allegiance to the Tokugawa. Their number varied over time but averaged about 265, while their size varied still more; some were very large, including the Satsuma domains in southern Kyushu and others in northern Honshu, whole others were a small fraction of their size. The Tokugawa domains were by a large margin the largest, including about a quarter of the productive agricultural land of the entire country and even more of its population. They stretched all the way west to and beyond Kyoto, and thus encompassed all of the main areas of population and production. The shogunate also directly administered the chief cities, including Edo, Kyoto, Osaka, and

Nagasaki. In 1606 Ieyasu's huge castle at Edo was finished, an impressive symbol of his power. His control was augmented by appointing other members of the extended family as *daimyo* of *han* located strategically around the central domain, at Mito, east of Edo, at Nagoya on the route to Kyoto, and at Wakayama to guard the southwestern approaches to Kyoto. These three collateral families were also charged with supplying an heir to the shogunate if the main branch was unable to do so. Other strategically placed *han* were put in the hands of *daimyo* who had been created by Ieyasu or his successors, mostly nobles who had supported Ieyasu's side or had been his vassals before 1600, or their descendants.

More distant areas were administered by what were called "outer *daimyo*," families which had become attached to Ieyasu only after his victory in 1600. Most of the outer domains were much larger than average and some of their *daimyo* still harbored resentment against the Tokugawa, but they were remote from the center of power. At the end of the Tokugawa they were to play a major role in its overthrow, but until then the system set up by Ieyasu worked well in insuring that Edo remained dominant and that no other regional group in Japan could challenge it. The *daimyo* managed the administration of their domains, which saved Edo from that burden and expense and made sense given the difficulties of

Tokugawa Japan

✶ Aristocratic Behavior in Japan ✶

The importance of hierarchical order in Japan is revealed in this 1615 decree of a shogun regulating the behavior of the feudal lords, or daimyo, and their retainers, the samurai. Note the obligation to be aristocrats rather than mere soldiers.

Literature, arms, archery, and horsemanship are to be the favorite pursuits. Literature first, and arms next to it, was the rule of the ancients. They must both be cultivated concurrently.... Drinking parties and gambling amusements must be kept within due bounds.... Offenders against the law are not to be harbored in the feudal domains. Law is the very foundation of ceremonial decorum and of social order. To infringe the law in the name of reason is as bad as to outrage reason in the name of the law....

The distinction between lord and vassal, between superior and inferior, must be clearly marked by apparel. Vassals may not ... wear silk stuffs.... Miscellaneous persons are not at their own pleasure to ride in palanquins.... Lately even sub-vassals and henchmen of no rank have taken to so riding. This is a flagrant impertinence.... The *samurai* throughout the provinces are to practice frugality. Those who are rich like to make a display, while those who are poor are ashamed of not being on a par with others. There is no influence so pernicious as this, and it must be kept strictly in check.

Source: D. Lach, *Asia on the Eve of Europe's Expansion* (Englewood Cliffs, N.J.: Prentice-Hall, 1965), pp. 157–160.

communication, but the costs were high, and in addition they had to furnish troops for the shogunal army and labor for big construction projects, including the building of Edo castle. The *shogun* could and did confiscate their lands if he found them disloyal or if they misgoverned, and kept a careful eye on any military buildup. *Daimyo* troops were limited by the shogunate, and any activity related to building up fortifications in their domains was quickly reported and checked. They were prohibited from making alliances with other *daimyo*.

As in feudal Europe, marriage ties were used to cement loyalty, but the special feature of Tokugawa control was the requirement for all *daimyo* to leave their wives and immediate heirs in Edo as hostages, and to personally attend at the *shogun's* court where they resided in alternate years, a system known as *sankin kotai* ("alternate attendance"). This involved the *daimyo* in the maintenance of a stylish and expensive residence in Edo, in addition to what they kept in their own domains, and they had to spend large sums of money also in making the journey from their home bases and back, accompanied by large retinues. These expenses were a heavy financial burden, as much as half of the income of most of them, leaving that much less for building their own strength. Their residence in Edo also tended to increase cultural unity in Japan, where even the remotest *han* followed the cultural and ideological lead of Edo. *Daimyo* processions to and from Edo, especially along the coastal road to and from Kyoto known as the Tokaido, also served to disseminate an increasingly national culture as well as stimulating commercial activity along the route. They also became favorite subjects for Japanese painters.

The Tokugawa Order

At Edo the *bakufu* continued to govern in the emperor's name, and treated the court in Kyoto with respect. Tokugawa funds and planning rebuilt the imperial palace and made over revenues for the support of the imperial court while retaining control over all court appointments and stationing a garrison in Kyoto. There was no question that the emperor and the nobility around him had a purely ceremonial role. *Bakufu* administration was headed by a council of elders, one of whom eventually was accepted as the head, or Great Elder, and a junior council of younger peers which supervised military affairs. Under the two councils were the usual and necessary branches of administration: commissioners of finance and tax collection (from the shogunate's own domains—the *han* paid no taxes to Edo), of temples and shrines, and of towns; the latter also supervised what foreign trade was permitted. Both open and secret police organizations kept order and checked on activities in the *han*; the Tokugawa secret police was a fearsomely effective operation. The internal administration of the *han* was similar in that in most of them there was also a council of elders, and a less formal use of lesser *samurai* to do the work of administration.

In the interests of further damping down forces for change and ensuring a smooth but rigid social order, the *bakufu* tried to freeze in place a class system which divided Japanese society into distinct and watertight groups. This reflected, and to a degree was sanctioned by, classic Confucian values, but the top class in Japan was the warrior-administrators rather than the scholar-bureaucrats of China. Peasants were essential producers, and as in China were considered the backbone of the system. Artisans, who mainly served the upper classes but whose work was obviously less basic or essential than farming, formed a third class, while merchants, regarded, as in the Confucian system, as parasites producing nothing and merely handling what was produced by others, were the fourth order. This was maintained despite the growing literacy, often cultivation, and wealth of merchants. The aristocratic class in Japan had retained Confucianism, and it was revived and strengthened under Tokugawa rule as suiting admirably their class-structured and hierarchical view of society and the stress on loyalty. Merchants were forbidden to wear the fine clothes or materials of the upper classes, to ride in sedan chairs (which the aristocracy used), or to omit the groveling and subservient bowing also required of peasants or artisans to *samurai* or other aristocrats whom they encountered, or when one of the *daimyo* processions passed. Those who did not bow low enough might have their heads chopped off by *samurai* guards or outriders.

Hereditary aristocrats, of various grades from rich to poor *daimyo* and lesser, even threadbare, *samurai*, totaled about 6 percent of the population, a relatively high figure compared with Europe (China had no hereditary aristocracy). In practice those who lived in towns, such as most merchants and artisans, tended to form a single group of "townsmen," or *chonin*. Peasants also often migrated to the town and became artisans or laborers, and some engaged in small-scale commercial dealings in the villages or in the production of goods for sale. Villages were largely self-governing, but did have to pay very heavy taxes, as much as half of the total output, for the expenses of *bakufu* and *han* administration and also for the support of the large *samurai* group as a whole. Private estates, except for those of the *daimyo*, were gone, and taxes had to support the whole structure, almost all at the expense of the peasants, who were cruelly squeezed. A much-quoted proverb at the time was, "Peasants are like sesame seeds. The more you squeeze, the more oil you get." But over 80 percent of the population were peasants, who suffered periodic famine while the court plus merchant culture flourished in Edo, Kyoto, Osaka, and other towns and cities and tends to dominate our image of the Tokugawa.

Another largely forgotten sector of Japanese society was the *eta* outcast group, altogether about 2 percent of the population, who performed essential services in disposing of dead animals but also served as butchers and leatherworkers, activities considered defiling since they violated the Buddhist doctrine against the taking of life. They were concentrated in Kyoto and westward and may have originated as people defeated in the wars of earlier times. They still exist, in roughly the same proportions, in modern Japan, and are still heavily discriminated against, although they are physically and culturally (except for their occupations in some cases) indistinguishable from other Japanese. Beggars, low-class prostitutes, and itinerant actors were also an outcast group, as in China and many societies.

The class divisions decreed by the Tokugawa and intended to be mutually exclusive did not thus accurately reflect reality. In addition, there were now really too many *samurai* to be adequately employed or to find sufficient support for. Some whose lords had lost out in the struggles of the sixteenth century and following decades or who were themselves natural losers and were no longer wanted or attached became a masterless group called *ronin* which was a source of trouble. But the major pressures working against the Tokugawa's too-neat divisions of Japanese society were generated by the continued evolution of that society, in spite of such determined efforts to prevent change of any kind. There were rural/peasant rebellions and townsmen revolts, which were relatively easily suppressed, but the continued rise of the merchant group could not so easily be dealt with. *Daimyo* expenses often outran their income, and *samurai* families clung to their aristocratic pretensions in the face of financial decline. The obvious solution, as in so many other societies, was to marry aristocratic daughters to rich merchant sons (sometimes also vice versa) and thus to save the family fortunes. In time and despite the official prejudice against them, rich merchants rose to prominence, especially in Edo and other cities. It was a quiet and nonviolent revolution, but eventually it fundamentally altered Tokugawa society and culture. There are of course parallels here with late medieval Europe and the rise to dominance of merchants there through intermarriage with money-hungry aristocrats. When the Tokugawa ended, Japan, like late medieval Europe, was poised for rapid change.

Tokugawa splendor: a view of the main audience hall at Nijo Castle in Kyoto. The superb screen paintings, beautifully set off by the plain *tatami* (rush mat) floor, are a fine example of early Tokugawa decorative art for the elite. (Anne Kirkup)

Tokugawa Ieyasu: Instructions to His Successor

Tokugawa Ieyasu was a careful planner, a good judge of men, and one who understood the virtue of patient waiting until the time was right for action. Here is one of the instructions he left to his successors.

The strong manly ones in life are those who understand the meaning of the word patience. Patience means restraining one's inclinations. There are seven emotions: joy, anger, anxiety, love, grief, fear, and hate, and if a man does not give way to these he can be called patient. I am not as strong as I might be, but I have long known and practiced patience. And if my descendents wish to be as I am, they must study patience.

Source: A. L. Sadler, *The Maker of Modern Japan* (London: Allen & Unwin, 1937), pp. 389–390.

The procession of a *daimyo* and his retainers along their journey from his local domains to take up required residence at Edo. (Marburg/Photo Resource)

Exclusion of Foreigners

As it was, the effort to block change from 1600 was greatly aided by the expulsion of foreigners and the policy of almost total isolation. Ieyasu had been anxious to maintain foreign trade, and he at first encouraged some Christian missions as well as permitting the Dutch and the English to establish trade bases at Hirado (see Chapter 12), since they were free of the missionary taint. Ieyasu agreed with Hideyoshi in seeing missionary efforts as disruptive and even a threat to the state. Originally the Japanese were more curious about and open to Westerners than the Chinese were, having long understood the value of learning from others, as in their long experience of adopting Chinese civilization. The combination of missionaries as traders and as possible agents or forerunners of foreign influence was disturbing to the smooth order Ieyasu had worked so hard to establish. In the years after his death in 1616, all missionaries were killed or expelled and converts were executed or forced to recant. Japanese suspected of having adopted the foreign religion were forced to step on a cross, a picture of

Christ, or other Christian symbol; those who refused were tortured to make them recant, or executed.

Ieyasu himself had issued anti-Christian decrees in 1606, and his immediate successor ordered those *daimyo* who had converted to renounce the new faith. In 1617 and again in 1620 many missionaries who still remained were executed, together with their converts. The persecution culminated in the suppression of a rebellion in western Kyushu by impoverished Christian peasants in 1637–1638, protesting against crushing taxation and led by a group of masterless *samurai*. This was the Shimabara Rebellion, taking its name from the Shimabara peninsula, not far from Nagasaki, long a center of trade with foreigners. The survivors were slaughtered and many crucified along the main roads, as an example. A few somehow escaped and kept Christianity alive on an underground basis until the appearance of Western missionaries in the 1860s. From 1640 all Japanese had to register periodically at Buddhist temples; clearly, the missionary effort had thrown a scare into the Tokugawa which they were anxious to avoid repeating.

In addition to the limited and tightly controlled trade with the Dutch and Chinese at Deshima in Nagasaki harbor, some controlled trade was permitted with Korea via the Tsushima Islands, which lie between the two countries, and with the Satsuma dependency in Okinawa. None of this trade even in aggregate amounted to much, and made little or no impact on the economy of Japan as a whole; Japan had in effect reverted to its pre-sixteenth century almost exclusive dependence on China for its contacts with the outside world. Chinese books continued to be imported, except for those which made any mention of Christianity, but Western books were banned for more than a century, like their nationals. Such artificially imposed isolation, just when Europe was beginning to produce the forerunners of the great scientific discoveries which were to give it wealth and power, was a terrible handicap for Japan, one for which it was to pay dearly in its long-delayed confrontation with the modern West in the nineteenth century. Most technological development was largely stagnated, and Japan turned inward on itself.

Economic Growth

Economic development, however, continued, and cultural life thrived, now even more in a distinctively Japanese mode. After the suppression of the Shimabara Rebellion, the country was at peace except for the chronic peasant and townsmen riots, all on a relatively small scale, but not real warfare. The *samurai* had to find nonmilitary occupations for the most part, which many of them did by becoming bureaucrats and living mainly in the towns and cities in the service of both *daimyo* and

bakufu. Their earlier warrior values became enshrined as *bushido*, "the way of the warrior," which was to be revived when Japan again went to war in the twentieth century, but under Tokugawa rule it had little scope. In 1663 the suicide of retainers who wanted to "follow their lord in death" was actually forbidden, although that did not save the famous "Forty-seven Ronin," celebrated ever after as exponents of *bushido* who came to a sad end. In 1701 a minor *daimyo* who felt he had been insulted by an Edo official drew his sword inside the Edo castle precincts; his domains were confiscated and he was forced to kill himself. Two years later 47 of his former retainers, now "masterless *samurai*," took revenge by assassinating the official who had humiliated their lord, upon which they were all forced to commit suicide, a drama still popularly retold as an echo of times past.

The fading of the warrior ethic and the transformation of many *samurai* into literate bureaucrats brought Japan more in line with the Chinese model in that important respect, and made the doctrines of Confucianism more attractive with their emphasis on public duty, responsibility, and leadership through morality. Even some of the Buddhist monks adopted Confucianism, and Confucian schools appeared. There was accordingly some tendency to recognize and reward merit on the part of bureaucrats, although this never displaced the strongly imbedded Japanese commitment to hereditary rank, and only those born into the upper classes served in administration. Honor and duty had always been central to the *bushi* code, and these qualities were now applied to more constructive ends. Confucianism was nevertheless originally a foreign import, and its renewed popularity may have helped to stimulate the continued importance attached to Shinto, which as an indigenous religion also fit the new sense of nationalism in a country which had cut most of its ties with the rest of the world and hence had reaffirmed its uniqueness, free of disruptive foreign influences. But religion as such was no longer the major element in Japanese society which it once had been. Especially with the new national scope of government, and the growth of trade and towns, society became far more secular, as it so thoroughly is today, where religion is used by most people for ceremonial occasions rather than as a guide to life.

Perhaps the chief benefit of the long Tokugawa order, apart from an end to the warfare which had disfigured Japan for so long previously, was the phenomenal growth of trade, which had struggled to maintain itself in earlier chaotic times and which now leaped forward. Despite *bakufu* and *daimyo* revenue needs, trade was only lightly taxed; it was agriculture and the peasants who paid the bills, perhaps consciously in keeping with Confucian and classical Chinese notions. The heavy expenses of the *sankin kotai* system led many of the *daimyo* to promote commercial production for sale outside their own domains: handicrafts, textiles, salt, dried seaweed or fish, timber, and in the far south of Satsuma, sugar. Rice was of course produced in every *han* and increasing amounts were sold to the growing towns and cities. *Sake* and soy bean sauce also became local specialties which traveled long distances to market and were relatively imperishable. In the past, Kyoto had been the only real city, but now Edo greatly exceeded it in size and by the middle of the eighteenth century may have reached one million, which would have made it the second largest city in the world at that time, rivaled only by Ch'ing dynasty Peking and bigger than any city in Europe (London and Paris did not reach a million until about 1800). This urban concentration in such a relatively small country, whose total population stabilized at about 25 million or a little more during the eighteenth century, resulted from a combination of administrative centralization and rapid commercialization. Edo and Osaka were the chief centers of what was becoming a national trade system and were the headquarters of large merchant groups.

EDO AND URBAN CULTURE

The requirement that *daimyo* had to maintain households in Edo, where they left their wives and heirs as hostages, further swelled the population, as did their regular formal visits every other year with their large retinues. *Daimyo* family estates, the large court of the *shogun*, and rich merchant families employed very large numbers of servants and artisans, who provided them with luxurious furnishings and works of art. Edo was also a major port and much of Japan's coastal trade passed through it in addition to what came by land. Much of the site had originally been swampy or prone to flooding and large new tracts were drained and reclaimed. Areas were set aside for *daimyo* and merchant residences and for shops and open air markets, temples, and amusement quarters around the landward sides of the castle. Thousands of soldiers based in Edo, as well as *samurai* bureaucrats, added to the numbers, as did the even more numerous laborers and suppliers to maintain such a huge population.

Merchants dominated the bourgeois (literally, "city people") culture of Edo. Rich commoners wore forbidden silk under their plain outer clothing, decorated their houses lavishly, and patronized the arts, as in Renaissance Italy two centuries earlier. The arts and amusements centered around what was called the Floating World (*ukiyoe*) of fugitive pleasures, an amusement quarter of theaters, restaurants, and geisha houses, lovingly portrayed in the wood-block prints (also known as

ukiyoe) which were produced in great volume, including, especially by the artist Utamaro (1753–1806), famous *geisha* and actors in *kabuki*, the popular drama which flourished in Tokugawa times and is still performed. *Kabuki* is less stiff and more lively than the *Noh* and deals with a wider range of human emotions, adventures, and foibles. *Kabuki* actors, richly costumed and accompanied by musicians, performed on revolving stages for quick scene changes and also along a walkway through the audience, which built a close interrelation and was good theater as well as enabling scenes along a road. Puppet plays (*bunraku*) were also extremely popular; women were forbidden on the stage, as in China, and puppets got around this, as did female impersonators among the actors, but puppets were artfully made and manipulated, creating an extraordinarily lifelike effect. The most successful and famous author of both *kabuki* and puppet plays was Chikamatsu Monzaemon (1623–1725), whose touch was sure and whose range was wide, from star-crossed lovers and love-suicides to moral dilemmas and drunken playboys. This was also the great age of the *haiku*, usually in three lines, which nearly all literate Japanese wrote but in gifted hands could be briefly and eloquently evocative, as in this sample:

> *All the rains of June:*
> *And one evening, secretly,*
> *Through the pines, the moon.*[1]

The flowering of the late seventeenth to early eighteenth century in Edo is called *Genroku* culture, more or less coincident with the life span of Chikamatsu (the name *Genroku* was derived from a calendrical period). The main pleasure quarter was at the northern edge of the city, outside the official limits, a district known as Yoshiwara. Patrons were mainly merchants, but *samurai* might sneak in to *geisha* houses, restaurants, and *kabuki* or puppet plays; retainers and artisans were freer to take part. Literature, theater, and art were not necessarily vulgarized by their bourgeois patrons, who in fact often insisted on high aesthetic standards in their prints, screens, clothing, porcelains, furnishings, books, and drama. It was a new urban age of great cultural vigor, reminiscent perhaps of Sung dynasty Hangchou, but distinctly Japanese in its taste. Many of the prints were purposely erotic, called "Spring Pictures," which circulated widely. In Japan, as elsewhere, notably in China and in Europe, tastes and influence were passing increasingly into bourgeois hands in a new, urban-dominated world. Like other Japanese cities, Edo was built almost entirely of wood except for the *shogun*'s castle and a few of the *daimyo* mansions, and fires could often not be controlled. The city burned down almost completely several times, but each time it was rebuilt on an even larger and grander basis.

✠ Japanese Women: An Outsider's View ✠

*From the early accounts of the Dutch at Deshima, some American authors
in 1841 compiled this account of the state of women in Japan.*

The position of women in Japan is apparently unlike that of the sex in all other parts of the East, and approaches more nearly their European condition. The Japanese women are subjected to no jealous seclusion, hold a fair station in society, and share in all the innocent recreations of their fathers and husbands. The minds of the women are cultivated with as much care as those of men; and amongst the most admired Japanese historians, moralists, and poets are found several female names. The Japanese ladies are described as being generally lively and agreeable companions, and the ease and elegance of their manners have been highly extolled. But, though permitted thus to enjoy and adorn society, they are, on the other hand, during their whole lives, kept in a state of tutelage: that is, of complete dependence on their husbands, sons, or other relatives. They have no legal rights, and their evidence is not admitted in a court of justice. Not only may the husband introduce as many unwedded helpmates as he pleases into the mansion over which his wife presides but he also has the power of divorce, which may be considered unlimited, since he is restrained only by considerations of expediency. The Japanese husband, however, is obliged to support his repudiated wife according to his own station, unless he can allege grounds for the divorce satisfactory to the proper tribunal; among which, the misfortune of being without children takes from the unhappy wife all claim to maintenance. Under no circumstances whatever can a wife demand to be separated from her husband. At home, the wife is the mistress of the family; but in other respects she is treated rather as a toy for her husband's amusement, that as the rational, confidential partner of his life. She is expected to please him by her accomplishments, and to cheer him with her lively conversation, but never suffered to share his more serious thoughts, or to relieve by participation his anxieties and cares. She is, indeed, kept in profound ignorance of his business affairs; and so much as a question from her in relation to them would be resented as an act of unpardonable presumption.

Source: P. F. Siebold, *Manners and Customs of the Japanese in the Nineteenth Century* (London: Murray, 1852), pp. 122–124.

Kyoto remained a large city, with about 400,000 people; like Edo, its size was augmented by the presence of the imperial court and a large part of its population were *samurai* and their retainers, plus artisans and servants to supply their needs and those of the court circle. The total number of hereditary aristocrats in the country as a whole seems disproportionately large, and represented a heavy drain on financial resources, but the aristocrats did support a graceful elite culture, increasingly with the help of marriage ties with merchant families. The chief commercial center of the Kansai region was however Osaka, also Japan's major port, at the head of the Inland Sea, and under Tokugawa rule it too reached approximately 400,000 and came to serve as the major market, especially in rice, for what was becoming a national economy. Elsewhere towns grew around most of the castles of the

daimyo, some 250 of them, originally inhabited mainly by resident vassals, who were however soon outnumbered by commoners providing services and goods and engaging in trade. Nearly all of modern Japan's cities began as castle towns, and under the Tokugawa some became true cities. Nagoya (part of the Tokugawa domains) and Kanazawa on the north coast opposite Nagoya probably grew to over 100,000, while some half dozen, including Kagoshima, Hiroshima, Okayama, and Sendai (in Tohoku), were over half that size, and several others well over 10,000. Other towns grew as way stations along the Tokkaido between Kyoto and Edo, and at strategic points along trade routes. Tokugawa Japan in the eighteenth century may have had nearly 10 percent of its people living in cities or towns, one more development which eased Japan's rapid transformation after 1868.

A *samurai* (note sword) takes his ease with *geishas* in a teahouse. This painting is by Okumura Masanobu (1691–1768). (Okumura Masanobu, Japanese, *Perspective Picture of Cooling-off in the Evening at Ryogoku Bridge*, Wood-block print, c. 1735–1740, 44.6 × 56.5 cm. Clarence Buckingham Collection, 1932. 1355 (Detail). Photograph © 1994 by The Art Institute of Chicago. All rights reserved.)

New commercial growth meant that money now displaced barter. The shogunate minted gold, silver, and copper coins, and merchant houses involved in both transporting goods and in banking and brokering as well as both retailing and wholesaling began to use paper certificates and letters of credit. Transport remained relatively crude, since the shogunate banned wheeled vehicles, partly to discourage the display of wealth by commoners and the possibility of more rapid military concentrations, and goods had to be moved along inadequate roads by pack animals and human porters. The coastal routes with which Japan is so well supplied, within the Inland Sea and between Osaka, Nagoya, Shizuoka-Shimizu, Edo, and Sendai, plus towns on the north and west coasts, were far more effective and were used wherever possible. Fortunately they linked all of the larger cities except for Kyoto. But merchants in Tokugawa Japan were not free of the Confucian prejudice against them. *Bakufu* and *daimyo* tried to control them (as the early Tokugawa had demolished the walls and the independence of merchant-dominated Sakai), extorted special levies from them when needed, and tried to punish those who forgot themselves so far as to display their wealth or to violate the sumptuary laws. The monopoly guilds which had developed were also taxed, periodically heavily.

The *bakufu* became alarmed at the rapid growth of cities and towns, and tried to check it by forbidding further migration to existing urban areas, although this tended to stimulate smaller-scale urban growth in previously rural areas. At best, *chonin* (townspeople) were an unruly lot, and the Confucian mindset was against them. But such pressures helped to spread the larger forces of commercialization and urbanization more widely, with rising rural literacy as an accompaniment. On the whole, despite the official disdain for merchants and trade, or perhaps in part because of such an attitude, the *samurai*-bureaucrats, like their Chinese counterparts, largely ignored the commercial sector except for occasional taxation or other levies, and left it to manage its own affairs. Great commercial families whose names became household words in modern Japan got their start in this period; Mitsui began as *sake* brewers and then moved into pawnbroking and banking and opened textile shops in Edo, Kyoto, and Osaka; Sumitomo grew on the basis of hardware and pharmacies in Kyoto and became dominant in the mining and smelting of copper, one of Japan's few major resources.

The Rural Sector

Agricultural production did not keep pace with trade increases, and this hurt the *samurai*, already living beyond their means, as well as most *daimyo*, since the income of both came largely from agricultural taxes. Nevertheless, overall farm output approximately doubled by the end of the Tokugawa as a result of increased intensiveness, new irrigation, fertilization, double cropping and improved seeds, and average yields exceeded those in China. The spread of literacy also made Japan by the mid-nineteenth century, and perhaps earlier, probably the most literate society in the world, a distinction which still marks contemporary Japan. Many rural areas lagged behind, of course, and widespread rural poverty often led to infanticide, usually of females, a process known euphemistically as *mabiki* ("crop thinning"). There was recurrent famine in the poorer areas, especially in Tohoku (northern Honshu) where 40 percent of the peasant population is said to have starved to death in the late eighteenth century, although disease may have helped to account for the deaths as well. It was an uneven picture, but as the economy in general grew, most people lived better, especially townspeople and aristocrats but also rural upper classes. Those at the bottom periodically revolted, although most such movements were more in the nature of demonstrations and protests against the very high taxes; as conditions worsened in some rural areas the protests became more violent.

As subsistence farming gave way in many areas to specialized crops for sale, peasants became tied to the market and hence more easily hurt by shifts in prices and demand. Tenancy increased greatly as better-off families concentrated their efforts on growing crops on their best land and rented out the less desirable parts. The wealthier families of course dominated village governments and were successful in shifting most of the tax burden to tenants and poor peasants. Those at the bottom, perhaps something like a third or more, did not have the means to invest in new ventures, such as local or village industries, which became very profitable to the rich landowners. Some peasants could not even afford to become tenants, and simply sold their labor on short terms for low wages to rich landowners, developments which were happening also in China and Korea, and for similar reasons. As elsewhere, some peasants, by good fortune and hard work, managed to profit from the changed conditions, becoming successful entrepreneurs and commercial producers who sold some of their output over some distances and offered competition for the much larger urban-based enterprises, producing goods like silk and cotton cloth as well as *sake*, soy bean sauce, and other traditional items. Some of these rural industries had already developed into genuine factories by the end of the Tokugawa, employing a hundred or more workers.

Literature, Art, and Society

The renewed enthusiasm for Confucianism among the *samurai* transformed into bureaucrats led to a return to Chinese rather than Japanese for the writing of "serious" books. There were most importantly histories, directly on the Chinese model, including even their titles;

the *Comprehensive Mirror of Our Country* appeared in 1670, and the *Veritable Records of the Tokugawa* between 1809 and 1849. Other *samurai*-scholars wrote new commentaries on Neo-Confucianism and reflected the work of the Ming scholar Wang Yang-ming (see Chapter 7), continuing in the tradition of the Sung philosopher Chu Hsi. But Japan's isolation and inward-centeredness stimulated new feelings of nationalism, despite the Tokugawa emphasis on Confucianism. Later historical writing stressed the uniqueness of Japan and its supposedly divine imperial line. More scholars began to study ancient Japan, before it was "contaminated" by Chinese influences, including its ancient and classical literature. Such writings were called "National Learning," and helped to build a vigorous national consciousness which served Japan well as it successfully organized to meet the foreign challenge in the second half of the nineteenth century. By the eighteenth century, most educated Japanese were trying to separate themselves from the Chinese model, for which in any case they now felt less reverence, in preference to the growing sense of their own, Japanese identity. Such trends naturally accelerated in the nineteenth century as China increasingly floundered, lost its aura, and suffered a series of humiliations at the hands of the West.

Popular religious movements which were essentially Shinto in nature developed, and even included some of peasant origin, some of which added faith healing and divine intervention to help believers. Women played a large part in many of these new sects, but in general, perhaps especially in elite society, women were more subject to men than in Heian times. The long centuries in which the warrior and his warfare dominated Japan had left too little place for women, who now were kept in the house; their role was to bear children, especially sons (for the same reasons as in China), and to manage the household. *Geisha* were perhaps a little freer, in the sense that they were not bound by the elite or more general social conventions, and with luck they might be bought by a rich patron, as a mistress or even as a wife. Like their Chinese originals, at least for those at the top, they were classically educated as well as trained in singing, dancing, and playing the *koto* (a small, flat harp) or the *samisen* (like a mandolin), both close copies of Chinese originals. For those less fortunate, often indentured by impoverished parents to the house where they served, life was hard and more like that of the run-of-the-mill prostitute in Western society. *Geisha* were divided into several grades, according to their accomplishments and reputation, with prices for their services to match. The same tradition still survives in contemporary Japan. Now that more of the population was literate, estimated as 45 percent of adult males and perhaps 15 percent of women, there was a boom in printing. It is interesting that Hideyoshi's expeditionary forces brought back Korean printers as well as potters, suggesting that the art was still more advanced in Korea, but the big increase in printing in Japan did not come until the eighteenth century. This included moral tracts and then more popular tales, about the adventures of the townsmen who by now were playing an important role in society but whose lives were shown as dominated by the quest for money—which their heirs then dissipated. There were also stories of adventure, some of which developed the form and length of a novel. There was also an erotic literature, notably the *Yoshiwara Pillow* of 1660—ratings of courtesans in the arts of love, with explicit illustrations. Like the warlords of the late sixteenth century just preceding them, and out of which they grew, the Tokugawa had flamboyant tastes and built in ornate style. This is best illustrated in the family shrines and temples built originally to commemorate Ieyasu, the founder, at Nikko in the mountains north of Tokyo (Edo), and in the design and decor of the Nijo castle, the *bakufu's* headquarters in Kyoto. Despite their baroque grandeur and the lavish use of color, both are kept within the demanding canons of Japanese good taste, and are still impressive to the tourists who flock there,

most of them of course Japanese. Nikko is an attractive escape from the summer heat of Tokyo, and is set in beautiful natural surroundings on a forested hillside surrounded by giant *cryptomeria* trees near a mountain lake and a waterfall emptying out of it.

Much Tokugawa-period painting followed these same trends, while continuing the styles of the Ashikaga period. But as literacy and urban-style culture spread more widely, some artists moved away from Chinese models and even began to paint in an almost abstract style. What are sometimes called the minor arts (usually defined as something other than painting, sculpture, and architecture, especially the making of small objects) flourished as never before, with the help of merchant patronage and their demand for fine things to furnish their houses. Things which we still associate especially with Japan, although the originals in both cases are Chinese, were turned out in quantity but of high quality: lacquer boxes and other ware, and folding screens (*shoji*) decorated with natural scenes, often of great beauty. Other objects included the small ivory fobs or toggles called *netsuke* used to fasten tobacco pouches or small purses, beautifully carved and often painted as well, and the similarly

Kabuki production

diminutive painted glass or porcelain snuff bottles, both now much sought after by collectors.

WOOD-BLOCK PRINTS AND HOKUSAI

The art of the wood-block print was brought to a peak of perfection in the late seventeenth century, especially in the use of several colors. Starting from an original painting, as earlier in China, an artist would make a number of different carefully carved blocks, each of which would then carry a different color or shading which would be successively printed on the final version. This brought art within the reach of a much wider public, since many copies could be made; this still makes it possible for people, in Japan and elsewhere, to buy them at a bearable price. They became extremely popular in Tokugawa Japan, and ultimately abroad, and became the most widely familiar form of Japanese art in the West. Perhaps the best known of Japanese wood-block printmakers were Hokusai (not his real name, which remains unknown), who lived from 1760 to 1849, and his rough contemporary Ando Hiroshige (1797–1858). Hokusai won fame for his "Thirty-Seven Views of Mount Fuji," and Hiroshige for his "Fifty-Three Post Stations on the Tokaido." Hokusai was born in Edo to unknown parents and was adopted at age three by a craftsman named Nakijima, who made mirrors for the shogunate. The boy seems to have shown a talent for drawing by the time he was five, and by age 13 had been apprenticed to a carver of woodblocks. Hokusai was a devout Buddhist and chose the name by which he is known, which means "north studio," to honor a Buddhist saint who was thought to be an incarnation of the north star. His early work centered on book illustration, and he also, like Utamaro before him, made many portraits of contemporary actors.

Limited and indirect trade with the West, via the Dutch at Deshima, had resumed by his time, even though other foreigners were excluded, and increased substantially after 1800. Japanese potters began to copy the Chinese blue-and-white porcelain ware which had proved so popular in Western trade with China; it became an important Japanese export, as did originally Chinese silk and tea later. It did not occur to the Japanese that Westerners would find their art desirable, and as for wood-block prints, they were turned out in large numbers and sold very cheaply. But the freshness, color, and simple lines of Hokusai's and Hiroshige's work appealed strongly to a Europe already impressed and influenced by Chinese art. The European craze for Chinoiserie in the late eighteenth and early nineteenth centuries was joined by an enthusiasm for "Japanoiserie." Many Japanese prints in fact arrived in Europe originally as wastepaper, used to wrap porcelain and

✠ Supernationalism in Japan ✠

Tokugawa Japan saw a new growth of nationalist feelings. Hirata Atsutane (1776–1843) asserted the superiority of Shinto over all other religions, and the superiority of Japan and the Japanese.

People all over the world refer to Japan as the Land of the Gods, and call us the descendants of the gods. Indeed it is exactly as they say: our country, as a special mark of favor from the heavenly gods, was begotten by them, and there is thus so immense a difference between Japan and all the other countries of the world as to defy comparison. Ours is a spendid and blessed country, the Land of the Gods beyond any doubt, and we, down to the most humble man and woman, are the descendants of the gods.... Japanese differ completely from and are superior to the people of China, India, Russia, Holland, Siam, Cambodia, and all other countries, and for us to have called our country the land of the Gods was not mere vainglory. It was the gods who formed all the lands of the world at the creation, and these gods were without exception born in Japan.... This is a matter of universal belief, and is quite beyond dispute.

Source: From R. Tsunoda et al., eds., *Sources of Japanese Tradition*, Vol. II. (New York: Columbia University Press, 1958), p. 39.

A *geisha*, titled "Beauty Wringing Out a Towel"; woodcut print by Utamaro, who loved to portray *geisha*. (The Asia Society, New York)

other goods for export shipment, but they soon became prized. Return trade to Japan brought among other things the color and materials for Prussian blue, which was soon used by the wood-block artists to brighten and enliven their work. Their style had a great influence on Western artists, especially the Impressionists in France and the American painter Whistler. Most of the Impressionists acknowledged this debt, and many of them painted pictures in an avowedly Japanese style during the craze for things Japanese after 1870. Vincent Van Gogh carefully copied prints by Hiroshige, perhaps the ultimate form of flattery.

Strains in the Tokugawa System

Cultural and economic change, and the rise of the merchant group, suggest an overall system which was dynamic despite the Tokugawa efforts to hold everything stable. They were able to prevent any significant political change, but pressures were building up. The original feudal system dominated by aristocrats whose origins were in the very different context of the preceding centuries of chronic warfare came to seem to most Japanese less and less appropriate. In an effort to control expenses, both the shogunate and the *han* reduced the stipends given to *samurai*, and drove many of them who were already on the edge into real poverty. *Ronin*, or masterless *samurai*, were of course the worst disadvantaged, but in general only those who had been able to find a functional role as bureaucrats, and not all of those, were saved from destitution. Already the less fortunate of these distressed and now threadbare aristocrats were being derisively called "sweet potato *samurai*," unable to afford rice and subsisting on the culturally despised sweet potato which had been introduced into Japan in the sixteenth century. There was even more widespread suffering in the rural areas, where the crushingly heavy taxes ground many peasants into the dirt; rural protests melded into riots and angry peasants began to attack the local representatives of both the *bakufu* and the *han*, as well as village elders and rich peasants. Their incidence rose steeply after the mid-eighteenth century, a sure sign that the system as a whole was in trouble, with large sections of the population feeling exploited, ignored, or just left out of the prosperity which many *chonin* or townspeople, mainly merchants, were enjoying.

And as seems to happen predictably in all political systems, those at the top, especially the *shoguns*, declined in competence and conscientiousness from the high level set by Ieyasu and his immediate successors. One who became famous for his eccentricity was Tsunayoshi (r. 1680–1709), the fifth *shogun*, who left matters largely to his Grand Chamberlain but who also debased the currency by merely minting more coins and alienated everyone by his quixotic policies in other respects. He is remembered most for his protection and patronage of dogs, in part through the use of Buddhist temples, and hence is known still as "the Dog Shogun." Fortunately he was followed by abler and more dutiful men who tried to repair the financial and other damage he had done, especially Yoshimune (1716–1745), the eighth *shogun*. But his reforms, while most were fully appropriate, and he himself a model Confucian ruler who set a good example of frugality and moral rectitude, took no account of the potentially revolutionary changes at work in Japanese society, and merely tried to reaffirm the original Tokugawa system and its rigidly controlled social order. He encouraged increases in farm output, true to his Confucian bias, but this had the effect of reducing rice prices, which hurt both the peasants and the *samurai* since the latter's income was mainly in rice. Thus the two sectors of the population already suffering most economically were further disadvantaged, not what Yoshimune had intended. Yoshimune had reduced the amount of foreign trade permitted, but Tanuma Okitsugu (1719–1788), more in tune with the times, allowed it to increase, and also increased the program of issuing licenses to merchants and their guilds as well as imposing some taxes on trade.

Unfortunately, successive *shoguns* modeled themselves on Yoshimune and reimposed strict limits on merchants and their behavior while paying totally inadequate attention to the worsening plight of most peasants. They relied on moral exhortation to force Japanese society back into its feudal mold, extracted forced loans from merchants, discontinued their government licenses, and tried to get peasants who had migrated to the cities to go back to their villages. Minting more coins, now supplemented by a silver coinage which in itself was an improvement, could not solve the *bakufu's* mounting financial problems, as it merely created new inflation. Some of the worst-off *samurai* were obliged to eke out their shrinking incomes in commercial activity, formerly and still officially despised. The urban poor suffered of course still more, and riots in the cities became more frequent. In the countryside periodic crop failures led to famine deaths and more unrest. It became increasingly clear to most Japanese that the Tokugawa were not managing the country well, much as Chinese felt that a dynasty in its last century, when similar problems surfaced, had lost the "Mandate of Heaven." Among the intellectuals, there was new interest in what was now unmistakably a big and growing Western lead in science and technology, and concern about the new power which this gave them. The aggressive Western record in the rest of Asia was beginning to be better known in Japan, and it was realized that Japan had totally inadequate means with which to defend itself against such determined enemies.

Dutch Learning

Western learning was known as "Dutch learning" (*rangaku*), since that was the source of nearly all the Japanese acquired, via the Dutch traders at Deshima. The Dutch were called the "Red-haired Barbarians" and were regarded by the few Japanese who encountered them with great curiosity. A surprising amount of information about the outside world filtered into Japan via Deshima, especially as a few Japanese scholars learned Dutch and began to translate the books they had brought. From 1720 the *bakufu* allowed the import of all books except those which dealt with Christianity, and the Dutch traders were required to come to Edo each year for an audience with the *shogun* (whom they mistakenly took for the emperor), where they were plied with questions and critically examined almost as if they were animals on display. Through the books they brought the Japanese began to learn something about the shape and nature of the world, noting that Japan was only a tiny part of it and on a remote edge, from the Western point of view. From samples of Western art, the Japanese also learned the technique of perspective and the general Western emphasis on realism, as they

A *bunraku* performance, showing the black-clothed puppeteers and the puppets. No one is disturbed by seeing the puppeteers so prominently; attention is concentrated on the puppets. (Japan National Tourist Organization, Chicago)

Haiku

The originally Chinese poetic form known in Japan as haiku *flourished during the Tokugawa. Here are a few samples, written by a variety of Tokugawa poets.*

On the moor; from things
Detached completely —
How the skylark sings!

My hut; in spring:
True, there is nothing in it —
There is everything!

A one-foot waterfall;
It too makes noises, and at night
The coolness of it all!

Source: Quoted in W. S. Morton, *Japan: Its History and Culture.* (New York: McGraw-Hill, 1994), p. 132.

learned about new techniques of gunnery, shipbuilding, and metalworking.

But it was Western medicine which attracted perhaps the greatest interest, and the anatomical illustrations in medical texts, such as Rembrandt's famous painting "The Anatomy Lesson." Japanese physicians compared these with the traditional Chinese medical texts on which they had relied, and through their own dissection of the corpses of executed criminals demonstrated as early as 1771 that the Dutch version was accurate, whereas the Chinese was not. The Chinese rejected dissection, taboo in light of the Confucian respect for the body and for one's parents who had bequeathed or created it. Such discoveries by the Japanese, and their new realization of the true extent of the world, led many to the conclusion that Western learning and power were superior, and that the Tokugawa system rested on ignorance and blindness. Some also pointed out that the *bakufu*, for all their supposed Confucian ethics, took too little action to try to relieve rural and urban poverty and seemed to ignore the sufferings occasioned by repeated famine. These were all highly seditious sentiments, and a few who were bold enough to publish or assert them too publically were punished and silenced. But it was increasingly clear that the existing order was no longer functioning effectively, that it was out of touch with changing reality, and that deep rifts had opened up in the traditional system. This included the tensions generated by the widening gulf between the few rich and the far more numerous poor, whose plight was steadily worsening. But it also included a more general realization that the legitimacy of the Tokugawa was fundamentally in question.

Confucian values were still uppermost in most people's minds, and the Tokugawa control system was still by-and-large effective. The riots which became more and more frequent in both urban and rural areas were easily put down, and the merchant community kept in check despite their still-rising wealth and their connections by marriage into the ruling aristocracy. It is possible that without the foreign threat, which finally came to a head in 1853 when an American naval squadron sent for the purpose forced Japan to open its doors to external trade and thus began the process of tumbling the apple cart internally, the Tokugawa might have continued in power with its tightly controlled feudal-style system still functioning for some decades to come. But by 1850, the pressures for change which had for so long been bottled up were building, and it was perhaps only a matter of time before they began to burst out. When the Americans kicked in the door in 1853, internal pressures found new support, and 15 years later the entire Tokugawa structure collapsed.

The New Western Challenge

For some time after the expulsion of foreigners by 1640, Westerners disregarded Japan, partly because they had no alternative, partly because in any case Japan was not thought to be worth the effort, as the English at Hirado had found even before the onset of the exclusion policy. It was after all remote and poor and offered few prizes. Meanwhile, the Western powers were occupied with the expansion of their trade and control in India, Southeast Asia, and, after 1842, in China. The Chinese experience did help to persuade many Westerners that Japan too should be made to open its doors, to trade and to the "blessings of civilization" Western-style, for their own benefit as well as that of the West. Western ships began to appear in Japanese waters, and the continued Russian expansion in their Amur valley and Pacific region brought them almost to Japan's doorstep, as Russian traders and fishermen began to make use of Sakhalin Island and the Kurile chain just north of Hokkaido. The Russians were thus the first to knock on the door, requesting the opening of official relations in Hokkaido in 1792 and at Nagasaki in 1804, although both requests were refused. The British were by far the dominant commercial power in East Asia, and their ships were nosing around the edges of Japan, including Hokkaido, Nagasaki, and in 1818 even into Edo Bay, but their pressures for an opening to trade were also rejected.

In the end it was the Americans who forced their way in, after over half a century of their own efforts to find an opening had failed. The Americans had become the predominant whalers in the Pacific as a whole, and American clipper ships were also active in the trade to and from Canton, with their great circle route passing close by the Japanese islands. Whalers and clipper sailors who were shipwrecked on the Japanese coast or who sought to replenish their supplies there were often roughly handled and the *bakufu* was slow to arrange for their repatriation. Some of the earlier efforts to establish some basis for dealings with Japan were aimed at rescuing these castaways or captives.

As steam began to replace sail, and given the very long haul across the Pacific, ships developed an urgent need for coaling stations along the route, and Japan was the obvious choice—if the government there could be persuaded to permit it. What was called in the United States "manifest destiny" seemed to provide a moral for American expansion across the Pacific, fresh from the American victory over Mexico and its grab of Mexican territory in the Southwest and California. But the *bakufu* response to all these foreign probings was to order the repulsion of all foreign ships and the destruction of foreign intruders. The sacred soil of Japan, and perhaps still more its carefully protected society, was to be kept free of any contamination. Some of the scholars who had studied Dutch books and understood something of the new power of the West realized that Japan was defenseless, and that these new "barbarians" were an aggressive lot who would not so easily be turned away.

The Americans now decided that force was the only way, and sent three new steam frigates and five other ships under the command of Commodore Matthew Perry, which arrived in Edo Bay in July of 1853. The Japanese were suitably impressed by these "black ships" which could move against tide and wind, and by their calculated demonstration of the power of their guns. Given this show of power, the Japanese were obliged to accept a letter to the "emperor" (by which the Japanese realized he meant the *shogun*) from Franklin Pierce, then president of the United States, in which, rather like George III to Ch'ien Lung, he requested trade privileges and "normal" diplomatic relations. The Japan-

✖ Merchants in Japan ✖

Rigid class distinctions were part of the Tokugawa system. Here is a passage from Chikamatsu's kabuki *play "The Uprooted Pine" which also suggests the rise of merchants.*

A samurai's child is reared by samurai parents and becomes a samurai himself because they teach him the warrior's code. A merchant's child is reared by merchant parents and becomes a merchant because they teach him the ways of commerce.... Money is so precious a treasure that it can even buy human lives. I am well aware that however much I begrudge spending my money, however much I hoard it, all that will be left me when I am dead is a single hempen shroud. But until I die I am bound to respect my gold and silver like the gods or Buddha himself—that is the way prescribed by Heaven for merchants.

Source: Quoted in C. Totman, *Japan Before Perry.* (Berkeley: University of California Press, 1981), p. 171.

ese realized that Perry's ships could easily blockade Edo and cut off its huge rice supply, most of which came by sea on barges. Leaving them to think things over, Perry and his fleet retired for the winter to Okinawa, saying that he would be back in the spring for his answer. The Japanese knew that there were even larger numbers of British ships in Japanese waters awaiting the outcome, and remembered also the results of the Anglo-Chinese war ("Opium War") of 1839–1842. They consulted the Dutch at Nagasaki, who strongly advised them to agree to the repeated foreign requests.

The *bakufu* in fact faced a dilemma; giving in to the foreigners would violate not only their country's carefully preserved isolation but the long-established Tokugawa policy, which it was feared would constitute a sign of weakness and also would open the door to sweeping changes which the *bakufu* had tried to prevent. Some of those in Edo argued one way, others another, while many of the more distant *daimyo* pulled in different directions. The head of the Council of Elders at Edo felt it was necessary to consult all of the *daimyo*, a major change in itself which of course invited discussion and criticism of all official policies. The dominant response was to resist all foreign pressures, however unrealistically, although a few realized that some concessions would have to be made on trade, which could after all be profitable to Japanese as well as to foreigners, and could make it possible to buy foreign weapons and strengthen the country's defenses.

But there was no real consensus, and far too little awareness of the overwhelming power of the Westerners. Nevertheless when Perry returned early in 1854 and presented his demands again at the coastal town of Kanagawa, now part of Yokohama, the *bakufu* felt obliged to agree to open two minor and remote or inaccessible ports, Shimoda at the tip of the mountainous Izu peninsula and Hakodate in distant Hokkaido, to American ships in need of provisions, and a limited amount of trade. They agreed to the stationing of an American consul at Shimoda, and the treaty signed at Kanagawa included the "most favored nation" provision begun by the Americans in their treaty with China in 1844, whereby all concessions granted to any foreign power were automatically granted also to the United States. Despite their reluctance to admit foreigners, the Japanese representatives showed their characteristic curiosity, visiting the ships once the treaty was signed and examining them carefully, while exchanging presents with the Americans and getting drunk together with much hilarity. The British negotiated similar treaties with the shogunate later in 1854 and the Russians early in 1855, with the addition of Nagasaki as an "open" port, and of another clause borrowed from the treaties forced on China earlier, extraterritoriality, whereby foreigners in both countries came under their own rather than Chinese or Japanese laws.

Impact and Response

The first American consul at Shimoda, Townsend Harris, pressed the *bakufu* to move toward a more adequate commercial treaty with the U.S. before a harsher agreement was imposed on them by what he asserted were the more aggressive European powers. Harris managed to get his treaty in 1858, which added to the list of "open" ports Kanagawa and Nagasaki, later extended by the addition of Niigata on the west coast and Hyogo (modern Kobe, west of Osaka). Foreigners were now permitted to reside at Edo and Osaka and to trade there, and the Dutch, Russians, British, and French extracted the same provisions in separate treaties in the following weeks. As in China, import and export duties were kept low according to these treaties so that foreign goods could more easily invade the Japan market and what the foreigners wanted more easily extracted for sale abroad. Foreign merchants tended to settle mainly at Yokohama, which rapidly grew into a major city around its excellent harbor, and at Hyogo (Kobe), which between them soon dominated Japan's foreign trade. The invasion of foreign currency largely destroyed the already creaking Tokugawa monetary system and stimulated new and disastrous inflation, especially as growing amounts of Japanese silk and tea were exported and new imports of Western manufactured goods, primarily cotton cloth, spread widely and involved Japan in extensive international monetary transactions. The long-suppressed Japanese merchants were as eager for this new trade and its profits as were the aggressive Western traders now established in their midst.

The presence of foreigners was offensive to some of the traditional-minded hotheads among the *samurai*. Several Westerners were attacked and killed in 1859 and 1861, and later in the same year the British legation in Edo was attacked and the consul, Rutherford Alcock, barely escaped with his life by hiding under a big wooden tub of the sort the Japanese used for bathing. Alcock, a typical "forward policy" imperialist of the period who had previously served in China, had outraged national sensibilities by climbing the sacred Mt. Fuji, which he could see from the legation. As they had done from their treaty-port bastions in China, the British walked and rode horseback in the hills around Yokohama, and four of them were attacked by *samurai* in 1862; one of them, named Richardson, was killed, and the *bakufu* had to pay a heavy indemnity to settle "the Richardson affair." Having been foiled in their effort to kill Alcock, firebrands burned down the British legation in 1863.

But this was not the underlying nature of the Japanese attitude. They were fortunately free of the cultural arrogance of China, and although they still felt that Japan was a special place, even a superior one, they easily recognized that the Westerners had much of value to offer them. Perhaps most importantly, they quickly saw that Japan was far behind the West in almost every respect, and could benefit from cultural borrowing. This was the same set of attitudes which had underlain the massive Japanese borrowing from Chinese civilization from the eighth century on, which also perhaps accustomed the Japanese to accepting that the outside world was something not to be haughtily rejected but to be learned from. At the same time, their long interaction with China had also taught them that borrowing ideas, techniques, and even institutions from abroad need not compromise their strongly held sense of separate and distinctive Japanese cultural identity. For them it was rational to be afraid of the West's new power rather than to dismiss it as "monkey tricks" as many Chinese did, and to apply the corollary of adopting many aspects of Western technology, without feeling that their strong national pride had been somehow besmirched. Japan began to see itself as mortally threatened, especially given the Western record everywhere else in Asia, and that the new sources of Western strength had to be adopted as the only way of defending the country against this threat. There were also many crosscurrents in late Tokugawa Japan, including growing dissatisfaction with the strict order and inflexibility of *bakufu* rule, and the spreading divisions within the society: merchants most importantly, with their own motives for welcoming Western traders, distressed peasants, unruly *chonin*, and even wide differences of opinion among the *samurai* and the *daimyo* about the best course to follow.

It took time for a coherent national policy to emerge, but Japan had the great advantage over China that it was small, with a population concentrated in a still smaller area which by the nineteenth century was effectively linked through the still-growing internal trade. The *sankin kotai* system which had *daimyo* and their large retinues moving back and forth along the Tokkaido and elsewhere, between Edo and all of the *daimyo* domains in every part of the country, meant that culture had become a largely national affair and that information and discussion of events at Edo spread rapidly to the rest of the country. Japan had the further advantage of a largely homogenous racial mix and the relative absence of strong feelings of separate regional identity or even of distinct regional dialects which crossed the border of intelligibility. All could feel that they were Japanese, members of a common culture and national identity. Even the *eta*, if not the few remaining Ainu, could share membership in this larger community. All of this helped to make it possible for Japan, once a coherent policy was decided on, to carry it out swiftly and effectively. It helped too that most Japanese saw the Tokugawa as increasingly ineffective in meeting the mounting problems which confronted it, and felt the need for change. Change was not a

new or fearsome idea in Japan as it was in China; Japan had been through many changes since the second or third century A.D. in which the whole institutional and ideological structure was altered several times. Also, the Confucian concept of the recognition and rewarding of individual merit and the proper governmental function of the scholar ran counter to the rigidly feudalistic system of the Tokugawa, as some Japanese scholars pointed out.

The imperial establishment in Kyoto had been effectively bypassed since the rise of the Kamakura warriors, and this too was seen by some as an insupportable contradiction of Japanese tradition. Hemmed in as it was by conflicting opinions, the *bakufu* even tried to get imperial approval of the Harris commercial treaty of 1858 in a desperate effort to create a national, sanctioned response, but this was not successful. The head of the Council of Elders tried to override this failure and punished a number of court officials who took a pro-imperial stance, but he was assassinated by a diehard *samurai* in 1860. Meanwhile some of the *daimyo* or their *samurai* agents now felt free to approach the court in Kyoto on their own, to seek support for their views. The slogan "Honor the Emperor, Expel the Barbarians" began to be widely heard, of course a strong implied criticism of Edo, especially after it felt obliged to sign the Harris treaty. In fact it really had no choice but to give in to the foreign demands, but this meant that it lost the support of many, perhaps most, Japanese.

The End of the Tokugawa

Among the outer *daimyo* domains, Satsuma in southern Kyushu and Choshu in western Honshu, appropriately far from Edo, continued to nurse anti-Tokugawa views, partly as a result of their defeats in the early days of the shogunate, and in any case remoteness weakened their supposedly feudal ties to Edo. Fortuitously, both were in better shape financially than the other *han* and certainly than Edo, partly because they had simply canceled their debts in the 1830s and in Satsuma had begun to make money from the sale of sugar from cane, which could be grown only in its subtropical climate but was in demand throughout the country. Choshu had become solvent largely through investing in the marketing of surplus rice to other *han* and through loaning money to them.

Rival conservative and reformist *samurai* factions in Choshu moved in and out of power, and tried to mediate between Edo and Kyoto, but that role was taken over by Satsuma, who in 1862 were asked to restore order in the capital and suppress the many *ronin* (masterless *samurai*) who had become a plague there and elsewhere in western Japan. More radical reformers became dominant in Choshu in support of the emperor, and obtained the blessing of the court. The Choshu contingent now stationed in Kyoto invited the *shogun* to visit Kyoto in 1863, and there obliged him to name June 25, 1863, as the date by which the "barbarians" would indeed be expelled, a promise which of course he had no hope of fulfilling. When the day passed without action, the Choshu men felt they had to do *something*; their forts on the Straits of Shiminoseki, between Honsu and Kyushu, fired on foreign ships; American ships returned fire and sank two new gunboats recently bought by Choshu at Nagasaki, while French ships sent landing parties which destroyed the forts and spiked their guns.

With Choshu thus humiliated, Satsuma troops drove the Choshu forces out of Kyoto. Rebuilt forts at Shiminoseki resumed firing on foreign ships, which provoked a joint expedition of Western forces who destroyed the forts again in 1864, forced Choshu to promise not to rebuild them, and demanded, from the shogunate, a large indemnity; defying the foreigners was proving unacceptably expensive. Nevertheless, Choshu began to build a Western-style army and navy and a peasant militia trained in the use of the then-new rifles. It was *samurai* from Satsuma who had assassinated Richardson outside Yokohama, and in 1863 the British sent a fleet to Kagoshima, the chief port of Satsuma at the southern tip of Kyushu, to force the payment of an indemnity. The Satsuma forts guarding the harbor of Kagoshima fired on the British warships, whose response was a devastating naval bombardment which largely destroyed the city. Satsuma paid up, but also learned at first hand what the new power of the West could do, and quickly began to build its own navy with ships obtained from Britain. Choshu meanwhile became involved in a civil war between conservative and radical forces, the latter incensed by the Choshu submission to the shogunate's demands that they apologize for their pressures on the imperial court and their demand that the *shogun* come there and name a date for the expulsion of foreigners. The conservatives accepted the Shogunate's terms, which included the disbandment of the new peasant militia, but these riflemen refused to comply; with some *samurai* support, they swept aside all opposition, captured the Choshu capital, and put the radical reformers back in power. It was a major break in the tradition of war as the preserve of the aristocrats, and in 1866 a punitive expedition from the shogunate was defeated by this new force, although it was outnumbered.

After its successful defiance of Edo, Choshu efforts to push for change were joined by the cooperation of Satsuma, its traditional rival but whose goals were similar. Satsuma was now led by two able men, Okubo Toshimichi (1830–1878) and Saigo Takamori (1827–1877), the latter especially forceful despite (or perhaps because of) his relatively lowly origins as the son of a poor *samurai* in reduced circumstances; Saigo was to play a major role in national affairs for the next decade. In 1867 a new *shogun*, Keiki, realizing the country's weakness in the face of mortal danger, tried to modernize the shogunate's armed forces and to build new ties with the most powerful *daimyo* by offering them in effect a role in the central government, but that effort failed. When the emperor died in 1867, Keiki handed over power to the new boy emperor Meiji and his Satsuma-Choshu advisers. The newly allied Satsuma and Choshu decided on a far more radical course. In January of 1868 their forces, with the help of others from Tosa on the island of Shikoku and some of the other domains of western Honshu, captured Kyoto and announced that the emperor was now restored to power. Although Keiki was inclined to go along with this *fait accompli* and withdrew his troops from Kyoto to Osaka, others at Edo determined to resist and sent the shogunal forces back to Kyoto to contest the coup. Once again, the new Satsuma-Choshu forces with their Western-style equipment and their *samurai*-led peasant troops were victorious, and went on to seize Edo itself, although the Tokugawa navy escaped to Hokkaido and the civil war did not end until 1869. This was the inglorious end of the shogunate, and the way was prepared for a wholly new Japan.

Achievements

The Tokugawa had presided over more than two centuries of internal peace and stability, during which impressive new economic growth took place. This in itself changed Japanese society despite their efforts at control, and paved the way for a complete remaking of the country after 1868. Before one dismisses their rigid control system as an increasing anachronism, it may be appropriate to consider the benefits of the peace and order which that ensured, and an important aspect of the top-down control system in the successful efforts to preserve the Japanese environment, especially against the pressures which built up as population increased. These were perhaps most pronounced in the large new demand for wood for building as the cities grew, and for fuel. But the Tokugawa understood the critical importance of tree cover to protect the steep slopes and thin soils of Japan, and were remarkably successful in preventing the kind of massive deforestation which continued to take place in China. Flooding did become more frequent, indicating that there was some excessive cutting, but the Tokugawa emphasis on regulation and their wise perception, shared by most of the Japanese elite, that short-term profit should not overrule long-term group interests generally prevailed and Japan's luxuriant forests were mainly preserved, in part through systematic replanting to replace what was cut. The Confucian emphasis on agricultural production as the chief support of society helped lead to an approximate doubling of total output from 1600 to 1850, as already pointed out, assisted by official encouragement and many pamphlets urging the increased use of night soil (much of it from the growing cities) and of fish and fish meal as fertilizer. The strong work ethic which was part of Confucianism helped to ensure that this intensification of cultivation was widely spread.

Thus despite its anachronistic characteristics, the Tokugawa system accomplished some good, and with the changes which took place despite their efforts to prevent them, left Japan in a strong position to move ahead rapidly once the traditional feudal shackles were taken off. The impressive achievement of modern Japan in fact owes a great deal to foundations established under the Tokugawa.

Note

1. From H. G. Henderson, *An Introduction to Haiku*. New York: Doubleday, 1958. p. 118.

Suggestions for Further Reading

Bellah, R. *Tokugawa Religion*. Glencoe, IL: Free Press, 1957.

Bolitho, H. *Treasures Among Men: The Fudai Daimyo in Tokugawa Japan*. Yale Press, 1974.

Boxer, C. R. *The Christian Century in Japan*. Berkeley: Unversity of California Press, 1951.

Cooper, M. *They Came to Japan: European Reports, 1543–1640*. California Press, 1965.

Dore, R. P. *Education in Tokugawa Japan*. Berkeley: Unversity of California Press, 1965.

Ellison, G. *Deus Destroyed: The Image of Christianity in Early Modern Japan*. Harvard Press, 1973.

Grilli, E. *The Art of the Japanese Screen*. New York: Weatherhill, 1970.

Hall, J. W., ed. *The Cambridge History of Japan*, Vol. 4, Cambridge University Press, 1991.

Hall, J. W., and Jansen, M., eds. *Studies in the Institutional History of Early Modern Japan*. Princeton Press, 1968.

Hanley, S. B., and Yamamura, K. *Economic and Demographic Change in Preindustrial Japan, 1600–1868*. Princeton Press, 1977.

Harrington, A. A. *Japan's Hidden Christians*. Chicago: Loyola University Press, 1993.

Hibbett, H. *The Floating World in Japanese Fiction*. Rutland, Vermont: Tuttle, 1960.

Jannetta, A. B. *Epidemics and Mortality in Early Modern Japan*. Princeton Press, 1987.

Keene, D. *The Japanese Discovery of Europe, 1720–1830*. New York: Grove, 1969.

_____. *World Within Walls: Japanese Literature 1600–1867*. New York: Holt, Rinehart, 1976.

Leupp, G. P. *Servants, Shophands, and Laborers in the Cities of Tokugawa Japan*. Princeton: Princeton University Press, 1995.

McClellan, E. *Woman in the Crested Kimono*. Yale Press, 1985.

Najita, T. *Visions of Virtue in Tokugawa Japan*. Chicago Press, 1987.

Nosco, P., ed. *Confucianism and Tokugawa Culture*. Princeton Press, 1984.

_____. *Remembering Paradise: Nativism and Nostalgia in Eighteenth Century Japan*. Harvard Press, 1990.

Ooms, H. *Tokugawa Ideology*. Princeton Press, 1985.

Perrin, N. *Giving up the Gun*. Boston: D. R. Godine, 1979.

Seigle, C. S. *Yoshiwara*. University of Hawaii Press, 1993.

Sheldon, C. D. *The Rise of the Merchant Class in Tokugawa Japan*. New York: Russell, 1983.

Smith, H. D. *Hokusai*. New York: Braziller, 1986.

Smith, T. C. *The Agrarian Origins of Modern Japan*. Stanford Press, 1959.

Toby, R. P. *State and Diplomacy in Early Modern Japan*. Princeton Press, 1984.

Totman, C. *Politics in the Tokugawa Bakufu, 1600–1843*. Harvard Press, 1967.

Wakabayashi, B. T. *Anti-foreignism and Western Learning in Early-Modern Japan*. Cambridge: Harvard Press, 1992.

CHAPTER 14

HUMILIATION AND RESPONSE IN NINETEENTH-CENTURY CHINA

The nineteenth century, or the period from the end of the Napoleonic Wars in Europe in 1815 to the outbreak of the First World War in 1914, was the heyday of imperialism. A handful of countries imposed their domination over large parts of the globe, primarily in Asia but also in Africa. Already by 1800 the British had established their primacy in India, which was complete by 1857. By the 1880s they also took over the whole of Burma and Malaya, having previously succeeded the Dutch in Ceylon (Sri Lanka). In 1886 the French completed their takeover of Vietnam, Laos, and Cambodia, and in 1898 the Americans took over the Philippines from a defeated Spain. In the course of the nineteenth century the Dutch extended and tightened their control over Indonesia, and completed it with their two-stage conquest of Bali in 1908, except for the northern fifth of Borneo, which remained British. China and Japan were forced to submit to Western domination under the "unequal treaties." Basing themselves on the Western model of imperialism, the Japanese then in 1895 took over Korea and Taiwan, and in 1905 replaced the Russians as the dominant power in Chinese Manchuria. The Russians had continued their eastward expansion and had also absorbed into their empire the series of Islamic states which had occupied central Asia north of Iran and Afghanistan: Kazakhstan, Uzbekistan, Turkestan, and several smaller ones.

Imperialism is perhaps best seen as a disease, which was highly contagious among rival powers and which was pursued despite its costs, which were never repaid by the returns to the home government, except in pride.

Individual traders and firms made profits, but it was governments which made decisions, carried out policies, and footed the bill. Basically, it was Western (and later Japanese) arrogance, fueled by the new power created by industrialization, which was the basic engine of imperialism, further stimulated by international rivalries and cheered on by the popular press. The nineteenth century saw a great expansion in so-called yellow journalism, dealing in sensationalism and the crudest forms of ultranationalism, avidly read by the uneducated. Power corrupts, and the new power of steam and steel fed Western and Japanese conviction that their countries and their civilizations were "superior" to others where industrialization had not yet spread, which were seen as "backward" and as needing the "blessings" which Western and Japanese civilization offered them. In the Western case, this had a moral and Christian basis also; the rest of the world was seen as "sunk in idolatry" and as retarded by their "outmoded" systems of belief and morality. Missionaries were often the most arrogant representatives of Western imperialism, and, perhaps ironically, often the most intolerant.

The creation of new national states in Germany and Italy after 1870 heightened the spirit of aggressive national rivalry. Great-power status was increasingly equated with the possession of overseas colonies, and empire became a matter of national "honor." Charles Darwin's careful exposition of the biological theory of selective evolution was misapplied to human affairs as "social Darwinism," and there was political talk about "the survival of the fittest." Aggression was glorified,

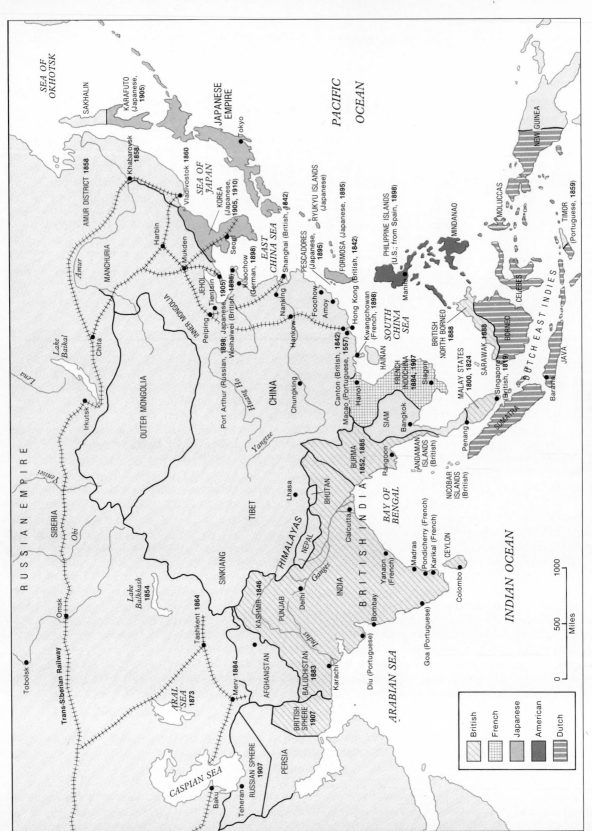

Colonial Empires in Asia

with strong and obvious racist overtones about who was "fittest" and who was "inferior." Policy makers often used economic arguments to justify the acquisition of colonies, but the facts suggest clearly that this was either wishful thinking or a smokescreen, as some of the Marxists argued. Nevertheless, even some of the socialists were enthusiastic about colonial expansion, and the general public, including workers and even trade union leaders, were vigorous supporters. Trade did not in fact "follow the flag"; most of the major colonial powers did more business, both trade and investment, outside their colonial holdings than within them, and any effort to measure the costs of conquering, holding, and administering colonies makes it clear that it was a losing proposition economically for the home governments, with the possible exception of the Dutch East Indies.

Many of the merchants urged their home governments to acquire more colonial territory or to increase their forceful presence, notably in China, where the Chinese government remained sovereign and understandably tried to stall outside efforts to obtain new concessions and privileges. Missionaries were often the most strident groups in urging retaliation when the missionaries were hampered by local resistance, or when some of them were killed by outraged mobs. China was by far the largest mission field, with the largest number of missionaries, 8,000 by 1914 and 10,000 by 1928, the majority of them American, and a large proportion were women, married and single. Missionaries were attracted by the immense size of the Chinese population—a huge potential harvest of souls—and by their conviction that China lacked what they considered a real religion of its own. Confucianism and Taoism were dismissed as systems of practical morality (inaccurate especially in the case of Taoism) rather than genuine religions, because they largely lacked any theology or doctrines about salvation and the afterlife. Buddhism, despite its similarity in some respects to Christianity, was rejected as "idolatry" and "superstition." China was therefore seen as a great opportunity for the spread of Christianity, and most missionaries could not understand why most Chinese showed so little interest. This proved nearly as true in Japan where, as in China, most people did not attach all that much importance to any sort of religion, especially not to the fervent evangelical brand of Christianity which most missionaries represented. East Asians had long been eclectic in what religion they did follow, taking bits from all of their religious traditions, but this was unacceptable to the far more rigid Christian missionaries, who thus lost many potential converts.

When Chinese did not pick up the mission message, many of its Western advocates turned against the people they had come to "save" and denounced them as stupid, backward, and "uncivilized," and as capable of understanding only the language of force. Some missionaries

became better acquainted with Chinese culture and had a more balanced attitude. Missionaries were in fact the first Western scholars of Chinese civilization and the first translators of the Chinese classics into Western languages, although of course their work began with translations of the Bible. But missionary derogation of Chinese and their culture was part of the larger Western arrogance toward other peoples. New discoveries in science and technology at home, and the increasing wealth which flowed from industrialization, gave Westerners a new sense of overwhelming self-confidence, and to some provided a mission, to spread the benefits of their "superior" civilization to less fortunate or "advanced" people elsewhere. "Be like us," the West has continued to say, "and you will succeed. Persist in your own backward ways and you will fail." The Western way, including its mores and belief systems, had proved its superiority. Surely no people would choose to remain "backward" once they had been shown the example of "progress," Western style. The Japanese picked up all of these notions as they followed the Western path of industrialization and consequent military power over the rest of East Asia, whose development was lagging. Japanese had always thought of themselves and their country as "special," and now felt that they had a "civilizing mission" to perform.

Economics and Illusions

Industrial economies also developed huge new appetites for raw materials, including tropical crops like sugar, rubber, cotton, tea, jute (from India), coconut oil, tin, and petroleum, which neither Europe nor Japan had in significant amounts. All of these were produced or extracted in Asia, mainly in South and Southeast Asia, and cheap labor in the colonies made their production or extraction especially profitable. There was also much talk about the need for protected markets for the industrial countries, and for profitable investments abroad. As indicated, such arguments may have been appealing but did not agree with the major patterns of international trade and investment. There seems little doubt that the industrial countries could have obtained both the raw materials and the markets they wanted through normal peaceful trade channels at a far lower cost than through acquiring colonies. But imperialism was never a rational business, rather the reverse. V. I. Lenin, the future leader of the Russian Revolution, wrote about imperialism as the last stage of a doomed capitalism as the industrial (capitalist) countries tried to dispose of their surplus goods and capital abroad, while preventing the rise of the living standards of their own workers so that they could not afford to consume adequately. Such an analysis is only partially accurate, since imperialism was primarily not an economic matter, but rather one of irrational arrogance, aggression, rivalry, and national pride.

Whatever the combination of reasons, imperialism caught the imagination of the European, and later the Japanese, mind, and it also responded to a popular thirst for the exotic. There was a vast popular literature in addition to the periodical press retailing stories of adventure abroad, tales of exploration, military exploits, deeds of derring-do, and accounts of strange cultures. Most of it reflected the Western conviction of their own superiority, mixed with their feelings about their "civilizing mission." The English writer Rudyard Kipling spoke of "The White Man's Burden" as the sacred duty of the "white" races; he actually addressed this poem to the Americans, as a piece of advice to a new colonial power from an older and more experienced one, on the occasion of the American takeover of the Philippines in 1898. But like many other Western writers, Kipling also reflected the widespread Western fascination with Asia, and its appealing aspects, as in these lines from his poem *Mandalay*:

> *Ship me somewhere east of Suez,*
>   *where the best is like the worst,*
> *Where there ain't no ten commandments,*
>   *and a man can raise a thirst.*[1]

As Kipling implies, Westerners in Asia, far from home, felt bound by none of their own domestic conventions and yet were also free of the morality of Asian societies; it was a paradise for adventurers, some of whom were failures or misfits at home but who could make out well as privileged colonialists. Westerners in Asia were often a law unto themselves, and became "little tin gods." No wonder so many of them came to admire, even to love, the Asian societies where they lived and worked and where they had both an easier and a more profitable life than they would have had at home, waited on by Asian servants and living very well. Many, perhaps most, of the missionaries, although they did not have such an easy life and often one of real sacrifice—certainly they were not in it for the money—found adventurous careers in the mission field and an exhilarating sense of being part of a great enterprise, which few of them could have found at home, since most of them were not very highly educated and often came from humble backgrounds so that the more glamorous professional careers at home were closed to them. Their lack of sophistication no doubt contributed to their subscription to the evangelical, fundamentalist version of Christianity which they preached, and also helped to close their minds to the virtues of Asian cultures. To most missionaries, all Asians were "godless" heathens—not an attitude calculated to win friends among potential converts. As we can observe in our own times,

fundamentalist religious sects tend to attract mainly the less educated, and their appeal is more to simple-minded faith than to reason. There were exceptions of course, and indeed it is not easy to generalize about missionaries, who included all sorts from evangelicals to scholars to dedicated followers of the "social gospel" who did much valuable constructive work.

The arrogance and the domination of Western imperialism were galling to Asians, especially given their own cultural pride, even arrogance, in their ancient traditions of greatness. Western imperialism in fact stimulated a revival of Asian tradition in many respects, and a determination to hold up their heads with pride against the Western dismissal of them as "backward." Being looked down on by "barbarians" was a role reversal which all Asians found deeply disturbing. In the glare of Western criticism, there were some efforts to eliminate or restrict aspects of traditional culture which had attracted unfavorable Western attention: footbinding, chaste widowhood, and concubinage in China, premarital promiscuity, mixed bathing, and more or less open pornography in Japan. The Chinese especially persuaded themselves that while the West might be temporarily ahead materially, the East remained superior spiritually and in the arts of civilization. After all, China had pioneered in science and technology, and this also made people feel better about their nineteenth- and twentieth-century humiliation at the hands of both aggressive Westerners and Japanese. China had led the world for so long that it was bitterly hard to accept its being treated as "inferior," with Chinese discriminated against even in their own country.

Westerners, and later Japanese, formed four different and often mutually antagonistic groups: missionaries (by far the most numerous), traders and businessmen, diplomats, and the small military forces (until the far greater numbers of the Japanese invasion of China in 1931 and 1937). They tended to be scornful of each other, with the missionaries often the target of the other three groups, while they themselves condemned the "immorality" of the others. Only the missionaries, and a few of the diplomats, bothered to learn the language. Some of the missionaries, given their mastery of the language, also served as diplomats, as did some of the merchants. But most found common ground in their feeling that if only the home governments would take a more forceful line, especially in China, or send another gunboat, trade would leap ahead, mission efforts would prosper, and China would be brought to "civilization." All were of course wrong, and very few understood what was happening in China or why, apart from surface manifestations. China continued to respond far more to its own internal circumstances and problems than to the presence and pressures of the small group of Westerners on the fringes of the country. China was immense,

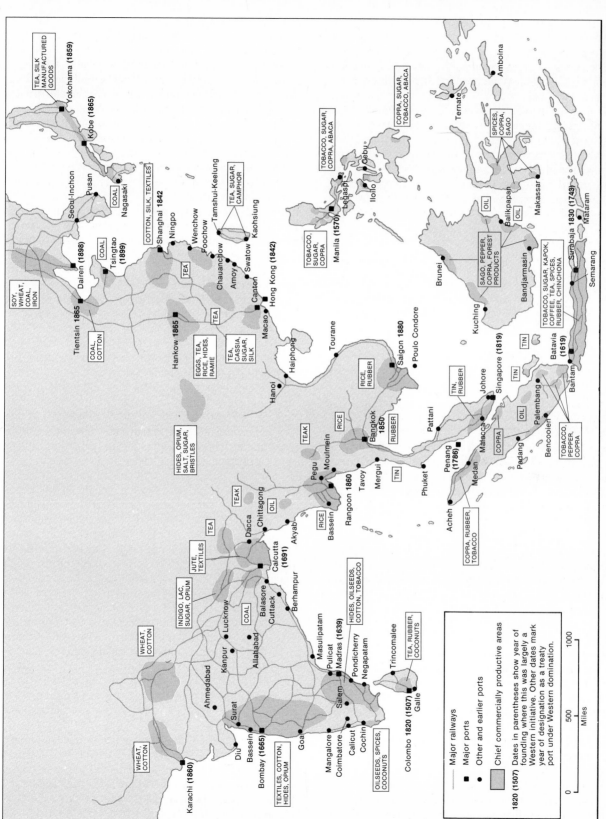

Major Ports and Commercially Productive Areas in East Asia, 1600–1940

and most Chinese never saw a foreigner; only the missionaries penetrated bits of the country beyond the foreign enclaves in the treaty ports. China continued to labor primarily with its inherited problems of overpopulation, declining per capita productivity, and increasing government ineptitude.

The most important consequence of imperialism was the growth of Asian nationalism, which ultimately destroyed colonialism. The great Asian empires and states of the past were cultural and bureaucratic structures different from the nation-states of modern Europe, whose national coherence and drive Asians rightly saw as a source of strength which they lacked, but which they must have if they were again to be masters in their own houses.

China Besieged

The Opium War of 1839–1842 (see Chapter 8), in which the British demolished the Chinese forces, did not yet make much impact on the country, its people, or their outlook on the world. The government in Peking was forced by the Treaty of Nanking in 1842, signed on board a British warship in the Yangtze off that city, to open Shanghai, Canton, Ningpo, Foochow (Fuzhou), and Amoy to British trade and residence, and to cede to Britain "in perpetuity" the island of Hong Kong. Other Western powers negotiated similar treaties in the following year giving them the same rights in the five mainland ports. The American Treaty of Wang Hsia, ratified in 1844, added a most-favored-nation clause whereby all concessions granted to any other power were automatically granted to the United States, a sort of insidious ratchet on the tightening of foreign domination which the other powers also quickly added to their treaties. The American treaty also added extraterritoriality, which meant that their (and other foreign) nationals were not subject to Chinese law but to their own domestic laws, administered by the respective consuls, who usually did not apply it with the severity practiced at home. The foreigners said that Chinese law was "barbaric" and only their own law was "civilized," conveniently forgetting that Western judicial practice, and their prisons, had only very recently evolved from late medieval conditions which were much the same as China's. They objected to the judicial use of torture to extract confessions, to the harsh punishments applied, and to the practice of collective responsibility whereby almost any individual could be punished for the misdoings of his family or other group.

This had been dramatically demonstrated in 1785 and again in 1821; in the first case a private British ship, the *Lady Hughes*, fired a salute near Canton and the

discharge from the firing killed two Chinese bystanders. It was unclear which man was at fault, but when the Chinese threatened to cancel all trade, the ship's captain surrendered one of the gunners, who then was strangled. The 1821 incident involved an American seaman on board the *Emily* by the name of Terranova who dropped a pitcher by mistake on the head of a Chinese selling fruit from a small boat; the blow knocked her overboard and she drowned. Again the Chinese threatened to stop the trade, Terranova was handed over, and he too was strangled in full view of the foreign factories (warehouses and offices—"factor" is an old name for "trader"). China in the past had expected foreigners who came there, notably Arab traders, to keep order among themselves through one of their own headmen. Extraterritoriality was thus not a new idea, and to begin with was not distressing to the Chinese—until it began to be used by Westerners to give them unfair advantages in their dealings with Chinese.

Sir Henry Pottinger, the British plenipotentiary who negotiated the Treaty of Nanking, declared that "The treaty has opened to British trade a market so vast that all the mills of Lancashire could not make stocking stuff enough for one of China's provinces."[2] Foreign trade immediately began an increase which continued until the world depression of the 1930s. Tea and silk remained the dominant exports and opium the main import, although it was overtaken after 1870 by cotton yarn, textiles, kerosene, and a variety of other foreign manufactured goods. The treaties further impinged on China's sovereignty by limiting import tariffs to 5 percent, opening the vast China market to Western goods. Although in fact China continued to provide most of its own needs and imports never became proportionately important, the "unequal treaties," as the Chinese nationalists later called them, reduced the country to semicolonial status. Peking's reluctance to comply with these terms led to a second war from 1858 to 1860, when British and French troops captured Tientsin (Tianjin) and Peking (Beijing) and burned the imperial summer palace in retaliation for what they saw as Chinese "treachery." The Chinese had fired on British forces, imprisoned the representative sent to negotiate under a flag of truce, broken successive agreements to observe earlier treaties, and refused to receive an ambassador in Peking. Lord Elgin, the commanding British general, said he had no wish to harm the Chinese people but chose instead to burn the summer palace as a symbol of Ch'ing government elitism and arrogance.

Nearly all of the treaty ports occupied sites purposely chosen to combine two characteristics: an existing center of trade with access to oceangoing shipping, and a position which was as much as possible surrounded by water. They had been wrested by force from an unwilling government, and the entire history of Westerners in

Foreign factories and their ships at Canton in the early days of steam. Oil painting by a Chinese artist. (Mark Sexton courtesy, Peabody Essex Museum, Salem, Massachusetts)

Asia had shown that their power lay overwhelmingly in their ships. They knew that the Chinese government remained hostile, and that they might have to defend themselves in their new settlements. Accordingly, these were selected so as to have navigable water around them as much as possible. The first British Consul at Shanghai, George Balfour, put it neatly soon after he arrived there in 1844: "By our ships our power can be seen, and if necessary felt."[3] The foreign settlement at Shanghai fronted on the Huangpu (Whangpoo) River, a tributary of the Yangtze which it joins about 12 miles below the city, but at the junction of the Huangpu with a smaller stream called Soochow (or Woosung) Creek. A still smaller stream at the then northern edge of the settlement was deepened and canalized to form what the foreigners called Defense Creek, between Soochow Creek, later called the Woosung (Wusung) River, and a creek which ran down to the Huangpu along the western edge of the settlement, completing the encirclement by water. The settlement at Amoy (Xiamen) was on an island, as of course was Hong Kong, while those at Canton, Foochou, Ningpo, and later Nanking, Tientsin, Hankou, Changsha, and Tsingtao (Qingdao) were clustered along the navigable waterfront. Only much later were treaty ports created in inland cities, and most of those were on a navigable river. At all the major treaty ports,

foreign warships were anchored prominently off the bund (an embankment to protect against flooding and to provide an unloading and loading area), ready to land troops if necessary but meanwhile to show the flag and to remind the Chinese of Western (and later Japanese) power.

At the time of the Treaty of Nanking the foreigners still knew relatively little about China beyond Canton. They did know from a few earlier observations that Shanghai was a major trade center, near the mouth of the Yangtze River, China's greatest internal trade highway. It grew by leaps and bounds, especially after the Tientsin Treaty of 1860 opened the Yangtze and its several major tributaries to foreign shipping, with new treaty ports at Tientsin, Nanking, and Hankou, plus others. Shanghai rapidly overshadowed and absorbed most of the trade of Ningpo, Foochow, Amoy, and even Canton, while Hong Kong, with the addition of Kowloon on the adjacent mainland peninsula ceded to the British by the 1860 treaty, soon became the dominant port of south China and served as an entrepôt or transshipping center for the trade of the entire coast. Beginning in 1860 under the new treaties, the foreigners were better able to identify and to claim as treaty ports the major Chinese trade centers, primarily those named above, since after all that was what they were there for, to tap the

✠ Through Each Other's Eyes ✠

After the Opium War, foreign arrogance increased. Here is a sample from 1858.

It is impossible that our merchants and missionaries can course up and down the inland waters of this great region and traffic in their cities and preach in their villages without wearing away at the crust of the Chinaman's stoical and skeptical conceit. The whole present system in China is a hollow thing, with a hard brittle surface.... Some day a happy blow will shiver it [and] it will all go together.

But the Chinese returned the compliment.

It is monstrous in barbarians to attempt to improve the inhabitants of the Celestial Empire when they are so miserably deficient themselves. Thus, introducing a poisonous drug for their own benefit and to the injury of others, they are deficient in benevolence. Sending their fleets and armies to rob other nations, they can make no pretense to rectitude.... How can they expect to renovate others? They allow the rich and noble to enter office without passing through any literary examinations, and do not open the road to advancement to the poorest and meanest in the land. From this is appears that foreigners are inferior to the Chinese and therefore must be unfit to instruct them.

Source: G. W. Cooke, *China: Being the Times Special Correspondence from China in the Years 1857–58* (London: Routledge, 1858), p. v; "A Chinese Tract of the Mid-Nineteenth Century," in E. P. Boardman, *Christian Influence on the Ideology of the Taiping Rebellion* (Madison: University of Wisconsin Press, 1952), p. 129.

---

trade of this immense and productive country and to find an outlet for their own exports. As at the other treaty ports, the foreign settlement grew outside the walls of the existing Chinese city whose trade had attracted the foreigners in the first place. During the period when Shanghai was surrounded by rebel groups which later merged with the Taiping Rebellion, the port stayed open and the city grew still more with the influx of refugees from the fighting, but the adjacent Chinese city was captured by rebel groups in 1853; they also captured the Chinese city at Amoy slightly earlier. The imperial Customs House was thus put out of action while the foreigners in both treaty ports successfully defended themselves.

The British and American consuls at both places agreed to collect the official customs duties owed by their own nationals during this supposedly temporary emergency. The imperial customs resumed operation later, but from the on-the-spot expedient arranged by the foreigners after 1853 there grew the Imperial Maritime Customs which by agreement recorded and levied dues on all foreign trade, leaving the Chinese customs to deal (never very effectively) with domestic trade passing through the ports. The new I.M.C. was based in Shanghai as the major port for foreign trade; it was an official organ of the Ch'ing government and remitted its revenues to Peking, but it was agreed that it should be headed by a national of the country whose trade with China was greatest. This was of course Britain, and although Japan surpassed it as the leading trader with China after 1910, the British retained the Customs leadership, partly as a legacy of the almost one-man creation of the efficiency and esprit de corps of the Customs Service by Inspector General Robert (later Sir Robert) Hart, known to foreigners as "the I.G." The Service was staffed at lower levels by Chinese, with the higher posts filled by a variety of foreign nationals in supposed proportion to varying national shares in China's foreign trade.

Hart, who retired only in 1908, and several successive Inspectors General stressed that all members of the Service were employees of the Chinese government rather than representatives of their respective countries. All foreign staff were required to learn Chinese, and the Customs Service stood out in a foreign-dominated and often exploited China as freer of special interest or blind arrogance toward things and people Chinese. Beginning in 1864, with the final suppression of the Taiping Rebellion, their trade statistics became more and more nearly complete, especially with the opening of successive treaty ports, in each of which a Customs man was stationed. In addition to recording trade and collecting the official duties, the Customs published annual and decennial reports on commercial and general conditions in the area of each treaty port which constitute one of the most important sources on the period. The Service also took responsibility for establishing and maintaining a system of lights and other navigational aids along the coast and major rivers, created and administered the first national postal and telegraph service, and lent its support to road building. Nevertheless, it acted also as manager of a system which imposed an arbitrarily low tariff on imports, agreed to in the treaties extracted from China by foreign governments eager to expedite the invasion of the China market by their own merchants. After the fall of the dynasty in 1911, the Service became simply the China Maritime Customs, but its operations continued without major change until the outbreak of the Pacific War in 1941.

Despite the increase in trade through the treaty ports from 1864 until the world depression of the 1930s, it never exceeded 1 percent of world trade, or probably 5 percent of China's gross domestic product, and came far short of Western trade dreams. In per capita terms, given China's huge population, it was negligible, probably smaller than that of any country in the world. Most of the foreign imports were consumed in the treaty ports and the immediately surrounding areas where Westernization spread, by the handful of foreigners and the very much larger numbers of Westernized Chinese. Exports were extracted from a small sector of the Chinese economy and involved a tiny proportion of it and of the total population. Westerners from the time of Marco Polo, especially traders, had seen China as the pot of gold at the end of the rainbow, but like the missionaries their hopes were never realized; although some individuals and some firms made profits, far more was earned by their Chinese agents, trade partners, and collaborators. Foreign merchants, not knowing either the language or the economy of the country, were totally dependent on Chinese agents to buy Chinese goods for export and to find markets for foreign imports, at the best prices. These *compradores*, as they were called (the word was originally Portuguese, from *compra*, "to buy"), of course charged for their services, often grew wealthy, and many became full partners in foreign firms, or set up in Western-style business on their own.

Traders and Missionaries

Missionaries often served as a forward wave for imperialism, building churches and preaching the gospel in the interior and then demanding protection from their home governments against Chinese protests or riots. Trouble encountered by missionaries or foreign traders might be answered by sending a gunboat to the nearest coastal or river port to threaten or shell the inhabitants, a practice known as "gunboat diplomacy." When missionaries or their converts were killed by angry antiforeign mobs, Western governments often used this as a pretext for extracting still more concessions from the weakening Ch'ing regime. Most Chinese resented foreigners with special privileges and protection encroaching on their

The treaty-port style: former headquarters of a foreign firm in Canton. Note the thick walls and the wide porches or galleries around the sides to help keep out the worst of the heat. (R. Murphey)

country. They did not understand the missionary practice of buying or adopting orphans for charitable and religious purposes, and assumed the worst of these strange barbarians. Stories circulated that they ate babies or gouged out their eyes for medicine.

In 1870 a mob destroyed a French Catholic mission in Tientsin and killed ten nuns and eleven other foreigners; gunboats and heavy reparations followed. Unlike the British, the French had no important trade with China and often used protection of Catholic missionaries as a means of increasing their influence. In 1883 they went to war with China over Vietnam when Chinese troops crossed the border to eject them. The French destroyed part of the brand new Western-style Chinese navy and the dockyards at Foochow on the south China coast, which they had earlier helped to build. China was humbled again.

The Taiping Rebellion

Meanwhile, the greatest of all uprisings against the Ch'ing government erupted in 1850, the Taiping Rebellion. Westerners tend to overemphasize their own role in China as the major influence on events after 1840. China was huge, Westerners were few, and their activities were sharply limited to the tiny dots of the treaty ports, plus outlying mission stations. China continued to respond primarily to its own long-standing internal problems, most importantly a population which had now long outgrown production and was falling into poverty in many areas. The Taiping leader, Hung Hsiu-Ch'uan (Hong Xiu Chuan), was a frustrated scholar who had failed the rigid imperial examinations several times, and then adopted a strange version of Christianity picked up from missionaries. In religious visions he saw himself as the younger brother of Jesus Christ. Hung became the head of a largely peasant group from the poor mountainous areas of south China, which had been excluded from the new commercial opportunities in the treaty ports. The rebels, now with a "Christian" ideology, were devoted to the overthrow of the Manchus as an alien dynasty of conquest. They picked up massive support as they moved north, and captured Nanking (Nanjing) in 1853. A northern expedition from there was turned back later that year near Tientsin, but their forces won at least a foothold in 16 of China's 18 provinces and dominated the rich Yangtze valley.

Taiping efforts at government were relatively feeble, but their system was primarily a traditional Chinese one. Factions grew among the Taiping leadership, and the "court" at Nanking was disorganized and increasingly given over to riotous living. Large-scale fighting against the Imperial forces continued nevertheless, without significant breaks until 1864 and with horrendous destruc-

tion and loss of life, until it was finally suppressed. As many as 40 million people died as a result of the Taiping Rebellion, and much of the productive lower Yangtze region was laid waste. During the same period, the Ch'ing also managed finally to put down three other mass uprisings, in the north, the southwest, and the northwest, the last two mainly Muslim rebellions against Ch'ing rule which were not finally defeated until 1873. As Tseng Kuo-fan (Zeng Guofan), the general who had finally defeated the Taipings, pointed out, these several revolts were a disease of China's vital organs, while the Western barbarians were a marginal affliction only of the extremities.

Self-Strengthening

One foreign power, however, was still advancing by land, the Russians. Sensing China's weakness and internal problems, they penetrated the Amur valley in northern Manchuria from which they had been excluded by the Treaty of Nerchinsk in 1689 (see Chapter 12). In the treaties following the war of 1858–1860 the Russians detached the maritime provinces of eastern Manchuria and added them to their empire, plus the port of Vladivostok which they had earlier founded on the Pacific Coast. Muslim rebellion in the northwest after 1862 led to Russian intervention in northern Sinkiang just across their own border, and their support of rebel Muslim leaders. The Ch'ing government decided that this threat must be met head on, raised an army under a highly effective general, Tso Tsung-t'ang (Zuo Zongtang), marched it 2,500 miles from its base in east China, and to everyone's surprise had defeated both the rebels and the Russians by 1878.

Suppression of the Taiping and other rebellions showed that, even in its last decades, the Ch'ing were still capable of successful action. They still refused to accept or to deal with foreigners as equals, but they had learned that adopting foreign military technology was essential if they were to defend themselves at all. After 1860 they began what they called "self- strengthening," including the establishment of new Western-style arsenals, gun foundries, shipyards, translation schools, and a new foreign office, the Tsung Li (Zongli) Yamen. These and other efforts to modernize were handicapped by government red tape and cross-purposes, but they made some slow progress. Several outstanding senior officials who realized the need for some changes and for more effective management rose to power, helped by the victories over the rebels and the now undeniable threat which foreigners posed. For a decade or two, the Ch'ing seemed to have a new lease on life and to show surprising vigor.

Unfortunately, it was not to last, nor were the reforms ever fundamental enough to be equal to China's problems. They never won full support from the still arch-conservative throne, or from most of the people. Both

✖ Self-Strengthening ✖

Li Hung-chang (1823–1901) was the chief architect of "self-strengthening" and made the case for it repeatedly.

The present situation is one in which, externally, it is necessary for us to be harmonious with the barbarians after China's humiliating defeats in 1840–42, 1860, and 1885, and internally, it is necessary for us to reform our institutions. If we remain conservative, without making any change, the national will will be daily reduced and weakened.... Now all the foreign countries are having one reform after another, and progressing every day like the ascending of steam. Only China continues to preserve her traditional institutions so cautiously that even though she be ruined and extinguished, the conservatives will not regret it. Oh heaven and man! How can we understand the cause of it? ... The Westerners particularly rely upon the excellence and efficacy of their guns, cannons, and steamships, and so they can overrun China.... To live today and still say "reject the barbarians" and "drive them out of our territory" is certainly superficial and absurd talk.... How can we get along for one day without weapons and techniques? The method of self-strengthening lies in learning what they can do, and in taking over what they rely upon.

Source: S. Y. Teng and J. K Fairbank, *China's Response to the West: A Documentary Survey* (Cambridge, Mass.: Harvard University Press, 1954), pp. 87, 109.

remained basically antiforeign, and opposed adopting barbarian ways even to fight barbarians. In 1862 a weak boy-emperor came to the throne, dominated by his scheming mother, Tz'u Hsi (Cixi), originally an imperial concubine, who plotted her way to the top. She was clever and politically masterful, but narrow-minded and deeply conservative, the opposite of the leadership China so urgently needed. In particular she had no understanding of or sympathy for what was required to strengthen China or to help it to deal more successfully and intelligently with foreign powers, whom she continued to see as unruly and hateful barbarians. China's first tentative efforts at change were thus mainly aborted. The Confucian reactionaries who now again dominated the government, with few exceptions, grudgingly acknowledged that the barbarians had a few useful tricks (weapons) which China might find useful, but there could be no thought of abandoning or even altering traditional Chinese culture or view of the world.

Treaty Ports and Mission Schools

Meanwhile, the treaty ports, which numbered over a hundred by 1910, grew rapidly, attracting Chinese as merchants, partners, and laborers. Nearly all of China's cities outside Peking became treaty ports, but only five or six—Shanghai, Tientsin (Tianjin), Hankou, Canton, Nanking (Nanjing), and Dairen (Dalien, in southern Manchuria) became major centers for foreign trade or foreign residence. Hong Kong, ceded outright to Britain, was technically not a treaty port but operated as an integral part of that system. These Western-dominated cities, although foreign residents were a relative handful in numbers, were an example of Euro-American-style "progress." Manufacturing also began to grow in the treaty ports, and increased especially rapidly after 1895 when the Japanese, who had defeated China in a war over the status of Korea, imposed a new treaty which permitted foreign-owned factories in the ports, producing mainly textiles and other consumer goods. This was the real beginning of modern industrialization in China, and was soon joined by Chinese entrepreneurs and industrialists, including many who had been blocked or discouraged by the conservative government until they entered the more enterprising world of the treaty ports.

As elsewhere in Asia, however, imperialist arrogance was growing, and Chinese found they were excluded from foreign clubs and parks and treated as second-class citizens. Given their ancient cultural pride, this was a bitter pill, but it fed the first stirring of modern Chinese nationalism, and a determination to purge

China of its century of humiliation. Such sentiments as yet affected only the few who lived in the treaty ports or encountered missionaries, and by no means all of them. Many treaty-port Chinese, like their Indian parallels in colonial Calcutta and Bombay, saw the Western way as the best for China and followed it increasingly in their own lives and careers. But they were the tiniest fraction of the Chinese people. Most of the few Chinese who ever saw a foreigner dismissed them as weird barbarians.

The total of Chinese Christians remained discouragingly small, probably about a million at most, out of a total population of some 450 million by 1910. Many, perhaps most, of them attended church for handouts rather than from sincere religious faith—"rice Christians," as they were called. But many of the missions saw that education and medical help were more attractive than Christian doctrine, and might be a better path toward the goal of conversion. Mission-run schools spread rapidly, as did their hospitals. The schools drew many, in time most of the young Chinese who wanted to study English and Western learning or science. They also got exposure to Christianity, but most graduates did not become converts, although they adopted Western ways of thinking in many respects, and Western-style nationalism as a source of strength which China lacked. Most twentieth-century Chinese nationalists were influenced by mission schools, and nearly all of China's universities before 1949 were founded by missionaries.

New government schools which included Western learning were also established, and in 1905, to mark the passing of an era, the traditional examination system was abolished. Missionaries and others translated a wide range of Western works, which were avidly read by the new generation of Chinese intellectuals. Many of them began to press for radical change, and for the overthrow of the Ch'ing. Ironically, they had to use the treaty ports, notably Shanghai, as their base, where they were protected from Ch'ing repression by living under foreign law. It was in the treaty ports, which were both an irritating humiliation and an instructive model, that the first stirring of revolution began.

Overseas Chinese

One consequence of the "opening" of China was great increase in the number of Chinese who went abroad. Most of them came from south China, primarily from Kwangtung (Guangdong), which had become especially overpopulated and which had a long tradition of overseas trade. Permanent colonies of Chinese merchants had been established as early as the Sung dynasty in the Philippines, Java, Vietnam, and Malaya, and these had

grown still more under the Ming and Ch'ing. The advent of steamships serving all Chinese ports, and the rapid growth of a new commercial economy of mines, plantations, and commercial cities in Southeast Asia in the nineteenth century needed workers and offered opportunity also for commercial entrepreneurs. Chinese went there in large numbers after 1850, many as contract labor under harsh conditions, but opportunities were more and more limited at home. The "coolie trade," as it came to be called, attracted severe criticism, was investigated by the Maritime Customs Service, and some of its worst excesses curbed. Other Chinese emigrants flocked to California after the opening of the 1849 gold rush there, where they worked as cooks and menial laborers. The Chinese name for San Francisco is still "Old Gold Mountain." Later Chinese provided the majority of the labor for building the western ends of the transcontinental rail lines in the United States, while Irish and Blacks built the eastern ends. By 1870 there was rising anti-Chinese prejudice in California, and periodic riots in which many Chinese were killed. Chinese, like Irish immigrants, were willing to work hard for long hours at low pay, and their competition for jobs was resented. Such feelings led Congress in 1882 to pass the first Chinese Exclusion Acts, forbidding Chinese immigration.

Chinese became known around the world as superb cooks; small restaurants offering various versions of Chinese food, and hand laundries, became Chinese specialties, both jobs requiring long hours of hard work for low pay. Chinese settlers in Southeast Asia as a whole totaled about 15 million by the 1930s; although the Chinese diaspora to the rest of the world was considerably smaller, there too they sent hard-earned money back to relatives at home. Most Westerners formed their images of Chinese from these downtrodden samples in their midst, with their "queer" ways.

Subjugation, Nationalism, and Humiliation

The Ch'ing tried to ignore its defeat by the British in the Opium War and to continue, as it had in the past, to refuse to deal with foreigners as equals or to establish what the British regarded as normal diplomatic relations. The Chinese had lost a "skirmish" with the hairy sea barbarians but saw no reason why this should change their position, their attitudes, or their traditional ways of doing things. The official accounts of the Opium War said that the sea barbarians had been driven off, with the implication that China would now return to dealing with its internal administration as usual. Many of the terms of the Treaty of Nanking were largely ignored, and difficulties placed in the way of the Westerners, against determined stonewalling by the Chinese. British diplomatic representation and residence in Peking were refused. It was almost as if nothing had happened in 1842.

Foreign impatience, now including the French and the Americans, grew, and there was a series of incidents, culminating in an undeclared war in 1856 when Chinese officials stopped a small Chinese-owned local ship, the *Arrow*, wearing by special registration a British flag, arrested 12 of the Chinese crew suspected of piracy, and hauled down the British flag. British protests and Chinese intransigence led to hostilities, which spread to a British siege of Canton, and then to an Anglo-French expedition to Tientsin (Tianjin), the port of Peking. In 1858 they extracted a new treaty confirming and expanding the terms of 1842 and opening ten new ports to foreign residence and trade. Much of the terms of the Treaty of Tientsin were also ignored by the Chinese, and in 1860 another Anglo-French expedition entered Peking and burned the Summer Palace in retaliation, as recounted earlier. The Ch'ing now had no choice but to accept foreign ambassadors at Peking, and to deal with them formally as equals. The foreign grip on China had tightened. Hong Kong, ceded outright in 1841, had been settled promptly and was flourishing as a trade entrepôt for the whole of the China coast. Its success attracted large numbers of adventurous Chinese eager for business Western-style and beyond the control of the bureaucratic state, as they were also in the coastal treaty ports.

From the Chinese point of view, these were still minor or even marginal matters, which the Ch'ing continued largely to ignore. With the beginning of the Taiping Rebellion in 1850 they also had other and from their perspective far more urgent problems, including the later Russian infiltration in Sinkiang, the Muslim Rebellions of the 1870s in the northwest and southwest, and a series of subsequent rebellions large and small which peppered the last half of the nineteenth century. It is understandable that the Ch'ing gave these problems top priority and were slow to recognize that the sea barbarians, a relative handful easily kept at arm's length in the past, had become the major threat to the country, with their now superior technology and their aggressive policies. One must remember that China was an immense country, in both area and population, and that even a more open-minded government would have felt it proper to put domestic concerns first.

Westerners have tended consistently to exaggerate the importance of their role in China, from the time of Matteo Ricci to the present. Most Chinese remained at best vaguely aware of their presence, if at all, and little if any affected by their activities, most of which were heavily concentrated in a few coastal and Yangtze river ports or at the capital in Peking. China was an overwhelmingly peasant country with few of its people living in or near the cities, to which the foreigners were largely limited. Even the mission stations in what the foreigners called "the interior" were necessarily in towns or small cities. The foreigners thought that their example of "progress" Western-style would transform China to follow a similar path, but the treaty ports made only the smallest impact on the main body of the country and its people. They did stimulate the growth of a new group, the Westernized treaty-port Chinese, originally agents for foreign firms (compradores), then merchants and industrialists in their own right, and in time Western-influenced intellectuals. But all told they were a tiny handful in this huge country and its masses of people, and they, like the treaty-port foreigners, were often cut off from close contact with the "real China" of rural peasants. Certainly they did not represent it, nor understand or respond to its problems and needs.

Foreigners have always dreamed about the profits to be won by selling to the huge China market, that pot of gold at the end of the rainbow, and multiplied what they

Prince Kung, after offering the dynasty's surrender to the Allies, Peking, November 4, 1860. (BBC Hulton Picture Library)

Tzu Hsi's infamous marble boat, resting in the mud at her newly built and lavishly rococo summer palace outside Peking. (R. Murphey)

could make from selling even a pair of socks by 400 million, or a billion, people. This goal has remained elusive, since China has continued to supply most of its own needs, as it traditionally did and mainly by traditional production methods, or used imports of foreign technology and machinery to build its own modern industry. The foreigners transformed the treaty ports, but touched the rest of the country hardly at all.

The major foreign impact was in ideas, much of it via mission-run schools and colleges, including the example of strength, organization, efficiency, and prosperity which China lacked but which the treaty ports exhibited. It was a combined message of the benefits of modern Western national states, technology, industrialization, the values of free enterprise, and the modern Western legacy of individualism, free expression, and democratic forms of government. Especially after 1917, the influence of originally Western Marxism and Russian Leninism became newly compelling, appealing to many patriotic Chinese as a better model of strength and success, but in any case a preferable alternative to their own traditional system, which they saw as having failed on all counts.

But it took much time for the lessons of China's humiliation to be absorbed, and for any substantial number of people with new ideas to emerge. Chinese had been

used to leading the world, for two thousand years or more. Their view of themselves, and of the appropriate response to the outside world, could not change quickly, even though to Westerners it seemed obvious that the world outside China had changed drastically and that Chinese responses had become disastrously, even maddeningly, out-of-date. In any case, it was hard to move a mass as immense as China and its peasant millions in an area larger than the United States, or even its small educated group, still schooled in the Confucian classics and still proud to the point of arrogance, finding anything foreign barbaric and distasteful if not contemptible. The new Western military technology was dismissed as "a few monkey tricks," which China need not stoop to copy. But slowly the message began to get through, even to some of the archconservative officials who dominated the Ch'ing government.

"Self-Strengthening" and Restoration

The final suppression of the Taipings was supervised by a dedicated scholar-official, Tseng Kuo-fan (Zheng Guo-fan, 1811–1872), who began by organizing a militia-style army to chase the rebels out of Hunan, his native

✳ Foreign Dreams ✳

Despite the disappointing trade figures, many foreigners continued to hope to find the pot of gold, and to transform China in the Western image.

The open ports are oases of light in a waste of darkness and stagnation.... All our modern ideas of progress and the possibility of improving their lot seem nonexistent in the official as well as in the popular mind.... Doubtless there is a leaven at work in our presence in China which will in time leaven the mass, and the more points of contact in the shape of treaty ports are created the quicker will be the advance, but to the outward eye only a small radius around each port has so far been affected.... A treaty port established ... means a concrete example of the gains to be derived from Western methods of progress.... The time must come when Western modes of thought will have taken hold.

Source: From Archibald Little, *Gleanings from Fifty Years in China.* (London: S. Low Marston and Co., 1910), p. 29–37.

province. He taught his Hunan Army discipline, built their morale, and made them into the government's major striking force, which took the offensive in many areas of central China. In 1860 Tseng was put in charge of all the middle and lower Yangtze provinces, where the now combined imperial forces began slowly to wear down the Taiping rebels. He encouraged his young protégé Li Hung-chang (Li Hong Zhang, 1823–1901) to build up a provincial army in Anhwei (Anhui) on the model of the Hunan Army. Li and Tseng bought foreign arms and established Western-style arsenals, with Western advisers, to make Western guns and steamships. An American adventurer from Salem, Massachusetts, F. T. Ward, organized a volunteer corps of foreigners to defend Shanghai from rebel attacks, soon joined by a larger Chinese contingent trained in Western arms and tactics. When Ward was killed in 1862, he was succeeded by Charles Gordon, on loan from the British army, known in the West as "Chinese Gordon." Like Ward, he was given Chinese military rank under Li Hung-chang, by now governor of Kiangsu (Jiangsu) Province, where both Shanghai and Nanking are located. Ward and Gordon won a number of engagements, but their contribution to the ultimate Ch'ing victory was slight, and Nanking was retaken from the Taipings in 1864 with no foreign help, nor was any used in the subsequent suppression of other rebellions. But the value of Western military technology had become clear.

A striking paradox of those years was the foreign assault on Tientsin and Peking in 1858–1860 while at the same time foreigners were fighting on the government's side in central China against the Taipings. Different Chinese government factions were in fact involved, and the foreign humiliation of the court in 1860 meant the defeat of that very conservative and antiforeign group, which in turn meant more scope for reformers like Tseng and Li. The foreigners did not understand this clearly at the time; they were merely defending themselves and their trade at Shanghai and nearby Ningpo, while dealing separately with what they saw as an intolerable set of bad relations with the government in Peking. After 1860 the foreigners increasingly saw their best interests would be served by keeping the weakened Ch'ing dynasty in power, propping it up as a client state which was unable to resist them and would do their bidding. The emperor fled from the Anglo-French forces who invaded the capital, and his brother, Prince Kung (Gong), concluded the final treaty settlement, which he saw as essential to save the dynasty. When the emperor died in 1861, Prince Kung took over as regent for the new boy emperor, whose reign title was T'ung-chih (Tongzhi), although he was obliged to share power with the boy's scheming mother, the young Empress Dowager Tz'u Hsi who had earlier won imperial favor as a concubine. Together they supervised the execution of rival antiforeign princes, and lent support to Tseng and Li in their anti-Taiping campaigns.

This was the beginning of the movement known as "Self-Strengthening," which consciously sought to adopt Western military technology, barbarian tricks to save China from the barbarians. The reign of the new emperor, from 1862 to 1875, came to be called the T'ung Chih Restoration, and China seemed to be at last on the right track. A new school to train Chinese interpreters in Western languages was established, and something like a foreign office, the Tsungli Yamen, to manage diplomatic relations. More effort was put into building arsenals for modern weapons and ships outside the foreign concession areas at Nanking, Tientsin, Shanghai, and, with French help, at Foochou (Fuzhou), including a naval dockyard.

But this was not Meiji Japan, despite the above similarities. China was still fundamentally conservative; the Manchu government was in its last half century and almost by definition had lost both the will and the ability to pursue change, while as an alien dynasty it felt obliged to maintain the traditional Chinese way in all things. The Ch'ing, and most Chinese, had a basic mistrust or even hatred of everything foreign, and of all change of almost any kind, except to spruce up the Confucian tradition, which in effect is what the T'ung Chih Restoration primarily aimed to do. In addition, the dynasty had been fundamentally weakened by the Taiping Rebellion and the enormous effort of its suppression— nor were such drains on the state's resources to cease until it finally collapsed in 1911.

Rebellions multiplied, and even the brilliant campaigns against the Muslim rebels in the west and the Russian schemes in Sinkiang under Tso Tsung-t'ang (Zuo Zongtang), trained in the Hunan Army under Tseng Kuo-fan, won only a brief respite, while exhausting the treasury. Revenues could not keep up with expenditures, even with the help of new taxes on trade. The growth of regional armies begun in the Taiping years signaled a trend toward regional diffusion of government authority and foreshadowed the warlordism

which was to consume the first decades of the twentieth century. In the face of such problems, the government could only repeat the Confucian formulas: respect for superiors, deference to authority, and hence the maintenance of harmony. Even Tseng Kuo-fan criticized what he saw as the money-grubbing merchants in the treaty ports, and felt that railways and the telegraph would disrupt the Chinese system and should be kept out.

The T'ung-chih emperor died in 1875, some said "assisted" by Tz'u Hsi, since he was only 19. She then had her own nephew, a boy of four, made emperor as Kuang-hsü (Guang-xu), but kept real power for herself, and in 1884 removed Prince Kung from office. Some projects of "modernization" continued, such as those promoted by Li Hung-chang, who became a governor-general, built up the arsenals, and promoted a number of other Western-style ventures. These included a highly successful steamship company, a modern-style coal mine, a telegraph company, and several modern textile mills. But they were insignificant ripples on the vast sea of the largely unchanged traditional economy, and most of the enterprises ran into financial trouble, in part because Li and many others siphoned off too many of the profits. They were supposed to be "government supervised and merchant operated" but they became largely inefficient bureaucratic operations, with a few exceptions. Li's coal mine at Kaiping, north of Tientsin, had a short railway line by 1883 to haul the coal to a port which was improved to handle bigger ships; the rail line was slowly extended to Tientsin, and even to the outskirts of Peking by 1896,

The first railway in China, from Shanghai to Wusung, built in 1876 and the next year bought and destroyed by the Chinese government. Note Chinese wearing a queue in front of the lead engine. (Courtesy, Essex Institute, Salem, Massachusetts)

but railway building elsewhere was even slower and often met with strong local resistance. A British firm in Shanghai built a short line to the outer harbor in 1876, but local opposition was so intense, especially after a man was run over, that the governor-general of the province in Nanking bought the line in 1877 and had it torn up and the rails shipped to lie rusting on a beach in Taiwan.

A few Chinese began to go abroad to study, helped by missionaries, but an educational mission which sent 120 college-age boys to Hartford, Connecticut, in 1872 was withdrawn in 1881, and on their return the students were treated with suspicion, as were all new things or change in any form, especially where there was a foreign connection. Those few official Chinese who urged Westernization, as the Meiji Japanese were doing full speed, were criticized or forced into retirement. Li Hung-chang was basically a conservative in his views; although he recognized the need for some change, he had to move cautiously, especially with the Empress Dowager. The same was true of another prominent governor-general who agreed that reforms were essential, Chang Chih-tung (Zhang Zhidong); but he was outspokenly antiforeign. His formula was widely repeated: use Chinese ways for fundamentals, and Western ways only as tools. Like most Chinese of his time, he failed to understand that the whole of the traditional Chinese system, including perhaps especially its "fundamentals," had to be changed if China was to escape from backwardness, poverty, and humiliation.

It was typical of the last decades of the Ch'ing that when Li tried to rebuild a fleet after the disastrous war with the French in 1885, much of the funds he needed were diverted by the Empress Dowager to build a garish new summer palace northwest of Peking, at mammoth expense. Eunuchs and other courtiers grew even richer on this new source of graft, and the new palace included an ornate two-tiered boat built of solid marble on the edge of a big lake; it became common knowledge that this was Tz'u Hsi's little joke—a marble boat for her instead of an adequate new navy for China.

When the new Japanese navy at a peak of efficiency attacked in 1894, there were too few Chinese ships to meet them, the Chinese admiral had no notion of modern naval tactics, many of the Chinese guns were supplied with the wrong size shells, and many of the shells proved to have been filled with sand by corrupt contractors. It was a humiliating defeat, matched by Japanese victory over the Chinese troops sent to Korea to defend their tributary "younger brother." At the peace negotiations for the Treaty of Shiminoseki in 1895, Li, who was head of the Chinese delegation, said to Ito Hirobumi (see Chapter 15), his opposite number:

"China and Japan are the closest neighbors, and moreover we have the same writing system. How can we be enemies? ... We ought to establish perpetual peace and harmony between us, so that our Asiatic yellow race will not be encroached upon by the white race of Europe." Ito replied: "Ten years ago I talked with you about reform. Why is it that not a single thing has been changed or reformed?" to which Li could only say: "Affairs in my country have been so confined by tradition that I could not accomplish what I desired.... I am ashamed of having excessive wishes and lacking the power to fulfill them."[4]

New Humiliations

The defeat by Japan was shattering to Chinese pride. Western powers were one thing, but Japan was almost like a younger member of the family, for centuries a patronized tributary state which had learned all the arts of civilization from China. Many conservatives, still in the great majority, repeated the phrase "Back to the Western Han!" as the cure for China's modern disaster. The Western Han (see Chapter 4) was long enough ago that people tended to remember only the good things about it, as an age of brilliant accomplishment and imperial glory when China ruled the world. It was typically Chinese to look to the past for guidance rather than to the present, and to try to make themselves feel better by remembering their ancient greatness. As the nineteenth century drew to a close, the Western powers, including Russia, seemed to be closing in for the kill, extracting new concessions, naval bases, leased territories, and "spheres of influence." What saved China from a complete colonial takeover was primarily the rivalry among the powers, including Japan; none of them were willing to see any one country become dominant in China, and it made no sense for often bitter rivals to try to run it collectively. In any case it would have been a colossal administrative headache, and even at the height of the imperialist fever few countries really wanted to take that on.

The scramble for new concessions included a relatively sudden rush for loans to and contracts with the Chinese government to build railways, mainly by private foreign companies although some had foreign government connections. A few major lines were completed, in a process which extended into the 1930s although after 1930 the Nationalist (Kuomintang-Guomindang) government (see Chapter 18) tried to keep control over all new lines. Railways were clearly a step forward, and badly needed for better national integration; even the Ch'ing government built and financed a few new lines. But the foreign involvement further increased their control and was much resented by many, as well as saddling successive Chinese regimes with new debt burdens. The customs revenues collected by the foreign-run I.M.C. were now put in a special account to pay interest on foreign loans, and on the huge indemnities imposed by the French after 1886, the Japanese from 1895, and the allied powers after the Boxer Rebellion. The imperial treasury was bankrupt. The Russians made Manchuria into their special sphere and began extensive railway building and mining operations there.

The Russian position and activities were taken over by the Japanese after their victory in the Russo-Japanese war of 1904–1905 (see Chapter 15). Under their direction Manchuria acquired a highly developed rail net and a major mining and industrial complex, but at the cost of any real Chinese authority there. Foreigners saw railway investment as profitable, but also as facilitating the supply of exports and the flow of imports, to and from the treaty ports. Foreigner steamships had become the major carriers on the Yangtze and its tributaries and along the coastal routes. Foreign naval vessels were anchored in every major treaty port, and patrolled the inland waters as well, to "safeguard foreign interests." Foreign banks dominated the financing of China's foreign trade and the highly profitable insurance business, an idea new to China but soon popular with many Chinese merchants.

Efforts at Reform

Some officials, scholars, and gentry urged that the Treaty of Shiminoseki be rejected, especially since the huge indemnity it imposed, three times China's annual revenues, would complete the utter ruin of the government's finances. K'ang Yu-wei (Kang Youwei), a vigorous Cantonese, became the leader of a group of graduates urging radical reforms, and was joined by his fellow Cantonese intellectual Liang Ch'i-ch'ao (Liang Qichao). No longer troubled by the apparent dilemma of how to save China by Westernizing it, the men had made the resolution reached a generation earlier by the Meiji reformers in Japan: at least in technology, education, and much of government, the Western way was the best way to promote national strength and prosperity. K'ang reinterpreted Confucius as a reformer, someone who preached "the right of rebellion" against unfit rulers, and who sanctioned change.

In late 1897 K'ang was recommended as a tutor to the Emperor Kuang-hsü, and in 1898 he presented a long list of reform proposals, including a national assembly and a constitution. From June 11 to September 21, 1898, prompted by K'ang and Liang Ch'i-ch'ao, the emperor issued over 40 edicts in what came to be called the Hundred Days of Reform, which aimed to remake the entire system of education, economy, and government. There was of course violent opposition from the official establishment. The Empress Dowager, who had temporarily "retired" at age 63, soon realized that K'ang had gone too far to win the support of most Chinese and that her reactionary views still rep-

Reform

Liang Ch'i-ch'ao (1873–1929), a student and associate of K'ang Yu-wei, was a tireless advocate of reform; he had this to say about China's situation in 1896, just after its crushing defeat by Japan.

Those who insist that there is no need for reform still say "Let us follow the ancients, follow the ancients." They coldly sit and watch everything being laid to waste by following tradition, and there is no concern in their hearts.... Now there is a big mansion which has lasted a thousand years. The tiles and bricks are decayed and the beams and rafters are broken up, its fall is foredoomed. Yet the people in the house are still happily playing or soundly sleeping. Even some who have noted the danger know only how to weep bitterly, folding their arms and waiting for death without thinking of any remedy. Sometimes there are people a little better off who try to repair the cracks, seal up the leaks, and patch up the ant holes in order to be able to go on living there in peace, even temporarily, in the hope that something better may turn up. [Liang means here the "self-strengtheners," still sticking to the old system.] These three types of people use their minds differently, but when a hurricane comes they will die together.... A nation is also like this.

Source: S. Y. Teng and J. K. Fairbank, *China's Response to the West: A Documentary Survey* (Cambridge, Mass.: Harvard University Press, 1954), p. 155.

resented a majority of the political elite. She engineered a coup on September 21, seized the emperor and forced him into seclusion, and executed six of the reformers, though K'ang and Liang escaped to Japan. When Tz'u Hsi finally died in 1908 she had managed to ensure that the emperor, presumably poisoned, died one day earlier, and arranged as his successor her three-year-old nephew Pu Yi, who "reigned" until the dynasty officially ended in 1912.

The Boxer Rebellion

Missionaries in rural areas continued to provoke antiforeign riots as their activities spread. In the late 1890s, an anti-Ch'ing group of impoverished bandits and rebels in eastern north China was adroitly turned by the Empress Dowager toward a different target: missionaries, and finally all foreigners, who were to be killed or driven into the sea. By early 1900 this group, known to foreigners as the Boxers (a crude translation of their name for themselves, "the fists of righteous harmony"), went on a rampage, burning mission establishments and killing missionaries and Chinese converts. Like most anti-Christian riots, it was masterminded by members of the gentry who resented the missionaries preempting traditional gentry roles in teaching and charitable works. Converts had always been resented because they often used foreign help, and sometimes gunboat diplomacy, to intervene in their disputes with other Chinese. The imperial court not only favored the Boxers, but saw them as the final solution to the barbarian question. By June 1900, with covert imperial support, they besieged the foreign legations in Peking, which barely held out until relieved by a multinational expedition in mid-August. Having earlier declared war officially against all the foreign powers, the court fled to Sian (Xian).

After brutal reprisals, the foreigners (now including a large Japanese contingent) withdrew, and a peace was patched up a year later, saddling China with a staggering indemnity on top of the one already extracted by Japan in 1895, but leaving the Empress Dowager and her reactionary councillors still in power. The Ch'ing dynasty was almost dead, but no workable alternative was to emerge for many more years. China had still to learn the lessons of national unity and shared political purpose, which had been unnecessary in the past when the empire controlled "all under heaven" and China had no rivals. The government finally fell in 1911, more of its own weight and incompetence than because of the small, weak, and disorganized group of revolutionaries whose mistimed uprising was joined by disgruntled troops. The fall of the Ch'ing was hardly a revolution, but it ended the dynastic rule by which China had been governed for more than 2,000 years, and opened the way for fundamental change in the years ahead.

A few of the more moderate reforms begun in the Hundred Days were retained, including the establishment of modern-style schools, and in 1905 the imperial examinations were abolished, ending an ancient institution which had outlived its time. The government moved slowly to create provincial and national "consultative assemblies," and promised a parliament by 1913, but it was too slow and too late to deflect the mounting pressures for change. The chief effort of the reformers, to create a revolution from the top, failed, primarily because most Chinese were not ready for such radical change despite the lessons of the years since 1842. Tz'u Hsi's answer to the foreign threat to China was to support the Boxers in their hopeless attempt to kill or drive away all foreigners. She and her government were lucky to survive that disaster, only because the foreign powers, now including Japan, saw no alternative, did not want to take on the job of administering China themselves, and had grown used to propping up the moribund dynasty as a compliant stooge.

For the most part, the efforts at reform, including the "Self-Strengtheners" of the T'ung-chih Restoration, were traditional answers to traditional problems. There was no significant industrialization, except on a relatively small scale in the treaty ports, most of it by foreigners, and little willingness to abandon institutions grown incapable of dealing with contemporary problems. China was still the Middle Kingdom, too successful in the past for too long to recognize the need for change or to learn from barbarians. No effective answer emerged to the dilemma of how to preserve the Chinese essence if that meant, as it clearly did, adoption of foreign technology *and* institutions. And yet the pride in being Chinese was never lost, nor was it to be when finally, after many false starts, failures, and betrayals, revolution came from the bottom up. The long Chinese sense of membership in a common culture had first to be augmented by a new sense of nationalism, irrelevant during the centuries when China was the empire which ruled "all under heaven" and only lesser people had "states." Now China had to learn the hard lesson that it too must become a modern-style state if it was to regain, not its old superiority, but a footing of equality in competition with other states which it had lost. Modern-style nationalism was to be the key to success, but political coherence was slow to grow beyond a few of the intellectual elite. It was to be another generation before such developments took place.

Notes

1. R. Kipling, *Complete Verse*. New York: Doubleday, 1939, p. 417.
2. Quoted in T. W. Bannister, "A History of the External Trade of China," in *Maritime Customs, Decennial Reports for 1921–1931*, Shanghai, 1932, p. 39.
3. Quoted in George Lanning, *A History of Shanghai*. Shanghai: Kelly and Walsh, 1923, p. 134.
4. Quoted in J. K. Fairbank, *The Great Chinese Revolution*, Harper and Row, 1986, p. 119.

Suggestions for Further Reading

Chesneaux, J., et. al. *China from the Opium War to the 1911 Revolution*. New York: Pantheon, 1976.

Cohen, P. *China and Christianity*. Cambridge: Harvard Press, 1963.

Cohen, P., and Schrecker, J., eds. *Reform in Nineteenth Century China*. Harvard Press, 1976.

Fairbank, J. K., ed. *The Missionary Enterprise in China and America*. Harvard, 1974.

Gardella, R. *Harvesting Mountains: Fujian and the China Tea Trade, 1757–1937*. California, 1994.

Gasster, M. *China's Struggle to Modernize*. New York: Knopf, 1982.

Gernet, J. *China and the Christian Impact*. Cambridge University Press, 1985.

Hao, Y. P. *The Commercial Revolution in Nineteenth Century China*. California, 1986.

Hsu, I. *The Rise of Modern China*. Oxford University Press, 1995.

Jen, Y. W. *The Taiping Revolutionary Movement*. Yale, 1973.

Kuhn, P. *Rebellion and its Enemies*. Harvard Press, 1970.

MacKinnon, S. R. *Power and Politics in Late Imperial China*. California, 1980.

Murphey, R. *The Outsiders*. Ann Arbor: Michigan Press, 1977.

Perry, E. J. *Rebels and Revolutionaries in North China, 1845–1945*. Stanford, 1980.

Peyrefitte, A. *The Immobile Empire*. New York: Knopf, 1993.

Schrecker, J. *Imperialism and Chinese Nationalism*. Harvard, 1971.

Seagrave, S. *Dragon Lady: The Life and Legend of the Last Empress of China*. New York: Vintage, 1993.

Wakeman, F. *The Fall of Imperial China*. New York: Free Press, 1977.

Wright, M. C. *The Last Stand of Chinese Conservatism*. Stanford, 1957.

CHAPTER 15

JAPAN'S RESPONSE TO NEW CHALLENGES

Japan's isolation was rudely shattered in the 1850s, as recounted in Chapter 13, and in the ensuing domestic turmoil the Tokugawa shogunate was replaced by a new government of radical reformers bent on rapid modernization and Westernization. Their aim was to give Japan the strength which industrialization had given to the West so that the country could defend itself against the threat of imperialist domination, under the slogan "Rich country, strong army." It was *samurai* from Satsuma and Choshu in southwestern Japan who had spearheaded the push for a more effective response to the Western challenge, and they dominated the new government. They represented a reassertion of strong national feeling which was to grow in strength and confidence until Japan's collapse in defeat in 1945. All of the Asian countries subjected to imperialist pressures or to outright colonialism resented it; no people anywhere likes to be dominated by outsiders. But the Japanese had thought of themselves from early times as a special people. Their distinctive culture and deep sense of separate identity, buttressed by their insular isolation and freedom from foreign invasion (except for the brief and unsuccessful Mongol attempts in the thirteenth century) had helped to build an equally deep sense of national pride. Despite the absence until 1600, with the victory of the Tokugawa, of an effective central government and the division of Japan into warring factions, Japanese had developed a version of cultural nationalism and a determination to keep Japan free of the taint of foreign pressures.

Japan's small size and largely homogenous culture, including language, was an important factor in this development, despite its political disunity. To a degree, Japanese nationalism was a natural growth which came easily, almost unthinkingly. It was a basic part of Japanese identity. All that was needed to make Japan into a Western-style nation-state was the creation of a strong central government. To some extent, that had been achieved under the Tokugawa despite the feudal structure on which it rested, but Tokugawa power was indirect in much of the country, where administration was left in local hands. There was no truly national bureaucracy, and poor communications slowed and dented central efforts at control, let alone the carrying out of national policy. The new government which came to power in 1868 soon had at its disposal railways, steamships, the telegraph, and a new postal system, all essential to establish a truly national order and to promote national policy as well as to coordinate the efforts of a centrally controlled bureaucracy to implement policy in every part of the country.

Throne and Political Leaders

It was bellicose *samurai* in Choshu and Satsuma, it will be remembered, who took the most aggressive actions against the Westerners who had entered Japan and its home waters, while others from these two *han* had been responsible for most of the attacks on individual Westerners in Tokyo, Kyoto, and elsewhere (see Chapter

13). These superpatriots were certainly expressing Japanese nationalism, and determination to keep Japan free of the foreign presence, let alone domination. For many centuries the emperor had been a symbolic figurehead rather than someone who wielded real power, but for the new oligarchs of the Meiji government he was a useful symbol of resurgent Japanese nationalism, including his supposedly divine descent and his legendary association with Japanese feelings about themselves as a people blessed by the gods. The emperor served the sort of function performed by kings in the West; both represented the essence of their respective countries, as Victoria did for example for England. The Japanese emperor was farther removed from worldly affairs, a sort of superhuman, and hence an even better focus for national feeling since his personal characteristics and foibles were not evident and he reigned purely as a sacred icon, like a national flag, on a level far above criticism, a rallying point for national sentiment. His name could be invoked, but everyone knew that decisions were made by political leaders; the emperor could not be faulted if anything went wrong. Use of the emperor as a symbol also helped to soften the impact of what was actually revolutionary change, by linking it with the traditional Japanese past.

The last emperor of the Tokugawa period, Komei, had died in 1867 and was succeeded by his 14-year-old son Mutsuhito, who took the reign title of Meiji ("Enlightened Rule") for the new "year period." Given his youth and his apparent willingness to go along with the tide of reform, he was the ideal patron, so to speak, of the radical reformers who formed the new government; he became a sort of personalized figurehead and a sanctification for the fundamental changes which the government now pursued. The Meiji era, which lasted until Mutsuhito's death in 1912, was in fact a period of astonishingly rapid change which remade Japan from top to bottom and left it at his death already a major industrial power, employing all the technology pioneered by the nineteenth-century West, and also an imperialist power, following the Western example in that respect as in so many others. It is probably more accurate to refer to what is called the Meiji Restoration (supposedly restoring the emperor to power, although his power was little if any greater than in the past) as a genuine revolution, which use of hoary Japanese tradition in the emperor's name and invoking of his sublime patronage helped to make more easily palatable, and more a *Japanese* regeneration than the wholesale adoption of Western technology and ideas which in fact it was.

The new Meiji oligarchs were mainly from Satsuma, including Okubo Toshimichi and Saigo Takamori, and from Choshu: Ito Hirobumi, Yamagata Aritomo, and Kido Koin. They were all relatively young, like most rev-

---

✳ The Meiji Spirit ✳

The revival of the emperor cult in Meiji Japan helped the cause of new national unity and sense of purpose, as the following 1868 communication to the throne from a group of the outer daimyo suggests.

There is no soil within the Empire that does not belong to the Emperor ... although in the Middle Ages the Imperial power declined and the military classes rose, taking possession of the land and dividing it among themselves. But now that the Imperial power is restored, how can we retain possession of land that belongs to the Emperor, and govern people who are his subjects? We therefore reverently offer up all our feudal possessions ... so that a uniform rule may prevail throughout the Empire. Thus the country will be able to rank equally with the other nations of the world.

Perhaps the best one-line statement of the mood of early Meiji is, however, the reply given to a German physician who visited Japan in the mid-1870s and asked a Japanese friend about his country's history. He replied:

We have no history. Our history begins today!

Source: R. Storry, *A History of Modern Japan* (London: Penguin, 1982), p. 105; W. W. Lockwood, "Japan's Response to the West," *World Politics*, Vol. 9 (1956): 32.

olutionaries anywhere, and had no stake in or commitment to the existing system. They had despised the old government's weakness and vacillation in the face of foreign pressures, and were scornful of the old guard establishment. Ito Hirobumi, who was to become the most important Meiji statesman, was only 27 in 1868. All of them had relatively humble origins; they could never have risen very high under the old system, but now with the old order suddenly swept away their personal abilities brought them to the top. All of this was part of their radicalism, and of their determination to build a new Japan.

They understood, all too well given the Satsuma and Choshu experiences with foreign retaliation for earlier efforts to defy them, that it was not possible to "expel the barbarians," but at least they could "honor the emperor" and try to build new Western-style strength which could ultimately keep Japan from becoming just another victim of Western imperialism. The "unequal treaties" which had been forced onto Japan as they had earlier on China: special privileges for foreigners, extraterritoriality, and an artificially low tariff of 5 percent on foreign trade, were from the outset more upsetting to Japanese than to Chinese or Thais, and from the early years of Meiji there was determination to bring about the revision of the treaties and an acceptance of Japan as at least a diplomatic equal rather than a "backward" nation which could be treated like an inferior. Chinese pride, even arrogance, about their own glorious past was more than matched by Japanese pride. The crucial difference was that Japanese pride did not include unwillingness to consider for adoption any foreign ideas which were thought to be useful. The long Japanese experience with cultural borrowing from China and Japanese open-mindedness to new ideas whatever their origin was to prove an enormous asset, while China floundered as its traditional system ran down and most Chinese set their minds against using any of the new "barbarian tricks" even to save China from the barbarians. The result was China's decline into weakness and humiliation, while Meiji Japan shot ahead, and by the end of the Meiji era had won treaty revision and taken its place as an equal in the larger family of nations.

The New Order

In the spring of 1868 the new revolutionary government had the emperor declare a "Charter Oath" which laid out Japan's future path. It declared a sharp break with the past, and the abolition of the class distinctions and limitations of the feudal past: "The common people, no less than the civil and military officials (all of whom had been aristocrats) shall each be allowed to pursue his own calling so that there may be no discontent." "Evil customs of the past shall be broken off and everything based on the just laws of Nature." "Deliberative assemblies shall be widely established and all matters decided by public discussion." And most quoted of all, "Knowledge shall be sought throughout the world so as to strengthen the foundations of imperial rule." This last was the prescription for Westernization as the source of strength. Earlier xenophobia and calls to "expel the barbarians" were suppressed, and the few who still pursued such a line were harshly punished. Representatives of foreign governments stationed in Japan were summoned to Kyoto for an audience with the emperor. This was all certainly revolutionary change, brought about with minimal violence or bloodshed.

New organs of administration were cobbled together under a Council of State, and a beginning made to attack the bankrupt financial situation inherited from the Tokugawa *bakufu*. To further mark the change, the capital was moved to Edo, which thus became Tokyo ("eastern capital"), and in May of 1869 the emperor was carried in a sedan chair from Kyoto to Tokyo and installed in Ieyasu's castle there, from then on the imperial palace. There was of course resistance on the part of many of the former *daimyo* domains to losing their previous autonomy to a new central government, but they were at least to begin with unable to act together whereas the new leaders had a coherent and concerted set of plans and a determination to carry them out. Their military forces, with the major support of modernized troops of the *han,* which were most active in pushing for change, had already bested those of the old order in the battles which led up to 1868, and they were clearly in the driver's seat.

They divided the area which had been ruled more or less directly by the Tokugawa into administrative prefectures, and followed this by applying the same system to the old *daimyo han.* This included most importantly the collection of taxes, and in the spring of 1869 the *daimyo* of Satsuma, Choshu, Tosa, and Hizen, whose *samurai* had taken the most prominent part in the overthrow of the Tokugawa, were persuaded to give over their domains to the emperor. By July most of the other *daimyo* had followed suit, anxious not to be left out. By the end of the summer the process was complete; *daimyo* now became simply prefectural governors. Such fundamental change could not of course have happened if sentiment had not been running so strongly in favor of it and in support of this new effort to remake Japan so as to give it the strength to resist a foreign takeover. As leaders in their areas, most *daimyo* saw the change as appropriate and were willing to play their parts in building a new and more effective *national* government.

After establishing at least the beginnings of a financial and taxation base, the first priority was understandably the creation of a new army and navy. This was begun in 1871 with the formation of an Imperial Force manned by 10,000 troops recruited from the former Satsuma, Choshu, and Tosa forces, most of whom had already been trained along Western lines and in the use of Western-style weapons. The new navy, put together at first from the small Tokugawa fleet plus ships from various domains, was dominated by men from Satsuma, while the new army was led mainly by Choshu men under the overall leadership of one of them, Yamagata Aritomo (1838–1922), just returned from a year of study in Europe where he had paid particular attention to military and naval matters. Yamagata prepared a new conscription system and became the first Army Minister.

All fit adult males were now liable for three years of service and four in the reserves, a revolutionary change in itself from the sharp class distinctions of the past where commoners were not even permitted to have weapons. It was a new, largely peasant army, which was to prove highly effective in the years to come. Despite the financial pressures on it, the new government felt it appropriate in effect to pay off the *daimyo* by allowing them to retain one-tenth of the former *han* taxes for their own support, which was more than ample since the central government now carried the full administrative burden of local government. There seems little doubt that this was a calculated generosity designed to dampen protest or possible rebellion, and it may have been influenced in part also by the revolutionaries' awareness that such momentous reversals of tradition and traditional loyalties should not be pushed too far too fast. *Samurai*, far more numerous and amounting to about 6 percent of the total population, were treated somewhat less generously, receiving about two-thirds of the stipends given them in the past. This swollen "gentleman-warrior" class was a legacy of the troubled past of chronic fighting and it amounted to a heavy burden on the rest of society. But the circumstances which had led to its growth were long gone, and it was reasonable to try to ease the *samurai* into more useful occupations, a course which in time most of them took, aided by their literacy and administrative experience.

Financial Problems

Payments to *daimyo* and *samurai* made the already serious financial plight of the new government worse. Some loans for railway building were obtained from Britain, but the Japanese were reluctant to put themselves too much in hock to the very foreigners from whom they were trying to free themselves. It was more palatable to extract loans from the big Japanese merchant firms, and to print more money, as hard-pressed governments everywhere have done, although this of course created new inflation and was especially hard on *samurai* living on already reduced fixed stipends. More important was the revision of the land tax, the chief support of most premodern governments, including the Tokugawa. It was changed from a percentage of yields, which of course varied from year to year and thus made budgeting a problem, to a fixed tax based on the value of the land. A new land survey established ownership, and at the same time cleared away most of the confusion and debris left over from the old feudal system. There had been considerable tenancy before (see Chapter 13), and this now shot up sharply as many peasant cultivators could not meet their tax payments in years of poor harvest and had to become whole or part tenants. By the end of the century tenancy was approaching 50 percent of all farmland. It was mainly agricultural taxes which paid the bill for the modernization of Japan in the Meiji era, as they had for the management of the Tokugawa system. But in time government finances were stabilized enough that it became easier for them to borrow money domestically and without special pressures.

Although they were a far smaller part of the population than the peasantry, the *samurai* contributed to the growing government stability by having their stipends reduced, by finding more constructive careers in both government and business, and in 1876 by being obliged to accept government bonds in place of their former stipends. This left most of them no longer viable economically, unless they could find gainful employment. Those who could not, or could not make the adjustment from entitlement to breadwinning, just merged with the larger population, a change one may say was long overdue. The *daimyo* were given government bonds at the same time instead of the former annual payments, but again their settlements were more generous and many of them invested their new wealth or used it to aid new careers in business and banking. In the same year of 1876 *samurai* were forbidden to wear their swords, for so long the potent symbol of their rank. The sufferings of most peasants seem however far more important. The fixed money tax on land worked great hardship on many of them, and they also saw the new conscription as a further extraction, which they referred to as a "blood tax." It was often disastrous to have a husband and/or son drafted into the army, leaving the family farm critically short of labor and those who remained on it, mainly women, children, and old people, unable to survive, or reduced to a cruelly marginal existence. There had been frequent peasant uprisings under the Tokugawa (Chapter 13) which had greatly increased in its last decades, but these now became far more frequent, and periodically bloody, although they were easily put down by the troops of the determined new government.

Overseas Aggression and the Satsuma Rebellion

It seems remarkable that with all it had on its plate, the new government should decide to embark on military adventurism abroad. Probably in the minds of some this had the appeal it often has to weak governments or those in trouble at home, as a way of drawing attention away from such problems. In the Japanese case, it was also seen as a way to employ some of the now restless *samurai*, and to express Japanese national pride. The absence abroad of many of the cooler heads in the government on a mission to the United States and Europe in 1871–1872 left an opportunity for the leaders remaining at home, especially Saigo Takamori, who had been a Satsuma firebrand in the last days of the Tokugawa, to plan a punitive expedition to Korea. The mission to the West returned in time to cancel that plan, resulting in Saigo's angry resignation, and to substitute a less dangerous expedition to the Ryukyu Islands where Okinawa lies, and to Taiwan. The Ryukyus had been part of the Satsuma domains which had been taken over by the new government in 1872, and the government chose to make an issue out of the killing of 64 shipwrecked sailors from the Ryukyus by the aborigines on the east coast of Taiwan in 1871. The punitive expedition to Taiwan was successful, but got the Japanese in trouble with China, who had earlier claimed the Ryukyus as tributary and was also sovereign in Taiwan. The Chinese, now greatly weakened under Western domination, accepted in effect Japan's claims to the Ryukyus and even paid an indemnity for the costs of the expedition to Taiwan. The Korean affair was settled Perry-style by a Japanese naval demonstration which forced Korea to open two ports to Japanese trade in 1876, in addition to Pusan where Japanese traders were already established.

But these expeditions could not employ most of the *samurai*, and in any case lasted only briefly, while the financial pinch continued to affect the majority. Mutinies began to break out in Choshu and Kyushu, but it was in Satsuma that the most serious rebellion occurred. When Saigo resigned from the central government in 1873 many of the Satsuma *samurai* went home with him. Early in 1877 they and others around him urged him to take the leadership of a genuine rebellion. The new government was obliged to confront this serious threat and there was hard fighting, ending with the defeat of the Satsuma forces by the new peasant army of Japan with its modern weapons, and the wounded Saigo asked to be beheaded by a comrade. The Satsuma Rebellion, as it is called, was the only major challenge to the new government, and once it was suppressed the way was cleared for continuing fundamental change. Clearly the issue of government bonds in 1876 in lieu of the former *samurai* stipends had left too many bitterly discontented; many also deeply regretted the abolition of the old social system which had put them and the *daimyo* at the top, and now opened careers to formerly despised commoners. The new opportunities for careers in business and government were not attractive to some, perhaps most, of this formerly privileged class not accustomed to the new work ethic in a society which to them had been turned on its head.

Economic Development

To complete the goals of "rich country, strong army," the Meiji leaders of course understood that the Japanese economy would have to grow and develop rapidly, especially in industry which could support the military. There the new government took the lead in starting and subsidizing heavy industries such as iron, steel, armaments, and shipbuilding, all along Western lines, carrying most of the original heavy expense and then later turning the management and ownership of these new enterprises over to private corporations at highly favorable rates. Such sweetheart deals did however tend to make corporations the loyal partners of government and helped to ensure that private and public sectors would work closely together toward the common goals. This partnership was the origin of the *zaibatsu* (corporate industrial/financial conglomerates) and their ties with the state, and the rise of the giant Mitsubishi firm, which now took its place with earlier originated firms like Sumitomo and Mitsui (see Chapter 13). Mitsubishi began its rise as a steamship company heavily subsidized by the government; its growth to dominance in the sea trade with China and then across the Pacific as the N.Y.K. (Nippon Yusen Kaisha) line, rising in time above most Western competition, resulted in part from the major boost provided by purchase from the government of the Nagasaki shipyards, the largest in the country, for far less than their value.

The government felt an equal urgency about the need to build modern internal communications, given their primitive state as of 1868. This too, especially railway building, was thought to be too expensive to expect private firms to undertake it, and as pointed out provided one of the few occasions for seeking foreign loans. The first rail line, between Tokyo and Yokohama (now in effect Tokyo's outport for deep-draught shipping) opened in 1872, and the analogous line from Kobe to Osaka in 1874, extended to Kyoto in 1877. By 1880 all major cities had also been linked by telegraph lines and a postal system. Roads remained few and crude, and indeed were still so into the 1950s, but all the important parts of the country were easily and cheaply connected by sea routes. The infrastructure thus laid down by the

A Japanese wood-block print of about 1860, showing an American ship in the harbor of Yokohama. (Chadbourne Collection, Library of Congress)

National Effort

Far more important in explaining the success of the Meiji drive for development was the very widespread understanding on the part of nearly all Japanese that it was urgently necessary for the country's defense and its escape from the humiliation of the unequal treaties. It was truly a national effort, aided of course by Japan's small size, the concentration of its population, the long tradition of direction by those on top, the new national administration even in local areas, and the rapid spread of communications, including the blossoming of the periodical press. Decisions reached in Tokyo were quickly announced everywhere in the country and rapidly and enthusiastically acted on, a totally different situation from China's with its vast distances, regional differences, and still politically uninvolved masses, under a government whose authority was now rapidly disintegrating. It was Japanese nationalism, its equivalent lacking so late in China, and the national commitment to hard work as a patriotic duty, which more than any other single factor explains the seeming miracle of Meiji Japan and its amazingly successful effort to lift the country by its own bootstraps.

The major exception, once the Satsuma Rebellion had been defeated, was peasant resentment of the taxes which bore so heavily on them, exemplified in the continuing rash of rural revolts. Resentment against conscription remained also, but in time the new peasant soldiers began to acquire their own pride in the army which they dominated numerically, and in its achievements as Japan's power began to make itself felt in East Asia. And despite peasant hardships, agricultural production had about doubled by the end of the century, thanks to government sponsorship of new irrigation, rising use of fertilizer, the beginnings of research producing better varieties of crops, the reclamation of new land from coastal areas, and the development of an extension service which continuously promoted all of these innovations. Development was masterminded from the top, but had its grass roots aspect as well, and rural Japan was organized and ready to apply new ideas in a way which most developing countries lacked and many still lack.

government, plus the building of new banking facilities to expedite commerce, a tax system which was relatively easy on business, and the development of a sound currency system, underlay the boom development of industrialization as the government began to hand over more and more enterprises to private ownership on give-away terms which ensured their continued loyalty. The giant *zaibatsu* firms were later to be targets of American criticism as the villains of Japanese imperialism and handmaidens of the expansionist Japanese government, but in the Meiji environment this private-public partnership made good sense and clearly accelerated Japan's development, allowing the most efficient firms and combinations to rise to the top, with government help.

Industrialization

In what was becoming a boom economy in heavy industry and railways, there was also new opportunity for small entrepreneurs, in traditional consumer goods, commercial cropping and marketing, and even foreign trade, most importantly silk, still largely a peasant and household operation. A Ministry of Industry was established in 1870 which encouraged private industrial and

Directions

In 1868, the boy emperor Meiji was given by the new reformers a document to sign which became known as the "Charter Oath." Although its five articles are rather general, more like exhortations than decrees, they do fit both the mood of the new Japan and the course which it took.

"Article 1. Deliberative assemblies shall be widely established and all matters decided by public discussion.

Article 2. All classes, high and low, shall unite in vigorously carrying out the administration of the affairs of state.

Article 3. The common people, no less than the civil and military officials, shall each be allowed to pursue his own calling so that there may be no discontent.

Article 4. Evil customs of the past shall be broken off and everything based upon the just laws of Nature.

Article 5. Knowledge shall be sought throughout the world so as to strengthen the foundation of imperial rule."

Source: Quoted in W.S. Morton, *Japan: Its History and Culture.* (New York: McGraw-Hill, 1994), pp. 149–150.

commercial development but which also developed modern-style coal and iron mines and built cement, glass, and brick factories. As in the West, textiles were the first consumer industry to prosper on a large scale: relatively easy and cheap to construct for producing a commodity, cloth and clothing, in universal use which could be made and sold at a relatively low price. Unfortunately, Western machine-made textiles were far in the lead and given the artificially low tariff easily invaded the Japanese market. Here was another case for government support and subsidy: state-owned factories to begin with, and low-interest loans to private entrepreneurs. The machinery had to be imported from Britain and the United States, but in time Japanese production drew even in quality and price, especially for the bottom end of the market, and by the end of the century had largely replaced foreign imports while at the same time invading markets in China and Southeast Asia.

Raw cotton too had to be imported, but silk was a domestic product, relatively easily improved by the development of steam filatures to unwind cocoons and wind the thread into hanks or reels. Most of this was done by the private sector, although there were some government loans, and careful state supervision to ensure uniform quality and to prevent the spread of diseased silkworm eggs which had badly damaged the Chinese silk industry. Japanese silk largely replaced Chinese in export markets as a result of such measures, and by the 1880s was earning over two-fifths of the country's precious foreign exchange. About the same time other Japanese exports, and the profits from the carrying trade, began to exceed imports and Japan was solvent in these terms at last.

Not so, alas, in domestic terms. The Meiji government had begun behind financially, and was then saddled with the maintenance of *daimyo* and *samurai*. Many of the vital industries started by the state were losing propositions, as is so often the case in the start-up stage, and the large military buildup was of course a dead loss economically. Issue of more paper money produced inflation, which hurt nearly everyone, as rice prices doubled and land values, which determined taxes, were debased. In 1880 a drastic series of measures began to deal with this crisis, beginning with the sale of all government industries to private interests except for those considered "strategic." They were made over at very low prices, despite the government's need, because it was well known that they had been losers and prospective buyers were few. The lucky buyers, most with existing government as well as *zaibatsu* connections, went on to reap handsome profits later as the industrialization boom resumed and the economy as a whole recovered its buoyancy and by the end of the 1880s bounded ahead again. But before that time the

The Japanese were quick to portray the Westerners who had forced their way into the country; like the Chinese, the Japanese clearly saw Westerners as savages. Here is an 1854 representation of Commodore Perry. (Smithsonian Institution)

government had put its financial house in order. The businessmen who benefited so largely from these transactions, including the giant *zaibatsu* firms, shared the patriotism which was so widespread a feature of Meiji Japan. They were not in it only for money, but felt they too had an important role to play in the building of national strength, and their managerial skills did make a contribution.

In 1876, as a reflection of new government confidence and financial solvency, the land tax was reduced; this lowered the risk of further peasant revolts, although they did occur, but also resulted in increased rural prosperity and the expansion of a number of rural nonagricultural enterprises. Osaka became the chief center of the modern machine cotton spinning and weaving industry. Kyoto, Osaka, Tokyo, and then other cities began in the 1890s to electrify lighting systems and to operate electric streetcars. A big new government iron and steel plant at Yawata in northern Kyushu, close to local coal

deposits, opened in 1901, producing fearful pollution but celebrated by the local residents as a proud symbol of "progress," as in the municipal "anthem":

> *Billows of smoke filling the sky,*
> *Our steel plant, a grandeur unmatched;*
> *O Yawata, Yawata, our city.*

The first major case of industrial pollution was the Ashio copper mine and refinery owned and operated by Sumitomo on a river in the mountains about 60 miles north of Tokyo. The mine had operated under the Tokugawa, but Sumitomo greatly expanded operations in 1870 and by 1880 toxic discharges were poisoning fish in the river; at the end of the decade rice crops irrigated from the river were poisoned too, and many of those who ate the rice. Local protests were ignored until 1901, when the central government ordered an investigation, but no action was taken to correct the problem. Some of the victims were offered token compensation by Sumitomo, in a pattern which was to become the dominant response to pollution, until the about-face of the 1970s.

Westernization

To begin with, the Japanese were not sure which aspects of the Western system had produced the Western strength they now sought to emulate for themselves, and so they tended to uncritically adopt all of Western culture, including clothing, diet, music, and manners. But part of the background was also their desire to be acceptable to Westerners and to be acknowledged as "civilized." As Sir George Sansom put it, they suffered from "a nervous dread of ridicule," so easily invited by their understandable clumsiness in manipulating things which were wholly strange to them. The diplomatic service adopted the striped trousers and cutaway coats then fashionable in Europe, and retained them until quite recently, while most other Japanese wore Western suits at least by day, though changing into more familiar and comfortable *kimono* once they got home. Most women stuck with their traditional kimono dress, but for fashionable occasions some wore the elaborate Western dresses of the time, and in the next century Western dresses became more widespread. The earlier Buddhist-induced vegetarianism gave way to meat eating, Western style, including the dish invented in this period called *sukiyaki*, centered around thin strips of beef boiled with vegetables. Public and domestic architecture of the time reflected the Victorian modes of the West.

A high priority was given to legal reform so that Westerners would not feel outraged by Japanese legal procedures and would be willing to give up their extraterritorial rights. The new law code, based mainly on

French and German models, was finally put in practice by 1896; judicial use of torture had been abolished 20 years earlier. One Western thing the Japanese refused to adopt was Christianity, but now Japan, like China, was invaded by missionaries, the first in 1859, who did somewhat better than in China and in time made converts of as many as 3 percent of the population, although this did not happen until the 1920s and was clearly related to Japanese admiration of Western culture in general. Meanwhile there was an official revival of Shinto as an obvious vehicle for Japanese nationalism, a state religion, including the cult of emperor worship. The newly reorganized education system incorporated daily bowing to a portrait of the emperor and periodic readings of his supposed pronouncements, which were actually the work of government officials.

Nevertheless, the main trend was away from any form of religion and toward spreading secularism. In keeping with the original Charter Oath of 1868 and its call to "seek knowledge throughout the world," large numbers of officials and students were sent abroad, and foreign experts brought to Japan as advisers in industrial and technological enterprises, including medicine. The chief promoter of Western knowledge was Fukuzawa Yukichi (1835–1901), who after study abroad founded in Edo even before 1868 a school which later became Keio University. He reached still more people through his writings, in which he extolled the institutions of the West. It was Fukuzawa who best articulated what many Japanese felt about the avalanche of Westernization transforming their country as they thought

for its own good: "If we use it, that will make it Japanese." A great many Western works, of all sorts, were translated into Japanese. The Imperial Tokyo University was founded in 1869 and soon became the country's premier institution, producing elite graduates for the foreign service and other branches of government. Other government universities followed, at Kyoto and elsewhere. Compulsory education for the first six grades, run according to a uniform centrally administered plan and with many Western-style subjects, had reached 95 percent of the population by 1905, and Japan soon became the world's most literate and best-educated society. Missionary and other private schools also grew, some to become universities such as Doshisha in Kyoto and Waseda in Tokyo. An Imperial Rescript on Education of 1890, also read aloud in the schools, stressed the importance of social harmony as urged by Confucius, and of loyalty to the emperor, and was followed by the return to the curriculum of Japanese and Chinese history, literature, and philosophy, appropriately enough. But the trend was toward education as indoctrination.

Western-style institutions of representative government were, somewhat reluctantly given Japan's past traditions, included in the plans for a new Japan, partly to impress the foreigners with Japan's progress toward the Western model, partly because for all the Japanese knew this might be part of the basis of Western strength. Despite the Charter Oath's promise of "deliberative assemblies," the government moved slowly. Already in the 1870s something like parties or "societies" had formed which criticized the government's absolutism, and in

The "iron horse" in Japan: early Meiji wood-block artists were fascinated by the new railways, as most Japanese were intrigued with the artifacts of the modern West that flooded into their country. (Asian Art Museum, San Francisco)

1875 the leaders prompted the emperor to issue a vague promise that eventually there would be a national assembly, while others pressed for a constitution. The first step taken was the creation of elected prefectural assemblies, which began to meet in 1879, although with an electorate limited to taxpaying males. Political ideas were widely discussed in the press, but some of this talk worried the government and it moved to prevent press attacks and later to limit public gatherings. In 1887 the government issued a "Peace Preservation Law" giving itself the right to expel from the capital anyone considered a "threat to public tranquillity," which was not defined and left the government virtually unlimited powers to deal with its critics. The parties which had formed collapsed under this blow.

The Meiji Constitution

The leaders realized that they would have to make some concessions, and asked Ito Hirobumi to chair a constitutional commission. In 1885 Ito replaced the former Council of State with a Western-style cabinet and himself became prime minister. Perhaps more significantly and a more radical departure from Japan's aristocratic past, an examination system for recruitment to the civil service was adopted in 1887. Ito's commission finally produced a constitution announced in 1889, which called for a national assembly in the following year and a two-house parliament called the Diet (the term is Western in origin, meaning "a political assembly"). The upper house, or House of Peers, was composed largely of high-ranking nobles, as in the British system, plus some other aristocrats and imperial appointees. The peers had in fact been created only in 1884 with this forthcoming constitution in mind, and were given ranked titles of prince, marquis, count, viscount, and baron, taken from those used in Chou China; most of these newly created peers were former *daimyo*, but they included the Meiji oligarchs too, who kept promoting themselves in rank; Ito became Prince Ito. It was of course an effort, however quaint (and was the object of some Western derision), to incorporate in the new order

The Meiji Constitution

The hurriedly drawn up constitution of 1868 was designed to make the Charter Oath more specific, which Article 1 of the Constitution merely restates. Most of the other articles echo Western models, at least in part to make a favorable impression on the imperialist powers and to hasten the time when they might give up their "Unequal Treaties." The following is a selection.

Article 2. All power and authority in the empire shall be vested in a Council of state, and thus the grievances of divided government shall be done away with. The power and authority of the Council of State shall be three-fold: legislative, executive, and judicial. Thus the imbalance of authority among the different branches of government shall be avoided.

Article 4. Attainment to offices of the first rank shall be limited to princes of the blood, court nobles, and territorial lords and shall be by virtue of (the emperor's) intimate trust in the great ministers of state.

Article 5. Each great city, clan, and imperial prefecture shall furnish qualified men to be members of the Assembly. A deliberative body shall be instituted so that the views of the people may be discussed openly.

Article 9. All officials shall be changed after four years' service. They shall be selected by means of public balloting. However, at the first expiration of terms hereafter, half of the officials shall retain office for two additional years ... so that the government may be caused to continue without interruption.

Source: Quoted in R. Tsunoda et al., eds., *Sources of Japanese Tradition,* Vol. II. (New York: Columbia University Press, 1958), pp. 137–138.

at least a gesture toward Japan's hierarchical, hereditary, aristocratic past. Most political power came to be exercised by the lower house, chosen by an electorate limited to adult male property owners, who were little more than 1 percent of the population. It was thus a highly qualified step in the direction of representative democracy, but the Diet as a whole had to approve the budget and freedom of speech and assembly were promised, "within limits not prejudicial to peace and order," a hedging in favor of the state which was to remain the basis of growing arbitrary power.

The emperor was also declared "sacred and inviolable," and was given supreme command of the army and navy, and the power to dissolve the Diet whenever he (really of course the government leaders) considered it desirable. The provision that the ministers of war and the navy must be serving generals and admirals was announced in an imperial decree shortly after the promulgation of the constitution, a move in which one can detect the strong hand of Yamagata, father of the new army, who had earlier insisted that the chiefs of staff were wholly independent of the civil government and acted only under the command of the emperor. Thus was foreshadowed the increasingly disastrous domination of government by the military, which put Japan on the path to Nanking, Pearl Harbor, and Hiroshima. The Meiji oligarchs were pragmatists, and perhaps judged correctly that Japan was not yet ready for and would not support a more legitimate form of democracy than the token form represented in the constitution.

This may have been so, but the leaders were clearly strongly authoritarian in persuasion; some, like Yamagata, more so than others, but as a group determined to safeguard government against popular opposition, and the military against even government efforts to control it. The legacy of this Meiji establishment of governmental forms, and the overtones clearly hinted at, was to be the ruin of Japan. Unfortunately but understandably, Japan's string of military successes beginning in 1894–1895 against China attracted strong popular support and tended to dampen down opposition. This was part of the goal the whole country had worked so hard for, and the fruits of victory in national pride were sweet.

Japanese Imperialism

Westerners are not, however, in a good position to criticize Japan for picking up from them the disease of imperialism (see Chapter 14) or for following their model in imposing their rule on other countries. Japanese had long had what one may call troubled relations with Korea, and as Japanese strength increased it was perhaps understandable that they should look there with newly ambitious eyes. Yamagata and some of his colleagues had clearly felt that it was part of the new Japan's destiny to express its strength in East Asia, and it will be remembered that as early as 1872 there were plans to invade Korea, and an actual expedition to Taiwan in 1874, followed by an expedition to Korea in 1876 to open Korean ports to Japanese trade. Korea was still a Chinese tributary, and China felt that it was responsible for whatever happened there. In 1882 an antiforeign mob attacked the newly established Japanese legation in Seoul, and both China and Japan sent troops. Two years later there was open fighting between the two sets of troops. Li Hung-chang and Ito Hirobumi agreed in 1885 at Tientsin in what was called the Li-Ito Convention that both countries would withdraw their troops and would notify each other before sending them back.

China was now at last trying to build up its military forces with Western weapons; Li was prominent in supporting the building of modern arsenals and of a modern navy, with ships bought abroad and constructed in Chinese shipyards. In 1894 a popular rebellion with earlier origins as the Tonghak movement broke out again in Korea, which was strongly antiforeign. The Korean king, against whom the revolt was aimed, requested help from China, but Japan sent a much larger force which seized control of the Korean government and forced it to declare war on China, which of course provoked a war between China and Japan. To Western surprise, the Japanese army routed the Chinese forces, occupied the whole of Korea, and moved on to invade Manchuria. The war at sea was even more disastrous for China. Its fleet was larger, but poorly supplied and led. Many of the shells did not fit the guns, and many of those which did were found to have been filled with sand by corrupt contractors. The admiral was a former cavalry commander who led his ships out in a line abreast like a cavalry charge. The Japanese ships were new too and were well supplied and led using modern Western naval tactics; they easily sank a large part of the Chinese fleet in a battle off the Korean west coast and damaged or routed the rest. It was a bitter humiliation, at the hands of an upstart country which had always been seen as a dutiful pupil, or at least as a sort of cousin within the East Asian family, albeit one long looked down on as less civilized, inhabited by "hairy sea dwarfs" and pirates. The victorious Japanese dictated the terms of the Treaty of Shiminoseki which ended the war, in a conference held of course on Japanese soil, and among other provisions extracted a heavy indemnity from China which was three times the annual income of Peking.

Nearly all Japanese were jubilant. The "Yamato race" had proved its superiority, and the new strength built by the Meiji leaders and by all the Japanese working together had paid off. Japanese dreams of their rightful dominance in East Asia were given new stimulus. Power always tempts those who have it to use it, and often provides its own justification, as Westerners justified their own use of power in the cause of "right" and the spreading of "civilization" as well as the glorification of aggression and the survival of the fittest. All of these delusions now fastened themselves on the Japanese mind, and at the same time encouraged them to see China, not inaccurately, as in decline from its former greatness, no longer either a model of superiority or a legitimate contender for the leadership of East Asia which it had aspired to in the past. China was increasingly now seen as "backward," "dirty," disorganized, and ineffective. Most Japanese felt that it was time for the Chinese to take a backseat and leave the leadership and the model behavior to Japan. Japan was in fact a far more appropriate model for Korea, which had tried to close itself off from all foreign contact while Japan had forged ahead through the use of Western ideas. Korea became from 1895 a Japanese sphere though nominally independent (i.e., from China), and was taken over as part of the Japanese empire in 1910. The Treaty of Shiminoseki, dictated by Japan, also gave it sovereignty over Taiwan and the nearby Pescadore Islands as part of the spoils of victory; this provided further scope for the application of the Japanese model of successful development, and fed new Japanese national/imperial pride.

Already the Japanese had their eye on Manchuria, next door to Korea, and the treaty granted them sovereignty also in the Liaotung peninsula of southern Manchuria, which they wanted for both commercial and strategic reasons; Port Arthur, built up by the Chinese near the tip of the peninsula (often referred to in Japan as Kwantung) was a valuable naval base within easy range of the China coast and occupying one edge of the Gulf of Pohai with Tientsin, the port of Peking, on its other (western) shore. A fleet based at Port Arthur could seal off access to north China and blockade much of the entire coast, while, adjacent Dairen (Talien), already a treaty port, was a valuable commercial base. But the Western powers, including Russia, were alarmed at Japan's astonishing success and its sudden grab of territory, especially of course its attempted intrusion into Manchuria, a Russian sphere of expansion ever since the Treaty of Tientsin in 1860. The Russians persuaded the Germans and the French soon after the Treaty of Shiminoseki was signed to "advise" Japan to give up Liaotung. Faced with such pressure, Japan was obliged to do so, but accepted a considerable increase in the indemnity, paid of course by China, which was still supposedly sovereign in Manchuria but was not involved in the Russian-German-French move known as the Triple Intervention. There was massive popular indignation in Japan over this "humiliation." The Emperor told his people that they must "endure the unendurable," a phrase which was repeated by his grandson Emperor Hirohito when he announced Japan's surrender to the Allies in 1945.

The British were not part of the Triple Intervention, and were later in 1902 to sign their own pact of friendship and alliance with Japan. But there was angry resentment against Russia, Germany, and France, many of whose institutions and culture had been faithfully copied by the Japanese and their countries respected. Now they were despised as hypocrites and oppressors. Within three years Russia took over Liaotung and Port Arthur, the Germans seized Tsingtao (Qingdao) in Shantung, the French Kuangchou Bay south of Canton, the British Wei-hai-wei in Shantung (which had originally been part of the Japanese claims), and the United States the Philippines and Hawaii. Japan had always feared Russia as a powerful and expansionist neighbor, and its plans for Manchuria conflicted head-on with Japanese plans.

Having denied it to Japan, Russia's new control of Kwantung (Liaotung) was followed by expansion of its de facto control in the rest of Manchuria with mining and railway rights. Much of this new imperialist grabbing was part of the fever pitch of the disease, at a time when China seemed largely defenseless. The Japanese defeat of China revealed Peking's weakness, and stimulated a new round of demands for additional concessions to the Western powers, as above. Western aggressiveness was accelerated by the Boxer Rebellion in 1900 when Chinese mobs with tacit imperial support besieged the foreign legations in Peking and were finally driven off only by an allied expedition, which included Japanese troops as about half of the total allied force. China was forced to pay yet another indemnity and Peking was occupied by foreign troops, the largest contingent of them Japanese.

It was understandable for the Japanese to conclude from all this experience that force was a very effective instrument of foreign policy, and in any case the army and the navy were now riding high. The British had noticed with grudging approval the military performance of the Japanese in 1894 and 1900, including their brilliant use of the ships bought from Britain, and they shared with Japan a deep concern about Russian expansion in Manchuria and their evident designs on Korea as well as on Britain's leading economic and diplomatic position in China. In 1902 the two countries signed an Anglo-Japanese alliance of mutual support; Japan accepted the existing treaty system in China, and Britain acknowledged that Japan had a special interest in Korea. This was Japan's first agreement with a Western power on equal terms, and it gave a great boost to morale, while reassuring the Japanese that if they attacked Russia the Western powers would remain "benevolently neutral."

✠ On Education ✠

The Imperial Rescript on Education of 1890 was much cited, and was regularly read aloud in the schools. Many Meiji officials contributed to its content and wording.

Know Ye, Our subjects: Our imperial ancestors have founded Our Empire on a basis broad and everlasting, and have deeply and firmly implanted virtue.... This is the glory of the fundamental character of Our Empire.... Ye, Our subjects, be filial to your parents, affectionate to your brothers and sisters; as husbands and wives be harmonious, as friends true; bear yourselves in modesty and moderation.... Pursue learning and cultivate the arts and thereby develop intellectual faculties and perfect moral powers; furthermore, advance public good and promote common interests; always respect the Constitution and observe the laws. Should emergency arise, offer yourselves courageously to the State, and thus guard and maintain the prosperity of our Imperial Throne coeval with heaven and earth. So shall ye not only be Our good and faithful subjects, but render illustrious the best traditions of your forefathers.

Source: Quoted in R. Tsunoda et al., eds., *Sources of Japanese Tradition*, Vol. II. (New York: Columbia University Press), 1958, pp. 139–140.

Conflict with Russia

The Russians had already advised the Japanese against building any fortifications on the Korean south coast, which could threaten Russian communications between Vladivostok, their Pacific naval base, and Port Arthur. The Japanese were incensed, and it increased their conviction that they would have to drive the Russians out of Manchuria and Korea. Ito seems to have been prepared to accept a Russian sphere in Manchuria, which they were already rapidly developing, in exchange for a Japanese sphere in Korea, but Yamagata and the cabinet which he then dominated were adamantly opposed and already planning to strike against the Russians. The Anglo-Japanese alliance fed Japanese national pride, and helped to make up for the "humiliation" of the Tripartite Intervention seven years earlier. After less than 50 years since Perry's "opening" of Japan, they had been accepted as an equal, and there was widespread celebration. It seemed that the Meiji government could not put a foot wrong.

The episode—it was not much more than that since it lasted only some 18 months—of the Russo-Japanese war was however what finally solidified Japan's position with the Western powers, and established it as an international power in its own right. Russia was probably the greatest land power in the world, especially with its huge army and industrial base, and it had besides a formidable fleet. When the Japanese attacked in 1904 most

Westerners assumed they had sealed their own doom. They caught the Russians off guard by attacking Port Arthur, sinking Russian ships on the Korean west coast, and occupying Seoul, the Korean capital, without a declaration of war, as they had done in 1894 and were to do again at Pearl Harbor in 1941, moves which obviously had to have been launched some days earlier and been long in the planning. Only after these first victories were complete did the Japanese declare war. Their armies then went on to besiege Port Arthur and to fight their way up the rail line from there to Mukden, the provincial capital of Manchuria. They lost 60,000 men at Port Arthur, and another 40,000 in the subsequent battle for Mukden; clearly they were willing to take heavy casualties, including the use of "human torpedoes" by volunteers who carried torpedo-shaped land mines and exploded them against the walls of Port Arthur. Port Arthur finally surrendered early in 1905 after an eight month siege; Mukden was taken by mid-March.

At sea the Japanese fleet bottled up the Russians in Port Arthur, after some losses, and then intercepted a Russian fleet sent out from home, which had had a long and difficult journey around Africa (the British had closed the Suez Canal to them). By the time the Russian ships reached Japanese waters marine growths on the hulls had slowed their speed, reduced their maneuverability, and left them low on food, water, and fuel. The Japanese admiral Togo met them in the Straits of Tsushima between Korea and Japan and sank all but two of them. The British were pleased at the performance of the Japanese navy, most of whose ships had been built in British shipyards and their officers trained or advised by the Royal Navy.

A week later the Japanese asked the American president Roosevelt to arrange a peace treaty with the Russians. A peace conference was held at Portsmouth, New Hampshire, and the treaty signed there recognized Japan's "paramount interests" in Korea, transferred to Japan the Russian rights in Kwantung (Liaotung) and the railway to the north, and ceded the southern half of Sakhalin, the island just north of Hokkaido, which the Japanese called Karafuto, together with special fishing rights. It was sweeping victory, and yet there was widespread indignation in Japan, where most people felt that Japan had not obtained what it deserved, especially in indemnity. The foreign minister, Komura, who had negotiated the Treaty of Portsmouth, had to hide from outraged assassins. On the radical side, groups which had courageously opposed the war and continued to hold antiwar rallies in Tokyo had 12 of their leaders executed in 1911, accused on the flimsiest "evidence" of plotting to kill the emperor. Others fled or died in prison.

In fact, the costs of the war had left Japan bankrupt and scraping the bottom of the manpower barrel, although the public was told none of this. The Russians were willing to settle also because they were having to confront at home in 1904–1905 the stirrings of revolution which was eventually to topple the Czarist regime. The war was generally unpopular and very expensive. Nevertheless the Russians had completed the last short link of the Trans-Siberian railway by 1905 and had earlier finished the rail link through Manchuria known as the Chinese Eastern Railway direct to Vladivostok with its southern branch to Mukden and Port Arthur. In time their far greater resources would have crushed the Japanese, who were lucky to escape as well as they did. But the early Japanese victories against the Russians astounded the world, and won them full acceptance as a great power. The British and the Americans saw Japan as an apt pupil who made all the right moves on the basis of Western teaching and example, and also as heaven-sent deliverers against the growing Russian threat to the British position in China, which implied a disruption of the multipower sharing of China's semicolonial domination. In 1899 and 1900 the Americans had issued two successive "Open Door" notes in which they tried, without much success, to get the other powers to agree to oppose the domination of China by any one of them and to keep trade open to all comers on an equal basis. Russian expansionism, its military power, and its location right next door to China, seemed to threaten all of this. The Japanese were thus cast as the saviors for the Anglo-American position, although a few saw their sudden rise as presaging trouble in the future.

Japan in Korea

The war had been fought in part over Korea, and before it was over the Japanese consolidated their hold there by forcing the Koreans to accept Japanese diplomatic and financial "advisers." In 1905 the Korean king was obliged to make over control of the country's foreign affairs to a Japanese Resident-General, a position filled by Ito Hirobumi. Understandable Korean reluctance to cooperate with this violation of their sovereignty led to new Japanese demands that they should approve all executive and legislative actions; the king abdicated and was succeeded by a crown prince who was more compliant. The Korean army was disbanded but there was massive and repeated rioting, which the Japanese brutally suppressed. Yamagata pressed for outright annexation of Korea, but Ito argued that Japan could and should try to win the Koreans over to the Japanese model of development. Nevertheless Korea was already in effect a Japanese colony, and they were of course bitterly resented. Faced with opposition at home to his policy of tact, Ito resigned in 1909, and later in the same year was assassinated by a Korean patriot. This gave Tokyo the pretext for complete annexation they had been looking for, and in 1910 Korea was declared to be an integral part of the new Japanese empire.

The heady atmosphere created in Japan by the victories over China and Russia further strengthened the prestige and dominance of the military in all aspects of Japanese life. General Nogi and Admiral Togo, the chief army and navy commanders against the Russians, became widely popular national heroes, revered in the schools and by the general public. A number of ultranationalist societies were formed in this period, most well known among them the Black Dragon Society (a translation of the Chinese characters for the Amur River), as pressure groups pushing for a more aggressive policy of expansion abroad and with close army connections. Japanese politics had long been marred by the assassination of political leaders whose policies displeased such groups, somewhat in the same way as late Tokugawa hotheads among the *samurai* had felt that the only acceptable response to foreigners on the sacred soil of Japan was to kill them. Assassination now became an all-too-common way for the new societies of superpatriots to eliminate politicians who did not conform to their ideas, and of course to use such acts as a threat to others. When the Meiji emperor died in 1912, General Nogi, accompanied by his wife, committed ritual hara-kiri; his will made it clear that this was to remind Japanese of the old *bushi* code and to condemn what he felt was happening in Japanese society as people were pursuing their own pleasure instead of sacrificing themselves to their national duty. The new emperor took the reign title of Taisho, but proved to be mentally deficient and most of his functions were in time performed instead by his son as a formal regent.

World War I

The Anglo-Japanese alliance of 1902 brought Japan into the First World War on the Allied side, but other considerations of their own immediate interest were clearly more compelling. The Germans had obtained from China the concession of the port of Tsingtao and some area around it in Shantung (Shandong) in 1898, plus railway building and mining rights. Japan moved immediately to take over the German position, and included German colonial property in the form of several strategic islands in the Pacific. There was sharp fighting against German resistance in Shantung, but the German forces were entirely cut off and the outcome was never in doubt. Shantung had long been part of the Japanese plans for East Asia, and they rationalized this power grab partly because the Germans had become enemies, and partly on the basis of the growing feeling that China was hopelessly backward and disorganized and that younger brother Japan should show its elder brother the way to "progress"; most Japanese came to believe that Japan, given its brilliant success, had somehow acquired the "right" to straighten out China.

The Japanese played no other significant role in the First World War, which was after all fought primarily in Europe, apart from sending a few destroyers to join the British Mediterranean fleet as a token of their support. What remained of a government in China (see Chapter 17) also, somewhat later, declared war against Germany and its allies, and sent a labor battalion of 200,000 men to support the bloody fighting in France, digging trenches and acting as a supply corps. Chinese felt that this should entitle them to Allied consideration when the war was over. Meanwhile, Japan reaped a golden harvest in trade and its stimulus to domestic industry as well as shipping, with Western competition largely removed as the European powers bled each other to death and focused all their efforts and resources on that struggle. In 1915 the Japanese government, in secret negotiations with the warlord regime in Peking, presented a list of 21 Demands, which would have turned China into a virtual Japanese colony. In addition to control of Shantung, Manchuria, the southeast coast of China Proper, and the Yangtze valley, the demands included the stationing of Japanese "advisers" in all branches of the national government and the requirement that China buy at least half of its munitions from Japan. There was an outpouring of

The first modern Japanese embassy abroad, sent by the Tokugawa to Washington and shown here in the navy yard there in 1860 with their American hosts. Notice that the Japanese are all dressed in *samurai* outfits, complete with swords. (Bettmann Archive)

Chinese popular anger and most of the provincial governors urged the then president, Yuan Shih-k'ai, to resist, but under renewed Japanese pressure he accepted most of the demands without consulting the legislature. Later the Japanese persuaded Russia, Britain, France, Italy, and the United States to recognize the 21 Demands, although the U.S. endorsement was vague and spoke only of Japan's "special position" in China.

At the peace conference at Versailles in 1919, Japan was given a seat at the table, while the Chinese delegation was excluded, despite Wilson's declaration of "self-determination of nations" and "open covenants, openly arrived at." They were however shown a secret agreement signed in 1918 by the then government in Peking in return for a Japanese loan whereby Japanese paramountcy in Shantung was accepted. This was to be the trigger of mass demonstrations in China and the first organized expression on a large scale of Chinese nationalism in the May Fourth movement of 1919 (see Chapter 17). But meanwhile Japan was riding high. The Russian Revolution of 1917 had been followed by civil war there, and in the general fear of communism elsewhere, the victorious Allies, including the United States, sent troops to Siberia and the Russian Far East to help the loyalist or "White" forces put down the Revolution. The Japanese sent 75,000 troops, three times the number sent by all of the Allies, and occupied Vladivostok and the eastern parts of the Trans-Siberian Railway. When the cause began to seem hopeless, the Allies withdrew their troops in 1919 but the Japanese remained until essentially forced out by the Western powers in 1922.

At home, war-caused inflation attendant on the economic boom hurt many people, especially since wages did not rise significantly, and rice riots broke out in cities, towns, and villages which had to be put down with army troops. A law of 1900 outlawed strikes, but urban riots among factory workers were often violent. Most Japanese remained relatively poor, and military glory was not enough to sustain them. Rice yields continued to increase, but taxes and tenant rents were heavy. The majority of factory labor was still peasant girls sent to the city to help out the family finances for a few years before their marriage. They were paid very little, worked extremely long hours, were housed in factory dormitories under close supervision, and could be laid off if business conditions warranted. Thus it was women and peasants who carried most of the burden of Japan's modern development.

The New Japanese Empire

Meanwhile, Taiwan and Korea were exploited to feed Japan's need for raw materials and food. Korea provided coal, iron, timber, and rice while Taiwan became an important source of sugar as well as rice. Taiwan was ruled somewhat less oppressively than Korea, in part because of its lesser strategic importance, plus the absence of the long history of conflict and mutual animosity between Japan and Korea. There were only some three million Chinese in Taiwan, never more than loosely governed by China and without their own tradition as yet of nationalism, unlike Korea. In both countries Japan built the first railways and modern coal mines, disseminated the same agricultural improvements, including irrigation and fertilizer, which had already revolutionized Japanese agriculture, built port facilities, developed hydroelectric plants and a new education system, and began an effective program of public health, like all the other colonial powers.

But Koreans especially were treated like inferiors and they and the Taiwanese considered only as loyal, if exploited and second-class, subjects of the Japanese empire. Japanese control was harsh, and the drain of raw materials and food actually led to a steep decline in Korean food consumption. Japanese policy in the new colonies, and in China, was pronouncedly racist, and the Japanese colonial record was decidedly bad in balance, developing its subject countries to feed the Japanese economy and repressing all protest. Later in Manchuria, Japanese policy was more constructive, investing large sums in the creation of a rail system, mines, factories, and a commercialized agriculture and thus creating the essential infrastructure for industrialization. Much of the fruits, including even the pig iron and steel produced in Manchuria, were drained off to Japan, but during their control Manchuria developed the largest heavy industrial complex in mainland East Asia, only then to be reabsorbed by Communist China before the heavy Japanese start-up costs had been fully repaid.

Meiji Culture and Accomplishments

By late Meiji times, in the flood of Western influence, Japanese had begun to write realistic novels as well as translating large chunks of modern Western literature. The French realist writer Emile Zola was especially admired, as were Western romantic models. Probably the best-known and still-valued writer of this period was Natsume Soseki (1867–1916). He had studied in England, and described himself as half Western and half Japanese. His poetry and even more his many novels, especially *Kokoro*, are still widely read. Many painters went even farther in imitating Western styles, especially those of the French impressionists and realists, including Kuroda Seiki (d. 1924), who shocked Tokyo by painting full frontal nude female figures in a style hard to distinguish from what was being painted in the West. By 1920 Japan had nearly 55 million people and nearly 100 percent were in school or had completed the primary grades. This provided a greatly expanded reading and viewing public, increasingly sophisticated in its tastes, concentrated in the booming cities but involving many in rural areas as well. As a reflection of Japan's success in Westernization, including its legal system, and also in response to its triumphs over China and Russia, the long hoped for relinquishment of extraterritoriality was accepted by Britain in 1899 and soon thereafter by the other Western powers; tariff autonomy was restored in 1911. In little more than a generation Japan had won its struggle for acceptance and equality with the West.

Credit for this achievement must be shared among the Meiji oligarchs but also with the Japanese people as a whole, for it was a truly national effort. Among the Meiji leaders, Ito Hirobumi stands out as a statesman, conservative like most Japanese of this period but open to new ideas. As a youth he wanted passionately to save his country from the foreign threat, and at age 21 tried to burn the newly established British embassy in Tokyo. But when he visited Britain the next year, he realized that it was impossible to drive the Westerners out, and returned to work for Japan's modernization. After the Restoration, he went with government missions to Europe and America to learn more from their example how to make his country strong. A later mission to Prussia convinced him that the Prussian constitutional monarchy was best suited to Japan, and Ito was the chief architect of the new constitution proclaimed by the emperor in 1889, which contained many Prussian ideas. He understood, however, that constitutional government, and the cooperation of the new parliament, could not be made to work without political organization and popular support. In 1898 he left office to form a political party for that purpose, which was dominant until 1941. In 1901 Ito gave the prime ministership to General Katsura, a fellow Choshu man and a follower of Yamagata.

Ito was an enthusiastic modernizer, especially after his visits to the West, but he also understood the need for compromise in politics and for adapting Western ways to Japanese traditions, circumstances, and values. In some ways, he remained at least as traditional as he was "modern." His objective was the preservation and development of his country, not its Westernization. He saw the need for many foreign ideas, but never at the expense of strong Japanese identity. He believed deeply in the restoration of the emperor's personal rule, and aimed to accomplish his ends by working through the throne. But he also understood the rising interest in a less authoritarian form of government, the need for political parties, a constitution, and a parliament. He was

Ito Hirobumi (seated left) with his family. (Library of Congress)

Viscount Katsura (1847–1913), prime minister of Japan three times between 1901 and 1913. He was a Choshu man, a general, and a protege of Yamagata. (BBC Hulton Picture Library)

both an enthusiast and a realist, a radical reformer and a traditional conservative, a promoter of change and a practical compromiser—in other words, a true statesman, who served his country well and who never let personal ambition or power cloud his judgment or his dedication to the public welfare.

With the goals of the national drive to modernize the country and obtain Western approval accomplished, and with the rise in living standards for most people (except for tenants, landless laborers, and most factory workers—altogether a substantial share of the population, but one with no real political power), attitudes and interests became more divided among divergent groups. The rise of the military in politics tended to form one such group, with their ultranationalist supporters. Those who hoped for a less authoritarian and externally aggressive alternative and pressed for a more genuine democracy formed another. The spread of universal public education and the rise of the universities produced a growing group of intellectuals who were, not surprisingly, heavily Westernized, as the education system was, and they tended to pull in conflicting directions but in general supported a liberalization of the rigid and autocratic system inherited from the Meiji period. The business community, including many who had become rich especially during the First World War, not only in the *zaibatsu* firms but in many smaller ones, tended to display their new wealth, sometimes garishly but in any case in increasing consumption of luxuries, representing a sharp departure from the Meiji ideals of frugality, self-sacrifice, and hard work.

These were the kinds of trends which General Nogi found distasteful in the testament he left behind on his suicide. But like the passing of all of the Meiji leaders, his death, followed by that of Yamagata as an old man in 1922, marked the end of an era. The Meiji oligarchs had offered strong leadership to a united country. Now that they were gone, there were really no comparable figures to succeed them, and there was not the same kind of national consensus which had supported their efforts. This was one reason for the rise of the military as the dominant power in the government, where authority rested on force, and the consequent slide of Japan into even more authoritarian government and, in time, further foreign aggression at the instigation of the militarists.

Before Japan's descent into what the Japanese call "the dark valley," there was a brief bloom of diversity, intellectual and artistic expression, and moves in the direction of a more democratic government and society, known as "Taisho Democracy" from the imperial era which spanned it. This, and its destruction by the rising military, will be considered in Chapter 18.

Suggestions for Further Reading

Barton, H. *Japanese Imperialism, 1894–1945*. Oxford: Claredon Press, 1987.

Beasley, W. G. *The Meiji Restoration*. Stanford Press, 1972.

———. *The Rise of Modern Japan*. New York: St. Martin's, 1990.

Colman, D. *The Nature and Origins of Japanese Imperialism*. London: Routledge, 1992.

Francks, P. *Technology and Agricultural Development in Pre-war Japan*. Yale Press, 1984.

Gluck, C. *Japan's Modern Myths: Ideology in the Late Meiji Period*. Princeton Press, 1985.

Hackett, R. *Yamagata Aritomo in the Rise of Modern Japan*. Harvard Press, 1971.

Hane, M. *Peasants, Rebels, and Outcasts: The Underside of Modern Japan*. New York: Pantheon, 1982.

Harashima, Y. *Meiji Japan Through Woodblock Prints*. Univ. of Tokyo Press, 1981.

Hunter, J. C. *The Emergence of Modern Japan*. London: Longmans, 1989.

Jansen, M. and Duus, P., eds. *The Cambridge History of Japan*. Vols. 5 and 6. Cambridge University Press, 1989 and 1993.

———. *The Emergence of Meiji Japan*. Cambridge: Cambridge University Press, 1995.

Jones, H. J. *Live Machines: Hired Foreigners and Meiji Japan*. Tenterden, Kent: Norbury, 1980.

Marshall, B. K. *Capitalism and Nationalism in Pre-war Japan*. Stanford Press, 1967.

Myers, R., et. al. *The Japanese Colonial Empire*. Stanford Press, 1984.

Nish, I. H. *The Origins of the Russo-Japanese War*. London: Longsmans, 1985.

Norman, E. H. *Japan's Emergence as a Modern State*. New York: IPR, 1940.

Pyle, K. B. *The New Generation in Meiji Japan*. Stanford Press, 1969.

Roden, D. F. *Schooldays in Imperial Japan*. California Press, 1981.

Samuels, R. J. *Rich Nation, Strong Army*. Ithaca: Cornell University Press, 1995.

Spaulding, R. M. *Imperial Japan's Higher Civil Service Examinations*. Princeton Press, 1967.

Wilson, G. M. *Patriots and Redeemers in Japan*. Univ. of Chicago Press, 1992.

CHAPTER 16

IMPERIALISM IN KOREA, VIETNAM, AND SOUTHEAST ASIA

Chapter 9 brought the account of the history of Korea up to the nineteenth century, with the Yi dynasty in its fifth century of existence and already tottering. Throughout Yi rule from 1392 Korea preserved a correct tributary relationship with China, which was often referred to by Koreans as "elder brother." Chinese influence strengthened throughout this long period, including new emphasis on Confucianism and the adoption of the Chinese examination system based on mastery of Confucian scholarship, philosophy, and morality. For a century or more there was a lively cultural growth on the Chinese model, including the printing of encyclopedias and extensive histories. The capital was fixed at Seoul and the country divided into eight provinces, subdivided into counties following the Chinese pattern, administered by a scholar-elite chosen from those who had passed the examinations.

Despite this system based on supposed merit, or in practice on conformity with the often rigid Confucian code, Korean society remained sharply hierarchical, based on hereditary class distinctions, as in Japan. All of those who served as officials came from the *yangban* or gentry group, which also monopolized all of the leading political posts. The unity and vigor provided by the Yi dynasty in its first centuries could not be maintained, and its authority was progressively weakened by chronic conflicts among rival bureaucratic and court factions. As recounted in Chapter 9, Korea was then devastated by the invasion of the Japanese warlord Hideyoshi at the end of the sixteenth century, and subsequently invaded by the Manchus in 1636 in preparation for their assault on Ming China. The government became more and more ineffective, while the economy and culture stagnated or declined. Korea was thus especially poorly prepared to meet the challenge posed by Western and then Japanese imperialists in the nineteenth century.

Rejection of Foreign Ideas

The Korean establishment and government were rigidly opposed to any and all foreign influences or presences, and had no interest in adopting Western technology even in self-defense. Catholic missionaries reached Korea late, at the end of the eighteenth century from China, but they and their converts were soon persecuted as both foreign and heretical—anti-Confucian—and Christianity was driven underground. Unfortunately for Korea, its position between the larger and more powerful states of China and later Japan, and in the later nineteenth century an expansionist Russia, exposed it to irresistible forces which it could not permanently resist, and also made it a battleground of competing foreign interests. It should however be remembered that Korea is the size and population of European states and with a far older sophisticated culture, a major civilization in its own right, though deeply in the shadow of China. Its seclusionist and antiforeign attitude led to its being called by Westerners "the Hermit Kingdom," but this merely increased foreign curiosity, and their determination to "open" the country to trade. The Korean government's response to the mounting foreign pressures after 1860 was in effect to pull the covers over their heads and hope the foreigners would go away. Shipwrecked mariners were treated roughly and expelled, while the Koreans fired on foreign ships which tried to establish contact and drove them off.

Christianity did spread despite persecution, which alarmed the government, and with it, through missionary priests, some of the Western learning and ideas which Jesuits and later missionaries had introduced into China and Japan. Followers in Korea called it "practical learning," and some began to urge fundamental change. There was a perhaps predictable backlash on the part of others who saw Western-inspired change as a threat to Korean values and identity. Bands of armed men called "tiger hunters" attacked foreigners and took part in the efforts to repel the still small-scale foreign expeditions. There was a major peasant-based revolt in the southeast in 1862 and 1863, in protest against mounting poverty and the ineffective government response, but also with antiforeign overtones.

In the 1860s a new religious cult arose called Tonghak, or "Eastern Learning," violently opposed to Western or "practical" learning and to all foreign influences. It was founded by a poor village scholar, Ch'oe Che-u (1824–1864), who had repeatedly failed the official examinations, and much like Hung Hsiu-ch'uan, founder of the Taipings in China (see Chapter 14), claimed to have had divine instructions to lead a new movement. His religion combined elements from Confucian, Buddhist, Taoist, Catholic, and indigenous Korean beliefs, including more than a touch of magic, but centered on

the creation of a new "way" which would conquer the Westerners and restore Korea to its ancient pride. He attracted widespread support from impoverished peasants, as with the Taipings, and there were renewed revolts. Ch'oe was arrested and executed in 1864 as a subversive, but after his death the Tonghak movement spread even more widely, for the time being on a more passive basis.

The government thus faced both domestic rebellion and foreign challenge. A regent known as the Taewongun or "Grand Prince" headed the government from 1864 to 1873 while his son who came to the throne in 1864 was still a child. He pursued a series of conservative reforms aimed to restore the "golden age" of the Yi dynasty's founder, nearly five centuries earlier. In a parallel to the T'ung-chih restoration in China during the same years (see Chapter 14), there was an effort to reduce corruption, strengthen the central administration, build new forts, and introduce a few modern arms. But the basically reactionary and exclusionist emphasis did not change. The government executed some French Catholic priests, and thus provoked a French naval attack in 1866. The Koreans managed to drive them off, and the commander lectured them in Confucian style, "How can you tell us to abandon the teachings of our forefathers and accept those of others?" Persecution of Christians was greatly increased, but the Koreans seem not to have realized even yet the potential or actual power of the Westerners, and continued to insist that their foreign relations be managed only through Peking, of which they remained a tributary state. In effect, they went on saying to foreigners who pressed for redress, or for admission and trade, "talk to my lawyer." Korea of

The Korean landscape. Note the largely bare hills, legacy of massive deforestation by the Japanese. Here, the exploding suburbs of booming Seoul have largely filled the lowland basin. (Cameramann International, Ltd.)

course counted on China to protect her, but with no understanding of China's deteriorating weakness or of Western strength and determination, soon to be supplemented by a resurgent Japan.

Foreign Contention for Korea

Japanese had continued to trade at the southeast port of Pusan, by special permission rather like the Dutch trade at Nagasaki under the Tokugawa. With the Meiji Restoration of 1868, Japan began to acquire new strength, and new ambition. The Japanese had had a long history of interaction with nearby Korea, and had even maintained footholds on the southeast coast in the past (see Chapter 10). Now they saw it as their first foreign opportunity to demonstrate their new power. But it was, after all, the Americans who had first succeeded in "opening" Japan in 1853, and in the growing rivalry over who would manage to do the same for Korea, the U.S. minister to China went in 1871 with five warships to the mouth of the Han River and sent his surveyors up river toward Seoul. The Koreans fired on them, wounding two. The Americans demanded an apology, and when none was forthcoming, destroyed five forts by gunfire and killed some 250 Koreans. But the government refused to deal with them and finally they had to sail away, leaving the Koreans sure they had won a victory. Japanese *samurai* soon decided to try to provoke a war with Korea and to detach it from the Chinese sphere into their own. Their first plan was stopped by the still cautious Meiji government, but in 1875 Japanese who landed from warships to survey the Korean coast were fired on, and the Tokyo government determined to use this as a pretext for demanding that Korea open its doors. A Japanese fleet anchored off Inchon, the port of Seoul, in early 1876, and forced the government to sign an "unequal treaty" patterned on those imposed earlier on China and Japan, opening the ports of Pusan, Inchon, and Wonsan to Japanese trade, and declaring Korea an "independent state."

The Taewongun, now formally out of power, nevertheless promoted an antiforeign riot in 1882, and a mob attacked the Japanese legation. Both China, still regarding itself as the ultimate legitimate authority, and Japan sent troops. Japan received an indemnity, and China removed the Taewongun and held him in China for the next three years. Li Hung-chang (see Chapter 17) took control of relations with and for Korea and tried to foster "self-strengthening" measures there. Li saw it was best for Korea to develop some counters to the overwhelming Japanese presence and ambitions and urged trade and diplomatic treaties with the Western powers. Such treaties were negotiated between 1882 and 1886, first with the United States, but the efforts at self-strengthening produced few results, blocked by Korean conservatism and by continuing factional conflict internally. The Chinese removal of the Taewongun left the arch-conservative Min family, especially the current queen known as Queen Min, in power, and they largely undid the few feeble efforts at rational change. Nevertheless, foreign influences increased, including those brought by a new flood of mainly American missionaries, and a Korean diplomatic mission was established in Washington in 1888.

But the major influence was still from Japan, whose example of modern development and strength since 1869 inspired most Korean patriots and reformers. They welcomed a larger role for Japan in Korea's overdue development, and when the Min faction at court blocked their efforts, they tried to stage a coup in 1884. In Japanese style, they assassinated several conservative ministers and seized the king. This had all been done with the knowledge of the Japanese legation, but their coup failed when the young Chinese commander in Korea, Yuan Shih-k'ai (see Chapter 17) defeated the guards of the Japanese legation and rescued the king. The affair was settled in 1885 by an agreement between Li Hung-chang and Ito Hirobumi (representing Japan—see Chapter 14), known as the Li-Ito Convention. Both powers agreed to withdraw their troops and military advisers and to notify each other before sending them back. Li proceeded to push for Korea's modernization, including a Customs Service, telegraph lines, and new military training.

But the Tonghak movement was still very much alive, and in 1894 it rose in rebellion, once again against unaddressed poverty and governmental ineffectiveness, including its inability to keep foreign influences out. China and Japan once more intervened, but now Japan was clearly superior militarily. In the brief undeclared war between the two, with China still attempting to act as Korea's protector, Japanese naval and ground forces won a quick and decisive victory (see Chapter 15). Korea was declared independent of China, but from 1895 it became in effect a Japanese sphere, and in 1910 was formally annexed as part of the new Japanese empire.

Korea would clearly have done better to have followed the Meiji pattern, or even that of post-1860 China or Siam (Thailand), letting in all foreign nations in order to balance each other out, while pursuing its own modernization along Western lines. As it was, Korea became Japanese property, and suffered terribly. Russian ambitions in Korea were ended with the Japanese victory over the Tsarist empire in 1905 (see Chapter 15), when Korea was officially declared to be a Japanese protectorate. The weak Korean king, successor to Queen Min, (who had been brutally murdered by the Japanese in 1895 because she was not compliant enough to suit them), was left nominally in power, but when he complained to Western powers of Japanese domination,

Tokyo forced him to abdicate and turn over the throne to his feebleminded son. Japanese now filled most official posts, and the Korean army was disbanded. Efforts at protest, which the Japanese labeled "riots," were brutally suppressed, killing over 12,000 people. Ito, from 1905 the Japanese Resident-General, was assassinated by a Korean patriot late in 1909, and Korea was officially annexed to Japan the following year, as the "Province of Chosen."

Korea Under Japanese Rule

Korea was perhaps more brutally exploited than any colonial country in the world, under an exceptionally harsh Japanese rule from 1910 to 1945. Living standards, already dangerously low, fell sharply during this period as Japan milked Korea of much of its raw materials and food. Modern mines, railways, roads, postal service, and factories were built for the first time, but most of the coal, iron, and food crops were shipped to Japan, and the forests stripped. Public health measures and an enforced civil order led to a substantial population increase, but with people living in increasing poverty. Koreans were obliged to take Japanese names; their language could not be used publicly or taught in schools. Most Koreans were denied even elementary education. Most nonmenial jobs, including even engine drivers, were filled by Japanese, while Koreans labored as near-slaves. A few found lower-level positions in the colonial bureaucracy, but Korean efforts at self-expression and movement for political reform and representation were ruthlessly suppressed, their supporters jailed, killed, or driven out as refugees. By 1945, there were too few Koreans with the education or administrative experience to form a viable government.

Even before Japan's victory over China in 1894–1895 and its consequent rise to dominance in Korea there had been strong resistance to the growing Japanese presence. After 1895 this became increasingly violent, and the Japanese response of brutal retaliation and counter-terror, including the burning of whole villages suspected of aiding insurgents, merely stimulated more determined resistance, as did the similar Nazi policies in occupied Europe 40 years later, and perhaps more directly, the cruel Japanese policies in the parts of China which they occupied after 1937. Japanese records show nearly 3,000 clashes involving nearly 142,000 insurgents in Korea between August of 1907 and June of 1911 alone, and this arbitrary period was generally typical of the entire span of Japanese control. The insurgents were helped by the mountainous terrain, but Japanese countermeasures were ruthless.

One of the worst aspects of the Japanese exploitation of Korea was their stripping of most of the country's tree cover for export to Japan, which left even the mountain hideouts exposed. The savage repression increased with the demonstrations of March 1919 (see below), and again as Japan entered the path to war mapped out by its now militarist-dominated government from 1931. A few Japanese were encouraged to move to Korea as farmers in addition to officials, engineers, and teachers, but Korea was never very popular as a home for most Japanese despite their favored position there. There were a few Korean collaborators, including some of the large landowners, but the biggest landowner of all was the semiofficial Oriental Development Company, which bought up and controlled a large part of Korea's rice land, worked by Korean tenants. Total rice production was increased with the application of the new technology already in place in Japan, but most of it was exported.

A mass demonstration of nationalist feelings and grievances took place on March 1, 1919, designed to make a point with the Western statesmen then meeting at the Versailles Conference, and appealing to U.S. President Wilson's call for "self-determination of nations." Over a million Koreans marched peacefully in Seoul, to be met by brutal Japanese force, killing or injuring over 20,000 and jailing a similar number. A few private schools continued to teach Korean subjects, but by 1929 they were forced to use only Japanese textbooks and language. Under all these conditions it is understandable that Korean nationalism flourished as never before. Japanese regarded Koreans as second-class Japanese, but in any case as inferior, and hence as proper subjects for exploitation. Cultural differences in diet, dress, speech, and behavior were cited as evidence of Korean "inferiority." Japanese spoke of them as "dirty" and as smelling of garlic. But they were now a conquered people and could be abused with impunity, forgetting Japanese civilization's heavy debt to Korea (see Chapter 10), which more and more Japanese came to deny. Koreans who fled to Japan in hope of a better material life, and the many others who went as forced labor, were crudely discriminated against, as they still are.

Western missionaries hung on in Korea, mainly American, and now began to make many new converts, who found the Christian message with its Western connections both an antidote to the Japanese and a consolation. In time, Korea became second to the Philippines as the Asian country with the largest Christian proportion of its population, nearly a fifth by 1950. Missionaries also founded schools and hospitals, as in China and elsewhere in Asia, and were periodically in trouble with the Japanese authorities, as were of course their converts. Many Korean nationalists, including the first postwar President Syngman Rhee (Yi Sung-man, 1875–1965), began their education in mission schools, although most, like Rhee, were imprisoned and tortured by the Japanese and then forced to flee. Marxist ideas also appealed to other Korean nationalists, and Russia was an obvious counter to Japan. The Korean Communist party was founded in 1925, but was kept ineffective by the Japanese police and their agents.

The Japanese colonial record in Korea ranks with the worst of those imposed elsewhere by Western powers. It left behind a deep legacy of bitterness, hatred, and resentment among Koreans which is still very much in evidence. Most Korean rice, the staple of the diet there as elsewhere in East Asia, was siphoned off to Japan to help feed the growing Japanese population. Koreans were forced to subsist, at greatly reduced nutritional levels, on cheaper and less desirable millet, sorghum, and barley, but the total was inadequate to their needs. Japanese investments in railways, mines, and factories did lay Korea's first modern infrastructure, but it was all for Japanese rather than Korean benefit. Korea was at least largely spared the fate of China as a theater of war from 1937 to 1945, but many Koreans were forced into the Japanese army or drafted as labor. By the war's end Korea was seriously impoverished, and many of its people on the brink of starvation. Korea had been cruelly oppressed under Japanese rule, but had still to face the arbitrary and damaging partition of the country, and the unprecedented devastation of the Korean War from 1950 to 1953 in which Korea suffered as a battleground of the Cold War between rival outside powers who cared little for the welfare of its people.

Imperialism and Colonialism in Southeast Asia

Southeast Asia has been so closely interrelated with both China and Japan, especially in the modern era, that it deserves our attention here. All of its people probably entered the area from south China, over a long period of mainly prehistoric time, and share many East Asian characteristics, especially of course in Vietnam but to differing degrees in every Southeast Asian country. Chinese emigrant settlers were also established there, beginning with Chinese traders in the Philippines and Java by at least the tenth century and subsequently in the rest of the region. In the nineteenth century as population pressure built up in south China and there was new economic expansion in Southeast Asia, large numbers of Chinese sought new opportunities there and became a major part of the population in Malaya and Thailand as well as the dominant group in the port city of Singapore.

The king of Annam, known as the Thanh-tai emperor (r. 1889–1907) with his three brothers. Note the French official towering over the group. The French found him not submissive enough, and exiled him as "insane" in 1907.

The Thais had originated in south China, and, after the thirteenth-century Mongol conquest of Yunnan and the Thai kingdom there, many more fled or migrated southward across the border, to be joined in the nineteenth century by new Chinese immigrants especially from the Canton area.

Burma had been invaded and briefly conquered by the Mongol hordes, and all of the Southeast Asian states became tributaries of the Chinese empire, sending regular missions to Nanking and then to Peking. The military power of the Ch'ing dynasty reached out to invade Burma briefly and to compel renewed recognition of vague Chinese overlordship through the tributary system. Vietnam had been subjected to direct Chinese rule under the Han and the T'ang, and though politically independent with the fall of the T'ang it remained a Chinese tributary, as did the state of Malacca in Malaya and successive kingdoms in Java. The great Khmer empire in Cambodia centered at Angkor had declined by the fourteenth century and much of it was absorbed by the expansionist Thais and Vietnamese. Finally, all of Southeast Asia except Thailand (which was forced to accept Japanese dominance) was briefly conquered by Japan from 1942 to 1945.

The British in Burma and Malaya

British interest in Southeast Asia, after their expulsion by the Dutch in the seventeenth century, was incidental to their concerns in India and their efforts to break into the China market. They first tried to found bases on the edges of Dutch power in Malaya, and made a settlement at Penang on the northwest Malay coast in 1786, where they hoped to attract Chinese traders. This was only moderately successful, and they established what soon became their major Southeast Asian trade base at Singapore in 1819. They had taken over Malacca from the Dutch in 1795, symbolizing the new shift of power (as the Dutch capture of Malacca from the Portuguese had done in 1641), but its harbor was small and it no longer controlled trade through the Straits. From the start, Singapore, with its large and excellent harbor commanding the southern entrance to the Straits, was a commercial center for all of Southeast Asia and not just for Malaya, which remained largely undeveloped economically and thinly populated until the end of the nineteenth century.

Meanwhile, Burma was next door to India and under the rule of an antiquated monarchy which was nevertheless expanding westward into areas claimed by Britain. It periodically made difficulties for English merchants, appearing to flout British power in a way which to some minds threatened their position in Bengal. A brief war from 1824 to 1826 gave the Company special rights in the important coastal provinces of Burma and checked Burmese expansion. Two more minor wars in 1852 and 1885–1886, largely provoked by the British, annexed both Lower Burma and the rest of the country. Burma was administered as a province of British India, with basically the same policies and results, until it was finally made a separate colony in 1937.

Burma and Malaya saw rapid commercialization after 1880 under British rule, which built railways and developed steam navigation. The Irrawaddy delta in lower

Steps to Control

In 1873, British policy in Malaya was stated in instructions to the governor as follows:

The anarchy which prevails and appears to be increasing in parts of the peninsula, and the consequent injury to trade and British interests generally, render it necessary to consider seriously whether any step can be taken to improve this condition.... Her Majesty's Government have no desire to interfere in the internal affairs of the Malay States [but] find it incumbent on them to employ such influence as they possess with the Native Princes to rescue, if possible, these fertile and productive countries from the ruin which must befall them if the present disorders continue unchecked.... You will report to me whether there are in your opinion any steps which can properly be taken by the colonial government to promote the restoration of peace and order and to secure protection to trade and commerce with the native territories.

Source: D. R. SarDesai, *Southeast Asia, Past and Present* (Boulder, Colo.: Westview, 1989), p. 149.

Burma, including much newly cultivated land, became a great exporter of rice. Upper Burma produced timber, especially teak, for export, and the central valley yielded oil from new wells drilled by the British. All this moved out for export through the port of Rangoon, which became a smaller-scale version of Calcutta and also served as the colonial capital. Rich deposits of tin were found in Malaya, a metal in great demand in the industrializing West, and toward the end of the century Malaya also became the world's major producer of plantation rubber. Labor for tin mining and rubber tapping had to be imported, since the local Malays, subsistence farmers, were not interested in such work. The gap was filled mainly by Chinese from overcrowded south China, who soon became nearly half of the population of Malaya, including the colonial capital at Kuala Lumpur, originally a miners' camp.

In time many of these Chinese immigrants, who also entered the booming commercial economy of Singapore, became wealthy. Chinese dominated the money economy of Malaya and there was growing resentment against them by Malays. Indians also came in, as laborers and as merchants, to the rapidly growing economies of Burma and Malaya. Chinese, Indians, and British dominated the commercial production and foreign trade of both countries. The colonial government, especially in Malaya where the locals had almost become a minority in their own country, tried to protect their culture and rights and ruled as much as possible through native sultans, but both countries were economically transformed under colonialism.

French, Dutch, and American Colonialism

Largely eliminated from India by the end of the eighteenth century, the French sought their own colonial sphere in Asia, and used the persecution of French Catholic missionaries in Vietnam as a pretext for conquering the southern provinces in 1862, including the port of Saigon. Later they annexed Cambodia and Laos, and in 1885 took over northern Vietnam, after defeating Chinese forces sent to protect their tributary state. There was bitter Vietnamese resistance at every stage, but southern Vietnam became a major exporter of rice and rubber grown in the delta of the Mekong River, exported through the chief port of Saigon, which was made the colonial capital. Cambodia and Laos remained little developed commercially. Northern Vietnam, the area around Hanoi, was already too densely populated on the Chinese model to have surpluses for export, but there was some small industrial growth there and in the northern port of Haiphong. The colonial administration tried to impose French culture on Indo-China (as Vietnam, Cambodia, and Laos are still called). Control was centralized in French hands and traditional institutions weakened. French rule was oppressive and often ruthless in squashing Vietnamese gestures toward political expression or participation. The army was augmented by special security forces and much of the apparatus of a police state, which executed, jailed, or drove into exile most Vietnamese leaders. These included the young Ho Chi Minh (1890–1969), later the head of the Vietnamese Communist party, who went to Europe in 1911 and later on to Moscow and Canton.

The Dutch left most of Indonesia to native rulers until late in the nineteenth century, content with their control of trade from their major base at Batavia (now Jakarta), the colonial capital on the central island of Java. Tropical Java was richly productive of plantation crops promoted by the Dutch: sugar, coffee, tea, tobacco, and a variety of others, plus rubber by the early 1900s, in production of which Indonesia was second only to Malaya. Oil was also found and exploited. The discovery of more oil, plus tin and prime land for rubber and tobacco, prompted the Dutch to increase their control first of Sumatra and then of the other islands of Borneo, Celebes (Sulawesi), the Moluccas, Bali, and the hundreds of smaller ones in the archipelago south of the Philippines. Tin and oil joined rubber as major exports, and new railways and ports were built to expedite trade.

Dutch rule became absolute despite fierce resistance on some of the islands, especially in Sumatra, but never tried to penetrate effectively into the mountain and jungle interior of Borneo. The northern coast of Borneo was divided between British colonial administration and nominally independent sultanates run as private preserves by British rulers, the Brooke family. Dutch control outside Borneo became increasingly oppressive, excluded Indonesians from participation in government, denied them more than basic primary education or free expression, and jailed protesters. Java was systematically exploited by forcing its peasants to grow export crops for Dutch profit. Production and population grew very rapidly, but living standards and quality of life declined.

In 1898 the United States won its war against Spain, and acquired the Philippines as its first overseas colony. In the 43 years of American control, more impact was made on the culture and economy of the islands than in 350 years of Spanish rule. The new imperialists built roads, railroads, hospitals, and an education system up to the university level. Literacy and health levels became the highest in Asia after Japan. But America's economic impact was exploitative. In partnership with rich Filipinos, it concentrated on growing commercial crops for export, especially sugar, and often neglected the basic needs of the people as a whole. Manila became a rapidly growing commercial center and colonial capital, and the

The Emperor Bao Dai with his prime minister and attendants, escorted by a French officer and in the background other French officials. (Stock Montage Inc., Chicago)

chief base of the rising Filipino middle class and educated elite. The American colonists were more idealistic than the French or Dutch and saw their goal as conferring their own type of democracy on their new subjects, whom they called "little brown brothers."

To a degree this was successful, but Philippine politics were dominated by a small elite drawing support from those who profited from the American connection and paying too little attention to the still predominantly rural and peasant population. Free public education and free expression were not something most peasants were able to pursue. Nevertheless, the United States promised speedy independence, and kept its promise in 1946, although on terms which diluted sovereignty economically and left huge American military bases in the Philippines.

Independent Siam

While the rest of Southeast Asia was being taken over by imperialist powers, the Thais kept their independence. Their country, called Siam until 1932, lay between the British in Burma and Malaya and the French

in Indo-China. Neither was willing to let the other dominate Siam. British preponderance in Thai foreign trade and investment was balanced by French annexation of Thai territory and claims in western Cambodia and Laos. British Malaya detached Siam's southern provinces. The Thai kings adroitly played the French off against the British and urged the advantages to both of leaving at least part of their country as a buffer state. They had to grant special trade, residence, and legal privileges to the colonialist powers, a system like that imposed on China, but there was no foreign effort to take over the government. Nevertheless, the Thai economy developed along the same lines as colonial Southeast Asia, with a big new export trade in rice from the delta area in the valley of the Chao Praya, followed later by rubber and tropical hardwoods. Bangkok, the capital, grew rapidly as virtually the sole port for foreign trade and spreading commercialization.

Overseas Chinese

Immigrant Chinese began to flood into all the commercially developed parts of Southeast Asia in growing

✠ Imperialist Designs ✠

British impatience and ambition over upper Burma, in the face of supposed French rivalry and the Burmese monarchy's resistance to British demands, are cleverly revealed in this passage from a letter by Sir Owen Burne, undersecretary of state for India, to the British Foreign Office in the fall of 1885.

I feel quite sure that some far more absolute action than we are yet aware of must be taken. I say unhesitatingly that we should now get any pretext to annex or make Burma into a protected state. King Theebaw's sins are many and great and I feel quite sure your able pen, aided by a few snarls from myself, could formulate a Bill of Indictment against him that would make every old woman in London weep.

Source: H. Aung, *The Stricken Peacock* (The Hague: Nijhoff, 1965), p. 9.

numbers after 1870, as plantation and mining labor and as traders. They soon largely monopolized the retail trade in all the cities of Southeast Asia, although they shared it with immigrant Indians in Burma and Malaya. In Bangkok they became over half of the population, and, as in Vietnam, controlled most of the large export trade in rice. They were understandably resented by Southeast Asians, especially since they also served as moneylenders and owned most of the shops, but were often welcomed by the colonialists as useful labor and commercial agents. In Siam, unlike the rest of Southeast Asia, most Chinese were quickly assimilated into Thai society through intermarriage and acculturation. Elsewhere, Chinese immigrants tended to stick to their own culture and residential areas and were discriminated against by the local people. Altogether, Chinese settlers in Southeast Asia, almost all in the cities, totaled about 15 million by the outbreak of World War II.

Plural Societies

Compared with India or even with treaty-port China, full colonialism came late to most of Southeast Asia. Dutch sovereignty over all of what is now Indonesia was not complete until the early twentieth century, more or less contemporary with the American conquest of the Philippines, from a loose Spanish control. Burma was not fully absorbed by the British until 1886, while they ruled Malaya "indirectly" through the traditional Malay Sultans who remained titular heads of the several small Malay states.

The British resident at each Malay Sultan's court slowly took over more and more responsibility for administration, and in 1896 the Malay states most important to the British were grouped into a Federation under a British Resident-General in what thus became the colonial capital of Kuala Lumpur. This was in a central location to administer the economically important west coastal regions where most of the tin and rubber were produced. Only then can one consider the British position in Malaya full colonialism, and even so it was modified by the same policies of indirect rule applied to the Princely States in India, on which it was in fact modeled. Penang, Malacca, and Singapore remained under direct British administration as the Straits Settlements. The remaining and economically less important Malay states were to a greater degree left alone; they came under British "protection" in 1909, but were allowed considerable autonomy, with British "advisers" rather than Residents.

It took time for most Southeast Asians to develop a national response to colonialism, and indeed it was not yet fully formed or well organized in most areas outside the Philippines by the outbreak of the Pacific War in 1941 which marked the end of colonialism in Asia, a scant half-century or less after it had been established in most of Southeast Asia. Outside Vietnam and Thailand, Western colonialism unified areas in much of Southeast Asia which had never been unified before, politically or culturally. Most were still composed of numerous different languages and culture groups with no tradition of living or working together and in many cases with a history of mutual antagonism. Under these circumstances, it is not surprising that modern nationalism and common effort were late and slow to grow, as they were in

India for similar reasons. As in India too, some Southeast Asians found the colonial system attractive and personally rewarding: the new Filipino commercial and political elite who profitably collaborated with the Americans, and smaller numbers of similar collaborators in the rest of Southeast Asia. Many of the minority groups included in the new colonial domains found especially the British concerned to protect them against pressures and exploitation by the dominant majority, as in the long conflict between the majority lowland Burmans and the quite different people of the Burmese hills and mountains, Shans, Karens, Kachins, and so on. Even the French and Dutch used ethnic minorities in Vietnam and Indonesia as makeweights against the dominant, and resented, Vietnamese and Javanese.

Malays saw the British, quite accurately, as their protectors against the Chinese who immigrated into their country, threatened to dominate it numerically, and monopolized its booming commercial sector. The British admired traditional Malay culture and tried to preserve it as well as its people; Chinese were forbidden to own land and hence did not intrude into the traditional agricultural economy except as plantation workers, while Malays were encouraged to preserve their own customs and to follow their traditional forms of law. Dutch policy in Indonesia was closely similar, based also on the belief that by keeping Indonesians fixed in their own traditional cultures, and also forbidding all outsiders to own land, the locals would remain more docile and less likely to unite against them or to catch the germs of nationalism and protest. Many Dutch also admired the traditional Indonesian cultures—and they were indeed, as throughout Southeast Asia, very appealing to romantic-minded Europeans. Unlike Indians, and in time Burmese and Filipinos, most Malays, Vietnamese, and Indonesians had extremely limited access to Western-style education, in Vietnam and Indonesia by explicit French and Dutch policy. All of these several factors helped to retard the growth of nationalism and of resistance to colonial control, despite its frequent ruthlessness. It is not surprising that nationalism emerged first in Vietnam, with its long self-conscious history of resistance to Chinese conquest, and then in the Philippines. Modern anticolonial nationalism was however earliest in the latter, after three centuries of Spanish rule, and indeed began to be expressed in the 1870s and to spill over in revolt in the 1890s.

Thailand (Siam) is a separate case, since it never became a colony, thanks in part to Anglo-French rivalry and their tacit agreement to leave it as a neutral buffer between British Burma and French Indo-China. Its independence was also due in part to a fortunate series of able Thai kings, most importantly Mongkut (r. 1857–68) and Chulalongkorn (r. 1868–1910), who used the British and the French against each other and at the same time promoted the modernization of their country. (Readers may recognize Mongkut as the ruler portrayed in *Anna and the King of Siam*, later the basis of the musical *The King and I*.) Siam nevertheless had to submit in the late 1850s to the now familiar set of unequal treaties and special privileges for foreigners, and was obliged to cede some territory to British Burma and Malaya on the west and south and to French Indo-China on the east. Siam was however almost homogenous in culture and language, especially once it had been obliged to give up the areas detached by Britain and France. The relative recency of Thai occupation of the country and of the Thai monarchy also meant that most Thais shared a common sense of their culture, history and identity, and a common reaction to foreign pressures, although there too many Thais profited from the commercialization after 1850.

Chinese might have become an important minority in Siam, and they were periodically resented or even the target of riots as they rose to dominate the new commercial economy, especially the export trade in rice, rubber, and hardwoods. But in Siam, unlike most of the rest of Southeast Asia, Chinese merged relatively peacefully with Thai society, married Thai women, took Thai names, and within a generation or less were no longer easily discernible as "minorities." In the Philippines the many immigrant Chinese before about 1850 were almost as easily assimilated by the same process, although more distinctions and discrimination were imposed on later arrivals.

The Plantation System

Colonial Southeast Asia became the world's major center of plantation agriculture, which in turn accounted for most of what economic development took place. In this tropical area with its year-long growing season and generally adequate and reliable rainfall, crops in great demand in the West could be profitably grown for export, drawing on local low-wage labor or on that of the streams of immigrant Chinese and Indians. Colonialism took over Southeast Asia after industrialization was well established in the West and had begun to generate an enormous appetite for tropical products such as rubber, sugar, palm and coconut oil, kapok, quinine, tea, and other crops. Rice, another major export (though mainly to the rest of Asia), was generally grown by peasants on individual farms in the Irrawaddy, Chao Praya, and Mekong deltas (in Burma, Siam, and Indo-China respectively) rather than on plantations, while teak and other tropical hardwoods were cut in existing forests. Tobacco and sugar also became important plantation crops, especially in Indonesia (Sumatra) and the Philippines. Hemp (abaca) was a staple Philippine export grown mainly by small-holders. Tin (west coastal Malay and northwestern Indonesia) and oil (central Burma and Indonesia) were additional major exports, but their existence was unknown until late in the nineteenth century, just when Western markets began to enormously increase their demand for both, along with rubber, as the age of the auto-mobile opened. Rubber plantations mushroomed in Malaya, Indonesia, and southern Thailand and Vietnam. But it was climate which offered the greatest attraction to Western colonialists to begin with, as in the time of the Portuguese and the spice trade; spices remain an important Southeast Asian export to the present.

French Indo-China

A plantation is a large unit of land under single ownership which hires labor to grow a single commercial crop, for sale or export, and which usually includes some processing facilities: preliminary or final sorting, curing, refining, and packing for shipment. It is run for profit only and usually grows no food crops for local consumption. The total amount of land occupied by plantations in Southeast Asia was never very large (see the map on page 448), but it was disproportionately productive. In most cases plantations did not displace food crops but made use of areas not previously cultivated. Many of the plantations concentrated on tree or bush crops which did well on slopes and did not need fertile soil: rubber, palms, kapok, quinine (from the chinchona tree, used for treating malaria), tea, and most spices. Rubber, a tree of the tropical rain forest, was introduced from Brazil where it had been gathered in the wild, but in Southeast Asia, with its closely similar climate, rubber trees were grown far more efficiently on plantations, where it was also easier to recruit low-wage labor, mainly immigrant Chinese and Indians. Southeast Asian rubber plantations soon destroyed Brazilian competition and dominated the booming world market, coagulating the milky sap tapped from the trees into sheets and shipping them out through the ports of Singapore, Batavia (the Dutch colonial capital of Indonesia, now Jakarta), Surabaya in eastern Java built up by the Dutch, Bangkok, and Saigon, the French colonial capital of Vietnam.

Sugar was sometimes a plantation crop in the Philippines, but mainly it was grown there, and in Java, the other major commercial producer, by individual peasant farmers, often as part of a crop rotation with rice; the deep rich volcanic soil of Java made this possible and gave both sugar and rice the nutrients they needed even under continuous cultivation; conditions on the island of Negros and in central Luzon in the Philippines, the major sugar producers there, were similar. The delta rice lands of lower Burma, Siam, and Vietnam were for the most part newly opened to cultivation, by clearing and drainage, and were thus very productive but without taking land from existing food crops. In Java, the much larger population—approximately 30 million by 1900—and the concentration on export crops, meant that rice to feed the people increasingly had to be imported, up to half of total consumption by the twentieth century. Rice was also imported to feed the booming port cities and coastal areas of India, China, and Japan.

Pluralism and Problems of Nationalism

Such changes affected only a small part of Southeast Asia, although they involved a larger share of its people. Nevertheless, most Southeast Asians remained subsistence farmers or sold only a part of their crop, and only a small proportion worked on plantations, mining enterprises, commercial rice farms, or served the labor needs of the export trade and the ports. The great majority of the area continued to be occupied, as for many centuries, by a variety of hill and mountain people who subsisted largely on shifting cultivation, clearing a patch of forest or jungle by fire and growing a quick crop there for a few years until the soil was exhausted or the patch of cultivation invaded by weeds. They then moved on to clear another patch, in a cycle that might take from 15 to 20 years or more before it returned to a plot which had been previously used. In that time the jungle would have taken over the plot in this tropical climate; rapidly decaying forest litter, plus the ash from burning, provided a brief fertility. It was thus a reasonably stable system, but it nevertheless involved the use of very large amounts of land of which only a small part would be in current use, and it produced almost nothing for sale, which invited the criticism of the colonialists. Some hill and mountain people lived in the forest as hunter-gatherers, and some of them did produce things gathered in the wild, such as honey, bark, medicinal roots and herbs, animal skins, and other forest products—and unfortunately also sometimes slaves.

The hill and mountain people were culturally and linguistically different from those of the lowlands, who referred to them by pejorative names such as "savages" or "barbarians" and often tried to subjugate them or raid them for slaves. In Burma, these hill people, some of them with their own literate and political tradition, make up about a third of the total population and have long been in chronic rebellion or disaffection from the dominant lowland Burmans. In Thailand, Vietnam, and Cambodia they are about a fifth. In maritime or oceanic Southeast Asia—Malaya, Indonesia, and the Philippines—lowland rice growers were or became numerically dominant too, but in each area, especially Indonesia and the Philippines, culturally different groups in bewildering variety occupied most of the land, concentrated in the hill areas but living also in the many islands of both countries, separated from the influences of Java or Luzon and chronically in conflict with each main power base, especially in the form of piracy, but in any case more dependent on the sea and its trade than on rice agriculture. Neither country had ever been politically unified before Western imperialism lumped them together in the late nineteenth and early twentieth centuries and their common or shared existence has thus been extremely brief, as was the case also in Burma. It is thus hardly surprising that common grounds for the growth of nationalism were few, and that traditional intergroup and interregional conflicts continue even now. There were also language barriers which divided most of these groups from each other and from the dominant lowland cultures, and a legacy of mutual dislike or hostility. Even Java itself was split between different regimes until the last years of Dutch control.

Into this already highly fragmented cultural landscape came many millions of permanent Chinese settlers, especially after about 1850, and smaller numbers of Indians in Burma and Malaya. With the qualified exception of Thailand, they were not absorbed into the emerging national cultures of each state and were generally resented and discriminated against. They clearly could not be drawn on as support for Southeast Asian nationalism, and indeed their presence tended to contradict it. The rise of cities and ports, where the Chinese lived almost exclusively, also generated a new urban culture sharply different from the traditional world of peasant rice growers and their hereditary overlords, while plantation workers and the few in factories or in menial jobs in the cities and ports, those who were not Chinese, formed yet another different group whose lives and interests shared little with those of peasants, hill farmers, or forest people. The cities began to generate a new class of intellectuals as well, deeply influenced by Western ideas and Western-style education among whom feelings of nationalism first began to grow and who led the nationalist movements which began to take shape after the First World War, people like Ho Chi Minh, the Philippine-educated elite, or *ilustrados*, and Sukarno in Indonesia. But except for Ho, who had the benefit of Communist organization and its effective propaganda machinery and thus was able to build a mass base, these emerging intellectuals were few in number and largely divorced from most of their fellow citizens or subjects. Ho succeeded in part because of the brutal oppressiveness of French rule, which nearly all Vietnamese experienced, and Sukarno drew strength from the similar consequences of harsh Dutch control and exploitation; but there and elsewhere it was a long uphill job to organize most Southeast Asians in the service of nationalism. The differences among them and in their situations and experiences were just too great.

The Rise of Southeast Asian Nationalism

Vietnamese resistance to the French conquest and subsequent rule has already been mentioned, but nationalism was nothing new to Vietnam. The first stirrings of

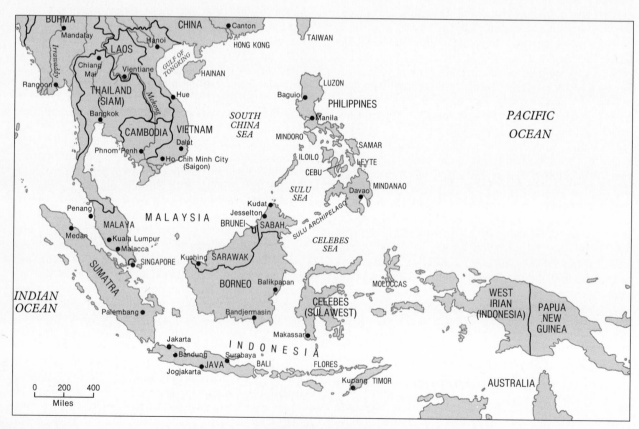

Southeast Asia

new anticolonial nationalism took place in the Philippines, where colonialism had a longer history than anywhere in the world. Three centuries and a half of Spanish rule had spread a common language and Catholic religion among the national elite, and there was an emerging middle class of educated people, the *ilustrados*, who were increasingly resentful of foreign rule. When their demands for reform beginning in the 1870s were met by harsh repression, they were first supplanted by and then joined outright revolutionaries led by Emilio Aquinaldo, who mobilized widespread popular support and declared an independent Republic in 1898. This would certainly have succeeded, making the Philippines the first Asian country to win its independence, if the Americans had not almost immediately intervened as part of their war against Spain.

Having promised the infant Philippine Republic its freedom in exchange for collaboration against the Spanish, the Americans then, once the Spanish had surrendered, turned on their Philippine allies and brutally suppressed Aquinaldo's forces in a long antiguerrilla war; the ruthless American military tactics were similar to those in Vietnam 50 years later. Bitterness over this betrayal faded relatively soon among the *ilustrados* as most of them made their profitable peace with the Americans as collaborators in the full-scale commercialization of the Philippines and the Americanization of its economic, legal, political, and educational systems. Increasing scope was provided for elective Filipino representation, and Manuel Quezon was elected first president of the Philippine Commonwealth, under an American High Commissioner. But the needs of peasants, still the great majority of the population, remained largely unaddressed.

Elsewhere in Southeast Asia the colonial experience, and the geographic political units created, had been too brief to allow similar developments. Most of the intellectuals who were troubled by foreign dominance began by reasserting their own traditional cultural identities, as in the General Council of Buddhist Associations in Burma,

---

✠ French and American Imperialism ✠

Jules Ferry, the imperialist-minded premier of France, urged that colonies were vital to French interests and, in 1881, justified the conquest of northern Vietnam as follows:

It is not a question of tomorrow but of the future of fifty or a hundred years, of that which shall be the inheritance of our children, the bread of our workers. It is not a question of conquering China, but it is necessary to be at the portal of this region to undertake the pacific conquest of it.

American Senator Henry Cabot Lodge probably spoke for most of his countrymen when he tried to 1899 to justify to the Senate the American takeover of the Philippines.

Duty and interest alike, duty of the highest kind and interest of the highest and best kind, impose upon us the retention of the Philippines, the development of the islands, and the expansion of our Eastern commerce.

The American General Shafter, in charge of the military campaign against the Philippine patriots under Aguinaldo in central Luzon, added this in 1900.

It may be necessary to kill half the Filipinos in order that the remaining half may be advanced to a higher plane of life than their present semi-barbarous state affords.

Sources: T.F. Powers, *Jules Ferry and the Renaissance of French Imperialism.* (New York: Octagon, 1972), p. 191; U. Mahajani, *Philippine Nationalism.* (Brisbane: University of Queensland Press, 1971), p. 225. F. Luzviminda, "The First Vietnam: The Philippine-American War," *Bulletin of Concerned Asian Scholars,* December, 1973, p. 4.

Ho Chi Minh (1890–1969), taken during a visit to India. (Bettmann Archive)

The Russian Revolution of 1917, the rise of Japan as an Asian power, and Gandhi's successes in building a mass movement against colonialism in India struck responsive chords among most educated Southeast Asians. The First World War had shown that Western civilization was deeply flawed and far from invincible. More and more Southeast Asian students now studied in Europe, India, and Japan, as well as at Rangoon University in Burma and a few at Hanoi and Batavia. Everywhere they went, these students learned the gospels of nationalism, which they brought home with them, including the organizational powers of modern political parties, and the need for modernization in all aspects of life as conditions for the independence many of them now aimed for. But there was still nothing approaching a mass base for such changes, nor was one to develop until after independence had been in effect created by the Japanese defeat of Western colonialism in Asia from 1941 to 1945. The Indonesian Communist party was founded in the early 1920s, but it remained a small and largely ineffective organization, especially given the ruthlessness of Dutch police control, which decimated it in several poorly prepared uprisings in 1926 and 1927. This happened also in Vietnam to both the Nationalist and Communist parties there, but the Communists, under Ho's better organization and strategy and with help from China, survived. In Burma, nationalist groups were divided between the traditionalists and the more modern reformers; partly for that reason, Burma never matched the effectiveness of the Indian independence movement under Gandhi and the Congress.

Apart from Ho, and the quite different group of *ilustrado* politicians in the Philippines, only one other figure emerged in the 1920s as a recognized nationalist leader, the man known as Sukarno (1901–1970: Indonesians usually use only one name). He was Dutch-educated in Java and Holland and picked up many Western ideas, but developed a personal and political mixture of Western, traditional Javanese, Islamic, and Marxist notions, blending them under the heading of Indonesian Nationalism. Like Ho and Sun, he had great personal magnetism and was an accomplished orator, although his true convictions were often clouded by a Messiah complex and a love of the limelight. He founded and headed the new Indonesian Nationalist party, but once in that prominent position he was an immediate target for the Dutch, who arrested and finally exiled him from Java; he did not return until the end of Dutch rule (see Chapter 21). Other Indonesian nationalist leaders were also banished or imprisoned, and the movement broke up into self-defeating factionalism.

In Burma, belated British concessions involved increasing Burmese representation in the colonial administration, and collaborators outnumbered those urging independence, as was to remain the case until the eve of the

and its Islamic parallels in Indonesia. Both became qualified mass movements, led by Westernized or Western-educated intellectuals, but moved only slowly to form viable political programs and demands for representation or independence. In Vietnam, the Chinese revolution of 1911 was an inspiration to many, and led to the founding of the Vietnamese Nationalist party, based on the ideas of Sun Yat-sen and his strong influence on Ho Chih-minh. The party attempted attacks on the French colonial government in 1929 and the early 1930s and was completely destroyed, leaving the field in effect to the newly founded Indo-Chinese Communist party led by Ho. In Malaya there was little or no resistance to colonialism, and the growing sense of Malay nationalism had far more to do with preservation of their Islamic religion and traditional Malay culture against what they saw as the threat from millions of immigrant Chinese and Indians. Even in independent Siam there was a renewed promotional interest in Buddhism, and in southern Vietnam a new sect, the Cao Dai, combining elements of traditional animism, Buddhism, and French-introduced Catholic Christianity.

Second World War. Then a new generation of radical nationalists centered at British-founded Rangoon University won over most politically conscious Burmese to the side of freedom—only then to be exploited and betrayed by the Japanese. In independent Siam, modernization had included a foreign-style education system, civil service, and military, but access to all these was limited to members of the widespread royal family and some of the court nobility. By the late 1920s this was no longer acceptable to the rest of the educated elite, including those who had studied abroad. In 1932, a group of army reformers forced the king to accept a constitution and changed the country's name to Thailand, which thereafter came under a militarized autocracy with the traditional monarchy retained as a national symbol. In the rest of Southeast Asia, the colonial orders seemed secure on the eve of the Pacific war. Although Philippine independence had been promised for 1946, and the movement toward self-government began in Burma, as in India, French and Dutch colonial regimes held firm and seemed impossible to dislodge. Their destruction would be accomplished by the Japanese.

Vietnam

Vietnam, as most closely in the Chinese orbit, merits fuller treatment. Where a disunited and disorganized Korea was overwhelmed by the Mongols, Vietnam, amazingly enough, beat off three successive Mongol efforts at conquest, fresh from their victories in China right next door. Later the Vietnamese repelled Ming and Ch'ing attempts to reincorporate them in the Chinese empire. Despite this history of bitter conflict, and consequent Vietnamese fear and mistrust of China, they, like the Koreans, adopted most of Chinese literate culture, including the writing system, Confucianism and Taoism, a state bureaucracy and examination system, classical literature, an imperial censorate and administration on the Chinese model, public granaries, and a system of imperial roads. Though even more closely related than the Koreans to the Chinese racially, culturally, and linguistically, especially to the Cantonese of neighboring south China, the Vietnamese nevertheless retained a strong sense of separate identity.

They had much in common with the rest of Southeast Asia, including the relatively high and free status of women and associated inheritance patterns, and the strong influence in their culture of originally Indian art forms and law, traceable to the early spread of Buddhism into Southeast Asia from India and the cultural influences which came with it. As in Korea, Chinese forms and culture tended to be concentrated in the elite and the political realm, while the basic and village-level culture remained clearly Southeast Asian, with Indian admixtures. Interaction with China continued, but Vietnam was at least equally involved in interaction with its neighboring Southeast Asian peoples and cultures.

While holding the Mongols and Chinese off from the thirteenth century A.D., an amazing feat in itself, the Vietnamese continued their own expansion southward, incorporating most of Annam by the fifteenth century and reaching the Mekong delta by about 1670, at the expense of the earlier inhabitants, primarily Chams and

Rubber plantation, Malaya. The tree is cut into to let the latex (sap) run down for collection in buckets, which then are taken to a processing station on the plantation where the latex is concentrated into sheets or balls for export. (Culver Pictures, Inc.)

Khmers. But French Catholic missionaries were already active in Vietnam, since the seventeenth century, and made more converts there than in all of China. As in Korea, the conservative Confucian-style government was opposed to foreign influences and especially to Christianity and its aggressive missionaries. In the nineteenth century, when they became alarmed at the growth of converts and mission efforts, they began a persecution of both, killing many priests and as many as 30,000 converts. This was the pretext the French had been waiting for. They captured Saigon, the southern capital, in 1859 and began to take over the surrounding southern provinces. A treaty in 1862 ceded the south to France, which then took over neighboring Cambodia as well. But French ambitions were not satisfied, and in 1882 they seized Hanoi, the northern capital, provoking a war with China which sent troops to protect its tributary state, as 11 years later in Korea against the Japanese invasion. The Sino-Vietnamese war against the French lasted from 1883 to 1885, and left the French in firm control; in 1893 they added Laos, formerly a Siamese (Thai) dependency.

The harsh French colonial rule was exploitative and aimed to impose French culture on the elite of Vietnam, while providing few educational opportunities and draining resources out to France rather than developing the Vietnamese economy, or preparing Vietnamese to play a role in the administration, education, or modernization of their country. In addition, the French period saw a rapid growth of landlordism and sharecropping; living standards for Vietnamese, as for Koreans under Japanese rule, fell. The French brutally suppressed all political expression, and many of the leaders of Vietnamese nationalism were jailed, executed, or forced to flee, like those in Korea. Among those thus forced out was Ho Chi Minh (1890–1969), who in 1911 went to France.

Ho helped found the French Communist party in 1920, studied in Moscow, and then worked with Sun Yat-sen and Michael Borodin, the Comintern agent, in Canton. Like other colonialists, the French developed a public health system but this resulted in the population increasing faster than the food supply, especially as much of the rice was exported. Most Vietnamese landholdings were small, but about half the cultivated land was owned by French or by their Vietnamese collaborators. In the south were many large estates or plantations where peasants worked as underpaid laborers, including rubber plantations. Railways and port facilities were built to serve this new commercial economy, but Chinese came to dominate the export trade, especially in rice, and became a major part of the population of Saigon, living in their own district known as Cholon. Although Vietnam was run as a police state, with the help of French secret police, educated Vietnamese acquired much of French culture, and learned about the French revolution and the ideals of liberté, egalité, and fraternité. But Vietnam under France offered no chance for reformist change; in the end, Communist revolution became the chief vehicle of Vietnamese nationalism and its struggle for independence, aided as in China by the Communist role in resistance to the Japanese after 1940.

From his base in Canton, Ho organized the Communist party of Vietnam in 1930, with support from the

Indonesian rice fields, Sumatra. Rice remains the major crop of lowland Southeast Asia, and much of Java and Bali resemble this scene, as do the lowland rice-growing areas of Burma, Thailand, Vietnam, Malaysia, and the Philippines. (Henri Cartier-Bresson/Magnum)

Comintern. The world depression and drought-induced famine were causing great suffering in Vietnam, and there was a military uprising later in the same year. After the bloody French suppression of the mutiny, and the virtual destruction of the Nationalist party, the Communist movement spread among impoverished peasants. The French called on their Foreign Legion, broke the Communist organization, and killed, executed, or exiled many thousands. Ho fled to Hong Kong, but the Communists continued organizing underground. The French were an obvious and hated target, uniting most politically conscious Vietnamese against them, and Marxism-Leninism provided an appealing anti-imperialist rationale. When the Japanese moved into Vietnam in 1940, they ran the country, plus Cambodia and Laos, through the Vichy French officials and police, until just before the end of the war, when they took over complete control. French rule was thus ended by the Japanese conquest, as elsewhere in colonial Southeast Asia.

It was the brief Japanese triumph at the beginning of the Pacific war which rang the death knell of Western colonialism in Asia, especially in Southeast Asia where all but Thailand had been incorporated into Western colonial empires. The Japanese victories destroyed the myth of Western invincibility and stimulated the continued growth of Southeast Asian nationalism, first against their erstwhile Western colonial masters and then very quickly against the Japanese themselves. Japanese policy and behavior in all of their conquered territories was at least as oppressive, even brutal, as the worst of the Western colonial regimes, and at least as racist, despite their slogan of "Asia for the Asiatics." They treated their newly conquered people as little more than slaves, gave them no voice in their government, and drained Southeast Asia of the resources which had attracted Japanese attention in the first place. With the defeat of Japan in 1945 and in the years immediately following, each Southeast Asian country except for Vietnam won its independence. The French tried to return to Vietnam as a colonial power, with American and British help, and when that effort failed in 1954, the United States moved in to take the French place and to try to hold Vietnam against the advance of communism.

Suggestions for Further Reading

Korea

Chandra, V. *Imperialism, Resistance, and Reform in Late Nineteenth Century Korea*. California Press, 1988.

Choe, C. T. *The Rule of the Tae Won'gun*. Cambridge: Harvard Press, 1972.

Deuchler, M. *Confucian Gentlemen and Barbarian Envoys: The Opening of Korea, 1875–1885*. Seattle: University of Washington Press, 1977.

Freseur, F. "Korea," in *The Politics of Colonial Exploitation*. in R. E. Elson, ed. Ithaca, NY: Cornell Univ., 1992.

Henthorn, W. E. *A History of Korea*. New York: Free Press, 1971.

Kang, Y. *The Grass Roof*. New York: Norton, 1975.

Kim, C. I. and H. K. *Korea and the Politics of Imperialism*. Berkeley: California Press, 1967.

Kim, K. Y. *The Last Phase of the East Asian World Order: Korea, Japan, and the Chinese Empire, 1860–1882*. California, 1980.

Lensen, G. A. *Balance of Intrigue: International Rivalry in Korea and Manchuria, 1884–1899*. Univ. of Hawaii Press, 1982.

McNamara, D. L. *The Colonial Origins of Korean Enterprise, 1910–1945*. Cambridge Univ. Press, 1990.

Southeast Asia

Adas, M. *The Burma Delta, 1852–1941*. Madison: Univ. of Wisconsin Press, 1974.

Brands, H. W. *Bound to Empire: The United States and the Philippines*. Oxford Univ. Press, 1992.

Buttinger, J. *A Dragon Embattled: Colonial and Post-Colonial Vietnam*. New York: Preager, 1972.

Chew, E. C. T. and Lee, E. *A History of Singapore*. Oxford Univ. Press, 1991.

Duiker, W. J. *The Rise of Nationalism in Vietnam, 1900–1941*. Ithaca: Cornell, 1976.

Jamieson, N. L. *Understanding Vietnam*. California, 1993.

Karnow, S. *In Our Own Image: America's Empire in the Philippines*. New York: Random House, 1989.

Kolko, G. *Anatomy of a War*. New York: Random House, 1990.

Kulick, E. F. and Wilson, D. *Thailand's Turn*. New York: St. Martin's, 1992.

McAlister, J. T. *Vietnam: The Origins of Revolution*. New York: Knopf, 1969.

Martin, M. A. *Cambodia*. California, 1994.

Maung, M. *The Burmese Road to Poverty*. New York: Praeger, 1991.

Osborne, M. *Southeast Asia: An Introductory History*. New York: Harper Collins, 1991.

_____. *The French Presence in Cochinchina and Cambodia*. Ithaca: Cornell University Press, 1969.

Patti, A. I. *Why Vietnam?* Berkeley: University of California Press, 1991.

Regnier, P. *Singapore*. Honolulu: University of Hawaii Press, 1992.

Reid, A. *Southeast Asia in the Early Modern Era*. Ithaca: Cornell University Press, 1993.

Rotter, A. J. *The Path to Vietnam*. Ithaca: Cornell University Press, 1987.

Sheehan, N. *A Bright Shining Lie*. New York: Random House, 1988.

Tai, H. T. H. *Radicalism and the Origins of the Vietnamese Revolution*. Cambridge: Harvard University Press, 1992.

Taylor, R. H. *The State of Burma*. Honolulu: University of Hawaii Press, 1988.

Werner, J. and Luv, D. H., eds. *The Vietnam War*. Armonk, New York: M. E. Sharpe, 1994.

Wijeyewardene, G. *Ethnic Groups Across National Boundaries in Mainland Southeast Asia*. Singapore: Institute of Southeast Asian Studies, 1990.

Wyatt, D. K. *Thailand: A Short History*. New Haven: Yale Universtiy Press, 1984.

CHAPTER 17

CHINA IN TATTERS, 1896–1925

New Foreign Plundering

The Boxer Rebellion, and especially its turning against foreigners, was clearly related to continued foreign pressures on China and to a new round of concessions in the 1890s, spurred on by Japan's seizure of Korea in 1895. British, French, and Russian banks loaned China the money needed to pay the huge Japanese indemnity imposed in 1895. In partial return, Russia obtained permission in 1896 to extend the Trans-Siberian railway across northern Manchuria on a straight line to Vladivostok, saving some 350 miles as against the route following the Amur River, still the border between Chinese and Russian territory. This new line was called the Chinese Eastern Railway, its Sino-Russian board headed by a Chinese but effectively under full Russian control. Later in 1896 Russia and China signed a secret alliance aimed at containing further Japanese expansion. In 1898 the Russians obtained a 25-year lease over the Liaotung (Liaodong) peninsula of southern Manchuria, including Port Arthur, where they stationed a fleet, and permission to connect it by rail with the Chinese Eastern Railway.

Using the pretext of the murder of two German missionaries by bandits in Shantung, the Germans occupied the harbor of Tsingtao (Qingdao) at the tip of the peninsula opposite Liaotung and Port Arthur in 1897. In the next year, not to be left out in this scramble for concessions, the French occupied the harbor of Kwangchow (Guangzhou) Bay south of Canton, close to their colony

in Vietnam. Britain added more adjacent mainland territory to Hong Kong, known as the New Territories, also in 1898, on a 99-year lease, and a naval base on the north coast of Shantung called Weihaiwei, to counter Russian, German, and French moves. The British also obtained an agreement from China that it would give no concessions to other powers in the whole of the Yangtze valley, which thus became a British sphere, to match the Russian sphere in Manchuria, the German in Shantung, and the French in Yunnan, adjacent to Vietnam. With the addition of railway concessions to the Western powers, China seemed on the point of becoming just another colony, although one with multiple foreign manipulators.

One response to this new increase in the plundering of China was the reform movement of 1898 described in Chapter 14. Another was the Boxer movement in Shantung, and its transformation by Tz'u Hsi into the antiforeign Boxer Rebellion. The protocol of 1901 with the foreign powers, signed by the aging Li Hung-chang two months before his death, called for the execution of ten high Ch'ing officials and the punishment of hundreds of others, not of course including Tz'u Hsi. She seems to have believed the Boxers' assertion that their magic rituals made them invulnerable to foreign bullets, but when the allied expedition was clearly winning the fight against them and the imperial troops which fought on their side, the court changed its line and declared the Boxers to have been a rebellion against the Ch'ing, as it originally was.

The dynasty was also saved in part through the actions of many of its regional officials who saw the Boxer

325

cause as hopeless, including Li Hung-chang, Chang Chih-tung, and the Manchu general Yuan Shih-k'ai. They and others assured the foreigners that they would keep order elsewhere and were not party to Tz'u Hsi's declaration of war. Thus most of China seemed to the foreigners to be in stable and cooperative hands, and left little to be gained from overturning the dynasty or punishing Tz'u Hsi as she deserved. She had escaped from Peking in disguise in a small cart without her usual retinue as the victorious foreigners were completing their mop up of the Boxers who had besieged the foreign legations and had begun widespread looting, eagerly joined by many Chinese. She and her court stayed in Sian for over a year and did not return to Peking until after the Boxer Protocol had been signed, providing for the permanent stationing of foreign troops at the capital. Another very heavy indemnity was imposed on China, and this time there was no hope of foreign loans to help pay it. The British later, and then the Americans following their lead, continued to collect the regular payments, which were secured on the Maritime Customs revenue, but put a large part of them into a fund—the Boxer Indemnity Fund—to support scholarships for young Chinese to study in Britain and the United States.

The dynasty's finances were, however, already in chaos, and the Boxer indemnity was over twice as large as Japan's had been in 1895. With the addition of the interest on existing foreign loans the two completely absorbed the Customs revenues and made it necessary to tap provincial revenues and the salt tax, leaving perilously little just to run the government, let alone invest in reconstruction and modernization as they had earlier been able to do. Fortunately for China's fiscal crisis, the Russian Revolution of 1917 and Germany's defeat in 1918 removed both from the list of creditors; other adjustments somewhat reduced the burden further, and some of the concessions granted in the 1890s for railway building were not followed up. But the Americans, previously free as they said of the taint of imperialism (conveniently forgetting their huge grab of land from Mexico and their enjoyment of all the foreign privileges in China won by British efforts), had succumbed to the disease in the 1890s and built a large new navy, which defeated the antiquated Spanish forces and took over the Philippines in 1898, while at the same time annexing Hawaii and the Pacific island of Guam.

The Open Door Notes

Such gross imperialist actions, which far exceeded those of any foreign power in China, did not prevent the Americans from attempting to trade on their supposedly pure anti-imperialist record in the Open Door notes of 1899 and 1900. The idea of trying to get the foreign powers to join in halting the scramble for new concessions and the creation of "spheres of influence" was originally British. John Hay, the U.S. Secretary of State, had earlier been ambassador to London and had discussed with the foreign office there British ideas on this matter, followed by conversations with Sir Robert Hart, the head of the China Maritime Customs. The British understandably saw the new foreign pressures on China as a threat to their own position as the dominant foreign power and the leading trader and investor there, but given their existing dominance felt that a counter gesture would come better from the Americans.

In September of 1899 Hay sent identical notes to all the foreign powers requesting that they not interfere with the existing treaty-port system, and that only the Chinese government, through the Maritime Customs as its agency, should collect trade duties. Hart's hand was clear in this, but the notes were aimed at preserving the status quo and equal access to trade by foreigners rather than trying to protect the Chinese state, as was often alleged. Britain, France, Germany, Italy and Japan gave rather evasive answers but said they would agree if everyone else did. The Russian reply was more negative, given their designs on Manchuria, which left everyone else off the hook, but Hay tried to put a good face on matters by notifying all concerned that his notes had been unanimously accepted and hence were "definitive."

Hay sent a second round of notes in July of 1900 as the foreign forces closed in on Peking, hoping for a solution which would bring "permanent safety and peace to China," protect foreign "rights," maintain Chinese sovereignty, and preserve for all "equal and impartial trade." This time, all agreed with this highly general declaration of virtue, and the Americans took full credit for having established an Open Door policy toward China, while at the same time brutally suppressing the Philippine nationalists and deposing the Queen of Hawaii. Unfortunately, everyone else gave the policy only lip service. More railway concessions continued to be extracted, and loans to build the lines. The Japanese were soon to begin their campaign to dominate China, after becoming the de facto rulers of Manchuria from 1905. The United States made no effort to back up its Open Door policy, and it was generally disregarded elsewhere, although it became a popular idea at home. Americans had always had a soft spot for China, primarily because of their missionaries, and the Open Door notes were at least well intentioned, if ineffective, while Americans increased their share of China's foreign trade under the provisions of the unequal treaties. They found new markets in China for their oil, imported mainly by the Standard Oil Company which also developed a cheap kerosene-fueled lamp giving a far brighter light than traditional vegetable oil, and were partners with the British in growing tobacco and making cigarettes, backed by a huge advertising campaign whose motto was "A cigarette in the mouth of every Chinese man, woman, and child." The British-American Tobacco Company imported seeds of Virginia tobacco and distributed them to peasants, especially in Shantung, to be fed to treaty-port factories; peasant producers and factory workers were badly exploited, but the new industry created some new jobs.

But there was long Chinese precedent for accepting what could not be changed, and specifically for accepting the membership of non-Chinese, like the people of the borderlands, other non-Chinese in East Asia, and indeed the Manchus themselves, as members of the greater Chinese empire of "all under heaven." The foreigners had forced China to accommodate them also, "barbarians" though they were, and in the course of the nineteenth century they too had made a place for themselves in the empire, whose continued sovereignty they recognized, as they served it in the Maritime Customs. The treaty system, one may say, institutionalized the foreign role in China and made them members of the whole. Although very few Chinese did not resent the foreigners, as they had resented other barbarians in the past and as many now resented the Manchus, they had become, like their barbarian predecessors, a fact of life like the Manchus, whom no one confused with Chinese. The Manchus themselves were of course well aware of their non-Chineseness, and indeed tried to preserve traditional Manchu culture, including language and the ancient Manchu homeland in Manchuria, where Chinese settlement was supposedly forbidden.

The Manchus were the *last* people to recognize or even tolerate the existence of Chinese nationalism, and indeed when it began to grow it was directed first of all against them as the immediate and obvious target. This would probably have happened eventually in any case, but as it was, foreign exploitation of China and treatment of Chinese as at best second-class people in their own country provided a new spark to Chinese nationalism, as the Japanese invasion was later to do. Politically minded Chinese increasingly blamed the Manchu dynasty for allowing China to be thus humiliated and plundered. In fact the Manchus had tried to defend the empire, and by diplomatic adroitness, foot-dragging, and playing off foreigners against each other ("using barbarians to control barbarians") they had preserved China despite its weakness and repeated defeats.

The Rise of Chinese Nationalism

Nationalism anywhere is often stimulated by frustration, defeat, humiliation, and of course by an external enemy; Germany after the First World War is one of many examples of the first, England against the Spanish Armada or France against European efforts to suppress the revolution of the second. Japanese nationalism was fed by foreign imposition of the unequal treaties. The foreign impact on China took longer, if only because China was so very much larger and more diverse, and because the foreign presence was so much less noticeable there. Chinese had no experience with what we recognize as nationalism in the modern world, still less with a modern nation-state. Confucianism, perhaps the most important cement of Chinese society, was a multinational or transnational institution shared with all other East Asians. The Chinese empire included all kinds of

One of the massive gates in the Peking wall, with foreigners in rickshaws passing under the p'ai-lo or ceremonial arch marking the approach to the gate, and a typical Peking cart on the left, taken soon after the Boxer Rebellion. (From the archives of the London Missionary Society)

people, and although the tributary system was more cosmetic than real, it perpetuated the notion that China was an all-embracing empire rather than a state; that designation was reserved for lesser kingdoms. The Celestial Empire had no rivals; the idea of nationalism is based on rivalry, and China had no rivals. It was dismissive of other peoples, largely on cultural grounds, and continued to feel that it was the only civilization. This sense of innate superiority helped China to accept the barbaric foreigners and to use their services in the treaty ports because they were not seen as a real threat to the supreme leadership of Chinese civilization, which had often in the past incorporated other barbarians within its system and even used them to help keep the peace along the frontiers against still other barbarians. The genuine political and military threat which the foreigners did represent was ignored or glossed over. China was unused to that form of confrontation or to rivalry on such a level; foreign strengths were dismissed and their potential totally underestimated because they were from the Chinese view such total outsiders, beyond the pale of the only civilization.

But with the combined shocks of cumulative foreign exploitation and the humiliating defeat by Japan in 1894–1895, a new sense of Chinese nationalism began to grow, first of course among intellectuals who lived in the treaty ports where they were daily exposed to the arrogant foreign impact. It too was humiliating, but the treaty ports also offered a model of order and strength through modern development which China so sadly lacked. As some intellectuals began to press for radical change and to plot the overthrow of the Manchus as alien conquerors who had failed China, they found refuge from the government police in the treaty ports under the protection of foreign law, an irony which disturbed many of them. It was there that secret societies formed, in the old Chinese tradition, dedicated to getting rid of Manchu rule, and there also that the first organized protests against foreign exploitation began. The first target of such protests, and accompanying boycotts in 1905, was the United States, not over the Open Door notes, but against the series of so-called Oriental Exclusion Acts passed by the U.S. Congress beginning in 1882 and extended in 1905, which forbade Chinese immigration (later extended to all Asians). This was a direct insult, less noticed or responded to to begin with but now intolerably offensive to the early stirrings of Chinese nationalism.

It was hard to see American behavior in China as having much to do with the ideals of the American Revolution: treaty-port merchants under the unequal treaties, missionaries, U.S. marines stationed in China from 1900, or U.S. gunboats on China's rivers. The moving message on the Statue of Liberty in New York Harbor now specifically excluded Chinese and other Asians with their "huddled masses yearning to breathe free."

Chinese immigrants had become some 8 percent of California's population by 1880, and many were killed in anti-Chinese riots. America was newly revealed as a racist country, and the insult was deeply resented by nationalist-minded Chinese, who for so long had had their own prejudice against "inferior" people, although it was predominantly cultural rather than racial. It was galling to have the tables turned on them. Widespread boycotts against American goods were organized in Canton, Shanghai, and most of the other treaty ports, where students, many of them returned from study abroad, joined Chinese merchant guilds and held mass meetings as well as using the press. American trade was hurt, but there was no softening of U.S. immigration policy.

The Last Years of the Ch'ing

Having survived the Boxer storm, Tz'u Hsi and her supporters at court then began to implement some of the reforms which K'ang Yu-wei had urged in the Hundred Days of 1898 even though she had executed all of those around K'ang whom she could catch. Chang Chih-tung, now governor-general of Hunan-Hupei, and Liu K'un-i, governor-general of Kiangsu-Anhwei-Kiangsi, presented the Empress Dowager with memorials in which they recommended such an about-turn, noting the strength of the foreigners and the spread of disaffection in China. At the top of their list, suitably enough for these survivors of the traditional Confucian emphasis on education, was

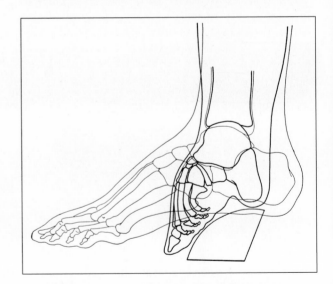

Diagram of a bound foot, superimposed on a normal foot. (From John K. Fairbank, Edwin O. Reischauer, and Albert Craig, *East Asia: Tradition and Transformation*. © 1989 by Houghton Mifflin Co. Used by permission.)

schools

a new program of schools to train officials, with the idea that eventually the old examination system would be discontinued. The old "eight-legged essay" (see Chapter 7) was abolished, but the new schools were intended to produce a new elite rather than to educate the people. They proved unpopular, even though in 1905 the old examination system was abolished and there was thus little demand for the academies and tutors of the traditional system. What did offer strong competition was mission schools, colleges, and universities, where most of the new generation of more modern-minded young men— and now women too—went. Some private Chinese-founded schools also appeared, with a "modern" curriculum and many Western subjects.

Missionaries had been pressing for what they called the emancipation of women, along Western lines, including of course their education. One of their crusades was against the custom of footbinding, begun in Sung times (see Chapter 6) and by the nineteenth century spreading to involve the daughters of most ambitious families in the torture which it inflicted, especially in north China, where even many peasant families succumbed to it in the hope of ensuring better husbands for their daughters. This foot fetishism had become part of the requirements in a bride, that she have a "lily foot"— and consequently be unable to do much beyond totter around the house, the bones of her foot broken within the tight bindings which produced a distorted stump like a bird's claw. The campaign against footbinding had in fact begun with Chinese reformers in the 1860s, although the Taipings had earlier inveighed against it.

The campaign made little headway even with the help of the missionaries, many of them women who were moved to help their Chinese sisters to escape from this bondage. But at least for the girls and women in their schools, the missionaries were successful, and helped to produce a new generation of women, few to start with, who were beginning on the long path to emancipation.

The Meiji Japanese example was inspiring in education as in its overall success. Chinese students, including some young women, began to go to Japan for their post-high-school education, and also learned at first hand what nationalism could do. Among them was Lu Hsun (Lu Xun, 1881–1936), the greatest of modern Chinese writers, who went to Japan to study medicine after his father had failed to be cured of tuberculosis by traditional Chinese methods. The Japanese had incorporated Western medicine in their new society and their medical schools followed that approach. While he was there, as he tells the story, an instructor filled up some time in class one day by showing a news film of the then current Russo-Japanese war. The film included the scene of a Chinese accused of spying for the Russians who was to be decapitated by the Japanese, while other Chinese stood around apathetically, waiting for the spectacle of an execution.

> Before the term was over I had left.... I felt that medical science was not so important after all. The people of a weak and backward country, however strong and healthy they may be, can only serve to be made examples of ... it doesn't really matter how many of them die of illness. The most important thing therefore was to change their spirit[1]

✠ Hope? ✠

Lu Hsun (Lu Xun) reports a conversation with a friend who came to urge him to write for the new magazine New Youth.

Hitherto there seemed to have been no reaction, favorable or otherwise, and I guessed they must be feeling lonely. However I said "Imagine an iron house without windows, absolutely indestructible, with many people fast asleep inside who will not feel the pain of death. Now if you cry aloud to wake a few of the lighter sleepers, making those unfortunate few suffer the agony of irrevocable death, do you think you are doing them a good turn?"
"But if a few wake, you can't say there is no hope of destroying the iron house."
True, in spite of my own convictions, I could not blot out hope, for hope lies in the future. So I agreed to write.... I sometimes call out, to encourage those fighters who are galloping on in loneliness, so that they do not lose heart.... I did not want to infect with the loneliness I had found so bitter those young people who were still dreaming pleasant dreams, just as I had done when young.

Source: Lu Hsun, *Selected Stories* (New York: W. W. Norton, 1977), pp. 4–5.

In time, with the passing of the old examination system, the new provincial schools in China too included many Western subjects, and educated Chinese read translations of a variety of Western works, many of them prepared by the classically educated scholar Yen Fu (Yan Fu, 1853–1921), who was one of the few in his time who saw a dynamism in Western civilization which China lacked and needed. Lu Hsun translated, and was much influenced by, Russian literature, but Yen Fu translated Western writers on liberal democracy, evolution, and political economy such as J. S. Mill, T. H. Huxley, Adam Smith, and Herbert Spencer, whose "social Darwinism" and ideas of individualism and individual freedom he came to support. He saw that Western rationalism, science, and legal and political systems had produced "progress," while China sank into relative backwardness following the very different Confucian path. Yen thus saw China as failing to take the road to wealth and power which the West had won for itself, and also as lacking the strength of true nationalism and the agency of the modern national state, so clearly evident in the West. Yen understood that talk of keeping the body of Chinese culture while using only some useful tools of Western origin missed the point. As the Meiji Japanese had realized early, the Western model worked as a package, part of which was its very differently conceived national state, and that if China was to survive it would have to pursue fundamental change.

But the country no longer had an effective central government, and what limited governmental effectiveness there was had progressively shifted to the provinces. Given the immense size of China it is not perhaps remarkable that with modern-style communications only beginning to spread no single power center could manage it all, any more than the traditional administrative system could penetrate most of the country except on a superficial basis. The rise of regional leaders and regional armies which had begun with Tseng Kuo-fan and his Hunan army in the suppression of the Taipings marked a development which became more marked after the 1860s. Even Li Hung-chang, though a loyal servant of the dynasty, had his own regional power base as a governor-general at the provincial level and his Anhwei army, led like the other regional armies mainly by local gentry who in turn had their own local networks. With the death of Li Hung-chang in 1901 and of Liu Kun-i, his fellow governor-general who came to head the Hunan army in 1902, Yuan Shih-k'ai, who had distinguished himself as a military man in Korea, emerged as the chief figure, at the head of his own Peiyang (Beiyang) army based at Tientsin (Tianjin) which became the most powerful military force in China.

Meanwhile, the growth of new economic centers in the treaty ports and of trade focused on them exerted a

The wreckage left after Anglo-French forces stormed the forts at Taku guarding the approaches to Tientsin and Peking in 1860. The guns had been made in China's early efforts to copy modern Western armament, but they were no match for those of the Westerners. (Time/Life Editorial Services/Chao-Ying Fang)

new centrifugal pull. The central government was slow to adjust to or compensate for these varied pressures which continued to dilute its effective power. Financially the government was still virtually crippled by the siphoning off of funds to pay the Japanese and Boxer indemnities or to meet interest payments on foreign loans. The revenue system was creaky and imperfect at best even without such drains, and far too much of what was collected either stayed in the provinces or somehow "leaked" out through corruption along the way. Basic change, not merely repair, was clearly needed, but the dynasty was old, deeply conservative, and now increasingly resented by rising Chinese nationalism.

Constitutionalism and Revolution

There were some efforts at the capital to move toward a new constitutional base and to overhaul the administrative system, but in general they foundered on the twin rocks of diehard Manchu reaction at court and cross currents among the provinces and between them and the central government. The Empress Dowager even promised a constitution in time, and in 1908 issued guidelines to prepare China for its coming and the creation of national assemblies. Her death later that year left the country still manipulated by the archconservative Manchu princes who had surrounded her. She is widely believed to have arranged the death of Emperor Kuang Hsü (Guangxu) a day before her own; if he had lived he might have resumed the spirit of basic change which he had exhibited in the Hundred Days of 1898; he was only 37, and was not unhealthy. The new emperor, Pu Yi, was a child, under the thumb of his father, the Manchu Prince Ch'un (Qun), as regent. Representatives from the newly constituted provincial assemblies urged Peking to move toward true parliamentary government; this was rejected, but the court reluctantly agreed later in 1910 to permit the convening of a national assembly, and the following year, with amazing unawareness of what was going on around them, appointed a cabinet in which there were eight Manchus, one Mongol, and only four Chinese.

It seems unlikely that this antiquated regime, already virtually dead in the water and either blind or determinedly opposed to the changes needed, could have lasted much longer, but matters were taken out of their hands by the revolution of 1911. There was growing anger in the provinces over the additional imperialist grip on China through the railways they built and controlled in Manchuria (Russian and Japanese), Shantung (German), and Yunnan (the French had completed their line from Hanoi to the provincial capital at Kunming in 1910), and which were accompanied by mining concessions along the routes. Other lines were being built by contract with foreign syndicates, in the form of loans to China but with whatever profits resulted going to the foreigners. Provincial leaders and gentry resented this new intrusion, and several of them tried to raise the capital to buy out some of the foreign interests. In May of

1911 Peking tried to steal a march on these provincial groups by decreeing the nationalization of all railway projects under central control, but there was widespread distrust of corruption in the central government and their new contract with a British-French-German-American banking consortium which would finance this project. Protests and mass meetings spread in the provinces; Szechuan (Sichuan), where no rail lines were in fact to be built until the 1950s, especially reacted in what local leaders saw as the defense of China against new imperialist encroachment; there was a major strike, and Szechuan stopped its central revenue payments.

Government troops moved in September, shot many of the demonstrators, and arrested many of the leaders. Szechuan, China's largest province but also one of its most isolated by distance and surrounding mountains, was the size of a European state and had always preserved a strong sense of separate regional identity, but with it there were now equally strong feelings of Chinese nationalism, influenced by what was happening in the foreign-dominated east coast and its humiliation of China, but largely free of this taint itself; its provincial capital at Chengdu had never been a treaty port. Many of the gentry leaders had studied abroad, and contrasted what they learned there with the corruption and ineptitude of the Ch'ing. They had also hoped to build and fund railway lines in Szechuan themselves and had already begun investing in projects, and anticipating profits. The largest number of them had gone to Japan and had come to admire the Meiji model of new strength.

Japan had its own interest in the impending collapse of the Manchus and the shape of what might follow it. K'ang yu-wei and Liang Ch'i-ch'ao had taken refuge there after the failure of the Hundred Days in 1898, and so had Sun Yat-sen, who was to become the leading figure of revolution and who depended importantly on Japanese support. K'ang remained in many ways a traditionalist despite his somewhat iconoclastic writings and his support for reform; he clung to the institution of the

A street in the small market town of Guanxian near Dujiangyan, Szechuan province. (Dennis Cox, ChinaStock)

emperor, perhaps because of his personal experience as a tutor to Kuang Hsü, while Liang and Sun moved far beyond this and pushed for more radical change, including especially for Sun the overthrow of the entire traditional system. Sun was the more radical of the two. Liang favored something more like enlightened despotism; as an elite scholar, he was not quite ready to trust the masses, feeling that they still needed to be led, and was unwilling to support violence. Liang's visit to the United States in 1903 left him unimpressed with the American version of democracy, its "mediocre" politicians, gross corruption, sensationalist press, and widespread violence. This was an elitist view to be sure, but it is usually enlightening to see ourselves as others see us!

Sun Yat-sen and 1911

Sun was born and educated more humbly, to a peasant family in 1866 near Macao, next door to Hong Kong. At age 13 he joined his older brother in Hawaii, where there was already a large Chinese community, made up largely of emigrant Cantonese like himself. Sun finished high school there and in those formative years became highly Westernized in the American version, accepted Christianity, and sang in the church choir. With his brother's support he then studied in Hong Kong and completed a medical degree there in 1892. His attempt to practice in Macao was thwarted by the Portuguese authorities there because he had no diploma from Portugal. Chafing over this rebuff, and over China's continued humiliation by foreigners, he turned first to reform, and then to revolution. Hung Hsiu-ch'uan, the Taiping leader, had been his childhood hero, and in his own life he not only had few ties with the traditional system but was in many ways more Western than Chinese. Indeed after he went to Hawaii he never again lived in China outside the treaty ports more than briefly, in the few years preceding his death in 1925. Macao and Hong Kong were not only formally foreign territory but quite untypical of the rest of China, part of the foreign establishment and its new ideas and ways.

In 1894, after some contact with the old Triad secret society, he founded his own, which he called the "Revive China Society." Sun was never very effective politically, and his first revolutionary plot in 1895 was discovered; he was lucky to escape to Japan, like K'ang and Liang before him, though most of his fellow conspirators were killed. He then returned to Hawaii, on to the United States, and to London, seeking support among overseas Chinese. He was kidnapped by the Ch'ing embassy in London, who planned to send him back to China for execution, but was freed after his former British medical teacher mobilized the Foreign Office and organized a press campaign, which brought him and his cause invaluable publicity.

A second attempt at an uprising in 1900, unrelated to the Boxer Rebellion but also designed to feed on anti-Ch'ing sentiment, fizzled. By now there were many other revolutionary societies, and Sun felt he had to build a new ideology and program, if only to meet this competition. His major base was now in Tokyo, beyond the reach of the Ch'ing police. Drawing from his diverse experience in Japan and the West, he announced Three Principles of the People: people's nationalism, people's democracy, and people's livelihood (San Min Chu-i in Chinese). This sounds, and was, vague, but also clearly derived from Western ideas; its vagueness helped to make it flexible in adjusting to changing circumstances. The notion of democracy implied an antitraditional egalitarianism, and Sun drafted a constitution to embody it, based on the American model but adding to the executive, legislative, and judicial wings two more: to supervise examinations, and an equivalent to the imperial Censorate to check on officials, both redolent of China's traditional past. Vaguest of all was "people's livelihood," which some equated with socialism but which mainly involved tax reform to curb speculators and big business rather than any radical restructuring of ownership. In Japan Sun was persuaded to join forces with Huang Hsing (Huang Xing), head of the chief rival revolutionary group, to form the T'ung Meng Hui or United League under Sun's overall leadership. He had become the best known of those working for revolution, and he seems to have had great personal charisma, despite his woolly thinking and his lack of political skill. He was able to ignite many with his revolutionary zeal (it was by now a popular cause) and to inspire them with his vision of a new China.

A revolt masterminded by another revolutionary group in Hunan in 1906 was suppressed, and in the next year Ch'ing pressure obliged Japan to expel Sun, who then went to Hanoi with Huang Hsing and tried to promote revolution from there in various parts of south China, until the French found all this revolutionary activity threatening to their own grip on Vietnam and they too forced Sun out. Sun went to the West again in search of support and funds, while Huang Hsing tried to foment revolution within the Ch'ing army, including a plot to capture the provincial office in Canton in April of 1911; this was a more hopeful tactic but it too was mismanaged and failed. By now, however, disaffection was indeed spreading within the army, there was growing economic distress, and provincial gentry like those in Szechuan were on the warpath.

It all came together on October 10, 1911, still celebrated as the date of the first Chinese revolution on the Double Tenth (10/10), but without any role by the

Sun Yat-sen and his young U.S.-educated wife, Soong Ch'ing-ling, in 1924. (Bettmann Archive/ Hulton Picture Library)

Sun was in America at the time still trying to raise money. He read an account of the events at Wuchang in a Chinese newspaper at the Denver Y.M.C.A. The revolutionaries, including now the T'ung Meng Hui, sent him a coded message telling him to return to China as its first president, but he had lost his codebook. Nevertheless he did return, and was finally inaugurated as president in January of 1912. Song Ching-ling (Soong Qingling), the woman he was to marry in 1915, was then a student at Wesleyan College in Macon, Georgia. She was the daughter of a Chinese emigrant who had returned from the United States, done well in treaty-port Shanghai, and sent his son and daughters to American colleges and universities. Song Ching-ling heard of the 1911 revolution, and wrote of it as:

> The emancipation of 400 million souls from the thralldom of an absolute monarchy.... The revolution has established in China Liberty and Equality.... Fraternity is the as yet unrealized ideal of humanity.... It may be for China, the oldest of nations, to point the way to this fraternity.[2]

In her youthful enthusiasm she exaggerated the success and the impact of 1911, but her remarks expressed views which were shared by many young Chinese intellectuals and at the same time showed the depth of Western influence on their thinking. The events at Wuchang were hardly a genuine revolution, but they fired the spread of Chinese nationalism in the modern sense for the first time. The end not only of Manchu rule but of more than 2,000 years of the dynastic order was certainly a big change, and the people who called themselves revolutionaries had some new and radical ideas. But they were too few and too politically inexperienced to establish an effective successor government. To make matters worse, it soon became clear that they were also split into factions.

Enter Yuan Shih-k'ai

Even Sun saw that he could not provide the unity and strong central government needed. The Ch'ing court had called on the help of their general Yuan Shih-k'ai, who however exacted his own terms as prime minister of a new government. Sun, Huang Hsing, and most of the other revolutionaries agreed that Yuan had the experience and the support, including his own Peiyang army, to pull the country together. In March of 1912 they turned the new presidency over to him. But Yuan, now turned politician as well as military man, was interested primarily in power rather than in shaping a new China, still less in the radical ideas of the revolutionaries. He set up a cabinet of ten, which included only four from the

T'ung Meng Hui; clearly, revolution was going to happen without, perhaps even despite, their "help." Some of the solders in the New Hupei (Hubei) Army stationed in the garrison at Wuchang (now part of Wuhan) had been talking revolution with sympathetic students. Their plot was discovered when a dog barked and a bomb they had made was found, a comedy of errors typical of earlier poorly organized revolutionary attempts. The army conspirators revolted on October 10, sensing they now had nothing to lose, and were joined by some of their fellows. Although the rebels were a small minority, the Ch'ing officials fled the city, which fell to the revolutionaries. Nothing succeeds like success, however rocky until the last moment, and not only most of the Hupei Army now joined the cause but most of the provincial governors and the new provincial assemblies by the end of the year; the absence of any significant amount of fighting makes it clear that most of China was ready for revolution.

T'ung Meng Hui, and a constitution which divided power between the president and the parliament; in practice Yuan called all the shots, and after a short time the T'ung Meng Hui members resigned in protest. Yuan tried to patch things up with Sun and Huang, but it was clear that he was unwilling to share power, or to tolerate any opposition. Nascent political parties, unheard of in the past, began to form, some of them with origins in the various secret societies which had pursued the cause of revolution but seldom acted together. A prominent T'ung Meng Hui member, Sung Chiao-jen (Song Jiaoren), who had resigned from the cabinet, persuaded most of the factions to join in a new alliance, the Kuo Min Tang (Guomindang), or National People's Party, in the summer of 1912. Elections held early in 1913 with a very small electorate gave the Kuomintang a clear majority in the new parliament, and Sung demanded that it should now also control the cabinet. Yuan's response was to have Sung assassinated in March, blaming it on Huang Hsing, and thus he hoped destroying the opposition.

Yuan's ploy was soon exposed, and he earned more hatred by his efforts to obtain money and support from foreign powers, in return for new concessions. This included a huge loan on onerous terms, from a six-power foreign consortium in 1913, and later Yuan's acceptance of Japan's 21 Demands (see Chapter 15). There was violent protest, and seven of the provincial governments declared their independence, but Yuan sent troops against them and reestablished his control. Sun, Huang, and other leaders again fled to Japan. Under threats from Yuan, the parliament elected him president to legitimize his position, and he then moved to outlaw the Kuomintang and dismiss all its representatives in parliament. Finally in early 1914 he dissolved both the parliament and the provincial assemblies and became in effect dictator with his powers confirmed through a new constitution which he simply announced. He silenced critics in the press, revived the state cult of Confucius, and conducted the ancient imperial rites at the Temple of Heaven like a new emperor. He now took to riding around in an armored car for fear of assassination by outraged patriots, but in fact most people were still willing to go along with his "strong man" rule, not ready yet to accept either the forms or the substance of democracy, with which they had had no experience, and feeling the need for control from the top, even one-man control, as for so long in the imperial past.

Actual treaties were signed with Japan accepting the gist of the 21 Demands in May of 1915, and adding the acceptance of Japan's "special interest" in the iron and coal mines and attendant iron and steel production in the Han-Yeh-P'ing combine in the Wuhan area, built in large part with Japanese loans and shipping most of its iron to Japan. There were fresh demonstrations, strikes, protests, and mass meetings, but the chief effect was to build more support for rising Chinese nationalism; boycotts of Japanese goods did damage their imports for the time being, but Yuan was immovable. One may argue that he had little alternative, especially given his pressing need for foreign funds and foreign support, and Japan's overwhelming military power. But his next step showed how out of touch he was with most political sentiment, and with the times; he began a campaign in the summer of 1915 to have himself declared emperor. In response to his own trumped-up propaganda, he agreed to accept the throne and a reign title, to begin in 1916. The response varied from cold to hostile. Eight southern and western provinces declared independence, there was

---

✠ Radical Change ✠

Ch'en Tu-hsiu issued a "Call to Youth" in 1915.

Chinese compliment others by saying "He acts like an old man although still young." Englishmen and Americans encourage one another by saying "Keep young while growing old." … Youth is like early spring, like the rising sun, like trees and grass in bud, like a newly sharpened blade…. I place my plea before the young and vital youth, in the hope that they will achieve self-awareness and begin to struggle…. It is the old and rotten that fills society. One cannot find even a bit of fresh and vital air to comfort those of us who are suffocating in despair. [But] *All Men are equal. Be independent, not servile. Be progressive, not conservative. Be aggressive, not retiring. Be cosmopolitan, not isolationist. Be utilitarian, not formalistic.*

Source: S. Y. Teng and J. K. Fairbank, *China's Response to the West: A Documentary Survey* (Cambridge, Mass.: Harvard University Press, 1954), pp. 240–244.

some inconclusive fighting, and in June 1916 Yuan died quite suddenly of a stroke. The emergence of a more modern, more nearly democratic China had moved agonizingly slowly since 1898, but it had already gone much too far to have the clock put back as Yuan tried to do. The protests against him still came almost entirely from the small educated and politically aware elite, but the ideas promoted by Sun and others of "the people" as the true basis of the emerging state had sunk deep roots and had begun to spread more widely.

The Warlords

With Yuan's death China collapsed into new chaos and division. These were the warlord years, which lasted until 1928, years that the locusts ate. Yuan himself was perhaps the first of the warlords, but at least for a time he controlled most of the country. Tibet fell away in de facto autonomy with an informal British guarantee, and Outer Mongolia the same, with Russian domination and later full independence as the Mongolian People's Republic (really a Soviet satellite), both ultimately acknowledged by treaties with Britain and Russia. Manchuria was tacitly accepted as a Japanese sphere. Sinkiang began to drift away from Peking's power, and the old Russian interest and intrigue there increased. But China proper was until early 1916 under a sort of central control, although the more distant provinces in the south and southwest were restive and maintained a good deal of local power, backed by the provincial armies. When Yuan died, regional military leaders with their own armies dominated the country. The headless government in Peking remained in place, represented the country abroad, and continued some essential services. The southern representatives in the parliament, most of them members of the Kuomintang, withdrew in protest against the growing power of Yuan Shih-k'ai's military lieutenants, generals in his Peiyang army. Sun saw this as an opportunity, returned to Canton in 1917, and formed a military government with the support of his Kuomintang colleagues, although it was dominated by the local warlords. Even Sun's new parliament was divided between those who favored cooperation with the local warlords and those opposed. Many of Sun's followers were assassinated on warlord orders, and Sun himself was forced to seek refuge in Shanghai in May of 1918. The north remained under the control of other warlords. China had been fragmented.

When the government in Peking decided to declare war on Germany in August of 1917, hoping to win some consideration in the peace settlement, it used that excuse to obtain large new loans from Japan but in fact used them to build up the northern army with Japanese instructors within a Sino-Japanese military alliance. Nevertheless, the north too was split by rivalries among different warlords and between political cliques in the government, periodically allied and then in conflict, often changing sides. It is a confusing period not easy to make clear. Most Chinese also had trouble understanding what was happening or sorting out the different factions, which frequently changed and differed from one area to another.

Warlords had a regional base and an army to match. Feng Yü-hsiang (Feng Yuxiang) and his "National People's Army" was dominant in Shantung, Honan, and the northwest. A large and colorful man, he was born a peasant who then acquired military training and experience, and became a baptized Christian. His missionary friends called him the Christian General, who was said to baptize his troops with a fire hose. He urged Protestantism, education, and a Y.M.C.A. version of social reform. Chang Tso-lin (Zhang Zuolin), who started out as a bandit and then allied himself with the Japanese against Russia, became a military governor and antileftist warlord of Manchuria but with power also in adjacent north China, especially the Peking area. Wu P'ei-fu (Wu Peifu), originally a Confucian scholar and then a military academy graduate, who with his army dominated the central Yangtze valley, was regarded by some as a moderate because of his classical education. And Yen Hsi-shan (Yan Xishan), who established his warlord kingdom in the province of Shansi (Shanxi), where he became known as the "Model Governor," and in fact anticipated many of the campaigns later pursued by the Communists, such as cleanliness and hygiene, discipline, local development projects, and civil order.

All the warlords claimed to be model rulers, "serving the people," but most of their energies were spent trying to overcome their rival warlords. There was chronic fighting, hardly a service to the people as armies marched back and forth over the countryside destroying and looting. The availability of modern weapons, some supplied by the Japanese to those they favored (they too were fishing in the troubled waters), and of steamship and railway transport for their troops as they invaded the territory of others, made them even more destructive. The warlords were mainly opportunists rather than leaders who offered any inspiration from their feeble ideology, and they were the obvious enemies of Chinese nationalism; they made a mockery of the national state. It was said that their armies never fought in the rain, before ten in the morning or after five in the afternoon, always took time out for lunch, and often acknowledged defeat without fighting at all if they found that the opposition had dominated the battlefield with a larger army and guns. The foreigners joked thus about them, but for all the jokes the warlord armies were a total plague on the land. Sun, still trying to pull the country together, attempted to play in their power games by siding with some warlords against others, supporting one side in the rivalry between southern warlord-governors, but to no lasting result. The warlords themselves continually switched sides and formed brief alliances to gang up on others. There was no talk by any of them of becoming supreme in China or of restoring the old imperial system. At most they hoped to build their regional power enough so that a new federal system would accept them as self-governing regional units.

Apart from their destruction and the taxation they imposed to maintain their campaigns, the warlords disrupted trade and slowed production and economic growth. The infrastructure, especially the still few railway lines, deteriorated as warlords requisitioned them to transport their troops but did little or nothing to maintain them. One particularly unfortunate consequence of warlord taxation was the recovery of opium production, just as it had begun to fade. Foreign imports had stopped in 1917 and domestic production languished, but now the heavy warlord taxes, especially in more remote upland areas where agriculture was at a disadvantage, obliged many areas to grow poppies since only the high returns could pay the taxes. Warlords became involved in the opium trade, exacting their own cut, and China again had the heavy burden of drug addiction to bear. Many of the warlords themselves were opium smokers, and most had a self-indulgent style with the trappings of a monarch, including a "stable" of women. Liang Ch'i-ch'ao, who had hung on in Peking politics hoping to exert a more positive influence, gave up in 1917 in despair and said that "In China today only cunning, crooked, vile, and ruthless people can flourish."[3] Equally serious was the cumulative neglect of the Yellow River dikes. These had been deteriorating in the last decades of the Ch'ing, and it was even said that in those corrupt years local officials would sometimes purposely make breaks in the dike in their area so that they could get government relief and could also profit corruptly from letting contracts for dike repair, but often and perhaps purposely on a shoddy basis so that new breaks could start the cycle again. In the 1920s this neglect and corruption came to a head in the catastrophic floods of the Yellow River which drowned many thousands and destroyed large areas of cropland, to be followed by famine.

New Social Mobility, and the New Culture Movement

In the past, such matters had been at least in part the responsibility of the local gentry, working together with imperial officials. With the end of the old examination system and the general demoralization, new local groups came to the fore, often without much education

let alone classical training, many of them simply local bullies or thugs with their own hired goons to collect exorbitant rents and terrorize the local people. Others found upward mobility by joining or working for warlords. There had been a remarkable degree of social mobility in the traditional past through the examination system, with as many as a third of each new generation of gentry rising into that group from nongentry origins—and necessarily of course a similar number moving vertically down out of the gentry group. The Western proverb, "rags to riches in three generations," fit the traditional Chinese pattern equally well, except that the Chinese noted also the other component of "riches to rags." The luxurious lifestyle of many of the elite was not good training for successive generations in the past, and now the same pattern was repeating itself. In more general terms, society was falling apart and losing the Confucian morality which had helped to hold it together in the past. More and more people were obliged to concentrate on simple survival and to follow a kind of "dog-eat-dog" morality.

The sad story of China's fate at Versailles has been told in Chapter 15. Despite the 200,000-man labor battalion sent to help the Allies in France, and despite President Wilson's Fourteen Points, the Chinese representatives sent to Versailles in 1919 were not even admitted, while those from Japan were seated at the table with the other Western powers. Although it was known that first Yuan Shih-k'ai and then successive warlord regimes in Peking had accepted most of Japan's 21 Demands, many Chinese hoped that the Versailles Conference would make a fresh start and would oblige Japan to return what it had grabbed in Shantung, if not in Manchuria, and would recognize the legitimacy of Chinese nationalism. When news reached China of the total sellout at Versailles, there was an explosion of popular protest. Students who had spent time abroad, including in Japan, joined others in Chinese universities in mass demonstrations. Most of this ferment centered in Peking University, the most prestigious and of course the one closest to politics. The best students were funneled to both private and state universities from both mission and government schools, including mission schools specifically for women. Students are natural activists everywhere, even revolutionaries, having little stake in the existing system and usually filled with idealism, including those returned from study abroad. In China they increasingly inherited the traditional role of the gentry as the educated elite who were best qualified to shape policy and to act politically.

The American remission of about two-thirds of their share of the Boxer indemnities in 1908, following the British lead, financed a number of Chinese to study in the United States, a flow which increased after 1924 when the balance of the indemnity was remitted and the funds thus increased. Earlier some Boxer funds had helped to found Tsing Hua (Xinghua) College (later Tsing Hua University) in Peking. Modern-style universities in every province, both mission- and government-founded, offered Western subjects. Shanghai was the largest Chinese city and the one most influenced by the foreign impact. There too schools and universities turned out a growing number of Westernized students, who like their fellows elsewhere in the country agonized over China's weakness and sought solutions. At Peking University Chancellor T'sai Yuanp'ei (Cai Yuanpei), who had studied in Germany and France, brought together beginning in 1917 a dynamic group of young intellectuals and emerging revolutionaries, men who had studied the classics and then had their minds opened by contact with the West. The most active of these was Ch'en Tu-hsiu (Chen Duxiu), who believed passionately in individualism and Western-style democracy. A former journalist, he edited an inspiring, largely political monthly magazine called *New Youth*, and continued to do so from his new base at Peking University, calling on young Chinese to realize a new vision of their country.

Among many others, he was joined by Hu Shih (Hu Shi), who after the usual classical education in China had gone to Cornell and Columbia where he became a student and disciple of the philosopher John Dewey. Hu Shih's main project was promotion of the popular or vernacular language, which he called *pai hua* (bai hua), supposedly the everyday speech of the common people, and he persuaded Ch'en Tu-hsiu to use it in *New Youth*. There had been novels and stories in the past written in something like the vernacular, and more recently missionary tracts designed to reach the masses, but most

Chinese remained either illiterate or semiliterate. Things written in the new *pai hua* were really not accessible to them, and those who wrote it, like Hu and Ch'en, could not forget their classical education as they used characters. But at least part of the point of the *pai hua* movement was to reach the common people with the message of change, and of course to teach them to be literate in this new, somewhat simplified language. It was certainly true that the classical written language was beyond most of them, the special preserve of the scholarly elite, and was often used to show off an author's classical learning. Hu and Ch'en wanted to produce a literature of "fresh and sincere realism," plainer, simpler, more "honest," and more related to people's everyday lives, a "people's literature."

By 1919 *New Youth* had been joined by several other similar journals with inspiring titles like *New Dawn* and *New China*, written in *pai hua* and pressing for change. They wrote about a variety of Western ideas and ideals, including socialism, anarchism, democracy, Dewey's pragmatism, Darwinism, liberalism, and utilitarianism. Ch'en declared that China needed the help of Western science and democracy, which he labeled "Mr. S. and Mr. D." He wrote that "Only these two gentlemen can cure the dark maladies in Chinese politics, morality, learning, and thought." Lu Hsun (Lu Xun) was one of those who wrote stories in these new journals. In 1918 he published his first story, "The Diary of a Madman," bitterly cynical like the rest of his work. It tells of an old friend whom he visited after a long separation who showed him his brother's diary, which Lu Hsun claimed to merely reproduce. The diary says that the people of

Cosmopolitanism in Shanghai, 1933. From left to right, the American journalist Agnes Smedley, the playwright George Bernard Shaw, Madam Sun Yat-sen, Ts'ai Yuanp'ei (a leading intellectual), and Lu Hsun. Shaw was on a visit to China and is being welcomed here by the founders of the China League for Civil Rights. (Eastfoto/Sovfoto)

his village are all man-eaters. When he tried to look up the history of cannibalism in earlier times he found that "scrawled all over each page are the words 'Virtue and Morality.'... I began to see words between the lines, the whole book being filled with the two words, 'Eat People.'" It is a powerfully convincing picture of paranoia, including the supposed actions and motives of those around him, even his own elder brother, who is in on the plot to eat him. When he spoke of "four thousand years of man-eating history" he meant it to characterize the old China with its Confucian morality of virtue and beneficence which was merely a cloak for the elite preying on others: oppressed peasants, oppressed women, and anyone outside their own charmed circle.

LU HSUN

Lu Hsun describes his own alienation, as a scholar, from the peasants in his moving story "My Old Home," and the plight of others like himself who cannot find in this deteriorating society any outlet for their own talents or energies. But perhaps his most bitter scorn is turned against the oppression of women, treated almost like animals or like pieces of property. His tragic story of "The New Year's Sacrifice" is about a peasant woman who is driven mad by her sufferings—the death of her husband, her forced remarriage merely to bring some marriage settlement money to her in-laws, the death of her son (for which she is cruelly and unfairly blamed), and her pathetic efforts to get some reassurance from the narrator, who is presumably Lu Hsun himself, the "I" of the story. The woman is not even given a name, but is called only "Hsiang Lin's wife." When near the end of her miserable life and taking to begging to survive, she encounters the narrator, "a scholar," who thus is supposed to be knowledgeable, and asks him if there is a hell, or a life after death, some hope to cling to. The narrator fumbles with his reply, but finally says "I am not sure," as Lu Hsun says, "a most useful phrase." Even these supposed leaders of society have no comfort to offer to the oppressed, and the story ends ironically with the people of the village busy with preparations for the celebration of Chinese New Year, to bring them "boundless good fortune."

Probably Lu Hsun's best-known story is the multi-incident account of a peasant character he calls Ah Q, which turns an equally sardonic eye on the masses. Ah Q is a poor illiterate, the village bum, who nevertheless is continually boasting of how "we used to be more prosperous." He loses all his fights with other villagers, cheats and lies but is invariably found out, and rationalizes his defeats by saying that since he is more virtuous he has won moral victories, against "unfilial sons." Ah Q

 Lu Hsun on the Breakup of China

Lu Hsun, in the year of his death (1936), commented favorably on the changed contents of the popular journals of the day which had picked up the nationalist (patriotic) message, but could not resist a characteristic touch of irony.

Most admirable of all is the fact that the "Spring and Autumn" supplement of the Shen Pao [a popular newspaper published in Shanghai] which used to refer with such relish to the Empress Dowager and the Ch'ing court, has also changed completely with times. In the comments at the beginning of one number, we are even told that when eating melons we should think of our territory now carved up like a melon. Of course there is no gainsaying that at all times, in all places and on all occasions, we should be patriotic. Still if I were to think like that while eating a melon, I doubt whether I could swallow it. Even if I made an effort and succeeded, I would probably have prolonged indigestion. And this may not be owing to my bad nervous state after illness. To my mind, a man who uses the melon as a simile when lecturing on our national disgrace, and the next moment cheerfully eats a melon, absorbing its nourishment, is rather lacking in feeling. No lecture could have any effect on such a man.

Source: Quoted in P. Lopate, *The Art of the Personal Essay.* (New York: Doubleday, 1994), p. 328.

Lu Hsun, part of a painting by Tan Hsia-ming, "The Struggle Continues." (Collection Viollet)

is a thinly disguised portrait of traditional China and its nineteenth-century humiliations. But when the revolutionaries come to Ah Q's area he joins the cause simply for the excitement; without understanding anything of what is happening, he is spurned by the revolutionaries and finally used as an example and shot for a robbery which, for a change, he did not commit. As in the film Lu Hsun describes when he was a medical student in Japan, a crowd followed the cart in which Ah Q was taken to the execution grounds hoping to see the spectacle of a beheading, but to their disappointment he was shot instead. "They had followed him for nothing."

Nowhere in his writings does Lu Hsun blame foreigners, even the Japanese, for China's plight, but rather the Chinese people: the Confucian elite, "man-eating" Confucianism itself, the ignorant masses, corrupt officials, the self-indulgent rich, the lack of compassion at every level. After 1921, although he continued to publish stories until 1926, he turned his attention more to writing political articles in the new journals. There as in his stories he spoke scathingly of the politics of the time, the warlords, the corrupt and ineffective political cliques, and the helplessness of his country. He was a total opponent of any form of censorship and of what he called tyrannical government. But he was equally scornful of mass democracy, feeling that it was only "the tyranny of many rascals instead of one" and "government by ignorant louts." These were perhaps reasonable descriptions of Communist China, but he did not live to see it; the Communists would quickly have silenced or eliminated him, as the Kuomintang tried to do (he lived most of his life after 1926

in the protection of the foreign concession of Shanghai), but he died of consumption and overwork in 1936. He sympathized with many of the Communist aims, but found other aspects of their program anathema and never joined the party, although after his death they celebrated him as one of theirs. He could never have accepted their version of China's future, although he would have applauded its early promise and some of its concrete results, as well as the Communist attack on the destructive aspects of Confucianism and the beginnings of a qualified liberation of women. But he would have been the first to speak out against Communist thought control, as he did against the Kuomintang, and against both parties' absolutism, corruption, hypocrisy, and oppression.

The May Fourth Movement

The mass protests which erupted in Peking on May 4, 1919, were thus part of a much larger movement and one with a longer history, going back at least to the changes at Peking University from 1917 and the founding of the magazine New Youth, and it continued well beyond the immediate protests into the early 1920s. Largely as a result of Hu Shih's work, it also came to be called the New Culture Movement. But on May 4, Chinese nationalism suddenly became a major force in politics, especially after the revelation of the secret agreements with all the major foreign powers by warlord governments in Peking to confirm the Japanese in Shantung. Student associations and labor unions all over China protested against this betrayal and against the powers meeting at Versailles, and on May 4 more than 3,000 college students from the Peking area assembled at T'ien An Men (Gate of Heavenly Peace) in front of the imperial palace. Demonstrations quickly grew violent as feelings ran high and students took courage from the large number of their fellow protestors. A pro-Japanese official was labeled a traitor and was badly beaten up by the demonstrators, who also burned the house of a cabinet member. What made May 4 even more effective, however, was that the students organized a union which kept political protest going, attracted massive support from similar groups around the country, and got the support of the press as well. As during the anti-U.S. boycott of 1905, the students were also joined by many patriotic Chinese merchants, and together they organized a very large-scale and effective boycott of Japanese goods. Student teams dealt directly with merchants to urge them not to stock Japanese imports, and put up signs in front of shops which had not joined the boycott, holding public rallies in the streets. Support came from Sun Yat-sen and the Canton government, and the move-

ment rapidly spread to nearly all Chinese cities, organized by local student groups. Student strikes closed down schools and colleges in over 200 cities.

The warlord government in Peking, clearly feeling threatened by this turmoil, tried to suppress it and arrested over a thousand students. Female students had been part of the movement from the beginning and many had become martyrs, killed by police repression, but in response to this action they now turned out in even greater numbers to demonstrate. Most of the merchants in Shanghai, where the movement had spread overnight, closed their shops for a week in protest, and many Shanghai factories were hit by sympathy strikes. This was the first large-scale involvement of women in political action, and many regarded that as the dawn of a new day of women's emancipation. With the country in such ferment, the jailed students were released. Three pro-Japanese officials were fired, the cabinet resigned in a body, and the government in Peking refused to sign the Versailles treaty. This was real victory and the students were ebullient. It was also the first truly effective action of the Chinese nationalism which had been growing since the early years of the century but had seen its hopes

✠ The Costs of Defeat ✠

Reparations extracted from China by foreign powers, after successive defeats:

(Note that the value of an ounce of silver varied widely over time; in 1887 it was worth U.S. $1.20 but by 1902 it had fallen to $0.62).

1842	21 million ounces of silver to Great Britain at the end of the 1839–42 war
1858	4 million ounces of silver to Britain and 2 million ounces to France
1860	8 million ounces of silver to Britain and 8 million ounces to France
1862–69	Approximately 400,000 ounces of indemnities cumulatively for violence against missionaries
1870	490,000 ounces of silver to France after the Tientsin massacre
1873	500,000 ounces of silver to Japan after the Japanese expedition to Taiwan
1878	5 million ounces of silver to Russia
1881	An additional 9 million ounces of silver to Russia as the price of Chinese reoccupation of the Ili valley in northern Sinkiang
1895	200 million ounces of silver to Japan
1897	30 million ounces of silver to Japan, for her withdrawal of troops from Liaotung
1901	450 million silver dollars to the Western allies as the Boxer Indemnity
1922	66 million gold francs to Japan, for her evacuation of part of Shantung

Source: Based on the table in J. Gernet, *A History of Chinese Civilization.* (Cambridge University Press, 1985), p. 609.

raised high by the revolution of 1911, frustrated first by Yuan Shih-k'ai and then by the warlords.

Once the demonstrations quieted down, the ferment of new ideas continued. It was not a movement which could maintain its momentum only through street rallies, but which drew its continuing strength from the widespread sense of the need for change. The campaign was carried on in the press and the new journals, and there was renewed attention to Western ideas. All in all, several hundred mostly short-lived journals were founded and eagerly read in which all of this was debated. John Dewey and the British socialist philosopher Bertrand Russell came to China to lecture and stayed on, Dewey for two years, Russell for one. Professors, other teachers, writers, and newspapermen all joined in this ferment, as many of them had in the earlier action. Like Lu Hsun, they attacked the old shibboleths of Confucianism, especially the subordination of "inferiors" to "superiors," the iron bonds of family, and the shackling and oppression of women. Confucianism was based after all on a hierarchical view of society which institutionalized great inequality. As Lu Hsun put it, "Chinese culture is a culture of serving one's masters, who triumph at the cost of the misery of the masses." The traditional rules and the bonds they imposed were angrily rejected by this new generation of young Chinese. Some of the scholars, including Hu Shih and Liang Ch'i-ch'ao, reexamined Chinese philosophy and tried to construct a new version of it, purged of the alien taint of Buddhism and promoting the egalitarian aspects of the Chou dynasty philosopher Mo-tzu (see Chapter 3) and the centrality of the vernacular novels of the Ming and Ch'ing. Such revisionism was upsetting to many of the more conservative scholars, who also saw the new turn toward political action and even revolution as disturbing and improper. Hu Shih led the fight against all "isms," as he labeled them, and advocated, like his mentor John Dewey, a pragmatic approach rather than a blind following of any particular school.

This was reasonable philosophy, but offered little concrete basis for political change. It was a waste of breath to appeal to warlords, as he and others did, to respect civil liberties and the rights of peasants. There was little precedent in Chinese history for such notions, or for the other ideals of Western liberalism, including the role of Western-style law with its acknowledgment of individual rights. That idea just made no sense to most Chinese, not yet. In effect Hu Shih and those like him were applying a Western medicine to China's ills, and it just didn't work. China would first have to build a modern nation-state. The students and others who made the May Fourth movement had begun to create a political role for Chinese nationalism. But despite their successes, they remained a relatively tiny handful, like their intellectual allies, reaching only a small part of the population and without any political organization or lasting power. They had plenty of ideology, but no army, while the warlords were the reverse. There were also those within the movement in the larger sense, like Hu Shih and Liang Ch'i-ch'ao, who were philosophically and temperamentally opposed to any form of violence, still more to revolution. For all its stirring appeal to educated youth, it was a movement which really was going nowhere. Intellectuals and writers in the big east coast cities, all but Peking part of the treaty-port system, lived and worked in a world apart from the mass of China. They debated in their journals and meetings mainly with each other rather than with other Chinese who were more representative of the country as a whole. The all too brief career of most of their journals, and their limited circulation, suggests that they lacked a mass audience. And despite the appeal of the *pai-hua* movement, the great majority of Chinese could not and did not read them in any case. The writers and intellectuals were talking to themselves.

Despite the continuing political chaos, there was some industrial growth, mainly in the treaty ports (much of the industry there was now Chinese-owned), but also in Japanese-financed iron and steel production and attendant coal mining in the Wuhan area (the Hanyehping project). Rail lines were further extended, including a loop through Inner Mongolia and most of the main north-south line from Peking toward Canton. Chinese textile and other light consumer goods industries boomed, although the scale of industrialization as a whole remained tiny in relation to China's size and population.

Russia and the Building of Party Organization

Other groups and other forces in the end took the lead away from the May Fourthers, more committed to building political organization and the strength for action. China needed such organization, but the two main forms in which it was generated, Communism and the increasingly conservative or even reactionary Kuomintang, were each a far cry from the Western-style liberalism which so enthusiastically exercised the May Fourthers. The Russian Revolution of 1917, "Ten Days That Shook the World," made a tremendous impression worldwide, nowhere more than in China. Russia was a relatively backward country ruled by an old-style despotism which had also fallen behind the rest of the West economically and technologically. If it could produce a successful revolutionary alternative, so could China, whose circumstances were seen as similar. The imperialist countries felt threatened by the Russian Revolution and its anticapitalist/imperialist rhetoric and lined up firmly against it, as in the Allied expedition to Siberia in 1919 described in Chapter 15. So-

✠ Soviet Help for China ✠

The Soviet diplomat Adolf Joff, acting as representative of the Comintern, met with Sun Yat Sen in 1923, and the two men issued a joint statement.

Dr. Sun Yat Sen holds that the Communistic order or even the Soviet system cannot actually be introduced into China, because there do not exist here the conditions for a successful establishment of either Communism or Sovietism. This view is entirely shared by Mr. Joff, who is further of the opinion that China's paramount and most pressing problem is to achieve national unification and attain full national independence, and regarding this great task, he has assured Dr. Sun Yat Sen that China has the warmest sympathy of the Russian people and can count on the support of Russia.

Source: Quoted in J. Spence, *The Search for Modern China.* (New York: Norton, 1990), p. 335.

viet anti-imperialism increased the appeal of the Russian model for China, while on other grounds as well it seemed to offer a sweeping solution to China's problems.

The other aspect of the Russian experience, especially under the leadership of Lenin, which appealed was the political organization of the Communist party and the methods by which it was built. If they worked so well in that vast and still mainly peasant country, perhaps they could be made to work in China and to give it at last the political cohesion is still lacked. *New Youth* began to publish articles on Marxism in 1919, pursued by study groups in Peking and Shanghai. Another in Changsha, the capital of Hunan province, was led by the young Mao Tse-tung (Mao Zedong), a native of Hunan who had drifted to Peking and become a student and library assistant at Peking University. His Peking mentor, Professor of Philosophy Li Ta-chao (Li Dazhao), had been converted to Marxism, as was Ch'en Tu-hsiu. In July of 1921, meeting in secret in Shanghai, Li, Ch'en, Mao, and 11 others founded the Chinese Communist party, with branches in Peking and most of the other big cities. Another intellectual, Kuo Mo-jo (Guo Mojo), had founded the Creation Society while a student in Japan, which now embraced Marxism. Kuo declared, "I have found the key to all the problems which appeared to me self-contradictory and insoluble."

But it was to be a long road ahead, and the way to Communist power was blocked by the far larger and stronger organization of the Kuomintang, now committed to its own version of "party dictatorship." For that, the Russian model of organization was appealing to the Kuomintang as well as to the Communists. Sun Yat-sen had complained that trying to get the Chinese people together was like trying to make a rope out of sand, a remark which reveals his own deep frustration. He too saw the Russian model and their experience as useful.

He concluded from the Chinese experience of May 4 that the Kuomintang must be reorganized to give it greater strength, and that an alliance with the Comintern (the Communist International, devoted to the cause of revolution around the world) would be helpful. Sun had been disappointed in his failure to get any significant support from the imperialist powers (except for a time from the Japanese) or any supportive response to his efforts to build a new China. Now he turned to the Russians, who readily offered help, and of a kind which was clearly needed: political organization. His Canton parliament had been a washout, plagued by factions, and his brief effort at alliance with local warlords had fizzled, enough so that he had had to take refuge in Shanghai. One thing which would clearly be needed was an army, and to this end he sent his military assistant, Chiang Kai-shek, to Moscow to study Soviet methods.

Comintern advisers were sent to China, most prominently Michael Borodin, who helped put together the new Kuomintang constitution and founded a political institute to teach organizers how to build mass support. The Communists, still small in numbers (less than a thousand members by 1923) and thus relatively weak, agreed that the Kuomintang should be "the central force of the national revolution." The Comintern representatives urged both parties to work together, under their advice, and to form a united front. Local Kuomintang cells were established, following the Soviet model, which took part in the election of delegates to a national party congress who chose a central executive committee. Sun issued a new version of his Three Principles which now, understandably enough, featured anti-imperialism and self-determination. Sun did not accept the Marxist-Leninist doctrine of class warfare, the generic link between capitalism and imperialism, or state ownership of the means of production, but he was clearly influenced in the Soviet direction, if only as a way to build political strength around his first principle of "People's Nationalism."

Chiang Kai-shek returned from four months in Russia and became head of a new military academy at Whampoa near Canton in 1925, with Russian advisers. The Communists too were represented there by Chou En-lai (Zhou Enlai, after 1949 the Premier of the Communist People's Republic), appropriately in the political education department. The Kuomintang, and the United Front with the Communists, at last began to build an army, which eventually would challenge and defeat the warlords and bring a measure of national unity. But Sun suddenly died of cancer in March of 1925, and the party lost his charismatic leadership. A new Nationalist government was formed at Canton as a military-party dictatorship headed by Wang Ching-wei (Wang Jingwei), an ambitious disciple of Sun. But Sun's chief political heir was really Chiang Kai-shek, his power built mainly on the army which Sun and the Soviet advisers had directed him to create. It was Chiang who largely turned the Kuomintang from a revolutionary party to a reactionary one, tried to eliminate completely his Communist allies, and ultimately lost the support of most Chinese through his repressive policies. He had some major early successes, first by eliminating most of the warlords and then by establishing the first real national government since the fall of the Ch'ing, at Nanking, his new capital, in 1927. In the ten years before the Japanese struck in 1937, the Nanking government did make some progress, but it moved farther and farther away from the ideals of Sun Yat-sen and those of May 4, in the name of building national unity, to which all else must give way. That story is told in Chapter 18.

Notes

1. From Lu Hsun, "Call to Arms," in *Selected Stories*. New York: Norton, 1977, p. 3.
2. From *China Reconstructs*. January, 1988, p. 26.
3. Quoted in Fairbank, J. K., et al., *East Asia: Tradition and Transformation*. Boston: Houghton Mifflin, 1989, p. 762.

Suggestions for Further Reading

Bays, D. H. *China Enters the Twentieth Century*. Ann Arbor: University of Michigan Press, 1978.

Bergere, M. C. *The Golden Age of the Chinese Bourgeoisie*. Transl., Lloyd, Cambridge University Press, 1989.

Buck, D. *Recent Studies of the Boxer Movement*. White Plains: M. E. Sharpe, 1987.

Chang, H. *Chinese Intellectuals in Crisis*. Berkeley: University of California Press, 1987.

_____. *Liang Chi-ch'ao and Intellectual Transition in China*. Cambridge: Harvard University Press, 1971.

Chang, S. H., and Gordon, L. *All Under Heaven: Sun Yatsen and His Revolutionary Thought*. Palo Alto: Hoover Inst., 1991.

Chen, J. T. *The May Fourth Movement*. Leiden: Brill, 1971.

Ch'i, H. S. *Warlord Politics in China, 1916–1928*. Stanford: Stanford University Press, 1976.

Chow, T. T. *The May Fourth Movement*. Cambridge: Harvard, 1960.

Elvin, M., and Skinner, G. W., eds. *The Chinese City Between Two Worlds*. Stanford: Stanford University Press, 1974.

Esherick, J., and Rankin, M., eds. *Chinese Local Elites and Patterns of Dominance*. Stanford: Stanford University Press, 1986.

Grieder, J. *Intellectuals and the State in Modern China*. Glencoe, Ill.: Free Press, 1981.

_____. *Hu Shih and the Chinese Renaissance*. Cambridge: Harvard University Press, 1970.

Huang, P. C. *The Peasant Economy and Social Change in North China*. Stanford: Stanford University Press, 1985.

Kapp, R. *Szechuan and the Chinese Republic*. New Haven: Yale University Press, 1973.

Kazuko, O. *Chinese Women in a Century of Revolution*. Palo Alto: Stanford Press, 1989.

Ko, D. *Teachers of the Inner Chambers*. Palo Alto: Stanford Press, 1994.

Lee, L. *Voices From the Iron House*. Bloomington: Indiana Press, 1987.

Li, L. *Student Nationalism in China*. Albany: SUNY Press, 1994.

Liu, K. C., ed. *Orthodoxy in Late Imperial China*. Berkeley: University of California Press, 1990.

Min, T. K. *National Policy and Local Power*. Cambridge: Harvard University Press, 1989.

Nathan, A. *Peking Politics, 1918–1923*. Berkeley: University of California, 1976.

Rankin, M. *Elite Activism and Political Transformation in China*. Stanford: Stanford University Press, 1986.

Saari, J. *Legacies of Childhood: Growing Up Chinese in a Time of Crisis*. Cambridge: Harvard University Press, 1990.

Schiffrin, H. Z. *Sun Yat-sen: Reluctant Revolutionary*. Boston: Little, Brown, 1980.

Schrecker, J. E. *The Chinese Revolution in Historical Perspective*. New York: Praeger, 1991.

Schwartz, B. I. *In Search of Wealth and Power: Yen Fu and the West*. Cambridge: Harvard University Press, 1964.

Sheridan, J. *China in Disintegration*. Glencoe, Ill.: The Free Press, 1975.

Wright, M. C., ed. *China in Revolution*. New Haven: Yale University Press, 1968.

Young, E. *The Presidency of Yuan Shih-k'ai*. Ann Arbor: University of Michigan Press, 1977.

CHAPTER 18

CHINA AND JAPAN: THE ROAD TO WAR

Chinese Nationalism

The United Front between the Kuomintang and the Communists, with Soviet advisers, set as its immediate objective the elimination of the warlords and the creation of a national government. To aid in this effort, and following Borodin's advice, the new political institute in Canton offered instruction in how to politicize the masses and how to organize mass support. The Communists were willing to serve under overall Kuomintang control, which they agreed was the "central force of the national revolution," but at the same time aimed in the long run to take it over from within. Meanwhile they developed their own mass organizations on the side. Sun Yat-sen endorsed the United Front, confident that the Kuomintang (KMT or GMD) would not be threatened by the relative handful of Communists, and anxious to tap all possible resources for the building of a national state, including the energy and effectiveness of student organizers, who had proved their value in the May Fourth Movement. The new army built up by Chiang Kai-shek after his return from Russia was indoctrinated with the new gospels of Sun's Three Principles, and dedicated to the creation of national unity.

Meanwhile the strength of emerging Chinese nationalism continued to grow, fed after May 4, 1919, by continued foreign dominance of China, especially in the treaty ports which were the chief centers of Chinese emotional response to the humiliations of imperialism.

Elsewhere foreign flags also still flew on the ships which dominated coastal and riverine trade, on the gunboats which patrolled these waters, and with the foreign garrisons still in Peking long after the Boxer Rebellion. Foreigners controlled the Chinese Maritime Customs and even the Post Office and Salt Revenue Board, and diverted their revenues to meet interest payments on indemnities and loans. Foreign banks dominated the financing of China's foreign trade and much of the modern-style industrial development. Foreign consortia built and controlled most of China's rail lines, while in southern Manchuria Japanese had become the de facto rulers. Most of the largest industrial enterprises, overwhelmingly in the treaty ports, were owned by foreigners, their Chinese workers, including many women and children, cruelly exploited. In part response, labor unions had begun to form, soon influenced if not dominated by the Chinese Communist party. The foreign establishment in China had for the most part supported or at least collaborated with Yuan Shih-k'ai, that betrayer of the revolution, and they represented, after all, the countries which had sold China down the river at Versailles. Life in the treaty ports provided daily reminders of China's subjugation, where its people were discriminated against and most lived in poverty while the Chinese collaborators and the foreign masters prospered.

There had been widespread protest strikes in the wake of May 4, and now they increased, accompanied by demonstrations against all that the foreign establishment represented. On May 30 the police of the Interna-

The Bund, Shanghai, 1986. Except for the vehicles, little has changed since Shanghai's heyday as a treaty port. Most of the buildings shown here date from the 1920s and 1930s. The Huangpu River and floating docks are on the right. (R. Murphey)

tional Settlement at Shanghai, led by British officers, fired on unarmed demonstrators and killed 13 of them, in what came to be called the May 30th Movement. Sympathy demonstrations, protesting against the same foreign grip on the country, broke out in Canton on June 23, where overreacting foreign troops again opened fire and killed 52 of the demonstrators. The two events sparked a 15-month strike and boycott of British goods, specifically the trade with Hong Kong, which as an outright British colony had come to dominate the trade of south China. Demonstrations erupted in other Chinese cities, fortunately without equivalent violence or killings, and the Communist party and its Comintern advisers found a new opportunity for involvement in mass organization and action. The Communists had started a Youth Corps, which by the end of 1925 enrolled about 20,000 young men and women who joined the Corps in large part as a result of the events in Shanghai and Canton, which had made them and many other Chinese newly dedicated foes of imperialism in all its forms, and newly dedicated also to the task of building the strength against it which only a national state could provide.

The Northern Expedition

Sun Yat-sen had long hoped to mount a military campaign against the warlords which could unify the country, and in July of 1926, still under the auspices of the United Front, the KMT's new army with its Communist allies moved rapidly north, preceded by political organizers to prepare the way for it, people who were either Communists or from the left wing of the KMT who saw

political organization and propaganda as the high road to power. This advance guard made the progress of what came to be called the Northern Expedition far easier and quicker, and before the end of 1926 they had reached the Yangtze, defeating or enrolling the series of warlord armies along the way in the name of Chinese nationalism. The KMT government now moved from Canton to Wuhan, where the success of the Northern Expedition greatly strengthened the already dominant KMT left wing. From Wuhan the expedition reached both down river to the Shanghai area and north toward Peking, where the biggest and strongest warlords were. The military side of the KMT, which was increasingly important in what was after all a military campaign, had always distrusted their Communist "allies," and the party soon split between a left and a right wing, the left under Wang Ching-wei (Wang Jingwe), a brilliant political lieutenant of Sun Yat-sen's, and the right under Chiang Kai-shek, although the two factions ultimately rejoined.

But first Chiang moved to eliminate his Communist partners in a brutal coup in Shanghai on April 12, with a good deal of foreign support (they were as anti-Communist as he was, still shaken by the Russian Revolution of 1917) and the help of Chiang's underworld gang connections. The British had stationed 40,000 troops to protect Shanghai and some of them aided Chiang's coup in the name of anti-Communist law and order, while others stood by. Chiang killed thousands in cold blood and nearly succeeded in destroying the Communists, including their labor union allies, but a few escaped the slaughter and others, including Mao Tse-tung (Mao Zedong) were not in Shanghai at the time and survived to keep the Communist party alive. Six days later, on April

18, Chiang established his new national government at Nanking. The left wing of the KMT based at Wuhan expelled its Communist members in July, but Mao, in defiance of the continued Soviet line to work with the industrial proletariat and seize power in the cities, went to the countryside. He supported a peasant strategy which was in the end to triumph, and coined a memorable phrase: "A single spark can start a prairie fire." China, especially peasant China, was ripe for revolution. Nevertheless his efforts to lead an "Autumn Harvest" uprising in his home province of Hunan failed, as did Communist-led coups at Canton and Swatow. What remained of the Communist organization was driven underground or forced to take refuge in the countryside and in mountain strongholds. Chiang had triumphed.

The Nanking Decade

The Nanking decade, as it is called, from 1927 to the full-scale Japanese invasion in 1937, was too short to constitute an adequate test of the effectiveness, or the long-term prospects, of Kuomintang rule. One thing it did accomplish was to alert the Japanese, who saw it correctly as a symbol of resurgent Chinese nationalism and the strength which that could provide. The Japanese had their own plans for China, and what successes the Nanking government achieved after 1927 increased the determination of the militarists who soon dominated the Japanese government to act on the mainland before it was too late. This was part of the Japanese strategy in their takeover of Manchuria in 1931, and the essential background for their ill-fated campaign to conquer the rest of China. The response of the other foreign powers in China to the Nanking government was more favorable. Their commercial interests had suffered in the chaos of the warlord years, and they saw advantages in the emergence of an effective central government. They also saw that a unified China could be a useful ally against an expansionist Japan, which so clearly threatened Kuomintang and Western interests in East Asia, and the KMT was also a bulwark against Communism and Soviet influence.

As an encouragement to the new government, the British voluntarily gave up their treaty-port concessions at Hankou (part of Wuhan) and at two other minor Yangtze ports, Kiukiang (Jiujiang) and Chinkiang (Jinjiang), followed by their surrender of Weihaiwei (see Chapter 17) and their concession at Amoy. The Northern Expedition assault on Nanking had killed six foreigners, and a British-American naval bombardment in response killed far more Chinese, but the incident was treated coolly by both sides. It began to be realized that the KMT had captured the leadership of Chinese nationalism, and that it hence had to be accepted and dealt

with. In 1928 the Northern Expedition forces took Peking and defeated most of the warlords in that area, which by the end of the year prompted all of the Western powers to recognize the Nanking government. Peking was renamed Peiping (peace in the north— Pei = north, King [or ching] = capital) since Nanking ("southern capital") was now the capital.

Nanking's control of the country was never complete. The old warlord Yen Hsi-shan remained dominant in Shansi; Feng Yu-hsiang, after a brief alliance with the Northern Expedition, retained major power in his warlord domains; Yunnan remained the stronghold of warlord Lung Yun. Other warlord figures broke with Chiang in the south in Fukien (Fujian) and Kwangsi (Guangxi), while Tibet remained beyond Chinese control and Sinkiang (Xinjiang) came under the dominance of local warlords there from the Ma family. Manchuria had been the political kingdom of warlord Chang Tso-lin (Zhang Zuolin); after his assassination by the Japanese in 1928, his son Chang Hsüeh-liang (Zhang Xueliang) succeeded him, and while formally allied with the new KMT government he continued to play a largely independent role, with his own army like the other surviving warlords. Altogether Chiang thus controlled in any direct or effective sense only about half of the country's area, although this included the majority of its population, and the Nanking government did represent the main stream. It attracted the support of most politically conscious and nationalist-minded Chinese, and recruited many able and dedicated people to its government agencies with hopes to build a new China, along largely Western lines.

But the KMT was fatally weakened by Chiang's inflexible conservatism, out of step with the rising tide of pressures for change among the heirs of Sun Yat-sen and the early promise of revolution, and out of accord also with China's now desperate need for basic reform, most of all on behalf of its peasant millions who had seen their livelihood deteriorate disastrously under the last decades of Ch'ing rule and then were the major victims of the warlord years. The 1920s, especially the first half, were particularly hard for north China, already economically marginal, as a series of first flood and then drought and famine years devastated the countryside and killed or starved millions, with no effective government response. There and elsewhere tenancy rates rose rapidly, and there was a sharp increase in the proportion of the peasants who were completely landless and were obliged simply to sell their labor. Western missionaries organized famine relief, built wells and roads, and established rural credit cooperatives, actions not matched by the warlord "government" in Peking or by provincial authorities. It was a true agrarian crisis, but the KMT, especially Chiang, mistrusted peasant organization, stonewalled or sidetracked what efforts there were by

Chiang Kai-shek flanked by warlords Feng Yu-hsiang (left) and Yen Hsi-shan (right), about 1928. (Hulton-Deutsch)

others to promote peasant literacy and rural reform, and especially feared anything with even a suggestion of popular democracy. His political base, and his own interests, were firmly on the other side. He presided over a political coalition of treaty-port Chinese who had done well in Western-style business, and large landowners (of which he was one himself in his home province of Chekiang (Zhejiang, just south of Shanghai). Neither group looked kindly on the idea of educating peasants or shaping policy toward rural development, especially not the now urgently needed land reform or the provision of rural farm credits for peasants to buy seeds and meet other expenses necessarily long before they had a crop.

Chiang was also a major investor in Shanghai, and though the evidence is shadowy, had close connections with an underworld gangster group called the Green Gang which made its money from protection rackets, prostitution, drugs, kidnapping, and other illegal but profitable activities, like all gangster groups. This too was hardly compatible with notions of social revolution. Ideologically, Chiang was an old-style Confucian, despite his un-Confucian links with the underworld and with rack-renting landlords. He seems to have felt that what China needed was a return to classic Confucian virtues, and he founded a youth group called the New Life Movement which stressed puritanism, old-fashioned morality, propriety, and integrity, somewhat like the Y.M.C.A. But he also founded a secret fascist organization he called the Blue Shirts, modeled on Mussolini's and Hitler's Brown and Black Shirts, which worked behind the scenes to promote militarization and the supreme leadership of Chiang. In 1927 he abandoned his first wife and married Soong Ch'ing-ling's (Mme.

Sun Yat-sen's) sister, Soong Mei-ling, who had been educated in the U.S. at Wellesley and was highly Americanized but, like her husband, extremely ambitious politically.

The third Soong sister, Ai-ling, married the treaty-port banker H. H. Kung, who later became the KMT minister of finance succeeding the Soong son, T. V., who preceded him as finance minister until 1933. T. V. had been educated at Harvard, including some business training, while Kung had gone to Oberlin College in Ohio. To please his new wife, a Christian, Chiang accepted Methodism, although it seemed to make very little impact on him or on his views. Chiang used these multiple family connections with the treaty-port Soong family to build relations with the United States, and to staff key posts in his government. T. V. especially was an able person, and deserves major credit for establishing a modern banking system centered around the Bank of China and three other banks which cut into the territory of the Western treaty-port banks and also helped finance the government. But for all the American training and experience of the Soongs and their family connection, they too seem to have left Chiang unchanged from his reactionary Confucian persuasion, deeply tinged with militarism and with more than a hint of European-style fascism.

Failures and Successes

Chiang was convinced that what China needed was unity and national strength under a single strongman, and that this could be achieved only through the build-up of his army. He employed German military advisers

Chiang Kai-shek in 1930. (BBC Hulton Picture Library)

in this effort, and thus strengthened his ties with what soon became Nazi Germany. For China's economic development he and his colleagues turned to more positive Western models. Most of the KMT officials had studied in the West or had been influenced by it. They saw that China had fallen far behind, its rail lines still only just begun, its roads little developed, its industrial plant still in the infant stage. The Western model paid scant attention to rural problems, or to a peasantry which was not part of the modern Western scene, and at least to that degree it did not well fit China's needs. But railways, industry, and a modern banking system were essentials too, and here the Nanking government made some progress, in the process attracting considerable support from the Western powers whose own earlier development was being echoed in China. Chiang was at least a genuine Chinese patriot, even though that did not include concern for the mass of its people. He had after all emerged out of the devastating warlord years, when military power was the key to political power, and now he saw the Communist menace, and soon the menace of an expansionist Japan, as making it necessary to put military power first, including the suppression of his Communist rivals in the name of national unity.

The army remained independent of the civil government and with no budgetary or other controls on it, under the direct leadership of Chiang himself, whom the foreign press came to call the Generalissimo. There was also a secret police to ferret out dissenters and suspected Communists, many of whom were executed or imprisoned and tortured. This was still the period of "political tutelage" prescribed by Sun Yat-sen, with elections held only within the party of the KMT, although even there party blocs or factions merely jostled each other, under what was in effect the dictatorship of Chiang. Peasant associations were suppressed, the press heavily censored, and there was not even a half-hearted effort at Western-style democracy, although the constitution provided for legislative, judicial, and executive wings, all really tools of Chiang within the party. Chiang held it all together through a combination of cronyism, payoffs, blackmail, pressure, and fear, and operated it as a police state dictatorship.

Nevertheless the Nanking decade produced some welcome achievements. Though dependent on foreign approval, Chiang was in line with most Chinese sentiment at least on the issue of anti-imperialism and the drive for the recovery of Chinese sovereignty which had been compromised so heavily by foreign privilege. T. V. Soong primarily engineered the recovery of tariff autonomy and promptly increased import duties, as part of his overall reorganization of China's finances. After all, he was a Harvard man, thoroughly Americanized, and thus someone whom the Western powers felt comfortable in dealing with almost as one of them, wearing Western clothing and speaking impeccable English, unlike Chiang. But financial reform did not include any new availability of funds for the rural sector, still the vast majority of the economy, nor anything to speak of for rural development programs. Many such programs were approved by the government, but virtually none were funded or carried out. Land reform and the limitation of rents landlords could charge were part of this package, but remained largely on paper. Chiang needed the support of his fellow landlords. The government concentrated the funds it had for investment in the urban-industrial sector, almost all in the treaty ports where its other political base was also centered. Taxation was highly regressive, taxing the poor at the same rate as the rich, including a long list of excise taxes on basic consumer goods like flour, salt, and kerosene.

But revenue remained far less than expenditure, and to fill the gap the government borrowed from its new banks and thus built up a new debt burden. The banks issued bonds, which of course only the rich—and government officials—could afford to buy, although many of them reaped a big profit from the high interest rates, and officials could often buy the bonds at very low prices. Business and industry were taxed heavily and

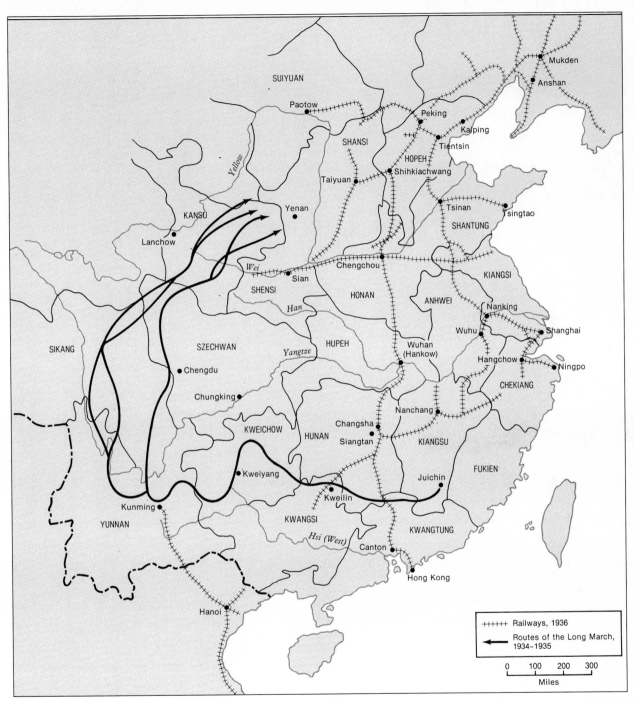

China in the 1930s

also suffered from new export taxes. It was thus not really, as it was sometimes called, a bourgeois regime. The government decided to leave the land tax, the state's traditional support, to the provinces, so the business community had to help make up the difference. One major achievement of the Nanking years was the building of at least the skeleton of a national rail system, masterminded by one of the ablest of the KMT officials, Chiang Chia-ngao, including the completion of the first through north-south line from Peking to Canton via Wuhan just two weeks before the Japanese invasion of 1937 forced the Chinese to blow up the bridges and put the line out of action. Beyond the few rail lines, transport remained primitive and expensive, often doubling the cost of goods after 50 or 100 miles. Waterways were helpful, and cheaper, where available. But otherwise goods moved by cart, pack animal, or human porter. The industrial base remained pitifully small, almost all of it in the treaty ports or in Japanese-owned Manchuria, while the countryside sank still further into economic misery, exploitation by landlords, and no improvement in the ancient technology which had changed little since medieval times.

Would the positive aspects of the Nanking years eventually have produced more genuine and more adequate development of the country as a whole, if it had not been for the Japanese attack? It seems unlikely, largely as a result of Chiang's stranglehold on party, government, and army and his total unwillingness to permit let alone pursue the fundamental change which was needed. It was a government run for and by a tiny privileged part of the population, many of whom quickly became corrupt, while they and their colleagues ignored China's real needs. It was thus inherently unstable. The growing Japanese cloud merely strengthened Chiang's conviction that military power was the only path, and that it must first be used to eliminate his Communist rivals.

After the bloody putsch in Shanghai in April of 1927 and the failure of successive uprisings in Hunan, Canton, and elsewhere, the remnants of the Communist party took refuge in two main mountain hideouts, one in the south in the mountain area called Ching Kan Shan (Jinggansshan) near where the borders of two provinces met (Kiangsi (Jiangsi), and Hunan), and a similar area in the upper reaches of the Han river valley in western Hupei (Hubei), plus others like these elsewhere. All had been used for centuries as bandit lairs, where they were relatively secure from central government forces and where overlapping provincial jurisdictions, vague at the edges and quick to pass the problem onto the neighboring officials, offered additional protection. Chiang tried hard, in five successive "bandit suppression" campaigns, to wipe out the Communists, but he was a notably poor military strategist despite his supposed training. In late 1928 the pressure of continued KMT attacks drove the Communists to a new mountain base on the border between Fukien and Kiangsi, from where they were finally driven out in October of 1934.

The Long March and the United Front

This was the beginning of the famous Long March, as a ragged column of Communists and their supporters twisted and turned through the rugged landscape of southwest China and the edges of Tibet, keeping a step or two ahead of pursuing KMT troops and heading for a

✠ Mao on Revolution ✠

Mao Tse-tung (Mao Zedong) made a study of rural conditions in Hunan Province in 1927 (and thus escaped Chiang's coup in Shanghai). His report, though still somewhat premature, showed his conviction that peasants could become the vanguard of revolution.

The present upsurge of the peasant movement is a colossal event. In a very short time, in China's central, southern, and northern provinces, several hundred million peasants will rise like a mighty storm, like a hurricane, a force so swift and violent that no power, however great, will be able to hold it back.... They will sweep all the imperialists, warlords, corrupt officials, local tyrants, and evil gentry into their graves.

Source: Mao T.-t., "Report on an Investigation of the Peasant Movement in Hunan," in M. J. Coye, J. Livingston, and J. Highland, *China* (New York: Bantam, 1984), pp. 213–214.

more secure base, which they finally found in 1935 in poor, remote northern Shensi (Shaanxi) after some 6,600 miles, where they were ultimately joined by their comrades from Hupei and from elsewhere. Chiang flew low above them in his private plane at many points along their tortuous route trying to plan their and his next move, but he never really caught up with them. To evade pursuit they went through the snows along the borders of Tibet, and then forced the passage of the upper reaches of a tributary of the Yangtze by capturing a chain suspension bridge under heavy hostile fire. The Long March paused briefly in the small Kweichou (Guizhou) city of Tsunyi (Zunyi) in January 1935, where in a strategy and policy conference Mao emerged as the unquestioned party leader, with Chou En-lai (Zhou En-lai) as his second in command, and Chu Teh (Zhu De) as military commander. The Long Marchers were by now out of touch with Moscow, and Mao's peasant strategy, the opposite of Soviet advice, was accepted at the Tsunyi Conference. The Long March took its place in legend, rather like Valley Forge in American history, as a time of heroic sacrifice, called on to inspire successive generations of Chinese. The figures we have are disconcertingly vague, but by one account about 80,000 began the Long March, and less then 10,000 finished; many died along the way from hardship and enemy fire, while others faded away and still others joined the marchers en route. Breaking out through the triple KMT lines around Ching Kan Shan, fighting occasional other KMT troops, warlords, and Tibetans also cut their numbers severely. Altogether something like 8,000 of the original Marchers reached northern Shensi in October of 1935, establishing their headquarters at Yenan (Yan'an) in December of 1936, where they were joined by local and more distant Communist groups making altogether some 15,000, increased to about 30,000 by later arrivals.

From then on they tried to build local support and abandoned the more radical policies followed in the area they had earlier controlled in Kiangsi, which had emphasized class struggle and forced redistribution of land and consequently alienated many peasants. In their new northwest base, they promoted collaboration with all groups and a more gradualist program of moderate reform and rent control, appealing to the peasants in this poor, arid, mountainous and remote area as a group which was on their side. But the main call for the collaboration of all was to build strength against the Japanese, who had already grabbed Manchuria, were present in force in north China, and were clearly preparing for an all-out assault. This was a popular cause, and it also showed up Chiang and the KMT who continued to temporize with the Japanese and to put civil war—the suppression of the Communists—ahead of resistance to Japan. Chiang planned to wipe out this now concen-

trated pocket of his mortal enemies, and ordered the army of the Manchurian warlord Chang Hsüeh-liang, at least nominally allied with him, to join with a northern KMT army to finish off the Communists. But the Manchurian troops became heavily influenced by the Communist program of a United Front against the Japanese, whose brutality they had already experienced in their homeland. In December of 1936 Chiang flew to Sian, the capital of Shensi, to urge them on against Yenan, but Chang Hsüeh-liang and his troops kidnapped Chiang where he was spending a few days at a hot spring resort (with a lady not his wife!) and demanded that he stop the civil war and join the new United Front in the cause of patriotic resistance.

Chou En-lai came down from Yenan as a negotiator, and in the end Chiang was released, on condition that he meet these demands and accept the Communists as allies against Japan. The Russians, and the Chinese Communists, felt that Chiang was too important as a leader figure to destroy him, and that top priority must now be given to the coming fight against the Japanese, in which Chiang and his army were essential. He did end the civil war for the time being, but continued his blockade of the Red area in the northwest. Chang Hsüeh-liang flew back with Chiang to Nanking as a hostage, but then was kept for the rest of his life in close confinement under house arrest. The Sian Incident, as it was called, helped to galvanize public support on both sides for the coming struggle,

Mao at Yenan in 1935, writing and working out his strategy. (Culver Pictures, Inc.)

although the United Front, renewed in 1937, was broken when a KMT army in early 1941 attacked a Communist army which they alleged was operating south of the line supposedly agreed to, although it was merely pursuing Japanese forces. For the rest of the war against Japan, the two Chinese sides remained split, with Chiang's troops guarding and blockading the borders of the Communist area and stockpiling weapons to be used against them in the final contest once Japan had been defeated.

The Communists, despite their smaller numbers, were the major resistance force after 1938, using a guerrilla strategy which perfectly fit their circumstances, sustained by the peasants in the areas they controlled, and harrying the invaders. They avoided direct conflict with those far superior numbers and weaponry, but destroyed bridges and rail lines by night, raided outlying Japanese posts, and pinned down a million Japanese troops. By the end of the war in 1945 there were 19 coordinated resistance bases in the Communist-controlled areas, some two million militia, and nearly a million regular Communist troops, their numbers swollen by their success in fighting the enemy, while after 1937 the KMT did almost nothing to contest the Japanese invasion.

Shanghai: The Model Treaty Port

While the Communists retreated to remote Yenan behind its mountain barriers and began to work out their program for a new China under the leadership of Mao

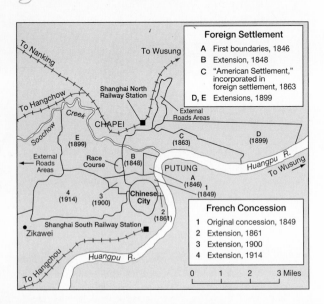

The Growth of Shanghai

Tse-tung, Shanghai remained a bastion of foreign privilege and Chinese collaborators. But it also harbored the growing group of Chinese dissidents, radicals, and revolutionaries, who lived there under the protection of foreign law. Chinese police could not pursue suspects in the foreign settlements, which were ruled by a foreign-dominated Municipal Council and its own police. The Chinese Communist party had been founded there in 1921 for that reason, by a small group of revolutionaries and writers who were part of the much larger numbers of such people living in Shanghai or using it as a refuge, many of them periodically hounded or captured and executed by the Kuomintang secret police. Chiang Kai-shek's military coup in 1927 killed many of them and drove some of the survivors out, but many remained in Shanghai semi-underground and continued to produce a long series of short-lived literary and political magazines with titles like "New China," "New Youth," and "New Dawn," avidly read by intellectuals in the rest of China. After Shanghai passed Peking as China's biggest city about 1910, it became the country's chief center of literature, publishing, and of cultural and political ferment. The May Fourth movement spread immediately from Peking to Shanghai; student organizers persuaded many Shanghai merchants to boycott Japanese, and later British, goods. Shanghai joined Peking as a major base for the "New Culture Movement," sometimes called the "Chinese Renaissance," and its efforts to remake Chinese society, as summarized in Chapter 17. Lu Hsun and many other New Culture writers lived in Shanghai.

At the same time, Shanghai remained by far the largest port and commercial center in China, through which over half of its foreign trade passed and which also contained over half of its modern industry. Chinese entrepreneurs, both traditional and Westernized, competed and collaborated with foreigners in trade, banking, and manufacturing, and many of them lived in Western style. The foreign settlements at Shanghai were replicas of the modern Western city, and looked physically like Manchester or Chicago. The muddy foreshores of the Huangpu (Hwangpu) River, a Yangtze tributary which ran along one edge of the city and constituted the harbor, were covered in the nineteenth century by an embankment known as the Bund. It became Shanghai's main thoroughfare, lined with imposing Western banks and hotels. Earlier the Westerners had imported a Scottish gardener who built a small park on the Bund where they could walk in surroundings designed to remind them of home. Signs (not a single sign as often said) were put up reading "No Dogs" and "No Chinese." This later became, understandably, a nationalist issue, as did the blatant racism and discrimination of foreigners in the treaty ports, as elsewhere. After all, whose country was it?

✠ Shanghai as an Affront to Chinese Pride ✠

Tai Chi-t'ao (Dai Jitao), an early member of the Chinese Communist party, spoke the mind of many Chinese intellectuals and revolutionaries in castigating the treaty ports and all they symbolized, although most of them were obliged to live there for their own security.

Tai's attitude toward Shanghai was the prime catalyst of his commitment to social revolution. For Tai and for the entire spectrum of Chinese revolutionaries as well, she was a bitch-goddess who gnawed at their souls, scarring them brutally and indelibly. Life in the Concessions was comparatively safe, for example, but the very security which Tai enjoyed there galled and tormented him at the same time. He, a Chinese, was being protected from fellow Chinese by the grace and scientific superiority of Westerners. His asylum rapidly crystallized into a personal confrontation with the entire legacy of China's humiliations at the hands of the West. [The Countryside] represented idyllic, uncontaminated China for Tai. There he saw Chinese living in a natural economy.... Thus while the workers of Shanghai were in hell, the handicraft worker-peasants of Hu-chou were in heaven.... He expressed grief that "old" Hu-chou, no doubt would soon be forced to enter the modern world under the impact of European civilization.

Source: Herman Mast, "Tai Chi-t'ao, Sunism, and Marxism," *Modern Asian Studies,* 5, 1971, pp. 227–250.

Nanking Road, the main shopping street, ran at right angles to it away from the river, and there were extensive residential areas with houses in Western style. Shanghai was famous as "sin city," with its wide-open prostitution, gambling, bars, and cosmopolitan glitter, a mix of nearly all the world's nationalities away from their normal bases, a sort of moral no-man's land, even for its Chinese inhabitants, most of whom were recent in-migrants. The foreign population peaked at about 60,000 in the 1930s, in a city which by then totaled about four million, many of whom lived outside the foreign concession areas in sprawling slums, or in the walled Chinese city next to the concessions.

But the commercial and industrial heart of Shanghai was largely run by foreigners (Japanese edged out the British as the majority by the 1930s) and they built it in the Western image. They were proud of Shanghai's impressive economic success in the "modern" mode, and saw it as a beacon of "progress" in a vast Chinese sea of "backwardness." Shanghai was described as "in China but not of it." They were two different worlds. The city drew most of its exports (silk, tea, other agricultural goods) from the Chinese hinterland and sent there some of its imports (metals, machinery, and manufactured goods), but Shanghai's economic example made relatively little impact, except in the other treaty ports.

Unlike the Indian experience, it was largely rejected as alien and as unsuited to China. The Communists labeled Chinese collaborators in Shanghai and the other treaty ports "running dogs" of the imperialists, and were contemptuous of their departure from Chinese ways in favor of Westernization.

Shanghai and the other treaty ports cut a deep wound of humiliation in the Chinese psyche, but also offered an example of the kind of strength which China must have. Shanghai played a major role in stimulating as a reaction the rise of modern Chinese nationalism and a determination to rid the country of its foreign oppressors. The foreign way was rejected, but its technological and industrial achievements were to be adapted to serve Chinese needs in a Chinese way. Those who lived in Shanghai, under foreign domination and protection, were of course the most affected by its example, and it was primarily there that China's modern revolution began. Shanghai foreigners called it "The Model Settlement," and felt convinced that its example of "progress" would transform China. In the end, it and all foreign privileges were swept away by the revolution, but Shanghai remains China's biggest city and most advanced industrial and technological center. Shanghai's example thus survived the expulsion of the foreigners, and shaped basic aspects of the new China.

Japan in the 1920s: Taisho Democracy and Its Fate

Hara Takashi (Hara Kei), prime minister from 1918 to 1921, was in the end assassinated by yet another young fanatic. He was deeply conservative, but he did widen the electoral base by reducing the tax qualification for voting. After his death Japan continued to move slowly in the direction of a more genuine constitutional government. The Taisho emperor reigned from 1912 to 1926, but he proved to be mentally retarded and the politicians and others simply worked around him while his son served as regent. His reign name is used to cover the period, especially in the 1920s. Japan had earned additional credits and recognition from the Western powers by its token participation in the First World War, and had profited immensely from the weakness of Western commercial competition during the war. With the final Japanese triumph at Versailles, the country was secure in its new prosperity and international acceptance. Joining with the Allies in 1914 increased the trend toward internationalism, and also the attractiveness of Western-style democracy, which had defeated German militarism. There was growing support for political liberalism, and for universal suffrage. Labor groups, Christians, students, leftists, liberal politicians, and intellectuals joined together in this new movement.

But in 1920 universal suffrage was blocked by Hara and there was a brief postwar recession, both of which left many Japanese disillusioned with the political process. Politics continued to be dominated by conservative leaders, aristocrats, bureaucrats, big business, the military, and landlords, none of them responsive to popular needs or sentiments and all basically opposed to change or to efforts to correct the gross economic inequality which had been even more accentuated by wartime prosperity for a few. Industrial workers were exploited and peasants had never shared in economic achievements after 1870, as tenancy greatly increased, reaching 50 percent by 1920. Silk exports, primarily a peasant household enterprise, had earned as much as a quarter of the foreign exchange needed to buy abroad things Japan lacked: machinery, but also coal, iron ore, cotton, and oil, all but the last from China. Price fluctuations for silk hurt peasant producers, but any government effort to improve their lot would tend to increase the cost of silk and thus hurt Japan's competitive advantage. Political parties had not been an important part of the Japanese system, and the Meiji effort at development had been a national one which required a united people pursuing agreed goals rather than the divisiveness which the leaders saw as the result of rival parties.

Political parties did nevertheless grow, partly as an aspect of Meiji Westernization, and now they began to represent, as in the West, different and usually opposing interest blocs: business, landlords, the military, and for some the needs of the downtrodden. Rice riots protesting the steep wartime rise in rice prices had erupted in 1918 which had to be put down by the army; the government was clearly at fault in offering only repression instead of efforts to improve the lot of factory workers and the urban poor. This further strengthened antiestablishment feeling and lent fuel to the continued drive for universal suffrage. A new political coalition won the elections of 1925, and its majority in the Diet finally approved universal suffrage (for males over 25 only—no females) in 1925, although this new electorate got its chance to vote for the first time only in 1928. Japanese were still unused to the ideas and the practice of electoral democracy, and extremists of both the right and the left continued to use violence or even assassination, that Japanese trademark, to press their cases. Three of the six party prime ministers (as opposed to bureaucrats or military men) between 1918 and 1932 were assassinated while in office. The passage of universal adult male suffrage was moreover linked to a new "Peace Preservation Law" which increased police powers and further limited freedom of speech and assembly, reflecting the long government obsession with "dangerous thoughts." The onset of the world depression in 1929, which hit Japan hard, led to an increase of labor agitation and to new demands for change from splinter parties which spoke for the masses, while many Japanese once again questioned the effectiveness of the democratic system, as people did in Europe and North America during the depression. In Japan too, there was greatly increased support for the ideas of socialism and communism and for parties which advocated them.

The Japan Communist party was founded in 1922, supported mainly by urban intellectuals as in both Russia and China, together with organized labor, but it never became more than a small movement, nor did the other opposition groups ever produce a significant dent in the elite establishment's grip on political power, despite the now greatly widened electorate and the opportunity this offered for new political party activity. The ideas of socialism had entered Japan around the turn of the century through Christian socialists among the missionaries, and appealed to many young Japanese who saw socialism's creed of universal brotherhood, redistribution of wealth, and the abolition of the class structure as the right prescription for a Japan which continued to support the opposites. The Socialist organization was crushed by the government and many of its leaders executed in 1911, but socialist ideas were revived following the rice riots of 1918, and socialists formed alliances with labor groups. They and the Communists never suc-

Concerns About Modernization

The novelist Natsume Soseki (1867–1916) speaks through a character in his novel, Passers-by, *about the disturbing pace of change, called "modernization," which reached full speed in twentieth-century Japan:*

You know, our uneasiness comes from this thing called scientific progress. Science does not know where to stop, and does not permit us to stop either. From walking to rickshaws [oddly enough, a foreign introduction], from rickshaws to horse-drawn cabs, from cabs to trains, from trains to automobiles … to airplanes—when will we ever be allowed to stop and rest? Where will it take us? It is really frightening.

Source: From E. McClellan, "An Introduction to Soseki," *Harvard Journal of Asiatic Studies,* 22 (1959), 205–206.)

ceeded in building an effective mass base, apart from their connections with labor unions, and of course their announced aims were simply anathema to the still conservative government. This led to chronic police repression and made an effective political role impossible. The first Communist party was utterly destroyed by police purges in 1923, and later in that year the great Tokyo earthquake and following fire which devastated most of the city and nearby Yokohama was used by the police to blame all "leftists" as scapegoats, thousands of whom were rounded up, of whom many died in prison. The Communist party was refounded in 1926, but again destroyed by police arrests in 1928 and 1929. A very few survived underground, but this was the effective end of the party, while all sorts of "dangerous thoughts," including almost anything which criticized or differed from government policy, were even more brutally hunted out and punished or suppressed.

Japan's brief and tentative steps toward a more legitimate democratic system were thus not allowed to get very far. The weight of Japanese tradition was against it, and new military adventurism from the late 1920s and the successes it produced added strength to the conservative establishment in its efforts to suppress dissent. But although political democracy failed at the national level, the 1920s did see a new surge of popular interest, especially among students and the younger generation in the cities, in all aspects of the contemporary West, including socialism, anarchism, realism in art and literature, female liberation, the sexual revolution and the ideas of Sigmund Freud, jazz, and the free-swinging world of what was called in the West "the roaring twenties." Japanese "flappers" appeared, and the type called in Japanese *moga,* a version of "modern girl," or "*modan guru,*" with bobbed hair and short skirts, accompanied

by equally stylishly dressed "mobo" or "*modan buoye*" (modern boy) who danced to the latest jazz tunes, played of course by Japanese bands, followed Hollywood styles, and read Scott Fitzgerald and other contemporary Western writers. Some of them had Bohemian lifestyles, and shocked most other Japanese of the older generation, who objected also to lipstick and cigarettes as improper, let alone free love or socialism. Tokyo had by now probably the world's largest student population at its many universities; students and graduates formed a large part of this new Westernized popular culture, which was in any case limited to the big cities. There was a feminist campaign for votes for women, won in the United States in 1920, but this was not to succeed in Japan until it was in effect imposed by the American occupation after the Pacific War. Golf, an Anglo-American game quite unsuited to Japan given its urban crowding and shortage of open space, became popular among the well-to-do.

The Taisho emperor died late in 1926, and was succeeded by his son, Hirohito, whose reign era was called *Showa* ("enlightened peace"), like most reign names a euphemism which soon proved the opposite of what actually happened. The clouds were already gathering which would lead Japan into the "dark valley" of war and final defeat. As already mentioned, the establishment of the Nanking government in 1927 and the achievement of qualified national unity in China while Chiang Kai-shek built up his army was taken by the militarists, who remained powerful in the Japanese government, and their supporters as an indication that they should prepare to strike now before China acquired more strength to resist them. In 1921–1922 Japanese representatives had met in Washington with those from Britain, France, and the United States to work out a "Four Power Pact" which attempted to produce a power equilibrium in the Pacific. Britain, with its worldwide empire, and the United States, with two coasts to defend (plus its colonies in the Philippines and Hawaii), agreed to limit their capital ships in the ratio of five British and five American to three Japanese; France (and Italy later) accepted a ratio for their big ships of 1.75. The Washington Conference accepted the existing foreign unequal treaty "rights" in China, and tacitly recognized Japan's "special position" in Manchuria, but also urged that there be no new pressure for concessions. Japan was thus to be enabled to defend itself, but not to take the offensive against Britain or the U.S.

Rise of the Militarists

The Washington Conference also marked the end of the Anglo-Japanese alliance, which had been renewed in 1905 and 1911, to be replaced by the far less satisfactory, from the Japanese point of view, Four Power Pact (Japan, the U.S., Britain, and France), something which was much resented and which built anti-British and anti-American feeling, which was to break out violently in 1941. However Japan did agree at Washington to withdraw from Shantung and return to China most of its interests there, taken from Germany in 1914, while retaining some economic concessions. The man primarily responsible for the necessary negotiations with China, the later Foreign Minister Baron Shidehara, was vilified and for years accused of a "weak-kneed" China policy. Japan recognized the new Russian government and also

withdrew from the northern part of Sakhalin Island, which it had occupied in 1905. Anti-American feeling was stimulated, on top of the Washington Conference, by the extension of the Oriental Exclusion Acts in 1924 to Japanese, deeply wounding to Japanese pride. In China the Japanese position in Manchuria, including their concession areas in the Liaotung peninsula, was bitterly resented, and Japan's imperialist role was part of Chiang's target of anti-imperialism and his goal to rid China of foreign domination. All of these factors helped to build support in Japan for a more aggressive policy abroad, especially in China, which many Japanese had come to see as somehow a legitimate sphere for Japanese influence, if not control. The effects of the world depression also fed sentiment in favor of Japan gaining control of Manchuria's, and China's, rich resources and possible settlement areas for its crowded population. Many Japanese favored the creation at home of what was called the "Defense State."

Japanese exports fell by half between 1929 and 1931, the depth of the depression, unemployment rose to three million, and workers' incomes plummeted. Rice and silk prices fell precipitately, which offered some help to the urban poor but which was very hard on the peasants, already the suppressed majority. A year of bumper harvests was followed by one of widespread crop failure, and many starved while others were reduced to begging or to eating bark. The government was blamed, not entirely unreasonably since it did next to nothing to alleviate the distress. Many Japanese found the Nazi model appealing, and lost their earlier enthusiasm for Western democracy, now failing to solve the economic problems and suffering

✠ Need for *Lebensraum* ✠

The Japanese used the same argument as the Nazis in asserting their need for expansion room to accommodate their population.

"We have already said that there are only three ways left to Japan to escape from the pressure of surplus population. We are like a great crowd of people packed into a small and narrow room, and there are only three doors through which we might escape, namely, emigration, advance into world markets, and expansion of territory. The first door, emigration, has been barred to us by the anti-Japanese immigration policies of other countries. The second door, advance into world markets, is being pushed shut by tariff barriers and the abrogation of commercial treaties. What should Japan do when two of the three doors have been closed against us? It is quite natural that Japan should rush upon the last remaining door."

Source: Quoted in R. Tsunoda et al., eds. *Sources of Japanese Tradition.* (New York: Columbia University Press, 1958), p. 289.

of its own depression. Germany had long been admired in Japan, well before its defeat in World War I; its system was also authoritarian and militarist, things which the Japanese felt at home with as they did not with democratic ideas or institutions. The army and navy, still revered for their brilliant earlier successes, were not included in criticism of the government, despite their already major involvement in politics. As the world economy showed its extreme vulnerability and unreliability, sentiment grew in favor of Japan creating its own dependent sphere in Manchuria and China, to add to what it already controlled in Korea and Taiwan, which could make it independent of the swings in world markets and also free of the need to pander to Western interests. Unemployment also suggested that many could find jobs in the military, for the greater glory and the greater good of the country.

In Manchuria, which most Japanese regarded as rightfully theirs, if only because of their victory over Russia in 1905, the military commanders had long operated with a good deal of on-the-spot independence. Japan's expeditionary adventure in Siberia from 1919 to 1922, continued against all logic, was one example, while at home military representatives or supporters frequently entered the fights in the Diet to ensure what they regarded as adequate appropriations. There was still much fear of Russia, greatly increased now that Communism had triumphed there. Japan dominated the foreign investment scene in Manchuria, and put a lot of money into development projects, including the South Manchuria Railway, which linked the port of Dairen (Dalien) with Harbin on the east-west Chinese Eastern. Agriculture along the line was commercialized with this new access to markets and sent growing shipments of wheat and soybeans to Japan, via Dairen, as well as into world markets, leaving the local population to subsist for the most part on less favored sorghum and millet. The port of Dairen was improved with storage and docking facilities. Nearly a million Japanese subjects now lived in Manchuria, although most of them were Koreans. Mining projects were also developed along the new rail routes, shipping coal and iron to Japan but also forming the basis of a big, new iron and steel industry centered in the Mukden (Shenyang) area, while dams were built on many Manchurian rivers to provide hydroelectric power and irrigation.

What the Japanese purposely overlooked was that Manchuria, especially its more fertile and productive southern half, had long been part of the Chinese empire since the Han dynasty (with breaks) and was claimed by successive Chinese government. To clinch the Chinese claim, Manchuria, originally with considerable Chinese settlement in the Liao valley since Han times, was massively settled beginning in the 1890s by migrants from the deteriorating scene in north China, a tide swelled by refugees from warlords, flood, and famine in the 1920s. From 1900 to 1940 about a million Chinese migrated to Manchuria each year, to a new and expanding economic frontier; some walked, others rode the trainlines which connected Manchuria to Peking via Tientsin and the pass at Shanhaikuan after 1901; still others made the trip in boats, many of them open, from ports on the coasts of Shantung. Most were destitute refugees, but the great majority found work and rising incomes in Manchuria. Some returned to north China after a year or two, but most remained as farm, industrial, and railway workers and even as entrepreneurs, bringing Manchuria's population to about 41 million by 1940, only a million of which could be claimed by Japan, and most of those, as pointed out, subject Koreans. There had been some thought that Manchuria could provide an outlet for Japanese overpopulation at home, but it was never popular and most Japanese who went there served as officials, engineers, or in the military. It was thus truly a Japanese colony, in the sense that foreign domination was imposed on another people, against the force of nationalism, which grew among the Manchurian Chinese as it was doing elsewhere. As in China, the Japanese disregarded this, eventually a tidal wave which swept away the entire structure of the Japanese empire.

Aggression in Manchuria

Officers of the Japanese Kwantung army assassinated their client Chinese warlord, Chang Tso-lin, in 1928, by blowing up the train on which he was returning to Mukden from talks in Peking. They acted without the approval of the Tokyo government, hoping to provoke a crisis which would be followed by military action, and also to find a more compliant successor to Chang Tso-lin who would better do their bidding. In that they were disappointed; his son, Chang Hsüeh-liang, turned out in the end to be at least as "difficult" from the Japanese point of view, a Chinese patriot whose role has already been sketched. He kept up a steady pressure on the Japanese for the recovery of Chinese rights in Manchuria. For the Japanese military, this just would not do, and bellicose sentiments were also rising at home, partly in response to a London naval conference in 1930 which limited Japanese auxiliary ships and submarines to what was felt to be unfairly low levels. Violence rose, including the assassination by a superpatriot of the Japanese prime minister Hamaguchi later in 1930. To its credit, the government felt that it was now appropriate to try to curb the army in Manchuria, and in September of 1931 sent a senior general there to urge that the army use "prudence and patience." But the army officers in the field learned in advance of this visit through their network of informers, and decided that they would act before the emissary's instruction could take the form of an order.

Under cover of darkness on September 18 they set off explosives on the rail line outside Mukden close to the main barracks of Chinese troops, hoping of course to fix the blame on them. In the ensuing confusion fighting broke out between Chinese and Japanese troops, and the senior Japanese officer ordered a full attack on the Chinese barracks and the capture of the city of Mukden. The army chief of staff in Tokyo sent ambiguous messages, and the Japanese consul in Mukden, when he tried to restrain the troops, was silenced by an officer who simply drew his sword. The cabinet in Tokyo urged restraint, but the Japanese commander on the spot in Korea ordered his troops into Manchuria. Chiang Kai-shek, feeling he lacked the force to repel the Japanese invasion, ordered Chang Hsüeh-liang (Zhang Xueliang), son and successor of Chiang Tso-lin, to withdraw his troops south of Shanhaikuan, the border with Manchuria, and the Japanese conquest was rapidly a fait accompli. The last Ch'ing emperor, Henry Pu Yi, now 25, who had been living since 1912 under Japanese protection in Tientsin, became the nominal ruler of the new Japanese puppet "state" of Manchukuo ("country of the Manchus"), which they promised would be independent of China. The League of Nations was slow to move, but in November ordered an investigative commission

under Lord Lytton to go to Manchuria and compile a report. The Lytton report was finally debated by the League early in 1933, recommended against acceptance of the Japanese grab, and rejected the in itself flimsy notion that Manchukuo was an independent state. The Japanese delegation rose in unison and walked out, never to return.

Meanwhile Japanese troops advanced into adjacent Jehol (Rehe), a northern border province of China, on the pretext that it was part of the "internal problem of Manchukuo"; in short order they conquered it as well, and occupied a strong defensive position at Shanhaikuan. The Japanese commander then felt it necessary to clear his southern line of Chinese troops, and ordered his forces into Hopei (Hebei), the metropolitan province around Peking, where they attacked and routed the Chinese army of that area. In May of 1933, the Chinese were forced to agree to a demilitarized zone in northeastern Hopei, under Japanese supervision. What the Japanese called simply the "Mukden Incident" of course stimulated renewed anti-Japanese passions in China, accompanied by a boycott of Japanese goods which was very effective. In January of 1932 Japanese marines were sent ashore in Shanghai, ostensibly to protect their concession area, and exchanged fire with KMT troops in the Chapei district. In response, the Japanese naval commander ordered the bombing of

✠ Japanese Militarism ✠

Japanese militarism had deep roots. Fukuzawa Yukichi, one of the chief Meiji reformers, observed, well before Japan's war on China of 1894–1895:

One hundred volumes of International Law are not the equal of a few cannon; a handful of treaties of friendship are not worth a basket of gunpowder. Cannon and gunpowder are not aids for the enforcement of given moral principles; they are the implements for the creation of morality where none exists.

When Inukai Tsuyoshi became premier late in 1931, the military already had the dominant voice in Japan's government. Although the emperor was effectively powerless, he warned Inukai about the military when he asked him to form a cabinet.

The army's interference in domestic and foreign politics, and its wilfulness, is a state of affairs which, for the good of the nation, we must view with apprehension.

Sources: J. K. Fairbank, E. O. Reischauer, and A. M. Craig, *East Asia: The Modern Transformation.* (Boston: Houghton Mifflin, 1965); p. 566, and R. Storry, *A History of Modern Japan.* (New York: Penguin Books, 1982), p. 190.

Chapei, which killed hundreds of innocent civilians, and followed this by a full-scale assault on Shanghai's Chinese defenders. An armistice in May forced the Chinese to accept a "neutral zone" around the city, but the Japanese retained the upper hand, and clearly demonstrated that despite their claims to be the agents of law and order in a disintegrating China they were quick to produce the opposite.

As often elsewhere, but in much more uncontrolled and disastrous terms, actions taken on the spot by military commanders, without the knowledge or approval of the government at home, committed Japan to policies of aggression which would not have been freely chosen by those in charge of policy. Matters were simply taken out of their hands. In the Manchurian case, Lieutenant-Colonel Ishiwara of the Kwantung Army told General Tatekawa of the Tokyo General Staff late in August, a bit more than two weeks before the event, that he planned to provoke an incident which would provide a pretext for Japanese conquest. He received no objection, nor did he when he told his commanding general in Manchuria. But these were all military men dealing with each other, and one must assume that all of them, like most of the military, saw aggression as the best policy and were impatient with pettifogging bureaucrats at home or with those who urged caution. The cabinet was split in 1931; a majority supported the fait accompli in Manchuria but opposed further expansion. When the cabinet resigned, the successor government was also split, but the new prime minister, Inukai Tsuyoshi, disapproved of the way the army had preempted the government's decision-making powers. He tried to get an imperial order restraining the army, and to negotiate directly with the Chinese, but he was consequently assassinated by ultranationalists in May of 1932. The military and their extremist supporters had tightened their grip on Japan.

Militarists in Command

A supposedly moderate admiral became the new prime minister, but he and his similar successors, both military men (Saito and Okada), were unacceptable to the army as too mild. The cabinet remained split into opposing factions, and although there was much criticism in the Diet of the new military expansionism nothing was done to check it. Ultraright societies now increased in number, urging not only support for Japan's aggression in Manchuria and China but also action against "traitors at the side of the emperor." Private societies of this sort were matched by the new growth of groups formed among young officers in the army or navy, critical of what they saw as both a corrupt and an ineffective government of party politicians and pushing for the contin-

uation of Japanese expansionism on the mainland. Civilian and military groups joined in the assassination of Prime Minister Inukai, and dealt similarly with top generals who opposed continued Japanese aggression. In February 1936 young army officers staged an open mutiny, attacking government offices and killing cabinet ministers; the mutiny was put down only after three days, by troops brought in from elsewhere. This was followed by a purge of generals accused of playing politics within the army, which brought to the fore General Tojo, who was to lead Japan into war with the United States. Clearly it took a brave person to try to speak against the army's actions on the mainland.

Official Japan succumbed to at least a degree of paranoia, accompanied by a need to show the extremists that they too were tough on leftists. There had never been any protection of civil or minority rights in Japan, and there was a sweeping purge of alleged leftists, with mass arrests and imprisonment and some executions. Professors and other intellectuals also came under fire, especially those who had questioned the supremacy or divinity of the emperor. Shinto was further institutionalized as the state religion, and controls over "dangerous thoughts" were tightened. Shinto and the cult of emperor worship became still more pronounced in the schools. The sufferings of the depression tended to increase the militarists' insistence on foreign expansion. The Diet funneled money to the army and navy. There were a few courageous voices raised, in the Diet and from splinter political parties as well as elsewhere, against the truly dangerous policies on which Japan was now bent, but the military grip on government had become unbreakable. Most Japanese came to accept what was happening, although many were disturbed over the ascendance of the military, and in the elections of 1937 on the eve of the war in China they supported mainly the parties which could be regarded as taking a relatively moderate position. But no one apparently could control extremist activists, or of course the officers in the field. In that sense, Japan had gone out of control.

The Meiji constitution had provided that the minister of war in any cabinet must be a serving officer, perhaps an important root of the drift toward militarism from 1928, but of course there were other factors, as outlined above. The nominally civilian government, though with a cabinet now dominated by military men, lined up with the Diet in support of the army and its foreign policy. At the end of 1936 Japan, which had always admired the German model, signed an anti-Comintern Pact with the Nazis, aimed of course at Russia, giving a further link with European fascism and qualified security for Japan's aggression against China. Thought control and police terror were widely used, but Japanese ideology was not revolutionized as Germany's and Italy's had been. Veneration of the emperor was intensified and schoolchildren were indoctrinated still more obsessively with the creed of Japanese nationalism, but these were hardly new ideas.

The developments in Japan were significantly different from German or Italian fascism, despite some obvious similarities. There was no one-man rule or dictatorship until General Tojo assumed some of that role with the outbreak of the Pacific War. Japan continued to be ruled by a coalition of military and generally compliant civilian officials. There was no scapegoat group such as the Jews (although Koreans in both Korea and Japan were treated extremely badly, and even blamed for the great Tokyo earthquake of 1923). No groups comparable to Mussolini's Brown Shirts, Hitler's Storm Troopers or Hitler Yugend, or even Chiang Kai-shek's Blue Shirts, emerged. Racism is unfortunately universal and is always intensified in wartime. In Japan, belief in the superiority of the Yamato race, as it was called, was both officially promoted and generally accepted, with dreadful consequences for Japan's victims everywhere. But for most Japanese the change from the qualified openness of the 1920s to the militarized Japan of the 1930s was not very abrupt, and did not represent any major departure from familiar values or institutions. In the 1936 elections, a "prodemocracy" group actually won the largest bloc of seats, and among the factions in the Diet were those who critized the ascendancy of military power in politics and policy. But these were never a majority, and the Diet, split as it was, no longer controlled foreign policy.

Many, perhaps most, Japanese felt that their country's cause was just and that first Manchuria and then China should properly submit to Japanese management. In effect, Japan was saying to the Chinese, "Oh get *out* of the *way* and let us, with our proven experience with development, put China in order and put its rich resources to use, for our mutual benefit." In a sense, that is what Japan did accomplish in Manchuria, and what they aimed to accomplish in China. There was a clear appeal in the Japanese "Greater East Asia Co-Prosperity Sphere," with Japan providing the technical and managerial skills and the rest of East Asia providing the raw materials and labor. What destroyed the appeal was the brutal and oppressive nature of the Japanese conquest, its blatant racism, and its total disregard of nationalist sentiment, first in China (or Korea) and then in the rest of East Asia which was soon conquered. There was also some attractiveness in the Japanese slogan, "Asia for the Asiatics," but in practice Japanese domination was far worse than anything the Western colonial powers had been guilty of. So Japan continued to drift toward war, or to be steered into it by the army and navy which had become almost wholly beyond civilian control.

Background of the "China Incident"

On the eve of the full-scale war in China, Prince Konoe was asked to form a cabinet after the elections of 1937. He was an old-line aristocrat and a writer, but he also had close ties with the army, with the political parties, and with the *zaibatsu*. He thus had support from nearly every important group. The war in China began only a month after he had put together his cabinet, but for all his connections he proved too weak to resist the pressures from the military and from the superpatriot groups in Japan. Despite the Anti-Comintern Pact of 1936, there was understandable anxiety about the possible role of Russia, as Japan pushed forward from Manchuria into Jehol and into north China, long-standing areas of Russian concern and influence. If it had remained in control of events or policy, the Japanese government would probably have followed a more cautious path. But once again events on the spot took matters out of their hands, and all-out war between China and Japan erupted on July 7, 1937, at the Marco Polo bridge in Peking (so called because it is described in Polo's journal), when Japanese troops stationed in the area clashed with Chinese troops in an incident which soon erupted into war. The Japanese army had been behaving as if it owned north China, and this was bitterly resented by all Chinese, most of all by the Chinese army. It would appear that the Japanese commander at the Marco Polo bridge clash tried to backpedal, or at least to cool tempers, but the Chinese were nursing a long grievance against Japanese aggression and belligerent behavior and could not be talked down, any more than could the Japanese troops. Both sides were in effect spoiling for a fight.

There was never a declaration of war against China, although the surprise and shock were a good deal less than in 1894, 1904, and later 1941, when Japan won an early advantage by attacking without any warning. The outbreak of full war in China was hardly a surprise; the Japanese continued until the end to call it simply the "China Incident," and at least to begin with hopes in Japan were high. Western opinion had began to turn against Japan over its seizure of Shantung, and became still more negative over the Japanese expedition to Siberia, kept there long after the Western powers had withdrawn. The Japanese saw the 1921–1922 Washington Conference and its limitations on their navy, together with the end of the Anglo-Japanese alliance, as anti-Japanese, and it was certainly the case that by then at least the British and the Americans did see Japan as a rising threat to their positions in East Asia. With the added blow of the U.S. Exclusion Act of 1924, Japan saw itself as still being treated like an inferior by the white imperialists. All of this helped to account for Japanese brutality against all Westerners (except their German al-

Celebrating the Tripartite Pact with Germany and Italy. General Tojo (in army boots) looks over at Foreign Minister Matsuoka raising his glass for a toast to this "pact for peace." (Kyodo News International, Inc.)

lies, who were treated rather ambiguously) once the Pacific War had begun at Pearl Harbor. It was an uneasy alliance between Japan and Nazi Germany, despite some similarities in their domestic systems, and neither side fully trusted the other. Japanese did not really admire Hitler, although when he foolishly attacked Russia in July of 1941, they breathed a sigh of relief since this further increased their security against the possibility of a Russian intervention against them in East Asia. The Japanese knew that Russians still resented their defeat by Japan in 1905 and the Japanese seizure of what had earlier been Russian territories and position in the area. But in the 1920s and 1930s fear of Russia, for the time being out of the power game as a result of the 1917 revolution, was replaced by fear and resentment of the British and Americans, who had so pointedly tried to fence them in.

To make matters worse, the United States, Japan's largest market after China, moved in the 1930s in the wake of the depression to pursue a high tariff policy, adding injury to the insult of the Exclusion Acts. The depression itself, although it hit Japan too, also tarnished the image of the Western democracies and made their political and ideological system seem much less attractive. Japan began to see itself as one of the "have-not" nations victimized by the "haves" with their far greater resources and wealthier economies. Faced as they saw it by a hostile or at least an unfriendly Western world, it was perhaps understandable that Japan should feel that its destiny lay instead on the Chinese mainland. Unfor-

tunately, although the cultural ties with China were deep and strong, China was now seen scornfully (and not entirely wrongly) as having degenerated from its earlier greatness and as needing the strong and competent hand of Japan. Ironically, given the ties between them, China and Japan might well have worked together cooperatively and to their mutual benefit. But the Japanese record of aggression and belligerency ever since the Sino-Japanese War of 1894–1895 and before, and their behavior in both Manchuria and China had made them the enemy in Chinese eyes. Japanese arrogance and domineering attitude toward China made them totally unacceptable to most Chinese as guides or partners. Despite all this, there had been much Chinese admiration for the Meiji achievements, and some interest in adapting the Meiji model of growth and national strength. Sun Yat-sen, Lu Hsun, and many others shared such a view, but the attractiveness of Japan was destroyed by Japanese behavior, especially with its seizure of Shantung and the events which followed.

Given the combination of the economic depression, the fear of Communism, the stories of political corruption among the parties, and the feeling that the West had turned against them, there was a growing sense that what the country needed was strong, authoritarian government and aggressive military buildup—the defense state." It left no place for dissidents, and centered on reverence for the emperor as the all-embracing national symbol. Party government was seen as having failed, and a more unified central direction as needed.

A sad farewell: a conscript entering the Japanese army being given a send-off by his former fellow students. (*Nihon hyakunen no kiroku*, Kodansha Publishers)

Patriotic societies mushroomed, most of them strongly rightist and urging unqualified support for the military, which was thought of as above the dirty arena of politics. Secret ultranationalist societies also increased in number and adherents; they had always advocated and used violence to advance their objectives, and now this became still more prominent. The easy success of the Manchurian takeover in 1931 brought general exhilaration at home. The political parties, with decisions in Manchuria taken out of their hands, felt that they had lost viability and the confidence of the country, and were thus the less reluctant to allow the drift toward the domination of the military at home to take its course. Military buildup also stimulated the economy (including the conscription of many more soldiers, mainly peasants from the rural sector) and helped Japan to recover from the depression, as rearmament in the West was to do a few years later. What was called "internationalism" was rejected as Japan determined to go it alone.

The ultimate clash with China certainly followed from the Japanese grab of Manchuria and their stationing of troops south of Shanhaikuan, but in 1937 Japan really stumbled into war, and without any very clear long-term objectives. The Japanese wanted China to submit to their direction, but they did not necessarily plan to conquer the country; it was Chinese resistance which made that necessary, and massive Japanese miscalculation of the strength of Chinese nationalism as well as the enormity of the task, which of course in the end defeated them. The "China Incident" became a morass into which Japan poured ever more resources and men without achieving any substantial results beyond their limited territorial conquests in the eastern part of the country, except for hardening the Chinese will to resist. Like both Napoleon and Hitler in their ill-fated invasions of Russia, they were stalled by the immense size of the country, its natural mountain defenses, and their lengthening supply lines, plus Chinese patriotic resistance. Unlike the Russians, the Chinese lacked an army big enough or well enough armed to defeat the Japanese, and also unlike the Russian army, the KMT forces were especially poorly led. Chiang Kai-shek was a disaster as a military strategist, and the Communist guerrillas in the north could only harry the enemy rather than confronting him head-on. So the war dragged on, never emerging from the stalemate the Japanese achieved early, by 1938. All of this might have been predicted in Japan, but the early successes increased their confidence and by 1938, when something might perhaps have been salvaged, too much had been invested to make it politically or psychologically possible for Japan to admit it had made a fundamental error and to withdraw.

The Growth of Japan's Empire

Suggestions for Further Reading

China

Ch'en Chieh-ju. *Chiang Kai-shek's Secret Past*. Boulder: Westview, 1994.

Clifford, N. R. *Spoilt Children of Empire: Westerners in Shanghai*. Middlebury College Press, 1991.

Coble, P. *The Shanghai Capitalists and the Nationalist Government*. Cambridge: Harvard University Press, 1986.

Cochrane, S. and Hsieh, A., eds. *One Day in China: May 21, 1936*. New Haven: University Press, 1983.

Dirlik, A. *The Origins of Chinese Communism*. Oxford University Press, 1989.

Eastman, L. *The Abortive Revolution: China Under Nationalist Rule*. Cambridge: Harvard University Press, 1974.

Hartford, K. and Goldstein, S., eds. *Single Sparks: China's Rural Revolution*. White Plains: M. E. Sharpe, 1989.

Hayford, C. W. *To the People: James Yen and Village China*. New York: Columbia University Press, 1990.

Hofheinz, R. *The Broken Wave: The Chinese Communist Peasant Movement, 1922–1928*. Cambridge: Harvard University Press, 1977.

Honig, E. *Sisters and Strangers: Women in the Shanghai Cotton Mills, 1919–1949*. Stanford: Stanford University Press, 1986.

Jordan, D. A. *The Northern Expedition*. Honolulu: University of Hawaii Press, 1976.

Kirby, W. *Germany and Republican China*. Stanford: Stanford University Press, 1984.

Luk, M. *The Origins of Chinese Bolshevism, 1920–1928*. Oxford University Press, 1990.

Meisner, M. *Li Ta-chao and the Origins of Chinese Marxism*. Cambridge: Harvard University Press, 1967.

Murphey, R. *Shanghai: Key to Modern China*. Cambridge: Harvard University Press, 1953.

Selden, M. *The Yenan Way in Revolutionary China*. Cambridge: Harvard University Press, 1971.

Snow, E. *Red Star Over China*. New York: Random House, 1938.

Sun, Y. *China and the Origins of the Pacific War*. New York: St. Martins, 1993.

Tien, H. M. *Government and Politics in Kuomintang China*. Stanford: Stanford University Press, 1972.

Wei, W. *Counterrevolution in China*. Ann Arbor: Univ. of Michigan Press, 1985.

Yang, B. *From Revolution to Politics: Chinese Communists on the Long March*. Boulder: Westview, 1990.

Japan

Arima, T. *The Failure of Freedom*. Cambridge: Harvard University Press, 1969.

Berger, G. M. *Parties out of Power in Japan, 1931–1941*. Princeton: Princeton University Press, 1977.

Crowley, J. *Japan's Quest for Autonomy*. Princeton: Princeton University Press, 1966.

Duus, P., et al., eds. *The Japanese Informal Empire in China*. New York: Columbia University Press, 1989.

_____. ed. *The Cambridge History of Japan: The Twentieth Century*. Cambridge: Cambridge University Press, 1986.

_____. *Party Rivalry and Political Change in Taisho Japan*. Cambridge: Harvard University Press, 1968.

Gordon, A. *Labor and Imperial Democracy in Prewar Japan*. Berkeley: University of California Press, 1991.

Iriye, A. *After Imperialism*. Cambridge: Harvard University Press, 1965.

Lebra, J., ed. *Japan's Greater East Asia Co-Prosperity Sphere*. Oxford: Oxford University Press, 1975.

MacPherson, W. J. *The Economic Development of Japan, 1868–1941*. London: Macmillan, 1987.

Marshall, B. K. *Capitalism and Nationalism in Prewar Japan*. Berekely: University Press, 1992.

Ogata, S. *Defiance in Manchuria*. Berkeley: University of California, 1964.

Tipton, E. *The Japanese Police State*. Honolulu: University of Hawaii Press, 1990.

Titus, D. *Palace and Politics in Prewar Japan*. New York: Columbia University Press, 1974.

Totten, G. O. *The Social Democratic Movement in Prewar Japan*. New Haven: Yale University Press, 1966.

Wynd, Oswald, *The Ginger Tree*. New York: Harper, 1991.

Yoshihashi, T. *Conspiracy at Mukden and the Rise of the Japanese Military*. New Haven: Yale, 1963.

CHAPTER 19

THE SECOND WORLD WAR IN ASIA

The war really began for China in 1931 with the Japanese invasion of Manchuria and their conflict with Chinese troops south of Shanhaikuan soon thereafter. Chinese rightly regarded Manchuria as part of their own territory, and the Japanese military presence in north China as an act of war. Although the Kuomintang (KMT) government was still too weak to challenge it in the field, this Japanese presence led directly to the Marco Polo Bridge incident which touched off full-scale war in July of 1937. Japan was prepared militarily, after several years of buildup, but amazingly unprepared in terms of any clearly defined goals, even in the minds of the military themselves. Wars usually begin with relatively clear objectives, however reasonable or unreasonable, and of course the clearest cases are those where a country tries simply to defend itself from an invader and to drive him out. But even external wars of aggression have their strategy and rationale, such as the seizure of territory. The Japanese began by biting off pieces of China, first Taiwan, then Manchuria, deluding themselves that these were somehow separate, non-Chinese areas not part of the Chinese state. It is possible that they might have been able to hold on to both for a time, until what one is tempted to call the inevitable Chinese revolution would surely have turned them out. But the Japanese invasion of China proper from 1937 greatly hastened the coming of that revolution, ensured that it would be led by the Communist party rather than the Kuomintang, and that it would be bitterly and violently anti-Japanese, determined to regain all of China's lost territories.

What did the Japanese have in mind when they invaded China in 1937? They had become captives of their own illusions: of Japan as all-powerful and all-competent, of China as hopelessly backward, weak, and disunified, needing and perhaps even wanting Japanese direction. Japan also assumed that once they had captured the Kuomintang capital at Nanking, and in the process overwhelmingly defeated the KMT army, China would agree to Japanese terms. When that too proved illusory, the next step or steps remained unclear and the war bogged down. Japanese terror tactics failed to persuade the Chinese to give up, and China's great distances and mountains helped to stall Japanese efforts to advance. Napoleon and Hitler had made the same mistake in Russia, prisoners of their own illusions, but nations, like individuals, seldom learn from the mistakes of others, and are often too slow to draw the correct conclusions from their own errors. There are lessons here for any superior power attempting to enforce its will on a weaker one. They were repeated in the Communist-Kuomintang civil war from 1947 to 1949, and then in first the French and then the U.S. effort to destroy the anticolonial (and also communist) resistance in Vietnam. Superior weaponry, even superior numbers, do not ensure victory, especially not when they are directed against nationalist, patriotic resistance, which in fact they serve to strengthen. Terror tactics only make it worse, as in repeated instances from Napoleon to Hitler to the Japanese to the U.S. in Vietnam.

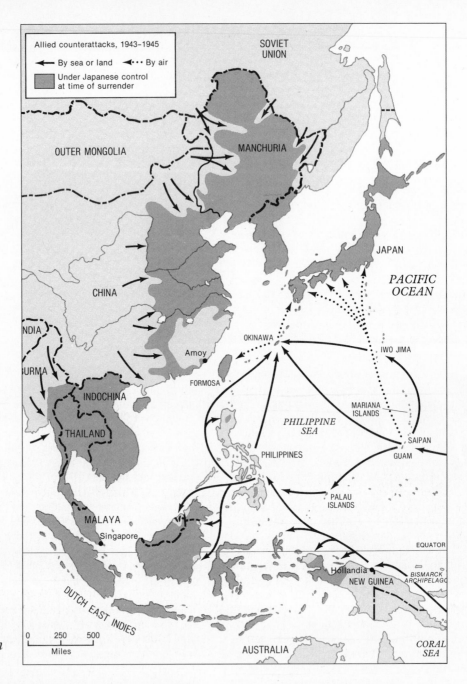

World War II in Eastern Asia

The Japanese Attack on China

It was perhaps inevitable that Japanese and Chinese troops, both stationed in the Peking area, should eventually clash. The Marco Polo bridge is about ten miles west of the city's center; Chinese troops stationed in that area decided to strengthen some defenses along the Yungting (Yongding) River there, especially since a new

railway bridge had been built next to it which linked Peking to Tientsin and in the other direction to Inner Mongolia and northern Shansi. The Japanese were aware of its importance, and periodically ran maneuvers in the area, provided for by the Boxer Protocol of 1901. July 7 was one such occasion. That night the Chinese troops fired into the Japanese concentration, and although they did not kill anyone, this alarmed the Japanese commander, who ordered an attack on the nearby rail junction of Wanping, where Chinese troops were gathered. On July 8 the Chinese unsuccessfully attacked the Japanese position, and although in the ensuing days there were negotiations and a general effort on both sides, including their home governments, to back off from war, both Japan and China mobilized their forces as a precaution and moved more troops into eastern north China. Again perhaps inevitably, or at least predictably, these reinforcements had the effect of raising the stakes, and of raising tempers on both sides. On July 27 new and fiercer fighting erupted around the Marco Polo bridge itself, which fell to the Japanese forces. By the end of July they held the whole Peking-Tientsin region.

At this point Chiang Kai-shek made one of his many fatal blunders by ordering an attack on Japanese forces in Shanghai, hoping to draw them from the north. Chiang had most of his best German-trained divisions in the Shanghai area, and for the moment they outnumbered the Japanese. On August 14 he directed his tiny air force to bomb Japanese warships riding at anchor right off the Bund at Shanghai. Their bombs all missed the ships and fell instead on the city, where they killed many hundreds of civilians. It was this foolish action which now brought full Japanese force to bear, still with no declaration of war nor even any recognition that what was happening in China was anything more than an "incident." Fifteen Japanese divisions moved in, and Chiang ordered his troops to defend Shanghai, his old personal base, at all costs. Shelled by the Japanese navy at close range, bombed by their planes, and assaulted by tanks and troops, the Chinese lost some 250,000 combatants, well over half of their best troops, at a cost of a mere 40,000 Japanese casualties. As the Chinese retreated in disorder toward Nanking in early November, Tokyo offered through Berlin to "settle the China incident." Chiang originally showed some interest, but it was soon too late, as the Japanese continued to extend their conquests in the north and now aimed to destroy the capital at Nanking. The Chinese fought mainly ineffective retreating actions, and Chiang vowed that Nanking would never fall, but it did so quickly, on December 13, partly because many or most of the defeated and demoralized Chinese troops who had

A famous newsphoto: aftermath of the Japanese bombing of Shanghai in 1937. (UPI/Bettmann)

escaped from their hopeless defense of Shanghai deserted. Chiang had earlier fled to Wuhan.

The Japanese had dropped leaflets on the city promising good treatment for all civilians there, but although there was little or no fighting to slow their occupation of Nanking, they now embarked on a campaign of terror which went on, with the full knowledge and approval of the commanders, for nearly seven weeks. This is best seen as the first major step in the Japanese effort to persuade China to surrender to save itself from even worse. The victorious Japanese troops went on an orgy of raping and killing, mainly of innocent civilians, including women and children. Women were bayoneted or impaled on stakes after repeated rapings, men and children stabbed or burned to death, pregnant women sliced open and left to die. Understandably, there are no accurate figures, but various estimates suggest that as many as 400,000 Chinese died in what became known as the Rape of Nanking. Looting and arson left much of the city in ruins. A contributing factor was probably the frustration of the Japanese troops, who had expected an easy triumph but had suffered far more casualties than had been anticipated, while their commanders' timetable had been disrupted. There was also resentment against China for refusing to give up or even to discuss terms. All Chinese were now seen as the enemy.

Koreans not seen as enemy

Retreat and Resistance

What remained of the KMT army retreated westward, hoping to regroup at Wuhan, where the government was established early in 1938. The Japanese rolled on westward, and when they captured the old Sung capital of Kaifeng at the bend of the Yellow River, with its rail line via Chengchou (Zhengzhou) south to Wuhan, Chiang, with little consideration for his people, ordered the destruction of the Yellow River dikes. The flood which resulted did stall the Japanese advance for nearly three months, but it also destroyed over 4,000 villages and their inhabitants and killed unknown numbers of peasants who were drowned without warning as the huge flood followed the old southern course of the river before the 1850s where dense agricultural settlement had grown up. The battle for Wuhan was thus delayed, at terrible cost, but the Japanese sent naval units up the Yangtze and brought in more troops and armor as well as aircraft, which bombed Wuhan heavily. They took the city in late October; Chiang had earlier had himself flown out to safety to his new base beyond the Yangtze gorges at Chungking (Chongqing), leaving the remnants of his army to fend for themselves or to find their own way west. Four days before the fall of Wuhan Japanese naval forces had seized Canton (Guangzhou), having earlier extended their control southward along the

coast from Shanghai to northern Kwangtung (Guangdong). Chiang had thus lost nearly all of the important east coast. There had been some active fighting against the Japanese advance westward from Nanking and even one or two temporary Chinese victories which inflicted heavy losses on the enemy, but these were essentially retreating actions and were the last of any consequence the Chinese were able to mount.

The war ministry in Tokyo had originally hoped to limit Japanese troops in China to 250,000, but this had become impossible, especially considering the losses, and already the army in China was overextended. Tokyo calculated that it might soon be needed elsewhere, and that it was important to prevent as much as possible any further losses. Ideally Tokyo would have preferred to disengage from China and husband its resources, but only on condition that the Chinese accepted some form of Japanese overlordship. When that was not forthcoming, Japan was trapped in a no-win situation of its own making. West of the great bend of the Yellow River in the north, and in pockets of mountainous Shansi and northwestern Hupei (Hubei), the Communists set up their guerrilla bases. There had been underground and guerrilla resistance to the Japanese earlier in Manchuria, and this continued throughout the full-scale war. As the Japanese pushed westward in north China their superior force and heavy equipment made it suicidal for the guerrillas to contest them head-on, but under cover of night they began to mount devastating attacks on outlying Japanese positions, and to systematically blow up bridges, rail lines, and roads. The guerrillas' successes were inspiring, especially to those who had suffered, as nearly all had, from Japanese brutality, and the Communist forces grew accordingly. They depended on peasants to provide them with food, for which they paid (unlike armies in the past), to offer them shelter, and to give them information on enemy concentrations or movements. Many worked ostensibly as simple peasants by day and as guerrillas or saboteurs by night, or served as guides and scouts. Guerrilla successes and their interdependence with peasants provoked savage Japanese reprisals, which often killed everyone in villages suspected of harboring the guerrillas, tortured others to make them confess their connections, and burned or flayed alive captured guerrillas.

Like the similar Nazi actions in Europe against the resistance there, this served only to harden the opposition against them and to build even stronger bonds between the guerrillas and the peasants, who knew they were fighting and dying in a common cause. Nothing unites people like a common invading enemy. The Communists were able to use this to build their strength in all the areas where they operated. They paraphrased the classical philosopher Hsun-tze (Xunzi, c. 300–235 B.C.): "The people are the water, and the ruler is the boat. The water

Chiangs defense actions lead to death

can support the boat, but can also overturn it." The Communist version was "The soldiers are the fish and the people are the water."[1] In effect, the Communists reversed the saying so as to emphasize interdependence rather than potential conflict. Their tactics against the Japanese included what they called "sparrow warfare," using small forces which struck by surprise at isolated enemy posts and then flitted away before a response could be prepared against them, and extensive "tunnel warfare." Tunnels enabled them to collect men and equipment undetected and then to emerge at night for a surprise attack. A network of tunnels was dug for this purpose on both sides of the Japanese lines, and was also used to store and plant explosives for use against Japanese positions. Japanese controlled the cities, and the rail lines by day, but the guerrillas controlled the countryside at night even in the supposedly conquered areas. In the course of the war, they built up their regular forces to well over 900,000 men, plus even more numerous local militias and their peasant allies. Most of their weapons they captured from the Japanese, or made themselves, including crude grenades and mines made from hollowed-out stones. What few supplies came from Russia to China went to the KMT, still a formal ally. The Communists coordinated their field actions through a simple but effective portable radio system, and soon were tying down about a million Japanese troops.

The KMT Side

The guerrilla effort in the north contrasted sharply with the KMT position in the areas west of the Japanese advance up the Yangtze and beyond their coastal conquests (see the map on page 366). From the new capital at Chungking, the KMT avoided clashes with Japanese forces. Chiang was not interested in organizing peasant resistance, fearing that it might be turned against him. In this he had some reason, since the full weight of his bureaucracy and conscription for his army now fell on what his government called "Free" China. He had lost all the major eastern cities and their revenues as well as nearly all of the income from taxes on foreign trade which had been so important before. The land tax had been given over to the provinces, but now in their greatly reduced base KMT tax collectors worked together with those representing the provinces; rapacious landlords added to the squeeze on peasants. In some areas it was said that rents and taxes were collected as much as 50 years in advance. Peasants, already oppressed and losing ground, sank still further into poverty, and there were periodic famines. The Communists were later to make much political capital out of these problems, and even turned the household and courtyard of one of the worst landlords in Szechuan into

a museum called "Rent Collection Courtyard" with lifelike statues of starving and beaten peasants and cruel overseers. But all even of "Free" China was not uniformly impoverished, and there were pockets of modest well-being, perhaps as many as the pockets of misery and famine.

The other major impact of the KMT on the countryside, where the vast majority of Chinese lived, was conscription. The very heavy army losses in the fighting for Shanghai and the engagements following had to be made up. China was still at war, whatever the Japanese called it, and Chiang also wanted to build his forces for what he was convinced would be the ultimate showdown with the Communists. Those with money or connections were able to buy their way out or through influence avoid being conscripted, but most people, and most peasants, had no such advantages. Press gangs invaded most villages and took the able-bodied who had not hidden or run away, operating on the basis of local quotas. The loss of a son, husband, or father was often disastrous to the family left behind without his labor, since so many were already living on the edge of survival. As many as a third of those conscripted died from mistreatment, starvation, and untreated disease or wounds, quite apart from battle casualties. One of the sights of wartime "Free" China was the straggling columns of the KMT army being marched from province to province to no apparent purpose, most of them ragged, starving, and brutalized by their officers, who stood over them with guns whenever they dropped out to relieve themselves, for fear they would run away. Officers rode horses while the men walked (as best they could), and often sold part of the men's rice rations. When given proper food, equipment, and training, they were fine soldiers, like those trained by the U.S. General Stilwell, who fought well in the reconquest of Burma, but with few exceptions they were unable to face the Japanese. After the fall of Wuhan the KMT mounted only a few retreating actions, most of which quickly deteriorated into a rout.

The figures are spongy, but Chiang had about five million men under arms by the early 1940s, though still saving his best troops and equipment for later use against the Communists. Morale deteriorated, not only because of the wretched treatment of conscripts but because there was no longer organized resistance against the Japanese. Chiang appointed his military commanders solely on the basis of their loyalty to him rather than for their competence, and very few of them were effective. Chiang himself insisted on directing operations and masterminding strategy and tactics from the security of Chungking, and his orders were often confused; all of the actual military engagements ended in disaster. One possible exception, although the fighting was on a small scale, was the front along the deep gorge of the

Salween River near the Burma border. Chinese and Japanese artillery fired at each other across the narrow gorge and there were occasional sorties, but no change in the line until the end of the war. Late in the war, in the summer of 1944, the Japanese pushed south from Wuhan and west from Canton and easily captured Changsha, Hengyang, Kuelin (Guilin), and Liuchou (Liuzhou), where the Chinese had built new airfields from which the Americans had begun to bomb Japan. Meeting so little effective resistance, Japanese columns probed westward and northward in the fall toward Kweiyang (Guiyang), provincial capital of Kweichou (Guizhou) and the road to Chungking. The Chinese troops fell back and there was panic in Chungking. But this was the high point of the Japanese advance in China and their drive was stalled by their overextended supply lines (especially for fuel) and the mountainous landscape, as well as the distances involved. They were obliged to withdraw, and their threat to Chungking was more psychological than real.

Earlier the Japanese had extended their position in Manchuria and north China by adding to their conquest of adjacent Jehol a new Mongol "autonomous" government in 1937 which theoretically controlled most of Inner Mongolia under Japanese domination, while in 1939 Japanese troops moving farther into Mongolia had become involved in a head-on clash with Russian-supported Mongol forces, now with tanks instead of their traditional cavalry. It was a major conflict, although never declared by either side, and it ended in a crushing Japanese defeat and withdrawal. Nevertheless they set up a puppet government in Peking, headed by a few old Chinese collaborators, and another in Nanking after the fall of the city, headed from 1940 by Wang Ching-wei, a former lieutenant of Sun Yat-sen's who was antagonized by Chiang's dictatorial leadership, and perhaps hoped to mitigate some of the severity of Japanese rule, as many collaborators elsewhere reasoned.

Refugees and Communists

Most Chinese in the occupied areas stayed where they were and tried to go on with their lives. The lot of refugees anywhere is a hard one, although it was hard too to live under Japanese rule, forced to bow or kneel to Japanese officers and beaten or shot if not sufficiently deferential, while many had their houses requisitioned, their women taken as "troop comforters," and their livelihoods eaten into by scarcity and inflation. It was worse in the areas of the north affected by guerrilla fighting, where noncombatants were slaughtered indiscriminately and the Japanese slogan, virtually a directive, was: "Kill all, Burn all, Loot all." Many ran from Japanese brutality to join the Communists in the north,

including many intellectuals. Others braved the risks and hardships involved in fleeing across the country to the new capital at Chungking, or to refuge in the southwest of Yunnan and Kweichou. With patriotic fervor to keep them going, workers left their factories in coastal cities and carried on their backs what equipment they could, to set up wartime factories in the west. Students and teachers evacuated their coastal universities and carried books and laboratory equipment on the long trek to Szechuan, Kweichou, and Yunnan, where the largest such concentration set up the wartime Lienta ("Combined") University in Kunming, the provincial capital. In general refugees from north China went to Yenan, those from central and south China to the KMT areas, but many of the latter became disillusioned with the ineffectiveness and corruption of the KMT and made their way to Yenan, while others still increased their sympathy for what the Communists were doing and trying to do. They seemed to many to be the true heirs of Sun Yat-sen, with the additional appeal of apparently genuine concern for peasant welfare.

In what the Communists called the Liberated Areas, where in time they controlled about 90 million people, there was no more talk of class warfare, the urban proletariat (not present in this poor agricultural area in any case), or party dictatorship, although such ideas were still clearly part of their ideology, and were to surface again once they won power in 1949. For the present they stressed common effort among all groups against the Japanese, tolerated private ownership, and promoted agrarian cooperatives to help the peasants. This relatively mild and progressive program won them much support elsewhere in China and abroad, where it was sometimes said that they were not really Communists but "agrarian reformers." Mao promoted a peasant and proletarian theme in art and literature, declaring that "art must serve politics" and "art must serve the masses," an aspect of what he called the "mass line." Many of China's intellectuals, writers, and artists had joined the regime in Yenan; they were welcomed, and asked to support the mass line, which most of them were quite willing to do. Artists produced wood-block prints for cheap mass distribution showing peasants as heroes and the nobility which often comes from poverty and sacrifice. Writers turned out stories in simplified language for a mass audience which were also accounts of peasant and soldier heroism. Efforts were made to spread literacy, usually in evening classes, and the rudiments of public health. Basic medical needs were served by local clinics staffed often by refugee doctors and by a few intrepid volunteer physicians from Canada (such as Norman Bethune, who died from blood poisoning after operating on an infected patient) and America (such as George Hatem—Ma Hai-teh). As the war dragged on and the KMT blockade of the Communist areas continued, casualties and other patients often had to be operated on without anesthetic and medical supplies of all kinds became scarce.

Mao circulated the text of several short pieces he wrote in Yenan during these war years, refining his ideas and hinting at the nature of a Communist regime in the future. They included "Evening Talks" at the Yenan Forum of Art and Literature, which presented the guidelines and the rationale for the new mass line to be followed by artists and intellectuals. Other articles were "On the New Democracy," and "On Guerrilla Warfare." The New Democracy was a multiclass coalition in which bourgeois elements, petty capitalists and landlords, and intellectuals formed a united front with peasants, under overall peasant-dominated leadership. It was to be followed by "socialist revolution" which would put peasants and workers in full control. The 1911 Revolution which toppled the Ch'ing had been, Mao said, only bourgeois (which was true), whereas his New Democracy would be part of the proletarian socialist revolution pioneered by Russia in 1917, and leading on to full state ownership. There were also pieces describing in simple terms the Marxist ideas of dialectical materialism, the primacy of conflict as a means to "progress," and the Marxist theory of the stages of historical evolution.

Mao and the other Communist leaders lived very simply, like most of the government and support personnel, in caves hollowed out of the low loess cliffs, holding their meetings outside in the warm weather and wearing the traditional thickly padded cotton gowns in winter. It was symbolically important that they shared the siege hardships and spartan lifestyle of the common people. Morale was high, and grew with their guerrilla successes. The cult of peasant virtue was part of the effort to awaken and politicize the masses. In addition to wood-block prints as the art of the common people, there was mass singing, the promotion of folk songs, and the elevation of a traditional peasant song and simple dance, the *yang-ko* (yangge), into a dance opera form which included propaganda stories as well as entertainment, in which nearly everyone participated. It was in the Yenan period that the chief slogan of the Communists emerged: "Serve the People." Party cadres (officials) lived in villages, worked with peasants, and shared their life. There was often discussion of policy, but under the direction of the party, and once a decision was reached, everyone had to go along with it. It was a party dictatorship, but with some aspects of what was soon called "people's democracy."

The radical nature of what was to happen after 1949 was inherent in the Communist party, but not yet made clear, although it had been anticipated more sharply during the period of the territorial bases such as Ching Kan Shan where radicalism tended to alienate people and was abandoned or softened in the Yenan period.

Mao was not an original thinker, and nearly all of his ideas had been stated earlier by others, Russian and Chinese, which of course is where he got them from. But he put them together into what purported to be a new doctrine, a development beyond Marxism-Leninism which had been tailored to fit the particular circumstances of China. Maoism became a cult, and loyalty to him and to his line was required and enforced for all, including the intellectuals who had grown up under the influence of Western liberalism and were now "reformed" or expelled. Most politically conscious Chinese (still a minority) realized that the coming struggle would be between the Communists and the KMT for the future of China. Some were concerned about the totalitarian as well as radical potential of the Communist side, but the KMT side was hardly a true democracy in almost any sense and was clearly failing to deal with China's real problems, either the present threat of invasion or the longer-term threat of economic deterioration and gross injustice. It was a dilemma for those caught in it, for whom we are obliged to have great sympathy, whichever side an individual chose to support. Already some of the demonic side of the Communists was apparent in their "rectification campaign" of 1942, which punished or drove to suicide alleged followers of Mao's rivals, and intellectuals, like the woman writer Ding Ling, who stepped out of line; her husband had been executed by the KMT, and after a time in Chungking she traveled to Yenan, like other writers, where she criticized cadres for insensitivity to women, and was sent down to labor in the countryside.

Chiang and the Americans

Two hundred thousand to four hundred thousand of the best KMT troops continued to blockade the Communist areas, especially after the United Front broke down again with the KMT attack on the Communist New Fourth Army in January of 1941, which they accused of operating south of the Yangtze in conflict with the supposed territorial division of forces. The lack of KMT action against Japan and their diversion of forces to watch the Communists disturbed the United States, especially after they too became involved in war against Japan after Pearl Harbor late in 1941. Both parties in China contributed to what was now a common effort by occupying some 40 percent of total Japanese forces, and at a time when Japan was engaged in the large-scale conquest and control of Southeast Asia, but the Americans were eager to have the huge KMT army play a more active role against the common enemy. Shortly after Pearl Harbor President Roosevelt sent General Joseph Stilwell to be Commander in Chief of the very small U.S. forces in

China, Burma, and India and to serve as liaison with Chiang Kai-shek. He arrived as the Japanese were defeating the British-Indian forces in Burma, but his efforts to coordinate the Chinese troops sent by Chiang, including most of what he had left of those with German training and equipment, were frustrated and Stilwell himself had to walk out from Burma to India to escape capture, while the KMT forces were decimated. This was the even more conclusive end of major KMT fighting efforts, and with the Japanese capture of Burma, the only supply route to the outside, the Burma Road, was cut. Chungking became almost as isolated as Yenan, although a small American military mission in the latter continued to report developments there.

The Burma Road had been built, after British delay in their anxiety not to antagonize the Japanese, mainly by conscript Chinese labor at terrible human cost, almost wholly by hand and without machines, from the Burma border near Lashio through the mountains of Yunnan to Kunming and on to Kweiyang (Guiyang) and Chungking. While it remained open, most of the time from December

2, 1938, to late April 1942, it carried a thin trickle of supplies (plus a good deal of illegal contraband and special consignments for KMT officials and army officers), but when it closed the only connection was by air, with very limited cargo capacity. Stilwell began to plan a new road from India direct from Assam around Japanese-held Burma, which finally did open late in the war, but meantime developed training programs in China and India for picked men from the KMT army who would be fed, instructed, equipped, and given a new morale. Their objective was the reconquest of Burma, or the Chinese role in that, where they eventually gave a very good account of themselves; but Stilwell, known familiarly as "Vinegar Joe," an old-fashioned, straight-talking and straight-dealing American, had trouble concealing his contempt for Chiang, whom he privately referred to as "Peanut." Chiang on his part hated Stilwell and everything he tried to do, but most of all Stilwell's position as Chiang's chief-of-staff and his continued insistence that the Chinese army must be made to fight. Stilwell had long China experience and was reasonably at home in the language, but was outmaneuvered by the American Air Force general Claire Chennault, who easily persuaded Chiang to support his alternative strategy of building airfields from which the U.S. Air Force could bomb Japan into surrender. Chiang was itching to be rid of Stilwell and persuaded Roosevelt to recall him in October of 1944, to be replaced by U.S. general Albert Wedemeyer, who despite his criticisms of Chiang and of the KMT army was more diplomatic.

The airlift from Calcutta and Assam over the "Hump" of the eastern edge of the Himalayas, which replaced the Burma Road, had often to carry more weight in fuel than in cargo, and to risk attack by Japanese planes en route as well as the dangers of forced landings in wild headhunter country in northeast Burma, but in time its capacity rose. Most of the heavy equipment used (with corvée labor) in building the new airfields for the bombing of Japan flew in over the Hump, and a growing stream of fuel and other military supplies. The irony of it was that soon after the first new airfields were finished, the Allied advance in the Pacific began to retake islands, beginning with the Marianas, which were within bombing range of Japan, and most of the new airbases built in China were used only briefly. The "Hump" remained a symbol of the fight against odds in the China war, like the Burma Road before it and, after the war, the Berlin Airlift, and it made Kunming for a time into the busiest airport in the world, on the edge of a small, traditional, walled city which was now also being hustled into the twentieth century by the arrival of thousands of American servicemen.

From bases in Vietnam (where the puppet Vichy French government allowed the Japanese to use their colony) and in east China, Japanese planes bombed the cities remaining under Chinese control in the west,

Chiang Kai-shek and Madame Chiang with the American general Joseph Stilwell in 1942. Stilwell was sent by President Roosevelt to try to reorganize the huge Chinese army and get it to fight the Japanese, but Chiang deeply resented Stilwell and had him dismissed in 1944. (Hulton-Deutsch Collection, London)

Japan Goes to War with the West

As war with the United States and Britain approached, Emperor Hirohito hinted at his own misgivings about Japan's course by reading at a conference on September 26, 1941, a poem by the Meiji emperor, his grandfather: "Since all are brothers in the world, why is there such constant turmoil?" After the attack on Pearl Harbor, he issued an imperial rescript declaring war.

We hereby declare war on the United States of America and the British Empire.... It had been truly unavoidable.... More than four years have passed since China, failing to understand the true intentions of Our Empire, disturbed the peace of Asia.... The regime which has survived at Chungking, relying on American and British protection, still continues its fratricidal opposition.... Both America and Britain have aggravated the disturbances of East Asia [and] have increased military preparations on all sides of Our Empire to challenge us. They have obstructed by every means our peaceful commerce and finally have restored to a direct severance of economic relations, thereby gravely menacing the existence of Our Empire.... Our Empire has no other recourse but to appeal to arms and to crush every obstacle in its path.

Source: Quoted in P. Calvocoressi and G. Wint, *Total War* (New York: Pantheon, 1972, p. 703.

mostly under the KMT, at will in the absence by now of any effective Chinese air force, which had been lost in the defense of Shanghai and Nanking. The raids killed many thousands of civilians, but had little or no effect on the war, except to further increase the will to resist, as indiscriminate bombing everywhere has always done. Postwar studies of the effects of bombing in both Europe and Asia make this clear, with the possible exception of the dropping of the atom bomb on Hiroshima and Nagasaki at the close of the war. Although large-scale fighting ended in 1938, Chinese estimates put the total number of war deaths, from 1937 only, at 21 million, most of them civilians. The Japanese occupying army was at least as ruthless as the Nazis in Europe. The Japanese record in the rest of Asia they invaded was equally bad, but in China they began much earlier, and they made no real effort to win Chinese support. Especially in Manchuria they conducted hideous medical experiments on Chinese prisoners, and there and elsewhere used them as live targets for bayonet practice. The Japanese were the only belligerents to use biological warfare, dropping germs of plague and other contagious diseases by air onto Chinese cities, although fortunately they did not spread widely. After the war the Americans offered many of those involved on the Japanese side immunity from prosecution as war criminals if they agreed to share the results of their work with the U.S. The Cold War had begun.

Chungking: Beleaguered Wartime Capital

The city sprawled in an untidy tangle over steep hills at the junction of the Chialing (Jialing) River and the Yangtze near the center of the generally hilly Red Basin of Szechuan (from the color of its soils), which was in turn surrounded on all sides by mountains. The steep and narrow gorges of the Yangtze, about halfway between Wuhan and Chungking where the river had cut its way through a mountain range along the provincial border, were blocked by a boom. These natural defenses kept Chungking secure from the Japanese army, but it had few defenses against air attack, and Japanese bombing caused great destruction and loss of life. Eventually more and better shelters were built, many hollowed out of the rock on which the city was built, others out of cliffs outside the city. An effective warning system was designed which responded to radio messages sent by Chinese behind enemy lines and at the borders who reported flights of planes by number and direction and gave time for most people to reach shelters when word came that the bombers were headed for Chungking. Sirens were supplemented by ball-shaped lanterns hung from tall poles on the highest hills; two balls meant bombers on the way, and when both dropped it warned everyone to take shelter. Air raids and alarms were called "chin-pao"; foreigners in town called the potent drinks made from Chinese spirits or whatever they could get, mixed with fruit juice or anything to make it palatable, "chin-pao juice." The power supply was increasingly inadequate for the city's swollen population and often broke down, or produced only a weak current. Those who tried to cope with this by installing more powerful lightbulbs would have them blown out by sudden power surges. Water mains, whose supply was minimal to begin with, were frequently disrupted by bombs, and the fires which followed often burned out of control.

Late in 1940, at Chiang's request, General Chennault, already in China as a special representative, was permitted to recruit U.S. pilots to fly American fighter planes as "volunteers" (at high pay)—to avoid breaking neutrality with Japan—a unit called the Flying Tigers, which in the course of 1941 greatly reduced the Japanese raids. They painted shark jaws on the noses of their planes and terrorized the Japanese bombers. America's final entry into the war with the Japanese attack on Pearl Harbor on December 7, 1941, gave morale another boost, and patriotic sentiment rallied to the symbol of the brave wartime capital, bloody but unbowed. But although it was not yet much talked about, part of the blood was that of alleged Communists or sympathizers, many of whom died in prison under torture. The head of Chiang's Blue Shirts, a fellow native of Chekiang named Dai Li, who also ran the secret police, engaged as well in

assassination of Chiang's rivals; the mere mention of his name struck fear into the hearts of many.

Disillusionment spread as the KMT army largely sat out the rest of the war and the increasingly corrupt government of Chiang and his cronies stockpiled men and weapons for use against the Communists. Chungking was notorious for its gray, cloudy weather and drizzle, suffocatingly hot in summer, cold and damp in winter. The city was painfully overcrowded; over a million people, including officials and army personnel, were added to the originally much smaller local population, and there were far too few additions to housing, water supply, and other basics. After the Japanese cut the Burma Road, the airlift over the Hump was Chungking's only link with the outside world. The main airport was a sandbank in the Yangtze hemmed in by steep cliffs on both sides and flooded every spring and summer by rising river levels. Approaches were usually obscured by dense, low clouds, but the summer airport was on the edge of a cliff above the river, and was equally dangerous. There were no railways anywhere in Szechuan, and people understandably felt isolated, if not forgotten. Prices for everything skyrocketed as a result of wartime shortages, the swollen population, and government ineptitude. The Szechuanese blamed it on "downriver people," who in turn were contemptuous of "ignorant provincials."

Tight "thought control" and the secret police suppressed all free political or even literary expression. The

Japanese troops entering a town in eastern China, where they generally followed their formula of "Kill all, burn all, loot all." (Hulton-Deutsch Collection, London)

press consisted of government handouts which rarely told the truth, including news about the "progress" of the war. Houses were searched for "improper" books and their owners jailed or executed. Those with money or connections lived luxuriously in guarded villas with American-made limousines, most of all Chiang and his wife, who often retreated from the steamy heat of Chungking to a large compound on the second range of hills across the Yangtze where it was noticeably cooler, surrounded by a wall and by armed guards who prevented any near approach. But most people in Chungking lived in poverty, mud, and squalor. Tuberculosis, that disease of poverty, bad housing, poor diet, and crowding, became epidemic. Already by 1940 inflation had begun to rise at about 10 percent per month, accelerating wildly after 1943 when the American military and diplomatic establishment had grown enough to add significantly to the competition for food and supplies of all kinds. Currency might lose half or more of its value between morning and afternoon, and people were obliged to carry it around in suitcases or wheelbarrows and to convert it into goods as quickly as possible. It resulted basically from wartime shortages, but the government "solution" was simply to print more money and in larger denominations, while its finance minister, H. H. Kung, Chiang's brother-in-law, illegally smuggled gold out of the United States for his own accounts in overseas banks, as did other KMT officials. Under the pressures of inflation and with salaries which quickly became inadequate, almost all officials, however idealistic to begin

with, succumbed to at least petty corruption in the form of bribery, if only to support their families, that Confucian imperative.

But salaries and wages for everyone fell hopelessly behind inflation. Furniture, clothing, books, works of art, and heirlooms were sold in a vain effort to stay afloat. In 1943 Chiang published a book titled *China's Destiny* which better than anything else revealed his "upright" Confucian exterior and his personal inconsistency with the sage's teachings. The book blamed all of China's problems on foreign exploitation under the unequal treaties, and celebrated the end of that era with the relinquishment of their special rights by the Western powers in the year the book was published. Chiang urged moral regeneration to save and rebuild China, along Confucian lines (overlooking its rejection by the May Fourth movement), but at the same time he presided over what most Chinese and foreign observers saw as a morally rotten government which showed little or no concern for China's people. He quoted Confucius on the central importance of virtue in the ruler, and added: "So long as we have a few men who will set an example, the people … will unconsciously act likewise."[2] Chiang was clearly oblivious to the irony. He also asserted that the government should set up collective farms whose peasant workers would be hardy soldiers (shades of the Legalists and Ch'in Shih Huang Ti!—see Chapter 4) and should control people's lives and limit their needs or wants to low levels. Here were clearly seeds of a

Kuomintang army supply train on the Burma Road inside China. The road was Nationalist China's wartime surface link with the outside world, but the Kuomintang soldiers were undernourished, diseased, maltreated by their officers, and with very poor morale. (S. Betterton)

new totalitarianism, which might have surfaced if the KMT had won the civil war and become as hateful as its Communist version.

The KMT government even before the Chungking years was dominated by two brothers, Ch'en Li-fu and Ch'en Kuo-fu, whose uncle had been Chiang's patron. They headed what was called the CC Clique, in close cooperation with Dai Li and his police network, and they too advocated a new Confucianism as China's best guiding principle, arguing that it was consistent with Sun Yat-sen's Three Principles and that it was the only way through which China could adjust successfully to the modern world and absorb new Western technology. Between them they ran the KMT political organization and operated the Central Political Institute in Chungking which trained civil servants. Others outside the KMT power structure saw them simply as henchmen of Chiang's whose chief function was the running of a police state. It was perhaps interesting that both they and Chiang should have reached far into the Chinese past for models, as successive dynasties had done, although none had tried to harmonize Confucianism with Legalism in this way. The point here is that turning to the past, although it might feed Chinese pride, was no longer a reasonable prescription for China's modern ills. This was something which virtually all politically aware Chinese had long since learned, but apparently not Chiang and his cronies. *China's Destiny* proved to be a big embarrassment for Chiang as both Chinese and foreigners criticized it as childish nonsense which showed better than anything else how out of it Chiang was. All copies which Chiang could commandeer were withdrawn, and the book is now hard to find.

By the end of the war there was universal demoralization and loss of faith in the KMT. The Chungking years were the death of Kuomintang hopes to remain the government of a China now sick of its ineffectiveness, cronyism, corruption, and reaction. In a way the jumble of shabby gray buildings scattered higgedly-piggedly over the cliffs and hills of Chungking became a symbol of failure and disillusionment. Given the frequent rain and the lack of almost any municipal services, the broken streets were often ankle-deep in mud, and rats ran rampant. In movie houses and theaters audiences still had to stand to attention at the beginning of any show while the screen showed pictures of Sun Yat-sen and then of Chiang and his wife posing inspiringly in front of the rippling KMT flag while the audience was supposed to sing along with a stirringly orchestrated version of the national anthem, San Min Chu I. No one dared to grumble or crack jokes about this, for fear of being reported by Dai Li's spies, but the image it aimed to present, of Chiang as China's savior (Führer?) fell increasingly flat, or merely aroused resentment.

The Coming of the Pacific War

As the Japanese misadventure in China ground on, to no result except more casualties on both sides and the brutalizing of the Japanese forces, Europe too moved toward war. Japan's chief fear was that the Soviet Union would try to reclaim the former Czarist position in East Asia and take revenge for the defeat by Japan in 1905. In 1936 the Russians had signed a mutual defense pact with Outer Mongolia (which was to be of critical importance in repelling the Japanese invasion of Mongolia in 1939), and there were already close ties remaining from the 1920s between the Soviets and China, specifically the KMT, although after 1936 the United Front with the Communists further cemented those ties. Japan withdrew from the international disarmament system in 1933, anticipating the similar moves by fascist Italy and Germany, and in 1937 began a new program of naval building to the point where the navy felt equal to any other power in the Pacific. Germany and Italy now seemed like Japan's natural allies against the Western democracies, and in the German case, against Russia. For the present at least, it was thought best not to antagonize Britain or the U.S.; Japan's plans were Asian, not global. The news of the German nonaggression pact with Russia in August of 1939 struck Japan like a thunderclap, and seemed to increase greatly the risk of Russian opposition to Japan's actions in China. Hitler was of course preparing the way for his conquests westward by protecting his rear, but Japan felt betrayed, and just as her troops were in effect at war with Mongol-Soviet forces in Mongolia.

As the Nazi armies advanced westward and the French surrendered in May of 1940 while Britain seemed doomed to fall after Dunkirk, Japanese opinion moved toward some kind of rapprochement with Berlin as the likely victor in Europe. The new foreign minister as of July, Matsuoka, was strongly pro-German and worked hard diplomatically to take advantage of these newly powerful potential allies, resulting in the Tripartite Pact between Germany, Italy, and Japan in September. A further possible advantage was Germany's new (since 1939) relations with Russia, which might ease the currently strained ones between the Soviets and Japan, using Germany as a kind of go-between. This proved to be a real advantage, and in April of 1941 Japan obtained a neutrality pact with the Soviet Union. The Russians now in their turn wanted to secure their own rear against what they feared was an imminent German invasion, which indeed took place in June of 1941 on a huge scale, and which eventually destroyed the Nazi power. Japan had thus as of 1941 obtained some security against Russian intervention in Asia against it, and lined up strong friends on its side in Europe as the Axis powers appeared to constitute the wave of the future. It was hoped also that this new set of agreements would serve to isolate the United States and Britain and make them less likely to interfere with Japan's plans for China, and for the rest of East Asia. It was a coup which was enthusiastically welcomed in Japan, and which prepared the necessary ground for the next stage of Japanese expansion in Asia.

On the other side of the Pacific, while the United States was by no means prepared to go to war against Japan, the Tripartite Pact tended to harden American opinion, since Japan had now formally joined up with the European fascists, already seen as the enemy by most Americans. Meanwhile the U.S. continued to trade freely (and profitably) with Japan, including most importantly in oil, scrap metal, and other sinews of war, although it was obvious that these things were being used to kill Chinese and that the Japanese military could not operate without them. Most Americans were on China's side as a matter of sympathy, in part because of the long American missionary involvement, but business interests were unwilling to lose profits and the government resisted steps which might antagonize Japan. The Nazi invasion of Russia left the Japanese feeling again betrayed, having used their German friends to help produce their neutrality agreement with the Russians but now left still allied to Germany, which asked the Japanese to open a front against the Soviet Union in the east. The Russian success in stopping the Nazi advance in the fall of 1941 led Japan to stick to the protection offered by its neutrality pact with the Soviets and to ignore the German request.

The chief worry remained Japan's dependence on imports from the United states, and Japan feared that these might be cut off at any time. The plans for expansion required especially oil, of which Japan had virtually none. American opinion was moving even more strongly against the Japanese actions in China. As long before as November 1937 the Japanese had bombed, strafed, and sunk the American gunboat *Panay,* clearly marked, as it was trying to evacuate embassy personnel from Nanking, which incredibly enough attracted only mild U.S. protest and no action. But finally now the mood had shifted, prompted in part by reports of the Rape of Nanking, partly by persistent missionary pleading as the record of Japanese atrocities against China dragged on, and partly by American reaction to the Tripartite Pact which linked Japan with Germany and Italy. There was oil, plus the tin and rubber also essential for war, in Southeast Asia. Japan still felt unable to extricate itself from China, and had long hoped to include Southeast Asia with its rich resources in what they now called Japan's New Order in East Asia, a label reminiscent of the Nazi Order in Europe. In preparation for its drive southward, Japanese military "observers" and then

troops were sent into French Indo-China soon after France fell to the Germans, in the summer of 1940, with the permission of the weak puppet Vichy government of France. Indo-China (Vietnam) was dangerously close to the American-owned Philippines, and the United States in response began to limit exports of critical material to Japan by a system of licenses. A year later, in July of 1941, the Japanese occupied the whole of Indo-China, and the Americans imposed a total embargo on all exports to Japan. What the sufferings of the Chinese people had failed to accomplish was thus brought about when Japan appeared to directly threaten the American position in the Philippines. But it was the China issue primarily which turned American opinion, and which was the crux of the negotiations in Washington in November and early December.

The Road to Pearl Harbor

Ambassador Nomura was joined in Washington by former ambassador to Germany Kurusu for talks with Cordell Hull, the U.S. secretary of state. The Japanese offered to withdraw their troops from Indo-China in exchange for oil, but Hull insisted that they also withdraw from China and Manchuria. That was refused, and indeed it had become politically and perhaps psychologically impossible, especially with the formation of what was in effect a war cabinet in October under General Tojo. The decision for war with the United States had in fact been made at an imperial conference on September 5, if the Americans refused to lift the oil embargo and if the negotiations in general had failed by November. Contingency planning already included the full-scale movement into Indo-China and detailed preparations for war in the Pacific. The attack on Pearl Harbor was practiced for months ahead of time at Kagoshima Bay in southern Kyushu. Admiral Yamamoto, the architect of the attack (sometimes labeled "the brilliant blunder"), had lived in the United States and knew more about it than most other Japanese leaders. He had argued against war with the U.S. as "waking a sleeping tiger," but like a good military man submitted to the collective decision, saying that he could give Japan a year, after which he feared it would be all down-hill. As it was, he was overoptimistic, but his plan, faultlessly executed, had the bad luck to find the four aircraft carriers of the U.S. Pacific fleet away on patrol. He had counted on getting them too, but their survival, almost alone among the big ships of the rest of the fleet, was to be crucial.

Nomura and Kurusu in Washington were told little of these preparations, and did not know that the Japanese attack force had left Japan a month before, awaiting at its rendezvous north of Hawaii the code message Tora Tora Tora ("Tiger Tiger Tiger") to launch its planes.

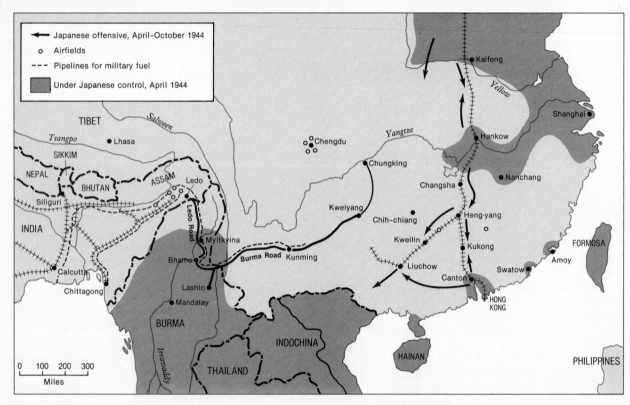

The China-Burma-India Theater in World War II

The attack was planned for just after dawn Honolulu time on Sunday morning December 7; planes out of the rising sun caught the defenders completely by surprise, most of them still in bed, or bleary-eyed from Saturday night revelry. A radar station on the coast picked up some Japanese planes approaching, but it was assumed they were American. It remains scarcely believable that the Americans so totally ignored a series of evidence and indirect warnings which should have had them prepared, including a last-minute message from Washington which in fact arrived too late. Nomura and Kurusu were sent a coded message which, given its secrecy, they had to decipher laboriously and then type up themselves in an English translation to pass on to Hull. By the time of their special Sunday meeting with Hull (it was now afternoon in Washington), word came through from Honolulu of the Japanese attack, without a declaration of war and while the negotiations in Washington were supposedly still going on. Hull was outraged, although the Americans had now broken the Japanese code and knew that Japan was preparing for war if the negotiations failed. The Japanese carriers had kept radio silence, and the Americans took it for granted that any attack would be aimed south, against Malaya or the Dutch East Indies. The carrier planes found nearly all the U.S. Pacific fleet lined up as sitting ducks in the anchorage at Pearl Harbor and sank or badly damaged nearly all of them, destroying most of the local air force as well. The Japanese fleet which had launched the attack remained undetected and returned safely to Japan.

Despite the mounting evidence which should have put the defenders on their guard, the Americans could not believe that the Japanese would attack them, foolishly confident that their own power superiority, and what they saw as Japanese "backwardness," made the whole idea out of the question. In fact the Japanese had not only built up their own navy in secret to a position of rough equality but had done so to very high standards. Their ships and aircraft were in every way the equal of their opponents' but the Americans dismissed them as no real threat, to their heavy cost. Yamamoto had not planned to attack without a declaration of war, but the delay encountered by Nomura and Kurusu in transmitting the message to Hull, which was in any case a last-minute affair, meant that the attack had already begun. The Japanese were condemned once again for their sneak tactics, as in 1895 against China and 1904 against Russia. Apart from whatever advantage that brought them, most Japanese (not including Yamamoto) believed that the Americans and British

✠ A Japanese View of Pearl Harbor ✠

The leader of one squadron of the torpedo bombers which attached Pearl Harbor gave an account of what he saw spread out before him.

Below me lay the whole U.S. Pacific Fleet in a formation I would not have dared to dream of in my most optimistic dreams. I have seen all the German ships assembled at Kiel Harbor. I have also seen the French battleships in Brest. And, finally, I have frequently seen our warships assembled for review before the Emperor, but I have never seen ships, even in the deepest deep, anchored at a distance of 500–10000 yards from each other. A war fleet must always be on the alert, since surprise attacks can never be fully ruled out. But the picture down there was hard to comprehend. Had these Americans never heard of Port Arthur?

Source: Quoted in P. Calvocoressi and G. Wint, *Total War* (New York: Pantheon, 1972), p. 698.

✠ Yamamoto's Misgivings ✠

Admiral Yamamoto, who designed the raid on Pearl Harbor, wrote of his misgivings at the time and afterword.

What a strange position I find myself in now—having to make a decision diametrically opposed to my own personal opinion, with no choice but to push full-speed in pursuance of that decision. Is that, too, fate?

Well, the war has begun at last. But in spite of all the clamour that is going on, we could lose it. I can only do my best.

This war will give us much trouble in the future. The fact that we have had a small success at Pearl Harbor is nothing. The fact that we have succeeded so easily has pleased people. Personally I do not think it is a good thing to whip up propaganda to encourage the nation. People should think things over and realize how serious the situation is.

Source: Quoted in P. Calvocoressi and G. Wint, *Total War* (New York: Pantheon, 1972), p. 704.

(whom they promptly attacked also at Hong Kong, Malaya, and Singapore) were soft and would not fight. If Japan succeeded, as they did, in knocking out most of the U.S. Pacific fleet, and soon thereafter in dealing a crippling blow to the British fleet off Singapore, they believed that both powers would negotiate, accepting the fait accompli and resuming oil supplies as the price of peace. The British had their backs to the wall, fighting alone against a German army which had conquered Europe and threatened to invade England. The U.S. was just beginning to recover from the great depression, but in any case lacked the *bushido* code of the Japanese, one of whom was thought to be the equal of ten spoiled Americans.

Only a few hours after the raid on Pearl Harbor, the Japanese attacked Clark Field in the Philippines. Again it is hard to believe that the defenders did almost nothing in response to the news from Honolulu, which they had in plenty of time. Most of their planes were destroyed lined up on the ground. Hong Kong was attacked the same day, and although it was indefensible and surrounded by vastly superior Japanese forces, Churchill ordered the garrison to fight. There were heavy casualties, including raw recruits just out from

Canada, but most of the defenders ended up in the notorious Stanley prison camp. Japan's conquest of Southeast Asia had been long planned. The day after Pearl Harbor Japanese carrier-based dive bombers sank the major capital ships of the British Asiatic fleet, the *Prince of Wales* and the *Repulse*, on patrol off Singapore and without air cover. This cleared the way for the invasion of British Malaya, from bases in Indo-China and Thailand, which had earlier, in 1940, agreed to Japanese occupation. The British had assumed that no army could move through the Malayan jungles, and what inadequate defense positions they had were centered on road and rail lines. But the Japanese army advanced rapidly southward along jungle trails, using bicycles to transport men and supplies, which were much more spartan than Western soldiers were used to. They took the colonial capital at Kuala Lumpar on January 11. Singapore's defenses did not allow for the possibility of a landward attack, trusting to the jungle barrier, and its guns and fortifications all faced seaward to protect its huge naval dockyard. The Japanese moved fast, and soon besieged the city, which surrendered on February 15, 1942. Many of those taken prisoner ended up working as slave labor, building a railway bridge near the Thai-Burmese border, a story well portrayed in the film "Bridge on the River Kwai."

The Philippines were invaded on December 10, 1941, most of the air force there having been destroyed. Manila surrendered on January 2, but a Philippine-American force held out in the mountain fortress of Corregidor on the Bataan peninsula in Manila Bay until it was starved into surrender. The commanding general, Douglas MacArthur, escaped by submarine to Australia, leaving his men to suffer through the infamous Bataan Death March as they were force marched, already malnourished, with inhuman brutality to a dreadful prison camp; many died along the way, and others from starvation and abuse in prison. Altogether, 5,000 to 10,000 Filipino troops died (the number is unclear, and many managed to escape along the way) and over 600 American; the few who survived did so as emaciated skeletons, with dreadful tales to tell. Sixteen thousand British and Indian soldiers died in the nightmarish horror of the bridge on the Kwai. With Singapore in their hands, the Japanese diverted most of their forces to the invasion of the Dutch East Indies (modern Indonesia), where they soon demolished the tiny Dutch naval and land forces, who surrendered on March 8. There too, in Java, prison camps were brutal places, especially for the Westerners, who were made special targets by the proponents of the "Yamato race." Other Japanese troops were diverted from conquered Malaya for the invasion of Burma, where British and Indian troops fought a more effective retreating action, but Rangoon, the colonial capital and major port, fell in early March and Mandalay, the traditional inland capital, in early May.

For the Japanese, the brutality of their treatment of both Southeast Asians and Westerners was an expres-

Building an airfield in the traditional way: mass human labor moving earth and rocks near Chengdu in 1942 to create a base for B-29s to bomb Japan. (General Library, University of California at Berkeley)

✠ A Soldier's Fate ✠

One of the songs the Japanese army sang as it went to war against the Americans and the British in 1941 was rather lugubrious, as many Japanese songs are.

Across the sea,
Corpses in the water;
Across the mountains,
Corpses heaped upon the field.
I shall die only for the Emperor;
I shall never look back.

Source: Quoted in P. Calvocoressi and G. Wint, *Total War* (New York: Pantheon, 1972), pp. 738–740.

sion of their own sense of "racial superiority," their hatred of their former Western masters, and their contempt for soldiers who surrendered even when their position was hopeless. Japanese soldiers were taught that surrender was disgrace, and that they themselves were instead to fight to the last man, as they often did. It was considered a privilege to die for the emperor. Japanese behavior to both Western and Asian civilians was equally horrendous and was part of official policy. All armies are brutal in war, especially as feelings mount and as armies have to face guerrilla resistance. Nearly all wars also stimulate feelings of racism. American and British wartime propaganda depicted the Japanese as treacherous, savage, "inferior," and hardly human, and as the war dragged on through bitter fighting and Allied troops learned of the horrors perpetrated by the Japanese against prisoners, there were Allied atrocities too, including the shooting of Japanese prisoners and of submarine crews who surrendered and the refusal to help survivors of Japanese ships sunk by Allied action. But the Japanese record in World War II is rivaled, although probably not equaled, only by that of the Nazis in Europe. "A man away from home has no neighbors," says a traditional Japanese proverb, and the Japanese army acted that out.

Most armies operate as a tightly controlled unit under orders, not as a group of individuals. After the war, many Japanese individually acknowledged the gross immorality of their wartime behavior, and gave accounts of the bayoneting and torture of prisoners and the uncontrolled killing of civilians. The Japanese military was very conscious of the traditional creed of *bushido*, the way of the warrior, and expected every soldier to live up to it and to be proud to die for his emperor. They boasted of their flouting of the Geneva Convention on the treatment of war prisoners, which they saw as a contemptible Western notion which had no validity for soldiers of the Yamato "race." Their racism also extended to Koreans, both in Korea and in Japan, despite the really minor differences between them and the Japanese and the early debt of Japanese civilization to Korea. Koreans were treated as an inferior people, conscripted as forced labor, and grossly discriminated against on racist grounds. One of the chief outrages of the Japanese army was its requisition of "comfort girls" from Korea, China, and Southeast Asia, to "service" Japanese soldiers, in a role far worse than prostitution. Long after the war, this horrible practice was finally but grudgingly acknowledged and some official Japanese apologies made, but this was of little help to the women, perhaps as many as 100,000 of them or more, whose lives had been ruined. Elsewhere, especially in China, rape was commonplace and Japanese soldiers simply helped themselves to women wherever they went, as they did later in Southeast Asia.

The Japanese had developed late in the 1930s a light, fast, maneuverable fighter plane, the Zero, made by Mitsubishi, which proved superior to any opponent until later in the war. Only the British Spitfire, instrumental in winning the Battle of Britain in 1940, could be compared with it, but the two rarely met in combat. The Zero, like the Japanese navy, was an outstanding example of how Japan had caught up with and even overtaken the West in military technology. The effectiveness of these military arms was a shock to the Allies, and it added to the shock of surprise attack. The Allies were psychologically unprepared to find Japan so formidable an enemy, and slow to adjust, as at Pearl Harbor and Singapore, to the brilliant Japanese use of strategy and tactics. In Malaya and Burma the Japanese pioneered jungle warfare and terrorized their opponents. But as the war progressed, the British and Americans developed new and better planes which progressively outclassed the Zero, became masters themselves of jungle warfare, and increasingly brought to bear the massive weight of their industrial and technological base. Japanese production of planes and ships had no hope of matching this, and in the end Japan was worn down by the sheer bulk of their opponents' power, primarily the United States, the "arsenal of democracy." This was what Yamamoto had feared when he spoke of "waking a sleeping tiger." In the early stages of the Pacific War with so much of the Allied fleets destroyed or out of action, submarines played a vital role in sinking Japanese naval units and supply ships, and their role remained important until the end, greatly outnumbering the Japanese submarines.

In addition to their conquest of Southeast Asia, the Japanese had occupied all of the smaller islands of the western Pacific by early 1942, and even installed a garrison in the western Aleutians off Alaska. They had no intention of invading the United States itself, but the west coast was alarmed, and Japanese submarines did destroy some shipping in the eastern Pacific. War hysteria and continued American racism were reflected in misguided and inhuman official policy which interned nearly all of the Japanese on the west coast, over 100,000 in all, including U.S. citizens born here. Their properties were confiscated and they were kept in desert camps behind barbed wire until after the war was over. Americans feared a long war as they began to build up their shattered Pacific fleet and prepared to fight on two fronts, against Germany (which had declared war right after Pearl Harbor) and against Japan. Apart from the Aleutians, there were no Japanese attacks on the U.S. itself, unless one wants to count the small loads of explosives carried on the prevailing winds across the Pacific on balloons launched as a patriotic gesture to help the war effort by Japanese schoolchildren. One or two actually made it, and killed a few people on the Oregon coast. After the war, some of these children, grown to adulthood, visited Oregon to apologize to the families of their victims, another example of how wartime hysterical behavior is seen very differently once the fighting is over.

But it was never part of the Japanese plan to invade, let alone conquer, the United States, but only to put pressure on them to settle, on Japanese terms. Apart from what had become their hopeless position in China, their great objective was the resources of Southeast Asia. They spoke of a Greater East Asia Co-Prosperity Sphere, under Japanese direction but theoretically in the interests of the other countries of East Asia (not including Korea, Manchuria, or Taiwan, which were regarded as integral parts of Japan despite the distinctions of their people from the Japanese). This idea had some merit, since it proposed to combine Japanese technological, industrial, and managerial skills with the labor and resources of the other countries. Japan was poor in natural resources and in agricultural land. Her supposed partners could fill that gap: oil, rubber, tin, sugar, and rice from Southeast Asia, iron and coal in China and the Philippines. The benefits to the supposed partners were never spelled out, but one could certainly argue that they needed the kind of experience and direction the Japanese offered and their own development could thus be assisted: raw materials in exchange for expertise.

✠ Call to Surrender ✠

The emperor's broadcast of August 15, 1945, calling on his forces and people to surrender was, like all his pronouncements, the work of several hands. It said in part:

The war situation has developed not necessarily to Japan's advantage…. The enemy has begun to employ a new and most cruel bomb, the power of which to do damage is indeed incalculable, taking the toll of many innocent lives. Should we continue to fight, it would not only result in an ultimate collapse and obliteration of the Japanese nation, but it would also lead to the total extinction of human civilization. We are keenly aware of the inmost feelings of all of you, Our subjects. However it is according to the dictate of time and fate that We have resolved to pave the way for a grand peace for all the generations to come by enduring the unendurable and suffering what is insufferable.

Source: Quoted in R. Storry, *A History of Modern Japan.* (New York: Penguin, 1982), p. 237.

But such benefits flowed back to them, if at all, only on the smallest scale, and Japanese rule was crudely exploitative as well as oppressively racist. Japan ignored and was clearly opposed to the rising force of Asian nationalism, first in China and then in her Southeast Asian conquests, where she quickly alienated political figures and the opinion of the general public, who to begin with welcomed the Japanese as liberators from Western colonialism. Almost from the beginning, racist arrogance and brutality made a mockery of "Co-Prosperity" and earned the Japanese bitter hatred everywhere, while feeding still further the fires of Chinese and Southeast Asian nationalism. Japan was now master of Asia, and all other peoples must bow to it, accepting an inferior position.

Soon after its early sweeping victories, the tide turned against Japan. What is referred to as "Japan's Hundred Days" was a brilliant success, and morale was sky-high at home. The turning point (about which the Japanese public was told next to nothing, as throughout the rest of the war) was the naval battle of early June 1942 off Midway, an American island base in the central Pacific northwest of Hawaii. The Japanese assembled a large fleet in the approaches to Midway hoping to destroy what remained of the U.S. Pacific fleet. The Americans had broken the Japanese code, which gave them a crucial advantage, and they also had the assistance of British-invented radar, which had helped turn the tide of the Battle of Britain (although both were, as indicated above, largely ignored at Pearl Harbor). In the battle, American carrier planes which had escaped the Pearl Harbor raid sank all four of the Japanese carriers and damaged other ships. It was a crippling blow. Soon thereafter began the Allied (British, Australian, and American) offensive in the south, first in the steamy Solomon Islands and the Bismarck Archipelago off New Guinea, then in the mountains and jungles of New Guinea itself, and on northward through an island-hopping campaign to the Philippines and beyond to the Marianas and Iwo Jima. There was bloody hand-to-hand fighting against Japanese defenders who often did fight to the last man. Casualties were heavy on both sides, including some Japanese-American troops, but by now the weight of numbers was on the Allied side and their naval and air forces were dominant. The Allies captured Saipan, within bombing range of all of Japan's big cities, in June of 1944.

The Philippines were retaken with massive naval support by early 1945, and then in June Okinawa, part of Japanese home territory. Fanatical Japanese troops now defending Japanese soil fought to the death and often had to be flushed out of their cave strongholds with flamethrowers. Their dwindling air force began to use what they called *kamikaze* ("divine wind") attacks by suicide planes loaded with bombs and purposely crashed onto Allied ships. Allied losses were severe, but were soon replaced. By now the Japanese fleet and supply ships were nearly all sunk and the air force largely gone. A last mission by the world's largest battleship, the *Yamato*, just finished, ended in disaster when she was sunk with all hands less than a day out of her home port. Indonesia was cut off from Japanese supply lines by Allied naval power and safely ignored.

Burma, and the End of the War

Apart from the Philippines, the other major campaign of the war in Southeast Asia was the battle for Burma, first the routing of the ill-prepared British and Indian forces in 1942, then the Japanese drive aimed at the invasion of India. This was turned back with heavy losses on both sides at Imphal just inside the Indian border early in 1944, to be followed by the successful Allied reconquest of Burma. After Imphal the British began to send commando units behind the Japanese lines for hit and run attacks to throw the Japanese off balance and remind them that a new army was coming, now trained and experienced in jungle warfare. By late spring of 1944 Indian troops under British command crossed into Burma and pushed steadily southward, despite the mud and downpours of the monsoon. As they took northern Burma they were joined by Chinese and American forces, taking Mandalay and finally Rangoon in May of 1945. The reconquest of Malaya was soon ready to start, but the Japanese surrender in August 1945 made it unnecessary. A frustrated Indian nationalist politician, Subhas Chandra Bose, who had been passed over for the leadership of the Congress party, saw his chance for power in alliance with the Japanese. He escaped from British arrest in 1941, made his way to Berlin, and then on by German and Japanese submarines to captured Singapore in 1943. There the Japanese gave him command of 60,000 Indian prisoners of war, which he called the Indian National Army for the "liberation" of their homeland. Instead they were used as coolies and as cannon fodder in the advance wave of the bloody and fruitless assault on Imphal. Bose escaped and was later killed in an air crash.

Japan was ready to surrender by early 1945, and had begun feelers through the still officially neutral Russians (their nonaggression pact with Japan had been signed in 1941 so as to concentrate their forces on the impending Nazi invasion). Approaches were also made through Sweden and the Vatican. U.S. bombers had destroyed nearly all Japan's cities. Incendiary bombs were used to start giant firestorms, which in one horrible night in Tokyo killed an estimated 120,000 people, twice the total killed in air raids throughout the war in England. Much of the surviving urban population was starving. The Japanese fleet and air force were almost all gone, and U.S. planes bombed at will around the clock. One relatively minor target remained: Hiroshima, a medium-sized city and army base. U.S., British, and European refugee scientists had developed a primitive atom bomb and tested it in the New Mexico desert on July 16, 1945, although they still had only a vague idea of its power, or of the dangers of radiation.

In February 1945 at the Yalta Conference between the Allied powers, Stalin had promised to attack Japan within three months after the defeat of Germany, which had come in May. Anxious to forestall the Russians and to show this awesome new power, the new American President Harry Truman decided to drop one of the two atom bombs they now possessed on Hiroshima on August 6, obliterating the city and killing over 100,000 people, nearly all civilians. Truman called it "the greatest thing in history." Russia declared war against Japan on August 8 and immediately invaded Manchuria. The next day, in an obvious response, Truman dropped the only other atom bomb, not wanting the Russians to think he had only one, on Nagasaki, where over 65,000 died. On August 15 the emperor announced Japan's surrender. The army in Japan was still in good order and might have fought fiercely against an invasion, supported by many civilians. Casualties on both sides would have been heavy. But in Japan's by now desperate situation, especially facing a Russian invasion, perhaps the emperor would have called for a surrender without the atom bomb—? Patriotic diehards were appalled at the emperor's decision, but obeyed his call, broadcast throughout the empire by radio.

A total of 2.5 million Japanese military had died in the war and nearly a million civilians in air raids. But Japan's defeat of Western colonial regimes had broken forever the myth of Western invincibility, while its own brutality had further fed the fires of Asian nationalism.

Notes

1. Both are quoted in J. K. Fairbank, *The United States and China*, Harvard, 1983, p. 292.
2. Quoted in J. K. Fairbank, *The United States and China*, op. cit, p. 59.

Suggestions for Further Reading

Boyle, J. H. *China and Japan at War, 1937–1945*. Sanford: Stanford University Press, 1972.

Braw, M. *The Atomic Bomb Suppressed: American Censorship in Occupied Japan*. White Plains: M. E. Sharpe, 1991.

Chi'i, H. S. *Nationalist China at War*. Ann Arbor: University of Michigan Press, 1982.

Conroy, H., and Wray, H., eds. *Pearl Harbor Re-examined*. Honolulu: University of Hawaii Press, 1990.

Cook, H. T. *Japan at War*. New York: The New Press, 1990.

Dower, J. W. *War without Mercy*. New York: Pantheon, 1986.

Goodman, G., ed. *Japanese Cultural Policies in Southeast Asia During World War II*. New York: St. Martins, 1991.

Harris, S. H. *Factories of Death: Japanese Biological Warfare and the American Coverup*. London: Routledge, 1994.

Hsiung, J. C., and Levine, S. I. *China's Bitter Victory: The War With Japan, 1937–1945*. Armonk, New York: M. E. Sharpe, 1992.

Hung, C. T. *War and Popular Culture*. Berkeley: University of California Press, 1994.

Iritani, T. *Group Psychology of the Japanese in Wartime*. London: Kegan Paul, 1992.

Neils, P., ed. *United States Attitudes Toward China*. Armonk, New York: M. E. Sharpe, 1990.

Renzi, W. A. and Roehrs, M. D. *Never Look Back: A History of World War II in the Pacific*. Armonk, New York: M. E. Sharpe, 1992.

Sakai, D., ed. *From Pearl Harbor to Hiroshima*. New York: St. Martins, 1994.

Selden, K. and M., eds. *The Atomic Bomb: Voices from Hiroshima and Nagasaki*. White Plains: M. E. Sharpe, 1992.

Spector, R. H. *Eagle Against the Sun: The American War with Japan*. New York: Free Press, 1989.

White, T. H., and Jacoby, A. *Thunder Out of China*. New York: Sloan Assocs., 1946.

Williams, P., and Wallace, D. *Unit 731: Japan's Secret Biological Warfare in World War II*. New York: Free Press, 1989.

Wint, G., Calvocoressi, P., and Pritchard, J. *Total War*. New York: Random House, 1991.

CHAPTER 20

CHINA SINCE 1945

The Civil War

With the Japanese surrender in August of 1945, China moved toward the civil war which had been brewing ever since the first United Front was destroyed by Chiang Kai-shek's coup in Shanghai in 1927. The Americans continued to regard Chiang as an ally, and made over to him the great bulk of the military equipment they had accumulated in China. That in itself does not seem unreasonable, especially since it made little sense to haul it back to the United States. But the Americans involved themselves from the start in the civil war with the Communists by using their large air fleet in China to transport KMT troops to Japanese-occupied east China and Manchuria in order to preempt the Communists. Japanese commanders were told to surrender only to the KMT forces, not to the Communists, although where the Communists had anticipated the KMT they pressured to take the Japanese surrender themselves. In Manchuria the occupying Russians, who had come in during the last week of the war, turned over much of their equipment and ammunition to the Communists, and in any case the latter had moved too swiftly to allow the KMT to upstage them, in part because their main forces were already in the north. KMT troops flown in by the Americans did manage to take most of the cities of Manchuria, but in time they found themselves beleaguered by Communist forces around them and they eventually surrendered. Chiang was advised against this diversion of his forces to Manchuria, but insisted on it, sending troops also overland from north China.

Meanwhile the Americans continued to press for some kind of political settlement between the two rival parties, hoping to avoid a civil war. At their initiative, Mao flew down to Chungking (the first time he had ever been in an airplane) for talks with Chiang which lasted into October of 1945 and which produced a reasonable-sounding set of common principles such as the need for political democracy, a unified army, and the convening of a People's Congress, but most of this was never implemented. Near the end of the year President Harry Truman sent General George Marshall as a special envoy to China in an effort to bring the two sides together. They soon agreed to a cease-fire, but it was quickly broken as both armies clashed in numerous incidents, with the KMT trying to alter the earlier agreements on the sharing of power so as to give themselves complete dominance. Those who protested against this, such as philosophy professor Wen I-to (Wen Yiduo) were simply shot in cold blood and even in public by the KMT, along with other "leftists" and liberals. Marshall pushed through another cease-fire in June, but it was overwhelmed by a new KMT effort to capture Manchuria.

The newly founded United Nations, through its agency the United Nations Relief and Rehabilitation Administration (UNRRA), was able to get more genuine cooperation from both sides in its successful operation to return the Yellow River to its northern bed (Chiang had blown the dikes to delay the Japanese advance in 1938), but the vast flow of U.S. and UNRRA supplies which poured into China, for a great variety of relief and reconstruction projects, fed enormous new corruption by KMT officials and businessmen (often with interconnections). Most of the supplies sent for the relief of the Chinese people never reached their goal but enriched the few with connections. Other KMT officials, sent ostensibly to take inventory of factories and businesses in the former Japanese-occupied areas, used the opportunity to ransack both. Many who had been collaborators with the Japanese went unpunished or were continued in office, while the KMT representatives often used their power to expropriate others (to their own profit) whose only crime was to have remained functioning under the Japanese. The currency system was in chaos, with exchange rates varying wildly from one city or province to another. The KMT was slow to restore some sort of order, and when it finally tried to do so its own currency issue was increasingly mistrusted. Despite Marshall's well-meaning but naive efforts, the conflict between the two parties deepened. Denunciations from both sides punctuated the continuing clashes, and in January of 1947 Marshall announced that his mission had failed and his liaison teams were withdrawn.

Where the KMT forces with their new American equipment were able to retake areas held by the Communists, as they did briefly in the Yenan area and many others in east China, they executed any suspected of Communist leanings or connections. In Manchuria, the People's Liberation Army (PLA), as the Communists now called their forces, began to isolate the KMT-held cities by cutting the rail lines connecting and maintaining them. As the KMT troops began to surrender they abandoned large supplies of equipment and weapons, which gave the PLA the additional strength they needed to intensify the siege and to narrow the ring around the cities. No reinforcements could now reach the KMT forces, and their morale sagged as that of the PLA mounted. KMT troops resented their officers, who lived luxuriously and enriched themselves while the soldiers suffered — the old story familiar from the anti-Japanese war. Instead of pursuing the PLA, they holed up in the cities and dug in. It was clear that Chiang's decision to fight in Manchuria was disastrous, like so much of his strategy, and that it would soon be lost, along with some of the best of his troops and equipment and the industrial bases built up in Manchuria by the Japanese. These had been pillaged of easily portable machinery by the departing Russians, but were still a major prize, and were to be vitally important in the Communist rebuilding of the economy after 1949.

In all of the KMT-controlled areas in China, the money system had reeled out of control. Of all the causes of Chiang's ultimate failure, this must be considered among the most important, not only because it largely paralyzed the whole economy but because it so heavily damaged livelihood and morale and built resentment against corrupt officials who protected themselves. Inflation had been destructive enough during the war (see Chapter 19), but now it soared even beyond those dimensions. The government continued simply to print more money as its response to exploding prices, which in turn were the predictable result of shortages, compounded by gross speculation by officials and their protegés and by rampant corruption. The failure to stabilize and regulate currencies in the former Japanese-occupied areas immediately after the war started the situation off in chaos. Demobilization of many soldiers and winding down of war industries produced new unemployment. There was a wave of strikes by industrial workers still employed as their wages fell disastrously behind the runaway prices. There was of course widespread hoarding, and efforts at price control failed. Prices rose a thousandfold between June 1947 and July 1948, 50,000-fold by February 1949. The government printed notes of larger and larger denominations, and Chiang continued to spend vast sums on the military, which predictably produced a huge deficit in the budget, itself a contributing factor to the economic deterioration. KMT officials, including many close to Chiang, sent gold out of the country to their overseas accounts.

By the spring of 1947 the Communists, aided by their guerrilla allies, controlled most of the countryside in the north, and in the following year they cut most of the rail lines. By late 1948 Manchuria had fallen and 400,000 KMT troops had surrendered with their equipment, most of them defecting to the other side. In a great battle at the end of the year where the Communists threw massive numbers of their army and captured equipment into the contest, they captured the vital rail junction of Hsuchou (Xuzhou) in northern Kiangsu (Jiangsu) despite the KMT's total control of the air. The battle lasted for some two months during which the KMT commanders were chronically hampered by wrongheaded and contradictory orders from Chiang, who insisted as so often before on directing the battle from a safe distance, and with the same disastrous results. About half of the KMT troops and their officers simply deserted to the Communist side, where morale was high and which was increasingly seen as the ultimate winner. In January 1949 the Communists took Tientsin (Tianjin), the biggest city of north China and its major port, and Peking surrendered at the end of the month. The Communist armies maintained their earlier record of paying for what they got from the people of the conquered areas; they strictly forbade looting and introduced a new gold-backed currency while forbidding all trading in precious metals and money, and all prices were stabilized.

Communist forces now outnumbered those of the KMT and had acquired much of the latter's heavy equip-

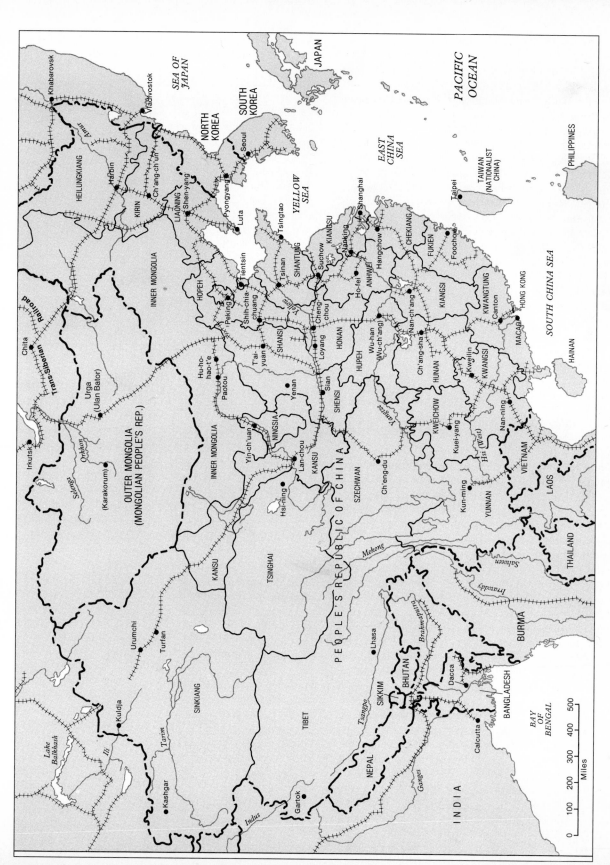

Modern China

ment. Already Chiang had fled to the island of Taiwan. Communist forces advanced southward, successfully crossing the barrier of the Yangtze and capturing Nanking without a fight on April 23, 1949, followed shortly by Wuhan and Hangchou, the old Southern Sung capital. Shanghai was thus cut off, and fell late in May with only token resistance, despite Chiang's earlier assertion that he would hold firm there and at Nanking. Other Communist forces moved west, capturing Sian, the old Han and T'ang capital, and by the end of the summer had taken Kansu (Gansu), Sinkiang (Xinjiang), and Inner Mongolia. Still others drove south, taking Canton in October, Kweichou, Szechuan, and Yunnan in November. In anticipation of this whirlwind victory, Mao Tse-tung (Mao Zedong) in his high, squeaky voice had announced from a podium in front of the Gate of Heavenly Peace (T'ien An Men) at the entrance to the Forbidden City in Peking the establishment of the People's Republic on October 1, still celebrated every year as an anniversary. Mao declared that "China has stood up," and the majority of Chinese responded with enthusiasm. Despite its offside location (less so with the modern development and key importance of Manchuria), Peking was again the capital, in line with imperial tradition. Chiang and his entourage, accompanied by about a million KMT troops, were now in Taiwan, which he declared to be the Republic of China, and the country's only "legitimate" government.

The KMT had started in its struggle against the Communists with vast superiority in numbers and equipment, much of it American, and it held all the major cities, against an enemy with no air force, no tanks, and only a little small artillery. It seems reasonable to lay most of the blame for this debacle on Chiang himself, and on the nature of the KMT government and army which he had created. With better strategic direction, the KMT might well have won the civil war. But what dragged it down to defeat was also its cumulative loss of popular support, extending even or perhaps especially to its soldiers, as political corruption, self-seeking, and failure to address the basic problems of the Chinese people all got worse rather than better once the anti-Japanese war was over, as China might now have concentrated its energies on rebuilding the country. The incompetence and callousness with which the KMT failed to deal with the problem of inflation, while its own high officials continued to live luxuriously and even sent money out of the country, was perhaps the final straw. Mao and several of the other Communist leaders came from peasant origins and their program emphasized peasant welfare and virtues ignored by the KMT. Most of the cities had been foreign-dominated treaty ports where Chinese collaborators grew rich, and were also the centers of KMT strength. Cities were thus an obvious target for the Communist revolution, although the Communists also promised a better life for oppressed urban workers and drew on their support.

Mao and the Mass Line

Success depended however on building a wide mass support base. This was achieved through land reform in the Communist-controlled areas, accompanied by campaigns to politicize the masses and organize them into action. As in Yenan days, intellectuals were at first welcomed to aid in this effort. Mao himself, though born in 1893 the son of a rich peasant turned grain merchant and hence familiar with the countryside, was primarily an intellectual. He quarreled with his father and left his home in Hunan to become at age 19 a student at a normal school in Changsha, the provincial capital, where he studied Western and Chinese philosophy and ethics. When he was 24 he published his first essay, urging Chinese to build their strength through physical education, as opposed to the sybaritic life of the traditional scholar. Other articles urged collective action, and the emancipation and mobilization of women. By 1919 he had moved on to Peking, the center of new ferment, and although not formally a student there attended the study group organized by Li Ta-chao (Li Dazhao, see Chapter 18). He supported himself by finding a low-level job in the university library, where he could still learn from his old Changsha teacher, who was now a professor at Peking University, but Mao also worked for a time as a laundryman.

Mao was well enough integrated into this small group of Marxist-oriented revolutionaries to be invited as the delegate from Hunan to the founding meeting of the Chinese Communist party in July of 1921 (he had returned to Changsha, where he established a Communist cell, late in 1920 as director of a primary school). He was thus hardly a peasant, and from his relatively early years a reader of books, a writer of articles, and a person who became increasingly convinced that China must have fundamental change. In organizing a peasant-centered revolution, Mao consciously followed an old Chinese tradition, with himself playing the role of the urban-based intellectual theorist and political organizer, as so many men of the gentry had done in the past in leading peasant rebellion. In time he was to play the role also of a new emperor as well as the source of wisdom and truth, celebrated in the widespread cult of Mao.

The close American connection with the KMT and its massive military support had troubled many Chinese patriots, probably weakened rather than strengthened its fight against communism, and left a legacy of anti-American bitterness. The revolution had been long delayed, beginning with the fumbling series of misadventures in 1911 when the old Ch'ing dynasty was overthrown. Many Chinese felt the need for radical change, only to

✠ Mao: The Revolutionary Vision ✠

The Communist revolution in China was in large part a peasant-based movement against the vested power of the cities. In 1939 Mao Tse-tung put it dramatically.

Since China's key cities have long been occupied by the powerful imperialists and their reactionary Chinese allies, it is imperative for the revolutionary ranks to turn the backward villages into advanced consolidated base areas, . . . bastions of the revolution from which to fight their vicious enemies.

Here is an equally famous statement made by Mao.

China's 600 million people have two remarkable peculiarities; they are first of all poor, and secondly blank. That may seem like a bad thing, but it is really a good thing. Poor people want change, want to do things, want revolution. A clean sheet of paper has no blotches, and so the newest and most beautiful words can be written on it, the newest and most beautiful pictures painted on it.

Still driven by his revolutionary vision, Mao the poet wrote in 1963, in traditional classic verse:

So many deeds cry out to be done,
And always urgently.
The world rolls on,
Time passes.
Ten thousand years are too long;
Seize the day, seize the hour,
Our force is irresistible.

Sources: Mao Tse-tung, *The Chinese Revolution and the Chinese Communist Party* (Peking: Foreign Languages Press, 1954), p. 17 (written in 1939); Red Flag, June 1, 1958, pp. 3–4; "Reply to Kuo Mo-jo" (dated February 5, 1963), in *China Reconstructs*, 16 (March 1967): 2.

see it aborted or betrayed by warlord regimes and then by the increasingly reactionary Kuomintang under Chiang Kai-shek after 1927. The effort at revolution had been led and joined almost exclusively by intellectuals, a tiny handful of the population. Now the Communists had finally succeeded in creating a mass base, with a peasant army forged in the fires of the anti-Japanese war, and a politicized people, who could carry out Mao's "mass line." The United States continued to support the KMT on Taiwan and to arm it, until the pressures of reality led belatedly to official recognition of the government in Peking in 1979, although unofficial ties with Taipei (the Taiwan capital) remained. Until his death in 1975, Chiang continued to urge "reconquest of the mainland," and there were brief artillery duels from islands off the coast still held by the KMT, who referred to the Communist regime simply as "bandits."

With the outbreak of the Korean War in June of 1950, and the subsequent entry of Chinese "volunteer" troops in October-November against a largely U.S. force under overall U.N. auspices, the U.S. and China were in fact at war, though it remained unofficial (see Chapter 21), and nearly a million Chinese died. The American role in Korea helped importantly to harden the line of the new Chinese government, to make it more radical, and to build a further legacy of anti-American feeling. It also greatly strengthened patriotic-national feeling, as the presence of an external enemy always does, and to make nearly all Chinese close ranks. The U.S. pushed through the U.N. a total embargo on trade with China, and enforced it by a blockade of the coast, further increasing the sense of encirclement and of the embattled new Chinese revolution standing against the world, now on the proud basis of "self-reliance."

The Outer Areas

Meanwhile in China the new government moved swiftly to repair the physical damage of the long years of war, in particular the reconstruction of the rail lines. Land reform and political education were extended into the newly conquered south and southwest. All over the country what was still called land reform became far more violent as party organizers, in an effort to create "class consciousness," encouraged peasants to identify and accuse their landlord-oppressors and to "speak bitterness." Many thousands, perhaps as many as a million, were killed by angry mobs, many after being paraded before a "People's Court" and confronted by their accusers. No doubt many were guilty as charged, but clearly, equally many were not, the predictable result of mob justice. In addition to the lands of those killed, lands of others classified as landlords were also confiscated for distribution among those classified as "poor peasants" or landless. The remaining categories of "rich and middle peasants" were for the present left alone because their continued production was essential, but the whole classification process was hasty and arbitrary. For the next many years, those classified as "rich" or even "middle" were under a cloud, and their children and even grandchildren severely discriminated against.

Firm central control was reestablished in all of the former empire, including Manchuria (now called simply "the northeast," given its troubled recent history), southern or "Inner" Mongolia, and Sinkiang, and an agreement made with Tibetan leaders to acknowledge Chinese sovereignty, although this was to be followed later by a brutal Chinese invasion (see below). Outer Mongolia had declared its independence in 1921 as the Mongolian People's Republic, but had become a Russian satellite; later, especially after the breakup of the Soviet Union, Chinese influence strengthened and there was large-scale Chinese settlement in Mongolia, many serving as technical advisers or managers. In Inner Mongolia, permanent Chinese settlers soon became about 90 percent of the population, and traditional Mongol culture seemed doomed to disappear, giving way to new industry and commercial stock raising and agriculture. In Sinkiang also there was heavy Chinese settlement, rising to about half of the total population, and much new heavy industrial development using Sinkiang's natural resources and concentrated in the capital at Urumchi (Ulumuqi), with other areas producing and refining petroleum and shipping most of it to China proper by both new rail lines and pipelines. Manchuria, with its huge Japanese-built industrial plant, became the chief engine of China's postwar industrialization, with major iron, steel, and engineering plants in the Mukden area (now called Shenyang) and oil newly

discovered in the 1950s from wells at Ta Ch'ing (Daqing) in north-central Manchuria. Ch'ang Ch'un (Changqun) in central Manchuria, which had served as the Japanese capital, became a major producer of vehicles, and Dairen (Dalien) saw vigorous new growth as a port and manufacturing center.

Tibet became a truly tragic case. Its people, culture, and language are sharply different from China's, and its dominantly pastoral economy (see Chapter 1) was politically incorporated in the Chinese empire only in the eighteenth century (Chapter 8). Chou En-lai (Zhou Enlai) met with the Dalai Lama, both the spiritual and temporal ruler, in Peking in 1950 and agreed that if Tibet accepted Chinese sovereignty (after the long lapse from before the fall of the Ch'ing) it would be allowed to manage its own internal affairs. But the Chinese began building roads up into Tibet to aid its development. Like so many works projects, this was undertaken by the P.L.A. Two of the three routes ran through Chamdo or eastern Tibet, where the Cham inhabitants had a long history of conflict with the advancing wave of Chinese settlement which had been moving up the valleys in search of farmland as part of the Ch'ing population expansion. The P.L.A. road workers were billeted in local households, and requisitioned their food supplies. It was not surprising that the Chams regarded all of this as an invasion of their country, and they began to shoot at the P.L.A. workers and to roll boulders down on their work sites. The Chinese government was not about to tolerate such open rebellion and moved in larger forces, who soon had the Chams with their backs to the wall. At this point the Chams appealed for help to their fellow Tibetans in Lhasa, the capital. The Dalai Lama was in a dilemma, correctly sensing that resistance to the Chinese juggernaut was futile but not willing to desert the Chams. Tibet was soon overrun by Chinese forces in the fall of 1950 and the Dalai Lama fled with some of his followers across the Himalayan border to India, where he set up a government in exile. The Chinese occupation of Tibet became ruthless enough to attract outside charges of genocide; they tried to suppress traditional Tibetan culture as an obvious vehicle for Tibetan nationalism/separatism, and Tibet has remained a most unhappy place, still seething with potential revolt.

The rebellion against Chinese occupation continued in remote alpine western Tibet, and to fight it the Chinese felt they had to build another road, from western Sinkiang; the only viable route through this wild mountainous country ran briefly on the Indian side of the line still claimed by India as its border with China. India was not even aware of the Chinese presence in this remote Himalayan region until the road was finished in 1962, when they foolishly fired on the Chinese and tried to eject them. The Chinese were there on a war footing and easily brushed off the ill-prepared Indian forces, advancing only to the line the Chinese claimed as the border, in a district known as the Aksai Chin. The dispute has still not been settled, but the two-week war clearly established China as the new arbiter of mainland Asia, while at the same time tightening their grip on Tibet. The Dalai Lama continues to appeal to Indian and Western sympathies, but any outside effort to "meddle" in the internal affairs of Tibet is resented and rejected by China, while its troops and police continue to impose an oppressive iron rule on the Tibetan people, against their frequent protest. In Sinkiang, where the Turkic Uighurs have long been the largest single group, the massive Chinese presence and dominance is also resented even though it means, as in Tibet and Inner Mongolia, "development" and all that comes in its wake, most importantly industrialization, new jobs, and a chance for the local people to rise within the greater Chinese system, as long as they follow Chinese ways.

The official fiction for these and other non-Chinese areas (non-Han) within the People's Republic is that they are "autonomous," a label applied also to smaller blocks of people and territory in the south and southwest where non-Chinese (non-Han) have managed to maintain themselves. This is a formula based on the Soviet Russian approach to their multicultural and multinational state, where Russians are now a minority, but Han Chinese are about 94 percent of China's population (the figure is spongy since so many people have claimed "minority" status or have married non-Hans in hopes of enjoying special privileges extended to minorities, especially to have more than one child). Clearly the non-Chinese (non-Han) groups cannot hope to stand against the Chinese steamroller, and are in addition scattered and divided. "Autonomy" is a farce, since all power is retained by the Chinese state, although in some cases shared with collaborators among the subject people. This is of course quite consistent with the long Chinese historical record on the subjugation of non-Chinese groups within the empire, and indeed with the record of virtually all other states (including the United States) as a single dominant population eliminates, conquers, or overwhelms all others and takes their lands.

To begin with, Mao spoke of the new government as a "democratic coalition" under Communist leadership, since he needed the support of all groups. But he also spoke of it as a "people's democratic dictatorship" which would hunt out "enemies of the people" and "counterrevolutionaries." For the present at least, intellectuals, whose talents were urgently needed, were welcomed, including those who had never been Communists, as were members of the business class, the "national bourgeoisie." Most of the intellectuals who had been studying abroad returned to lend their skills and enthusiasms to building a new China. A National People's Congress was essentially window dressing and had no real power, which remained in the hands of the Communist party and its central committee, but newly invigorated mass organizations such as labor unions and youth and women's groups helped to make the connection between government and the people and to indoctrinate the populace.

The leaders of Communist China in 1965, on the eve of the Cultural Revolution. From left to right, Chou En-lai, Chu Teh, Mao Tse-tung, and Liu Hsiao-ch'i. (Eastfoto/Sovfoto)

Here was the mass line in action, and it soon began to mount mass campaigns against selected targets. The first was the "Resist America, Defend Korea" campaign in late 1950 and after, followed by others against "rightists" and soon accompanied by a rapid reorganization of the agricultural system. Land reform was succeeded by the formation of farm cooperatives, complete for most of the country by 1956. These in turn were transformed into collectives along the Soviet model, and the next year into communes as part of the "Great Leap Forward" (see below). By 1956 Mao felt that support for the new government was wide and deep enough to permit criticism. In a famous speech he declared "Let a hundred flowers bloom, let a hundred schools of thought contend"; this was not an invitation to total free expression, but to criticism of the party, as long as it was not "antagonistic" or "counterrevolutionary," that convenient pretext for repression. He probably also intended this as a move to smoke out and punish opposition. Many intellectuals and others, including many of the ethnic minorities, responded with a torrent of criticism. Most of it was pronounced "destructive" and counterrevolutionary, and many of the critics were arrested and jailed or even executed. Mass campaigns identified many thousands as "rightists" or counterrevolutionaries," who were also imprisoned or killed.

The Great Leap Forward

Despite the evidence of dissent, Mao still felt secure enough in the support and radical fervor of the majority of his people that he moved swiftly to collectivize all land. By 1958 he moved beyond the Soviet model of collectivization and organized most land into new "communes"; private ownership was abolished and all enterprises managed collectively. Communes varied widely in area and population but averaged about 15,000–25,000 people and incorporated large numbers of originally separate villages. Several villages made up a "Production Team," several Teams a "Production Brigade," and several Brigades a commune. Communes were supposed to include industrial enterprises also, to bring industrialization to the rural areas. Urban communes were also set up in the cities, but added little to existing factories, departments, or offices, which remained the major units, and the urban communes did not last.

Mao announced that 1958 would be the year of "The Great Leap Forward" in which China would overtake Britain in industrial output by the united efforts of a galvanized people—the mass line in action—who would "go all out" within the commune structure to achieve the decreed goals. Communal dining halls were set up so that families need not lose work time by preparing meals. Backyard steel furnaces sprang up all over the rural landscape, using local iron ore and coal or other fuel. Communes were given quotas for production of specific agricultural and industrial goods, but too little attention was paid to the nature of local resources or to rational organization more generally.

The Great Leap was a dismal failure, and the country collapsed into economic chaos in 1959. Peasants had been driven to exhaustion in pursuit of unrealistic goals and inefficient combinations of tasks and resources. Nearly all of the iron and steel from the backyard furnaces was of unusable quality and had to be thrown out, as well as much of the other industrial output. Crops were neglected or failed as labor was shifted arbitrarily to different tasks, and for at least three years there were massive food shortages and widespread famine. Probably at least 30 million people died of starvation or malnutrition. It was the worst famine in world history. Mao's radical policies had brought disaster, and for several years other more pragmatic measures and more moderate leaders such as Chou En-lai (1898–1976) and Liu Hsiao-ch'i (Liu Shaoqi, 1894–1971) had a greater role and for the time being eclipsed Mao, although he remained the party chairman.

The Sino-Soviet Split

The Russians were alarmed by what they saw as the radical excesses of the Great Leap and its departure from the Soviet pattern. They were annoyed also by Mao's assertion that his version of socialism was superior to theirs, his continued support of Stalinist policies after they had been discredited in the U.S.S.R., and his accusations that Russia had now become ideologically impure or "revisionist." The Russians saw Mao's bellicose stand on the reconquest of Taiwan, for which he requested Soviet nuclear aid, as a threat to world peace, and there were inevitable tensions arising out of the large scale Soviet aid program and Soviet advisers in China. In 1959 the Russians withdrew their aid and advisers and moved toward a more antagonistic relationship with China. The next 15 years saw revived territorial disputes and armed border clashes between the two former allies on the very long frontier which divides them, especially in the Amur region of northern Manchuria and along the northern border of Sinkiang.

No longer sharing a common ideology (except in its historical origins) and as rival models of true socialism, with each claiming to be the heir of Marx and Lenin, long-standing substantive conflicts between them surfaced. These dated back to the early Tsarist expansion into northeast Asia, Russian dominance in Manchuria, and their threatening role as one of the Western imperialist powers during China's years of political weakness. On the other side, China's billion people, next door to thinly settled Siberia and the Soviet maritime provinces and driven as they seemed to be by radical fanaticism, led to Russian fear, and to preparations which China found threatening. The rhetoric of mutual accusation mounted on both sides, and troops were stationed along the frontiers. But China could not stand alone against the world, and her leaders began indirect overtures to the United States. More than a decade later, with the end of their misadventure in Vietnam in sight, the Americans finally responded late in 1971, beginning a cautious restoration of contact when their president visited Peking. This slowly led to the establishment of diplomatic relations, with full U.S. recognition and the exchange of ambassadors in 1979.

The Cultural Revolution Decade

China first had to pass through perhaps the greatest cataclysm in world history, measured by the hundreds of millions of people involved in mass persecution and suffering, the Great Proletarian Cultural Revolution, as Mao called it, from 1966 to his own death in 1976. The failure of the Great Leap had necessitated more moderate policies and a period of recovery from economic disaster. By 1966 Mao judged recovery complete and launched a new campaign to reradicalize a revolution which he saw as slipping into "revisionism," complacency, opportunism, and self-seeking on the part of party officials, managers, and all people in positions of authority. Mao remarked that he felt like "an ancestor at his own funeral and at the burial of his hopes." Basically, his message was the old one of "serve the people," with its clear echoes of Confucian responsibility, but the methods employed by the Cultural Revolution had devastating results. The chief targets were the elite: Party officials, teachers, writers, all intellectuals, all those who were "tainted" by foreign influence or "bourgeois" lifestyles, and all whose "class origins" were not poor peasant or manual worker.

Millions of officials, managers, writers, and teachers were hounded out of their jobs. Artists and musicians who showed any interest in Western styles were attacked. Many of the intellectuals, and others who were labeled "counterrevolutionaries," were beaten or killed, others jailed, sent to corrective labor camps, or assigned to the lowest menial tasks, as both punishment and "reeducation." Opera stars and concert violinists were set to cleaning latrines. All foreign music, art, literature, and ideas (except for Marxism, Leninism, and Stalinism) were banned, and even Chinese books disappeared or were burned, except for the ever-present works of Mao himself and "The Little Red Book" of his sayings. Those who had studied abroad, especially valuable for China's efforts at national reconstruction, were particu-

lar targets. People were encouraged to inform on friends, colleagues, and even family members, causing immense bitterness, separation, and suffering.

Those accused, often without evidence, of "rightist" or bourgeois tendencies were jailed, sentenced to corrective labor, or driven to suicide. Few had the courage to try to help them, for fear that they themselves would meet the same fate. Teachers were attacked and beaten by their students in a brutal reversal of traditional respect for learning; musicians and artists had their fingers broken. The official line was that it was "Better to be Red than Expert"; most of China's relatively small group of urgently needed professionals ("experts") in most fields were hounded, jailed, or killed. Almost no one in this immense country beyond the age of one escaped the turmoil, which wrecked the lives of hundreds of millions of people and killed unknown millions. The rural communes were not exempt, and there too there were repeated radical campaigns and terror.

All universities and colleges were closed for several years, as breeding grounds for a new elite. When they slowly began to reopen it was only to the children of peasants, workers, and party faithfuls still in power, but with a curriculum which concentrated on "political study." Most high school graduates in the decade after 1966, and in the big cities practically all, were assigned to "productive labor in the countryside," where they were told to "strike roots permanently." This was partly a leveling alternative to the now closed or restricted universities, partly a means to ease unemployment and housing shortages in the cities, and partly a way to reeducate those too young to have shared the early Yenan years of hardship and sacrifice. Now they would learn from the peasants the meaning of hard work instead of following the upwardly mobile path which education has always meant to Chinese, and thus becoming both elite and bourgeois "experts."

Some 17 million young people were sent down in this program, until it was largely discontinued in the late 1970s. Most of those sent to the countryside saw it as ruinous to their own ambitions and career plans, for which their urban origins and education had prepared them. Nor were most of them very helpful in rural agricultural or other development work. Their training had not in most cases been very relevant, and indeed it had tended, as in China's past, to make them think of themselves as an educated elite who looked down on peasants and on manual labor. The program was understandably unpopular with peasants, too, since they had to feed and house disgruntled city kids who, despite their higher level of education, were both incompetent and uninterested in farm work. All white-collar workers were also required to spend at least two months each year doing manual labor, mainly in the countryside, a far more sensible idea but one which not

Revolution, Chinese Style

From the beginning of their revolutionary victory, the Chinese asserted that their principles and experience should be the guide for the rest of the world, not the Russian way. Here is Liu Shao-ch'i in 1949.

The road taken by the Chinese people in defeating imperialism and in founding the Chinese People's Republic is the road that should be taken by the peoples of many colonial and semi-colonial countries in their fight for national independence and people's democracy.... This is the road of Mao Tse-tung.... This is the inevitable road of many colonial and semi-colonial peoples in the struggle for their independence and liberation.

Lu Ting-i, director of propaganda of the Central Committee, added in July 1951:

Mao Tse-tung's theory of the Chinese revolution is a new development of Marxism-Leninism in the revolutions of the colonial and semi-colonial countries.... It is of universal significance for the world Communist movement.... The classic type of revolution in colonial and semi-colonial countries is the Chinese revolution.

The Russians replied, in the words of Y. Kovalev, a leading propagandist.

The decisive prerequisites for the victory of the Chinese revolution were the October Socialist Revolution and the victory of socialism in the U.S.S.R., and the defeat of Japanese and German imperialism by the Soviet Union in World War II.... Stalin's analysis of the peculiarities of China as a semi-colonial country was taken as the basis for the working out of the strategy and tactics of the struggle for an independent and democratic China by the Chinese Communist Party.

Stalin's successor, Nikita Khrushchev, lectured Mao in 1958, after Mao suggested that the combined numbers of China and Russia could overcome the capitalist West.

Comrade Mao Tse-tung, nowadays that sort of thinking is out of date. You can no longer calculate the alignment of forces on the basis of who has the most men. Back in the days when a dispute was settled with fists and bayonets it made a difference who had the most men.... Now with the atomic bomb, the number of troops on each side makes practically no difference.

But the Chinese stuck to their insistence that theirs was the only true way. This editorial, in characteristic Cultural Revolution style, appeared in Liberation Army Daily *in May 1966.*

The thought of Mao Tse-tung is the sun in our heart, the root of our life, and the source of all our strength. Through it one becomes unselfish, daring, intelligent, and able to do anything; no difficulty can conquer him, while he can conquer any enemy. The thought of Mao Tse-tung transforms man's ideology, transforms the fatherland.... Through it the oppressed people of the world will rise.

Sources: I. Hsu, *The Rise of Modern China* (New York: Oxford University Press, 1975), pp. 810–813, 859.

surprisingly also met with resistance from high status professionals and others.

As shock troops for the Cultural Revolution, Mao called on teenagers and students, often natural "revolutionaries" in all societies, with little stake in the status quo, filled with idealism, easily diverted from their studies, and welcoming their exciting new role as a lark. Mao called them "Red Guards," who abandoned their families, jobs, and studies to roam the country ferreting out "rightists" (often including their own family members, another especially harsh denial of long-standing Chinese values) and harassing everyone in responsible positions. Red Guards invaded the homes of all suspected of "bourgeois tendencies," destroyed books and artworks, and beat up the residents. Millions rode free or commandeered trains and buses to Peking where cheering crowds of Red Guards were addressed by Mao at mass rallies, and to other cities, bastions of the elite. For a time the Red Guards even took over the Foreign Ministry and tried to direct China's foreign policy. Mao and those supporting him promoted the even more extreme spread of a personality cult; huge pictures and

statues of "The Great Helmsman" and copies of his "Little Red Book" mushroomed everywhere. Rival warring factions quickly emerged among the Red Guards, each claiming to be following the "true" line, and pursuing what amounted to gang warfare. Groups and individuals welcomed the opportunity to pay off old grudges and to denounce others or to accuse them anonymously. There was uncontrolled violence, including large-scale street warfare in many cities.

To prevent continued chaos, Chou En-lai finally prevailed on Mao to call in the army in 1968 and put down the Red Guards, thus creating a new embittered group who felt they had been betrayed, a "lost generation." But the nightmare went on even after the Red Guards had been sent to the countryside. Even those at the top, except for Mao himself, were attacked for alleged "deviations" from the correct line, which changed unpredictably and was involved with political power plays. Liu Shao-ch'i, originally picked by Mao as his successor and an old revolutionary comrade, was removed, accused of "rightist revisionism" because of his efforts to rebuild the economy after the disaster of the Great Leap Forward,

The mass line in action: some of the 100,000 people involved in building, largely by hand, a new irrigation dam outside Peking. This is in fact an ancient system; similar armies of mass labor built the Great Wall, the Grand Canal, and other monumental public works in the long past. (*China Reconstructs*)

✠ Attack on the "Revisionists" and "Imperialists" ✠

At the Tenth Party Congress in 1973, Vice-Chairman Chou En-lai gave a long address in which he castigated the Russian "revisionists" and lumped them together with the American "imperialists."

There were many instances in the past where one tendency covered another and when a tide came, the majority went along with it, while only a few withstood it.... We must not fear isolation and must dare to go against the tide and brave it through. Chairman Mao states: Going against the tide is a Marxist-Leninist principle.... The West always wants to urge the Soviet revisionists eastward to divert the peril toward China, and it would be fine so long as all is quiet in the West. China is an attractive piece of meat coveted by all. But this piece of meat is very tough, and for years no one has been able to bite into it.... The U.S.-Soviet contention for hegemony is the cause of world intranquillity.... They want to devour China but find it too tough even to bite.... U.S. imperialism started to go downhill after its defeat in the war of aggression against Korea.... [Khrushchev and Brezhnev in Russia] made a socialist country degenerate into a social imperialist country. Internally it has restored capitalism, enforced a fascist dictatorship and ... exposed its ugly features as the new Czar and its reactionary nature, namely 'socialism in words, imperialism in deeds'...." If you are so anxious to relax world tension, why don't you show your good faith by doing a thing or two—for instance, withdraw your armed forces from Czechoslovakia or the People's Republic of Mongolia and return the four northern islands to Japan [the Kurile archipelago north of Hokkaido]? China has not occupied any foreign countries' territory. Must China give away all the territory north of the Great Wall to the Soviet revisionists in order to show that we favor relaxation of world tensions? ... The Sino-Soviet boundary question should be settled peacefully through negotiations free from any threat. We will not attack unless we are attacked; if we are attacked, we will certainly counterattack.

Source: I. Hsu, *The Rise of Modern China* (New York: Oxford University Press, 1975), pp. 878–879.

and died as a prisoner after public humiliations and beatings. Other high officials suffered similar fates. Professionals in all fields were scrutinized for their political views and activism. Absence from the endless daily political meetings, or silence during them, was evidence of "counterrevolutionary tendencies." No one at any level felt safe or free to say what they really thought.

The Chinese revolution remained ostensibly a peasant movement, a Chinese rather than a foreign-style answer to China's problems. This was appealing also on nationalist grounds, especially since nearly all the cities had been tainted by semicolonial foreign dominance while the great bulk of the country's people remained in the agricultural countryside. What little industrialization there was before 1949 was almost entirely in the cities, particularly in the foreign-run treaty ports or in Japanese-controlled Manchuria. There was thus both a pronounced antiurban bias to the revolution, and a determination to exalt the countryside, to put the peasants in charge and to concentrate efforts at develop-

ment in the rural areas, the supposed source of all revolutionary values.

This was the theme of both the Great Leap Forward and the Cultural Revolution, and both included ambitious plans to bring the benefits of industrialization to the countryside. And, since the mid-1950s, all movement of people was controlled, especially to the cities, where housing and ration books for food and household supplies were allocated only to those who were assigned jobs there. Jobs could not be chosen by individuals, who worked where the state sent them, including school and college graduates. In the 1970s and 1980s there was a growing number of illegal migrants to the cities, living underground or on forged papers. Most of them are still there, their numbers apparently greatly increased; urban unemployment has become a major problem. Despite the official denigration of cities, they remained the places where most people wanted to be, seeking wider opportunities for personal advancement as well as the excitement of any city. This was all disapproved of as "bourgeois" or even counterrevolutionary, but is understandable enough and indeed has been the common experience of all modern societies.

In the countryside, each commune was designed to be as much as possible self-sufficient, and "self-reliant." Under the Cultural Revolution there was a much larger growth of small-scale rural industry, especially what were labeled "the five smalls": iron and steel, cement, fertilizer, agricultural goods (including tools, machinery, and irrigation equipment), and electric power. There was also much production of light consumer goods for local use. Manufacturing in each area, using only local resources, did of course reduce the load on an already overburdened road and rail system, and saved transport costs, while providing employment and experience to the masses of rural people. But in most cases such production was considerably more expensive than in larger-scale and better-equipped urban-based plants, as well as being of much lower quality. Rural industry has been thought about by many in the West and in India as an ideally preferable alternative to the crowding, pollution, and dehumanization of industrial cities since the eighteenth century in nearly all industrializing societies. But the economies of scale ("the bigger the cheaper") have meant that it is seldom fully practical. Like others of his policies, it was part of Mao's utopian vision, appealing in many ways but pursued at dreadful cost, while China lagged still farther behind the rest of the world technologically and educationally.

Mao had said that the major goals of the revolution should be to eliminate the distinctions between city and countryside, between mental and manual workers, and between elites and peasants or workers; all three goals were of course closely related. In pursuit of these aims, workers or janitors became plant managers and university officials, poor peasants were elevated to power in commune "revolutionary committees"; professors, technicians, and skilled managers were humiliated, downgraded, or reduced to the lowest menial jobs. This was all in large part a reaction against the strongly hierarchical and elitist structure and values of traditional Chinese society, and a desire for change according to the egalitarian ideals of Communism, further strengthened by the nature of the revolution which had succeeded in 1949. That had been based largely in the peasant countryside, and was in any case aimed against the old established order as well as against the cities. Nevertheless, Mao drew heavily on traditional ideas in emphasizing the duty of those in positions of power and responsibility to serve the masses, and he, like the Confucians, used moral example, slogans, and simplified philosophical sayings to inspire and mold group behavior in the common interest.

As an intellectual himself, in the long Chinese tradition, he was a noted poet and calligrapher, like many emperors. But he relied also on the new technique of the mass campaigns, to galvanize people into action in the service of revolutionary goals. Some were constructive, like the campaigns to eliminate rats and flies or to build new dams and irrigation canals. But most were more politically inspired and were aimed at "rightists" and "counterrevolutionaries." The Cultural Revolution was the last and the most devastating campaign. Most revolutions go through an extreme radical phase, like the Terror in Paris in the 1790s. The Chinese revolution's radical phase lasted longer and went to greater extremes than any other, but in time it too faded, if only because the Chinese people were exhausted by constant political campaigns and by the terror itself. Mao's death in 1976 removed the chief obstacle to a return to more normal conditions, and China turned away with relief from its long ordeal.

One of Mao's less attractive traits was his penchant for women. In addition to the three he married, he had endless affairs, many of them one-night stands, perhaps in emulation of imperial models in the past. As "the great helmsman" he had only to indicate his interest in

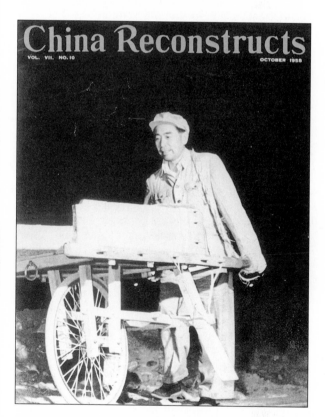

Chou En-lai setting an example, pushing a wheelbarrow at the Ming Tombs Reservoir Project near Peking in 1958. (*China Reconstructs*)

what he thought of as likely-looking young women to have them brought to his bed, whether they were already married or not. On his frequent trips around the country he would requisition a different woman every night from among the locals, who of course were told that this was a great honor(?), but in any case did not dare to refuse. There is no record of how many pregnancies resulted, or of what was done about the consequences. Supposedly a great philosopher and statesman, Mao behaved in fact like so many power-hungry politicians everywhere, and having achieved power clearly thought of himself as above both law and moral codes. China remains even now a far more prudish society than most in the West, and the memory of Mao's violations of such a code still stings, like his remark that "political power grows out of the barrel of a gun," and his turning on old comrades whom he thought of as departing from his line or threatening him as a rival.

Marshall Lin Piao (Lin Biao), a veteran, like Liu Hsiao-ch'i, of the Long March and then a highly successful general in the civil war against the KMT, saw what had happened to Liu, and then was designated by Mao as his new successor, his "close comrade in arms." But Mao soon became jealous of him as well and began to attack him obliquely. Late in 1971, he apparently decided to flee, and died when his plane crashed, perhaps on the way to Russia (?)—somewhere in Mongolia. The official story was that he had betrayed Chairman Mao and plotted to take his place, with Soviet help, but the full story remains most unclear. Another hero of the Long March and the civil war, Marshall P'eng Te-huai (Peng Dehuai) had the audacity in 1959 to criticize the Great Leap, for which he was dismissed as a "right opportunist," although he escaped the fate of Liu and Lin, probably because of his immense popularity. In one of his many secret (not published) speeches, Mao boasted that he had outdone the Ch'in dynasty emperor Shih Huang Ti, who buried supposedly 600 scholars alive, by saying that he, Mao, had killed thousands of them.

China After Mao

As Mao lay dying in 1976, a few months after Chou En-lai had died of overwork and exhaustion trying to hold the country together, the radical faction led by Mao's widow, Chiang Ch'ing (Jiang Qing), tried to continue his extreme policies. But the country was sick of radical politics. In 1978 a new, more moderate leadership emerged under Hua Kuo-feng (Hua Guofeng), whom Mao had designated as his successor. Chiang Ch'ing and three of her associates, the so-called Gang of Four, were tried and convicted of "crimes against the people" and sentenced to jail. China began to emerge from its nightmare, and to resume cautious interchange with the rest of the world after 30 years of isolation which had cost it dearly, especially in technology. The universities and their curricula were slowly restored for students who now had to pass entrance examinations rather than merely to demonstrate proper "class origins," and there were efforts to provide somewhat greater freedom for intellectuals, writers, teachers, and managers.

Many Chinese have long been quick to stereotype women with access to political power as dangerous, selfish, and an omen of degeneracy, or even of the inglorious end of a dynasty. Among others they remember the T'ang emperor Hsuan Tsung's favorite consort Yang Kuei-fei to whom they attributed the decline of the T'ang through her "evil influence," the notorious Empress Wu who usurped the throne earlier in the T'ang dynasty, and the truly evil Empress Dowager Tz'u Hsi. Chiang Ch'ing, Mao's third wife, had been a minor movie star before she married him in Yenan in 1939. This gave her, she felt, a role in shaping party cultural policy, and with the Cultural Revolution in 1966 she emerged publicly as a member of the party's Central Committee in charge of cultural affairs. She was personally responsible for the persecution of writers and artists and for decreeing what was acceptable in music, art, literature, and drama. It was said that she used her power to pay off old scores against professional rivals, and that she increasingly ignored or countermanded her husband's advice. She was often vituperative and spiteful in her personal style and ruthless in carrying out the line she favored. Both traditional and foreign works were banned, in favor of a new and rigid "socialist realism" with a heavy political message designed to appeal to the masses of peasants and workers.

During Mao's last years, when ill health and senility obliged him to withdraw from the day-to-day management of affairs, Chiang and her radical colleagues increased their power and were probably the chief architects of the Cultural Revolution after about 1968. At her trial she insisted that she alone had been faithful to Mao's vision, but most Chinese had come to fear and hate her and she is still seen as the arch-villain of China's dark years.

The new mood in the country continued to move away from the madness of the period from 1957 to 1976. Hua Kuo-feng was peacefully replaced with the return to power of the old party pragmatist Teng Hsiao-p'ing (Deng Xiaoping) in 1981 as the real head of state and chief policy maker. Most of Mao's policies were progressively dismantled. The new government acknowledged that China was still poor and technically backward, that it needed foreign technology and investment, and that to encourage production its people needed material incentives rather than political harangues and "rectification campaigns."

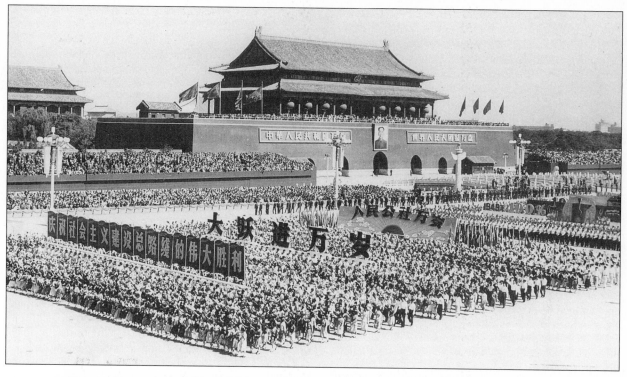

Tien An Men square, in front of the main gate to the Forbidden City. This is where the massacre of June 4, 1989, took place, but shown here is a parade to mark the tenth anniversary of the People's Republic on October 1, 1959. (Bettmann Archive)

The communes were quietly dissolved in all but name. Agriculture, still by far the largest sector of the economy, was largely organized on a "responsibility system" whereby individual families grew, on land still nominally owned by the commune, the crops which they judged most profitable in an economy which was now market-oriented. The state still took its tax share of farm output, but peasants were free to sell the rest in a free market which was encouraged as rewarding those who performed best. Those who did well under this system, and urban entrepreneurs who prospered in the small private businesses now permitted, felt free once again to display their new wealth. Expensive houses with television aerials sprouted here and there in the countryside, and in the cities motor scooters, tape recorders, washing machines, televisions, and refrigerators became more common. The new rich and even party officials began to indulge their personal tastes in clothing, including colors and Western-style or even high-fashion outfits instead of the drab uniform wear decreed in earlier years.

Some rural industry remained, where it was economically rational, but renewed emphasis was placed on large-scale and urban-based industrial production and on catching up with world advances in technology to make up for the lost years. Many factory and office managers and workers were now rewarded on the basis of productivity and profitability. Technological, managerial, and educational elites also reappeared, and with them the bourgeois lifestyles so feared by Mao as the antithesis of revolutionary socialism. In earlier debates during the Cultural Revolution, Teng Hsiao-p'ing had said "I don't care if a cat is red [socialist] or white [capitalist] as long as it catches mice," and he now put this dictum into practice. He insisted, however, that although performance should be central, China was still a socialist country under a Communist government which planned and managed the economy and which aimed to provide social justice. And all too soon, after 1986, he was to suppress the growing movement by students and intellectuals for freer expression and what they rather ambiguously called "democracy."

There has been no decline in government control over people's lives, direct and indirect, and the system in other respects, including the at least nominal state ownership of most means of production, is certainly socialist. For a time it was no longer so highly politicized or ideological and became flexible enough to include, especially in economic matters, provision of individual incentives as an aid to production and some other patterns

Small-scale rural industry: a commune hydroelectric plant. (R. Murphey)

which one may call capitalist, though one could argue that such things have long existed in nearly all economies, of varying political stripes. In any case, China's revolutionary fervor, and the utopian madness of 1966–1976, cooled, as all revolutions have in time. It was acknowledged that although Mao had been a great revolutionary leader before 1957 (some said before 1949), he had made major mistakes later which set the country back many years. He too largely ignored economic development and the basic need for "modernization," which were sacrificed to ideology, or as Mao put it, "politics in command." The dilemma remained how to "modernize" and yet retain the country's strongly held sense of distinctive Chinese pride and identity.

Most Chinese were weary of politics and ideology; those who had survived or were still redeemable wanted to get on with their lives and their careers, make up for what they called "the wasted years," and help to further China's aborted development. Despite the overdose of Maoist rhetoric, most Chinese still cared about their country, still wanted it to catch up and perhaps, one day, again lead the world as it had for so long in its glorious past. Most Chinese are phenomenally hardworking people. Under a more rationally organized system, perhaps Mao will be proved right after all, that over a billion Chinese, about one-fifth of the world, can indeed move mountains.

Achievements, and the Future

The years from 1949 to 1978 were by no means all chaos, and in fact the mass line, plus revolutionary fervor, national pride, organized group effort, and central direction accomplished a great deal. China remained poor, but there was encouraging growth in agriculture (except for 1958–1964) due to new irrigation and later better seeds and fertilization, and more rapid though uneven growth in industry, from a very small and limited base to begin with. In 1964 China tested a nuclear bomb and joined the ranks of the major powers. Thousands of miles of new railways and roads were built, and China became a major industrial power. As in India, where similar developments were taking place in these years, gains in production, especially in agriculture, were only a little greater than continued increases in population. One of China's greatest successes was in delivering basic health care to most of its people, including the system of so-called barefoot doctors who traveled even to remote villages, and the clinics established in every commune.

As in India, this greatly reduced the death rate, while the birthrate remained high, so that the population grew rapidly, nearly doubling from 1949 to the first real census in 1982. In the 1970s, China belatedly realized that this was perhaps its greatest problem, in terms of the per capita welfare by which real economic growth must be measured. Mao had declared that any talk of overpopulation was counterrevolutionary and anti-Chinese, but from 1983 families were severely discouraged from having more than a single child, an extreme, if temporary, policy which was seen as necessary for perhaps a generation if China was to escape from poverty. One-child families were rewarded, and those who had more were punished with economic sanctions. The task of providing enough basic necessities, let alone amenities, for the well over a billion Chinese already born is dismaying, let alone for future population increases. The population growth rate has been slowed, but over 20 million babies are still born every year.

Meanwhile there have been some substantial economic gains. Poverty at the bottom has been reduced (though far from eliminated) by increased production, better distribution, and the collective welfare system of communes and factories. Health levels, thanks in part to better nutrition as well as better medical care, have been greatly improved. Literacy has more than doubled, and about half the population now get as far as the early high school grades, although there are places for only about 3 per cent in the universities.

Living standards in the cities have risen far more rapidly and substantially, except for the overcrowded and inadequate housing, than in most rural areas. The growing urban-rural split in lifestyles and attitudes is a worrying problem for the heirs of a rural and peasant revolution, although it is one shared by all the rest of the developing world. Areas with poor soil, mountainous, semiarid, and remote areas lagged far behind the more productive ones, and in some of them there was widespread malnutrition. China's cities are not yet disfigured by masses of visibly homeless or unemployed, as are cities elsewhere in the developing world, but only because rigid controls on all movement and employment still prevent most rural people from moving cityward, as most of them clearly would like to do, despite the rhetoric of the Maoist vision. The cities are dangerously polluted, as bad as any in the world, the air a choking mixture of smoke and gases the Chinese call "Yellow Dragon" and the rivers and wells full of chemicals and heavy metals—the price of rapid industrialization. Progress in other respects too has been won at the cost of state and collective social controls and the suppression of personal choices. This is not as disturbing to most Chinese as it might be to most Westerners, since the subordination of individualism to group effort and group welfare has long been central to their tradition.

China's past achievements, and its revolutionary progress, were due in large part to the primacy of responsibility and the pursuit of common goals over privilege and self-interest. Nevertheless there have been protests and even demonstrations against the continuing controls on free expression and free choice of employment. As China opened its doors to more normal interchange with the rest of the world, more Chinese have come to see their political system as repressive. Many would argue that it has other important virtues, and that some controls remain necessary. But China needs to make up for the years of isolation and destructive ideological aberrations, rebuild its education and technological systems, and move ahead with what it now calls "modernization," recognizing that this must include a large infusion of foreign technology and foreign ideas— and perhaps also a greater scope for individual creativity.

The liberation of women, one of the goals of the revolution, is still relatively far from attainment, although there has been considerable progress. Women are no longer as oppressed as they were under the old society, but they are still far from equal, even less so than in the contemporary United States. The new marriage law of 1950 gave them equality with men in marriage rights, divorce, and the ownership of property, which was a major step forward, and Mao declared that "women hold up half the sky." The traditional extended family—three generations living under one roof—has largely gone, especially in the cities, and with it the authority of the oldest surviving grandparents. A grandmother, and sometimes a grandfather, may live with a son's family but now serves more commonly as baby-sitter, shopper, and general household help, representing the family on neighborhood committees while the wife goes out to work. Nearly all adult women in China have full-time jobs outside the home, but they are usually not paid equally with men, and at the end of the workday it is usually they who cook the meals, clean the house, and care for the children. On the other hand, employers or the state provide extensive child-care facilities for working mothers, far more than in the United States. The top positions in government, business, industry, and education are held almost entirely by men, with occasional token female representation on committees. At the same time, just about all occupations and professions are open to women; they are probably a higher proportion of professionals than in the United States, but most Chinese women work in lower-level or even menial jobs. And despite government efforts to persuade people that daughters are as good as sons, most families still give sons the first priority since only they will continue the family line and can provide some security for aged parents, as daughters still become members of their husband's family at marriage.

There are considerable differences between city and countryside in all these respects, with the rural areas clinging more to traditional values and patterns—including the production of more children in the effort to have

"Women hold up half the sky," as Mao said, and since 1950 have entered many occupations previously reserved for men. *(China Reconstructs)*

a son or sons. Nearly all urban and now most rural women do at least keep their own names after marriage, and there is in general a major change from the old society in the status of and attitudes toward women. But China, like Japan, and like most of the rest of Asia outside the Southeast, still has a long way to go before women are truly equal members of society.

Renewed Demands for Liberalization

In 1987, 1988, and 1989 the government under Deng Xiaoping became increasingly repressive in its response to growing disaffection and protests against "thought control." Meanwhile inflation mounted, badly damaging

most people, and there was widespread and bitter resentment of the unchecked corruption of party officials and those, especially businessmen, who had "connections" to them. In May of 1989, crowds of students began to demonstrate in Tien An Men square in Peking, Communist China's chief parade ground and ceremonial center where Mao had once addressed a million cheering followers waving his "Little Red Book." Now the students were asking instead for "democracy" and eventually even built a cardboard statue of "The Goddess of Liberty" modeled on the statue in New York Harbor. Their demands were vague, and there were few attempts to make them more specific, but they were clearly inspired by the recent increases in contact with the rest of the world, especially with the United States, as well as reflecting unhappiness with censorship, controlled job assignment, inflation, corruption, and political dictatorship. Communist China's 25 *million* officials, or more, had become a terrible burden, hated by most people as well as resented, as China had become the most closely controlled state in world history. The student demonstrations, briefly joined by a few of the local population, were never violent, but the government regarded them as a threat, and after some two weeks of hesitation as different responses were debated, the hard-liners in the government won out. On the night of June 3 and the following day, the army and its tanks moved in to crush the demonstrators, killing perhaps as many as a thousand unarmed students.

The demonstrators had challenged an all-powerful state, and it responded as it had so often before. China has never had parliamentary democracy, free expression, or the rule of Western-style law—nor have Western states responded very differently in the past to similar direct challenges. But the brutality of what soon came to be called "The Peking Massacre," enacted in front of the world's television cameras, sent shock waves around the world, as the Soviet Union and eastern Europe were entering an exciting new phase of liberation. China stood out as isolated and condemned, except for continued U.S. support. In the wake of June 4, the government imprisoned many of the surviving demonstrators, as well as many thousands of "liberals," executed several, and resumed full force its earlier policies of censorship, suppression, the apparatus of the police state, and strident denunciations of all forms of Western influence and lifestyles. Meanwhile it continued its brutal suppression of protests in Tibet against Chinese efforts to stamp out expressions of Tibetan identity and requests for a more genuine role in the administration of their supposedly "Autonomous" Area.

Officially, all religions were tolerated in China after 1950, despite the Communist stance against religion.

✠ The East Is Red ✠

Like a symbol of the Unequal Treaties, the clock on the foreign-built Customs House on the Shanghai Bund rang the Westminster chimes every quarter hour, familiar to Westerners but alien to Chinese. Early in the Cultural Revolution, in 1966, these were replaced by chimes which played instead "The East Is Red," from a popular patriotic song of the time.

Over a century ago the Western colonialist robbers crashed the gates of China. By controlling China's Maritime Customs they drained away the blood of the Chinese working people. The heavy church-like chimes of the big clock on the customs building ... were a constant reminder of this imperialist exploitation. Control of the Maritime Customs was taken back by the Chinese people in 1949 when Shanghai was liberated, but the imperialist chimes stayed on. Then came China's great cultural revolution ... clearing away the remnant traces of filth left over from the old Shanghai.

Source: From the account published in *China Reconstructs*, Peking, Vol. 16, Feb. 1967, p. 10.

But Christianity, which survived for perhaps a million Chinese and minority adherents, was "purged" of its foreign connections, all foreign missionaries expelled, and the church put in charge of Chinese clergy, dependent only on local financial support. There are said to be more Christians now than ever in China's past, including "unofficial" church groups. After 1978, Christians and their churches became more acceptable and visible, as did Buddhists, Taoists, Muslims, and their temples or mosques, with qualified official approval. The approval was especially qualified in strongly Lamaist-Buddhist Tibet, where there had been earlier Chinese efforts to eradicate Buddhism as a badge of Tibetan separatism. Muslims remained by far the largest religious group, including perhaps 50 million Chinese Muslims, often indistinguishable from other Chinese except by avoidance of pork, in addition to the Uighurs and other Turkish Islamic groups.

As of late 1995, the future of the present regime in Peking remained cloudy. The death of Deng Xiaoping was anticipated by many as being followed by a power struggle, openly or behind the scenes, among the different factions in Chinese politics representing different approaches to the country's problems, and different responses to the very widespread discontent. Most state enterprises, the core of the economy, were poorly managed, and most lost money as they fell even further behind technologically, although there was considerable improvement after 1992. But there was strong growth in the expanding private sector, and with it destructive inflation from the overheated economy. Unemployment, open and disguised, remained a major problem. There was a floating population of some 80 million construction and factory workers in the booming cities, trucked in daily or weekly from the countryside, housed in shacks and poorly paid, but this was still more attractive than the limited opportunities and even lower pay in most of the rural sector. Unknown but very large numbers remained in the cities as illegal immigrants.

Exports soared as "market forces" triumphed everywhere, especially in the new free-trade zones in and around several coastal cities. Southeast Kwangtung (Guangdong) adjacent to Hong Kong became one of the fastest growing economic areas in the modern world, along with Hong Kong itself. But some of the exports also came from prison labor, and there were said to be at least 20 million prisoners in China, many of them political. Figures which show the growth rate of the Chinese economy as the world's highest are thus somewhat misleading, and do not adequately reflect the bulk of the country or its population, which remains rural-agricultural and includes major pockets of genuine poverty.

The "free-market" policies continue to spawn vast corruption, a huge illegal underground economy, and more "bourgeois elements." There were discos, nightclubs, and beauty parlors in most cities and even a nightclub owned by the People's Liberation Army in Canton. Mao would be horrified.

Meanwhile the push for economic growth at any cost accelerated further destruction of the remaining forests and further hastened erosion, while the cities and their water supplies grew even more polluted. The economic "reforms" beginning in the 1980s with the rise of the free market and the failure or reduction of many state-owned enterprises generated massive unemployment, especially with the abandonment of the "iron rice bowl" of guaranteed employment in the state sector. This was accompanied by a growing wave of crime, especially by juveniles (under 18) who by the 1990s were over 75 percent of all criminals.

The Chinese people have suffered terribly under successive regimes: the last decades of the deteriorating Ch'ing dynasty, the warlord years after its collapse in 1911, the reactionary, oppressive, and ineffective Kuomintang, and the long nightmare of Maoism, some of which was revived after 1986; "foreign influences" were again reviled, "bourgeois" and "rightist" tendencies declaimed against, and from 1989 "political study" was again required of all students.

✠ Trial by Mob ✠

At the height of the Cultural Revolution in 1967 Red Guards often took it on themselves to attack, or "struggle with" as they called it, people identified as rightists. Sometimes they carried to extremes orders originating higher up. Here is part of an account of the mob arrest and trial of Liu Hsiao-ch'i's wife, Wang Kuang-mei; her clothes and "bourgeois lifestyle" made her a target.

More and more big character posters, cartoons, and slogans appeared [on the campus of Tsinghua University in Peking] attacking Liu Shao-ch'i's wife Wang Kuang-mei.... With material on Liu himself far too scanty, the central authorities had granted the Red Guards permission to check all the files on Liu's visits to foreign countries.... It was here that a hole in [his] armor was found: his wife was a capitalist-class member.... "Wang Kuang-mei is caught in the net!" The news spread swiftly.... Using the only loudspeaker still under their control, the Headquarters announced a mass meeting ... to struggle with "capitalist element Wang Kuang-mei."... Wang's daughter ... was taken by surprise in a classroom and forced by the Red Guards to accompany them to the Peking Medical College, where she called her father's home ... and was made to tell her mother that she had been seriously injured.... Because of her deep love for her daughter, Wang rushed to the hospital ... and was captured—as easily as that.... [At the mass meeting] The chairman [said] "Drag out capitalist-class element Wang Kuang-mei to face the people!" Instantly a deafening roar of slogan shouting began.... She was in a blue cadre uniform, modest and plain.... There was a trace of a smile on her pale face. She was guarded by four girl Red Guards who walked her ... across the stage several times so that everyone could have a good look at her. From time to time the Guards tugged at her hair, making her lower her head.... Wang lowered her head and confessed her crime and apologized ... in a barely audible voice.... She admitted ... that her awareness had been poor.... The chairman cut her short, denouncing her poor attitude.... There were shouts from the audience: "Let her show off her ugly look. Make her put on the [dress] she wore in Indonesia! We want to see this stinking woman's pose!" ... She stood shivering in her bright silk dress, her head shrunk in her shoulders ... the collar of the dress was yanked open ... her hair was tousled like a mop.... We heard her sobbing voice: "Did Chairman Mao ask you to do this? ... [The chairman pronounced sentence.] The party central authorities [should] immediately dismiss her from all her posts. In addition she should undergo reform-through-labor in earnest and further expose the crimes of her husband in order to redeem her own crimes.... But no one was listening any longer to her reply.

Source: K. Ling, *The Revenge of Heaven: Journal of a Young Chinese* (New York: Putnam, 1972), pp. 198–214.

Here come the barefoot doctors, carrying basic medicines and treatment to remote villages. Unfortunately, the program was discontinued in the 1970s as medical services became more and more concentrated in cities and towns. (*China Reconstructs*)

A symbol of the new China: proletarian poster art showing a peasant moving the mountains. (*China Reconstructs*)

Taiwan

The island of Formosa (Taiwan) had been taken over by the Japanese in 1895 after their victory over China (see Chapter 13) as part of their colonial empire, but with Japan's defeat in 1945 it was returned to Chinese sovereignty. In 1949 Taiwan became the sole remaining base for the defeated Kuomintang, defended against the Communist mainland by American military power, including the U.S. Seventh Fleet patrolling the Taiwan Strait. Some two million mainland Chinese, including units of the Kuomintang army and government, fled to Taiwan, where they largely excluded the Taiwanese from any political power. The island was settled mainly by Chinese from Fukien (Fujian) Province, just across the narrow strait which separates it from the mainland. They retained their Chinese culture but developed some separate regional feeling, especially under Japanese control; their language, known as Taiwanese, is in fact Fukienese, not mutually intelligible with standard Chinese.

This heightened feelings of difference, as did their relatively frontier circumstances compared with overcrowded south China as they cleared and settled Taiwan, under very loose and often ineffective control from distant Peking. Taiwanese had fought underground against Japanese rule, and welcomed the mainlanders in 1945, hoping to work with them in forming an administration for the island, now again a Chinese province. But after brutally repressive actions against them in 1947 and the massacre of most of their political leaders by the

Mao's Farewell

At the end of his life, Mao wrote a poem to the dying Chou En-lai in 1975 that looked back over the past 40 years and anticipated his own end.

Loyal parents who sacrificed so much for the nation
Never feared the ultimate fate.
Now that the country has become Red,
Who will be its guardians?
Our mission, unfinished, may take a thousand years;
The struggle tires us, and our hair is gray.
You and I, old friend,
Can we just watch our efforts being washed away?

Source: Quoted in M. Meisner, *Mao's China* (New York: Free Press, 1977), pp. 380–381.

Kuomintang, they tended to regard their new masters as oppressors even worse than the Japanese. The mass influx of 1949 tightened Kuomintang control and excluded Taiwanese from power, as "carpetbaggers" from the mainland dominated the scene.

Nevertheless, Taiwan in the 1950s began a period of rapid economic growth, at first with heavy American aid and then by the early 1960s on its own. An American-directed land reform program, ignored by the Kuomintang while it was in power on the mainland, gave farmers new incentives, plus increased supplies of fertilizer, new crop strains, and new irrigation. Growing rural prosperity was matched and, by the 1970s, exceeded, by boom industrial growth as Taiwan developed into a smaller-scale version of the Japanese "economic miracle." Taiwan's path was much the same, including its technological achievements and both light and heavy manufacturing, beginning with textiles and other consumer goods and moving rapidly into electronics, high-tech products, shipbuilding, and industrial goods. As in Japan earlier, many components were made on a small scale or even household basis, and brought new prosperity to rural as well as urban areas. Living standards rose sharply, and most Taiwanese became relatively affluent, as well as well educated. As elsewhere, the two were causally linked. This was some recompense for their lack of political voice, but slowly Kuomintang domination became less rigid and Taiwanese began to play a fuller part in the political life of the island. Industrial development exacted a price, as in Japan, in dangerous pollution, especially in Taipei, the capital, lying in a basin surrounded by hills and by the 1980s one of the world's most polluted cities.

Taiwan's trade with the rest of the world quickly exceeded that of vastly larger mainland China, as it still does. Taipei became a huge, overcrowded city, and was joined by other rapidly growing industrial and port centers. Prosperity, wider relations with the rest of the world, and an unspoken acceptance of political realities in China and East Asia began by the 1980s to help soften somewhat the harsher aspects of Kuomintang control, and to end earlier goals to "reconquer the mainland." The Maoist economic disaster, contrasting so dramatically with Taiwan's new prosperity, bolstered confidence. More representation and more positions were offered to the Taiwanese, and the beginnings of more freedom of expression. These trends accelerated after the death of Chiang Kai-shek in 1975, and under his son Chiang Ching-kuo, who succeeded him as president, until his death in 1988. The vice president, Li Teng-hui, then became president, as the first native-born Taiwanese to do so, and was later confirmed by the Kuomintang party. He was inaugurated in 1990 as the head of what was becoming a multiparty democracy with an active political opposition, which won a substantial number of legislative seats in the first islandwide and largely free elections of 1986. Li supported continuing liberalization within the Kuomintang, and encouraged the further growth of private and interpersonal travel and economic contacts with the mainland, while indirect trade with the People's Republic, via Hong Kong, continued to increase. Reunification remained a distant goal, but both sides began to make formal and informal overtures to each other. Taiwan was shocked by the brutal crackdown in China in June of 1989 and after, and moves toward some qualified reconciliation were abruptly slowed. Much will depend on what happens to Hong Kong under Chinese rule from 1997, but in 1994 opposition candidates won more seats than the KMT.

Deng Xiaoping and President Jimmy Carter sign an agreement in 1979 providing for scientific, technological, and trade exchanges. (UPI/Bettmann)

Hong Kong

The tiny and mountainous island of Hong Kong, just off the mouth of the West River which leads to Canton, had been ceded in perpetuity to the British in 1841 as an incident of the so-called Opium War. Adjacent Kowloon, on the mainland peninsula across the harbor, was also ceded permanently in 1860 at the Treaty of Tientsin. In 1898, additional adjoining territory on the mainland, called "The New Territories," was leased for 99 years, to supply Hong Kong with food and water and to provide some room for expansion as Hong Kong grew rapidly in the nineteenth and twentieth centuries. Although under British control as a Crown Colony, Hong Kong remained an overwhelmingly Chinese city like the coastal treaty ports, peopled by immigrants from overcrowded south China who brought with them their interest and skill in commerce and their capacity for hard work. Hong Kong flourished mainly as a trade entrepôt, a duty-free port serving all of the China coast, and as a center for international banking, finance, and insurance. With the Communist victory in China, Hong Kong was isolated from its major market, for which it had served as a leading foreign trade port. At the same time, it was flooded by waves of refugees from the mainland.

The city and its resourceful people survived the crisis by developing a highly successful array of light manufacturing industries, first in cotton textiles and then in a wide range of electronics and high-tech consumer goods. All these were necessarily dependent on imported raw materials but were made profitable by low-wage labor and efficient factories, plus the advantages of a duty-free port for imports and exports. Hong Kong also continued to serve as an international shipping, banking, and financial center, and despite the great decline in direct trade with China, handled indirectly about half of China's foreign trade. It also served as China's window on the rest of the world, and through the stream of refugees provided much information about the catastrophic events after 1949, when foreigners and the foreign press were excluded. One of the grisly measures of the violence during the Cultural Revolution was the bodies which floated down the West (Hsi or Xi) River to Hong Kong, many of them with hands or feet bound and throats slit, despite efforts by the Chinese authorities to fish the bodies out before they reached Hong Kong waters.

Hong Kong's swollen population was in time housed more or less adequately in both government and private apartment blocks, another achievement to the credit of the government and people of Hong Kong, although crowding was high and in many cases one or more families lived in one room. Hong Kong became probably the most densely crowded city in the world. At the same time, with virtually full employment, it joined Japan, Taiwan, and South Korea as one of the fastest growing economies in the world. The city has little heavy industry and has thus avoided the worst pollution, helped still more by usually strong winds off the sea, but rising incomes have also been accompanied by heavy vehicular traffic, both private cars and trucks and buses. To help ease traffic congestion, a vehicular tunnel has been built under the harbor between Hong Kong Island and Kowloon, and preliminary work begun on a new airport on another island, Lan Tau, linked to the mainland by causeway. Hong Kong's harbor, shielded from wave

Hong Kong in 1990. The building boom continues as reabsorption by China approaches. Although that may be disastrous politically and for human rights, most people foresee little change in Hong Kong's vigorously growing economy. (Superstock, Inc.)

age, with much of the shipments between them going by water.

Like its analogues in Taiwan, Japan, and South Korea, Hong Kong puts great stress on education, and its economic success is clearly attributable to that major investment. By the 1960s Hong Kong became even more prosperous than it had been before World War II, and as China began to resume trade outside the Communist bloc, Hong Kong regained its former role as a major shipping, distribution, commercial, and financial center for East and Southeast Asia, a function which it shared with another exclave Chinese city, Singapore. By 1995 the city and its small, adjacent territories approached a population of six million. But the Chinese government announced, and Britain perforce agreed in 1985, that when the lease of those territories expired on June 30, 1997, they and all of Hong Kong (plus Portuguese Macao) would be reclaimed. It remains to be seen how this citadel of capitalism will be integrated with the still supposedly socialist system of the People's Republic. Hong Kong has flourished since its founding as a kind of "alternate China," a base for revolutionaries and dissidents (including Sun Yat-sen), and an arena where Cantonese and later Shanghainese entrepreneurial talents have found a free field unhampered by traditional government, Confucian restraints or prejudice, or Communist controls. The events of June 1989 shocked Hong Kong even more than Taiwan, given its imminent absorption. As June 1997 approaches, there have been repeated anti-Peking demonstrations and last-minute efforts by the British colonial government, working with Hong Kong representatives, to introduce some elements of democratic government previously largely ignored, seemingly by mutual agreement. The business of Hong Kong has always been to make money, and little else has mattered. But Hong Kong has been highly profitable to China, and is also an outstanding example of the kind of economic success China badly needs. Much of the Hong Kong model has spilled over the border into southeast China, and has helped to give the P.R.C. for the past several years the highest economic growth rate in the world. By 1997, a more enlightened government in Peking may feel it has much to learn from Hong Kong's example and may make a fuller place for it within an evolving Chinese system.

action by many islands and with plenty of deep water, is one of the finest in the world, and given the volume of its trade, since 1978 overwhelmingly with China, it has become the world's largest container port. In many respects it serves as the deepwater port or outport for Canton, whose harbor is small and shallow, some 40 miles up the West River and well above the estuary where silting makes for problems. There is now through rail and road service from Kowloon to Canton, but the two cities have always functioned in a close link-

Suggestions for Further Reading

Bonavia, D. *The Chinese.* New York: Harper and Row, 1984.

Chan, M. K., ed. *Precarious Balance: Hong Kong Between China and Britain.* Armonk, NY: M. E. Sharpe, 1994.

Chang, Jung. *Wild Swans: Three Daughters of China.* New York: Simon and Schuster, 1991.

Chen, Jo-hsi. *The Execution of Mayor Yin.* Bloomington: Indiana Univ. Press, 1982.

Cheng, C. Y. *Behind the Tienanmen Massacre.* Boulder: Westview, 1990.

Ching, F. *Hong Kong and China.* New York: The Asia Society, 1985.

Cooper, J. F. *Taiwan.* Boulder: Westview, 1989.

Dietrich, C. *People's China: A Brief History.* Oxford: Oxford University Press, 1994.

Dikkotter, F. *The Discourse of Race in Modern China.* Stanford: Stanford University Press, 1992.

Evans, R. *Dengxiaoping and the Making of Modern China.* New York: Viking, 1994.

Fairbank, J. K. *The Great Chinese Revolution.* Cambridge: Harvard University Press, 1986.

———, et al., eds. *The Cambridge History of China, Vol. 14, 1949–79.* Cambridge: Cambridge University Press, 1987.

Goldman, M. *China's Intellectuals and the State.* Harvard, 1987.

Goldstein, M. C. *A History of Modern Tibet.* Berkely: University of California Press, 1989.

Harding, H. *China's Second Revolution: Reform after Mao.* Washington: Brookings, 1987.

He, Bochuan. *China on the Edge: Crisis of Ecology and Development in China.* San Francisco: China Books, 1992.

Hsu, I. C. Y. *China Since Mao.* Oxford Univ. Press, 1990.

Lardy, N. *China in the World Economy.* Washington: Institute for International Economics, 1994.

Li, Y. N. *Chinese Women Through Chinese Eyes.* Armonk, NY: M. E. Sharpe, 1992.

Liang, H., and Shapiro, J. *Son of the Revolution.* New York: Knopf, 1984.

Liu, Binyan. *China's Crisis, China's Hope.* Cambridge: Harvard University Press, 1990.

Long, S. *Taiwan: China's Last Frontier.* New York: St. Martins, 1991.

Meisner, M. *Mao's China and After.* New York: Free Press, 1986.

Nathan, A. *China's Crisis: Dilemmas of Reform and Prospects for Democracy.* New York: Columbia University Press, 1990.

Rubinstein, M. A., ed. *The Other Taiwan.* Armonk, NY: M. E. Sharpe, 1994.

Schram, S. *Mao Tse-tung: A Preliminary Reassessment.* New York: Simon and Schuster, 1984.

Schrecker, J. *The Chinese Revolution in Historical Perspective.* New York: Praeger, 1991.

Simon, D. F., and Kau, Y. M., eds. *Taiwan: Beyond the Economic Miracle.* Armonk, NY: M. E. Sharpe, 1992.

Smil, V. *China's Environmental Crisis.* Armonk, NY: M. E. Sharpe, 1993.

Sutter, R. G. *Taiwan: Entering the Twenty-first Century.* New York: University Press of America, 1989.

Thurston, A. *The Ordeal of the Intellectuals in China's Great Cultural Revolution.* Cambridge: Harvard University Press, 1988.

Ts'ai, I. F. *Hong Kong in Chinese History.* Berkeley: University of California Press, 1993.

Vogel, E. *The Four Little Dragons.* Cambridge: Harvard University Press, 1992.

Watson, R. S., and Ebrey P. B., eds. *Marriage and Inequality in Chinese Society.* Berkeley: University of California Press, 1991.

Wolf, M. *Revolution Postponed: Women in Contemporary China.* Stanford: Stanford University Press, 1985.

Woronoff, J. *Asia's Miracle Economics.* Armonk, NY: M. E. Sharpe, 1992.

Wu, H. *Laogai: The Chinese Gulag.* Boulder: Westview, 1992.

Yahuda, M. *Hong Kong: China's Opportunity.* London: Routledge, 1996.

CHAPTER 21

JAPAN AND KOREA SINCE 1945

Meeting at Potsdam near Berlin on July 26, 1945, the victorious Allies, who had defeated Germany, called on Japan to surrender "unconditionally," an unwise move which stiffened the Japanese will to resist and which proved in the end to be inaccurate, since the surrender which was later accepted retained the institution of the emperor, a major Japanese concern. Tojo, the wartime prime minister, had been replaced as the tide turned strongly against Japan in July 1944, and the successor government was uncertain of the meaning of "unconditional"; it sent an ambiguous reply, but meanwhile prepared for the worst. Hiroshima, the Russian invasion of Manchuria, and Nagasaki led to an imperial conference in which Hirohito, the emperor, broke the deadlock in favor of surrender. Late on August 14 he recorded his message calling on all Japanese to lay down their arms, which was broadcast by radio on the 15th all over Japan and the occupied territories. He spoke in the old court language of Heian Japan and many had trouble following it, but the gist was clear. The Allies quickly agreed to allow the continuation of the emperor as ceremonial head of state though without real powers, as had always been the case; his name and authority had been vital in ensuring compliance with his call to surrender. Many Japanese kneeled and/or bowed to his voice as they heard the broadcast. The Allies now correctly saw the institution of the emperor as providing essential continuity under their military occupation, and even as adding some sanction to their authority, ensuring the co-operation of the Japanese people. Breaking imperial precedent, Hirohito called on General MacArthur, the Occupation commander, at his downtown office, took on himself full responsibility for the war, and allowed himself to be photographed, like an ordinary person, although formally dressed, standing beside the general in his casual outfit. He also denied his supposed divinity, as the Allies wanted him to do.

The Revival of Japan

Japan, especially its cities, had been more completely destroyed by the war than any of the other belligerents. In addition to Hiroshima and Nagasaki, Tokyo and Yokohama were largely flattened and burned out, as were all large and most smaller cities, except for Kyoto, the old imperial capital, which was preserved by the intervention of American scholars in art history. The government, and what remained of the army in the home islands, were still however in good order and discipline, and there was a smooth transfer of power to the American military government of occupation. Japan had surrendered to the Allied forces, including Britain, China, Australia, Canada, New Zealand, and the Soviet Union, all of whom had contributed to Japan's defeat. But MacArthur permitted only token representation from each of the other allies in his SCAP (Supreme Commander Allied Powers) regime of occupation, over which he

Modern Japan

knew the Japanese language and were thus far more dependent on the conquered people than in the Occupation of Germany.

Occupation and Americanization

Relief on finding the occupying forces bent on reconstruction rather than revenge was soon joined by gratitude for American aid. Most Japanese had lived at best on an austerity diet during the last years of the war, and many were half starved, living in makeshift shelters in the bombed-out cities. The winter of 1945–1946 would have been far harder if the Americans had not flown in emergency supplies of food, and got the main rail lines working again to transport fuel and essential building supplies. Having expected far worse from their new

Emperor Hirohito of Japan with General MacArthur at the U.S. Embassy in Tokyo in 1945. (Bettmann Archive)

presided like a new emperor, in control of a wholly American enterprise.

With very few exceptions, the Japanese people, including officials, officers, and troops as well as other civilians, accepted their emperor's pronouncement of surrender and his call to "endure the unendurable." Japan had never known defeat in war by foreigners, and for many it was a bitter experience. But most felt primarily relief that the disastrous war was over. They soon found that the occupying Americans were not the devils which some had feared, and saved their bitterness for their now discredited military leaders who had so nearly destroyed the nation they were sworn to serve. In general, the years of the Occupation, from late August 1945 to late April 1952, were peaceful, constructive, and impressively cooperative, with Japanese doing most of the work of government except at the highest level, under American supervision. Very few Americans rulers, the Japanese were pleasantly surprised. Many were even enthusiastic about the institutional changes which SCAP began to decree so as to root out militarism and implant American-style democracy.

The big prewar industrial combines (*zaibatsu* firms) were broken up, although they were subsequently revived even before the end of the Occupation. Thousands of political prisoners who had been accused of "dangerous thoughts" by the military-controlled government of the 1930s and 1940s were released. Other Japanese who were identified—sometimes wrongly—as too closely associated with the Japanese version of fascism or with armed expansion abroad were removed from their posts, including a number of senior officials, altogether about 200,000 people, although most of these "purgees" reentered public life after 1952 when the Occupation ended. Several hundred other Japanese were identified as suspected "war criminals," and most were tried by a special tribunal in Tokyo which included Allied representatives. Seven were executed, including the wartime prime minister, Tojo, and 18 others sentenced to prison terms. Nearly a thousand "minor war criminals" in Japan and Southeast Asia, largely military men, were executed for gross cruelty to prisoners or to inhabitants of conquered countries. This contrasted with the far more lenient treatment and in some cases even protection of all but the top Nazi leaders by the United States and its allies in Europe, and prompted charges of racism.

A victor's justice in the aftermath of a bitter war is easily criticized, but most Japanese accepted the tribunal's verdict as inevitable, and perhaps even appropriate punishment; most blamed their failed leaders rather than their new masters. The national ability to accept what cannot be helped, and to change direction in keeping with new circumstances, had been demonstrated often before, most recently in the sweeping changes carried out after Japan had been forced by Western powers to open its doors in the 1850s. But it impressed the Americans, who had expected a sullen and resentful populace and found instead that they were both liked and admired. Americans were admired because they had won, and because not only their relief and reconstruction efforts but their moves toward the "democratization" of Japan were generally popular. The Japanese people had suffered terribly from militarism and its police state and were ready to follow new paths. American ways were sought after by many uncritically, but the basic political reforms of the Occupation struck a deeper responsive cord.

Most of the changes were reaffirmed after the Occupation ended, except for the *zaibatsu* dissolution, and have struck firm roots in contemporary Japan, or perhaps more accurately were grafted onto earlier Japanese efforts to adopt Western institutions of government, law, education, and culture which had been in eclipse during the years from 1931 to 1945. In addition to a revitalization of electoral and party democracy, government was decentralized by giving more power to local organs. Public education, formerly supervised closely by the central government, was also decentralized and freed as much as possible from bureaucratic control. The American system of 6–3–3 grades was followed and coeducation became the norm. Post-high-school institutions proliferated and in time Japan became second only to the U.S. in the proportion of its population going on to higher or further education. One of the most successful and permanent changes was the SCAP-directed land reform, which put a ceiling of ten acres on individual holdings and compensated the large owners whose property was expropriated. The land was sold at low prices to former tenants, in a way the last blow to the surviving traces of Tokugawa feudalism. Japanese society began to move rapidly toward its present very considerable social equality, where status results from achievement rather than birth.

The new constitution drafted by SCAP officials retained the emperor as a figurehead but vested all real power in a legislature and prime minister elected by universal suffrage. The constitution, adopted by the Diet in 1946, stated that sovereignty rested not with the emperor but with the people of Japan. The emperor was defined as a symbol of the state—a limited monarch similar to British or Scandinavian patterns, although the Japanese emperor has remained much more aloof from the public. There was a detailed Bill of Rights for the protection of individuals against arbitrary state power. Women aged 20 and over were given the right to vote, and there was a new bureau to protect the rights of women and children. Primogeniture was abolished as a hangover from the feudal past, although this was easily got around by those who wanted to, through indirect arrangements. Article Nine of the constitution forbade Japan to have any armed forces except for police, and denied it the right to go to war. To most Japanese this was not only reasonable but welcome, given the ruin that arms and warfare had brought on them. Japan, many felt, should set an example to the rest of the world of the folly of war. More than anything else, what soured the Occupation was the shift in American policy beginning in 1948, as the Cold War intensified, toward rebuilding Japan's military capacity and using it as a base of American military operation. This and other changes like the crackdown on labor unions, originally promoted by the Occupation as part of "democratization," but now suspect as "leftist," was referred to as "reverse course."

The goal of making Japan a Cold War ally of the United States soon became more important than reform. The Berlin blockade, the final Communist victory in

✠ MacArthur: An Assessment ✠

*Most observers described General MacArthur as a vain man, ever con-
scious of his public image. Here is a leading Western historian's assess-
ment of MacArthur in his role as the head of SCAP from 1945 to 1951.*

A tendency toward complacent self-dramatization was encouraged by the adulation of a
devoted wartime staff that he took with him to Japan.... They took almost ludicrous care
that only the rosiest reports of the occupation should reach the outside world. In their
debased opinion the slightest criticism of SCAP amounted to something approaching
sacrilege. MacArthur took up residence in the United States Embassy in Tokyo. Each day at
the same hour he was driven to his office in a large building facing the palace moat; at the
same hour each day he was driven home again.... He never toured Japan to see things for
himself.... The irreverent were heard to say that if a man rose early in the morning he
might catch a glimpse of the Supreme Commander walking on the waters of the palace
moat. There is no doubt that this aloofness impressed Japanese of the conservative type....
But it may well be doubted whether this kind of awed respect was compatible with the
healthy growth of democratic sentiment.... The Japanese perhaps learned more about
democracy from MacArthur's dismissal than from anything he himself ever did or said.

Source: R. Storry, *A History of Modern Japan* (Harmondsworth: Pelican Books, 1982), pp. 240–241.

China in 1949, and the Korean War all further hardened
the American line. Although MacArthur was fired by
President Truman in April 1951 for his irresponsible
management of the Korean War, Cold War considerations continued to dominate American policy, and when
the Occupation ended in 1952 Japan was bound to the
United States by a security treaty which permitted the
buildup of a Japanese "self-defense force," the stationing
of American troops, and their use of several major bases
in Japan. American pressures for Japanese rearmament
have continued, and the bases remain, but Article Nine
of the constitution still has the support of most Japanese.

The Occupation was after all a military government,
and it is not perhaps surprising therefore that free
speech was suppressed, despite SCAP pronouncements
and the official line that Japan was to be "democratized."
All Japanese publications were censored, as was all information coming into or out of Japan, especially about
SCAP itself, where only the most laudatory accounts
were permitted. With few exceptions, only American
journalists were allowed to function in Japan, and they
risked expulsion if what they wrote offended SCAP,
most of all its chief, MacArthur, whose own antecedents
had been highly conservative, and who now functioned
like a dictator. The Japanese of course saw this, but they
were no strangers to authoritarianism or to controls on
free speech, and in some ways the self-aggrandisement

of MacArthur and his dictatorial ways as well as his
aloofness from day-to-day affairs and from the Japanese
public fitted in with their notions of the way rulers of
Japan in the past had behaved. MacArthur never bothered to leave his well-protected office in downtown
Tokyo to see how the Occupation programs were doing,
or how they were responded to by Japanese. In this too
he was like a Japanese emperor, supposedly above the
dust of politics, but his own conservative point of view
was strongly represented in everything the Occupation
did, including the removal of restrictions on the *zaibatsu*
when Cold War pressures made it seem that the Japanese economy must be rebuilt if Japan were to become a
powerful ally.

Even the existence of SCAP censorship was "classified," but perhaps its worst transgression against free
speech was its total cover-up of the effects of atomic
bombing at Hiroshima and Nagasaki, where thousands
continued to die of radiation sickness long after the ex-
plosions. Many of those who were in Hiroshima or Nagasaki continue to suffer from it and to die prematurely,
but during the Occupation it was forbidden to report any
of this. Originally it was felt that labor unions, suppressed under the former Japanese government, were
an important part of "democratization," but they proved
to be highly political as well as infiltrated by Communists, whom the Occupation purged, as well as putting
sharp restrictions on the right to strike.

✖ Democratization Under the Occupation ✖

The new constitution imposed by the American Occupation, but prepared by the new leaders and ratified by the Diet, set up a cabinet drawn from the majority party. The vote was extended to all men and women age 20 or more, there was an independent judiciary, and the standard Western rights of assembly, free press, and free speech were guaranteed. The emperor was retained as a national symbol, "deriving his position from the will of the people with whom resides sovereign power." Article 9 declared:

The Japanese people forever renounce war as a sovereign right of the nation and the threat or use of force as means of settling international disputes.... Land, sea, and air forces, as well as other war potential, will never be maintained. The right of belligerency of the state will not be recognized.

In fact, the 'self-defense force' has grown over the years and is now a formidable assembly of warships, armed troops, and planes, most of the arms being supplied by the United States.
The peerage was abolished, and Article 20 stated that:

All of the people are equal under the law and there shall be no discrimination in political, economic, or social relations because of race, creed, sex, social status, or family origin.

Source: As summarized in W. S. Morton, *Japan*, New York: McGraw Hill, 1994, p. 206.

Economic and Social Development

Whatever the political shifts and the change in attitudes as the Occupation wore on, economic reconstruction was almost miraculously rapid. By 1950 the shattered cities and rail lines had been largely rebuilt, and most of the factories. By the end of 1951 industrial production was about equal to what it had been in 1931, but now from new and more efficient plants. The Korean War (see later parts of this chapter) added an additional boost as Japan became the chief base and supplier for American forces in Korea. By 1953, with reconstruction complete, personal incomes had recovered their prewar levels and Japan was entering a new period of boom development. Some credit is due to American aid in the hard years immediately after the war, but "the Japanese economic miracle," as it is called, was overwhelmingly the result of their own hard work, organization, and a national pursuit of success through group effort, no longer military but economic and corporate. The growth of production and income in Japan from 1950 (the first "normal" postwar year) to 1975 was faster than has been measured in any country at any time; in those twenty-

five years, output and incomes roughly tripled. Yet the Japanese continued to maintain a very high rate of personal savings, much of it invested in various forms in economic growth, demonstrating again the close relationship between the level of saving and economic growth rates.

At the same time, production quality also rose impressively, and in many respects Japanese goods became the best in the world market, notably cars, cameras, sound reproduction equipment, optics, and many electronics. This was a tribute to advanced Japanese technology and design, as well as to the efficiency of an industrial plant which was necessarily newly built since the devastation of the war. The same factors were active in the postwar recovery of Germany, while the victorious Allies were saddled with their older and less efficient plants. After 1953 Japan dominated world shipbuilding, though giving ground in the 1980s increasingly to South Korea. By 1964 Japan had become the world's third largest producer of steel, and by 1980 had overtaken both the U.S.S.R. and the United States in steel as well as becoming a major producer and exporter of automotive vehicles. Japan also invaded European and American markets on a large scale with its high-tech and industrial goods, and became the largest trade partner of the People's Republic of China.

As Japan's economy expanded into world markets, many in the U.S. leveled charges of unfair collusion between Japanese government and business, especially in the Ministry of International Trade and Industry, generally known as MITI. In fact there was very little government subsidy of businesses, but only a coordinating effort and research to identify key industries and overseas markets. The connection was not nearly as close as it had been during the Meiji era, and government intervention or assistance was no more prominent in Japan than in many European countries. Japan is small enough to make national coordination of effort much easier than in the U.S., but vigorous competition has remained among different Japanese companies. Japan sells its products abroad, including in the U.S., because they are of high quality and in wide demand, as they have kept up with market changes. It is not reasonable to demand that they buy a fixed amount of U.S. or other foreign goods in order to help balance the trade deficit resulting from an excess of exports over imports. The government can hardly enforce this, and cannot ask its people to buy goods, often of lesser quality, which they would not freely choose to buy. Some adjustments can be made to lessen Japanese import restrictions, and will be made increasingly as negotiations continue. After a widespread crop failure in the 1993 rice harvest, Japan began, for example, to import large amounts of American rice.

But the charges that Japan's economic success is the work of what is called "Japan Inc." are largely without validity. The shortage of domestic natural resources, unlike the United States, means that Japan must import nearly all of its oil, most of its coal, and many other raw materials; although these come in by cheap sea transport, production has had to be highly efficient in order to compete in world markets. Some growth industries and some so-called "infant" industries are still protected by tariffs, quotas, and bureaucratic red tape designed to minimize foreign competition, but protectionism is not unique to Japan and is a factor in American trade policy too.

As industry boomed after 1950 people increasingly moved to the cities, leaving many rural areas almost empty, while the proportion of the population still engaged in agriculture fell steadily nearly to an American level, or less than 3 percent. Some factories sprang up in formerly rural areas, and new houses departed from traditional styles, while the cities continued to spread over the surrounding countryside as Japan became the most highly urbanized country in the world. Farming was highly commercialized and mechanized, more a business than ever before; it used huge amounts of chemical fertilizers and pesticides, which was in itself worrying to those concerned about long-term effects on the environment, but continued to lead the world in the per-acre

yield of most of its crops in most years. Urban and even many rural residents acquired however a taste for food items which had to be imported: coffee, tropical fruits, increasing amounts of meat, and indeed the whole panoply of choices displayed in supermarkets in Japan as in the U.S. or western Europe.

The Japanese economy suffered a severe recession, along with nearly all of the West, from 1991 as part of the global business cycle and the rising competition of lower-cost producers like South Korea and Taiwan. Unemployment, normally minimal, rose, and there were severe cutbacks generally. But employment with a Japanese company is usually for life, or until retirement, which is standard at age 55 although many go on working in other jobs as a kind of phased retirement. One of the bases of Japan's economic success has been the loyalty of employees, who generally like the protective paternalism of the company and the security it offers. This however does make companies less able to adjust to market shifts and of course tends to increase costs; both have contributed to economic problems in the 1990s, but while there have been some layoffs they remain on a much smaller scale than in other countries. The pattern of lifetime employment is fast changing, however, and it never covered more than about 30 percent of the workforce; most young workers now say they are ready to change jobs for a better opportunity.

Hong Kong, Taiwan, South Korea, and Singapore later followed essentially the Japanese path to development, first in light industry and consumer goods and going on to high-quality precision goods. It is clearly not coincidental that all of these East Asian countries developed, like Japan, out of an originally Chinese tradition (minus the more recent irrationalities of state communism and Maoism) which emphasized disciplined hard work and organized group effort, and which placed the highest value on education, as the Japanese have done. The unspoken commitment to group identity, interest, and effort has been a powerful asset. For East Asians, education is a family priority; fathers, mothers, and older siblings work with children to help them excel. Failure, like social deviance, brings shame on the family or other group as success brings credit. East Asian children at virtually all levels outperform their American counterparts in nearly every field, as most East Asian adults outperform them in the workplace. The two are obviously connected, not only through differing emphases on education but through the East Asian consensus about the importance of the work ethic and of group or family loyalty in the service of group or family advancement.

Japanese democracy, American-style, has remained a healthy growth, although politics was long dominated by a conservative coalition with no effective rival parties. High school education is virtually universal, and literacy the highest in the world. The press has remained of high quality, and avidly read by a public which also buys and reads more books than in any other country, about ten times the figure for Americans. Nearly half of young Japanese continue with post-high-school education, in a great variety of colleges, universities, and other institutions, and the Japanese are now probably the best-educated population in the world.

Investment in education continues to be a major basis for Japan's spectacular economic success. Economic growth also largely eliminated poverty and unemployment, the only major country in the world to be virtually free of these scourges. With the postwar disappearance of what aristocratic survivals remained from Tokugawa and Meiji times, Japan became a nation of prosperous, middle-class people in an orderly society largely free of slums, violent crime, and social despair. Japan's murder rate is less than 1/200 of that in the United States. The very low rate of crime, especially interpersonal violence, results from the absence of poverty and from the sense of group responsibility; individuals are unwilling to bring shame or disgrace to their families or work groups by antisocial or reprehensible behavior. As another measure of well being, Japan achieved by 1980 the world's highest life expectancy.

Japan has been largely unencumbered by the crushing economic burden of maintaining the huge military establishment undertaken by most other large countries in the postwar world, and this has paid off handsomely. Money has been invested instead in economic growth, new technology, full employment, education, and a wide range of social services. Japan is virtually alone in the world in having escaped from most of the cankerous problems which breed in poverty, such as violence, hopelessness, and drugs. The national ethics of work, achievement, and high standards, now in the service of personal and group goals of economic advancement rather than of imperial ambition, have produced a new and more constructive conquest.

The chief figure in Japan's early postwar recovery and the establishment of democratic government was Yoshida Shigeru (1878–1967), who became prime minister in April of 1946. Like many Japanese, he was not happy about many of the reforms of the Occupation, but did his duty as a good public servant. Before the war he had also been opposed to the ties with Germany and favored instead links with Britain and America, but events outran him. He protested against the seizure of Manchuria, and later supported the group which argued for early peace negotiations with the Allies. For this he was arrested and jailed, which of course made him even more acceptable as a postwar leader. He had had an elite education at Tokyo University, entered the foreign service (for which a Tokyo University degree is still almost a requirement), and served as ambassador to England, so that he was at home with Anglo-Americans. A conservative domestically, he strongly supported Japan's disarmament and its avoidance as far as possible of any involvement in the Cold War.

The restoration of democracy saw a great increase in the number and variety of political parties, still a distinctive feature of Japanese politics, but from 1955, after Yoshida's last government had fallen, a single party, the Liberal Democrats (LDP), won a plurality and dominated the political scene until the summer of 1993, when it finally lost its position in the elections, to be replaced by a seemingly less conservative coalition. However there continued to be frequent changes of prime minister throughout this period. There are no doubts about the genuineness of Japanese democracy, its frequent free and fair elections, and (after SCAP) its freedom of speech and expression. Part of the reason for the LDP's long run, and for Japan's general stability, has been simple prosperity, where most people were not inclined to vote for change and tolerated the paternalism and corruption which came to characterize the LDP as a typical political machine, familiar in many of the big cities of the U.S.

One of the things which led to the ultimate defeat of the LDP in 1993 was the manifold charges of corruption. Some Japanese turned away from politics, and some of those who felt left out of the new prosperity or who regretted the passing of the traditional society and its values founded or followed new eclectic religions. These

Schoolchildren in front of the Heian Shrine in Kyoto. Japanese students wear uniforms, the boys' in military style and dating from Meiji times. (Steve Elmore)

drew on Shinto (technically outlawed under the Occupation), Buddhism, Christianity, or a mixture of these. Modern Japanese society is highly secular and most Japanese probably pay less attention to religion than do Americans or Europeans, although Buddhist or Shinto priests usually appear at marriages and commonly at funerals, which are often held in Buddhist or Shinto temples. The most successful of the new religious groups, the Soka Gakkai, or "Value-Creating Society," was founded in the early 1950s and grew very rapidly, especially among the less well off, such as small shopkeepers, miners, laborers, and taximen.

As it grew, it attracted increasing numbers of other Japanese, including many from the younger generation who, like their fellow joiners, were looking for something to give meaning to their lives. Soka Gakkai preached national and individual salvation through faith in the Nichiren sect of Buddhism, and spread through local group associations which offered mutual aid, practiced faith healing, and created a sense of belonging. But the new faith also allowed the importance of getting on materially in this world, the opposite of the Buddha's original message, and indeed its religious character tended to become less important than its group basis. Something like 8 percent of the population were carried on Soka Gakkai membership lists, and the sect organized frequent parades and mass meetings, generally condemning or regretting the wave of "modernization" and urging a return to traditional culture and its virtues.

In 1964 Soka Gakkai founded a new political party which it called the Clean Government party, which as its name suggested was against corruption but tended to be vague about other issues. It did very well at the polls, winning nearly 11 percent of the vote in 1969, although its share slowly declined thereafter and it in effect joined the many other minority parties which did not present any serious threat to the LDP. Before the latter's final collapse in the elections of 1993, it lost its majority in the upper house of the Diet in 1989 but retained a plurality. In this changed situation, the Socialist party, which had been in existence from the start, rose to new prominence under its woman leader, Doi Takako, who became a major figure in Japanese politics, the first woman to do so. The women's vote had become a more important element, and the new cabinet following the elections of 1989 included two women. But the LDP was not finished yet, despite continuing financial scandals involving bribery and payoffs, and soon regained its majority—until 1993. The LDP was finally defeated in the elections of 1993 by a coalition of opposition parties, and in 1994 formed an alliance with the Socialist party, resulting in the Socialist Murayama Tomichi actually becoming prime minister, although there was little real change in government policies, nor was there when Murayama was succeeded as head of a new coalition government by the LDP figure Hashimoto Ryutaro early in 1996.

No society is free of problems. Japanese society is generally high-pressure, and the drive for achievement exacts a toll, on schoolchildren as well as on adults. Pressures begin even for admission to the "right" kindergarten, so that one can move on to the "right" elementary school, middle school, and college or university, all of which are carefully status-ranked. Each stage is accompanied by examinations in which the competition is fearsome. Childhood, after the age of five, is a stressful time for most Japanese, although the juvenile suicide rate is less than in the U.S. Extreme urban crowding and cramped living space add further burdens. Population density in the urban corridor from Tokyo to Hiroshima, which contains three-quarters of

✠ Value-Creating Society ✠

The most popular of the new religious societies in postwar Japan was the Soka Gakkai, or Value-Creating Society. The founder, Kiromizu Munetada, had been born in 1780, became a Shinto priest, and had a mystical experience of becoming one with the sun, which he interpreted as a sign from heaven. Converts recited his Great Purification Prayer:

The heavenly deities will push open the heavenly rock door ... and pushing aside the mists of the high mountains and the low mountains ... in the lands of the four quarters under the heavens, each and every sin will be gone.... Beginning from today, each and every sin will be gone. Cleanse and purify! Cleanse and Purify!

Source: Quoted in W.S. Morton, *Japan.* (New York: McGraw Hill, 1994), p. 265.

the Japanese people, is the highest in the world. Commuting time for those who work in downtown Tokyo *averages* nearly two hours each way, and is only somewhat less for other big Japanese cities. Parks and recreation facilities are extremely limited. Housing is fearfully expensive, and most urban Japanese, over 80 percent of the population now, live in tiny apartments with minimal amenities. As one of the best informed and widely traveled people in the world, most Japanese know that they are generally very well off; but they also know that they are very cramped by comparison with others elsewhere. There seems no prospect that most Japanese will ever have adequate living space, privacy, or the kinds of comforts and elbow room which middle-class people in Western countries take for granted. Subway commuters crammed into overloaded cars are pressed against ads promoting various products using a backdrop of an alpine meadow, a country lawn, or a beach, all empty except for one or two lone figures—things which most Japanese can see only abroad.

Rush hour at Shinjuku station, a major Tokyo junction. (David Madison)

Apart from the very small group of urban poor, many of them dropouts from society, two minority communities in Japan are still severely discriminated against: the *eta* or *burakumin* group of "untouchables," and the sizable Korean minority. *Eta* form about two percent of the population, and are physically indistinguishable from other Japanese, but are still looked down on; they are avoided as neighbors, employees, or, most of all, as marriage partners, because of their traditional occupations, and they live in segregated ghettoes. In the dominantly Buddhist society of traditional Japan, the *eta* disposed of dead animals, cured the hides, and made leather goods, as well as butchering and eating animals, all forbidden by Buddhism. As with untouchables in India, this made them "unclean." Such religiously based distinctions are long gone, but Japanese prejudice and discrimination remain.

Many Koreans migrated to Japan to escape the forced poverty and repression at home under Japanese domination from 1895. Many more were taken to Japan as forced laborers. Japanese prejudice against Koreans as an "inferior" people grew with Japanese imperialism, and those who lived in Japan were badly treated despite Japan's long-standing debt to Korean civilization (Chapter 10). Many of them drifted into illegal or shady activities, which strengthened Japanese prejudice against them. It is still very hard for anyone of Korean origin to obtain citizenship in Japan, as it also is for all other foreigners, or to receive anything approaching equal treatment. There are about half a million Koreans resident in Japan, many of them born in Japan or having lived there for generations, but still denied full acceptance or equal treatment.

Japanese society has always been strongly hierarchical, divided into different status groups. Given the postwar openness to the West and the other changes at work in the society, this now strikes many Japanese as onerous, especially the subordinate status of women. Deference to superiors or elders, and of all women to men, bothers particularly younger people as stultifying, although these and other traditional forms and values have changed a good deal in the postwar years. The coming generation of Japanese may well reshape their society on somewhat freer lines, but most would agree that it will be a long time before women achieve anything close to equality. In the workplace most women serve in subordinate or service roles, as secretaries, receptionists, or tea-makers, collectively known as "O.L's"—"office ladies." Meanwhile married women are often the real powers within the family and household. They usually have control of the family finances and have the preponderant role in the upbringing of children, since many fathers work long hours and commuting time means that they often get home only after the children are in bed. Nevertheless, about half of adult Japanese women work outside the house, close to the current American figure, although this is often managing a small family business or neighborhood store. Equality

✠ Stresses of Westernization ✠

Many Japanese, especially of the older generation, still fell torn between traditional Japanese culture and the flood of both Westernization and the culture of the new generation of Japanese. No less a person than Ogura Kazuo, director of cultural affairs at the Japanese Ministry, wrote in 1991:

People sense that the old pattern has yet to change. Those on the U.S. side are still leaning heavily on Japan, never reflecting on their own country's shortcomings, and those on the Japanese side are still bowing before the American demands, as if doing so was Japan's fate.... For many Japanese the concepts of freedom, democracy, and the market economy do not have a home-grown feeling. Although they have taken deep root in Japan, they give us a vaguely unsettling sensation, as if we were wearing a new suit of Western clothes. The consequence is that it is very difficult for the Japanese to believe that fighting to the death for these concepts is their natural duty as Japanese.

Source: From Kazuo Ogura, "Japan and America: Pride and Prejudice," *The New York Times,* Nov. 24, 1991.)

in the professions remains a distant goal. Nearly half of Japanese women get some form of post-high-school education; much of it is vocational, and relatively few attend the prestige universities. Many women attend college for reasons of social status, or to find a husband.

In the 1950s and 1960s most marriages were still arranged, or at least set up, by go-betweens, and were still seen as interfamily alliances. By the 1990s go-betweens were still used as a last resort, but most couples met each other on their own or through friends, and now lived apart from their parents whenever they could afford it. In the highly restricted space of most housing, intergenerational strains were and remain a problem where two or more generations, each with its different standards and tastes, share cramped quarters. Those born after about 1960, now a majority of the population, grew up in a world sharply different from that of their parents or grandparents; they became culturally highly Americanized, devoted to U.S.-style pop culture in its many forms, generally permissive, and much freer than their parents or grandparents in sexual matters. Many now meet their future spouses as fellow students or in the workplace, and no longer feel beholden to their parents.

Such newer lifestyles, including a rising divorce rate as well as rising age at first marriage, common to most of the Western world as well, meant changes also for the lot of the aged. Traditionally, parents and grandparents lived with married children, usually the eldest son, as in China. With most of the population in Japan urban, it was a strain to provide anything like adequate space for three generations, as it was in urban China, and more

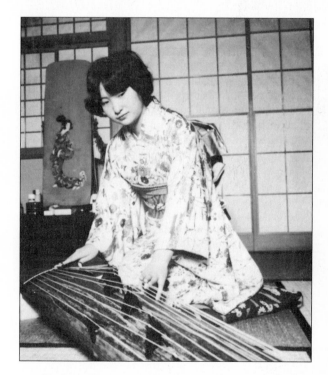

Modern Japanese women still learn traditional arts, and playing the *koto* is one. Koto players must wear kimonos, and usually practice in a thoroughly traditional setting, such as that shown here, kneeling on a tatami in a traditional-style room. (Shashinka Photo, Inc.)

Tradition meets modernity: woman at a bus stop in Tokyo dressed in traditional kimono. (Ira Kuschenbaum/Stock, Boston)

and more elderly Japanese have moved into retirement homes, although half or more still stick to the old pattern. As the birthrate has come sharply down, Japan's population is rapidly aging, which presents a still largely unresolved problem, especially as the traditional East Asian respect for age has increasingly given way to "liberated youth." Individualism is on the rise as young people seek to escape from social restraints, and there is growing use of drugs, linked to increasing crime and violence, though Japan is fortunately much less afflicted with these problems than are Western countries.

Japan's Global Role

Japan's rising sun now extends economically even more widely than its former military successes, but despite their major global stature, the Japanese have been reluc-

tant to function as a world power in other terms, a role which has brought them such tragedy in the past. They have been uncomfortably aware of this inconsistency between their technological and economic power and their far more hesitant posture abroad in political terms. On several occasions they have felt ignored in the maneuverings of Cold War diplomacy, especially by the abrupt American reversal of policy toward China in 1971. As an American client and bulwark against neighboring Communist states, Japan was dumbfounded when Washington suddenly renewed contact with China, in part as a move by both sides against the Soviet Union, without even informing the Japanese, despite Japan's role as the major American military base in Asia. The Japanese still refer to that event as "Nixon shock," and there have been many others like it when the Japanese have felt slighted or ignored by the big countries in their power games.

It seems likely that in time Japan will come to play an international diplomatic role more in keeping with its economic role, and this has already begun to happen, but most Japanese continue to hope that this can take place without their having to add new military power. As on many issues, there are crosscurrents, and some Japanese openly favor rearmament so that Japan can occupy a more "appropriate" place in a world unfortunately now dominated by those with the greatest military power. If that should happen, Japan's neighbors and former victims of her imperialist adventures would be deeply concerned. And although the Americans have pressed for it, a rearmed Japan would no longer be their client, which is indeed why some Japanese favor it. More positively, by 1988 Japan had become the world's largest donor of foreign aid, far outdistancing the much larger and richer United States. Japanese aid is also entirely economic and developmental rather than military.

One other way in which modern Japan has led the world is its success in the 1970s in limiting industrial pollution. Japan is small, and most of its population, cities, and industry are crowded into a narrow coastal corridor only about 400 miles long. Industrial concentration is higher there than anywhere in the world, and hence Japan was the first to notice the lethal effects of air and water pollution, as one consequence of its postwar industrial growth. There were many deaths and many more health casualties from heavy metal toxins and from air pollution, all traced to specific plants or industrial operations and their poisonous discharges into water bodies or the atmosphere. Once this became clear and mass publicity and pressures became a political issue, national and municipal governments quickly passed stringent control legislation beginning in 1969 with the city of Tokyo. Controls were strictly enforced, with the help of new technology designed to limit emissions and effluents from coal and oil power plants, industry, and from vehicles. Japanese cars became out-standingly low in their polluting effects, as well as fuel-efficient, and went on to dominate world markets. The big car-making companies had been reluctant to change, as in the United States, but in Japan public opinion and government were firm in enforcing the new controls; the car companies designed cleaner-burning engines, and everyone benefitted.

As industrial growth continues, concentration and crowding will go on generating the same problems, as elsewhere in the world; pollution levels are building up again, while controls have remained incomplete or in some cases relaxed. But Japanese organization, efficiency, and technology have demonstrated that the problems are manageable, given the willingness to confront them. The technology needed to control or even eliminate pollution was quickly developed, and the added cost involved in pollution controls was extremely modest, estimated at between 1 and 2 percent of total production costs.

There were strict controls on the disposal of all hazardous wastes, and on all industrial operations which could not be made to meet the new environmental standards. The Japanese solution has been to "export pollution," as it is described, sending wastes abroad for disposal by agreement with other countries, primarily the Philippines and Indonesia, and establishing abroad also some of the worst polluting operations, which are accepted in these other countries with their far less stringent environmental legislation or enforcement. Japan's forests have also been carefully preserved for the most part, which is in itself commendable, but the huge Japanese market appetite for wood and wood products has led to devastating inroads on the highly vulnerable forests of Southeast Asia by Japanese companies or with Japanese financing, and it is they who are primarily responsible for the rapid shrinkage of the Southeast Asian tropical forests, with possibly catastrophic consequences for the global climatic balance. The Japanese are also the most resistant nation to global efforts to restrict the slaughter of whales, and are one of the few holdouts from the international agreements on this issue. This is perhaps irrational, since despite their governmental claims, an insignificant number of Japanese are still dependent on whaling, and the contribution of whale meat to their diet is infinitesimal, while Japanese recalcitrance on this matter has earned them bitter criticism abroad.

Japan also led the way in reducing energy use, through more efficient plants and better designed engines, reacting both to world energy shortages and price rises and to its own determination to reduce pollution. Nearly all trains are electrified, including the heavily used highspeed line connecting Tokyo with all major Japanese cities to the south, southwest, and north to

Hokkaido. Trains leave Tokyo every 15 minutes for Osaka, making the 310-mile trip in three hours, including stops at Nagoya and Kyoto, and running at speeds up to 140 miles per hour.

Population increase has been sharply reduced, by personal and family choice, and is close to stabilization. As with high-income and better-educated groups in other countries, especially in cities, couples prefer to limit the number of their children so as to provide better for them, including their education. But the coastal area from Tokyo to Osaka and on to northern Kyushu has been rapidly becoming one vast urban-industrial zone. Although the rural Japanese landscape is very beautiful, especially the mountains which cover most of the country, most of it is increasingly empty as people have flocked to the cities in search of wider economic and cultural opportunity. On weekends and holidays there is a huge rush of urbanites to natural beauty spots, temples or shrines, and resorts nearest the big cities, which are often overrun by excessive crowding. Then there is the long journey back, crammed onto overloaded trains or buses where most passengers must stand for hours, or locked into gigantic traffic jams on the highways. Much of traditional Japanese culture has been lost or discarded in this avalanche of modern change. Although many Japanese regret such a price for development, their sense of national identity has remained strong, bound together with many symbolic survivals of traditional culture: the sharply distinctive Japanese food, at-home clothing, many houses or at least rooms in traditional style, gardens, shrines and temples, the keen

Pollution: Tokyo billboard, which automatically prints out the parts per million (PPM) of sulfur dioxide, particulates, nitrous oxide, and an overall ambient air quality rating, changing as traffic changes. This proved one of several effective devices to alert people to what was happening to their environment. (R. Murphey)

Japanese aesthetic sensitivity, and the commitment to order, self-discipline, and group effort in the pursuit of excellence.

Tokyo and the Modern World

By about 1965 Tokyo had become the world's largest city, and a symbol of Japan's new economic leadership. The urban area had grown outward to merge with that of previously separate cities in the same lowland basin, including Kawasaki and Yokohama. By 1990 this vast unbroken conglomeration of dense settlement, commerce, industry, and government measured 50 miles across and included over 30 million people and the world's largest and most efficient subway system. Almost nothing is left of the Edo described in Chapter 13, most of which had been in any case periodically destroyed by fires. Modern Tokyo was also largely ruined by a catastrophic earthquake in 1923, and then again by American bombs and firestorms in 1944 and 1945.

The only part of the city which has survived all of these cataclysms unscathed is Tokugawa Ieyasu's massive shogunal castle, surrounded by its moats and stone walls, originally built in the early seventeenth century and since 1869 used as the imperial palace. In the middle of a huge and strikingly modern city of glass, steel, skyscrapers, and expressways, with urban traffic flowing around it, the palace still stands as a symbol of Japan's traditional past, both as a Tokugawa monument and as the home of a still-enthroned emperor, whose lineage and ceremonial functions date back to before the dawn of Japanese written history. The death of the aged emperor Hirohito in 1989 and the accession of his son Akihito as the new emperor, with all the traditional rituals, signaled no change and reaffirmed Japan's commitment to its past and to its distinctively Japanese tradition.

Among Japan's many big cities, Tokyo still plays the role of the brash modernist, the focus of change, the center of everything new, but even in Tokyo Japanese do not forget their past. The palace, and its medieval walls and moats, is an anachronism, but it is nevertheless an appropriate focal point for the capital of Japan, more than the parliament or other government buildings, more than the banks, offices, skyscrapers, factories, and other symbols of Tokyo's Western-style modernity. For all its apparent focus on the streamlined or frantic present and future, Tokyo is also a city of the traditional Japanese style.

That aspect of the city's character becomes clear beyond the immediate downtown and government areas. Except for the industrial clusters around the fringes of each originally separate municipality, Tokyo is primarily a vast collection of neighborhoods. Many are grouped around a surviving or rebuilt temple, shrine, former daimyo estate, or park-like garden. Wandering through the back streets and alleys of these neighborhoods, it is easy to imagine one's self in Tokugawa Edo. Clouds of steam escape from public bathhouses, enveloping patrons who include many dressed in traditional *kimonos* and walking in wooden clogs, especially in the evening after work. Inside countless tiny restaurants and teahouses with their *tatami* straw mats, low tables, and scrolls on the wall, little seems to have changed since Ieyasu's time, including much of the food. Many of the tiny houses or apartments maintain miniature Japanese-style gardens the size of a small tabletop, or lovingly tend potted plants set out to catch the sun by the doorway or on small balconies. Street vendors with their traditional chants peddle roasted sweet potatoes, chestnuts, or *yakitori* (Japanese shishkebob).

Crowds of *kimono*-clad worshippers, or just people on an outing, throng the courtyards of traditionally rebuilt temples and shrines, especially on festival days. Similar crowds fill the narrow streets and patronize street vendors or shops selling traditional as well as modern goods: fans both manual and electric, silks and nylons, horoscope fortunes and stock market guides, tea and beer, lacquer and plastic, scrolls and comic books. Like Japan, Tokyo is both very modern and very traditional, very Japanese and very Western. Few people seem to be torn by this dichotomy. The Japanese sense of national and cultural identity rides serenely through it all.

Japan's Relations with Its Former Enemies

The end of the Pacific War did not produce a peace treaty between Japan and the Soviet Union. This was primarily because the Soviets remained in occupation of the Kurile island chain stretching northeast from Hokkaido, as well as of the southern half of Sakhalin Island to the north, which the Japanese had taken after their defeat of Russia in 1905. Japan was willing to let southern Sakhalin go, but the Kuriles had long been Japanese property; they and the waters around them, from which Japanese were now barred, were of major importance to the Japanese fishing industry. Japanese efforts to negotiate with the Russians continued to break down over this issue, which remained unresolved, but a new Russia since 1992 may return the Kuriles. Anti-American feeling, which had grown during the later years of the Occupation, as was only to be expected, peaked again in 1954, just after the signing of a U.S.-Japan Mutual Security Treaty, when a Japanese fishing vessel named Lucky Dragon was heavily contaminated by fallout from the American nuclear testing on Bikini atoll in the western Pacific. The catch of tuna had already entered the market when the boat and its crew were found to be dangerously radioactive; some of the crew later died. Japan panicked, especially since fish, including tuna, were so important a part of the diet, but panic was mixed with anger. Hadn't the Japanese suffered enough at American hands, the only people in the world (until the Bikini tests) victimized by nuclear weapons?

Meanwhile successive conservative governments pursued what was now also called a "reverse course" as in the later years of the Occupation, undoing as much as possible of the democratic reforms of the Occupation and building up the "Japan Self-Defense Force," really a cover for rearmament. This did not represent the views of many, perhaps most, Japanese, and the Socialist party won more votes, but remained a largely powerless minority politically. The conservatives of the ruling Liberal Democratic party (LDP) had built a strong coalition of business and landed interests, including most farmers, who benefited from the high government price supports for rice. This was clearly against the interests of urban dwellers, the vast majority, but the LDP political machine proved hard to challenge, until 1993.

National morale was boosted when Japan was admitted to the United Nations in 1956, where it slowly began to play a role, though still not commensurate with its new economic stature even by the 1980s. The U.S.-Japan Mutual Security Treaty was renegotiated in 1960, extended for another ten years, and retained the huge American bases in Japan. It was planned to have the then President Eisenhower visit Japan, but when ratification of the new treaty was forced through the Diet by strong-arm tactics, mass demonstrations erupted and there was widespread violence and attacks on and by police. Eisenhower's secretary, who had come as an advance guard for the president's visit, was trapped with the U.S. ambassador in a car at Tokyo's airport and rocked by an angry mob. Eisenhower's visit was canceled. Bitterness remained, but the violence faded. Attention shifted to the Olympic games, held for the first time in Japan in 1964 in Tokyo, and to a World's Fair in Osaka in 1970, when with relatively little discussion or public protest the security treaty with the United States was renewed for another ten years. Growing affluence for most Japanese had made them more complacent, and more inclined to support the Conservative LDP, despite a long series of scandals involving successive prime ministers accused, with ample evidence, of taking bribes and of other financial and moral corruption.

Textbooks for use in schools were now approved by the national Ministry of Education, and periodically brought out in new editions to keep up with the times. Part of the changing times was changing Japanese attitudes, about themselves and about their role in the Second World War. There were vigorous protests from South Korea and from China over successive reeditions in the 1980s which progressively toned down earlier critical statements about Japanese actions in both countries in the past. As for domestic affairs, the 1980s also saw the revision of textbook accounts of the sordid history of pollution; officially, the pollution problem was now "solved." The Chisso Chemical Company, which had been responsible for the worst offenses, including mercury and cadmium poisoning at Minamata and Niigata, was successful in having its name removed from

Bullet train (Shinkansen) passing Mt. Fuji. (R. Murphey)

the textbook accounts. The Keidanren, or Japanese Businessmens' and Industrialists' Association, was anxious to project a positive image of the Japanese economic miracle and to favor the big corporations who had played such a large part in that success.

The Americans had continued to occupy Okinawa, important to them as a military base, and had resisted repeated Japanese requests to return it. Finally in 1972 it was handed back, although the major American bases in Japan, notably at Yokosuka near Yokohama and Sasebo near Kobe, were retained. Many Japanese protested against this, and especially against the introduction of nuclear weapons on U.S. warships using those bases or patrolling in Japanese waters. Apart from Japan's own tragic history with nuclear warfare, it made their country a more important target for any external enemy. There were tensions also inevitably resulting from the presence of foreign troops and their interactions with local people, especially women, but there were no signs that the Americans were planning to pull out, especially not after the destruction and abandonment of their

bases in the Philippines as the result of a major volcanic explosion in 1992. The Japanese response to the American rapprochement with China in 1971–1972 was the visit to Peking of Prime Minister Tanaka in 1972 and Japan's subsequent recognition of the People's Republic. Japan became China's major trade partner, as was only logical, and to cement this relationship, Prime Minister Kaifu visited Peking in 1991, the first visit by a major head of state since the Peking massacre of June 1989.

But Japanese in general became more confident, and more assertive, as they became richer and as Japan became a major economic power in the world. People grew more conservative and more willing to support the LDP despite continuing financial and even sex scandals which forced several prime ministers and cabinet ministers to resign. In these and perhaps other respects, Japan was becoming more and more like the contemporary United States, on which its political system had, after all, been modeled. But despite such considerations, and despite the continuing whirlwind of Westernization in so many aspects of Japanese culture and life, Japanese clung to their identity, and could now add to it a new and perhaps better-earned national pride.

A mobile computer bus stopped at Tokyo kindergarten, with children learning how to operate personal computers. (Reuters/ Bettmann Newsphotos)

Divided Korea

Korea had been grossly exploited as a Japanese colony, and although this included the creation of a modern infrastructure of rail lines, highways, mines, factories, hospitals, and schools, Korean material welfare had suffered severely. The country and its people had been dragged into the modern world at heavy human cost. So oppressive was Japanese rule that few Koreans had the opportunity to obtain higher education or administrative/managerial experience, serving instead mainly as menial labor and low-level clerks. Some had low- or middle-level experience in the colonial bureaucracy or in business and industry, but their number was limited. Korea had been promised its independence by the Allies, and with the defeat of Japan, Koreans who had fought underground against the Japanese emerged to form a provisional government. In the south, the Americans who moved in to supervise the surrender of Japanese troops some three weeks after the emperor's broadcast (it took time to assemble the necessary forces from Japan) swept aside this provisional government on the grounds that it was "too radical." It had already begun to promote land reform, and to take measures against Koreans who had allegedly collaborated with the hated Japanese, including many large landowners who did in fact owe their position to the colonial administration. The Americans were already paranoid about communism, and did not want to see their half of Korea go that way.

In the frenzied weeks after Japan's surrender in August 1945, what was thought of as a temporary arrangement among the victorious Allies agreed to have Russian troops already in Manchuria next door accept the Japanese surrender in the northern half of the country, above the 38th parallel, pending a more permanent settlement. American troops were to do the same for the southern half. But the deepening Cold War led to a hardening of the artificial division and the emergence of rival Korean political regimes. Extremists on both sides, fed by Cold War ideology, eliminated the few moderates in both north and south. A Soviet-dominated Communist government ruled the north from its capital at Pyongyang, and a U.S. client government, strongly anti-Communist, ruled the south with its capital at Seoul. Both cities had served as national Korean capitals in the past.

The Americans installed as head of the government of South Korea a political refugee, Syngman Rhee (Yi Sung-man, 1875–1965) an early Christian convert who had fled Korea in 1911 after imprisonment and persecution by the Japanese colonial administration and had not been back since. He lived in Hawaii until 1936, having earlier studied at U.S. universities, but had returned to Korea briefly before the formal Japanese absorption of Korea in 1910 as a Y.M.C.A. worker until such activities, and his association with the Korean independence movement, antagonized the Japanese and obliged him to escape to Hawaii. His career thus paralleled that of Sun Yat-sen, but where Sun picked up the more democratic or radical aspects of the American model, Rhee was more influenced by its conservative or even reactionary side. It was perhaps understandable that, given the situation of his country in 1945, he should be fervently anti-Communist as well as anti-Japanese, which was what made him attractive to the Americans in this early phase of the Cold War. But his rule in South Korea was strongly repressive and he set up what amounted to a police state.

Americans had dominated the Western missionary movement in Korea, especially the Presbyterians, and it was in one of their schools that Rhee became acquainted with the West and with English. Christianity appealed to nationalist-minded Koreans as a counter to Japanese rule as well as a means to acquiring Western learning; it was both a solace in those difficult years and a path for future Korean development, with close Western rather than Japanese ties. For these and other reasons, missionaries won more converts in Korea than in any other Asian country except for the Philippines, but from the Japanese point of view it was on the edge of subversion, especially as so many Korean nationalists were converted or educated by Western missionaries and used their Christianity as a support group against Japanese oppression. Rhee was certainly a Korean patriot, but he was long out of touch with his home country, and his arrogant one-man rule antagonized most people, as did his police-state methods.

Marxism had spread underground in Korea, and more openly among Koreans living in eastern Manchuria. Their anti-Japanese sentiments also provided some common ground with the Russians, but in Korea itself the fearsomely effective Japanese police drove the Communist party, founded in 1925, to a

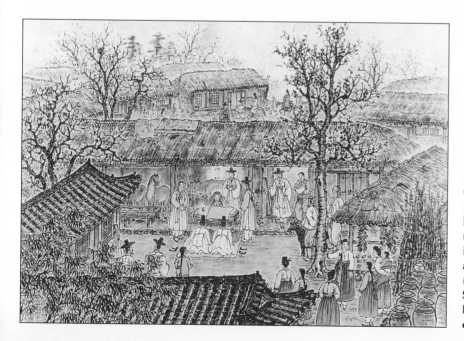

Korean nativity scene, by Hye Ch'on Kim Hak-soo, a modern Korean Christian artist. The human figures are wearing traditional Korean clothing, including the black "stovepipe" hats and the dresses of the women. (Yonsei University Collection, Seoul; courtesy of the United Board for Christian Higher Education in Asia, New York)

largely ineffective underground organization. Nevertheless, the ideas of Marxism, Leninism, and the apparent promise of the Russian Revolution of 1917 were attractive to many, if only as a different counter to the strongly anti-Communist and anti-Russian trend in Japan. Thus both rival models and ideologies of the new superpowers who divided Korea in 1945 had their supporters, and in both parts of the country, but of course Russian occupation of the north and their establishing of their client government there ensured that communism would be dominant in Pyongyang and the area it controlled.

About a million Koreans, unwilling to live under a communist government, migrated south, and a much smaller number whose sympathies ran the other way moved north. Kim Il-sung, who for unclear reasons took his name from that of a former guerrilla leader in the resistance against Japan (although he himself had been active in the resistance) was the Russian candidate for head of state from the beginning. He and his new government, the Democratic People's Republic of Korea (the south was called simply the Republic of Korea) established mass organizations for mobilizing the population and ran the familiar campaigns of political indoctrination supervised by the Communist party. Land reform confiscated landlord estates and distributed the land to peasants; manufacturing and eventually all enterprises were nationalized beginning in 1946. In the south too the Americans found that the interim Korean government had set up local people's committees everywhere and proclaimed a "People's Republic" with a program of reform. This government was not given any chance to show its more permanent nature, as the Americans refused to deal with or recognize it and imposed instead their client regime under Syngman Rhee, who built his own political organization and police allies.

The United Nations Commission on Korea continued to urge reunification and pressed for national elections. Rhee won the elections in the south in May of 1948, with support from conservatives and big landowners, many of them former Japanese collaborators, and subsequently became president of the New Republic of South Korea, thus ending the American military government. The north held its own elections in September and unanimously chose Kim Il-sung as its head. In the course of the following year Russian and American troops were withdrawn from both halves except for a token presence. As of 1950, the north was ahead industrially, given its near monopoly of industrial resources (coal, iron, hydroelectric power) and the Japanese developments based on them, mainly in the Pyongyang area, and it had stronger military forces, thanks to Soviet aid, although the south had also been armed by the Americans. Both sides appeared to be jockeying for advantage, and there seems little doubt that each was

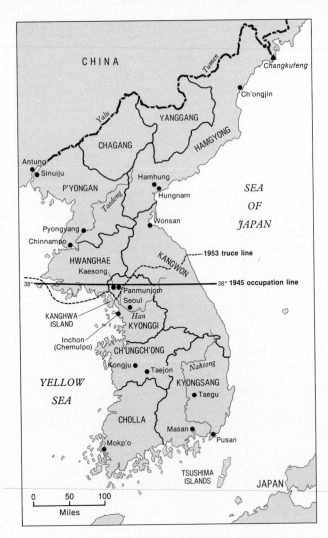

Modern Korea

preparing to strike against the other to enforce Korean unity under its rule.

As it happened, the north struck first, on June 25, 1950, it seems without consulting their Russian patrons but using the new military equipment the Soviets had given them. The south was inadequately prepared, and was obliged to retreat, abandoning the capital at Seoul after early battles and air strikes as north Korean forces struck deep into the south. The United Nations Security Council of the major powers condemned this action, aided in this case by the absence of Russia, which had boycotted the organization in protest against its recognition of the KMT regime on Taiwan as the legitimate government of China instead of the government in Peking, still a Russian ally, and hence was not present to cast a veto. At the urging of the United States, the U.N. agreed to confront this aggression and to send a substantial force under an American general (MacArthur-U.S. troops were already next door in Japan) which numerically dominated the U.N. army, although some troops were sent from Britain, France, Turkey, and altogether 13 U.N. countries. The Russians stayed out of it, perhaps signaling their displeasure with the north Korean action but in any case unwilling to seek a direct confrontation with the Americans. The forces which in time confronted the north Koreans were thus about half American and slightly less than half south Korean, with some 40,000 from other U.N. countries, totaling about a million all told. The north Korean drive was halted as the U.S.-U.N. forces built up, via Japan and the major southeastern port of Pusan, along a perimeter just short of that city, and then was slowly driven back in heavy fighting, through bomb-shattered Seoul, across the 38th parallel, and nearly to the Chinese border.

MacArthur's orders were to stop at 38°, which would have made the repulsion of the north Korean invasion legitimate, but he defiantly directed his forces to keep advancing, presumably in the hope of completely destroying the north Korean regime. China began to send a series of indirect warnings that they regarded the presence of a clearly hostile force close to their borders as a threat, and that they would intervene if necessary. Their sense of threat was greatly increased when MacArthur, instead of trying to allay their fears, issued provocative statements about his possible need to bomb the Manchurian military and industrial bases or areas along the Chinese side of the border which might be used for supply and refuge for north Korean forces, which he said might even have to be invaded and occupied. He brushed aside the Chinese warnings and continued with the advance, and American planes began to fly survey missions over eastern Manchuria. Beginning in October and continuing into November, the Chinese moved large numbers of troops called "volunteers," since they still pulled back from a direct confrontation with the U.S., into Korea under cover of night and hidden from daytime reconnaissance until they totaled nearly half a million men. In late November sudden and massive Chinese and north Korean attacks drove the U.N.-U.S. forces south again during the harsh Korean winter, far south of Seoul, which was again devastated.

In April 1951 President Truman fired MacArthur for his dangerously irresponsible and insubordinate behavior, and replaced him in Korea with General Matthew Ridgeway. Under Ridgeway's command the U.N.-U.S. forces were strengthened by reinforcements from Japan and the U.S., and slowly they fought their way north again. What was left of Seoul was retaken in a campaign which destroyed areas already fought over and heavily damaged three times, and eventually a stalemate was established along a jagged line close to 38° just north of

Seoul. Truce negotiations were begun in 1951, but agreement was finally reached to end the fighting only in October of 1953. Meanwhile both sides suffered heavy casualties in contesting small bits of ground so as to improve their position at the negotiating table. The settlement in 1953 left things as they had been since 1945, give or take a few square miles.

The war caused enormous destruction in both halves of the divided country, greatly set back Korean economic growth, and left about 800,000 North and South Korean combatants dead, nearly 800,000 Chinese out of the roughly 2.5 million "volunteers" who served over time, and about 56,000 United Nations troops, mainly Americans. It also left a legacy of heightened North-South bitterness, tension, and mutual paranoia. There were streams of displaced refugees, over three million driven from their homes, and uncounted but enormous civilian casualties, probably about four million killed or wounded. Both sides continued to build up their military strength, with fresh support from the two superpowers. If the U.N.-U.S. forces had not intervened, there seems little doubt that Korea would have been united under Northern direction, as a Communist state. In the Cold War rhetoric of the 1950s, that was unthinkable, but one may now legitimately wonder if the sacrifices and losses summarized above were worth it, especially since both of the two Koreas continued as repressive police states. The U.S. has belatedly come to accept a Communist government of China, among others. It is not easy to argue that a unified Communist Korea would have been worse for Koreans than the massive destruction they suffered, and the legacy of division and tension.

Korea Since 1960

Korean culture, language, and national consciousness have however remained unitary. They increase the tragedy of the country's artificial division, like the diversion of scarce resources into both military establishments. This has been a greater sacrifice in the less developed North than in the South, which included most of the best agricultural land and most of the newer industry. The North was earlier the industrial leader since most of Korea's industrial raw materials are in the area controlled by Pyongyang, developed under the Japanese. By the 1960s the South had begun to recover from the war, and by the 1970s to leap ahead economically, following the same path of rapid industrial development earlier pursued by Japan, and then by Taiwan. In the North, economic growth was severely handicapped by a rigid Communist ideology and a faithfulness to the irrational Maoist policies being followed by China, who had largely replaced Russia as the North's Big Brother, especially after the valiant Chinese effort to defend the North against the Allied invasion. North Korea with its government-controlled press remained almost entirely closed to outsiders, but there was some modest economic growth after 1980.

Syngman Rhee was forced to resign as the Southern president in 1960, after his dictatorial style had alienated not only his rivals but many of his supporters. Rhee was a supporter of the status quo, and a domineering ruler who was willing to use terror tactics to enforce his way and was ruthless with those who opposed him. The Korean War, beginning with the attack by the North, left the South paranoid, determined to build its military strength with American arms aid, and to press for order and anti-communism rather than for democracy or civil rights. The government became more and more a military autocracy. A year after Rhee's forced retirement, a group of young military officers led by General Park Chung-hee seized power. Park was subsequently confirmed as president in the elections of 1963, and ruled until 1979, when he was assassinated by the Korean Central Intelligence Agency, a secret military police which he had helped to build up as a feared and hated power over peoples' lives. Another military group then seized control, led by General Chun Doo-hwan. There were widespread protests and demonstrations against this sorry denial of responsible government, and the army and police killed many hundreds of demonstrators.

There was a judiciary and an elected legislature or National Assembly, more or less on the American pattern, but both were largely ignored by the authoritarian executive from the beginning. The president appointed all cabinet ministers, judges, governors, and public university heads, while the military carried out his orders. Most cabinet posts were given to military men, or to archconservative economists or loyal bureaucrats. Government took a leading role in promoting the economic development and industrialization of the South, on the Meiji Japanese pattern, and that effort became very successful as South Korean development prospered and multiplied, including its private sector. There was a vocal political opposition, but when it seemed to garner too much of the popular vote it was subjected to severe government harassment, as in the repeated arrests and imprisonments of Kim Dae-jung, the main opposition figure. Student protests and demonstrations also continued against governmental authoritarian policies, met by riot police, clubs, and tear gas.

But there was also a growing urban middle class, professionals and businesspeople whose numbers and stake in society were stimulated still further by the economic boom which gathered force in the 1970s and 1980s. The benefits of South Korean economic growth were in fact fairly widely distributed, as in Taiwan, although to a lesser extent. Most industrial workers re-mained poorly paid, and there were increasing protest demonstrations from them, often met with violence, as well as support for opposition parties. But many who had begun as workers or even as poor peasants also moved into the middle class, especially as they acquired new education, always a Korean priority. Both workers and middle-class people, as well as many Christians (often the same people) moved increasingly toward support for some alternative to the militarized and authoritarian government, more responsiveness to people's needs and regard for human rights, and a more democratically responsible rule.

The elections of 1987 offered the chance for the first time for a direct vote for president, after massive demonstrations in favor of this change. Unfortunately, the opposition parties remained divided, and the presidency was thus won by a minority candidate, Roh Tae-woo. He was the first president in nearly 30 years to enter office by vote rather than military coup, although there was widespread voting fraud and the other two opposition candidates together won a majority. Roh said he would work with them, and South Korea began to move toward a more democratic order. Such trends were reinforced by the new wave of material prosperity for most as Korean economic development followed the Japanese model, first in light consumer goods using low-wage labor, and then increasingly in heavy industry and high-tech products: shipbuilding, steel, electronics, and automobiles, all of which became competitive in world markets. In South Korea too, vertical conglomerates like the Japanese *zaibatsu* firms emerged, such as Hyundai and Samsung, and especially the larger businesses were closely tied to government and dependent on various forms of subsidy. New consumer goods spread widely among a now generally prosperous population, and many Koreans even owned cars. Life expectancy rose almost to the Japanese level, and, as in Japan, education remained all-important and literacy virtually universal. It was a replication of the Japanese "economic miracle" 20 years earlier, and rested on the same basis of hard work, a national drive to succeed, and a high priority on education. The same economic success produced a similar rise to dominance of the middle class, which in turn, as in Japan, became the chief bulwark of a more democratic society and polity.

The close linking of government and business stimulated massive corruption in both, especially under the dictatorship of Park Chung-hee and his successor Chun Doo-hwan but were continued under Rho Tae-woo. Cut off from the industrial base of the North, South Korea rapidly industrialized on its own, with capital investment and technological help from the United States. Such progress was interrupted by the Korean War from 1950 to 1953, and in fact the economy lost considerable ground, including its industrial output. The resumption

✠ South Korea Indicted ✠

Kim Dae-Jung, the most prominent of the minority politicians in South Korea and the chief spokesman for Western democracy, was a prominent critic of the military dictatorship of the 1960s, 1970s, and early 1980s. In a speech delivered at the University of Michigan on November 18, 1983, he had this to say:

The United States has maintained a close relationship with my country for over 100 years. Christianity first came to Korea from America; the United States liberated Korea from Japanese colonialism in 1945; it came to the rescue of the Korean people during the Korean War; and it supported the April 19, 1960, Student Revolution which ushered in a brief period of democratic expression. But with the advent of the Park Chung Hee dictatorship, the United States used the pretext of security as the rationale for ignoring popular aspirations for democracy.... Following his assassination, General Chun Doo Hwan was allowed to ... massacre Kwangju citizens and suppress popular democratic aspirations. These slain patriots had advocated American-style democracy.... Some American leaders have supported the South Korean government's argument that democratic development will have to yield to the imperatives of economic growth. But [despite our new prosperity] we enjoy none of the democratic freedoms.... A recent national survey revealed that 80 per cent of the South Korean people desire democratic development even if it would mean slowing down economic growth. President Reagan's recent visit to Korea has disappointed the South Korean people. Though he expressed the importance of democracy and human rights, his visit did not bring the release of political prisoners, the relaxation of suppression of the mass media, nor a lift on the ban on many politicians.... Even though hundreds of democratic figures were put under house arrest because of his visit, he didn't make sufficient effort to have them freed.... I worry that Mr. Reagan's visit may result in fanning the flames of anti-American sentiment now smoldering among our people.

of growth after 1953 was rapid, and generated destructive inflation until prices were more or less stabilized by 1960, by which time exports also began to grow. Agricultural investment was relatively neglected as capital went into the rebuilding of industry, and rural areas remained impoverished and technically backward while the cities, especially Seoul, boomed. From 1965 the Korean economy grew about as fast as Japan's, but still had to import much of its food. Park tried to achieve self-sufficiency in food, and pushed the development of export-oriented industries. Unemployment was greatly reduced, but serious inflation remained, while those who complained or in other ways stepped out of line were harshly suppressed. Unions were blocked except for those controlled by the government, and worker incomes continued to fall behind. Bribery and favoritism favored the big enterprises, especially those who supported Park. The ten largest conglomerates wholly dominate the South Korean economy and account for some two-thirds of GNP and some 70 percent of exports. By the early 1990s prices and interest rates had

come down somewhat, although widespread corruption and payoffs continued and the rural areas lagged far behind the cities in development and in average incomes. New elections in 1994 brought a new president to office, Kim Young-sam, who has pledged to change all this, to further spread the fruits of economic growth, and to check or reduce the very large scale of corruption.

The North followed a separate path; it has not attempted to invade overseas markets and has not notably departed from its original emphasis on heavy industry. Information is scanty from this tightly controlled system, but it seems clear that incomes, standard of living, and the availability of consumer goods, now so plentiful in the South (where television sets, for example, are nearly universal even in rural households), are far behind the South. Nevertheless the North has done better than most other Communist states outside the Soviet Union, although now lagging behind former Communist Czechoslovakia or East Germany, and is still somewhat ahead of China in per capita output. In 1980 Kim Il-sung's son, Kim Jong-il, was named to succeed his

✠ A Korean Story ✠

Here are some passages from a short story, "Bird of Passage," by the noted Korean writer O Yongsu, first published in 1958 and set in the years just after the Korean War. The story captures some of the hardship and pathos of that time.

Minu had been teaching at W. Middle School in Pusan, where he stayed until the recapture of Seoul. They called it a school, but it was a makeshift affair, just a group of tents. All kinds of peddlers came there, but the shoeshine boys were the worst.... To Minu, whose responsibility it was to keep the campus in order, fell the futile task of ejecting the shoeshine boys, only to have them reappear once his back was turned.... One day one of the shoeshine boys [Kuch'iri] held out his stool and said ... "There are too many shoeshine boys here.... I'll shine all the teachers' shoes for just twenty *hwan*, if you will make it so that I'm the only one allowed to shine shoes here." ... it made sense.... The other boys protested: "Aren't we all refugees together here?" ... Minu managed to quiet the boys. Yet he could not help feeling moved when they said they were all refugees together, for Minu himself was a refugee school teacher who had left his home in the North... . When a new principal was appointed Minu left the school and went to Seoul. He forgot about Kuch'iri [But Kuch'iri turned up later in Seoul and found him].... One day Kuch'iri said, "Teacher, your shoes are all worn out, [but] don't buy any. I'll get you some high-quality American ones from a guy I know.... It's okay if they're second-hand, isn't it?" ... After that Kuch'iri worried about his offer each time he shined Minu's shoes. "I saw the guy yesterday and he says he'll get them soon"—and then mutter something to himself. [But then he disappeared, and] another boy took over the spot [who told him that Kuch'iri had gone with some other boys to] an American army base up near the DMZ [demilitarized zone along the 38th parallel].... It would be autumn before they returned.... One day as leaves were beginning to fall Minu glanced up as a flock of geese flew by in a neat V.... "Kuch'iri too will be coming back soon," he thought.

Source: P. H. Lee, ed., *Flowers of Fire: Twentieth Century Korean Stories* (Honolulu: University of Hawaii Press, 1986), pp. 191–204.

father ultimately and placed in top party jobs, but the father still carried on as head of state. Kim Jong-il appears to be as rigidly doctrinaire as his father, and in 1994 the rest of the world became concerned that North Korea had the capacity to produce nuclear weapons, which given the extreme position of the regime politically caused special worry in the South. Kim Il-sung has long been the subject of an adulatory cult even more pronounced than that of Mao at its height. The press is filled with worshipful references to the "great leader"— and with little else, since it is completely a government mouthpiece. The rest of the world can have only the smallest glimpse of life in the north, and little or no insight into what its government may or may not do. Some families divided by the 38th parallel have recently been permitted to cross it for brief meetings, but other outside observers have only the most limited access. Korea has thus not lost its role as a focus and potential battleground of the Cold War, even as the Cold War itself has ended. Indeed one of its most tragic aspects remains the polarization and unnatural division of Korea. In July 1994 Kim Il-sung suddenly died and was succeeded by his son, Kim Jong-il, but by late 1995 there was no marked change in North Korean policy.

Violent clashes between students or workers and riot police continued in the South, while Seoul, grown to giant size as an industrial center as well as political capital, became one of the most badly polluted cities in the world. It lies, like Taipei, in a lowland basin surrounded by hills, but is far larger and more overcrowded, despite some government efforts at dispersal. As the Cold War began to thaw elsewhere, notably in Europe and in relations between the two superpowers for whom Korea was a major battleground, there were some signs of hope for a qualified reconciliation between North and South, and the withdrawal of at least some of the U.S. troops still stationed in the South. But the goal of unity, which nearly all Koreans continued to want, remained elusive. While Korea remains divided between two hostile governments supported by external power rivalries, the peace of this chronically troubled part of the world will continue at risk, and the welfare of its people will suffer.

Suggestions for Further Reading

Japan

Bestor, T. C. *Neighborhood Tokyo.* Stanford: Stanford University Press, 1989.

Brinton, M. C. *Women and the Economic Miracle: Gender and Work in Postwar Japan.* Berkeley: University of California Press. 1995.

Cohen, T. *Remaking Japan: The American Occupation as New Deal.* New York: Free Press, 1987.

Dore, R. *City Life in Japan: A Study of a Tokyo Ward.* Berkeley: University of California Press, 1994.

Gordon, A. *Postwar Japan As History.* Berkeley: University of California Press, 1993.

Hane, M. *Modern Japan.* Boulder: Westview, 1986.

Hendry, J. *Understanding Japanese Society.* London: Routledge, 1988.

Hideki, R. *The Price of Affluence: Dilemmas of Contemporary Japan.* Tokyo: Kodansha, 1985.

Immamura, H. E. *Urban Japanese Housewives.* Honolulu: University of Hawaii Press, 1986.

Lebra, T. S. *Japanese Women: Constraint and Fulfillment.* Honolulu: University of Hawaii Press, 1984.

Lynn, R. *Educational Advancement in Japan.* Armonk, New York: M. E. Sharpe, 1988.

Minear, R. *Victor's Justice.* Princeton: Princeton University Press, 1971.

Okata, S. *Japan in the World Economy.* Tokyo: Tokyo University Press, 1990.

Peak, L. *Learning to Go to School in Japan.* Berkeley: University of California Press, 1991.

Reischauer. E. O. *The Japanese Today.* Cambridge: Harvard University Press, 1988.

Saso, M. *Women in the Japanese Workplace.* London: Hilary Shipman, 1990.

Schonberger, H. B. *Aftermath of War, 1945–1952.* Kent, Ohio: Kent State University Press, 1989.

Shield, J. J., ed. *Japanese Schooling.* University Park: Penn. State University, 1989.

Sumiko, I. *The Japanese Woman.* New York: Free Press, 1993.

Ui Jun, ed. *Industrial Pollution in Japan.* Tokyo: U.N. University Press, 1992.

Van Wolferen, K. *The Enigma of Japanese Power.* Oxford: Oxford University Press, 1990.

Zinn, R. B. *Winners in Peace: MacArthur, Yoshida, and Postwar Japan.* Berkeley: University of California Press, 1992.

Korea

Amsden, A. *Asia's Next Giant: South Korea and Late Industrialization.* Oxford: Oxford University Press, 1992.

Cotton, J., and Neary, I. *The Korean War in History.* London: Humanities Press, 1989.

Cumings, B., and Halliday, J. *Korea: The Unknown War.* New York: Columbia Press, 1983.

Eberstadt, N. *Korea Approaches Unification.* Armonk, New York: M. E. Sharpe, 1995.

Foot, R. *The Wrong War.* Ithaca: Cornell University Press, 1990.

Foss, R., and Sullivan, J., eds. *Two Koreas, One Future?* New York; University Press of America, 1987.

Jacobs, N. *The Korean Road to Modernization and Development.* Chicago: Univ. of Illinois Press, 1985.

Lone, S., and McCormack, G. *Korea Since 1850.* New York: St. Martin's, 1993.

Macdonald, D. S. *The Koreans.* Boulder: Westview, 1990.

Pae, S. M. *Korea Leading Developing Nations.* New York: Univ. Press of America, 1992.

Song, B. N. *The Rise of the Korean Economy.* Oxford: Oxford University Press, 1990.

Stueck, N. *The Korean War.* Princeton: Princeton University Press, 1996.

Vogel, E. *The Four Little Dragons.* Cambridge: Harvard University Press, 1991.

Woronoff, J. *Asia's Miracle Economics.* Armonk, New York: M. E. Sharpe, 1992.

CHAPTER 22

SOUTHEAST ASIA, VIETNAM, AND THE U.S. IN EAST ASIA

Southeast Asia Since World War II

China's revolutionary resurgence sent shock waves especially through Southeast Asia, where there were also some 15 million permanent Chinese residents (see Chapter 16). The Japanese had helped to destroy European colonialism in Asia, but China now offered to many a different and more appealing model. In neighboring Vietnam the Chinese example encouraged and aided the Communist party under Ho Chih Minh (1890–1969) in its struggle first against French colonialism and then against an American invasion in support of a U.S.-linked government in the south. The Philippines saw a peasant Communist uprising, the Hukbalahaps, remnants and offshoots of which still continue. In Indonesia, fear of an alleged plot by Indonesian Communists and Chinese led to a counterstrike by the military in 1965, with American CIA support, and to mass killings of innocent Chinese and suspected Communists, probably over half a million. In Malaya, an insurrection occurred from 1943 to 1957 by a small group of Chinese residents there, using Mao's example of guerrilla warfare. It was aimed first at the Japanese occupiers, and then at the restored British colonial government. It was finally put down as virtually the last act of the colonial government when most Malayan Chinese, who had done well in the flourishing commercial economy of the country, refused to join it,

and help from China did not materialize. In Burma there were major Communist-led revolts from 1948 to 1950.

Neighboring Thailand was wary, but there was no rebel effort by Thai Chinese, who had assimilated into Thai society much more successfully than in any other Southeast Asian country except perhaps the Philippines, where Chinese settlement and intermarriage with the locals are also long-standing and widespread. In Burma, chronic tension existed between the majority Burmans of the Irrawaddy valley and the numerous minority groups in the surrounding uplands and mountains. The small Chinese minority in Rangoon was largely expelled with Burmese independence from Britain in 1947. The military government which came to power in 1962 under General Ne Win (1911–) followed the Chinese example by cutting nearly all of Burma's ties with the rest of the world and attempting to promote domestic development along "the Burmese way to socialism."

In most of Southeast Asia colonial rule left too few educated people to form a stable political base, and too few with any political experience. Parliamentary government was tried in Indonesia and Burma but the lack of an adequate base and the political inexperience and ineptitude of leaders led to its collapse and a takeover by the military. But nowhere in Southeast Asia has Western-style democracy flourished, and in nearly every country power is exercised to varying degrees by a police state, a military-dominated government, or a Communist regime.

432

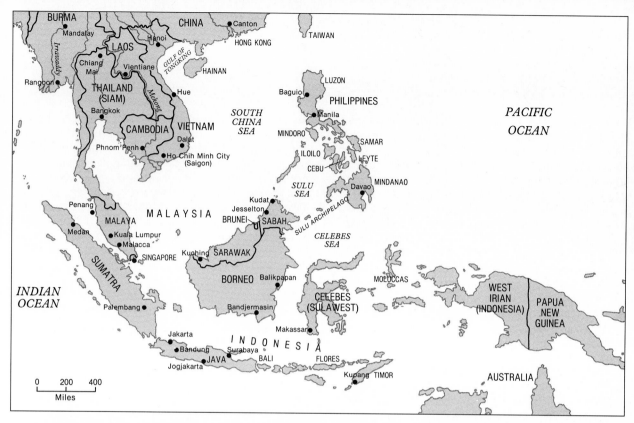

Southeast Asia

Vietnam's 30 Years of War

When the war ended in 1945, Ho and his followers were ready to take over the government. They had been organizing from bases in south China since 1941, where they set up a united front with other Vietnamese nationalists called the Viet Minh, or League for the Independence of Vietnam, and by 1944 the Viet Minh had infiltrated much of the northern part of the country and was mounting guerrilla resistance to the Japanese. Their commander, General Vo Nguyen Giap, entered Hanoi with his troops soon after the Japanese surrender, and in September of 1945 Ho proclaimed the independent Democratic Republic of Vietnam. A great famine in the north in 1944 and 1945 had the effect of building Communist strength. Ho's government controlled most of the north, and tried to extend its support southward, but its dominantly Marxist line, appealing to poor peasants, was resisted by many of the wealthier and more educated. Ho dissolved the Communist party in November, and brought into the Viet Minh and the government in Hanoi many more non-Communists, hoping to broaden his appeal.

But meanwhile the French returned, with British and American arms and support, and occupied Saigon in September of 1945. By the end of the year they had reoccupied most of the south. Protracted talks with Ho and the Viet Minh ended in stalemate. In November of 1946, French naval units bombarded Haiphong, the port of Hanoi, killing as many as 10,000 civilians, and landed troops. What has been called the "endless war" had begun. General de Gaulle, by now president of France, had declared that "France's sword shall shine again," after his country's humiliation by Germany, and mindful of the long French tradition of "la gloire." But France, prostrate after the war, now operated necessarily with American-supplied arms. Cold War pressures had convinced the Americans that communism must be fought even half-way around the world in Vietnam, and that the French were a useful ally. Neither France nor the United States appeared to realize that colonialism in Asia was dead, and that the struggle was one for Vietnamese independence.

With their superior American equipment, the French had reconquered all of the cities by early 1947. The Viet Minh, taking a leaf from the book of the Chinese Communists and following the same guerrilla strategy against a superior enemy, took to the countryside, from which they harried the French positions, especially at night, and disrupted road and rail traffic, while at the same time extending their political support against the hated foreign enemy. It was very like the Chinese Communist strategy against the Japanese, and a few of the more far-seeing observers realized that it would have the same ultimate outcome. In an effort to bolster their legitimacy, the French installed the former Vietnamese "emperor" Bao Dai in 1950, as the Japanese had used Pu Yi (see Chapter 18) in Manchuria. Cambodia and Laos were reincorporated as "associated states" within the French Union of Indo-China. For most politically conscious Vietnamese, Ho Chi Minh remained the prime symbol and leader of their national strivings. After 1949, economic aid, training, and arms came to the Viet Minh from China next door. China's revolutionary success, and the pressures of the anti-French war, strengthened the Communist leadership of the Viet Minh. The French foolishly diverted a major part of their forces to a large base in the mountains of the northwest at Dien Bien Phu, to try to hamper a Communist invasion of Laos. This gave the Viet Minh an opportunity to pick them off. General Giap hauled siege equipment to this remote mountain bastion, and in 1954 the French garrison surrendered.

At the international conference in Geneva which followed, with China, India, and the major Western powers represented, the French agreed to give up their struggle. Vietnam was temporarily partitioned between north and south, along the 17th parallel just north of the old capital at Hué, with the Bao Dai government in the south, led by Ngo Dinh Diem as premier. The Geneva agreements called for the withdrawal of all foreign troops and for na-

tionwide elections to be held the following year, but Diem and his American supporters refused, fearing that the Viet Minh would win hands down. Diem deposed Bao Dai in 1955 and made himself president of what he called the Republic of Vietnam, supported by many, including Vietnamese Catholics who had fled from the Communist-dominated north. But there were even more supporters of Hanoi in the south, and Diem attempted to suppress them. In 1960 Hanoi organized what it called the National Liberation Front (NLF) to meet this threat, composed mainly of southerners but under northern direction at the top. Guerrilla warfare spread in the south, and the United States began to send "military advisers." Diem's forces, with growing American help, increasingly lost out in the struggle against the NLF, and in 1963 he was assassinated, with American CIA collusion, by a military clique. American ground troops began to augment the South Vietnamese forces more openly, 75,000 by 1965, and over half a million by the late 1960s. Successive military regimes proved both ineffective and unpopular, and the United States became in effect the real power in the south.

At the end of January 1968, over Vietnamese New Year or Tet (the same as Chinese New Year), North Vietnamese forces mounted a surprise attack on 15 cities in the south, fighting together with the NLF. The counterattack by southern and U.S. troops hurt the NLF badly, and from then on they and the northerners returned to a guerrilla strategy. But it had become a very bloody and ruthless war, on both sides. Southern and U.S. forces tried to wipe out NLF and Viet Minh supporters, a guerrilla group known as the Viet Cong, often by killing villagers suspected of aiding them, and by

---

✠ A Warning to France ✠

As it became clear that France intended to reestablish its colonial rule of Vietnam, Bao Dai, whom the French had earlier installed as their puppet, appealed to General de Gaulle on behalf of Vietnamese nationalism, in part as follows:

You would understand better if you could see what is happening here, if you could feel the desire for independence which is in everyone's heart and which no human force can any longer restrain. Even if you come to re-establish a French administration here, it will no longer be obeyed; each village will be a nest of resistance, each former collaborator an enemy, and your officials and colonists will themselves ask to leave this atmosphere which they will be unable to breathe.

Source: E. Hammer, *The Struggle for Indochina* (Stanford, Calif.: Stanford University Press, 1954), p. 102.

forcing other villagers to live in fortified encampments called "strategic hamlets" begun earlier in the war where they could have no contact with the guerrillas. NLF, Viet Minh, and Viet Cong forces used similar terror tactics against those they suspected of collaborating with the other side. Much of the American actions was televised for audiences back home, and news leaked out of the massacre of an entire village at My Lai by American troops, only one incident of many such. American public opinion began to turn strongly against a war which seemed to violate so much of American values and ideals and which could not easily be won. By 1969, U.S. forces in Vietnam were being slowly reduced, although the tide had by no means turned in their favor. At the same time, the Americans bombed Hanoi almost to rubble, mined the harbor of Haiphong, and spread the war into Cambodia in an effort to prevent its use by northern forces as a refuge, or as part of their supply route to the south, the so-called Ho Chi Minh Trail.

Ho died in 1969, still short of his goal of Vietnamese unification and independence, but the United States was growing weary of this "endless war" and the terrible price it exacted. Peace talks had begun with the North Vietnamese in Paris in 1968; the bombings of Hanoi and Cambodia were designed to "put pressure" on the North and weaken their negotiating position. The agreements finally signed in Paris early in 1973 were limited to provisions for the safe withdrawal of the remaining American troops, who in effect deserted their erstwhile southern allies and their civilian collaborators. The final evacuation of the last U.S. diplomatic personnel in 1975, by helicopter from the roof of the American embassy in Saigon as frantic Vietnamese collaborators and their dependents fought to get aboard, was an unedifying spectacle viewed by millions of Americans on their television sets. The NLF and northern forces overwhelmed the South. Saigon fell in 1975, and in 1976 the country was formally reunited as the Socialist Republic of Vietnam, with its capital at Hanoi; Saigon was renamed Ho Chi Minh City. The Americans had tried to replace the French as a new foreign power attempting to deny the unity and independence of Vietnam, roles which many Americans too found uncomfortable despite the prevailing mood of the "crusade against communism." In any case, although they had vast superiority in high-tech weapons and firepower, the Americans were unable to defeat guerrilla-based nationalism, as the Japanese had found earlier in China. In the course of the long struggle, the Vietnamese communists became even more the leaders of their country's fight for independence, again following the Chinese pattern.

In the American phase of the war, beginning in 1964, U.S. forces lost nearly 58,000 dead and some 300,000 wounded, in a conflict whose purpose and meaning were understood by very few on the American side, including those in Vietnam. In an effort to use firepower rather than men, the Americans dropped more bombs, by a large margin—some say twice as much tonnage—on Vietnam alone than in the whole of World War II in both Europe and Asia. But the losses were overwhelmingly greater on the Vietnamese side. From the beginning of their war in 1945 to its end in 1975, they lost nearly two million dead, mainly military personnel but including very large numbers of civilians; nearly four million, soldiers and civilians, were wounded or maimed, and there were well over a million refugees driven from their homes by the fighting. Longer-run effects included the massive devastation of many of the cities and much of the countryside, and the American spraying of the forests to defoliate them with the herbicide Agent Orange, to deny the shelter of their leaves to guerrilla forces. Agent Orange caused human casualties on the American side too, but its consequences for Vietnam and its people were enormously more serious and longer lasting; soil as well as people became poisoned.

It was part of an American strategy reflected in the much-quoted remark of a junior officer, "We had to destroy the village in order to save it." Like the village's inhabitants, who were also destroyed, the "saving" of Vietnam from communism, by a power from the other side of the world with no stake in Vietnam otherwise, came to seem at best inappropriate, to both Vietnamese and Americans alike. This was especially so given the terrible costs of that effort, and it became increasingly clear that it was in any case futile. Guerrilla-based nationalism had proven its power in the 2,000-year Vietnamese struggle against the might of the Chinese empire, and now it had humbled the greatest power of the modern world. American policy makers would have done better to study Vietnamese history, and to try to understand the true force of Vietnamese nationalism. The fact that the nationalists were dominated by Communists, who predictably became more hard-line as the war progressed, was far less important to most Vietnamese, and to the outcome of the war. China and the Soviet Union supplied arms to the north, but no troops. It was a Vietnamese victory, and, perhaps only incidentally, a Communist one.

Politically also, the war exacted a high price. One can rarely safely predict, but it seems at least possible that if Vietnam had been given its independence, like nearly all of the rest of Asia after the end of World War II, a Communist regime under Ho Chi Minh might have developed more openly, less rigidly, and with greater freedom for non-Communists and others than it did after 30 years of struggle. The long and bitter war for independence, which became in effect a civil war, divided northerners and southerners, Communists and non-Communists, into opposing camps of mutual suspicion and hatred, much of which still remain. Vietnam after 1976

Refugees in Vietnam being forcibly evacuated from their village by the U.S. forces for resettlement in a guarded camp. Their village area will then be defoliated, to deny the rice crop to the Viet Cong who have infiltrated it. (UNIPIX)

Declaration of Independence

The Vietnamese declaration of independence on September 2, 1945, was consciously modeled on that of the United States. Here are some sample sentences.

All men are created equal.... They are endowed by their Creator with certain inalienable rights.... Nevertheless for more than eighty years the French imperialists, abusing their "liberty, equality, and fraternity," have violated the land of our ancestors.... They have deprived us of all our liberties. They have imposed upon us inhuman laws.... They have built more prisons than schools. They have acted without mercy toward our patriots.... They have despoiled our ricelands, our mines, our forests.... They have invented hundreds of unjustified taxes, condemning our countrymen to extreme poverty.... [But] we seized our independence from the hands of the Japanese and not from the hands of the French.... A people which has obstinately opposed French domination for more than eighty years.... who ranged themselves on the side of the Allies to fight against Fascism, this people has the right to be free.... All the people of Vietnam are determined to mobilize all their spiritual and material strength, to sacrifice their lives and property, to safeguard their right to liberty and independence.

Source: H. J. Benda and J. Larkin, *The World of Southeast Asia* (New York: Harper & Row, 1967), pp. 270–273.

was politically rigid, tolerating no opposition or divergent views. In part because of its doctrinaire policies, and suffering from a U.S.-led international trade and aid boycott, economic development lagged far behind most of the rest of Asia, and the devastating destruction of the "30 Years War" from 1945 to 1975 was still not fully made up by 1995.

The Americans were slow to accept their defeat, imposed an embargo on impoverished Vietnam, and blocked its access to the rest of the world, except for China and Russia, and to the United Nations. Negotiations for a peace treaty were stalled by American insistence on a full accounting and the return of the remains of their military personnel missing in action until 1975, the so-called MIAs. However much one may sympathize with the American families concerned, the number of men at issue was far smaller than in any modern war, including both World Wars, estimated by the Americans at some 2 percent of their forces, whereas nearly 20 percent were in that category in the Second World War and 30 percent in the First, another reminder of the terrible chaos and human tragedy of warfare. Some 300,000 Vietnamese are still MIA. Vietnam's recovery from its unprecedented devastation continued to be slowed by its isolation from normal trade and interchange with the rest of the world, though by 1990 there were a few signs that the U.S. position might soften somewhat, and in 1993 limited American trade with and investment in Vietnam were resumed. From the late 1980s, Vietnam also began to follow the same path as China, toward a market-oriented system and away from ideological rigidity. Its economy has begun to grow rapidly and may well become another "little dragon" together with Taiwan, South Korea, Hong Kong, and Singapore. Partly in acknowledgment and eager not to miss out on trade opportunities being vigorously pursued by most other countries, the U.S. lifted its embargo on Vietnam and moved toward normal diplomtic relations in 1994.

Bloody Cambodia

The French reoccupied Cambodia in 1945, and presided over a series of ineffective puppet governments. At the Geneva Conference of 1954 (see above), Cambodia was given what amounted to independence, and the country came under the virtual one-man rule of Prince Norodom Sihanouk, formerly king. There was also a small Cambodian Communist party. Sihanouk's rule was largely benign, and Cambodia was for the present spared the ordeal of Vietnam, enjoying a modest prosperity and considerable foreign development aid. After 1965, Cambodia sold rice to North Vietnam and transported Soviet and Chinese arms from its port of Sihanoukville on the Gulf of Siam. A peasant uprising in 1967 was savagely re-

pressed, and Sihanouk's popularity began to wane; he began to spend much of his time producing and starring in films, and traveling abroad. In 1969, the Americans began their so-called secret bombing of Cambodia, in an effort to block the flow of supplies from North to South Vietnam and to disrupt troop sanctuaries. While Sihanouk was out of the country in early 1970, he was deposed by his own army. A new military regime under General Lon Nol took over Cambodia with American support, but in May American and South Vietnamese forces invaded the country and laid waste the border area with Vietnam. Nevertheless, and despite repressive efforts by the Lon Nol government, Communist insurgents controlled about two-thirds of the country by the end of 1972.

With the American withdrawal from Vietnam in 1973, Cambodia became their target, in a campaign of "carpet-bombing" which in eight months (until it was stopped by Congress) dropped twice the explosives dropped on Japan in the whole of World War II, and on a country with which the United states was not even at war. The civilian casualties were enormous, but the effect of the bombing was to further strengthen the Communists, as might have been predicted from experience in Germany and in Vietnam, and to help them recruit more support among the embittered survivors. Phnom Penh, the capital, was hopelessly overcrowded with perhaps two million refugees from the bombings. In 1975, it and the whole country were taken over by the Communists, under the man who called himself Pol Pot; as Saloth Sar he had given up teaching school at age 32 and became a high official in the Cambodian Communist party. His forces, soon to be known around the world as the Khmer Rouge, ordered almost the entire population of Phnom Penh and of the second city, Battambang, probably about three and a half million altogether, to leave their homes and work indefinitely in the countryside. This was an idea, in distorted form, borrowed from Mao Tse-tung and his antiurban gospel; Maoist and Chinese influences were strong with Pol Pot and the Khmer Rouge.

There was indescribable suffering on the part of these newly created refugees, and mass murder of middle-class, professional, and educated people, accurately portrayed in the films *The Killing Fields* and *Swimming to Cambodia*, although they told only a small part of the horror. Others were driven or worked until they dropped or died of exhaustion and starvation. Perhaps as many as two million Cambodians died in this holocaust in 1975 and four following years, over a quarter of the total population. Cambodia was cut off from all foreign connections or influences (except for China) and things like cars, libraries, and other "alien" symbols destroyed. Cambodia too announced a "Great Leap Forward," with much the same consequences in human suffering and economic chaos as in China a decade earlier.

The police chief of South Vietnam executing a Viet Cong suspect on a Saigon street. This and other similar pictures were widely circulated abroad and helped to build opposition to the war in the United States and elsewhere. (AP/Wide World Photos)

Pol Pot's agents continued to torture and murder many thousands, including especially teachers and alleged "counterrevolutionaries" and political opponents whom the paranoid Pol Pot saw everywhere.

By 1978 there was growing opposition to these hideous policies, especially in the eastern areas and with some Vietnamese support. Early in 1979 the Vietnamese army intervened, meeting no resistance outside of the retreating Khmer Rouge forces, which holed up in forest sanctuaries along the Thai border. A pro-Vietnamese government was installed at Phnom Penh, with the title of the People's Republic of Kampuchea. The United States and China, plus Thailand, all implacable enemies of Vietnam, recognized, supported, and continued to send arms to the Khmer Rouge and Pol Pot, on the theory that "the enemy of my enemy is my friend." Pol Pot's murderous government continued to represent Cambodia, or Kampuchea, in the United Nations. Under these circumstances and with sanctuaries across the Thai border, the Khmer Rouge held on and could not be eliminated by the Vietnamese. Under international pressure, and with the hope of restoring relations with the United States in particular, the Vietnamese withdrew their forces in 1989. American policy began slowly to move away from total anti-Vietnam hostility and vindictiveness, but China especially remained adamant.

In 1979, to "punish" Vietnam for its intervention in Cambodia, China had invaded its northern provinces in a brief campaign in which the Vietnamese again proved their ability to defeat their ancient antagonist, and without pulling troops back from Cambodia. There were heavy losses on both sides, but the Chinese soon withdrew. After the Vietnamese left Cambodia in 1989, the Khmer Rouge greatly expanded the area it controlled and even threatened the cities, still abetted and supplied primarily by China, and some said covertly by the U.S. CIA. Cambodia has been for nearly two decades a bloody battleground, and its future remained dark while it continued to be used as a pawn in wider power struggles. By 1990 official American opinion was at last edging away from support of Pol Pot; there was some hope for a compromise settlement and an end to Cambodia's nightmare. But as of late 1995 there was no stable resolution of Cambodia's future.

Laos: The Forgotten Country

In tiny, mountainous, and isolated Laos too, there has been little peace since 1945. After the end of the Japanese occupation, chronic internal struggles, continued through the repressive French reoccupation, ended in the emergence of a Communist government in 1975, still with its capital at the old base of Vientiane. American aid for non-Communist groups in the 1950s and 1960s had little effect, and successive governments largely ignored the problems of the rural areas, where most Lao lived. By 1963, Laos was engulfed in a bloody civil war. Vietnamese support for the Communists, and their use of Lao territory along the frontier as part of their supply route to the south, led to a massive and immensely destructive American bombing of Laos, producing uncounted casualties and nearly a million refugees. Communists in the then coalition government in Vientiane gained new strength from this example of "capitalist-imperialist aggression," and took over in 1975. The Vietnamese were confirmed as an ally, with a strong influence on Laos. Many Lao, especially the educated elite, and many minority tribespeople such as the Hmong, fled to Thailand or the West to escape collectivization and "reeducation," although the government's policies were far from being as severe as in Cambodia. But Laos, a poor country to begin with, still suffered from the destruction of chronic warfare, and from its use as a pawn in contests between outside powers.

Burma, Thailand, Malaya, and Singapore

The rest of mainland Southeast Asia has had a varied history since 1945, but only Burma has failed to win internal order, or to benefit from rapid economic growth, while Thailand, Malaysia, and Singapore have been among the most rapidly growing economies in the world.

Burma

The Japanese at first used a few Burmese anticolonialists in their campaign against the Indian and British troops, and allowed the organization of a small Burma Independence Army. But once the campaign was over, it was largely demobilized in July of 1942 and the remnant referred to simply as a defense force. The Japanese permitted a show of participation in administration by Burmese, but that did not prevent the drafting of forced labor. Underground resistance spread, and as Indian and British troops advanced southward in 1944 and 1945, many Burmese cooperated with them and fought the Japanese. Many politically conscious Burmese had joined an Anti-Fascist People's Freedom League, led by Aung San. The British effort to resume colonial control and delay the granting of independence led to demonstrations and strikes organized by the AFPFL, and it was finally agreed that independence would follow national elections. The AFPFL dominated the voting, and independence came in January of 1948, six months after India.

Meanwhile, Aung San, the chief Burmese political figure, was assassinated by conservative opponents in mid–1947, together with seven of his close associates, and the AFPFL Vice President U Nu became the first independent premier in 1948. But the death of Aung San had removed the only figure who could command the support of most Burmese, and of the non-Burman mi-

nority groups who lived in the hills and mountains surrounding the Irrawaddy plain, most importantly Shans, Karens, and Kachins. The colonial government had protected these major ethnic minorities, who feared a reassertion of Burman dominance when the British withdrew, and many of them were Christians. Communist groups also opposed the U Nu government, and chronic rebellion soon broke out. By 1949 the government controlled only the cities, with fighting often even in the suburbs of Rangoon. Slowly the government gained the ascendancy, and held fresh elections in 1951, but was never able to put down rebellion in the remoter mountain districts. Both the AFPFL and the varied opposition groups were split, and Burma made little or no economic progress as the central government was increasingly paralyzed by divisions and by bureaucratic ineptitude.

U Nu was a charismatic figure and an interesting one, a devout Buddhist who disliked both violent and nonviolent conflict and who periodically retired to a monastery, "to keep his vision clear." Most Burmese remained Buddhists, and his wing of the AFPFL, named the Union party, won a strong majority in the elections of 1960, but his authority and that of the government continued to deteriorate, with no institutional or adequate political base. In 1962, the army general Ne Win seized power. U Nu fled into exile while Ne Win suspended the constitution and imprisoned most of the remaining political opponents, under the auspices of a "Revolutionary Council," staffed mainly by military men.

The Council nationalized all foreign and the larger domestic firms, expelled the several thousand Indians remaining in the country, monopolized all internal and external trade, and progressively cut Burma's ties with the outside world, including most imports, under the banner of "the Burmese Way to Socialism." This was a strange mixture of Marxism-Leninism, Buddhism, and Burmese traditionalism, which condemned greed and claimed to further instead the cultivation of spiritual values. In fact, Burma became a police state, and student and worker demonstrations were harshly suppressed, as troops fired on unarmed demonstrators. Education at all levels was suspect and declining, and foreign or even domestic books hard to find. The economy slowed even more, and there was much unemployment, especially among educated groups. Armed rebellion continued in the north, especially among the Karens and the Kachins, the latter periodically allied with the Burma Communist party.

It was reasonable for Burma to avoid alignments with any of the major powers and hence to avoid being drawn into wider conflicts, but in other terms its self-imposed isolation from the rest of the world, including foreign investment and imported goods and technology, cost it dearly economically and further weakened its schools and universities. Maintenance and basic services deteriorated, especially in increasingly tattered Rangoon, and tourist visas for foreigners were limited to one week. The patient, gentle Burmese still smiled, and of course there were nonmaterial rewards in preserving tradition against the avalanche of "modernization" elsewhere in the world, but life was hard for many, eased for some by a vigorous black market, especially in imported goods. But Burma turned its back on "progress," a path which had both pluses and minuses. Peasants were less severely affected, and, where the civil war did not spread, were able to preserve their traditional way of life, but the slow or stagnant pace of agricultural development left them little if any better off, and there were occasional food shortages as population continued to grow. Ne Win hung onto power despite cosmetic gestures about retiring, and in 1989 the military government changed the spelling of the country's name to Myanmar, linguistically or phonetically equivalent to *Burma*. In May of 1990 elections in which opposition parties were permitted to compete produced a sweeping victory for a Socialist party headed by Aung San's daughter Suu Kyi, who had been kept for the previous year under house arrest. The government was clearly taken aback by the vote, and it remained unclear whether it would in fact step down, and whether Burma might regain at least a degree of political freedom. In early 1991 the military government outlawed the Socialist party, the National League for Democracy, which had won the elections the previous May, and by late 1995, although Aung San Suu Kyi, who had won the Nobel Peace Prize was released, there was no change in the government's police-state policies.

Thailand

The Thais were fortunate in having few ethnic minorities within their borders except for the Chinese immigrants, who as pointed out in Chapter 16 were for the most part peacefully assimilated into the larger society and in a generation tended to become Thai. Forced collaboration with the Japanese had saved the country from the destruction suffered by most of the rest of Southeast Asia, but the immediate postwar government proved ineffective and unpopular. A military group seized power in 1947 with a generally conservative policy, sending troops to fight in the Korean War and attempting to build American favor and support. The growing success of the Viet Minh in Vietnam helped to ensure such an outcome as Thailand became an American supply base, but the military government's repressive actions domestically led to its overthrow in a 1957 coup and the effort to establish parliamentary rule. This in turn had a short life; the army found it "indecisive," and military rule was reimposed in 1958. Once again opposition groups were suppressed, but the new government under General Sarit built wide political support by effectively promoting economic development, and also education.

Thailand remained at least nominally a monarchy despite the reforms of 1932 (see Chapter 16), but General Sarit encouraged the king to play a more active role in public life, and the monarchy became more popular and a focus for Thai nationalism. Sarit died prematurely in 1963, but by then the Vietnam War had become the country's major concern. Thailand gradually became an increasingly open ally of the United States in its effort to defeat the Viet Cong. Vietnam was feared for its past history of expansion, and its ambition to dominate Cambodia and Laos, Thailand's immediate neighbors which had been detached from the Thai sphere by the French. Thai troops fought under the Americans in Vietnam, and U.S. air bases in Thailand were of major importance. Forty thousand American military personnel were stationed in Thailand, and it was heavily used as an "R and R" base. U.S. spending in all these respects was huge, and the

Buddhist Burma: a monk with shaven head and yellow robe in the courtyard of the Shwedagon pagoda in Rangoon. (Jean-Claude Lejeune)

economy prospered, much as Japan had benefited from being used as a supply base in the Korean War. Bangkok was the chief beneficiary, but there were also U.S. bases upcountry; provincial towns grew too, and national economic growth soared. The government sponsored extensive development projects in the northeast, in the provinces bordering Laos and Cambodia. But there were rebellions there, fueled by poverty and organized by the small Thai Communist party. In 1971, after its brief revival in 1968, the constitution was again set aside by a military coup. Protests and demonstrations against the government mounted, especially among students in Bangkok. In 1973 General Thanom was forced to flee the country and a civilian government came to power.

But it proved difficult to satisfy all of the now vocal and periodically violent protestors, demonstrating for a more genuinely democratic government. In 1976 troops, police, and vigilantes went on a veritable orgy of violence against rioters at Thammasat University in Bangkok, lynching, beating, burning, and shooting scores of protesting students. Shortly thereafter the army moved in again and the military ruled the country for most of the ensuing decade. A brief period of elected government in the 1980s was ended by another military coup early in 1991. Dissent was repressed, but Thai society had been transformed by economic development. Bangkok had become a huge, overcrowded city of industry and trade, with a burgeoning new middle class. Elsewhere, development meant that by 1990 most Thais were no longer farmers but industrial or transport workers, bureaucrats, or businesspeople at various levels. Investments by successive military governments in education had also created a very large new group of well-educated people, over two million of them university graduates. Future efforts to restore constitutional government seemed likely, but the army retained real power.

Malaysia and Singapore

Malaya, like Burma, had suffered a brutal Japanese invasion and occupation, with the Chinese of Malaya especially resisting underground and through guerrilla actions while more Malays became collaborators, in part because the Japanese were not as brutal to them as to the Chinese. Chinese were nearly two-fifths of the total population, not counting dominantly Chinese Singapore, and the arrangements for the independence of Malaya, which all parties agreed was appropriate, were long delayed as Malay and Chinese groups worked out their compromises. Meanwhile the Communist party, largely Chinese, decided to resort to armed insurrection by mid-1948. The battle of the colonial government against what was called "The Emergency" lasted nearly ten years, although the Communist guerrillas holed up in the jungles saw their numbers and support dwindle after about 1950, in part because general prosperity deprived their somewhat vague radical program of much of its appeal. The Emergency heightened anti-Chinese feeling; many Chinese were forcibly resettled in fortified villages to deny their alleged support to the guerrillas, and about 10,000 Chinese were deported to China.

The most effective counter to the guerrilla opposition was however speedy progress toward independence for Malaya, and general prosperity. A coalition between the Malay and Chinese political organizations won nearly all the seats in a Legislative Council elected in 1955, and worked out the details of an independence agreement with the British which took effect in August of 1957. Malays were given the dominant position in the new state, including a virtual monopoly of political office, the civil service, and university education, while it was understood that the Chinese would continue their dominance of the economy, in which most of them had done very well. A group of wealthy Chinese then founded a Chinese university in Penang. Efforts were made to rediscover and revitalize traditional Malay culture, long in eclipse under colonial influence, but entrepreneurial activity had never been an important part of that culture, and foreigners, including Portuguese, Indians, Indonesians, Arabs, and British, as well as Chinese, had for centuries managed most of Malaya's trade and commercial sectors. The new government also made successful efforts to diversify an economy too heavily dependent on rubber and its export, and developed important production of palm oil and timber for world markets.

Singapore had been left out of the new Malayan state, mainly because the Malays feared to add still more to the Chinese share of the population, which would then have been almost equally balanced between Chinese and Malay. But the economic logic of union was powerful, and in 1963 Singapore joined Malaya, only to be ejected again by the Malayan government in 1965 on the same old communal grounds. The brief union with Singapore was accompanied by the inheritance of the former British colonial territories along the north coast of Borneo, never controlled by the Dutch and hence not part of Indonesia. (The tiny Sultanate of Brunei became independent, and rocketed to wealth when rich oil deposits were discovered there.) There had been heavy Chinese settlement in north Borneo too, especially in Sarawak and Sabah and in the commercial towns and cities on the coast, but they remained a large minority, outnumbered by a great variety of indigenous peoples. There were also many Malays, so that in balance incorporating these areas into what was now called the state of Malaysia would strengthen the Malay and non-Chinese share of the total population.

Nevertheless, bitterness and periodic conflict continued to divide Malays and Chinese, and there were outbreaks of communal violence in which hundreds, mainly Chinese, died. Chinese were about 32 percent of the Malaysian population, Malays about 47 percent, with the balance split among Indians and other smaller ethnic groups. Islam had been made the official state religion, and now it became even more a Malay nationalist and communal badge. In the later 1980s the government began to put pressure on non-Muslims, and to press for an orthodox Islamic line in all things, attempting to limit or emasculate even traditional Malay art, literature, and music. Although there continued to be violent Malay-Chinese clashes, Malaysia did very well economically, and the parliamentary system, with minimal Chinese representation, proved stable, unlike Thailand or Burma. There was also a growing industrial sector, including some high-tech electronics and other consumer goods, and some Malays began to enter the business world as well as becoming skilled workers.

Singapore became an even more striking success story economically, thanks largely to its dominantly Chinese population (plus the entrepreneurial skills of its Indian minority) and its duty-free port status as a small city-state, a parallel to Hong Kong. Separated from Malaysia in 1965, it went on to achieve a very high economic growth rate, serving as an entrepôt, processing, servicing, and financial center for much of Malaysia and Indonesia. The forms of parliamentary democracy and courts were preserved, but the government remained dominated by its vigorous and strongly conservative British-educated prime minister, Lee Kuan Yew. He tolerated no opposition or criticism, censored the press, and enforced law and order according to his own views, to which there was no significant political opposition in what became a one-party as well as virtually a one-man state. Electronics and other light manufacturing joined earlier processing industries, and Singapore became a major banking as well as trade center. Most Singaporeans were prosperous, and indeed their living standards were second in Asia only to Japan, far ahead of the rest of Southeast Asia. The government also invested in public housing and maintained an enviable range of social services as well as a highly developed education system, a traditional Chinese priority. It was a bargain which most Singaporeans found attractive, economic security for nearly all, affluence for many, in exchange for some losses in free expression and personal liberties. Lee's official retirement in 1991 and his replacement have not been accompanied by significant change.

Indonesia and the Philippines

The Dutch, with British and American support, ill-advisedly tried to reestablish their colonial control of the East Indies after the Japanese surrender. Java especially had suffered under a harsh Japanese occupation, but their invasion had destroyed the colonial order. The chief Indonesian leaders, Sukarno and Mohammed Hatta, actively collaborated with the Japanese, but were ineffective in moderating their brutality or preventing their conscription of slave labor, most of whom were worked to their deaths. Sukarno and Hatta announced Indonesia's independence as a republic two days after the Japanese surrender, with themselves as president and vice president. But there was no mass base, no organized government, and few Indonesians with any education or administrative experience, thanks to repressive Dutch colonial policies in the past. Negotiations with the Dutch were accompanied by Dutch reoccupation, and a "Police Action" which brought most of Indonesia under their control by 1948 and captured Sukarno and Hatta. But the Indonesians had put together an army, and patriotic youths flocked to it. Their guerrilla actions against the Dutch were increasingly successful. The Americans and the United Nations withdrew their support for the Dutch, and at the end of 1949 they were obliged to grant full independence.

But the former Dutch East Indies, now called Indonesia for the first time, was a hodgepodge of different ethnic, religious, and linguistic groups with no common tradition except oppression by the Dutch and no experience of working together, still less of sharing a state. The territory was scattered over some 3,000 separate islands stretched along more than 3,000 miles. About 3 percent of the population was Chinese, concentrated in the cities and dominating the commercial sector and the export trade. In the rural areas, local hereditary elites and village headmen retained their power and often ignored the dictates of the new central government based in Jakarta, the former Dutch colonial capital of Batavia. There was also deep resentment in the outer islands against the dominance of Java, traditionally the major power center, the richest area, and with by far the largest population. Christianity had spread widely in many of these outer islands, promoted both by Portuguese and later by Dutch and American missionaries, and this increased resentment of largely Muslim Java, while Bali remained Hindu-Buddhist, a survival of earlier Indian influence which had also covered most of Java until the seventeenth century. The Javanese language was foreign to the rest of the new Indonesia, which spoke a great variety of other tongues. The new government created a new national language called simply Indonesian, based largely on Malay, which had been a widespread trade language. Most Indonesians thus became bilingual, in Indonesian (taught in all schools) and in their own local language.

The new government understandably had trouble establishing its authority, and in managing the economy

✠ Guided Democracy ✠

Sukarno supported what he called "guided democracy," based on "una-nimity," which he said derived from traditional village patterns.

The only way in which it can function satisfactorily is by means of unanimity arising out of deliberation.... Deliberations should not be held in such a way that there is no contest between opposing points of view, no resolutions and counter-resolutions, no taking of sides, but only a persistent effort to find common ground in solving a problem. From such deliberation there arises a consensus, a unanimity, which is more powerful than a resolution forced through by a majority of votes, a resolution perhaps not accepted, or perhaps resented, by the minority.... The nationalism we advocate is not the nationalism of isolation, not chauvinism as blazoned by people in Europe ... who say there is none so great as Germany, whose people, they say, are supermen, corn-haired and blue-eyed 'Aryans' whom they consider the greatest in the world, while other nations are worthless. Do not let us hold by such principles, do not let us say that the Indonesian nation is the most perfect and the noblest while we belittle other peoples. We must proceed towards the unity of the world, the brotherhood of the world.

Source: Sukarno, *Towards Freedom and the Dignity of Man* (Djakarta: no date), p. 14.

---

after the devastation caused by both the Japanese and the Dutch. As the Dutch withdrew, there were far too few Indonesians who had the technical competence or the experience to manage the basic infrastructure of transport, industry, finance, or basic administration. By 1957 the effort to establish parliamentary rule collapsed, and there was widespread rebellion. The army took power, and in 1959 Sukarno reemerged as head of state, in alliance with the Indonesian Communist party and the army, under the banner of "Guided Democracy." To draw attention from the seriously deteriorating economy and runaway inflation, Sukarno campaigned successfully to recover from Dutch control the western half of New Guinea, which he renamed West Irian, and launched a "Confrontasi" (Confrontation) with the new state of Malaysia over the status of several small islands which lay between them. His Communist allies began to push radical land reform and rent reduction, alarming many of the traditional local elites. Then in 1965 a group of junior officers assassinated six senior generals in an attempted coup, claiming Sukarno's leadership. The coup was officially interpreted as a Communist plot to seize power, although the evidence for that is poor. It was quickly suppressed by the army under General Suharto, and the army then went on to wipe out the Communist party and all who were suspected of sympathy with it, aided by bands of youths and local mobs. The victims included many thousands of Chinese, who were suspected because China had gone Communist,

but were also turned on as targets for long-standing ethnic resentment against them as alien exploiters. In this horrendous bloodbath, probably at least half a million unresisting people were killed, some say a million. Sukarno was forced into retirement, and General Suharto took over.

Suharto successfully sought foreign economic aid and investments, and slowly began to rebuild the shattered economy. In 1968 he was elected president, and confirmed in subsequent stage-managed elections in 1971, 1977, and 1982, with respectable majorities. Despite this show of democratic procedures, Indonesia has remained largely a police state, suppressing free expression, jailing or torturing dissidents, including even major writers, and operating a brutal police system. Suharto ruled virtually as a dictator. He also invaded East Timor, an island in easternmost Indonesia, when the Portuguese withdrew in 1965, and cruelly suppressed the nationalist movement there, killing an estimated 200,000 or more. Suharto built further close ties with the United States and Japan, encouraged investment by multinationals, and eased the way for large Indonesian-Chinese businesses by providing Indonesian "partners" with payoffs. Bribery became even more widespread, but the economy began to recover and in many years posted very high growth rates. Chinese were still resented, and the government forbade the use of Chinese language or even the import of books in Chinese. While profiting from Chinese commercial skills,

Sukarno, in a characteristic pose, announcing the end of the struggle against the Dutch, in 1950. (United Nations)

the government continued to discriminate against them and to prevent their assimilation into what was after all already a multiethnic society. On their part, the Chinese had little choice but to stick to their own communities and to retain their traditional culture. A new bureaucratic, if not commercial, Indonesian middle class began to grow, nourished by the huge government bureaucracy and by considerable corruption, and there began to be a number of Indonesian professionals as well. Oil production from Java, Sumatra, and Borneo (Kalimantan) and its export were increased under the government monopoly firm Pertamina, and provided an augmented boost to the economy.

But most Indonesians remained poor, especially outside Java, and even there, as population continued to grow rapidly. After about 1970 economic growth was substantial but it was not equitably distributed, especially not in the burgeoning urban slums and squatter towns or among poor peasants, still the great rural majority, while landowners enjoyed relative prosperity. Public health measures became more effective and widespread, but this lowered the death rate and added more mouths to feed each year. Education was strictly controlled, but the level and extent of literacy gradually rose. Java had become dependent on food imports under the Dutch plantation system centered on cash and nonfood crops, but in the 1980s there were determined government efforts to spread the Green Revolution of better seeds and higher-yielding crop strains, aiming to make the country self-sufficient in rice. To sustain the higher yields, however, required heavy investment in fertilizers and irrigation, things which only the richer peasants or landowners could afford. Many poor and landless peasants migrated to the already overcrowded cities, especially Jakarta, to seek work as scavengers, street vendors, or prostitutes and living in vast squatter encampments. But the disastrous decline of the Sukarno years was reversed, and as economic growth continued there was some hope that the rising tide might in time lift all boats, or at least most of them, and that this might also bring new support for a return to a more democratic system.

The Philippines

Most Filipino politicians collaborated with the Japanese, but most Filipinos supported or joined the resistance forces, and many died in guerrilla actions or at the hands of the Japanese military police. Anti-Japanese struggles were also mixed with peasant struggles against the rampant landlordism which had thrived under American colonialism. The Hukbalahap (People's Anti-Japanese Army) was involved with both, mainly in central Luzon, the main island of the Philippine archipelago, where they benefited from the disruption of the war and occupation and attracted many supporters. Most of the politicians who had collaborated with the Japanese had returned to public life and to public office by 1948. The granting of independence in 1946, as promised before the war, was welcome, but Filipino gratitude was heavily mixed with resentment about the niggardly American aid, its tying to the special American concessions in property and trade which were retained, and its insistence on keeping and building up the huge military bases at Clark Field and Subic Bay. As communism triumphed in China and Vietnam and appeared to threaten Malaya, and later Cambodia and Laos, the Americans became fearful for the Philippines and lined up in support of successive conservative governments after 1946, no longer troubled that the people in power were in many case the same as those who had welcomed the Japanese. Filipinos admired and copied much of American culture, including baseball, and blended it with their Spanish colonial heritage to make a kind of Latin American parallel. As one often quoted remark put it, Philippine culture was the result of 350 years in a Catholic convent and half a century in Hollywood.

There was enormous corruption, a trademark of Philippine politics, and the government was unable to control destructive inflation, rebuild the shattered economy, or defeat the Huks. By 1950 the country was in crisis on all these fronts. But the elections of 1953 brought to power a different kind of politician, Ramon Magsaysay, who had earlier, as secretary of defense, reorganized the army. He assembled around him a group of intelligent and dedicated younger men, and in a relatively short time had put down the Huk rebellion and begun land reform in the areas of their earlier support, easing the burdens of tenancy and helping to cut the ground out from under Communist appeals. Unfortunately he was killed in a plane crash in 1957 (some said it was not an accident). Successive members of the old conservative political elite restored the former oligarchy, dependent on family ties, corruption, and even violence, while economic development, especially for the population as a whole, languished as the few at the top earned new wealth. Magsaysay's early efforts at land reform were shelved, especially as rich landowners were an important political support for those in power. Multinationals were encouraged to invest in the Philippines, and there was some new economic growth, but its benefits were not widely shared. Manila boomed, American-style, but its slums and shanty towns grew at least as fast.

In 1965, Ferdinand Marcos, a former senator, won election as president, and was reelected in 1969. By now the flow of new American investment had begun to create a period of prosperity, for a few, but Marcos felt that democracy was inefficient, wasteful, and in the Philippine case especially, corrupt. He pushed instead for what he called "constitutional authoritarianism," and in 1972 declared martial law, but without making it very clear on what grounds. It soon became clear that his aim was to wipe out all forms of opposition and dissent. The press was controlled, many thousands were arrested, jailed, and tortured; normal legal procedures were suspended, and the army was built up, citing the danger of a "Communist takeover." Marcos' power was already being challenged by other members of the old oligarchy, especially the Lopez family, owners of the daily *Manila Chronicle* and of television stations. In 1973 Marcos pushed through a new constitution, rigged the courts, and proclaimed the "New Society." A "referendum" authorized him to continue indefinitely as president, and another to be both president and prime minister. An election in 1978, with widespread fraud, voted in a compliant National Assembly which rubber-stamped his actions. Government became even more dominated by cronyism and associated corruption, most of all by Marcos and his wife, Imelda.

Times Square in Manila, a scene typical of developing urban Southeast Asia. (FPG International)

All of these flagrant abuses, the neglect of rural areas, and the worsening plight of most Filipinos, understandably provoked both resentment and rebellion. The Philippines are predominantly Christian (Catholic), but in the southern island of Mindanao, much of the Muslim community there, known as Moros, joined an armed rebellion of guerrilla warfare, although Marcos was able to buy off some of the leaders and the rebellion remained relatively small and local. Elsewhere, a reorganized Communist party formed a radical guerrilla wing called the New People's Army, which attracted growing numbers of supporters especially in Luzon, where the old Huk territory had been. In 1981 Marcos technically ended martial law, but only technically, in deference to worldwide criticism. His policies and actions remained largely unchanged, except that he now permitted a somewhat freer press, and pointed to it as evidence that he presided over a genuine democracy. In fact his power over all dissent was as great as ever, and many of those who spoke out or tried to oppose him continued to be jailed, tortured, or shot. In 1983 this included his chief political opponent, Benigno Aquino, who had been released from jail to visit the United States and was shot down at Manila airport when he returned. This blatant action began to turn Filipino opinion against Marcos and his wife, whom many feared would succeed him as his health continued to deteriorate. Many Filipinos fled the country with their capital, which contributed to a general economic collapse and uncontrolled inflation.

The elections of 1986, called by an overconfident Marcos, ended in his defeat, despite extensive vote-buying, intimidation, and other fraud, and the victory of Corazon Aquino, Beningo's widow. Marcos claimed that he had won, and clearly intended to hang on, but a faction of the army deserted his cause and refused to fire on the crowds of demonstrators demanding that he leave. The Americans, having long supported Marcos and even praised him as a "great democrat," now persuaded him to emigrate to the United States (where he died in 1989), and Corazon Aquino became president.

Mrs. Aquino inherited an impoverished, ravished, and bankrupt country, still dominated by a few rich and powerful families and their political networks, and by a large and powerful army. She was not able to break her ties with either of these groups, and indeed depended on them. She herself came from a rich, landed family, the great granddaughter of a Chinese immigrant who had prospered as a trader and sugar grower, and she necessarily operated as president in the long Filipino tradition of family politics. She survived six army rebellions, the most serious in 1989, but was unable or perhaps in part unwilling to push for the kinds of basic change the Philippines needed if it was to escape from mass poverty for most, corrupt privilege and wealth for a few, and a political system notorious for its cronyism and inefficiency. She chose not to run for reelection in 1992, when Fidel Ramos succeeded her. By 1995 Ramos had made some progress in containing rebellion, attack-

---

✠ Revolutionary Filipino Ideas ✠

Louis Taruc (born 1913) became a Communist and then head of the Hukbalahap, a guerrilla group that fought against the Japanese occupation and, after the war, against the independent Filipino government. Here are some passages from his Born of the People.

For over half a century the Philippines has become largely the private landed estate of a handful of big business men who live ten thousand miles away in the United States…. To guarantee their profits, American imperialism has kept us a backward, colonial people, with the majority living in the misery of poverty and ignorance…. It has claimed that it trained us in the ways of democratic government, but today [1949] the most corrupt regime in our history, with American approval, massacres the people…. The Filipino moves about in an American-made world. The clothes he wears, the cigarettes he smokes, the canned food he eats, the music he hears, the news of the world he reads are all American…. The Americans solved their problem by getting Filipinos to rule for them … the landlord-*ilustrado* class, the landed gentry … they were an integral part of the new American pattern of rule.

Source: L. Taruc, *Born of the People* (Manila: International Publishers, 1953), pp. 265–271, 274–275.

ing corruption, and stimulating healthier economic growth. Gross inequality, and poverty for most Filipinos, remain major problems for the future.

The United States and East Asia

Americans entered the trade with East Asia early, even before independence. Their sailing and trading skills won them a place in the Canton trade, and then in 1784 the *Empress of China* sailed from Brooklyn for Canton. Merchant families in Salem, Boston, New York, Philadelphia, and Baltimore grew rich on the China trade, and furnished their houses with Chinese porcelains, rugs, and paintings. American ship designers perfected the clipper ship, and their captains held records for the fastest voyages to and from Canton. It was hard to find Asian markets for American goods. For some years ice cut on New England ponds and packed in sawdust in the hold, necessarily crossing the equator twice, sold profitably in Canton. Furs were another export, including sea otter from the American northwest coast. American merchants were prominent in the opium trade both before and after 1842, and it was by far the largest commodity as well as the most profitable, although most of it was bought in Persia and Turkey, given the British monopoly in India. In time, American oil and kerosene became our leading exports to East Asia, marketed by the Standard Oil Company, and later some American machinery and minerals. Tobacco was another export, at first seeds of Virginia tobacco and then, through the British-American Tobacco Company, production on a large scale in north China for manufacture into cigarettes. U.S. trade with East Asia was never very large, as part of U.S. or of Asian trade as a whole, and remained a small fraction of Britain's and later Japan's. But in the missionary field Americans outnumbered those from any other country in China, Japan, Korea, and the Philippines.

In the East Asian mind, America represented wealth and power which they hoped to emulate, but also democracy and—that elusive concept—"freedom." East Asian hierarchical traditions had no place for such notions, but they were appealing to many, and for even more America was the country of Thomas Jefferson, Tom Paine, and Abraham Lincoln, the country which had created a revolution and "fired the shot heard round the world." A major part of the American model for East Asians was its opposition to imperialism and colonialism (despite our grab of Mexican territory in 1845–1848)— until the American conquest of the Philippines in 1898–1900 revealed the U.S. as just another imperialist nation. Our record in the Philippines as a colonial

power, after our brutal suppression of the Philippine nationalists, does perhaps compare favorably with that of any other colonial power, especially with the Japanese, French, or Dutch. But the greatest shock to Asian sensitivities was the series of so-called Oriental Exclusion Acts beginning in 1882 which barred first Chinese and then all other Asians as immigrants to this country. The stirring lines from the poem by Emma Lazarus at the base of the Statue of Liberty erected in 1886: "Give me your tired, your poor,/your huddled masses yearning to breathe free/I lift my lamp beside the golden door," did not, it seems, include Asians. Strong resentment against East Asian immigrants, mainly Chinese, had already erupted into race riots in California and elsewhere in which many Asians had been killed.

Despite our imperialist venture in the Philippines, we did try to protect China from further imperialist encroachment (but mainly to protect our own share of the trade) by other powers in the Open Door notes (Chapter 17), but then sent our own troops to help the other powers put down the Boxers and maintained, like them, a permanent garrison at Peking. The U.S. had been quick to take advantage of the Unequal Treaties imposed on both China and Japan, in China by the British, in whose wake we followed without taking part in any of the fighting. It was the American Treaty of Wang Hsia in 1844 which first imposed extraterritoriality on China, later extended to Japan, and Americans profited from the most-favored-nation provisions of the Treaty of Nanking in 1842, as it was our missionaries who benefited from the Anglo-French War which produced the Treaty of Tientsin in 1860. The fleets of American steamship companies were prominent on the Yangtze and other Chinese rivers, while American gunboats also patrolled them and enforced the special privileges they enjoyed under the Unequal Treaties. The missionary effort did more than preach the gospel, and in particular pioneered the spread of Western medicine and through their schools and universities opened Western learning to young Chinese, including nearly all of those who later become politically prominent, together with a fuller picture of what the United States was all about, much of which was appealing.

Our self-image as a friend of China began to suffer severely as we backed Japan as a useful client in 1905, again at Versailles in 1919 (despite Wilson's "Self-determination of nations" and his other 14 Points), and then as Japan prepared for war and attacked China in 1931 and 1937 we served as their principal supplier of essential oil, scrap metal, and other war materials used to kill Chinese. We belatedly cut off these supplies only in the summer of 1941, less because of our genuine concern for the suffering Chinese than because the Japanese had occupied French Indo-China and thus threatened our colony in the Philippines. After Pearl Harbor we interned Japanese living in this country, many of them American

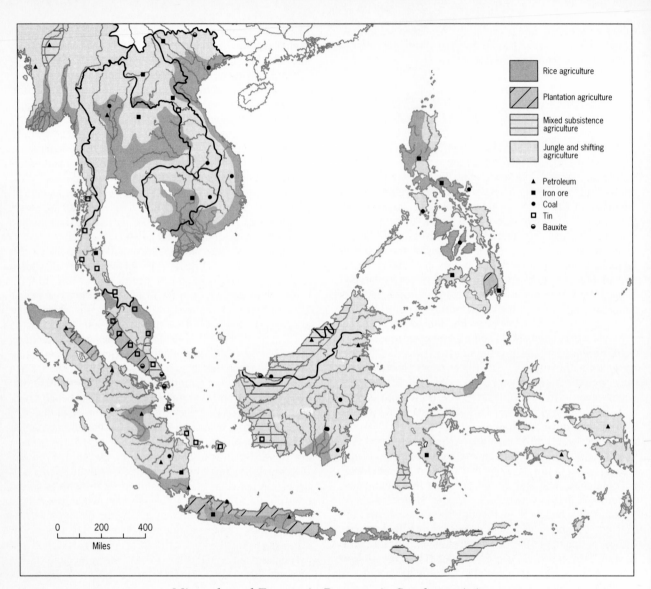

Minerals and Economic Patterns in Southeast Asia

citizens by birth, for the duration of the war; this inhuman, racist, and vindictive action was apologized for and some compensation paid only in 1992. At the war's end we established huge American military bases in Japan and the newly independent Philippines as part of our Cold War strategy, and imposed a seven-year military occupation of Japan, although the occupation was on the whole a positive and successful enterprise which helped to encourage a new and more peaceful Japan, still tied to the U.S. as a Cold War ally. Our misguided intervention in the Chinese civil war, on the predictably losing side, and our continued support for the defeated KMT on Taiwan earned us the bitter resentment of the Chinese government and people at a time when we should have been

building a more constructive relationship with what was clearly becoming the greatest power in Asia.

From 1950 in Korea we were at war with China, and relations were further set back, as they were to remain until 1971. Our intervention in Korea was responsible for the devastation of that country and its unnatural division into two antagonistic halves which still threaten the peace of the world. In all of these policies we have followed what we saw as our own strategic interest in the Cold War rather than considering the interests of the people of East Asia. The greatest and most tragic error was however our intervention in Vietnam as part of our crusade against communism, largely in ignorance of the situation there and in total disregard of the welfare of the people of Vietnam. In a war which could not be won and which was motivated entirely by Cold War considerations, we devastated Vietnam even more completely than we had Korea, and as in Korea, with nothing to show for it beyond the dismaying casualty lists except a hardening of the Communist regime we had tried to destroy and another legacy of bitterness. Vietnam was our "dark valley," although it was infinitely worse for Vietnam and the Vietnamese.

Despite this at best mixed record of the United States in East Asia, there is still a reservoir of Asian admiration for American ideals, however much they may have been ignored by our actions, still some resonance in the Asian mind of the inspiring goals of our founding fathers, enough so for example that the Vietnamese declaration of independence in 1945 closely paraphrased or adopted Thomas Jefferson's ringing words of 1776. We are also still admired for our undoubted successes, in technology and in economic development; for some that is the major attraction of the American model: wealth, and power. On our side, Americans have consistently viewed East Asia as a huge potential market of some one and a half billion customers, and as a similarly immense pool of potential converts, to Christianity and to "the American way." China has served as the biggest such lure since the time of Marco Polo and after him the Jesuits, a kind of pot of gold at the end of the rainbow. This combination of missionary and mercantile ambitions ("moral superiority" and simple greed?) is not perhaps the best basis for building a relationship with this large and important part of the world. East Asia contains over a quarter of the world's population, and its importance

economically continues to increase rapidly. The coming century will be dominated by Asia in these terms even more than it already is. We Americans, despite our wealth and our power, are less than 4 percent. It behooves us to understand more than we have done about what makes East Asia tick, in its various parts, and to begin to consider more adequately the welfare of its people, the only sound basis for any long-term relationship.

We must first accept that East Asians' values and goals differ from ours. They are as entitled to theirs as we are to our own, and it is not reasonable, despite the Americanization of much of East Asian culture since 1945, to expect that they will simply become like us. It helps to remember that there are a great many more of them than there are of us, and that their cultures rest on many centuries of tradition and on strong senses of nationalism and national/cultural identity. They are as proud of their distinctive identities as we are of ours, and as determined to keep them so and to resist any efforts at foreign domination or manipulation. We have tended since we became a superpower to treat East Asians as enemies (China, North Korea, Vietnam), as our pawns in the Cold War, or as people whose markets we must penetrate with American goods. We must try to build a relationship with this major part of the world on more positive grounds, in our own interest as well as theirs, based on mutual respect and on our mutual stake in ensuring cooperative support for peace, stability, and growth in the world of the coming century. The positive parts of our heritage can be important assets in such an endeavor: our belief in self-determination, in responsible government, in respect for human rights and the rule of

Aerial view of Kawasaki. Originally a separate city, Kawasaki is now engulfed in the expansion of Tokyo, which has become a vast industrial complex outside the old city of Edo. Note the smoke and the elevated highway. Both air and water are dangerously polluted, as in all Asian cities. (R. Murphey)

law, and in the common humanity which binds us all together. We must come to deal with East Asians as friends and partners rather than as objects. We must put racism behind us, together with our own cultural arrogance, and must try to learn from our mistakes in the past. Only thus can we play the kind of role in East Asia which we would like to play, and of which we can be proud.

East Asia and the Future: A "Pacific Century"?

As we approach the end of the twentieth century, there seems little room for doubt that East Asia will dominate the coming century even more than it does now. The United States is a major trade partner of each East Asian country, and trade across the Pacific, which by 1980 had exceeded trade across the Atlantic, continues to enlarge that lead. There is also heavy East Asian investment in the United States, and many of our citizens are from East Asia; their numbers continue to grow. U.S. trade with East Asia remains unbalanced; we import far more from there than they buy from us, a problem which has led to tensions and to efforts to persuade East Asian markets, especially China and Japan, to open more equitably to American goods. Our trade deficits with China and Japan are the largest we have, and although this gap may be reduced through ongoing negotiations, the volume of our trade with East Asia will clearly continue to rise.

The biggest single reason is that East Asia offers the world's largest market, and one which is growing faster than any other, not only in numbers of people but in its economic growth rates, far in advance of any other part of the world, including our own. It is these trends which suggest that we may be entering what has been called the "Pacific Century," where North America (including Mexico) on the eastern side of the Pacific and East Asia on the other side continue to build a dynamic commercial relationship in which East Asia, if only because of its size and its vigorous economic performance, will be the major component. When China takes over Hong Kong in July of 1997 it seems unlikely that this will slow Hong Kong's economic growth more than temporarily, or that of the adjacent southeastern sector of China whose growth has been stimulated by Hong Kong. Together they have posted in recent years the highest economic growth rates in the world, approached only by Korea, Taiwan, and Singapore, with Malaysia, Thailand, and Indonesia close behind them. Vietnam may well join that pattern as it follows, like China, the dictates of "market forces," and in the process provides a largely new market and trading partner for the United States.

Technologically, following the lead of Japan, East Asia has joined the rush of change which has engulfed most Western countries. In many respects, Japan in particular has surged ahead of its former teachers technologically and has won a strong global position in a number of high-tech goods such as semiconductors, microchips, sound reproduction equipment, microprocessors, and others, to add to its early leadership in optics and automobiles. The other "Little Dragons" of East Asia, Korea, Taiwan, Hong Kong, Vietnam, Singapore, and now Thailand and Malaysia plus Indonesia, are following the same path. It is no longer, as it once was, a trade mainly in raw materials or primary goods such as oil or wheat from North America and tea or hides from East Asia, but predominantly one in manufactured goods, in both directions. And we are no longer East Asia's teachers as we once were as they came to terms with the modern world and followed our lead. That gap has been largely closed, more than closed in Japan, and we trade with East Asia for the most part increasingly as technological equals. East Asians have long been consummate traders, since at least the time of the Sung and Ming expansion of overseas commerce, the boom growth of Shanghai and Hong Kong, the dramatic economic expansion of Japan since 1868 and, especially in the world of the last few decades, the prominent role of overseas Chinese in trans-Pacific and inter-Asian trade. Chinese and later Japanese commercial skills are second to none.

When this is combined, as it still is, with the originally Confucian ethic of education, hard work, and organized group effort, the results are impressive and have much to do with the striking economic success of East Asia. It is sometimes referred to as "Confucian capitalism," but it has much less to do with Confucianism than with the common East Asian heritage. This has always put a high value on education and still does, making a strong asset for economic growth, especially important as East Asia has so successfully kept abreast of or even exceeded the sweeping technological changes of the modern world. Education is a family priority in East Asia, and usually also a family enterprise in which parents and older siblings work with and offer an example for younger children. This is part of the group ethic, but beyond it the larger society also operates as a series of nested groups, where group welfare and advancement take precedence over individual ambition, or subsume it in the service of the group. East Asia led the world in the past for all of these reasons, and now is forging ahead in the modern world, thanks in part also to the East Asian awareness that nothing is accomplished without hard work and their long experience of putting that into practice.

With all of these long-standing characteristics, East Asians are formidable competitors, but commercial partnership with them makes good sense. Their role in the emerging global economy seems certain to increase, as we enter the "Pacific Century."

Suggestions for Further Reading

Ablin, D. A., and Hood, M., eds. *The Cambodian Agony.* Armonk, NY: M. E. Sharpe, 1987.

Andaya, A. *A History of Malaysia.* London: Macmillan, 1982.

Atkinson, J. M., and Errington, S. *Power and Differences: Gender in Island Southeast Asia.* Stanford: Stanford University Press, 1990.

Aung, S. S. K. *Aung San of Burma.* Edinburgh: Kiscale, 1991.

Brands, H. W. *Bound to Empire: The U.S. and the Philippines.* Oxford: Oxford University Press, 1992.

Chandler, D. A. *A History of Cambodia.* Boulder: Westview, 1983.

———. *The Tragedy of Cambodian History.* New Haven: Yale University Press, 1992.

Chew, E. C. T., and Lee, E. A. *A History of Singapore.* Oxford: Oxford University Press, 1991.

Drake, C. *National Integration in Indonesia.* Honolulu: University of Hawaii Press, 1989.

Gibson, I. *The Perfect War.* New York: Vintage, 1994.

Harrison, J. P. *The Endless War.* New York: McGraw Hill, 1983.

Hawes, G. *The Philippines State and the Marcos Regime.* Ithaca: Cornell University Press, 1988.

Hayslip, L. *When Heaven and Earth Changed Places.* New York: Doubleday, 1989.

Hood, S. J. *Dragons Entangled: IndoChina and the China-Vietnam War.* Armonk, New York: M. E. Sharpe, 1994.

Jackson, K. D. *Cambodia, 1975–1978: Rendezvous with Death.* Princeton: Princeton University Press, 1989.

Jamieson, N. L. *Understanding Vietnam.* Berkeley: University of California Press, 1993.

Karnow, S. *In Our Own Image: America's Empire in the Philippines.* New York: Random House, 1989.

Kolko, G. *Anatomy of a War.* New York: Random House, 1990.

Kulick, E. F., and Wilson D. *Thailand's Turn.* New York: St. Martin's, 1992.

Martin, M. A. *Cambodia.* Berkeley: University of California Press, 1994.

Maung, M. *The Burmese Road to Poverty.* New York: Praeger, 1991.

Osborne, M. *Southeast Asia.* New York: Harper Collins, 1991.

———. *Sihanouk.* Honolulu: University of Hawaii Press, 1994.

Patti, A. I. *Why Vietnam?* Berkely: University of California Press, 1991.

Regnier, P. *Singapore.* Honolulu: University of Hawaii Press, 1992.

Rotter, A. J. *The Path to Vietnam.* Ithaca: Cornell University Press, 1987.

Shawcross, W. *Sideshow: Nixon, Kissinger and the Destruction of Cambodia.* New York: Simon and Schuster, 1979.

Sheehan, N. *A Bright Shining Lie.* New York: Random House, 1988.

Steinberg, D. *The Philippines.* Boulder: Westview, 1994.

Taylor, R. H. *The State in Burma.* Honolulu: University of Hawaii Press, 1988.

The U.S. and East Asia

Chan, S. *East Asian Dynamism.* Boulder: Westview, 1990.

Iriye, A. *Across the Pacific.* New York: Harbrace, 1967.

McCord, W. *The Dawn of the Pacific Century.* New Brunswick, alt.: Transaction, 1991.

Rozman, G., ed. *The East Asian Region: Confucian Heritage and Modern Adaptation.* Princeton: Princeton University Press, 1991.

Schaller, M. *The U.S. and China in the Twentieth Century.* Oxford University Press, 1993.

Simone, V., and Feraru, A. T. *The Asian Pacific.* White Plains, New York: Longman, 1995.

Thomson, J. C., Stanley, P. W., and Perry, J. C. *Sentimental Imperialists: The American Experience in East Asia.* New York: Harper, 1981.

Watts, W. *The U.S. and Asia.* Lexington: University of Kentucky Press, 1982.

Werner, J., and Luv, D. H., eds. *The Vietnam War.* Armonk, New York: M. E. Sharpe, 1994.

West, P., et al., eds. *The Pacific Rim and the Western World.* Boulder: Westview, 1987.

ACKNOWLEDGMENTS

The following works, from which substantial portions are quoted in this book, are protected by the copyright law of the United States and International copyright laws.

Basham, A. L. From *The Wonder That Was India* by A. L. Basham. Reprinted by permission of Macmillan General Books.

Benda, H. J. and J. Larkin. From *The World of Southeast Asia* by H. J. Benda and J. Larkin. Reprinted by permission.

Collis, M. From *The Land of the Great Image* by M. Collis. Reprinted by permission of Faber and Faber Ltd.

Crump, J. I., Jr. From *Song-Poems From Xanadu,* trans. by J. I. Crump, Jr. © 1993 by Center for Chinese Studies, The University of Michigan. Reprinted with permission.

de Bary, William Theodore. From *Sources of Chinese Tradition* edited by William Theodore de Bary. Copyright © 1960 by Columbia University Press. Reprinted with permission of the publisher.

de Bary, William Theodore. From *Sources of Japanese Tradition* edited by William Theodore de Bary. Copyright © 1958 by Columbia University Press. Reprinted with permission of the publisher.

Eoyang, Eugene. Poem, "An Old Charcoal Seller" translated by Eugene Eoyang in *Sunflower Splendor,* Liu Wu-chi and I.Y. Lo, editors. Reprinted with permission of Eugene Eoyang.

Fairbank, J. K. From *Trade and Diplomacy on the China Coast* by J. K. Fairbank, Cambridge, Mass.: Harvard University Press, Copyright © 1953 by the President and Fellows of Harvard College. Reprinted by permission.

Fairbank, John K., et al. From John K. Fairbank, Edwin O. Reischauer, and Albert M. Craig, *East Asia: Tradition and Transformation,* Revised Edition. Copyright © 1989 by Houghton Mifflin Company, Reprinted with permission.

Gernet, Jacques. From *A History of Chinese Civilization* by Jacques Gernet. Reprinted by permission of Cambridge University Press.

Grousset, Rene. From *The Rise and Splendour of the Chinese Empire* by Rene Grousset, English translation by A. Waterson-Gandy and T. Gordon. Permission granted by the Regents of University of California and The University of California Press.

Haeger, J. W. From *Crisis and Prosperity in Sung China,* edited by J. W. Haeger. Reprinted by permission of the University of Arizona Press.

Hammer, E. From *The Struggle for Indochina* by E. Hammer, 1961. Reprinted by permission of Stanford University Press.

Henderson, Harold G. From *An Introduction to Haiku* by Harold G. Henderson. Copyright © 1958 by Harold G. Henderson. Used by permission of Doubleday, a division of Bantam Doubleday Deli Publishing Group, Inc.

Jones, Borton and Pearn. From *The Far East 1942–46* by Jones, Borton and Pearn, Royal Institute of International Affairs, O.U.P., 1955.

Keene, Donald, From "The Tale of Heike" from *Japanese Literature* by Donald Keene. © by Grove Press, Inc. Used by permission of Grove/Atlantic, Inc.

Keene, Donald, from *The Tsurezuregusa of Kenko* translated by Donald Keene in *Columbia University Records of Civilization #78.* Copyright © 1967 by Columbia University Press. Reprinted with permission of the publisher.

Lach, Donald F. and Carol Flaumenhaft. From *Asia on the Eye of Europe's Expansion* by Donald F. Lach and Carol Flaumenhaft. Reprinted by permission of the author.

Lee, P. H., ed. *Flowers of Fire: Twentieth Century Korean Stories.* Honolulu: University of Hawaii Press, 1974, 1986, pp. 191–204.

Ling, K. *The Revenge of Heaven: Journal of a Young Chinese* by Ivan and Miriam London with K. Ling. Copyright © 1972 by Ivan London. Reprinted by permission of Sterling Lord Literistic, Inc.

Lopte, Phillip, *The Art of the Personal Essay* by Phillip Lopte. New York: Doubleday, 1994, p. 328.

Mast, Herman. From "Tai Chi-t'ao, Sunism and Marxism" by Herman Mast, *Modern Asian Studies,* Vol. 5 (1971). Reprinted by permission of Cambridge University Press.

McClellan, Edwin. Reprinted with the permission of the editors from "An Introduction to Soseki" by Edwin McClellan, *Harvard Journal of Asiatic Studies* 22 (1959): 205–206.

McCullough, H. C. From *Yoshitsune: A Fifteenth Century Japanese,* translated by H.C. McCullough. Reprinted by permission of the University of Tokyo Press.

Morris, Ivan. From *The Pillow Book of Sei Shonagon* translated by Ivan Morris. Copyright © 1991 by Columbia University Press. Reprinted with permission of the publisher.

Morris, Ivan, *The World of the Shining Prince.* New York: Alfred A. Knopf, Inc., 1964, p. 206.

Murasaki, Lady. Excerpt from *The Tale of Genji* by Lady Murasaki, translated by Arthur Waley. Copyright, 1929. Reprinted by permission of Houghton Mifflin Company and HarperCollins Ltd. All rights reserved.

Ogura, Kazuo. From "Japan and America: Pride and Prejudice" by Kazuo Ogura, *The New York Times,* November 24, 1991. Copyright © 1991 by The New York Times Company. Reprinted by permission.

Potter, John Deane. From *Admiral of the Pacific* by John Deane Potter. Copyright John Deane Potter. Reprinted by permission of Reed Consumer Books (William Heineman, 1965) and John Johnson Ltd.

Reid, A. From *Southeast Asia in the Age of Commerce: The Lands Below the Winds* by A. Reid. Reprinted by permission of Yale University Press.

Sadler, A. L. From *The Makers of Modern Japan* by A. L. Sadler. Reprinted by permission of Routledge, Chapman & Hall Ltd.

Sansom, G. B. From *A Short Cultural History* by G. B. Sansom. Reprinted by permission.

Sansom, George. From *A History of Japan, 1334–1615* by George Sansom. Reprinted by permission of Stanford University Press.

Storry, Richard. From *A History of Modern Japan* by Richard Storry. (Penguin Books 1960, Fifth revised edition, 1982) copyright © Richard Storry, 1960, 1961, 1968. All rights reserved. Reprinted by permission of Penguin Books, Ltd., U.K.

Taruc, L. *Born of the People* New York: International Publishers, Inc. 1953, pp. 265–271, 274–275.

Teng, S. Y. and J. K. Fairbank. From *China's Response to the West* by S. Y. Teng and J. K. Fairbank, Cambridge, Mass.: Harvard University Press, Copyright © 1954 by the President and Fellows of Harvard College. Reprinted by permission.

Totman, Conrad. From *Japan Before Perry* by Conrad Totman. Permission granted by the Regents of University of California and the University of California Press.

Waley, Arthur. From *The Way and Its Power* by Arthur Waley. Reprinted by permission of George Allen & Unwin, an imprint of Harper/Collins Publisher Limited.

Wu-chi, Liu. From *An Introduction to Chinese Literature* by Liu Wu-chi. Copyright © 1966, Indiana University Press. Reprinted by permission of Indiana University Press.

INDEX